HANDBOOKS

W9-AJS-212

CROATIA & SLOVENIA

SHANN FOUNTAIN ČULO

Contents

▶ **Discover Croatia
  & Slovenia** **6**
  Planning Your Trip 8
  Explore Croatia & Slovenia 14
  • The 14-Day Best
    of Croatia and Slovenia 14
  • Pick Your Paradise:
    The Southern Dalmatian
    Islands 15
  • Movable Feast: A Culinary
    Tour of Istria and Kvarner 17
  • Vines and Wines............. 18
  • Village Life 20
  • Kid-Friendly
    Croatia and Slovenia 22
  • Sailing the Croatian Islands.... 23

▶ **Zagreb** **25**
  Sights......................... 30
  Entertainment and Events....... 42
  Shopping..................... 44
  Sports and Recreation.......... 46
  Accommodations 49
  Food......................... 50
  Information and Services 55
  Getting There and Around....... 57
  Around Zagreb 59

▶ **Inland Croatia** **63**
  Zagorje 66
  Međimurje.................... 71
  Slavonia...................... 79
  Karlovac Region 90

▶ **Istria** **97**
  Labin 100
  Pula 104
  Brijuni Islands 111
  Rovinj........................ 112
  Poreč 117
  Istrian Interior 124

▶ **Kvarner Gulf**................. **131**
  Rijeka........................ 134
  Opatija Riviera................. 140
  Kvarner Islands 146

▶ **Northern Dalmatia** **167**
  Zadar........................ 170
  Islands Around Zadar.......... 177
  Paklenica National Park........ 179
  Plitvice Lakes National Park..... 181
  Murter and the Kornati Islands... 183
  Šibenik....................... 185
  Primošten.................... 192
  Trogir........................ 194

▶ **Southern Dalmatia** **199**
  Split 202
  Omiš 211
  Makarska Riviera 213
  Southern Dalmatian Islands 216

▶ **Dubrovnik** **234**
  Sights 238
  Entertainment, Shopping,
    and Recreation 246
  Accommodations 248
  Food 250
  Information and Services 252
  Getting There and Around 253
  Around Dubrovnik 254

▶ **Ljubljana** **259**
  Sights 262
  Entertainment and Events 269
  Shopping and Recreation 272
  Accommodations 274
  Food 275
  Information and Services 278
  Getting There and Around 279
  Around Ljubljana 281

▶ **Inland Slovenia** **282**
  Pohorje Region 285
  Pomurje Region 291
  Savinjska Valley 292
  Savinjske Alps Region 294
  Dolenjska and Bela Krajina 296
  Julian Alps 300

▶ **Coastal Slovenia
  and the Karst Region** **309**
  The Coast 311
  The Karst Region 316

▶ **Background** **320**
  The Land 320
  History 323
  Government and Economy 328
  People and Culture 330

▶ **Essentials** **333**
  Getting There 333
  Getting Around 336
  Visas and Officialdom 340
  Recreation 341
  Accommodations 343
  Food 345
  Tips for Travelers 349
  Information and Services 354

▶ **Resources** **358**
  Glossary 358
  Croatian Phrasebook 359
  Slovenian Phrasebook 364
  Suggested Reading 369
  Internet Resources 371

▶ **Index** **373**

▶ **List of Maps** **390**

Discover
Croatia & Slovenia

Croatia and Slovenia may only occupy an area slightly larger than the state of Maine, but the countries pack a lot into the small space. The cities are winding amalgams of Roman, Venetian, art deco, and modern architectural styles. Snow-capped mountains give way to fertile green valleys and thick fairy-tale forests. Then there are the barren rock-covered hinterlands, rimmed by sparkling turquoise waters, and islands, scattered like pebbles along the coast.

These two countries share a turbulent history of rulers, wars, and invading empires that have all left their mark. But instead of obliterating the local flavor, they only added another layer to the rich cultures of Croatia and Slovenia. The amphitheater in Pula is an enduring reminder of the Romans, the bustling cafés and wedding-cake architecture in Zagreb and Ljubljana are reminiscent of Vienna, and much of Istrian and coastal Slovenian cuisine is greatly shaped by their Italian neighbors. Despite all these influences, Croatia and Slovenia are clearly countries with a strong sense of self, reflected in their enduring villages, festivals, and crafts.

Though the tourists have been coming en masse – especially to the beautiful Dalmatian coast – since the countries' independence in the early 1990s, there are still plenty of spots off the beaten track. The charming old towns of Ljubljana and Zagreb are still relatively empty of camera-wielding

tourists. Visiting one of the coast's sleepy fishing villages or pristine islands can feel like discovering a private gem. Croatia's Slavonia region is dotted with typical wooden village houses and wineries, while Slovenia's interior has everything a sports fanatic could want, from rafting on mountain streams to skiing to exploring a vast network of caves. Istria is home to black and white truffles, *agroturizam* restaurants, and one-of-a-kind farm stays.

Perhaps the best thing about a trip to Croatia and Slovenia is that it really can be whatever you make of it. It's possible to go skiing one day and have dinner on the coast the next evening. There are also hundreds of museums, churches, and castles to explore.

But if you come to Croatia and Slovenia, come for the people – strong, resilient, and proud of their relatively recent independence. Don't be shy to learn a few words of their language and start a conversation. They are always willing to answer questions and give their advice. You'll find it's the people that make the region what it is: beautiful, warm, and welcoming.

Planning Your Trip

▶ WHERE TO GO

Zagreb

Croatia's capital is the cultural and social heart of the country yet it's overlooked by most tourists, who miss the buzzing vibe of this charming city. Social life revolves around the bustling squares and streets of Donji Grad (Lower Town). For the softer side of town, head to Gornji Grad (Upper Town) with its quiet, winding cobblestone roads, stunning churches, and excellent museums. Bridging old and new is the delightful Tkalčićeva street with its boutiques and cafés. Mount Sljeme, a national park just out of town, has hiking trails and mountain huts where you can while away an afternoon with a beer and a bowl of bean stew.

Inland Croatia

Beginning in the mountainous Gorski Kotar and stretching across Croatia's long eastern arm, inland Croatia is definitely the country's undiscovered find. The region is dotted with picturesque villages, excellent restaurants, and

the Croatian National Theater in Zagreb's Donji Grad

IF YOU HAVE . . .

- **FIVE DAYS:** Visit Ljubljana, Bled, Zagreb, and Plitvice.
- **ONE WEEK:** Add Šibenik and Kornati Islands.
- **TWO WEEKS:** Add Split, Dubrovnik, Hvar, and Korčula.
- **THREE WEEKS:** Add Opatija, Grožnjan, Pula, Cres, and Rovinj.

seoski turizam establishments, where you can sleep like a local and wake up to the rooster's crow. Don't-miss destinations include the vineyards that dot the countryside, the riverside town of Osijek, and the stork-filled Lonjsko polje. The easternmost regions around Vukovar are only now recovering from the Homeland War, and you'll find friendly people, eager to show off their towns to visitors.

Istria

This tiny peninsula, wedged between Croatia and Slovenia and only a stone's throw from Italy, packs a lot of punch into its small size. You can sun yourself on a rocky beach in the morning, retreat to the green hills for lunch, and finish off the day with dinner next to a rushing stream or in a seaside medieval town, depending on your mood. Istria is most famous for three things, and you shouldn't miss any of them: the Roman amphitheater in Pula, the region's wines, and its truffles. But there's more to unearth here, from almost

perfect little villages like Brtonigla and Hum to a taste of faded Tito-esque grandeur in the Brijuni National Park.

Kvarner Gulf

Home to the grand Austro-Hungarian coastal playgrounds of Opatija and Lovran and the laid-back port town of Rijeka, the Kvarner Gulf is less than a two-hour drive from Zagreb. Its real jewels are the stunning islands just off the coast, such as Rab, with its preserved old town and colorful festivals; Krk, drawing a younger, party-loving crowd;

genteel Veli Lošinj; and Pag, with its famous lace and cheese and 24-hour party beach near Novalja. The true don't-miss islands are relatively undeveloped Cres, with its refuge for griffon vultures, and Susak, whose clay cliffs jut into the remotest portions of Croatia's Adriatic.

Northern Dalmatia

The coast is full of Roman-Veneto architecture, starting with the impressive old towns of Zadar and Šibenik, snaking down to precious little Trogir and the Kaštela fishing villages. Beaches can be filled to capacity in the summer, but you should be able to find a relatively roomy one by hiring a boat to take you to one of the little islands just off the coast, each with a culture and personality all its own. Also included in this region are the stunning Plitvice Lakes, slightly inland, one of the most-visited destinations in Croatia for good reason.

Southern Dalmatia

Split is the border between north and south on the Dalmatian coast. It's important not only because it's the second-largest city in Croatia and for its dozens of connections to the Croatian islands, but also for the hauntingly beautiful Diocletian's Palace in the heart of town. Celebrity-laden Hvar has already made a name for itself in the press, but along Croatia's most stunning coastline it's not alone in its beauty. From the former pirate stronghold, Omiš, to the birthplace of Marco Polo on Korčula, to diving the

Lastovo village, on the island of Lastovo, near Dubrovnik

Adriatic's clear blue waters or rafting the Cetina Gorge, there's something for every traveler.

Dubrovnik

Dubrovnik is Croatia's most famous city, and it's easy to see why. The dramatic beauty of the walled city on a cliff, the sunny cream stone and red-tiled roofs contrasting with the blue Adriatic Sea, and the grand architecture are a few of the qualities that make Dubrovnik hold its own with other European destinations. The city's popularity has translated into masses of tourists, but there's also a less seen side of Dubrovnik, including aristocratic Trsteno and the shady island of Lokrum. The restaurants and wineries of the Pelješac Peninsula and the nearby islands of Lastovo and Mljet, with a lake at its center, are great escapes not far from town.

Ljubljana

Ljubljana may be small, but with a cultural menu to rival much larger capitals, a funky nightlife, and a strong sense of self, it is a city not to be overlooked. It's impossible to ignore the influence architect Jože Plečnik had on the city; his touch is all over Ljubljana, including its famous Tromostovje (Triple Bridge), the colonnaded market, and many of the city's tree-lined promenades. Ljubljana is the cultural and social as well as political capital of Slovenia, and it's here that you'll find an impressive selection of museums and galleries. If you'd like to take a peek into a more hidden part of Ljubljana, the 15th-century quarter of Krakovo is a peaceful little distraction.

Inland Slovenia

Filled with mountains, lakes, rivers, and caves, Slovenia's interior is an ideal region for sports enthusiasts. For those interested in quieter

herding settlement on Velika Planina, in inland Slovenia

pursuits, there is also food, culture, and history to be discovered, including wineries, Roman ruins, herding settlements, and centuries-old churches and castles. The region's most famous town is Bled, with a church-topped island in the center of the mountain-rimmed lake. To the east of Ljubljana is the town of Maribor, with a sweet historic center. Those into rafting and adventure sports will be happiest around the Triglav National Park and Bohinj, with plenty of adrenaline-pumping activity.

Coastal Slovenia and the Karst Region

While not as grand as the Croatian coast, the coast of Slovenia has many charms of its own, from stunning architecture and unusual medieval frescoes to coastal walking paths to towns filled with winding cobblestone streets. Venetian-influenced Piran is the pride of the Slovenian coast and a starting point for those exploring the region. Caves like Postojnska Jama and Škocjanske Jame are worth a peek for their underworld glory. And a trip to the area wouldn't be complete without sampling the Karst's famous wind-cured *pršut* (prosciutto).

Piran, on the coast of Slovenia

► WHEN TO GO

The coast of Croatia and Slovenia has a Mediterranean climate with hot summers and relatively mild winters. Inland locales will bring warm to hot summers and cold winters, though snow accumulation has dwindled in recent years.

July and August are the busiest months on the coast—beaches and nightclubs are packed, and many of the coastal towns hold colorful festivals. But all in all they're probably the worst months to visit Croatia and Slovenia, with hotels filling up even at the most expensive high-season rates and inland capitals void of locals (who've joined all the foreigners by the sea).

June and September are ideal for visiting the coast or cities in the interior. The waters are warm enough for swimming, and the biggest influxes of tourists are sandwiched between these relatively peaceful months. If swimming's not your thing, then March, April, May, and October are possibly even better—an early-morning ramble around town may make you think you're the first to discover a destination.

Autumn is a great season for visiting Istria and inland Croatia and Slovenia: Wine is harvested, leaves turn to shades of gold, and the crisp air is invigorating.

Winter, when most hotels and restaurants are at their cheapest, is best suited to Southern Dalmatia. Keep in mind, though, that some hotels and restaurants will be closed, particularly on the islands. Inland Croatia and Slovenia are very cold and gray in winter, but December festivities and markets bring life to Zagreb and Ljubljana.

springtime in Croatia's Krka National Park

▶ BEFORE YOU GO

Visas and Officialdom

To enter Croatia, U.S., EU, Canadian, Australian, and New Zealand citizens will need only a passport; no visa is required for stays up to 90 days.

To enter Slovenia, U.S., Canadian, Australian, and New Zealand citizens will need only a passport; no visa is required for stays up to 90 days. Citizens of the EU, Switzerland, and Croatia can visit for up to 30 days with only a national identity card.

Citizens of other countries should check visa regulations for Croatia and Slovenia.

Getting There

Getting to Croatia and Slovenia is easier than ever before, particularly in summer when low-cost airlines offer flights from major European hubs such as London and Frankfurt and ferry services connect the countries with Venice and Trieste in Italy.

If you're flying, you'll find Croatia and Slovenia's main air carriers (Croatia Airlines and Adria Airways, respectively), supplemented by companies such as easy-Jet, Ryanair, and Germanwings, offer many flights accommodating a variety of budgets. Though the low-cost carriers generally deposit travelers in the most popular coastal regions, it's easy to get off the beaten track by taking trains or buses into the interior. Croatia's main airports are located in Zagreb and Split, though Dubrovnik, Pula, and Rijeka see their share of travelers during the summer months; Slovenia's only major airport is in its capital, Ljubljana.

Train service is frequent and reliable in both Slovenia and Croatia, with at least two to three daily trains linking capitals Ljubljana and Zagreb with Italy, Austria, Hungary, and Serbia. Bus service is good as well, though buses have been known to deposit regular

a horn-masked sheepskin costume – part of the Kurentovanje festival in Ptuj, Slovenia

customers close to their homes, making the journey a little longer than planned from time to time.

In the summer, ferries connect cities like Split, Dubrovnik, and Pula in Croatia and Portorož and Piran in Slovenia with Venice and the northern Italian coast.

Getting Around

If you'll be sticking to larger towns, public transportation is an excellent option for getting around both Slovenia and Croatia. Buses and trains are frequent, safe, and reliable. Islands are well connected via ferry.

However, if you're planning on exploring smaller villages or following the regions' wine routes, you'll find renting a car to be a lifesaver. Arranging for the car before you come usually secures a better price.

As most roads lack bike lanes, as well as drivers used to sharing the road, you'll find bicycle use best suited to sleepy coastal islands, some devoid of cars.

Explore Croatia & Slovenia

▶ THE 14-DAY BEST OF CROATIA AND SLOVENIA

Day 1

After landing in Ljubljana, take it easy the rest of the day. Refresh at your hotel before heading out in the evening for a stroll and dinner in Ljubljana's Old Town, capping off the day with a view from the town's castle, Stari Grad.

Day 2

Head to nearby Bled for a tour of the castle and church-topped lake, ride on a *pletna* (a gondola-like boat) or in a horse-drawn carriage while admiring the scenery. Adventurous types can switch the strolling for a spot of white-water rafting or hiking around the lake. Have an afternoon coffee and *kremšnite* (cream cake) on a hotel terrace overlooking the lake and dine on some of the area's fresh trout for dinner, preferably at a cozy fireside table.

Day 3

Head to Zagreb, stopping for a late lunch at the Golf Hotel Castle Mokrice, a castle just before the Croatian border. After dropping off your bags at your hotel in Zagreb, catch at least one or two museums in the lower town before dinner and people-watching along Zagreb's buzzing Bogovićeva.

Day 4

After breakfast at the historic Regent Esplanade (if you stayed in another part of town have breakfast at the market), make a

Lake Bled, Slovenia

PICK YOUR PARADISE: THE SOUTHERN DALMATIAN ISLANDS

Southern Dalmatia is covered with rocky beaches, sun-washed towns, and some of the prettiest destinations in Croatia. With dozens of islands to choose from, which ones do you pick? Though each has its charms, here are four to stick on your don't-miss list.

MLJET

Legend has it this is the island that seduced Odysseus to stay for seven years on his way back from Troy and it's not hard to see why. This **heavily forested island** near Dubrovnik has **two saltwater lakes.** An island in the larger lake holds a 12th-century Benedictine monastery. Bike rentals are available for exploring Mljet, and the island also offers **excellent diving** with a 3rd-century Roman shipwreck and a sunken WWII German torpedo boat right off the coast.

HVAR

Since the 4th century B.C. many countries have laid claim to Hvar's sun-drenched stone buildings, lavender and rosemary fields, rich vineyards, and deep blue waters. These days it's the tourists who seem to have conquered. Frequented by famous actors, models, and gossip-mag regulars, Hvar Town offers **pulsing summer nightlife.** The island's staple club, Carpe Diem, and any of the many other bars and discotheques radiating from the main square promise prolific diversion. During the day, **St. Stephen's Cathedral,** built during the 16th and 17th centuries, and the **Fortica,** a Venetian fortress with a grand view of the harbor, beckon travelers. Hvar's summer music festival is host to classical, jazz, and folk concerts. It's worth a visit to the winery of **Zlatan Plenković** in Sveta Nedjelja to sample its award-winning wines.

KORČULA

Famous as the birthplace of Marco Polo and often dubbed a **mini-Dubrovnik** due to its charming walled city, the island of Korčula is also home to sandy shaded coves with some of Croatia's **best beaches.** Korčula Town's 15th-century cathedral displays an early work by Tintoretto, and Moreška sword dancers give colorful performances in July and August.

VIS

First settled in Neolithic times, Vis was closed to the public shortly after World War II, when it became a Yugoslav military base. Opened to tourism in 1989, this **tranquil island** has slowly seen an increase in visitors. The town of Vis is filled with narrow leafy streets, perfect for meandering and admiring the limestone villas built by wealthy seafarers. The **Archaeological Museum** showcases many island treasures and offers leaflets suggesting walks past the city's ruins.

the island of Vis

beeline for Dolac market and then Zagreb's Gornji Grad for a long morning of sightseeing and coffee sipping. Head to fairy-tale-like Tkalčićeva for lunch and shopping. Have dinner at Bistro Apetit.

Day 5

Leave fairly early this morning to make it to Plitvice before lunch. Take your time walking around the majestic cascading lakes and chow down on sausage stew at Lička kuća before driving on to Šibenik and a late-night drink in its stunning old town.

Day 6

Snag a table overlooking the cathedral at Pelegrini for breakfast before hitting a few of Šibenik's sights. Then drive to nearby Jurlinovi Dvori for lunch and a tour of a typical Dalmatian village. In the evening have

Plitvice Lakes National Park, Croatia

a drink in the Medieval Mediterranean Garden of St. Lawrence's Monastery before choosing a spot for a seafood dinner.

Day 7

Get up early this morning for a day trip to the Kornati Islands to see the stark beauty of the national park, swim and soak up some sun, and likely eat some grilled fish. Not an early bird? Choose an excursion to the islands of Zlarin or Prvić instead. Get back to Šibenik in the early evening and immediately head out for Split to get an early start on sightseeing there in the morning.

Day 8

Start the day with a tour of Split's major attraction, Diocletian's Palace. After a light lunch head out to the Marjan Peninsula and absorb Meštrović's mammoth house and artwork before whiling the evening away in a lively bar crawl through the narrow, busy streets of the palace, hopefully catching a bit of jazz or live music.

Day 9

Take the catamaran to Hvar, fitting in a tour of Hvar Town's sights before dressing up and heading to dinner and a drink at the famed Carpe Diem or some wine tasting at the Pršuta Tri Wine Bar.

Day 10

Even if you're not a wine connoisseur, taking today to visit some of Hvar's inland wineries is a great way to see a less-touristed side of the island. Make sure to visit the vineyards of Zlatan Plenković and lunch at his waterside Bilo Idro restaurant. Save room for dinner in Stari Grad, though, where the historic restaurant Jurin Podrum will impress you with top-quality cuisine.

Day 11

Head to Korčula in the morning, touring the mini-Dubrovnik's cathedral and art galleries with a break for a sweet treat from local legendary bakery Cukarin. In the evening dine on fresh fish and mussels.

Day 12

Head to the Pelješac Peninsula this morning for laid-back beach lounging or winery-hopping before having an early dinner at Kapetanova kuća and heading to Dubrovnik for a quiet drink at your hotel. If you're still going strong, take a walk along the Stradun with an ice-cream cone in the late evening when all the day-trippers and cruise passengers have left the city.

Day 13

Start your day with a tour of the town walls before heading to the town's galleries, the Sponza Palace, and the Rector's Palace. Have a quick sandwich at Buffet Škola, saving a visit to the Franciscan Monastery for later in the day when the crowds have begun to thin. After changing at your hotel, have a cocktail-with-a-view at the Sunset Lounge before splurging on dinner at Gil's under a starlit sky.

Day 14

Buy a few snacks in the Old Town's market before heading for one last swim on the island of Lokrum. Early flight? Have coffee and a pastry at the historic GradsKavana and savor a bit more of the bustle of grand Dubrovnik

Diocletian's Palace, Split, Croatia

and perhaps one last look at the shimmering Adriatic before heading to the airport.

▶ MOVABLE FEAST: A CULINARY TOUR OF ISTRIA AND KVARNER

Though you'll find great food throughout Slovenia and Croatia, the Istria and Kvarner regions are the most concentrated centers of gourmet finds. From restaurants that compete with big names like Ducasse to wineries to prized lamb specialties, every day should bring a couple of discoveries for even the most experienced palates.

Day 1

Start your tour on the Opatija Riviera, where you'll find a treasure trove of top restaurants. An absolute must is the famed Plavi Podrum in Volosko, often included on "world's best" lists and winner of multiple awards and honors. Also worth checking out are Kukuriku in the village of Kastav and Le Mandrać, yet another of Croatia's top restaurants.

Day 2

Head into Istria, stopping for lunch on the terrace of the Humska Konoba in Hum, supposedly the smallest village in the world. Top off your meal with a bit of the town's mistletoe brandy, said to aid digestion. Don't have more than a sip since you'll need to save your tolerance for wine tasting at the winery of Livio Benvenuti near Motovun, perhaps getting in a bit of sightseeing while you're in the area. Later have dinner at Zigante Tartufi, the truffle king, in Livade before heading up to Grožnjan to spend the night.

Day 3

Get a good look around Grožnjan and its art galleries before slowly making your way

VINES AND WINES

Motovun, a hillside town in Istria, the region where Croatia's best-organized wine roads are found

Slovenia and Croatia are both perfect destinations for wine aficionados. Vineyards dot the hills of both countries and the region boasts a very long winemaking history, dating from Roman times. The wines produced vary in quality and taste, but are inexpensive in general, and stopping to sample homemade vintages along the wine roads is a fun way to get to know the countryside. Some excellent wines never make it to the West, selling out their small stock locally.

CROATIA

In Croatia, mostly white wines have dominated, though red wines have had a strong showing in recent years as well. The most popular award would likely go to Istria's light white **Malvazija.** Istria's other indigenous wine, **Teran,** is an earthy red, well loved locally but little embraced by foreign palates. The small peninsula, reminiscent of Tuscany, is dotted with excellent small winemakers with dozens of varieties to try.

The Dalmatian coast is another well-known wine-producing region, particularly the Pelješac Peninsula, where the local **Plavac Mali** grape is responsible for some of the country's best red wines.

The interior of Croatia is perhaps the country's lesser-known wine-growing region. Međimurje, which hugs the Hungarian border, produces mostly whites, a bit acidic for most tastes. Some very good Croatian whites come from little-traveled Slavonia, from the vineyards around Slavonski Brod to the far eastern corner of Ilok, where solid reds, particularly **Burgundy,** are produced as well.

Many of the areas are covered with marked wine roads, though the best organized and promoted are those in Istria. More information about Istrian wine roads can be found at www.istra.hr.

SLOVENIA

Like Croatia, Slovenia's winemaking history traces its roots to Roman times. Today, the country's wines have garnered a solid reputation, but to try many of the local products, mostly produced for personal consumption and regional sales, you'll need to get out and visit the small vineyards in person. Slovenian white wines, particularly **Beli Pinot, Šipon, Chardonnay,** and **Sauvignon Blanc,** are high in quality. The country is most known for its Beli Pinot and Šipon and for the red **Kraški Teran** in the Karst. Slovenia also makes something similar to a rosé, called **Cviček,** and a couple of decent sparkling wines. The three main regions producing wine are Podravje (Pohorje and Pomurje regions), Posavje (Bela Krajina and Dolenjska regions), and Primorska (coastal region).

Slovenia has an excellent and well-marked network of wine routes for driving or biking. More information can be found at www.slovenia.info.

Croatia contains more than 300 geographically defined wine regions.

to Brtonigla and the Hotel San Rocco, where you can sip local wines by the hotel pool before having dinner in the top-notch restaurant and taking a walk around the charming village.

Day 4

After a late checkout, drive to Novigrad for lunch at Damir i Ornela for their creative Mediterranean take on sushi. In the afternoon drive up to the vineyards of Moreno Coronica near Umag for wine tasting or take to the *vinske ceste* (wine roads) in the area for a look at some more mom-and-pop vineyards to see what's on offer.

Day 5

Stop in at Poreč for a peek at the city's magnificent basilica before driving to Pula. Tour the amphitheater and its interesting display on Roman winemaking, then head to Restoran Milan for coffee and cake or a late lunch. Save room for dinner at the superb Valsabbion, also a great place to spend the night and enjoy walking the marina and admiring the shiny yachts.

Day 6

Take a ferry to Cres, where you should have lunch at the unassuming Bukaleta to feast on some of the island's specialties, particularly lamb. After lunch walk around the twisted forest paths of the Caput Insulae Eco Centre and hopefully catch a glimpse of the protected griffon vultures.

Day 7

Going over to Mali Lošinj, make sure to eat at Konoba Corrado in between lazing on the beach. Walk the pretty promenade to Veli Lošinj, stopping to admire the aristocratic homes overlooking the water, before continuing to Trattoria Bora Bar for dinner prepared by an Italian-born, U.S.-trained chef.

▶ VILLAGE LIFE

Traveling to less-touristed parts of Croatia and Slovenia, you'll be rewarded with typical village accommodation, winery hotels, cozy restaurants, and quirky museums. Want to see the talked-about sights too? Just add in a couple of days to peruse the capitals of Ljubljana and Zagreb or combine the trip with a jaunt to the coast, since the tour has you headed in that direction anyway.

Day 1

Leaving Ljubljana, head to the small town of Bovec, at the edge of Triglav National Park. Spend the afternoon walking the paths around the rushing turquoise river before getting a good night's sleep at either the Dobra Vila hotel or the more rustic Pristava Lepena, in the middle of the mountains.

Day 2

Head to Idrija, famous for three things: the Čipkarska šola (Lace-Making School), the excellent restaurant Gostilna Lectar, and the Kendov Dvorec, an elegant castle hotel that happens to be one of Slovenia's best. A night at the hotel is worth the excursion alone.

Day 3

Cruise the Upper Dolenjska Wine Road or practice your swing at the Hotel Grad Otočec.

Day 4

Passing through Zagreb, head east on the highway to Kutjevo, where you can visit centuries-old cellars before unpacking your bags at the inn of modern-day winemaker Enjingi. Spend the afternoon wine tasting, eating on the terrace overlooking the vineyards, and picking the vintners' brains on everything there is to know about viticulture.

Day 5

You've got about a two-hour drive to Osijek, where you'll tour the Tvrđa before eating local specialties like frog legs or stew at atmospheric Kod Ruže. Tonight you'll sleep in the red-themed guest house of Crvendać, just outside of Osijek.

lace-making in Idrija, Slovenia

Dolenjska, one of Slovenia's wine-producing regions

Day 6

This morning take a tour of Kopački rit before heading to the Baranja for a trip through local wineries. Eat dinner at Baranjska kuća, taking a peek at the restaurant's ethnographic museum, and stay at the 1910-era Sklepić house.

Day 7

Don't leave the Sklepić house before riding in a typical Slavonian horse-drawn carriage (arrange in advance). After the ride, drive to Ilok for winery visits and dinner at the Odescalchi castle.

Day 8

Today you can drive to Slavonski Brod, stopping at the Vinarija Zdjelarević, a combination winery/restaurant/hotel, or continue on to the Lonjsko polje to search for storks and swimming furry pigs. Dine and stay at the Ravlić house, a thatched-roof cottage filled with antiques, sure to make you feel like you spent the night inside a fairy tale.

Day 9

Drive to Samobor, nowadays essentially a suburb of Zagreb, for small-town charm and a slice of the city's famous *kremšnite*. Walk around the town's museums and churches or go for a hike in the area to stretch your legs after today's drive.

Day 10

This morning you'll drive to the Gorski Kotar, stopping at the picturesque village of Fužine. There's plenty to do in the area but there are three things you shouldn't miss: the endearing Muzej Žaba (Museum of Frogs) in Lokve, lunch at Konoba Volta for local specialties, and a night at Tito's former hunting lodge Bitoraj. Tomorrow you can continue on to Kvarner and Istria or turn around and return to Zagreb for a flight out.

▶ KID-FRIENDLY CROATIA AND SLOVENIA

Lake Bled and its church-topped island, Slovenia

Thought traveling through Europe with kids was hard? Think again. Croatia and Slovenia are very family friendly, with lots of attractions that seem made for kids and laid-back locals who love to see young faces and the sound of happy noise.

Day 1

Starting in Ljubljana, tour the Old Town (kids tend to want a picture with the dragons on the Dragon Bridge), perhaps fitting in a child-friendly attraction like the Železniški Muzej (Railway Museum), the Hiša Eksperimentov (House of Experiments), or the clock at the Lutkovno Gledališče (Puppet Theater), which puts on a free show every hour during the day. Older kids will probably enjoy the novelty of staying in the Hostel Celica, a former prison. The hostel offers private cells in addition to typical hostel accommodation or tours if you were planning on somewhere more luxe.

Day 2

Head to Bled, where the castle and the deep blue lake are the main attractions, though kids should like a horse-drawn carriage ride or taking a *pletna* boat to the lake's church-topped island. In season, taking the steam train to nearby Bohinj is a fun excursion as well.

Day 3

Driving to Zagreb in the early morning, take a tour around the Gornji Grad and walk down the city's Brothers Grimm–like Tkalčićeva street, stopping for cake and hot *kakao* (hot chocolate) at Ivica i Marica. If you have time, add a day to visit Maksimir's tiny zoo or hike up Mount Sljeme with older kids to have a hearty lunch of bean stew and roast chicken at the outdoor picnic tables.

Day 4

Head into the Gorski Kotar, stopping at Fužine. Visit the village of Lokve's Muzej

paddling on Lake Bohinj, Slovenia

Žaba (Museum of Frogs) and walk along the river. Stay at the Kuća Sobol, in a peaceful valley populated by numerous butterfly species.

Day 5

Today is your family's introduction to Istria, stopping at the village of Hum, claiming to be the smallest in the world. Young ones will like lunch at the cozy Humska Konoba or in nearby Kotlić, where you can dine beside a rushing stream (perhaps a too-precarious choice for very young children).

Day 6

Head to Rovinj, taking a tour of the old town.

Child-friendly attractions not to miss are the Kuća o batani, a small but charming museum about the town's indigenous *batana* boat, and the market, a fun place to shop for homemade souvenirs. Later make your way to the beaches, tailor-made for kids and even strollers, with lots of shady forests just behind to escape the sun if it gets too strong.

Days 7 and 8

Head south to Pula, where kids of all ages will enjoy the Roman amphitheater. From here you'll want to take an excursion to the Brijuni Islands, with a zoo safari park and lots of wild nature to fascinate the whole family.

► SAILING THE CROATIAN ISLANDS

Sailing the islands in the Adriatic is a relaxing way to spend a week (or more). This itinerary is one of the most popular with sailors, with stops at some of Croatia's top destinations.

Days 1 and 2

Set sail from Split to Milna on the island of

Brač. The next morning, take a short hop to Bol, lounging on the beaches at Zlatni Rat and noshing on *gregada*, or fish stew.

Day 3

Docking at the uber-popular Hvar Town on the island of Hvar, spend the day seeing the

Hvar Town, on the island of Hvar

sights and the evening partying with other yachting types at Carpe Diem.

Day 4

Today's destination on the island of Vis, Komiža, is the perfect place to rest after splurging in Hvar Town. The laid-back fishing village has a few must-sees for seafaring sorts, including the Ribarski muzej (Fishing Museum) and the Gospa Gusarica (Our Lady of the Pirates) church. Dine at Konoba Jastožera, a former lobster-storage facility turned upscale restaurant.

Day 5

Today it's time to sail to the islet of Biševo with its famous Modra špilja (Blue Cave). Then cruise the southern side of Vis to Senko's, a famous restaurant in a small cove around nowhere. It's definitely worth the mooring for some of Senko's fabulous cooking.

Day 6

Today it's up to Vis Town, where you can stop at some museums and a Greek cemetery before dining at Pojoda, one of the island's top seafood restaurants.

Days 7 and 8

Head back to Split, where in addition to Diocletian's Palace there's a don't-miss for sailing fans—the Hrvatski pomorski muzej (Croatian Maritime Museum), with lots of historical model ships, costumes, uniforms, and maritime memorabilia.

Komiža harbor, on the island of Vis

ZAGREB

On the surface, Zagreb seems like a modern, bustling city. And in many ways, it is. The streets prowl with luxury cars and designer duds. Large international corporations have attached their logos to shiny new office buildings. And don't be surprised if you hear German, French, or Chinese: Over 45 embassies are located in the rather small capital of approximately 790,000 (closer to one million in the metro area).

Zagreb is the country's business capital, but as you cruise the streets you'll soon realize that much of this business is done over a cup of strong coffee or a long lunch. The cafés are swarmed, particularly on pretty days when it just seems natural to take a meeting outside. At night the socializing continues, from old men in a small bar kicking back a *rakija* (brandy)

to young people in a disco pulsing to the latest U.S. dance tunes.

As you delve a little deeper, you'll see a city that changes only what it wants to and at its own pace. At Dolac (Zagreb's main fresh market) the ritual of the daily market remains among the urbanization. Some locals stop for a quick prayer in the Kamenita vrata, just as *zagrebčani* have done for over 250 years, and for the Saturday-morning promenade everyone gets dressed up to see and be seen while they stroll the streets around Cvjetni trg (Flower Square).

Zagreb is perhaps the perfect European capital. With a charming Old Town, a lively café culture, and the requisite cathedral, but without the loads of tourists à la Prague or Vienna, the city is easy to explore in a day before

HIGHLIGHTS

◖ Tržnica Dolac: Get into the thick of things, bumping shoulders and bargaining for fresh produce in the city's largest fresh market (page 31).

◖ Tkalčićeva Street: This fairy-tale-like street with cafés, restaurants, and local artisans is perfect for strolling, sitting, or window-shopping (page 32).

◖ Kamenita vrata: Inside this 13th-century stone gate is an ornate shrine where the faithful pray surrounded by flickering candles (page 33).

◖ Muzej grada Zagreba: Zagreb's city museum is well presented and the best way to get a thorough overview of the history and culture of the capital city in just over an hour (page 33).

◖ Cvjetni trg: You can't spend time in Zagreb without taking part in the citizens' favorite pastime, a long leisurely coffee (*kava*) on one of the streets near this square while watching the passersby; it's the busiest on a sunny Saturday morning (page 36).

◖ Trg maršala Tita: A beautiful square dominated by the wedding cake-like Croatian National Theater, Marshal Tito Square is also home to the must-see Museum of Arts and Crafts, a treasure trove of design and interiors objects in a stunning art nouveau space (page 36).

◖ Mount Medvednica: Head to the park's most popular peak, Sljeme, to spend an afternoon on the mountain topped off with a mug of beer and a bowl of steaming *grah* with the locals (page 47).

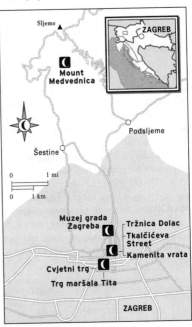

LOOK FOR ◖ TO FIND RECOMMENDED SIGHTS, ACTIVITIES, DINING, AND LODGING.

traveling on to the coast. The museums, while not housing great works of art, are well done and intimate, with exhibits on topics like naive art, local sculpture, and local history. Zagreb boasts glorious Secession architecture, some impeccably restored, some often going unnoticed on decaying gray facades.

Though the city is home to a quarter of Croatia's population, it's easy to get off the beaten path and mix with the locals. The Paris-style parks or the hike up Mt. Sljeme for fresh air, folk music, and great cheap food, are worth

staying an extra day for, and several wonderful towns with culture, history, and almost no tourists are easily accessible for a day or even half-day trip.

You'll find the city easy to maneuver. It's not too large and practically everyone under 40 speaks English—often outstandingly good English, better than you'd find in nearby Italy or Germany. The people are friendly, too, and happy to lend a hand or a recommendation.

The city is what you make of it. You can live the glamorous life with the city's high rollers, surrounded by a crowd that's probably dressed better than you are, or share a plate of fried sardines with the locals in a standing-room-only bar. There's the old and the new, and for the most part, it's all good.

Moving west instead of east, Zagreb is changing. It has been changing every year since Croatia's independence. But the core of Zagreb—the buzzing social vibe that moves like honey—remains the same. So whether you spend your time in the museums or in the nightclubs, by far Croatia's best, you can't leave Zagreb without ordering a coffee in a café. Just remember to drink it slowly. It's part of the experience.

HISTORY

In a nutshell, it's amazing that Zagreb has developed into the vibrant town it is today, having been threatened by wars (not to mention some fires and the occasional plague) in almost all nine centuries of its history.

Zagreb is thought to have been settled way back in the Iron Age, but the city wasn't officially established until 1094 when King Ladislaus of Hungary developed a diocese to gain more control over northern Croatia. A settlement called Kaptol developed around the diocese buildings, while Gradec, an area controlled directly by the Hungarian king, sprang up on the neighboring hill.

The two towns fought with each other over land and mills almost from the beginning. On top of that, they had to deal with outside invaders. In a particularly bitter fight with the Mongols in 1242, Gradec was so ravaged that King Bela IV granted Gradec an exemption from jurisdiction, even though he did not exempt them militarily. The exemption, called a "Golden Bull," freed Gradec's citizens of many taxes in order to entice others to move there.

Kaptol wasn't so happy about Gradec's good fortune and escalated the rivalry in 1247 by erecting a tower on Gradec's land; the two communities fought bitterly for decades. Several blows in the 16th century, including the loss of Kaptol lands to the Turks, the defeat of Kaptol by Hapsburg troops, and Gradec's

loss of free jurisdiction, diminished the fighting and the two began to be referred to collectively as Zagreb.

Zagreb established itself as the capital of Croatia and Slavonia when the Croatian viceroy Nikola Frankopan moved his headquarters there in 1621. The 17th and 18th centuries were devastating for the city despite its new role as capital. Warfare, several fires, and two bouts of plague almost obliterated Zagreb, with the capital packing up for Varaždin to the north in 1776 and leaving less than 3,000 residents by the end of the 18th century.

The 19th century was the most prosperous for the town. The capital had centered itself in Zagreb once again and, fueled by developing industries, the city added museums, theaters, and schools.

The city continued to thrive until the formation of Yugoslavia in 1918, when the central government moved to Belgrade. And Zagreb underwent a significant transformation in the 1950s and '60s when mayor Većeslav Holjevac built giant apartment complexes across the banks of the Sava River, adding an entire section, called Novi Zagreb (New Zagreb), to the city.

After Croatia's independence in 1991, the city struggled through the war; in the years that followed rampant corruption stagnated the country's growth. Fortunately, the city has finally begun to move forward and is quickly developing into a vibrant capital.

PLANNING YOUR TIME

It only takes a day to get a good overview of Zagreb with a walk through Gornji Grad, visits to a couple of the better galleries and museums, a nice lunch, some window-shopping, and an evening out. If you have two days, though, make sure to spend the second day hiking around Sljeme or visiting one of the cities in the surrounding area, like the sugary little Samobor, on the verge of becoming a suburb of Zagreb.

You'll probably want to use Zagreb as your base for exploring the area; the city's transportation system makes it pretty easy to whiz

ZAGREB

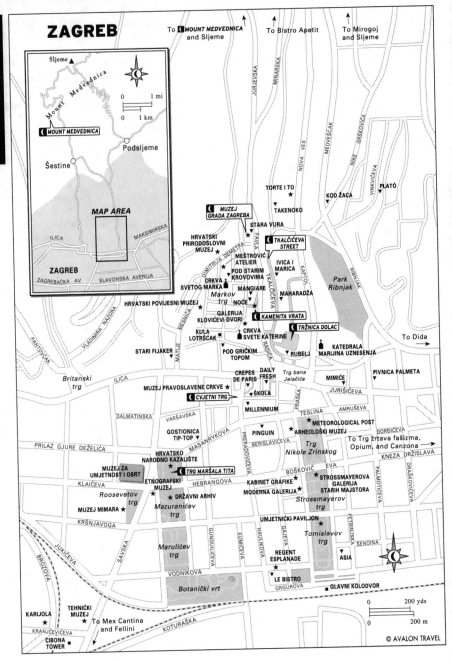

© AVALON TRAVEL

around to most of your stops by tram. If you plan on only spending one day in Zagreb, you'll probably get more for your money at hotels in Samobor (about 30 or 40 minutes by bus from Zagreb's center, depending on the traffic). However, if you don't like traveling on a bus or want to experience some of Zagreb's laid-back nightlife, skip the savings and splurge on a place in town.

Zagreb's main attractions are all within walking distance of each other, though you'll do a lot of walking if you want to traverse both the upper and lower towns in a day. The best plan is to see the highlights and fit in a few other stops that suit your interests, whether that's art or history or shopping, and skip the rest. Architecture buffs might really enjoy making time to see the stunning art nouveau interior at the State Archives.

From September to May, you'll probably find yourself alone in Zagreb's museums, save for the occasional group of schoolchildren. However, tourists are slowly beginning to discover the city, and in summer you'll see the tall flags of tour groups as travelers squeeze in a tour of the old town between their flight and a week on the coast.

Remember that almost everything is closed on Sunday (save for most museums) and most of Gornji Grad's museums are closed Monday. In addition most museums have shortened hours on Saturday and Sunday. Should you find yourself in town on a weekend afternoon, this is the day to head to the slopes of Sljeme or the wide promenades of Maksimir, though on a nice day it may seem the entire city had the same idea.

Winter is usually gray day upon another gray day, though if you happen to end up in town in winter, look on the bright side: You'll have the town's tourist attractions practically to yourself and the city looks quite romantic in winter. Just be sure to grab a bite in the restaurants described as light-filled or sunny. You can also head up to Sljeme, a good choice almost any time of year, for a bit of snow-packed fun.

Spring, early summer, and fall are the best times to visit Zagreb. Though fall can sometimes be rainy, it also gets its share of crisp, sunny days that somehow make the town really shine. Summer is usually bearable, but you may want to avoid town in August, when all the locals are on the coast and the city is empty save yourself and some other tourists traipsing around town.

ORIENTATION

Zagreb can be divided into dozens of neighborhoods, but the two most important for the traveler are Gornji Grad (Upper Town), which comprises the old town and many of the city's most charming attractions, and Donji Grad (Lower Town), rarely referred to as such since it *is* Zagreb—the part of the city where much of the daily hustle and bustle as well as shopping, socializing, and business is carried out. It's also in Donji Grad that you'll find most of the accommodations and restaurants as well as Zagreb's green horseshoe, a network of squares laid out in the 19th century, home to quite a few more important buildings and museums. However, recent development has reduced some of Donji Grad's importance, with business towers being built slightly south of town and Western-style shopping malls popping up in the west toward Samobor and to the south in Novi Zagreb.

Novi Zagreb sprang up in the 1960s, across the Sava River, and is mostly an amalgam of soulless multistory apartment buildings, though the area has come into its own recently with the addition of a new shopping mall and a renovation to the riverside Bundek park, a nice place for a stroll on a sunny day.

However, it's the northern suburbs, toward Sljeme, where the upper middle class live (and the very rich in the Tuškanac area, worth a drive if you're a fan of old houses). The hills, as they are referred to by locals, are bordered on the east by leafy Maksimir park and in the north by Sljeme, a favorite haven of city dwellers on the weekends.

Sights

TRG BANA JELAČIĆA AND KAPTOL

Trg bana Jelačića is the city's main square and a useful base for exploring the town. The **Kaptol** neighborhood that stretches north of the square around the cathedral is filled with restaurants, cafés and shops, culminating in a swank shopping center, Centar Kaptol.

Trg bana Jelačića
Ban Jelačić Square

Trg bana Jelačića has been a meeting point for centuries of locals. Before being officially designated the main square in the 1850s, it served as a point for tax collections and was known as "Harmica" (after the Hungarian *harmincad,* which means a thirtieth).

Today the square is flanked by some beautiful, if not a little over-the-top, examples of classicist and Secessionist architecture sporting ugly signs for multinational corporations on their roofs. What the square lacks in charm it makes up for in convenience. As the city's largest tram stop, it's the perfect departure point for seeing the sights and is a popular meeting place for visitors and locals alike. Before heading off, you can stop at the main **tourist office** (Trg bana Jelačića 11, tel. 01/481-4051, www.zagreb-touristinfo.hr, 8 A.M.–8 P.M. Mon.–Fri., 9 A.M.–6 P.M. Sat.–Sun. June–Sept.; 8:30 A.M.–8 P.M. Mon.–Fri., 10 A.M.–5 P.M. Sat., 10 A.M.–2 P.M. Sun. Oct.–May), located on the southeastern edge of the square.

The square is rimmed with cafés, including the city's legendary **Gradska Kavana,** opened in 1925, long a watering hole for Zagreb's older elite, politicians, and writers, as well as unsuspecting tourists who will find

ONE DAY IN ZAGREB

No later than 8:30 A.M., have breakfast at the Regent Esplanade hotel and imagine you're an Orient Express passenger from the era of luxe rail travel. A little before 10 A.M. walk up through the stunning tree-lined **Zrinjevac** to **Trg bana Jelačića,** Zagreb's main square. Follow the row of fresh flower stands topped with red umbrellas and climb the stairs to **Dolac Market** to join the pre-noon crowd bargaining for fresh produce. After you're through with haggling, take a peek at the **Katedrala Marijina Uznesenja** (Cathedral of the Assumption of the Blessed Virgin Mary) and then double back to historical **Tkalčićeva Street** with its petite colorful buildings straight out of a Brothers Grimm tale. The street is crowded with places to stop for lunch, then take a coffee and dessert at **Ivica i Marica** and do a little window-shopping.

From here take the **Stube Bartola Felbingera,** a set of steps marked with a street sign, to the Gornji Grad. Stop for a photo of the colorful roof of **Crkva svetog Marka** (St. Mark's Church) and continue on to visit **Meštrović Atelier** and the **Muzej grada Zagreba** (Zagreb City Museum), adding the **Hrvatski muzej naivne umjetnosti** (Croatian Museum of Naive Art) if you have time. Instead of taking the funicular, take the long way back down by passing through the 13th-century **Kamenita vrata** (Stone Gate).

Have dinner in the lower town, preferably around **Cvjetni trg** (Flower Square), and for dessert stuff your face with gelato at **Millennium** or savor a French-style crepe, locally called *palačinke,* at **Crepes de Paris** – both places are located on or near the square. From here you don't need to look far to find some nightlife. Sip coffee or have a beer with the hundreds of revelers sitting at outdoor cafés along **Bogovićeva.** If the day's history lesson hasn't worn you out, the night is young – at 10 P.M. in Zagreb the party is just getting started.

the prices almost double those of other locations. Trg bana Jelačića is also the site of loud free concerts, political rallies, homecomings for sports figures, and several markets, the largest of which is held at Christmas, with wooden huts selling gifts, souvenirs, and homemade cookies.

Presiding over the square is the **statue of Ban Josip Jelačić,** sculpted by Viennese artist Antun Fernkorn in 1866. Ban Jelačić is a national hero, a Croatian count and general who abolished serfdom and broke ties with Hungary during a rebellion in 1848. The statue used to face north, with Jelačić's saber pointing in rebellion against the Austro-Hungarian empire. The Socialist government dismantled the statue in 1947 and it remained in the Academy of Arts and Sciences until 1990, when it was returned to the square, now facing south, presumably in defiance of its neighbors.

◖ Tržnica Dolac
Dolac Market
North of Trg bana Jelačića, Zagreb's main square, follow the row of fresh flower stands topped with red umbrellas and climb the stairs to Tržnica Dolac (until around 2 P.M. daily), the city's main market since 1930. If you're looking for the heart and soul of Zagreb, you'll find it here. Old men drink tiny glasses of brandy at the old cafés along the market's edges and watch the crowd bargaining with the headscarved vendors for fresh produce, herbs, eggs, and homemade cheeses. The atmosphere is warm and friendly and you'll find that even those who can't speak English will try and converse and are always happy to dole out advice and recipes. This is also a great spot to search for souvenirs. From the more predictable embroidered tablecloths, some in good taste and some not, to the quirky elixirs and health remedies, you should be able to find something worth sticking in your suitcase. My recommendation is to buy a fresh *burek* from one of the bread shops on the edge to eat right away, and pick up some local olives or a jar of domestic honey seasoned with lavender or rosemary for the trip home.

Dolac Market, the city's main market

Katedrala Marijina Uznesenja
Cathedral of the Assumption of the Blessed Virgin Mary

The tall, lacy spires of the Katedrala Marijina Uznesenja (Kaptol 31, tel. 01/481-4727, open 7:30 A.M.–7:30 P.M. daily, mass at 7, 8, and 9 A.M. Mon.–Fri. and 7, 8, 9, 10, and 11:30 A.M. Sun., free) can be seen from many parts of Zagreb and though the church is grand, it seems a bit out of place with its more modest surroundings. Built on the site of a small Romanesque church built in 1217 by King Ladislaus, the present cathedral, constructed in the last half of the 13th century, is now a largely neo-Gothic structure. A planned renovation to the cathedral in the 19th century became a near rebuilding of the church after a catastrophic earthquake in 1880. The Viennese architect Hermann Bollé integrated the design of the church, which had suffered from a mish-mash of styles following years of raids, various archbishops, and subsequent renovations that had all left their mark. Four Renaissance choir stalls and a few medieval frescoes are all that remain of the cathedral before the earthquake. Other items of note: the carved panels on the side altar by Albrecht Dürer and a subtle relief by Ivan Meštrović, marking the grave of the controversial Archbishop Alojzije Stepinac. Flanking the southern side of the cathedral, the 18th-century **Archbishop's Palace** is also quite different than the original structure. All that remains today are the medieval-like turrets. Wind around the palace down Vlaška Street and make a left turn where you'll find **Ribnjak** park. Though it's slightly off the beaten tourist track, the sweet little well-maintained park in the heart of the city is a nice spot to eat your finds from Dolac. Once exclusively for the use of Kaptol's priests, the park was opened to the public in 1947.

Gliptoteka Hazu
Glyptotheque of the Croatian Academy of Sciences and Arts

Though this warehouse-like space houses mostly plaster replicas of sculpture and even medieval gravestones, there are a few original pieces, and the whole collection is so well presented that it might be worth the trip if you have some extra time or are in the area. The Gliptoteka Hazu (Medvedgradska 2, tel. 01/468-6050, www.mdc.hr/gliptoteka, 11 A.M.–7 P.M. Tues.–Fri., 10 A.M.–2 P.M. Sat.–Sun., 10Kn) also has exhibits of photography and architecture throughout the year. Check their website or the tourist office to see what's on.

◖ Tkalčićeva Street

Just south of the Gliptoteka in the direction of Trg bana Jelačića, you'll find **Centar Kaptol** (Nova ves 11, tel. 01/486-0241, www.centarkaptol.hr, 9 A.M.–9 P.M. Mon.–Sat.), a shopping mall that houses a multiplex cinema as well as several chic cocktail bars and restaurants frequented by the city's young elite. If you have time, have a slice of cake at local addiction **Torte i to.** As you continue further south, the street runs into Tkalčićeva Street, marked by the beginning of a pedestrian zone. Often

© SHANN FOUNTAIN CULO

statue of Marija Jurić Zagorka

KRVAVI MOST (BLOODY BRIDGE)

The street called Krvavi Most was once a bridge spanning Medveščak Creek (today Tkalčićeva Street). The creek served as a border between the settlements of Kaptol and Gradec, who rarely got along. Residents from both sides had mills along the creek and often got into skirmishes. However, the bridge really got its name from a 1667 battle in which the soldiers of Viceroy Zrinski attacked the citizens of Gradec, resulting in so many injuries and deaths that the waters of the creek supposedly ran red. The bridge was demolished in 1899 after the creek was filled in, but the tiny street's name keeps a piece of town history alive.

referred to simply as Tkalča by the locals, the street is one of the city's social hubs, packed with bars and restaurants.

But what is now a stream of people was once an actual stream bed, forming a boundary between the cities of Gradec and Kaptol. The stream was rerouted due to sewage issues and in the 18th century it became a center for manufacturing, its length lined with workshops making soap, stonework, and liquor, as well as a leather factory.

Today the street's petite colorful buildings with gingerbread windows look like something straight out of a Brothers Grimm tale. However, don't let Tkalčićeva's old world charm deceive you. It is also home to many up-and-coming Croatian artisans. Spend some time shopping the street's jewelry ateliers, galleries, and clothing boutiques.

As you stroll, stop for a photo with the sculpture of **Marija Jurić Zagorka,** one of Croatia's first female journalists and writers.

GORNJI GRAD
Upper Town

Gornji Grad is the heart of Zagreb and the oldest part of town. The area is full of charm and character and has a good portion of the city's best museums and galleries.

Kamenita vrata
Stone Gate

Forming the eastern entrance of the city walls, the cavern-like Kamenita vrata, built in 1241 by the Hungarian King Bela IV, is the only gate that remains of the original four that led into the city. The gate has survived renovations, fires, and various motions by the city to tear it down. The last fire, in 1731, spared a small painting of the Virgin Mary and locals considered it a miracle. A small shrine was formed, with an intricate Baroque iron gate to protect the painting inside a small niche. Candles flicker against the dark space, lit by those who come to pray and seek help from the Virgin of the Stone Gate, whom the archbishop of Zagreb proclaimed a special protector of the city in 1991.

The rooms in the building that line the city gate were originally used as storage areas, but in the 17th century they were converted into small shops. The **pharmacy at Kamenita Street 9** continues the apothecary tradition started in the 14th century, when a pharmacy occupied the same space. A plaque on the building claims that the grandson of the famous author Dante worked in the apothecary in 1399.

Muzej grada Zagreba
Zagreb City Museum

Following the city's development from prehistory to the 20th century, Muzej grada Zagreba (Opatička 20, tel. 01/485-1358, www.mdc.hr/mgz, 10 A.M.–6 P.M. Tues., Wed., and Fri., 10 A.M.–10 P.M. Thurs., 10 A.M.–2 P.M. Sat.–Sun., 10–20Kn) is definitely worth a visit to get a feel for Zagreb's origins and history. Located in the 17th-century convent of the Poor Clares, the museum houses a good mix of exhibits, including portraits, regional dress, everyday objects, socialist posters, and several scale models of Zagreb throughout the centuries. Children will enjoy the re-creations of early 20th-century storefronts and a room dedicated to Croatian animation. Most impressive though is the somber yet exquisite reconstructed portal of the cathedral before its 19th-century renovation.

Just up the street from the museum is **Ilirski trg,** a small square unremarkable save for a café called Palainovka that has a nice gravel terrace and dates from 1846. The area is usually quiet save for occasional bursts of classical music drifting from the windows of the School for Classical Ballet across the street.

Meštrović Atelier
Meštrović Studio

The Meštrović Atelier (Mletačka 8, tel. 01/485-1123, www.mdc.hr/mestrovic, 10 A.M.–6 P.M. Tues.–Fri., 10 A.M.–2 P.M. Sat.–Sun., 20Kn) is in the Zagreb home where Ivan Meštrović lived between 1924 and 1942. This cozy little museum is not only home to some 300 sculptures and drawings by the famous sculptor, but is also an intimate look into the life of the artist. His sunny studio is light-filled even on a rainy day and is so simple and beautiful that it may be hard to leave.

Markov trg
St. Mark's Square

Crkva svetog Marka (St. Mark's Church, Trg svetog Marka 5, tel. 01/485-1611, 11 A.M.–4 P.M. and 5:30–7 P.M. daily, posted hours not always observed, free) just might be one of the most photographed buildings in Croatia. Its colorful roof tiles, the most unique feature of the church, depict the coat of arms of Zagreb (the white castle on a red background) and the Triune Kingdom of Croatia, Slavonia, and Dalmatia (on the left if you're facing the church). You'll probably recognize the red and white checkerboard design, called

IVAN MEŠTROVIĆ, CROATIA'S MOST FAMOUS SCULPTOR

The sculptor Ivan Meštrović was born in 1883 in Slavonia, though he spent most of his life in Drniš in Dalmatia. His family was poor and daily chores left no time for him to go to school, though he managed to teach himself to read and write. He was an excellent self-taught artist and managed to land an apprenticeship with a stonemason in Split, where he was discovered and sent to study at Vienna's prestigious Academy of Art.

Meštrović's talent gained him success almost from the start and soon his work was a part of important exhibitions and he was receiving commissions for pieces like *The Well of Life,* in front of the Croatian National Theater. His early pieces reflect the influence of Rodin, whom he knew in Vienna, but his work quickly developed a style all his own.

Meštrović is an important figure not only for his talent as a sculptor but also for the political impact he had as an artist. Committed to the idea of a unified Slav nation, Meštrović began his artistic political statements by including a sculpture of the Serbian hero Kraljević Marko in a 1910 exhibition (today it's in his studio in Zagreb) and placing his work in the Serbian Pavilion at the Rome International Exhibition in 1911 as a statement in support of a unified Slav state.

Meštrović returned to Croatia in the 1920s, turning away from political themes and producing the Račić Memorial Chapel in Cavtat and the statue of Gregorius of Nin for the city of Split.

Imprisoned by the Ustaše in 1941, he was later freed and allowed to leave the country. Although Tito tried to get Meštrović to return to his homeland, the sculptor opted to work as a professor in the United States, where his 1924 sculpture of two Native Americans on horseback decorates Grant Park in Chicago.

Most of the work in his later life revolves around religious themes. He died in 1962 and was laid to rest in the Church of the Holy Redeemer in Otavice, which he had built as his family's resting place years before.

the *šahovnica,* from the modern-day Croatian flag. It has been a symbol of Croatia since medieval times. Dalmatia is represented by the three lions' heads and Slavonia by the animal, actually a marten or *kuna,* the national animal of Croatia and also its currency's namesake.

The Romanesque window on the south side of the church helps support the claim that the church may have been built as early as the 13th century, but earthquake, fire, and well-intentioned reconstructions have left little of the original structure. The simple Gothic church has a rather pretty south portal, original to the church, the work of 14th-century sculptors from Prague.

Outside the church on Markov trg, if you have the feeling you're being watched, you probably are. The square is home to Croatia's government, and men in dark suits protecting the country's politicos are a regular fixture here, explaining the proliferation of sleek black cars parked in the square. At the corner of the square and Cirilometodska Street is the **Town Hall,** now used only for meetings of Zagreb's Town Council. The **Sabor,** or parliament, is housed in the buildings on the eastern side of the square and the **Banski dvor,** the former Baroque residence of the civil governor of Croatia, is now the official seat of the government.

Hrvatski povijesni muzej
Croatian History Museum

Housed in a refreshed Baroque mansion, the small Hrvatski povijesni muzej (Matoševa 9, tel. 01/485-1900, www.hismus.hr, 10 A.M.–6 P.M. Mon.–Fri., 10 A.M.–1 P.M. Sat.–Sun., 10Kn, free Mon.) shows interesting and well-presented temporary exhibitions pulled from the museum's collection of over 140,000 items.

Hrvatski prirodoslovni muzej
Croatian Natural History Museum

The Hrvatski prirodoslovni muzej (Demetrova 1, tel. 01/485-1700, 10 A.M.–5 P.M. Mon.–Fri., 10 A.M.–1 P.M. Sat.–Sun., 15Kn) houses mediocre temporary exhibits, but the most interesting displays are the permanent collections on the 2nd floor. Skeletons, specimens in glass bottles, and stuffed birds and mammals showcased in old-fashioned glass cabinets provide an experience from another era; it's even a little creepy if you happen to be the only visitor. The most amazing display is the 26-foot basking shark, found in the Adriatic in the 1930s.

Hrvatski muzej naivne umjetnosti
Croatian Museum of Naive Art

The small Hrvatski muzej naivne umjetnosti (Sv. Ćirila i Metoda 3, tel. 01/485-1911, www.hmnu.org, 10 A.M.–6 P.M. Tues.–Fri., 10 A.M.–1 P.M. Sat.–Sun., 10Kn) is a don't-miss,

NAIVE ART IN CROATIA

The naive art movement in Croatia was started in the late 1920s and 1930s by an academically trained artist, Krsto Hegedušić, who found similarities to French naive painter Henri Rousseau in a small group of painters in the village of Hlebine. With his support, self-taught artists like Ivan Generalić and Franjo Mraz began exhibiting more widely and started using a traditional technique of painting on glass with oil.

Though their work does include a few jaunty pictures of village life, most of Generalić's and Mraz's work is dark and sometimes gruesome, portraying the hardships of peasants and the realities of war. The strong political messages and socialist exhibitions by the Hlebine painters came to an ugly end when Mirko Virius, an artist with a no-holds-barred approach to depicting rural poverty, was killed by the Ustaše in a concentration camp.

The movement then entered a surrealist phase, with works by Ivan Generalić and a new generation of naive painters that included his son Josip and another artist, Ivan Rabuzin, displaying often distorted dreamlike pieces.

Much of naive art today is more decorative than artistic, though the village of Hlebine remains a haven for the purest form of the craft.

if only for the simple, almost organic art it displays. The artists, all untrained, depict sometimes lively, sometimes depressing, scenes of peasant and village life. Most of the works are by the movement's most famous painter, Ivan Generalić, though other artists—even those from outside of Croatia but who embody the naive style—are also on display.

Jezuitski trg
Jesuit's Square
Galerija Klovićevi dvori (Klovićevi dvori Gallery, Jezuitski trg 4, tel. 01/485-2117, www .galerijaklovic.hr, 11 A.M.–7 P.M. Tues.–Sun., 20Kn), once a 17th-century Jesuit monastery, hosts important exhibitions, often of well-known international artists such as Picasso and Chagall. Jezuitski trg, marked by the fountain depicting a fisherman wrestling a snake, spills over into Katarinin trg, where 17th-century **Crkva svete Katerine** (Jesuit Church of St. Catherine, 10 A.M.–1 P.M. daily, free) is a jewel-box Baroque church that is worth a peek. Built between 1620 and 1632, it is the earliest example of Baroque religious architecture in Zagreb.

Kula lotrščak
Burglars' Tower
The Romanesque Kula lotrščak (Strossmayerovo šetalište 9, tel. 01/485-1768, 11 A.M.–8 P.M. Tues.–Sun. May–Oct., call for winter hours, 10Kn), dating from the 13th century, was built by the people of Gradec to protect the city from the Tatars and thieves. At the time, loud bells warned citizens of fires, storms, and the closing of the city gates every evening. In the 19th century a 4th floor was added and later a cannon, to help the churches' bell-ringers know when it was noon.

The cannon is still fired every day at noon, these days letting locals know it's time for lunch. Hike up the narrow staircase for a red-tiled roof view of Zagreb's lower town.

In front of the tower you'll find the **Strossmayerovo šetalište,** or Strossmayer's path, a promenade named after Josip Juraj Strossmayer, bishop of Đakovo. It's worth a stroll to see the magnificent city views.

At the base of Lotrščak tower, the **uspinjača** (funicular, Tomićeva ulica, tel. 01/483-3912, every 10 minutes 6:30 A.M. to 9 P.M. daily, 3Kn one-way) transports passengers—some 750,000 a year—down to the lower town (and back up again if they wish). The 66-meter-long funicular, the shortest in the world, is one of the oldest forms of public transportation in the city, established only one year after the first horse-drawn tram appeared on Zagreb's streets.

DONJI GRAD
Lower Town
Though Donji Grad is slightly younger and a lot busier than the cobblestoned Gornji Grad, the area is a must-see for its museums, its charming network of squares, and most of all, for a taste of bustling Zagreb life. Don't leave without a coffee on Cvjetni trg among the locals.

From the bottom of the funicular that runs from the upper town it's just a short walk south to Ilica, a busy street filled with shops that connects the main square, Trg bana Jelačića, with Britanski trg to the west. Cross over Ilica (watch for trams when you cross) and make your way to Cvjetni trg and the café-lined Bogovićeva for a peek into the social side of the city.

◖ Cvjetni trg
Flower Square
Locals almost never refer to this square by its official name, Preradovićev trg (Preradović's Square), but instead call it Cvjetni trg since it was the site of a Parisian-style flower market until the 1980s, and is still the home of several florist stands. The streets that branch off of the square are the place to be seen on Saturday mornings; sunny days seem to bring out all of Zagreb to the cafés along Bogovićeva and Preradovićeva. Before leaving Cvjetni trg to have a coffee yourself, peep inside the small **Pravoslavna crkva** (Serbian Orthodox Church, hours vary, free). The quiet icon-filled space is a tranquil respite from the activity outside.

◖ Trg maršala Tita
Marshal Tito Square
The **Hrvatsko Narodno Kazalište** (Croatian

TITO SENTIMENT

The tiny village of Kumrovec is all but deserted on a typical day, leaving the birthplace of Josip Broz Tito, his statue in front of the barn, and the rest of the small town rather abandoned and forgotten. But come to town on May 4 (the anniversary of his death) or May 25 (the anniversary of his birthday, long celebrated in former Yugoslavia as Dan Mladosti, or Day of Youth) and you'll see a different story as people gather in the Zagorje village to remember and celebrate Tito. In fact, in 2005, 25 years after Tito's death, there were over 10,000 attendees, from Croatia, Serbia, and Bosnia.

As the years have passed since Tito's death in 1980, the opinion of the former dictator of Yugoslavia has been increasingly positive. Close to half of Slovenians polled in 2000 referred to their opinion of Tito as "excellent" or "good," with only 10 percent responding "poor." There are also plenty of Croatians who remember him fondly, with 60 percent of those polled voting to have his body moved from Belgrade back to Kumrovec (which has not happened, by the way). All this enthusi-asm may seem hard to imagine given all of the bad things that went with his regime: The oppression of even a word against Tito, the tendency to throw people into prison over nothing, the Bleiburg massacre, the repression of the Church (state employees were not allowed to attend if they wanted to keep their jobs), and the Croatian Spring debacle are just a few examples.

But people tend to remember the good, such as how Yugoslavians were the wealthiest and freest in Eastern Europe, putting them above their neighbors. Neighbors like Hungary and the Czech Republic have turned the tables on the former Yugoslavia since the fall of the Berlin Wall, and that makes some people nostalgic. Some also miss the security of a state job and a state-provided apartment. Yet plenty remember the hardships of living under the Tito regime. And so for the time being, there will still be one or two news stories a year about people fighting to have the name of Tito Square changed and people fighting to keep it the way it is.

National Theater, Trg maršala Tita 15, tel. 01/482-8532, www.hnk.hr), a massive yellow neo-Baroque wedding cake of a building, dominates the center of the square. Built by Viennese architects Ferdinand Fellner and Herman Helmer, who designed 40 theaters in Europe, the Croatian National Theater was opened in 1895 by the Emperor Franz Josef I, who beat on the balcony above the main entrance with a silver hammer. Inside the domed ceilings, frescoes and gilt-laden balconies are just the right environment for taking in an opera or a ballet, a must if you want to get a peek at the interior. Or, just walk up and see if it happens to be open.

The square is also home to two sculptures, Ivan Meštrović's beautiful 1905 piece *Well of Life,* in front of the theater, and, tucked amongst the trees in the southwestern corner, a piece by Fernkorn of St. George killing a dragon.

On the western side of the square is the **Muzej za umjetnost i obrt** (Museum of Arts and Crafts, Trg maršala Tita 10, tel. 01/488-2111, www.muo.hr, 10 A.M.–1 P.M. Mon., 10 A.M.–8 P.M. Thurs., 10 A.M.–10 P.M. Tues.–Wed. and Fri.–Sun., 20Kn). A veritable wonderland for anyone who loves interiors, its impressive exhibits range from furniture to porcelain to religious art, and the space itself, with its central atrium rimmed with intricate cast-iron handrails, are truly a don't-miss for design fans.

The northern and eastern sides of the square are flanked by the beautiful buildings of Zagreb's **Law Faculty,** holding their own against the theater with their more austere but equally glorious Austro-Hungarian facades. Another of Meštrović's sculptures, *History of the Croats,* stands in front of the yellow building in the northwest corner.

Muzej Mimara
Mimara Museum

Housed in a sprawling 19th-century building, once a local high school, the Muzej Mimara (Trg Franklina Roosevelta 5, tel. 01/482-8100, 10 A.M.–5 P.M. Tues.–Sat., Thurs. until 7 P.M., 10 A.M.–2 P.M. Sun., 40Kn) is the collection of Ante Topić Mimara, who made money abroad and donated the artwork he amassed to the nation. There's lots of controversy surrounding the Mimara, from just who Ante Topić Mimara was, to how he made his money, to whether many of the pieces are real or fake.

With close to 4,000 works of art and some big names attached (no one has ever proved the works are fake, by the way) like Van Gogh, Rubens, Renoir, and Manet, plus prehistoric artifacts, glassware, and sculpture, the museum displays just about everything that falls under the heading "art."

However, unless you're a raging art fan or have never been to a large national museum with famous works of art, you'd probably be better off spending your time visiting places that can only be found in Zagreb, like one of the intimate museums housing local paintings, crafts, or history.

Etnografski muzej
Ethnographic Museum

One of the most under-visited museums in town, the Etnografski muzej (Trg Mažuranića 14, tel. 01/482-6221, www.etnografski-muzej.hr, 10 A.M.–6 P.M. Tues.–Thurs., 10 A.M.–1 P.M. Fri.–Sun., 15Kn, free Thurs.) not only has an impressive collection of regional costumes from around the country, but the building itself, with a gorgeous art nouveau cupola, is worth checking out.

Marulićev trg
Marulić Square

Most people would bypass the **Državni arhiv** (State Archives, Marulićev trg 21, tel. 01/480-1999) on Marulićev trg with only a passing nod to the beautiful building, built in 1913 as the University Library. However, if you have the time it's really worth catching the daily guided tours (noon, 1, and 2 P.M. Mon.–Fri., 20Kn) to see the interior of one of the city's most impressive art nouveau buildings. The building is full of elaborate marble and dripping, decadent crystal chandeliers. Best are the reading rooms, full of soaring ceilings and leaded-glass windows, particularly the Professor's Reading Room. A sort of chapel to academia, the cozy wood-paneled room is filled with its share of opulence, particularly the art nouveau paintings of nudes celebrating higher learning. Behind the building, facing the Botanical Gardens, is a statue of Marko Marulić, the 15th-century poet the square is named after.

Botanički vrt
Botanical Gardens

The land for the Botanički vrt (www.hirc.botanic.hr, 9 A.M.–7 P.M. Tues.–Sun. Apr. 1–Nov. 1, free) was given as a gift to the University of Zagreb from the city in 1889 on the condition that its gates would be open to the public free of charge. Over 100 years later, the university still honors the promise and provides a green oasis for locals and visitors to stop and reflect in the center of the city. Open spring through fall, the winding gravel paths pass through nicely maintained flower beds and hundreds of specimens of trees and shrubs. You'll see families out for a stroll, young couples meeting for a chat during their lunch break, or those who just decided to take a greener detour amid the car-packed city streets. Don't miss the beautifully restored **Exhibition Pavilion,** which as recently as 2004 was decaying into ruin.

Tomislavov trg
Tomislav Square

Continuing east from the Botanical Gardens and passing the grand **Regent Esplanade hotel,** a long stretch of green signals your arrival at Tomislavov trg. In this square named for the first Croatian king a statue of the 10th-century Tomislav on horseback greets travelers spilling out of the **Glavni kolodvor** (Main Train Station). At the other end of the square is the yellow-hued neoclassical **Umjetnički**

REGENT ESPLANADE HOTEL

Even if a night at the Regent Esplanade is out of your budget, this landmark of rail travel deserves a stop to admire the marble and mirrored art nouveau lobby and perhaps have a drink in the piano bar before continuing on your tour of the city.

Built in 1925 for Orient Express passengers when Zagreb was a stop on the original Venice-Simplon Orient Express, the hotel has a long list of famous people who enjoyed its glory days – past guests include Josephine Baker, Charles Lindbergh, Sir Laurence Olivier, and Louis Armstrong.

The hotel has been home to many local scandals since its debut, but the hotel saw its darkest days as the last guests disappeared at the beginning of World War II, only to be replaced by hundreds of German officers when the gestapo chose the hotel as its headquarters in the area. The hotel was neglected during its years as part of Yugoslavia but was tastefully renovated in 2004, regaining the same aura it had so long ago.

paviljon (Art Pavilion, Trg kralja Tomislava 22, tel. 01/484-1070, www.umjetnicki-paviljon.hr, 11 A.M.–7 P.M. Mon.–Sat., 10 A.M.–1 P.M. Sun., 20Kn, free Mon.), designed by Viennese architects Ferdinand Fellner and Hermann Helmer. Opened in 1898, it still hosts temporary art exhibits and special functions.

Strossmayerov trg
Strossmayer Square
The **Strossmayerova galerija starih majstora** (Strossmayer Gallery of Old Masters, Trg N. Š. Zrinskog 11, tel. 01/489-5111, www.mdc.hr/strossmayer, 10 A.M.–1 P.M. and 5–7 P.M. Tues., 10 A.M.–1 P.M. Wed.–Sun., 20Kn) is an impressive collection of rich paintings, including works by Tintoretto and El Greco. The most important Croatian work on display is the 11th-century **Bašćanska ploča** (Baška tablet), found on the island of Krk. It is the oldest example of Glagolitic script, the writing of the medieval Croatian church. A statue by Ivan Meštrović of Bishop Juraj Strossmayer, the founder of the Yugoslav Academy for Arts and Sciences, is located behind the building.

Across the street from the Strossmayer Gallery is the **Moderna galerija** (Modern Gallery, Andrije Hebranga 1, tel. 01/492-2371, 10 A.M.–6 P.M. Tues.–Sat., 10 A.M.–1 P.M. Sun., 20Kn), with a nice permanent exhibition entitled *200 Years of Croatian Art*. There are plans to move the museum to Novi Zagreb but work on the building has currently stopped.

Nearby is the **Kabinet grafike** (Graphic Art Gallery, Strossmayerov trg 12, 10 A.M.–6 P.M. Mon.–Sat., admission varies), which holds temporary art exhibitions, some better than others.

Zrinjevac
Possibly the prettiest of Zagreb's squares, lined by giant trees with crackled white and gray bark and surrounded by some of the city's prettiest architecture, Zrinjevac was used as the city's cattle market when it was moved from Trg bana Jelačića in 1830. The square was turned into a park in 1872, the same year the now-massive plane trees were planted, using seeds from Trieste, Italy. It was designed by Milan Lenucij, who went on to design the other squares (Strossmayer, Tomislav, Starčević, Marulić, Mažuranić, Maršal Tito) that form the city's green "horseshoe." Soon Zagreb's elite were constructing mansions along the square; the grand buildings are a great sampling of the city's most prominent architects during the late 19th and early 20th century. In the summer, classical music concerts are often held in the music pavilion and the fountain designed by Bollé still patters with water. However, perhaps the two most interesting features of the square are the **meteorological post,** donated by a local doctor in 1884, where you can check the ever-changing weather, and the **portrait** by Oton Iveković of the square's namesake, Nikola Zrinksi, at No. 20.

While you're there, the **Arheološki muzej** (Archaeological Museum, Trg N. Š. Zrinskog 19, tel. 01/487-3101, www.amz.hr, 10 A.M.–5 P.M. Tues.–Fri., 10 A.M.–1 P.M. Sat.–Sun., 30Kn) is worth a visit. Within an interesting art nouveau building is an impressive collection, from prehistory finds around northern Croatia to the pottery of Greek settlements on the Adriatic coast. The most interesting exhibits are likely the local pottery and jewelry from the Bronze Age, including the famous Vučedol Pigeon, a pouring vessel iconic to the country. There is also an interesting Egyptian exhibit and an exposed mummy, its linen wrappings laden with Etruscan text displayed on the wall beside it. In the summer months, a café serves drinks in the museum's garden.

Trg žrtava fašizma
Victims of Fascism Square

If Zrinjevac is Zagreb's most beautiful square, then Trg žrtava fašizma is its most political. It was christened Trg hrvatskih velikana (Square of Great Croatians) in 1990, but anti-fascist groups protested until the former name was returned. The large circular structure at the square's center, **Dom hrvatskih likovnih umjetnika** (House of Croatian Artists, 11 A.M.–7 P.M. Tues.–Fri., 10 A.M.–2 P.M. Sat.–Sun., admission varies), was completed as an art gallery in 1938, based on a plan by Ivan Meštrović. In 1941 it was turned into a mosque, complete with three minarets, to build Bosnian Muslim support for the NDH, a pro-Nazi puppet state that was in power at the time. In 1945 it became the Museum of People's Liberation; the minarets were pulled down four years later. In 1991 the building was returned to its original purpose and currently houses excellent contemporary art exhibitions.

OUTSIDE THE CENTER
Savska

Though Savska Street is still considered the center by many locals, it's a bit of a trek from the most-frequented sights. If you're at the Mimara Museum, just keep heading south along Savska towards the cylindrical window-filled Cibona

NIKOLA TESLA: A GENIUS FOR INVENTION

Nikola Tesla was born in the village of Smiljan, near Lika, in 1856, the son of a Serbian Orthodox priest. He studied in Karlstadt, Graz, and Prague before beginning his career as an electrical engineer in Hungary. He worked in Paris for the Continental Edison Company, then accepted an offer to work for Thomas Edison in New York in 1884.

His letter of introduction to Thomas Edison, written by a Mr. Batchelor, said, "I know two great men – one is you and the other is this young man."

Tesla and Edison later had a falling out. The reasons for the argument are unclear – some say the issue was money and others claim it was an argument of direct current versus alternating current to power long-distance transmission.

Tesla teamed up with financial support from Westinghouse, ultimately winning the battle of the currents and demonstrating the use of alternating current at the Chicago World's Fair in 1893.

Tesla realized many other achievements, such as designing the first hydroelectric power plant at Niagara Falls in 1895 and inventing the Tesla coil, widely used in radio and television sets, in 1891.

He registered over 700 patents worldwide, though much of his genius did not earn him recognition or money, largely because he did not want to reveal his secrets. For instance, Tesla was the father of long-range radio-wave transmissions but did not demonstrate this feat publicly, allowing Guglielmo Marconi to receive credit first (the U.S. patent office later recognized Tesla as the inventor). He also claimed some far-fetched inventions, like a supposed death ray, that caused many to see him as slightly delusional. Yet when Tesla died in 1943 the FBI confiscated his research, leaving his fans to speculate as to what he was really working on.

DRAŽEN PETROVIĆ, BELOVED BASKETBALL STAR

Croatia is a tiny country full of successful athletes, from Wimbledon-winning tennis stars to Olympic gold medalists. But basketball player Dražen Petrović was in a league of his own. Born in Šibenik in 1964, he grew up playing basketball and soon moved from Zagreb's Cibona team to Spain's Real Madrid and finally to the NBA, at a time when European players were the exception rather than the norm. He played for the Portland Trail Blazers and the New Jersey Nets, where he earned the title of team MVP.

In the summer of 1993, after his best NBA season ever, he traveled to Poland to play with the Croatian National Team in a qualification tournament. He made the fateful decision to drive back to Croatia with friends and was killed on the German autobahn in a high-speed crash on June 7, 1993.

The impact his death had on the country was intense. Seeing a wonderful player and a great person struck down in the prime of his life would have been enough cause for sadness. But the death of a role model at a time when young men were still dying for Croatia's independence on the front lines that summer brought the grief to a much deeper level.

The entire nation mourned the death of Dražen Petrović, with over 200,000 people showing up for his funeral. His tomb at Mirogoj is still visited daily by fans who will not forget him.

Tower. Just before reaching Cibona, you'll find the **Tehnički muzej** (Technical Museum, Savska cesta 18, tel. 01/484-4050, www.mdc.hr/tehnicki, 9 A.M.–5 P.M. Tues.–Fri., 9 A.M.–1 P.M. Sat.–Sun., 10Kn), with an interesting array of machinery, engines, a transportation exhibit, and even a WWII submarine. There's also a planetarium and reconstructions of a mine shaft and Nikola Tesla's laboratory. It's worth a stop if you're a big fan of science or have never made it to the Smithsonian. If the above two don't apply to you and you're short on time, feel free to skip this stop.

The rather unattractive **Cibona Tower** marks the home of Zagreb's basketball team, Cibona, which plays next door in the Dražen Petrović Basketball Center. You can also visit the **Dražen Petrović Memorial Center museum** (Trg Dražen Petrović 2, www.drazenpetrovic.net, tel. 01/484-3146, 10 A.M.–5 P.M. Mon.–Fri., 20Kn) for a peek at the life of one of Croatia's most beloved athletes. On display are his jerseys, awards, honors, and photographs that chronicle his rise in basketball.

If you're in the area, make sure to stop at nearby Karijola for one of their excellent pizzas.

Mirogoj

Though it may seem morbid to spend one's holiday poking around a cemetery, Mirogoj (www.gradskagroblja.hr, dawn–dusk daily, free) is not only considered one of the most beautiful memorial parks in Europe, but it is also a major Zagreb landmark. It looks like a fortress for the dead, with its high brick walls topped by cupolas that appear to guard the graves beyond. Known for its grand architecture (the main building was designed by Bollé) and the famous Croatians buried there, it is also interesting for its example of religious tolerance, with Catholic, Orthodox, Muslim, and Jewish tombstones lying side by side. The place is vast—it is the final home of some 300,000 people—but the most outstanding features are found along the arcades that extend from either side of the main building, with their haunting cast-iron lanterns and magnificent, somber sculptures watching over the graves of Croatia's most famous historical figures. To get there from the center take bus #106 from the cathedral or tram #14 going east toward Mihaljevac and get out at the fourth stop (Gupčeva zvijezda) and walk about five minutes uphill.

Remete

Though Remete is quite close to Mirogoj, if you're lacking a navigation system or have a fear of passing giant city buses on curvy roads about the width of a pencil, the best way to get to this leafy suburb of Zagreb by car is to take Bukovačka cesta from Maksimir Park (by bus, hop on #226 from Mirogoj or #203 from Mirogoj's crematorium; ask the driver to alert you to the stop for Remetska crkva) and follow it to the top of the hill. As you begin your descent, you'll see **Crkva svete Marije** (Church of St. Mary, tel. 01/450-0500, generally open dawn–dusk daily, free), a Gothic structure with a salmon and white Baroque facade. The church is swamped with the faithful on Marian feast days, particularly August 15 (Assumption, locally known as Velika Gospa). The interior of the church is stunning in an eclectic way, with an over-the-top marble altar, whose 15th-century wooden statue of the Madonna is said by many to bestow miracles. But the most beautiful feature of the church is the delicate, fading frescoes by Ivan Ranger, the famed monk whose artwork graces many north Croatian churches.

Entertainment and Events

NIGHTLIFE
Bars

The over-20 set can easily start a bar-hopping tour of the city around Bogovićeva. The nearby **Maraschino** (Margaretska 1, tel. 01/481-2612, 7 A.M.–1 A.M. Sun.–Thurs., 7 A.M.–4 A.M. Fri.–Sat.) is a good place to start; its tables are jammed with a young professional crowd from weekday mornings to weekend nights when the bar amps it up with DJ music. **Bulldog** (Bogovićeva 6, tel. 01/481-7393, 8 A.M.–11 P.M. daily) is a pub around the corner with lots of outdoor seating and a pretty impressive wine selection from its sister bar, **Bulldog XL** (same location, same times). Just down the street, slightly hidden **Škola** (Bogovićeva 7/2, tel. 01/482-8196, www.skolaloungebar.com, 10 A.M.–1 A.M. Mon.–Sat., 11 A.M.–midnight Sun.) fills up its gallery-like space with the beautiful people after dark.

Zagreb has several lounge bars with comfy chaises from which to strike a pose. The most popular downtown spots are the ultra-chic **Khala** (Nova Ves 11, tel. 091/321-1338, 8 A.M.–1 A.M. Sun.–Thurs., 8 A.M.–3 A.M. Fri.–Sat.), which also functions as a wine bar, in Centar Kaptol, and **Hemingway** (Trg maršala Tita 1, tel. 098/980-5000, www.hemingway .hr, 7 A.M.–3 A.M. daily), a lounge bar opposite the HNK (Croatian National Theater). Further afield, **People's** (Hektorovićeva 2, tel. 01/604-0521, www.peoples.hr, noon–1 A.M. Sun.–Wed., noon–3 A.M. Thurs.–Sat.) and **Spoon** (Slavnoska avenija 6, tel. 01/631-0860, www .spoon.hr, 10 A.M.–2 A.M. daily) cater to plenty of in-crowd primp and show. Keep in mind that some of these spots don't get going until at least 11 P.M.

Thirtysomethings who like to pretend they're in their twenties will enjoy **Movie Pub** (Savska 141, tel. 01/605-5045, www.the-movie-pub .com, 7 A.M.–2 A.M. Mon.–Wed., 7 A.M.–3 A.M. Thurs., 7 A.M.–4 A.M. Fri.–Sat., 6 P.M.–2 A.M. Sun.), with lots of beers on tap in a huge space that manages to fill up on weekends and karaoke on Wednesday and Thursday. Literary types should try **Sedmica** (Kačićeva 7A, 7 A.M.–11 P.M. daily), where the patrons, instead of the decor, give the bar an artsy vibe.

Students might want to try **Spunk** (Hrvatske bratske zajednice, tel. 01/615-1528, 7 A.M.–midnight Mon.–Sat., 6 P.M.–midnight Sun.), outside the National University Library, which doesn't look that promising but is still filled with laid-back people and good music with occasional live bands. **Krivi put** (Runjaninova 3, no phone, hours vary), whose name means "wrong way," is a smoky college bar with cheap drinks and a terrace for summer swilling. For something edgier (at least in Zagreb terms),

Dobar Zvuk (Gajeva 18, tel. 01/487-2222, noon–11 P.M. Mon.–Sat.) is a serious rocker bar that doesn't take itself too seriously.

Live Music and Dance Clubs

Close to the center, **Gjuro II** (Medveščak 2, tel. 01/468-3367, www.gjuro2.hr, 9 P.M.–2 A.M. daily) has a small dance floor, theme nights, and a crowd that grows younger as the week goes on. **Kset** (Unska 3, tel. 01/612-9758, www.kset.org, 9 A.M.–3 A.M. Mon.–Fri., 10 P.M.–3 A.M. Sat.) has a cult-like following for its great jazz and DJ mixing. It's popular with students and a slightly alternative older crowd.

Fans of jazz will like **B.P. Club** (Nikole Tesle 7, tel. 01/481-4444, www.bpclub.hr, 10 A.M.–2 A.M. daily) or **Sax!** (Palmotićeva 22, tel. 01/487-2836, www.sax-zg.hr, 9 A.M.–4 A.M. daily); Sax! hosts blues and rock bands as well. Both places have a good drinks menu and lots of places to sit if you're not into shaking your thing. **Tvornica** (Pavla Šubića 2, tel. 01/777-8673, www.tvornica-kulture. hr, 9 A.M.–10 P.M. Mon.–Fri., 10 P.M.–4 A.M. Sat. and during events) is a quirky club in a large space near the bus station. The entertainment varies widely from gypsy tunes to rock to fashion shows, but the bands are usually high quality. Call or check the website to find out what's on before heading out. For really late nights, head to **Ritz Cabaret** (Petrinjska 4, tel. 099/660-7182, 10 P.M.–6 A.M. Wed.–Sat.). Full of luxe vibe, it caters to a thirty-something, slightly flashier crowd with VIP tables available by reservation.

If you're in the mood for some club hopping, make a beeline to Jarun, where **Aquarius** (Matija Ljubeka bb, Jarun, tel. 01/364-0321, www.aquarius.hr, 9 A.M.–6 A.M. Thurs.–Sat.) brings in big-name DJs and local stars and **Piranha Bar** (Jarunska obala, tel. 091/462-9234, www.piranha.com.hr, 8 A.M.–2 A.M. Wed.–Thurs., 8 A.M.–4 A.M. Fri.–Sat., 8 A.M.–midnight Sun.–Tues.) swarms with well-dressed kids.

Closer to the center, **Boogaloo** (Ulica Grada Vukovara 68, tel. 01/631-3021, www.boogaloo .hr, 8 P.M.–4 A.M. Tues.–Sun.) is an all-purpose dance club with popular tunes and salsa nights. And if your feet need a break from boogying, Boogaloo has a lounge room with comfy couches and a bar for refreshments.

THE ARTS
Theaters and Dance

Break out the opera glasses at **Hrvatsko Narodno Kazalište** (Croatian National Theater, Trg maršala Tita 15, tel. 01/482-8532, www .hnk.hr, box office 10 A.M.–7:30 P.M. Mon.–Fri., 10 A.M.–1 P.M. Sat. and 1.5 hours before performances), also known as **HNK,** where drama and ballet are staged in a beautiful gilt and frescoed atmosphere. **Exit** (Ilica 208, tel. 01/370-4120, box office 4:30–8 P.M. Tues.–Sat.) is a small studio theater with some good contemporary plays. Both theaters stage performances almost exclusively in Croatian.

Opera and Classical Music

The **HNK** (Croatian National Theater, Trg maršala Tita 15, tel. 01/482-8532, www.hnk .hr, box office 10 A.M.–7:30 P.M. Mon.–Fri., 10 A.M.–1 P.M. Sat. and 1.5 hours before performances) has opera performances, while **Koncertna dvorana Vatroslav Lisinski** (Vatroslav Lisinski Concert Hall, Trg Stjepana Radića 4, tel. 01/612-1167, www.lisinski.hr, call or go online for a list of concerts) brings in big names like Cesaria Evora on occasion as well as regular performances by the Zagreb Philharmonic and the Croatian Radio Symphony Orchestra.

Film

The best thing about seeing a movie in Croatia is that they are all in the original language, save for some animated features, with Croatian subtitles. Zagreb has three big multiplexes but the two located closest to the center are **Continental Movieplex** (Nova Ves 17, Centar Kaptol, tel. 01/486-0777, www.movie plex.hr), at the end of Tkalčićeva in Centar Kaptol, and **Cinestar** (Branimirova 29, tel. 01/468-6600, www.blitz-cinestar.hr), in Branimir Centar near the Sheraton. You can often catch a show in town at the old **Europa** (Varšavska 3, tel. 01/487-2888, www.kino europa.hr) on Cvjetni trg, which screens mostly art-house films.

FESTIVALS AND EVENTS
Animafest: World Festival of Animated Films
This 30-year-old festival, now held on a yearly basis, screens excellent feature-length and short animated films from international filmmakers, including categories for student films and short films made for the Internet (late May–early June, www.animafest.hr).

International Folklore Festival
Teeming with colorful costumes from all over Croatia, Trg bana Jelačića comes alive with dance and music performances and stands selling hundreds of handicrafts during the International Folklore Festival (last weekend in July, www.msf.hr).

Zagreb Summer Festival
Though much of Zagreb empties out during summer, the Zagreb Summer Festival (mid-July–mid-Aug.), featuring orchestral and chamber music, still plays to good-sized crowds who come to enjoy the wide range of international performers.

International Festival of Puppet Theater
Featuring wonderful puppet productions from all over central and eastern Europe, the International Festival of Puppet Theater (late Aug.) is a must-see for kids, and has a few shows aimed at adults as well.

Zagreb Film Festival
A relatively new film festival that is already gaining in importance, the Zagreb Film Festival (Oct., www.zagrebfilmfestival.com) screens some 70 films from around the world in three Zagreb cinemas.

Shopping

ANTIQUES AND FLEA MARKETS
Hit **Britanski trg**'s antiques market (8 A.M.–2 P.M. Sun.) for old postcards from the region, interesting jewelry, and various knickknacks from another era. You'll find some of the same things for less than half the price at **Hrelić** (Sunday morning, pros arrive at 7 A.M. or earlier), the city's flea market in Novi Zagreb, fittingly located near the trash dump where three quarters of the stuff should have gone before it was fished out for sale by the vendors. However, if you're willing to peruse the items on blankets strewn about the ground, you'll probably find something worth taking home. Common finds are intricately carved brass Turkish coffee grinders and long wooden bowls used for kneading dough.

SOUVENIRS
Though some items are a bit overpriced, **Bakina kuća** (Strossmayerov trg 7, tel. 01/384-3805, www.bakina-kuca.hr, 8 A.M.–9 P.M. Mon.–Fri., 9 A.M.–5 P.M. Sat.) is a one-stop shop for sweets, *rakija,* souvenirs, and herb-based cosmetics.

For a practical item that will also remind you of your trip to Zagreb, **Cerovečki Kišobrani** (Ilica 49, tel. 01/484-7417, www.kisobrani-cerovecki .hr, 8:30 A.M.–8 P.M. Mon.–Fri., 8:30 A.M.–3 P.M. Sat.) sells the same red handmade Šestine umbrellas that cover Dolac market stands.

Dolac itself is a spot to pick up embroidered tablecloths and other handicrafts in the stalls at the back of the market, near the fish section and up the stairs.

For kids, **Hlapićev dućan** (Katančićeva 3, tel. 01/481-7224, www.hlapic.net, 9 A.M.–7:30 P.M. Mon.–Fri., 9 A.M.–5 P.M. Sat., also in Centar Kaptol shopping center) stocks toys and knickknacks from the well-loved Croatian book character Hlapić, created by author Ivana Brlić Mažuranić.

FOOD AND WINE

There are lots of places to get your gourmet on in Zagreb. Among the best are **Pršut Galerija** (Vlaška 7, tel. 01/481-6129, 9 A.M.–8 P.M. Mon.–Fri., 9 A.M.–2 P.M. Sat.), selling all sorts of home-cured ham, similar to Serrano ham, and **Vinoteka Bornstein** (Kaptol 19, www.bornstein.hr, 9 A.M.–7 P.M. Mon.–Fri., 2–7 P.M. Sat.), a great wine shop in a dark Kaptol (the neighborhood, not the mall) cellar, with a strong showing of Croatian wines. The owners are also local emissaries for all things Istrian and are a great source of info if you're headed that way.

Franja (Vlaška 62, tel. 01/455-6391, www.franja.hr, 7 A.M.–8:30 P.M. Mon.–Fri., 7 A.M.–5 P.M. Sat.) sells the local Franck brand of coffees, and while real coffee connoisseurs will not be impressed, it makes a decent souvenir.

If you're dying for real tea, which is a rare find in Croatia, stop by **Kuća Zelenog Čaja** (Ilica 14, tel. 01/483-0667, www.kuca zelenogcaja.com, 9 A.M.–8 P.M. Mon.–Fri., 9 A.M.–3 P.M. Sat.) for a good selection of loose-leaf tea.

FASHION

Since the tie was actually invented by Croats, a necktie is a nice souvenir from the country. **Croata** (Ilica 5—inside the Oktogon, tel. 01/481-2726, www.croata.hr, 8 A.M.–8 P.M. Mon.–Fri., 8 A.M.–3 P.M. Sat.), Croatia's "official" tie store, has a good selection and purchases are packaged with a little history of the cravat.

Zagreb is the home of some interesting and unique fashion design. A couple of stores to check out are **Boudoir** (Radićeva 25, tel. 01/481-3464, www.boudoir.hr, 1–8 P.M. Mon.–Fri., 9 A.M.–3 P.M. Sat.) and **Stolnik** (Vlaška 58, tel. 01/461-7000, www .moda-stolnik.com, 9 A.M.–8 P.M. Mon.–Fri., 9 A.M.–3 P.M. Sat.). For jewelry, head to Tkalčićeva, where **Lazer Rok Lumezi** (Tkalčićeva 53, tel. 01/481-4030, www .nakit-lumezi.hr, 10 A.M.–8 P.M. Mon.–Fri., 10 A.M.–3 P.M. Sun.) designs unique pieces that will surely get you noticed. If you're

shopping for bargains at Dolac Market

not looking for wearable art so much as some fun jewelry to take home to friends, **Lapis** (Tkalčićeva 32, tel. 01/481-0255, 10 A.M.–6 P.M. Mon.–Fri., 10 A.M.–2 P.M. Sat.) has colorful, wiggly pieces that make great presents.

ENGLISH-LANGUAGE BOOKSTORES

Algoritam (Gajeva 1, tel. 01/481-8672, www.algoritam.hr, 8:30 A.M.–9 P.M. Mon.–Fri., 8:30 A.M.–3 P.M. Sat.) has several stores throughout Zagreb, but the main location at Gajeva near Trg bana Jelačića has the best selection of books, DVDs, and computer games. They also carry a range of foreign newspapers and weekly magazines, though sometimes a day or two behind (or a week or two in the case of gossip rags), if you're itching to read the *New York Times*. If Algoritam doesn't have what you're looking for, **Profil Megastore** (Bogovićeva 7, tel. 01/487-7300, www.megastore-profil.hr, 9 A.M.–10 P.M. Mon.–Sat.) is just a short walk away and has an in-store café and a large selection of stationery supplies. If you're traveling around Europe, it's worth checking out the English bookstores in Zagreb as they offer an even better selection than you'll find in large cities like Frankfurt.

Sports and Recreation

CYCLING

Cycling on Zagreb's city streets, particularly on weekdays, is not recommended. Though the city has installed some designated bike lanes in the past few years, you'll usually find quite a few cars parked along them and drivers aren't used to sharing the narrow roads with cyclists. If you'd like to bike in parks like Maksimir and Jarun, you can rent a bicycle from the **Fumić Bicycle Shop** (in Jarun near *ulaz petrine*— Petrina entrance, tel. 01/466-4233, www .fumic-bicikli.hr) for 80Kn per day or 20Kn per hour. Mr. Fumić also organizes bike rides from his shop in Jarun, starting at 9 A.M. on good-weather Sundays. Rides traverse the surroundings of Zagreb and are 80 to 120 kilometers long.

SKIING

Sljeme has decent skiing for beginners or for those that just want to keep their skills from getting too rusty. During the ski season more info can be found by calling 01/455-5827 and online at www.sljeme.hr. Local outfitter **Sport4You** (Ilica 213, tel. 01/377-0150, www.sport4you.hr, 9 A.M.–5 P.M. Mon.–Fri., daily equipment rental approx. 140Kn) offers ski lessons (with English-speaking instructors) and equipment rental on Sljeme. Call ahead to make arrangements.

PARKS
Maksimir

While it may not be a must-see, Maksimir (tram nos. 11 or 12, direction Dubrava, dawn–sunset daily) should make the top of your list if you have any extra time in Zagreb for a leisurely stroll. Located about a five-minute drive east of Trg bana Jelačića, the park was founded in 1774 by the Bishop Maximilian Vrhovac and was originally constructed in the Baroque French style, with three radial paths that still exist today. Subsequent Bishops Aleksandar Alagović and Juraj Haulik expanded on his design, incorporating many English features. Despite its wide, straight promenade, there are dozens of smaller forested paths where you can lose an afternoon. The park is also home to the small but well-thought-out **Zagreb Zoo** (tel. 01/230-2198, www.zoo.hr, 9 A.M.–8 P.M. daily May–Sept., 9 A.M.–4 P.M. daily Oct.–Apr., 20Kn), and children will appreciate the **Echo Pavilion,** built in 1840, located near the zoo's entrance. When you're done with exercise, join a crowd of locals at the **Gazebo** (no phone, hours vary), rising above the end of the main promenade, for a peaceful view of the park and a little liquid refreshment.

Jarun

A 15-minute drive west from the center (direction Samobor) will take you to Jarun (tel. 01/303-1888, www.jarun.hr, from Trg bana Jelačića take tram #17 to Jarun), a popular spot for *zagrebčani* to while away a weekend afternoon. With two lakes and six different islands, the 585-acre park complex, built for the 1987 University Games, has a variety of recreational and water sports available. There is also a nice network of flat paths, perfect for in-line skating (rent by the hour from the Fumić Bicycle Shop, described earlier) or biking around the lakes. For those who like to fish, the lake is well stocked and a daily fishing license is available. But Jarun is perhaps best known as a nightlife destination for Zagreb's younger crowd, with a strip of bars and clubs lining the lakeshores—perfect for party-hopping types.

Bundek

A lake just off the banks of the Sava River in Novi Zagreb, Bundek (from Trg bana Jelačića take tram nos. 14 or 6, direction Novi Zagreb, to stop Sopot, from there a short walk) experienced a rebirth in 2006. The area, once ridden with unsavory types lurking about and the litter they left, is now a clean, busy, family-friendly park with impeccably maintained flower beds, great paths, one of the nicest playgrounds in Zagreb, and a pebbly beach serviced by a few waterside cafés. If it's a hot day, it's a pleasant place to take a dip.

◖ Mount Medvednica

With its densely forested slopes and endless trails, an excursion to the Mount Medvednica range is great almost any time of the year. The range stretches along the northern side of town, from the western suburbs to slightly east of the center; its highest peak and most developed mountain, **Sljeme,** is reached by driving along Ribnjak out of the center until you see signs pointing right to Sljeme via Gračanska cesta. By tram, take #14 to Mihaljevac and then #15 to the last stop at Dolje. From there it's a short 10-minute walk to the cable car station (*žičara,*

© SHANN FOUNTAIN ČULO

Sljeme, a popular outing from Zagreb

A DAY ON SLJEME

Winding your way up Mount Sljeme on a fall day, leaves trickle onto the pavement as you pass hikers and cyclists all basking in the flickering light that filters through the forest of beech. Fall – or any other time of year for that matter – is perfect for enjoying one of Zagreb's traditional weekend outings. Since the 19th century, *purgeri* (the local name for people from Zagreb) have been visiting the mountain for rest and relaxation.

You can choose the easiest way to climb towards the summit of the highest peak of the Medvenica mountain range – a car. For those more athletically inclined, the steep hike or bike ride will still challenge your hamstrings. And if you're not afraid of heights, the cable car offers panoramic views of the golden treetops.

It is difficult to imagine you're only minutes from the city center, with its crowded cafés filled with designer-clad individuals wielding the latest models of mobile phones. Here you can enjoy a moment's quiet reflection, appreciate the local flora and fauna, and take a time out from the busyness of city life.

However, the most charming attractions of Sljeme are the many stops where you can replenish your reserves for the return journey. Many of these alpine-style huts, with names like Željeznički Dom (Railway Home) or Dom Grafičar (Home Grafičar), were built by state-run companies during communism for their workers to enjoy. My favorite place to visit is **Puntijarka** (9 A.M.-7 P.M. daily except major holidays), the restaurant of the Mountaineering Society. Old and young gather to share bowls of beans (locally called *grah*) and

mugs of beer at dozens of picnic tables outfitted with holes to accommodate walking sticks. The lively sounds of the musicians' accordion and *tambura* accompany the crowd's appetite. Beginning outside, a long line forms to sample simple but enchanting entrées including roast chicken, sausages, and walnut cake.

On a crisp day you'll see young and old, biking enthusiasts sharing tables with children in strollers, though it's the established set that draws the most attention. Old men with coordinating scarves, alpine hats, and pants similar to jodhpurs are out in large groups – they take their hiking seriously. Feel free to sit down at any table with a free spot and start a conversation over some mulled wine.

For those desiring to experience times past, an outing to a place like Puntijarka is certainly not to be missed. The spirit of community and equality that enthuses the cool air today is a stark contrast to the new Eastern Europe, where the middle class is a minority. In some ways it reminds one of the intriguing and romantic Croatia at the beginning of its independence. Gone are the threadbare art deco booths of Zagreb's Theater Café and the communist white shoes of its waitresses. The blue trams that once circled the town in uniformity now zip past advertising movies and soft drinks. Gray, crackling facades are being colorfully restored one by one to their Austro-Hungarian glory. Many things are changing, most for the better, in the new, more Western Croatia. Yet this sense of society, of the communing of the people, may be one remnant of the old regime worth preserving.

8 A.M.–8 P.M. on the hour daily, 11Kn one-way, 17Kn round-trip) or about a three-hour trek to the top. In nice weather, a hike or an outdoor lunch near the top are reasons enough to go. In snowy weather, there are some bunny slopes and spots for sledding to keep you occupied.

Four kilometers southwest of Sljeme is the 13th-century **Medvedgrad** fortress. Built to defend against Tatar attacks, it was abandoned

in 1571 and remained neglected until it was rebuilt in the 1990s. An **Oltar domovine** (Homeland Altar) with an eternal flame surrounded by sculptures in the form of tears looks somewhat out of place in its medieval surroundings, though it's an important photo stop for Croatian politicians. There are some great views from here and a restaurant serving typical dishes. From Sljeme, follow the marked paths from the Tomislavov dom hotel or take about an hour's walk from Šeštine church.

SPECTATOR SPORTS
Soccer

The **Maksimir stadium** (Maksimirska 128, tel. 01/484-3769) across from Maksimir Park is home to games of the Croatian National Team and the local Dinamo, whose fans deck out in the team's signature blue for loud and exciting matches. The main season is August to May (with a break in January and February) and tickets run a cheap average of 30Kn and can be purchased from kiosks near the entrance.

Basketball

Cibona draws pretty decent-sized crowds to watch quality basketball at the **Dražen Petrović Basketball Center** (Savska cesta 30, tel. 01/484-3333, around 30Kn at the door) from September through April.

WELLNESS CENTERS

Zagreb is full of spas and wellness centers, though none offer out-of-the-ordinary services. **Wellness Centar Coner** (Trpimirova 2, tel. 01/539-0555, www.coner.hr, 6:30 A.M.–10:30 P.M. Mon.–Sat., 9 A.M.–10:30 P.M. Sun.), in the Sheraton, offers a full range of massages, facials, and pedicures as well as an indoor pool, fitness center, and sauna. Just across from Centar Kaptol are some of the best facials in the city at **Murad** (Medvedgradska 1C, tel. 01/466-6473, call for hours), run by a doctor of dermatology.

Accommodations

Some of the cheapest accommodation can be found by staying in a private home or renting a short-term apartment. Several companies offer these sorts of accommodation, starting from 150Kn; try **NEST** (Boškovićeva 7A, tel. 01/487-3225, nest@nest.hr, www.nest.hr), **InZagreb** (Remetinečka 13, tel. 091/652-3201, info@inzagreb.com, www.inzagreb.com), or **Evistas** (Augusta Šenoe 28, tel. 01/483-9554, evistas@zg.t-com.hr, www.evistas.hr).

Since Gornji Grad is currently devoid of formal accommodations, you'll need to sift through these agency's offerings to find rooms or apartments located in the oldest part of Zagreb. Be aware that not all of these apartments have air-conditioning—definitely a consideration in the height of summer. Otherwise, hotels and hostels are found in the lower part of town, with most being quite expensive for what you get in return.

TRG BANA JELAČIĆA AND KAPTOL
Under 700Kn

The **Fulir Hostel** (Radićeva 3A, tel. 01/483-0882, fulir@fulir-hostel.com, www.fulir-hostel.com, 139Kn per person) opened in 2006, just off Trg bana Jelačića in a quiet location with multi-bed rooms.

700–1,400Kn

Though the rooms are a bit worn, the location of **Hotel Dubrovnik** (Gajeva 1, tel. 01/487-3555, reservations@hotel-dubrovnik.hr, www.hotel-dubrovnik.hr, 1,066Kn d., including breakfast) can't be beat. It's right on Trg bana Jelačića and has a friendly staff and a decent buffet breakfast.

DONJI GRAD
Under 700Kn

If you don't mind staying in a private home, **Ilički Plac Private Accommodation** (Britanski trg 1, tel. 098/419-231, ilicki@email.t-com.hr, www.ilicki.com, 426Kn d.) is a great value, with the added bonus of getting a feel for living in one of the center's high-ceilinged apartments. It's also conveniently located on Britanski trg for fans of Sunday-morning antiques-hunting.

Billed as Zagreb's first design hotel, the

modern **Arcotel** (Branimirova 29, tel. 01/469-6000, allegro@arcotel.at, www.arcotel.at, 575Kn d.) is slightly out of the way, but has good jazz in the lobby bar two nights a week. The **Best Western Hotel Astoria** (Petrinjska 71, tel. 01/480-8900, info@hotelastoria.hr, www.bestwestern.com, 568Kn d., including breakfast) is a fairly new hotel in a convenient location to the tram station and within a 10-minute walk of Trg bana Jelačića.

700–1,400Kn

The historic **Palace** (Strossmayerov trg 10, tel. 01/489-9600, palace@palace.hr, www.palace.hr, 1,024Kn d., including breakfast) has Secession charm, in particular the art nouveau lobby, and a super location—however ask for a renovated room if you want to get your money's worth.

Though the comfy **Sheraton** (Kneza Borne 2, tel. 01/455-3535, www.sheraton.com, 1,150Kn d., including breakfast) is a favorite with the business set and has a great spa and decent indoor pool, if you're looking for luxury, skip it (it's out of the way for the price and notorious with taxi drivers looking to rip off unsuspecting foreigners).

Instead, stay in the (**Regent Esplanade** (Mihanovićeva 1, tel. 01/456-6666, info .zagreb@rezidorregent.com, www.regenthotels. com, 1,074Kn d., including breakfast), built for Orient Express passengers in 1925 and fastidiously renovated.

OUTSIDE THE CENTER
Under 700Kn

The **Hostel Lika** (Pašmanska 17, tel. 01/618-5375, info@hostel-lika.com, www.hostel-lika .com, 96Kn per person) looks depressing from the outside but consistently gets good reviews from backpackers.

The **Ravnice Youth Hostel** (Ravnice 38D, tel. 01/233-2325, www.ravnice-youth-hostel .hr, 121Kn per person), near Maksimir Park, is a bit more secluded but a slightly more upscale version of the traditional hostel.

Leave the center to find the best deals on accommodation. The **Hotel Fala** (Trnjanske ledine 18, tel. 01/611-1062, hotel-fala@hotel-fala.zg.hr, www.hotel-fala.zg.hr, 476Kn d., including breakfast) has basic but clean rooms about a half-hour walk from the center.

Food

TRG BANA JELAČIĆA AND KAPTOL
Cafés and Desserts

(**Torte i to** (Nova Ves 11, tel. 01/486-0691, www.torte-i-to.hr, 9 A.M.–11 P.M. daily, 25Kn) is a bit hard to find, tucked in the back of the 1st floor of Centar Kaptol shopping mall, but it's worth the effort to sample the best cakes in Zagreb. *Torta ledeni vjetar* (cold wind cake) is the unofficial house specialty, though the cheesecake is stupendous too.

Behind a gingerbread facade at **Ivica i Marica** (Tkalčićeva 70, tel. 01/481-7321, www .ivicaimarica.com, 10 A.M.–11 P.M. Mon.–Fri., 9 A.M.–11 P.M. Sat., 11 A.M.–8 P.M. Sun., 20Kn) you might be expecting to find a cheesy tourist locale, but you'd be wrong. Locals love the place for their healthy no-preservative cakes and cookies and the nonsmoking atmosphere.

Fine Dining

Unless you eat dinner really early, you'll need to make reservations for **Takenoko** (Nova Ves 17, tel. 01/486-0530, www.takenoko.hr, 11 A.M.–1 A.M. Mon.–Sat., 11 A.M.–6 P.M. Sun., 85Kn), Zagreb's first sushi restaurant and in-crowd favorite. The sashimi and wok bowls are quite nice, but the American-style rolls are a bit overpriced for what you get. No reservation? Try snagging a seat at the bar.

If you can't figure out exactly what you're in the mood for, **Mano** (Medvedgradska 2, tel. 01/466-9432, www.mano.hr, noon–11 P.M. Mon.–Sat., 100Kn) can probably help you out with a menu featuring dishes influenced by Indian, Asian, Mediterranean, and local cuisines. Some of the dishes try just a bit too hard (and rarely impress) but the atmosphere—a candlelit brick-walled warehouse space—is one of the best in the city.

International

If your craving is for curry, pop by **Maharadža** (Opatovina 19, tel. 01/481-4305, noon–11 P.M. Tues.–Sun., 60Kn), an intimate and pretty good, if not very busy, Indian restaurant.

Once the sun goes down, **Plató** (Nova Ves 17, tel. 01/486-0721, 9 A.M.–1 A.M. Mon.–Sat., 60Kn) becomes a hip lounge space for throwing back cocktails. But if you're looking for breakfast, lunch, or dinner, the light-filled space (perfect for dining on a rainy day) has a good menu inspired by varied cuisines. From shrimp tempura to a club burger, it's all good, particularly the hot chocolate cake with vanilla-bean ice cream.

Local Cuisine

I've seen travelers walk away from the restaurant at **Ivica i Marica** (Tkalčićeva 70, tel. 01/481-7321, www.ivicaimarica.com, 10 A.M.–11 P.M. Mon.–Fri., 9 A.M.–11 P.M. Sat., 11 A.M.–8 P.M. Sun., 70Kn), located beside its excellent café, afraid the traditionally costumed waitstaff and homespun flavor of the wood-beamed restaurant spell tourist trap. But it's actually a favorite of locals too, with well-prepared regional dishes and quite a few vegetarian options.

Technically, it's a slight detour from Kaptol to ◖ **Kod Žaca** (Griskovićeva 4, tel. 01/468-4178, noon–midnight daily, 90Kn), or Žac's Place, but it's not far off the beaten tourist track. Look closely or you'll miss the small plaque that marks this little gem. Ask the owner, Žac, for his recommendation; if you're lucky you can try the duck raised by his mother. The atmosphere is traditional and the flavor is local, but the international clientele includes heavy-hitting business executives and local celebrities.

Quick Bites

City Kebab (Tkalčićeva 27, 10 A.M.–11 P.M. daily, 20Kn) is the definition of "hole in the wall." This miniscule place is where to go for *doner* kebabs, mystery meat sandwiches that taste really good (the level of satisfaction tends to escalate with your level of drunkenness) and are slightly addictive.

Mangiare (Tkalčićeva 29, tel. 01/482-8173, 10 A.M.–11 P.M. Mon.–Sat., 1–11 P.M. Sun., 40Kn) is a cozy little pizzeria with a pleasant atmosphere and tasty brick oven–baked pizzas.

You'll find **Rubelj** (Dolac Market, 10 A.M.–midnight daily, 35Kn) restaurants all over Zagreb. Rubelj is almost synonymous with *čevapčići*, slightly spicy ground-meat rolls eaten with doughy bread. They also have a good selection of pizzas and other grilled meat dishes. The location next to Dolac has a large terrace for eating on the run in nicer weather.

For a really quick (and cheap) snack, pick up a *burek* from one of the bakeries lining **Dolac Market** or a piece of fresh fruit and a small bag of nuts from one of the vendors.

A much-needed addition to Zagreb's fast-food scene, **Daily Fresh** (Frane Petrića 1, at the corner with Ilica, tel. 01/639-7111, 8 A.M.–11 P.M. daily, 35Kn) makes sandwiches and salads as well as to-go coffee (a relatively new concept in town). The chain has several locations across town but the most convenient for tourists is located steps from Trg bana Jelačića on Ilica.

GORNJI GRAD
Fine Dining

Built into the old city walls just steps from the Kamenita vrata, **Noće** (Kamenita 5, tel. 01/485-1394, www.noce.hr, noon–midnight Mon.–Thurs., noon–1 A.M. Fri.–Sat., 85Kn) serves up Italian-inspired dishes like homemade green ravioli with lobster crème, a good grilled chicken salad, and lots of yummy crostini and bruschetta options for a young, hip crowd.

Though actually a short drive out of the upper town, ◖ **Bistro Apetit** (Jurjevska 65a, 01/467-7335, 9 A.M.–midnight Tues.–Sun., 90Kn) is a chic slow-food restaurant in a modern light-filled space. Don't let the description scare you off, though. The place is elegant but

a place to wet your whistle in Gornji Grad

© SHANN FOUNTAIN ČULO

unpretentious, and the out-of-this-world food is worth the not-outrageous prices.

Local Cuisine

Pod grićkim topom (Zakmardijeve stube 5, tel. 01/483-3607, 11 A.M.–midnight Mon.–Sat., 150Kn) serves up slightly overpriced Croatian comfort food just steps from Kula Lotrščak, or Burglars' Tower. The terrace is the best spot to dine in nice weather, with a great view of the lower town. The restaurant has been heavily covered in guides and articles, though, so if you're looking for an insider find, this is not it.

It seems apropos that **Stara Vura** (Opatička 20, tel. 01/485-1368, www.stara-vura.hr, noon–midnight Mon.–Sat., 110Kn) shares an entrance with the Zagreb City Museum. The ancient brick domed interior is like a medieval cellar. The dishes are good, though a bit expensive. You'll get the most for your money if you dine here on Friday or Saturday night when a band of Gypsy *tambura* musicians descend on the place, singing lively folk music.

Didov san (Mletačka ulica 11, tel. 01/485-1154, www.konoba-didovsan.com, 10 A.M.–11 P.M. Mon.–Sat., 10 A.M.–10 P.M. Sun., 95Kn) is filled with regional touches, from the dark-wood and embroidered-tablecloth interior to the food. Specializing in Dalmatian cuisine, there's a good selection of fish dishes and even a couple of escargot options for gourmands. The *janjetina ispod peke* (oven-baked lamb) is worth ordering ahead.

Quick Bites

Claiming to be the oldest café in Zagreb, **Pod Starim Krovovima** (Basaričekova 9, tel. 01/485-1342, 8 A.M.–11 P.M. Mon.–Sat., 18Kn) has been serving guests since 1830. Today the space is bright and friendly with a new exhibition of art on its walls every month. Have a beer and snack on *hrenovke* (hot dogs), *kranske* (a type of regional sausage), or a sandwich.

DONJI GRAD
Cafés and Desserts

If you're window shopping on Ilica, stop at **Vincek** (Ilica 18, tel. 01/483-3612, www.vincek.com.hr, 8:30 A.M.–11 P.M. Mon.–Sat., 20Kn), a long-running Zagreb institution, for cakes, cookies, and ice cream.

Crepes filled with banana and vanilla sauce might just be the closest thing to dessert perfection at **❰ Crepes de Paris** (Oktogon br. 5, tel. 091/400-1033, 7 A.M.–11 P.M. Sun.–Thurs., 7 A.M.–midnight Fri.–Sat., 18Kn) on Cvjetni trg (Flower Square). The little stand offers a lot of other options for filling *palačinke,* the local name for crepes, like chocolate sauce, nutella, nuts, and fruity jams.

Pass on the cakes at **❰ Millennium** (Bogovićeva 7, tel. 01/481-0850, 8 A.M.–11 P.M. daily, 8Kn). They're good, but they can't come close to the creamy gelato-style ice cream in dozens of flavors.

Fine Dining

While it might be a slight stretch to say the cuisine of **❰ Škola** (Bogovićeva 7/2, tel. 01/482-8196, www.skolaloungebar.com, 10 A.M.–1 A.M. Mon.–Sat., 11 A.M.–midnight

ZAGREB'S SOLAR SYSTEM

© SHANN FOUNTAIN ČULO

Prizemljeno Sunce, the center of Zagreb's solar system

When you're having a drink or snack on Bogovićeva, make sure to look out for the large golden ball, actually a sculpture by Ivan Kožarić, titled *Prizemljeno Sunce* (Grounded Sun). First exhibited in 1971, the ball, almost seven feet in diameter, changed location several times before it landed in one of Zagreb's busiest pedestrian streets in 1994. In the early years of the new millennium, Dawor Preis began placing models of the planets of the solar system around town with little or no publicity. Even most locals aren't aware of his installation, entitled *Nine Views*. The size and distance of all the models are in scale with the "sun," the *Prizemljeno Sunce*. If you'd like to discover all nine models, someone has tracked them down at www.phy.hr/~mpozek/planeti.

Sun., 70Kn) classifies as gourmet, the restaurant gets bumped into this category if only on the basis of bang for the buck. With excellent food, attentive waitstaff, and an ultra-modern gallery-style space, this lounge bar/disco by night, restaurant by day and evening is one of the city's most overlooked eateries. A small black sign near the Millennium ice-cream parlor will lead you behind the Profil Megastore in a building that used to be a school, hence the name.

International

Located in a dark but swank space at the bottom of Branimir Centar, **Opium** (Branimirova 29, tel. 01/461-5679, www.opium.hr, 11 A.M.–midnight Mon.–Sat., 11 A.M.–11:30 P.M. Sun., 70Kn) offers food that won't blow you away, but if you're in the mood for Thai it's your only option.

If you ask locals for their favorite Chinese restaurant, they'll almost always say **Asia** (Šenoina 1, tel. 01/484-1218, noon–midnight daily, 70Kn). It so happens several Chinese nationals in Zagreb say the same. If you're a big fan of Mandarin cuisine, feel free to order dishes not listed on the menu.

Local Cuisine

The interior of **Purger** (Petrinjska 33, tel. 01/481-0713, 7 A.M.–11 P.M. Mon.–Sat., 50Kn) is pretty basic, but the hearty local dishes are well prepared and well priced. There's also a terrace.

At **Pivnica Palmeta** (Palmotićeva 5, tel. 091/579-4120, 10 A.M.–10 P.M. Mon.–Sat., 55Kn), a block's walk from Trg bana Jelačića, near the Jurišićeva post office, the food is hearty and good and the service is informal and cheeky. Sophisticated it is not, but it's hard to knock its value for money and the '70s communist vibe, disappearing fast in a city bent on keeping up with the rest of Europe. You'll leave with your stomach full and your wallet not much lighter.

For a more upmarket local experience, **Stari Fijaker** (Mesnička 6, tel. 01/483-3829, www.starifijaker.hr, 7 A.M.–11 P.M. daily, 85Kn) has Croatian staples like *punjeni paprika* (stuffed peppers) and *sarma* (pork and rice wrapped in cabbage leaves).

Quick Bites

Donji Grad is filled with good options for fast food. If late nights and panini-style sandwiches are your thing, **Pinguin** (Nikole Tesle 7, tel. 01/481-1446, 8:30 A.M.–5 A.M. Mon.–Sat., 7 P.M.–3 A.M. Sun., 18Kn) will satisfy, with huge hot circles of bread filled with basic toppings like ham, cheese, and fresh tomatoes.

Ham Ham (Varšavska 8, tel. 01/483-0483, 9 A.M.–11 P.M. Mon.–Sat., 35Kn) was serving burgers to locals long before McDonald's came to town. The restaurant, a bit hidden at the back of a passage, was recently renovated and looks more like a chic lounge than a fast-food place. Burgers with Ham Ham's special sauce are served on china plates and you get a real glass with your drink. Ham Ham is also the best place to get a good, reasonable breakfast or brunch, with eggs any style, bacon, and a side of fresh tomatoes.

Flores (Frane Petrića 1, tel. 01/481-9272, 7 A.M.–11 P.M. Mon.–Sat., 9 A.M.–11 P.M. Sun.,

30Kn) is a chic café that also sells a few good sandwiches for a meal on the go.

Less than a block from Trg bana Jelačića is **Mimiće** (Jurišićeva 21, 8 A.M.–9 P.M. Mon.–Fri., 8 A.M.–5 P.M. Sat., 20Kn), a fish restaurant that is low on atmosphere but high in character. If you don't mind standing up, this Croatian version of fish-and-chips is a great value.

For those who'd like a chair with their fish, **Gostionica Tip-Top** (Gundulićeva 18, tel. 01/483-0349, 7 A.M.–10 P.M. daily, 40Kn), locally known as Blato (mud), serves excellent and very well-priced fish dishes. The unpretentious *kavana* was very popular with Croatian artists and has immortalized the poet Tin Ujević on the front window. The cuisine comes from the island of Korčula, with dishes like *pašticada* and *bakalar* (cod) every Friday. There's also a good selection of Dalmatian wines.

A bit on the pricey side for quick bites, but worth a mention for the sunny French bistro–style atmosphere and super brunch-type dishes, **Le Bistro** (Mihanovićeva 1, tel. 01/456-6666, 9 A.M.–11 P.M. daily, 85Kn) in the Regent Esplanade hotel is a great way to while away a Sunday morning.

Vegan

A macrobiotic restaurant in a small but sleek space, **Nova restoran** (Ilica 72, tel. 01/481-0059, www.biovega.hr, 9 A.M.–10 P.M. Mon.–Sat., 55Kn) offers an impressive range of vegan dishes with dozens of delicious spins on tofu, seitan, and vegetables.

OUTSIDE THE CENTER
Fine Dining

Marcellino (Jurjevska 71, tel. 01/467-7111, noon–11 P.M. Mon.–Sat., 120Kn) has long been Zagreb's only truly fine-dining restaurant (read: small portions and creative cuisine), though Bistro Apetit is giving it a run for its money. The space is large and modern and prettiest at night when the trees outside the large windows are lit from below. The food is very good, with what seems like four chefs participating in every dish (you can see them working from the dining room), but the prices are high.

Dubravkin Put (Dubravkin put 2, tel. 01/483-4975, 10 A.M.–midnight daily, 115Kn) is the city's nicest fish restaurant with food to match. The decor is simple but the vibe is luxe to the extreme.

International

Mex Cantina (Savska cesta 154, tel. 01/619-2156, www.asker.com/mex-cantina, 9 A.M.–11 P.M. daily, 70Kn) has the most authentic Mexican food in Zagreb and if you want a fajita, it's probably worth the hike out to Savska. If you're planning on partying at Movie Pub, it's practically across the street.

A tiny Italian restaurant, **Fellini** (Savska 90, tel. 01/617-7545, www.fellini.hr, 11 A.M.–11 P.M. Mon.–Fri., noon–11 P.M. Sat.–Sun., 60Kn) is usually full with patrons who know the food and service are consistent and the wine list isn't too shabby either.

Local Cuisine

If you can't make it to Dalmatia, a meal at **Dida** (Petrova 176, tel. 01/233-5693, 9 A.M.–11 P.M. Mon.–Sat., 9 A.M.–10 P.M. Sun., 100Kn) is the next best thing. With a rustic coastal interior and fish you select from a bed of ice before it's cooked, Dida serves meals that are pricey but always excellent quality.

Quick Bites

Near Cibona Tower, **Karijola** (Kranjčevićeva 16a, tel. 01/366-7044, 9 A.M.–midnight daily, 45Kn) serves pizza, but not the kind you ordered at 2 A.M. for sustenance during a study session. Their clay oven–baked pizzas have a thin crispy crust and super-fresh ingredients. The pizza with mozzarella, tomato, and fresh basil hits the spot on a hot summer day.

Only a couple of blocks from the Sheraton, **Canzona** (Ivana Šveara 9, tel. 01/461-7777, 9 A.M.–11 P.M. Mon.–Sat., noon–11 P.M. Sun., 55Kn) is as cute as restaurants get. The walls are painted to depict quaint buildings, and in the lantern light it really does feel like you're eating in an Italian courtyard. The pasta and pizza dishes are very good and their tiramisu is a sweet ending to your meal.

Information and Services

TOURIST AND TRAVEL INFORMATION

The main **tourist office** (Trg bana Jelačića 11, tel. 01/481-4051, info@zagreb-touristinfo.hr, www.zagreb-touristinfo.hr, 8:30 A.M.–8 P.M. Mon.–Fri., 9 A.M.–5 P.M. Sat., 10 A.M.–2 P.M. Sun.) is located on Trg bana Jelačića and provides some nice color brochures, featuring maps and walks around town, free of charge. The office also provides information on events and happenings around town and sells the Zagreb Card (90Kn), which includes free city transport, a 50 percent discount on museums and tours, and discounts at other locations throughout the city during a 72-hour period.

GUIDED TOURS

If you'd like someone to take you around town, the tourist office can hook you up with a private guide or you can hop on the **Zagreb City Tour** (tel. 01/369-4333, www.ibus.hr, 10 A.M. daily Apr. 1–Oct. 31, other times by arrangement, 165Kn per person, discount with the Zagreb Card), run by iBus; the tour departs from Bakačeva Street near the cathedral.

A slightly quirkier option is the **Segway City Tour** (tel. 01/301-0390, www.segwaycitytourzagreb.com, from 300Kn depending on tour and number of people), which offers several pre-planned tours or custom tours depending on your interests. The tours start and end at the Regent Esplanade hotel and more information is available from the concierges at the Regent Esplanade and the Best Western Hotel Astoria as well as the tourist office on Trg bana Jelačića.

BANKS AND CURRENCY EXCHANGE

It's best to avoid changing money at hotels due to the usually poor exchange rate; most banks will exchange money, as will exchange offices (look for the *mjenjačnica* signs), who take about a 1.5 percent commission. Major banks are Zagrebačka Banka, Privedna Banka (PBZ), and Raiffeisen. If you need to exchange money outside of business hours, head to the bus station or the post office next to the train station for 24-hour service. Also, ATMs (labeled *bankomat*) around town accept most major cards. There's one conveniently located on Trg bana Jelačića, as well as many other locations around the center. Don't expect to find one in Gornji Grad, however.

INTERNET ACCESS AND COMMUNICATIONS

The main post office (Branimirova 4, 24 hours) is located next to the train station. Here, as well as at the post office at Jurišićeva 13 (7 A.M.–9 P.M. Mon.–Fri., 7 A.M.–7 P.M. Sat., 8 A.M.–2 P.M. Sun.) have metered booths for international telephone calls. Other post offices are located around town—just look for the yellow Pošta signs.

While more and more hotels and hostels are offering free Internet connections, there are several places to go if you're in a pinch.

For the whole package (computer and access) with an alternative, gay-friendly vibe, try **M.a.m.a.** (Preradovićeva 18, tel. 01/485-6400, www.mi2.hr, 10 A.M.–10 P.M. Mon.–Sat., 4–10 P.M. Sun., 10Kn per hour), which also has fax and copying services on the premises. **Sublink Internet Centar** (Teslina 12, tel. 01/481-1329, www.sublink.hr, 9 A.M.–10 P.M.

Mon.–Sat., 3–10 P.M. Sun., 15Kn per hour, student discount) is another option nearby, with an in-house café if you need a shot of caffeine. If you have your laptop or wireless handheld with you, order up a drink at **Škola Lounge Bar** (Bogovićeva 7, tel. 01/482-8196) and surf using the bar's Wi-Fi Internet access. Wi-Fi is beginning to pop up at more and more locations around town.

LAUNDRY SERVICES

Washing, dry-cleaning, ironing, and basic mending services can be found at **Doratex** (Draškovićeva 31, tel. 01/461-2990, 7 A.M.–7 P.M. Mon.–Fri., 8 A.M.–noon Sat., 6–18Kn per item) or **Petecin Zdenka** (Kaptol 11, tel. 01/481-4802, 8 A.M.–8 P.M. Mon.–Fri., 8 A.M.–3 P.M. Sat., 6–20Kn per item).

LEFT LUGGAGE

The main bus station (Avenija M. Držića bb, tel. 060/313-333, www.akz.hr, 6 A.M.–10 P.M. daily, 1.20Kn for up to 15 kg per hour) and train station (Trg Kralja Tomislava 12, tel. 060/333-444, 24 hours) have left luggage offices with cheap rates for stowing your bags.

EMERGENCY SERVICES

Croatia's emergency number is 112, though you can also dial each service directly: ambulance (94), fire (93), and police (92). The main police station (tel. 01/456-3311) is at Petrinjska 30. If you find yourself in need of a doctor in the middle of the night, the clinic of the Sveti Duh hospital (Sveti Duh 64, tel. 01/371-2111) is open 24 hours. There are several all-night pharmacies in Zagreb though the most central is at Ilica 43 (tel. 01/484-8450).

Getting There and Around

GETTING THERE
Air

Located 17 kilometers from the center, Zagreb's small Pleso Airport (tel. 060/320-320, www.zagreb-airport.hr) is easy to find your way around, and out of. Croatia Airlines (tel. 01/487-2727 or 01/616-0215, www.croatia airlines.hr) is the major carrier to and from the airport.

From the airport, a taxi to the center should cost around 200–250Kn. If you take a taxi, make sure the driver starts the meter and ask for a receipt. A cheaper option is to take the Croatia Airlines bus, which leaves the airport every half hour or hour (check the schedule at www.plesoprijevoz.hr/schedulezg.htm). The price is only 30Kn, payable to the driver, and takes about 30 minutes to the main bus station.

Train

Zagreb's main train station (Trg Kralja Tomislava 12, tel. 060/333-444) is conveniently located in the center of the city; unlike in many European cities, it is located in a safe area. Trains, run by Hrvatske željeznice (Croatian Railways, tel. 060/333-444, www .hznet.hr), are usually on time and are a great way of getting around the Zagreb area. You can also pick up multiple daily connections to regions around Croatia and Slovenia. Inter-Rail passes are valid in Croatia, though Eurail is not.

Tickets should be purchased at the ticket counter to save a little money; tickets bought from the conductor will be slightly higher. You should also be aware that there are slow trains (*putnički*) that stop at every station along the way, and inter-city trains (IC), which are more expensive but usually worth the money in time savings.

You can purchase a timetable at the station, though your best bet is to check out Croatian Railways' website. Make sure to give yourself a few extra minutes to board since the Zagreb train station can be more than a little confusing at times.

Bus

The city has a large and busy bus station (Avenija M. Držića bb, tel. 060/313-333, www .akz.hr) with lots of connections. Though the inter-city buses are run by multiple companies, the system actually runs pretty smoothly, as long as you don't get ruffled by the occasional unscheduled stop to drop regular customers off closer to their houses.

Car

Highways into Zagreb from Slovenia are quite good, with most of the Ljubljana to Zagreb highway (A3, approximately 1.5–2 hours between the two capitals) having been recently completed. From the Ljubljana border, drive straight until you see white signs marked with the word Centar, directing you toward the center of town. If you're traveling from Zagreb to Maribor, take the A2, also about a two-hour journey between the two cities.

GETTING AROUND
Tram and Bus

Since Zagreb's trams only operate in the central zone of the city, you need not worry about getting too lost. The main hubs for trams are at the train station and Trg bana Jelačića, with large maps displayed at these major stops to help you find your way. Buses will take you into the suburbs of Zagreb.

Regular service for both buses and trams is from early morning to 11:20 P.M., when night services take effect. During the day, tram service is very frequent (around every 10–15 minutes), though night trams and buses are terribly confusing to figure out, with crazy schedules and different routes than those on the regular service route. If you find yourself needing a bus or tram late at night, the best thing to do is ask. As Croatians are usually friendly people and a large percentage of the population under 40 speaks English, you shouldn't have a problem.

To travel on buses and trams, buy tickets at newspaper stands or directly from the driver. You can buy tickets per journey (6Kn from the kiosk, 10Kn from the driver, valid one-way for 90 minutes) or per day (*dnevne karte*, 25Kn), or buy a **Zagreb Card** from the tourist office—this includes city transport for 72 hours as well as discounts to museums. Once you board the tram or bus, simply validate your ticket by punching it in the machine onboard.

Taxi

There are numerous taxi stands in Zagreb. The two most central and convenient taxi stands are on Trg bana Jelačića next to the Varteks department store and on Gajeva next to the pedestrian zone. You'll also find them in front of the main train and bus stations as well as in front of hotels. Alternatively, call 970 or 01/660-0671 to reserve a taxi. (You will not find taxis driving around waiting to be flagged down—the person wildly gesturing at cabs from the sidewalk is easily pegged as a tourist.)

Taxis in Zagreb are incredibly expensive, and unfortunately some drivers like to get the best of foreigners. The standard rate is 25Kn to start and 7Kn for every kilometer thereafter (rates are increased at night and on Sundays and holidays). If you try using a few words of Croatian you'll lessen your chances of being taken for a more expensive ride than you planned. Also make sure the driver turns on the meter and ask for a receipt.

Most drivers, however, are friendly and honest. While tipping is not standard, it is customary to round up when paying your fare.

Car

While driving on Croatia's highways is quite easy and comfortable, driving in-town is often a stressful, wild tangle of cars. Traffic in Zagreb is nearly always bad from 8 A.M. to around 6 or 7 P.M., unless of course you visit in July and August when it seems like the entire city is at the coast. The major tips for in-town driving: Pay attention and remember that the majority of drivers do not obey the rules.

If you need to rent a car in Zagreb, Budget Rent-a-Car (www.budget.hr) and Avis (www.avis.com.hr) have locations in Pleso Airport and the Sheraton. The wonderful service Rent-a-Smart (Ivana Kukuljevića 32, tel. 01/487-6172, www.rentasmart.com.hr, 10 A.M.–8 P.M. Mon.–Sat.) rents Smart cars from one day to one year, making getting around town a cinch.

Parking in Zagreb is scarce and not for those averse to parallel parking, so you'll want to find somewhere to leave the car and traverse the city center by foot or with the help of trams (if you chose the Smart car, however, you'll find a few more spots to leave the car). If you do need to park in Zagreb, remember that each zone is subject to different rules, with first-zone areas allowing a maximum of only one hour. Find a parking meter, placed at intervals along the street, and pay, then place the receipt on your dashboard from inside the car. Or pay your parking via cell phone—send your license plate number via a text message to 101 (Zone 1, one-hour maximum), 102 (Zone 2, two-hour maximum), or 103 (Zone 3, three-hour maximum). It is charged to your cell phone immediately; it's either added to your bill or, if you have a prepaid card, deducted from the balance. Lately the city has been quite tow-happy, so make sure the place you park is legal.

Around Zagreb

SAMOBOR

Since the early 19th century, Samobor has lured travelers to its charming streets and the tranquil mountains that surround it. Though today it is mainly a destination for Zagreb residents looking to get away from it all, in the past its importance and culture rivaled that of its much larger neighbor.

There are a few things in this gingerbread town that are considered typical Samobor. The most famous is the *kremšnita,* a flaky square of crust topped with vanilla custard, though its name suggests the origin may be Austrian (but don't mention that to the locals). They also make a big deal over their crystal, though you'd probably be better off toting home some local *bermet,* touted as an aperitif—or a digestif, which might be a better term given how strong it is, or *samoborska muštarda,* a very sharp mustard with a hint of grape.

One of the best times to come is during **Samoborski fašnik,** or carnival, when the town hosts hundreds of revelers with all kinds of performances and lots of activities for kids. Samobor's version of carnival is decidedly more family-friendly than its better-known cousins.

If you miss *fašnik* there are several other festivals worth checking out. The Samoborski proljetni sajam (Samobor spring fair) features stands with local food products and handiwork, while the square is popping with fireworks on Dan Grada (Day of the Town, July 26), and Samoborska glazbena jesen, Samobor's autumn music festival, brings some excellent musicians to town. Check with the **tourist office** (Trg Kralja Tomislava 5, tel. 01/336-0044, www.tz-samobor.hr, 8 A.M.–7 P.M. Mon.–Fri., 9 A.M.–7 P.M. Sat., 10 A.M.–7 P.M. Sun.) for more information.

Sights

After admiring the pretty buildings and the mountains from **Trg Kralja Tomislava,** the main square and center of the tiny town, head to the **Gradski muzej** (Town Museum, Livadićeva 7, tel. 01/336-1014, 9 A.M.–3 P.M. Tues.–Fri., 9 A.M.–1 P.M. Sat.–Sun., 12Kn) next to the Hotel Lavica. The museum was home to composer Ferdo Livadić, who once hosted his friend Franz Liszt here. There's not too much to see here, besides some furniture and decorations from local families and a decent exhibit of agricultural tools.

Heading back across the square towards the parish church you'll pass the **Muzej Marton** (Marton Museum, Jurjevska 7, tel. 01/332-6426, www.muzej-marton.hr, 10 A.M.–1 P.M. Sat.–Sun., 15Kn), which will delight fans of glass and porcelain with a large display including pieces by Meissen, Sèvres, and plates that once belonged to Tsar Nicholas I.

The **Fotogalerija Lang** (Langova 15, tel. 01/336-2884, 11 A.M.–1 P.M. and 4–7 P.M. Sat.–Sun. and by appt.), tucked in an alleyway, hosts surprisingly good contemporary

Samobor's Gradski muzej

© SHANN FOUNTAIN ČULO

© SHANN FOUNTAIN ČULO

view of mountains from Samobor's town center

photography exhibits. A short walk away, on the northeastern side of the square, is the **Galerija Prica** (Trg Matice hrvatske 3, tel. 01/333-6214, 9 A.M.–3 P.M. Tues.–Thurs., 1–7 P.M. Fri., 10 A.M.–1 P.M. Sat.–Sun., 15Kn), which displays paintings by primary-color fan and local artist Zlatko Prica, and haunting photography from his equally talented daughter Vesna.

The town has two nice Baroque churches worth a peek if you have the extra time: the 17th-century **Crkva Sv. Anastazije** and the 18th-century church of the **Franjevački Samostan** (Franciscan Monastery). But if you're tight on time, make a beeline for the **Anindol** forest on Tepec Hill. It's full of paths to explore, but the best two are the winding **Križni put,** which puts you at the tiny **Kapelica sv. Jurja** (Chapel of St. George) in less than half an hour, or the path to Samobor's **Stari Grad.** Stari Grad is really just the ruins of the town's 13th-century castle, but the view is worth the hike and the ruins are quite peaceful.

If you really want to explore the excellent **hiking** options around town, pick up a *planinarska karta* (mountain map) from the tourist office on Trg Kralja Tomislava.

Samobor is the entrance to the Žumberak region of inland Croatia, with a wonderful nature park (www.ppzsg.org) and some great eco-tourism sites.

Accommodations

If you have a car, staying in Samobor, where you'll get more for your money, can be a much better option than Zagreb.

The **Hotel Livadić** (Trg Kralja Tomislava 1, tel. 01/336-5850, www.hotel-livadic.hr, 455Kn d., including breakfast) is the nicest accommodation in Samobor, with quaint rooms right on Trg Kralja Tomislava, the main square.

The **Hotel Lavica** (Ferde Livadića 5, tel. 01/336-8000, www.lavica-hotel.hr, 291Kn d., including breakfast) is somewhat more basic but the price is better and the location is only a few steps away from Trg Kralja Tomislava.

Food

For local flavor at lunch or dinner, the **Samoborska Pivnica** (Šmihenova 3, tel. 01/336-1623, www.samoborska-pivnica.hr, 9 A.M.–11 P.M. Mon.–Fri., 9 A.M.–midnight Sat.–Sun., 70Kn) serves up stomach-filling dishes in a cavelike space. The **Hotel Lavica** (Ferde Livadića 5, tel. 01/336-8000, www.lavica-hotel.hr, 75Kn) restaurant is even nicer, with a dark-wood interior and a quiet location next to the Town Museum.

Zeleni Papar (Ante Starčevića 17, tel. 01/336-3893, www.zelenipapar.hr, 11 A.M.–11 P.M. Mon.–Sat., closed Aug., 80Kn) doesn't look all that special, but it has some of the best food in Samobor, with homemade *kulen* (salami), wine goulash, and super *biftek* (steak).

For a quicker bite, try the **Pizzeria Napoli** (Grada Wirgesa 6, tel. 01/336-0072, noon–10 P.M. Mon.–Sat., 40Kn) for pizzas and pasta dishes.

Information and Services

Located conveniently on Trg Kralja Tomislava

© SHANN FOUNTAIN ČULO

Trg Kralja Tomislava, the main square in Samobor

the **tourist office** (Trg Kralja Tomislava 5, tel. 01/336-0044, www.tz-samobor.hr, 8 A.M.–7 P.M. Mon.–Fri., 9 A.M.–7 P.M. Sat., 10 A.M.–7 P.M. Sun.) sells maps, including special versions for hiking. They also hand out free brochures and information and can help you arrange accommodation.

Getting There and Around

Samobor is a little over 20 kilometers west of Zagreb. If you're driving, take the A3 toward Ljubljana. The trip should take about 30 minutes, but heavy traffic on the road sometimes makes it a bit longer. Buses run by the Samoborček company (tel. 01/333-5170, www.samoborcek.hr) leave Zagreb's main bus station and the Črnomerec tram terminal. There are dozens of connections daily, taking about 45 minutes, and costing around 35Kn each way depending on where you get on. When you get to Samobor, from the bus station it is only a five-minute walk to the main square, Trg Kralja Tomislava.

PLEŠIVIČKA WINE ROUTE

The best wine route in the area is the Plešivička Wine Route. You can pick it up at Rude, a few kilometers southwest of Samobor. The roads

are well marked; you can get additional information and a list of wineries online at www.zagrebacka-zupanija.hr/vina/eng. However, it's best not to plan too much and just enjoy the drive of around 20 or so kilometers through vineyards and villages. The wineries are marked with little signs declaring *vino*. Though none of them hold regular opening hours, despite some claiming they do, it's a nice drive hunting down a spot to buy some wine.

Most of the growers will offer you a tasting before you buy, which is important given that the quality of the wine will vary greatly. However, it's pretty cheap and if you happen to be traveling the road in autumn, you'll run into Portugizac Plešivička, the local version of Beaujolais Nouveau.

There are two nice places to stop for lunch along the way: **Restoran Ivančić** (Plešivica 45, tel. 01/629-3303, call for hours) with its vineyard-view terrace or **Boltina Hiža** (Pl. Prekrižje 12, tel. 01/629-3115, call for hours, closed Mon.).

ZAPREŠIĆ

The main attraction in the small town of Zaprešić, 18 kilometers northwest of Zagreb, is the **Jelačić Novi dvori,** a well-preserved feudal estate that covers 50 acres. There's also a small museum, the **Matija Skurjeni Museum** (Aleja Đure Jelačića 8, tel. 01/331-0540, www .muzej-matija-skurjeni.hr, 10Kn), with a cheerful display of naive art, an impressive manor house, a chapel and the grand **Jelačić family tomb.** Hours are 9 A.M.–3 P.M. Tuesday and Thursday, noon–6 P.M. Wednesday and Friday in summer and 11 A.M.–5 P.M. Wednesday and Friday in winter, 9 A.M.–2 P.M. Saturday, and 9 A.M.–noon Sunday.

Nearby is a well-maintained **golf complex,** though it's really little more than a driving range. A short drive south, the **Zajarki Lake** has a nice fish farm and fishing society.

If you'd like to stay in Zaprešić or just want a bite while you're there, the **Trajbar Team** (Ulica bana J. Jelačića 199, tel. 01/331-0838, info@kk-trajbar-team.hr, www.kk-trajbar-team.hr, 312Kn d.) horse farm offers nice meals and rooms in a rural setting. If you'd like to try out your equestrian skills, the farm also offers lessons for beginners and trail rides for the more experienced.

Zaprešić is accessible by bus and train, with frequent connections since many people work in Zagreb. It's a 30-minute drive from Zagreb (take Ilica out of town and follow the signs for Zaprešić).

MARIJA BISTRICA

Thirty-two kilometers north of Zagreb is Marija Bistrica, whose hilltop **Hodočasnička crkva Marije Bistričke** (Pilgrimage Church of St. Mary of Bistrica, tel. 049/468-380, www .info-marija-bistrica.hr, contact tourist board for hours and pilgrimages) has turned into a destination for the devout, particularly between Whitsunday (Pentecost) and the end of October. The church itself is attractive, designed in the late 18th century by Bollé, who built Zagreb's cathedral. But the pilgrims come not so much for the church as for the **Black**

Madonna, a 15th-century dark wooden statue of the Virgin. Legend has it that the statue was bricked into the church wall in the 17th century to protect it from the Turks. Some three decades later, a beam of light revealed its hiding place. Locals declared it a miracle and the bishop of Zagreb spread the news, hoping to promote the town as a spiritual center for pilgrims.

His efforts paid off and today the Black Madonna, who also survived an 1880 fire that only added to her aura, brings busloads of tourists to the otherwise tiny town.

Behind the huge **amphitheater,** built for a visit by the pope in 1998, a path leads up **Kalvarija** (Calvary Hill), passing the Stations of the Cross to a very nice view of the town at the top.

If you have time and your own car, take a leisurely drive north to **Belec** to visit the gorgeous 1675 Baroque church of **Marija Snježna** (Our Lady of the Snow). The outside is plain and unassuming but the inside is filled with paintings, gilt, and heavily carved statues and altars. Though the church is only officially open on Sundays, knock at the white house just below the front gate of the church and ask for Ivo, the bellringer. It's his job to unlock the church for visitors, so don't be embarrassed.

The rooms at **Lojzekova hiža** (Gusakovec 116, Gornja Stubica, tel. 049/469-325, info@ lojzekovahiza.com, www.lojzekovahiza .com, 199Kn d., including breakfast), west of Marija Bistrica, are pretty basic, but the typical Zagorje farmhouse, the warm and friendly owners, and their soul-warming comfort food make an overnight in the area a pleasing idea.

If you'd like to visit Marija Bistrica, there are multiple connections by bus daily to and from Zagreb (40 minutes). To visit the church at Belec, about 15 kilometers north of Marija Bistrica, follow the road to Zlatar and then follow signs for Belec.

INLAND CROATIA

If you're the type of traveler who loves to discover not-in-the-guidebook destinations, you must go to inland Croatia. With nary a tourist, despite charming Baroque enclaves, funky art galleries, and outstanding wineries, inland Croatia offers charms as varied as its landscape.

Zagreb sits within this area, divided into several regions, each with its distinct culture and geography. For avid sightseers, Zagorje has plenty of castle-topped hills to visit and Međimurje is filled with Baroque palaces and festivals. Slavonia's little villages are great places to get into deepest Croatia, a Croatia you would likely have found 60 years ago: Farmhouses hug the main road, many displaying signs for fresh eggs, lamb, wine, or even hogs, 100 kilograms and up. Where Slavonia

stretches toward the Danube are some of the best wineries in the country, plus the area's largest towns like Osijek and Vukovar, just pulling out of the economic stagnation caused by the war.

For the more active traveler, the Žumberak, not far from Zagreb, has a network of winding trails for hiking, or the Gorski Kotar's mountainous, almost alpine, geography makes way for skiing, climbing, and rafting excursions. The Lonjsko polje and Kopački rit are two nature preserves with loads of wildlife, worth taking a boat or jeep tour to spot wild storks and swimming swine.

While each area is distinct, one thing they all have in common is their impressive range of *seoski turizam* (village tourism), where visitors can stay overnight and get a real taste

INLAND CROATIA

HIGHLIGHTS

◖ **Varaždin:** In this gentile Baroque city there's lots for lovers of the style to gawk at, even a park-like neo-Baroque cemetery (page 71).

◖ **Hlebine:** Artists still keep tradition alive in this charming town, birthplace of the Croatian naive art movement. The galleries show off the masters, but you can also sometimes arrange a meeting with locals at work in their studios (page 78).

◖ **Tvrđa:** The fortress in Osijek is criss-crossed with centuries-old cobblestone streets and hopping with chic cafés and restaurants. It's also at the heart of the city's cultural rebirth, with more buildings under restoration for education and the arts (page 84).

◖ **Kopački rit:** One of Europe's best wetlands, this park is a must-see for bird-watchers (page 86).

◖ **Ilok Wineries:** This tiny medieval town is home to several old wine cellars and the surrounding countryside is just right for getting out on the open road. Consider joining a guided cycling tour to discover the region (page 89).

◖ **Fužine:** Smack dab in the middle of nowhere in the Gorski Kotar, this often overlooked village on the road to Rijeka has some great food and a hotel in a former Tito hunting lodge. It's also a great jumping-off point for adventure sports (page 94).

◖ **Lonjsko polje:** Wildlife fans shouldn't miss this nature preserve not far from Zagreb, where you can see hundreds of nesting storks and furry swimming pigs or stay amongst a cluster of preserved 19th-century wooden houses (page 96).

LOOK FOR ◖ TO FIND RECOMMENDED SIGHTS, ACTIVITIES, DINING, AND LODGING.

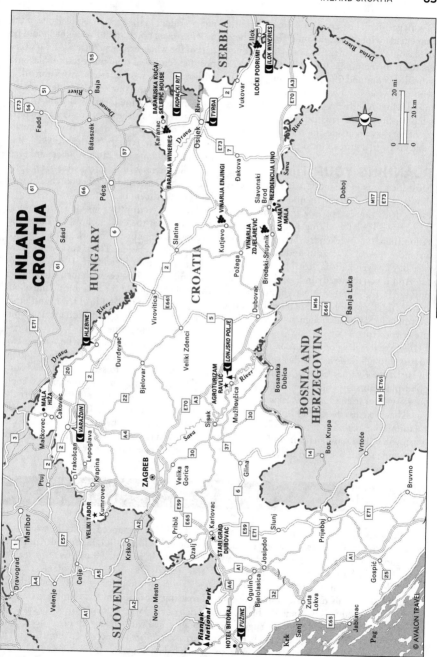

INLAND CROATIA

of village life. They are also brimming with homemade wines (though you'll find the best in Slavonia), with vineyards and wine producers open to the public for tastings and occasionally accommodation, where you can chat with the owners and learn all about the making of wine. Another common thread are the people—hospitable, friendly, and welcoming to visitors—who assure the traveler a memorable visit and a taste of local culture.

PLANNING YOUR TIME

Most locations in inland Croatia are an easy day trip from Zagreb. In one day you can easily fit in three stops in Zagorje by car, or one or two if you're taking public transportation (harder at weekends when connections are more scarce). Varaždin and Karlovac are nice day or even half-day trips from the capital. And if you're already in Samobor, outside of Zagreb, the Žumberak is right around the corner. You'll probably need to plan at least one overnight in Slavonia, though, to make the best use of your trip.

If you're traveling on to the coast, you have to pass through Karlovac whether you're headed to Istria, the Kvarner Gulf, or Dalmatia. It's a good place to stop and have lunch. And on your way to or from Opatija, Rijeka, and Istria, you'll have to cross the Gorski Kotar. The leafy, mountainous region is a restful prescription when you've had too much sun and sailing.

Slavonia requires a special trip, with at least one overnight in the area. If you pick one of the *seoski turizam* hotels, that overnight should be part of the whole experience itself. And it's very possible you spend your entire tour of Slavonia without seeing another tourist from abroad.

How you plan your time also depends on your interests. Wine lovers will want to rent a car and take to the wine roads of Slavonia for two or three days, while adventure fanatics should head straight to the Gorski Kotar for rock-climbing and rafting. There are even a couple of crazy film festivals for artsy sorts and all the castles and ancient churches history buffs could dream of.

Those traveling by bus or train should take note that the castles of Veliki Tabor and Trakošćan are not the easiest to access with public transportation. The same goes for most of the wine roads listed here. If you'd like to see some of these places without a car, contact the tourist boards in the area to find out about guided tours, organized bike trips, and other arrangements to avoid losing too much of your precious traveling time.

Whatever your choice may be, taking two or three days to see inland Croatia is a great decision. You'll get to see a side of the country that few tourists bother to explore. People are friendly all over the country but perhaps even more so in towns like Osijek and Vukovar, where the area is just beginning to recover from the war and the kind locals are thrilled to share the best of the region with visitors.

Zagorje

Bucolic little villages, winding hillside roads, and medieval storybook castles . . . When traveling in Zagorje it's hard to believe you're just a stone's throw from the bustling capital of Zagreb.

Zagorje is also home to a rather distinguished political history. The launching spot for the 1573 Peasants' Revolt and the birthplace of Josip Broz Tito (the leader of Yugoslavia from 1945 to 1980) are both located here.

It's a nice place for cycling if you're so inclined. Well-marked paths between the major sights like Veliki Tabor and Kumrovec make taking to a bike a nice way to see the area; rentals are available in Zagreb.

Zagorje is the place to really relax, slowly browsing a castle and then going for a long lunch of local specialties like *štrukli* (a pasta-ish dough filled with creamy cottage cheese) and *purica z mlincima* (turkey with *mlinci*, a sort of thick baked noodle).

© SHANN FOUNTAIN ČULO

rural life in Zagorje

For souvenirs, pick up the little *licitari,* or bright-red gingerbread hearts, that are meant as an ornament rather than a sweet. They're synonymous with the area and have been adopted by Croatia as one of the country's iconic symbols.

The **tourist board** (Tourist Board of Krapina-Zagorje County, Zagrebačka 6, Krapinske Toplice, tel. 049/233-653, info@ tz-zagorje.hr, www.tz-zagorje.hr) can provide more information for planning your visit.

KUMROVEC

Though it's famous as the birthplace of Yugoslavian leader Josip Broz Tito, Kumrovec's **Muzej Staro Selo** (Old Village Museum, www.mdc.hr/kumrovec, 9 A.M.–7 P.M. daily Apr.–Sept., 9 A.M.–4 P.M. daily Oct.–Mar., 20Kn) is intriguing in its own right. Some 20 cottages and outbuildings, including Tito's childhood home, have been restored and opened to the public; the museum starts behind the large parking lot on the right if you're coming from Klanjec. The best thing about the museum is that while the displays are interesting and informative, it bears no resemblance

to most tourist villages. Here you actually feel like you are in an early 20th-century village, with chickens and geese running wild and still occupied homes that are only distinguishable from the museum ones by the paraphernalia and occasional child in the yard.

If you're interested in **biking,** there's a nice marked trail from here to Veliki Tabor, about 15 kilometers north.

The **Pansion Zelenjak** (Risvica 1, Kumrovec, tel. 049/550-747, zelenjak@zelenjak.com, www .zelenjak.com, 149Kn d., including breakfast) has clean rooms on the shores of a rushing mountain stream and some good freshwater fish dishes in the restaurant.

Kumrovec is 40 kilometers northwest of Zagreb. To reach Kumrovec, take a train from Zagreb to Savski Marof, where five buses continue to Kumrovec's train station, a little less than half an hour's walk from the museum complex. The train and bus take around an hour and cost approximately 35Kn. By car, take the A4 direction Maribor, exit at Krapinske Toplice, and follow signs to Kumrovec. The drive takes about 45 minutes.

the preserved village of Kumrovec

© SHANN FOUNTAIN ČULO

VELIKI TABOR

When most people think of a medieval castle, something like Veliki Tabor (tel. 049/343-963, www.velikitabor.hr, 10 A.M.–6 P.M. daily Apr.–Sept., 10 A.M.–3 P.M. daily Oct.–Mar., 20Kn) is what comes to mind. It's the sort of castle you drew in school, with huge circular towers looking over the surrounding countryside from a hilltop. The main structure, a pentagon-shaped tower, was built in the 12th century; the cone-roofed circular towers were added in the 15th and 16th centuries. Some historians claim the castle sits on the site of an earlier Roman fortress from the 2nd century.

There are several varied exhibits including medieval weaponry, glazed sections of old stove tiles, and a smattering of furniture. The real draw here is the architecture of the castle, which looks like the setting for a movie about knights and fair maidens. There's also the castle's most famous exhibit, the purported **skull of Veronika Desnićka,** a local beauty who caught the count's son's eye. They ran off together, but the count disapproved of the marriage and had his son imprisoned. The unlucky Veronika was drowned and her body holed up inside the castle. In 1982, renovations uncovered a skull, now displayed in the castle's chapel.

Not all sections of the castle have been restored. Long-term renovations are ongoing, and it is difficult to say which rooms will be next. In the summer months there are performances of sword-fighting and hawking, particularly interesting for children.

There's a restaurant nearby, **Grešna Gorica** (tel. 049/343-001, www.gresna-gorica.com, daily, 50Kn), though the hilltop setting is far better than the food. Even so, it's usually packed on the weekends with day-trippers having lunch among the turkeys and chickens that wander around. Near the village of Desinić, a short drive away, there's the lovely **Seljački Turizam Trsek** (Trnovec Desinićki 23, tel. 049/343-464, josip@trsek.hr, www.trsek.hr, 242Kn d., including breakfast), a rustic bed-and-breakfast sort of place with excellent food and cozy charm.

About 50 kilometers northwest of Zagreb, Veliki Tabor can be reached via the A4

MATIJA GUBEC AND THE PEASANTS' REVOLT

In 16th-century Zagorje, peasants were stretched thin between ever-increasing feudal obligations and constant battles with the Ottoman Empire. The peasants complained but the emperor didn't listen, so in 1573 they decided to rebel.

When the rebellion broke out, they elected the charismatic Ambroz Matija Gubec as leader in a plan to develop a government, led by peasant officials, that would answer only to the emperor. Their revolutionary ideas alarmed the nobility, who raised armies to defeat them.

The poorly armed peasant army fought hard but eventually lost a decisive battle at Stubičko Polje in February 1573 when the bishop of Zagreb, Juraj Drašković, defeated Gubec and his men in a bloody battle, capturing Gubec.

Gubec was executed in St. Mark's Square

in Zagreb. On the accusation that he had been elected "king" by his followers, he was crowned with a scalding ring of iron.

The revolt and execution of Gubec became the stuff of legend in Croatia, inspiring poets and writers and even politicians. Tito and his partisans embraced Gubec's cause as their own, naming one of their brigades in World War II after the famous peasant leader.

The village of Gornja Stubica, where the revolt was launched, has the **Muzej seljačkih buna** (Peasants' Revolt Museum, Samci 64, tel. 049/587-880, www.mdc.hr/msb, 9 A.M.-5 P.M. daily Oct.-Mar., 9 A.M.-7 P.M. daily Apr.-Sept., 20Kn), which presents items that give a sense of everyday feudal life, with captions in English, as well as a hilltop statue of Matija Gubec.

highway, direction Maribor. If you're taking the bus, there are several daily connections from Zagreb to the nearby village Desinić (2.5 hours). It's about a five-kilometer walk from the station to the castle.

KRAPINA

The busy border town of Krapina is most famous for the 1899 discovery of Neanderthal remains, which put the city on the map. Today, a modern **museum** (Šetalište Vilibalda Sluge bb, tel. 049/371-491, www.krapina.com, 9 A.M.-5 P.M. daily June-Sept., 9 A.M.-3 P.M. Tues.-Sun. Oct.-May, 20Kn) displays nice exhibits on Stone Age life in the area. A short path takes you to the exact spot where the bones were found, marked by some statues depicting a Neanderthal family—a good spot to take a photo.

Gostionica pod Starim Krovovima (Trg ljudevita Gaja 15, tel. 049/370-536, 6 A.M.-10 P.M. daily, 45Kn) has tasty local dishes like freshwater fish and schnitzel, plus several clean rooms at good prices. Just north of town is **Gostionica Preša** (Tkalci bb, tel. 049/372-664, 6 A.M.-11 P.M. Mon.-Thurs.,

6 A.M.-1 A.M. Fri., 6 A.M.-5 A.M. Sat., 7 A.M.-10 P.M. Sun., 55Kn), where you can munch on Zagorski specialties while taking in some great views of Krapina and the surrounding hillsides lined with vineyards. A short drive out of Krapina, **Pansion Vuglec Breg** (Škarićevo 151, tel. 049/345-015, info@vuglec-breg.hr, www.vuglec-breg.hr, 526Kn d., including breakfast) is a slightly more upscale form of rural accommodation. The re-created village offers clean rooms, nice meals, and homemade wines from the surrounding vineyards. It's less authentic and pricier than some other *seoski turizam* establishments in the area, but it has nice atmosphere.

Krapina, 56 kilometers north of Zagreb, is easily reached via the A4 highway toward Maribor. It takes about one hour to reach town. The town is also easily reached by train (1.5 hours) for around 39Kn. From the train station (F. Galovića 8, tel. 049/371-012), it's a short walk north to the town center.

LEPOGLAVA

Though Lepoglava's main claim to fame is being home to the country's largest prison,

LEPOGLAVA LACE

The art of lace-making was introduced to Lepoglava by 15th-century Pauline monks. The local village population started making the lace, using narrow strips of linen thread. Lace-making became a mini-industry for Lepoglava, supported by local aristocracy, the Paulines (who used the lace for church clothing and decoration), and the sale of pieces at local fairs.

A lace school, the Banovinska čipkarska škola, kept the tradition alive by teaching the art in the first half of the 20th century while introducing new techniques to the women who practiced the skill. Lepoglava bobbin lace is still made the way it has for centuries – on a cylindrical pillow, winding the thread around small wooden sticks, or bobbins. The most common designs are geometrical or depict plants and animals.

The town is working hard to keep the tradition alive, with lace-making classes in elementary schools, the founding of a society, and the county fair-style **Međunarodni festival čipke** (International Lace-Making Festival, late Sept., contact Lepoglava tourist office for more details, 10Kn), which brings exhibitions of European laces, workshops, and cultural performances to the little town every September.

the little town has some interesting tourist stops. The city's **tourist office** (Trg 1. hrvatskog sveučilišta 3, tel. 042/791-090, cell tel. 091/570-0491, turizam@lepoglava-info.hr, www.lepoglava-info.hr, hours vary, feel free to call cell for assistance) can help with maps and information as well as arrange guided tours. The **prison**, located in a former Pauline monastery that sustained substantial damage in World War II, counts dozens of famous historical figures including Tito, Croatia's first president Franjo Tuđman, and the Cardinal Stepinac as former inmates.

However, Lepoglava was also home to painter-monk Ivan Ranger, who left his touch on churches across northern Croatia. The **Crkva Blažene Djevice Marije** (Hrvatskih

pavlina bb, tel. 042/792-566, hours vary, open daily, free) is a beautiful Gothic church with lots of Baroque touches, including some outstanding frescoes by Ranger. You can visit the church's **Galerija Ivana Rangera** (Gallery of Ivan Ranger, inside the Crkva Blažene Djevice Marije, hours vary, open daily, donation appreciated) to see photos of his other frescoes if you don't have time to travel Ranger's Way, heading north out of Lepoglava.

It's somewhat quirky, but perhaps the most interesting exhibit of artwork in Lepoglava is that created by the prisoners. Their work is displayed in the **Galerija zatvorskih radova** (Gallery of Prisoner's Work, by arrangement with the tourist office, 20Kn).

Lepoglava is approximately 70 kilometers north of Zagreb. There is at least one daily bus from Zagreb (2 hours 10 minutes, 76Kn), but traveling to Lepoglava is easiest via Varaždin, 26 kilometers to the northeast; it has many more connections via train and bus, taking about 45 minutes. The train is the cheaper method, running around 25Kn each way.

TRAKOŠĆAN

Trakošćan castle (tel. 042/796-281, www .mdc.hr/trakoscan, 9 A.M.–6 P.M. daily Apr.–Sept., 9 A.M.–3 P.M. daily Oct.–Mar., 30Kn) is a bit of a national icon. This is the castle you'll find on many postcards from Croatia—it's a must-see field trip for Croatian schoolchildren, and certainly the country's most famous. Built in the 13th century as a small and rather unimportant fortress, the castle was given by King Maximillian to the Drašković family in the 16th century. They owned the castle for almost 400 years and remodeled it to more closely resemble Bavarian castles of the day. The interior exhibits consist mainly of possessions of the great family, including weaponry, paintings, furniture, and a nice display of lead soldiers.

Outside, there's a beautiful Romanticist park designed in the 19th century. In nice weather, it's a great place for a leafy walk around the lake.

At the entrance to the castle, there's a small café offering drinks and a light lunch, or try

TRAVELING RANGER'S WAY

Ivan Ranger was born in 1700 in Tyrol. Joining the Paulist Monastic Order as a child, he began painting at a young age in northern Italy and in southern Germany. In his twenties he moved to Lepoglava and became a prolific painter of Baroque frescoes in churches throughout northern Croatia, decorating their walls with his colorful and stylistically original murals. He died in Lepoglava in 1753 and is buried inside the church.

From Lepoglava, traveling Rangerov put (Ranger's Way) is a nice way to see the countryside. With five stops in chapels and churches, the 8.5-kilometer journey can be taken by car or as a pleasant two-hour journey on foot. The stops include:

· Crkva Sv. Marije (Monastery and Church of St. Mary), Lepoglava

· Kapelica Sv. Ivana (Chapel of St. John), Gorica

· Kapelica Sv. Juraja (Chapel of St. Juraj), Purga

· Kapelica Majke Božje Snježne (Chapel of God's Mother of Snow), Žarovnica

· Župna crkva Pohođenja Blažene Djevice Marije (Chapel of Visitation of the Blessed Virgin Mary), Višnjica

The tourist office in Lepoglava has maps in their office (Trg 1. hrvatskog sveučilišta 3) as well as on their website (www.lepoglava-info.hr) that can help guide you in following Ranger's footsteps.

---

the nearby **Hotel Coning** (Trakošćan 5, tel. 042/796-224, www.coning-turizam.hr, 6 A.M.– 11 P.M. daily, 45Kn) for more hearty fare.

Trakošćan is 80 kilometers northwest of Zagreb. The only way to reach Trakošćan is by car (via Krapina) or by bus from Varaždin. By car, head out of Zagreb on the road to Ljubljana, and exit on the road for Maribor/Krapina. At Krapina, you'll head northeast towards the village of Bednja, just a kilometer or so from the castle. The drive should take around 1.5 hours. By bus, there are multiple daily connections from Varaždin taking about 45 minutes.

Međimurje

Hugging the borders of Slovenia and Hungary, Međimurje has a flavor all its own and plenty of pretty countryside to explore. The region technically begins above Varaždin, in Čakovec, a small town that was once home to a powerful family, the Zrinskis. The regional distinction for Varaždin is not clear, even among locals, who don't consider themselves to belong to Međimurje or Zagorje and will heatedly debate their side. And to be fair, Varaždin is certainly a city unto its own. The chocolate-box town is filled with immaculate Christmas-village buildings and is a must-see in the area. But getting out into the countryside is worthwhile, too. The low rolling hills of the area are covered with vineyards and tiny villages, perfect for a sunny day's drive, topped off with a leisurely late lunch and a bottle of local wine.

◖ VARAŽDIN

A neat little Hapsburg town 80 kilometers north of Zagreb, the city of Varaždin was first mentioned in 1181. The town was always an important military outpost, occupying a prime spot on the Hungarians' route to the sea and key for fending off later attacks by the Turks on Hapsburg and Hungarian lands. The wealthy city was even Croatia's capital from 1765 to 1776, when a disastrous fire forced the government to move back to Zagreb. After the fire, the

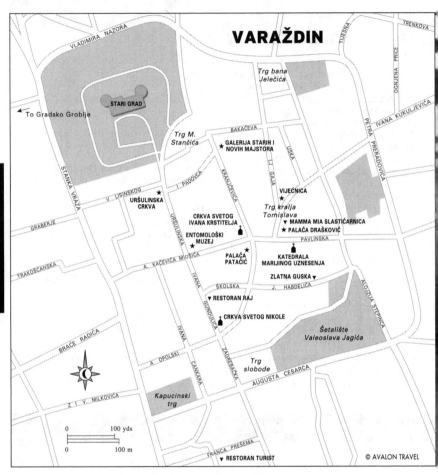

VARAŽDIN

© AVALON TRAVEL

town rebuilt its palaces, their intricate Baroque facades creating an almost amusement-park feel to the refined provincial town.

Sights
TRG SLOBODE AND NORTH
Freedom Square

A good starting point on a sightseeing tour is the Gothic church, **Crkva svetog Nikole** (Church of St. Nicholas), on Trg slobode. It is thought to date from Romanesque times (beginning of the 11th century through the 12th century) though the current structure is a 15th-century rebuild of the original. Further up the street is the **Entomološki muzej** (Entomology Museum, Franjevački trg 6/I, tel. 042/210-474, 10 A.M.–5 P.M. Tues.–Fri., 10 A.M.–1 P.M. Sat.–Sun., 20Kn), with an exhibit of over 4,500 insects. Even if you're not into bugs, the artistic use of mood lighting to draw attention to the creepy crawlies is interesting in itself.

Heading up Uršulinska, the **Uršulinska crkva** (Ursuline Church) is worth a quick peek. Though it doesn't house any important works behind its pink Baroque facade, the interior is a pretty blend of Gothic and Baroque touches.

© SHANN FOUNTAIN ČULO

Crkva svetog Nikole, a Gothic church

STARI GRAD

A touch further north of the Ursuline Church is Stari Grad (Strossmayerovo šetalište bb, tel. 042/658-754, www.varazdin.hr, 10 A.M.–6 P.M. Tues.–Sun. April–Sept., 10 A.M.–5 P.M. Tues.–Fri. and 10 A.M.–1 P.M. Sat.–Sun. Oct.–Mar., 20Kn), better known as Varaždin's castle, which is also home to the **town museum** (same hours, entrance included with ticket to Stari Grad). The museum is home to a decent collection of weaponry, local crafts, and old furniture, helpfully captioned in English. The castle was built as a fairly standard Hungarian fort in the 12th century and transformed in the 16th century into a Renaissance castle complete with two concentric moats. At the end of the 16th century it was acquired by the counts Erdödy, who made significant structural changes to turn it into a residence, where the family lived until 1925.

If you have time to take a short detour, a leisurely five-minute walk west takes you to the **Gradsko Groblje** (City Cemetery, Hallerova aleja, dawn–dusk, free). It is one of the most beautiful cemeteries in Croatia and worth a visit if you enjoy gardens. Laid out in the early 20th century and inspired by Versailles, the cemetery has rows of tombstones lined with 7,000 trees and shrubs and somber sculptures, making it feel more like a park than a graveyard.

TRG M. STANČIĆA
M. Stančić Square

Slightly east of the Stari Grad castle complex, walk through the 15th-century **Kula stražarnica** (Watchtower), which has an interesting ethnographic collection, to the Trg M. Stančića. If the weather's nice, stop for a coffee on the square for a nice view of the castle. When you're finished head to the tri-colored **Palača Prassinsky-Sermage,** a 17th-century palace unlike most of that period's architecture (the facade seems rather Shakespearean) that houses the city's **Galerija starih i novih majstora** (Gallery of Old and New Masters, Trg Miljenka Stancica 3, tel. 042/214-172, 10 A.M.–2 P.M. Tues.–Fri., 10 A.M.–1 P.M. Sat.–Sun., price varies) to view seasonal art exhibits from the city's vast collections.

FRANJEVAČKI TRG
Franciscan Square

Near the Trg M. Stančića is Franjevački trg. The square isn't square at all, but rather a very wide rectangular street. On the northern end is the **Crkva svetog Ivana Krstitelja** (Franciscan Church of St. John the Baptist), a pleasing 17th-century church with a gilded altar and a copy of the statue *Grgur Ninski* by Ivan Meštrović.

Just across the square is the frothy rococo **Palača Patačić** (Patačić Palace), one of the city's most impressive mansions from the late 18th century.

TRG KRALJA TOMISLAVA
King Tomislav Square

Located at the eastern end of Franjevački trg, Trg kralja Tomislava is Varaždin's unofficial main square. The **Palača Drašković** (Drašković Palace) is on the eastern side, the

INLAND CROATIA

© SHANN FOUNTAIN CULO

Stari Grad, Varaždin's castle

former home of Suzana Drašković, a woman who had a significant impact on Varaždin's history. When her husband died in 1765, the viceroy of Croatia moved his court to the city (purportedly to be closer to her, though Zagreb had also been declining in the 18th century), making Varaždin the capital of the country. The palace itself is rather ho-hum, save for its heavy stone portal presided over by a shiny gold crest.

The **Vijećnica** (Town Hall) at the northern end of the square acquired its present appearance in the late 18th century, after renovations. The structure was actually built in 1523, though parts of the building are Romanesque, likely remnants of a previous building. The town hall lends a theme park–like appearance to the square, with its crisp white facade and neat flower-filled balcony topped by a huge clock tower. Every Saturday between 11 A.M. and noon the **changing of the town guard** takes place, with uniformed volunteers bringing back a bit of Austro-Hungarian flair to Varaždin.

At the southern end of the Trg kralja Tomislava, turn onto Pavlinska headed east toward Varaždin's cathedral, built in 1647. Despite the imposing name, the exterior of the **Katedrala Marijinog Uznesenja** (Cathedral of the Ascension, Pavlinska 5, free) doesn't look much grander than the other churches in town, though its gilt-laden interior tries hard to live up to its name; it's usually open during the day, and there are morning and evening masses daily.

Entertainment and Events

On Saturday from April to October, Franjevački trg turns into the **Square of Olden Trades and Crafts,** featuring everything from potters to weavers and ironsmiths, plus musical performances and a children's puppet show. The city's arts festival **Špancirfest** (late Aug., www.spancirfest.com) holds street and open-air theatrical and musical performances as well as some interesting costume parades. And during September there's the refined **Varaždinske barokne večeri** (Varaždin Baroque Evenings, late Sept., www.vbv.hr) with lovely Baroque music concerts performed by both local and international musicians. The town's Baroque settings make the concerts all the more satisfying.

But if a Baroque concert is a little too cultural for your tastes, September is also the month the city hosts the small, off-beat **Trash Film Festival** (www.trash.hr), focusing on low-budget and sometimes flat-out weird action movies.

Any time of the year you can check out the city's **concert** schedules at the Erdödy Palace or the Croatian National Theater.

For sports enthusiasts, the city's first-division soccer team, **Varteks** (www.nk-varteks.hr), has home games that can really get you into the spirit of the town.

Accommodations

Though the rooms aren't as promising as its charming exterior, the **Hotel Istra** (Ulica, Ivana Kukuljevića 6, tel. 042/659-659, www.istra-hotel.hr, 845Kn d., including breakfast) has an excellent location steps off Trg Kralja Tomislava. The rooms are a bit bland and on the small side for the price, but the hotel is new and has flat-screen TVs and air-conditioning for the warm summer months.

The **Hotel Turist** (Aleja kralja Zvonimira 1, tel. 042/395-395, www.hotel-turist.hr, 490Kn d., including breakfast) might be exhibit B under communist hotels from the outside, but the rooms inside are fresh and clean after a renovation.

For a more bed-and-breakfast feel, try the **Pansion Garestin** (Zagrebačka 34, tel. 042/214-314, www.gastrocom.hr, 334Kn d., including breakfast), run by a restaurant group in town and offering simple rooms with air-conditioning, television, and private bathrooms. The **Pansion Maltar** (Preševorna 1, tel. 042/311-100, info@maltar.hr, www.maltar.hr, 398Kn d., including breakfast) is a nice little bed-and-breakfast a short walk from Trg Kralja Tomislava. **T-tours** (Gundulićeva 2, tel. 042/210-989, t-tours@vz.tel.hr, 8:30 A.M.–7:30 P.M. Mon.–Fri., 8:30 A.M.–12:30 P.M. Sat.) can help you book a private room in town.

INLAND CROATIA

© SHANN FOUNTAIN ČULO

Baroque architecture in Varaždin

Food

The **Mamma Mia slastičarnica** (Trg kralja Tomislava 2, tel. 042/320-519, 15Kn) on Trg kralja Tomislava not only offers desserts and coffee but also has pizza slices and sandwiches for a quick bite. Slightly out of the center, but still close by, **Pečenjarnica čevap** (Vidovski trg 17, tel. 042/312-674, 7 A.M.–11 P.M. Mon.–Sat., 25Kn) is a sit-down fast-food option with grilled meats and the ubiquitous *čevapčići*.

Perhaps the best deal in town, **Restoran Raj** (Ivana Gundulića 11, tel. 042/213-146, 8 A.M.–10 P.M. Sun.–Thurs., 9 A.M.–midnight Fri.–Sat., 35Kn), in the center, is a slightly shabby art nouveau cafeteria with great values on soups and hot main dishes starting at only 15Kn. In nicer weather you can sit on the restaurant's terrace and fill up for very little money.

For slightly more upscale eats, follow the stone staircase to the tucked away **Domenico** (Trg Slobode 9, tel. 042/212-017, 8 A.M.–11 P.M. Sun.–Thurs., 8 A.M.–midnight Fri.–Sat., 50Kn) for good pizzas and pastas in a cozy atmosphere.

The rather uninspiring **Restoran Turist** (Aleja kralja Zvonimira 1, tel. 042/395-395, www.hotel-turist.hr, noon–11 P.M. daily, 65Kn) in the Hotel Turist actually boasts two chefs who have been awarded some of Croatia's top honors for their good-quality regional dishes. At **Zlatna Guska** (Juraja Habdelića 4, tel. 042/213-393, www.zlatna-guska.com, 7 A.M.–midnight daily, 75Kn), an attractive yet a bit gimmicky medieval-style restaurant in one of the city's more run-down palaces, the menu is full of heavy meat dishes and local wines. Order the cream soup with nettles if it's on the menu.

Information and Services

The **tourist office** (Ivana Padovca 3, tel. 042/210-987, info@tourism-varazdin.hr, www.tourism-varazdin.hr, 8 A.M.–6 P.M. Mon.–Fri. and 9 A.M.–1 P.M. Sat. Apr.–Oct., 8 A.M.–4 P.M. Mon.–Fri. Nov.–Mar.) has maps and the staff is happy to answer questions. For English books, head to **Algoritam** (Ivana Kukuljevica 7, tel. 042/302-422) just off Trg Kralja Tomislava.

Getting There and Around

The bus station (Zrinskih i Frankopana, tel. 060/333-555, www.ap.hr) is about a five-

traveling green in Varaždin

minute stroll from the town center. Buses connect almost hourly with Zagreb, a little under two hours away (about 100Kn). The train station (Kolodvorska 17, tel. 042/213-740) is slightly farther out on the conveniently named Kolodvorska (it means railway street). Slow trains to Zagreb take about 2.5 hours but are very scenic and the price is hard to beat (about 80Kn). If you're driving from Zagreb to Varaždin, the trip is about 80 kilometers (approx. 1.5 hours) on the A4 highway.

Around town, the best form of transportation is your feet. The city is rather small, particularly the touristed sections, and much of it is pedestrian-only. If you do find yourself in need of a taxi, though, simply dial 970.

ČAKOVEC

There's not a lot to see in this largely modern town except the 17th-century **castle,** famous because it was home of the Zrinskis, one of Croatia's most powerful noble families. You'll see the Zrinski name, attached to a family of powerful warrior barons, once favorites of the Hapsburgs, all over Croatia—from street names to restaurants. The unassuming little Čakovec was their home from 1546, when the castle was given to Nikola Šubić Zrinski by Emperor Ferdinand I. The Zrinskis came to an unfortunate end when their loyalty to Austria waivered and Petar Zrinski was executed in 1671.

A Baroque palace inside the castle walls houses the **Muzej međimurja** (Museum of Međimurje, Trg Republike 5, tel. 040/313-285, www.mdc.hr/cakovec, 10 A.M.–3 P.M. Tues.–Fri., 10 A.M.–1 P.M. Sat.–Sun., 20Kn). There are some exhibits about the Zrinskis, as well as Iron Age finds, and brightly embroidered regional dress.

Today Čakovec is the departure point for a wine-roads tour of the region.

Katarina (Matice hrvatske 6, tel. 040/311-990, 10 A.M.–11 P.M. daily, 60Kn), in the center of town, has nice *međimurski* regional dishes in a brick-walled atmosphere. If you're looking for something besides meat and potatoes, **Trattoria Rustica** (I. G. Kovačića 6,

tel. 040/311-207, 8 A.M.–11 P.M. Mon.–Fri., 8 A.M.–midnight Sat.–Sun., 55Kn) is a good choice for Italian staples. Four kilometers north of town, **◖ Mala Hiža** (Mačkovec 107, tel. 040/341-101, www.mala-hiza.hr, 9 A.M.–11 P.M. daily, 75Kn) looks like a gingerbread house in the middle of nowhere, but the flashy cars out front will tip you off to the well-known restaurant inside that brings people from miles around to munch on gourmet dishes in rustic surroundings. In the summer the terrace on the 1887 house is also nice for a glass of wine and a leisurely lunch.

Čakovec is 12 kilometers northeast of Varaždin. You can get to Čakovec by bus or train from Varaždin (15–20 minutes) or Zagreb (2.5 hours by bus, 3 hours 15 minutes by train). The bus station (Tome Masaryka 26, tel. 040/313-947) is only a two-minute walk north of the Trg Kralja Tomislava. The train station (Kolodvorska 2, tel. 040/384-333) is slightly further away, about a 10-minute walk to the southwest. If you're driving, simply follow the roads to Čakovec from Varaždin.

MEĐIMURJE WINE ROADS

Driving northwest out of Čakovec in the direction of Štrigova, you'll start to see signs for *vinska cesta* (wine road), leading you through peaceful countryside, with rolling hills strung with rows of vineyards. Before heading out, visit the **tourist board** (Turistička zajednica Međimurske Županije, Ruđera Boškovića 3, tel. 040/390-191, info@tzm.hr, www.tzm.hr) in Čakovec for maps and directions. You'll need a car to navigate the routes, though the brave might be able to travel by bicycle (with a lot of safety gear).

The wines you'll find will be of varying quality, but most people will let you taste before you buy. And if you're the type who feels guilty trying and not buying, bottles are usually available for a not-too-steep 30–40Kn. If you get stuck with a bad one, just add some fizzy mineral water to your glass and say *življeli* (cheers).

Sights

Though the main attractions are the lovely

winding roads and vine-covered hillsides, in the middle of the small village of Štrigova, northwest of Čakovec almost at the Slovenian border, is a nice dual-towered church, the 18th-century **Crkva Sv. Jeronima** (Church of St. Jerome). If you're lucky enough to find the church open, check out its beautiful frescoes by Ivan Ranger.

Wineries

It seems every other house along the route has a handpainted *vino* sign, alerting you to homemade wine. You can stop and try your luck if you feel like it, but there are a couple of wineries on the routes worth singling out. **Vinogradarstvo i podrumarstvo Bobnjar** (Robadje 130, Štrigova, tel. 040/851-431, call for hours) is run by a lovely couple who have been producing wine since 1952. With a great selection of whites (all made without additives so they're a bit acidic) the couple counts at least two Croatian presidents as customers. **Vino Lovrec** (Sv. Urban 133, Štrigova, tel. 040/830-171, call for hours) produces a very honest wine with no added sugars and has a really great rustic tasting area.

Accommodations and Food

Međimurski Dvori (Vladimira Nazora 22, Lopatinec, tel. 040/855-763, info@medjimurski-dvori.hr, www.medjimurski-dvori.hr, 65Kn), northwest of Čakovec in Lopatinec, is a destination restaurant, the sort of place you can easily spend several hours lingering over the chef's duck specialties or a more common north Croatian dish like turkey with *mlinci*.

Terbotz (Železna Gora 113, Štrigova, tel. 040/857-444, www.terbotz.hr, 11 A.M.–11 P.M. Fri., 11 A.M.–1 A.M. Sat., 75Kn), amidst seemingly endless vineyards on the surrounding hills, has some nice local dishes, with a good selection of game, and a collection of regional wines to choose from. The wine cellar area is probably the best spot to sit and order up a few glasses.

Most of Croatia's hot springs are marked with unappealing and decaying communist hotels, but **Toplice Sveti Martin** (Grkaveščak bb,

tel. 040/371-111, info@toplicesvetimartin.hr, www.toplicesvetimartin.hr) is a new complex with indoor and outdoor pools, waterslides, a makeshift beach, and some really good spa treatments and massages. If you'd like to use the facilities, tickets are about 60Kn depending on the season. The hotel (due to open in June 2009) and several apartments (from 243Kn per night) with kitchens are available for those who'd like to stay a little longer. Sveti Martin is 15 kilometers almost due north of Čakovec but is easily reached on the road from Štrigova (Sveti Martin is only a couple of kilometers southeast) if you'd like some pampering after all that wine.

◖ HLEBINE

The small town of Hlebine is where the naive art movement was born. It's not hard to find your way away around the town's one main street. The **Generalić Gallery** (tel. 048/836-430, www.generalic.com, call ahead to arrange a visit) is located in the former studio of Ivan Generalić, the genre's most well-known painter, though it also exhibits work by his son Josip and grandson Goran. The gallery is open on request only, so call in advance if you would like to visit. The **Galerija Hlebine** (Community Gallery Hlebine, Trg Ivana Generalića 15, tel. 048/836-075, 10 A.M.–4 P.M. Mon.–Fri., 10 A.M.–2 P.M. Sat., 10Kn) has some nice pieces by various village artists. It's located in a modern building on the road to Koprivnica and you can ask at the gallery about other artists in the area willing to open up their studios.

There's not really anywhere to eat in Hlebine, so head to the nearby **Podravska Klet** (Starogradska cesta bb, tel. 048/634-069, 10 A.M.–10 P.M. daily, 70Kn) in Koprivnica. It is one of the best restaurants in the entire region, with a warm local atmosphere and homey dishes like beef goulash on the menu. On weekends, it's a good idea to book ahead.

Almost at the Hungarian border, Hlebine is approximately 80 kilometers northeast of Zagreb and is accessed via Koprivnica, about 16 kilometers away. Monday to Friday there are six buses a day from Koprivnica to Hlebine (30 minutes, 20Kn), but service gets highly irregular on the weekends. Koprivnica is connected by bus with Zagreb (1.5 hours, 80Kn) and Varaždin. Even simpler is to take the slow train to Koprivnica (1.5 hours, 46Kn) and then take the bus for Hlebine. If you're traveling by car, the simplest route is to take the A4 toward Varaždin and exit Koprivnica and follow the signs.

Slavonia

A vast stretch of rich agricultural land, Slavonia (Slavonija) doesn't get many of Croatia's tourists, who typically turn west toward the coast and skip this part of eastern Croatia, stretching out its green arm leisurely toward the Danube. Its geographical position, sharing borders with Bosnia, Serbia, and Hungary, has led Slavonia to be bounced between different rulers and kingdoms on and off since the 11th century. The Homeland War, Croatia's fight for independence from Yugoslavia in the 1990s, affected the area significantly with some towns, like Vukovar, suffering mass destruction and loss of life.

Today the region is rebounding quickly and Slavonia is doing a great job of promoting the things that make it unique. This is the place to stay in a *seoski turizam* hotel, get a ride in a *fijaker* (carriage), and explore the local cuisine, heavy in pork but also characterized by freshwater fish. *Fiš paprikaš* is a must-eat while you're here, but also be sure to try some of the spicy *kulen* (salami) and sausages made after the annual pig slaughter in November.

POŽEGA

Požega is one of Slavonia's prettier small towns, with a long row of one-storied typical homes

sheep grazing near Požega

WINE ROADS TOUR OF SLAVONIA

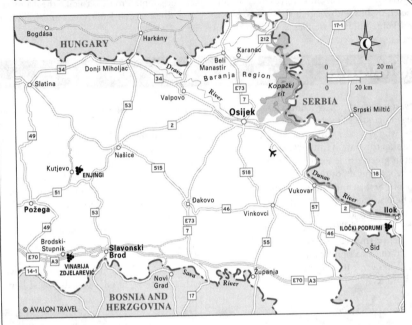

DAY 1

Drive from Zagreb to **Požega,** taking a quick look around the pretty town before heading out to the **Enjingi** winery, one of Croatia's best, for some serious kicking back with a bottle and some local *kulen.*

DAY 2

Slowly make your way to **Slavonski Brod,** where you should stop for a coffee at the town's central **Kavana Mala.** Then head on to **Vinarija Zdjelarević,** whose vineyards were the inspiration for famed Croatian writer Ivana Mažuranić's Hlapić storybook character. The Slavonian home cooking here might even be good enough to make you forget about the wine for a few minutes.

DAY 3

Spend the morning touring **Osijek** or **Kopački rit** before holing up for the night in Osijek's historic **Hotel Waldinger.**

DAY 4

Wind your way through the wineries of the **Baranja,** arriving at the **Sklepić house** in the early afternoon for a ride in a typical Slavonian horse-drawn *fijaker,* a great meal, and a night in the 1910 village cottage.

DAY 5

Spend your last day roaming around the medieval town of **Ilok** and the surrounding wineries with a lingering lunch at the **Odescalchi castle.**

barbecue, Slavonian style

lining the main road in and out of town. On the town's main square, **Trg svetog Trojstva**, the **Crkva svetog Duha** (Church of the Holy Spirit) was once used as a mosque by the Turks, who occupied the town between 1536 and 1691. The 14th-century **Crkva svetog Lovre** (St. Lawrence's Church) has some nice Gothic frescoes and the **Gradski muzej** (Town Museum, Matice Hrvatske 1, tel. 034/272-130, www .gmp.hr, 9 A.M.–3 P.M. Mon.–Fri., 10Kn) has a small collection that's worth a peek if you're in town. For a quiet escape, the **Šetalište Stari Grad** is a nice walking path through the ruins and site of the early 13th-century town.

In May Požega hosts a quirky **Hrvatska revija jednominutnih filmova** (Croatian Festival of One-Minute Films, www.crominute .hr), with creative takes on 60 seconds from around the globe.

Wineries

Twenty-seven kilometers from Požega is **Enjingi** (Hrnjevac 87, Vetovo, tel. 034/267-200, www.enjingi.hr, 391Kn d., including breakfast), one of Croatia's best wineries. It's open to the public for tastings (8 A.M.–5 P.M. Mon.–Fri., 8 A.M.–3 P.M. Sat.) but it's even better to spend a night here, chatting with the owners over a glass of wine and some local *kulen* with fresh bread.

Nearby are the 800-year-old **Kutjevo cellars** (Kutjevo, tel. 034/255-041, 8 A.M.–8 P.M. Mon.–Sat., 50Kn admission and tasting), where you can taste several wines as well as learn a bit about local wines in the guided introduction. An additional sum (50Kn) buys you lunch as well as local salami and cheese. Kutjevo produces several varieties of wine, but be sure to sample its specialty, ice wine, made from grapes harvested when the temperatures are well below freezing, giving it a distinct flavor, as well as its aged wine, de Gotho.

Accommodations and Food

Grgin Dol (Grgin Dol 20, tel. 034/273-222, 334Kn d., including breakfast) and **Vila Stanišić** (Ulica Dr. Franje Tuđman 10, tel. 034/312-168, www.vila-stanisic.hr, 400Kn d.), the former a set of rooms above a candy store, have basic rooms at reasonable prices. For food,

Restoran Tomislav (Vjekoslava Babukića 25, tel. 034/274-066, 7 A.M.–11 P.M. daily, 50Kn) is a reliable choice for good sit-down fare, heavy on local pork specialties.

Getting There and Around

You can reach Požega by bus (Industrijska 2, tel. 034/273-133) or train (Franje Cirakija 7, tel. 034/273-911); both stations are at the northern end of the town. There are several bus and train connections daily (the bus takes 2.5 hours, the fast train takes 3 hours, and the slow train takes up to 5 hours), though the trains are a bit cheaper—a one-way ticket on the train is 88Kn versus 110Kn by bus. By car from Zagreb it's about 150 kilometers east. Take the Autocesta towards Slavonski Brod and exit Nova Gradiška. From here you'll find road signs that will point you into town.

SLAVONSKI BROD

Though there's not a lot to see in this mainly industrial town, the city's small 19th-century waterfront center is a nice place to stop for a bite to eat and there are a couple of good options for overnight stays before moving on through Slavonia. If you're here mid-June, be sure to stop for the **Brodsko Kolo Festival** (www.fa-broda.hr) for the superb displays of folk dance, *tamburaše* musicians, and exhibits of village life.

Sights

The main square, **Trg I.B. Mažuranić,** faces the Sava River and the town of Bosanski Brod, today a peaceful place on the other bank—though less than two decades ago, shots rang across the river into town. Walk down the riverside walkway **Šetalište braće Radić** to the Baroque **Franjevački samostan** (Franciscan monastery). On the western side of the square are the remnants of the **Brod Fortress,** once a giant star-shaped fortress built in the early 18th century to defend Slavonia against the Turks.

Going out of town, **Dilj mountain** is a lovely place to take a hike, with some beautiful old weekend homes, including one once occupied by Croatian children's author Ivana

AGATHA CHRISTIE AND CROATIA

Famed mystery author Agatha Christie had more than one connection with Croatia. In 1928, after a painful divorce, she set out from London to Baghdad, taking the Venice-Simplon Orient Express. She said she had always wanted to take the famous train. She described it as "Allegro con fuoco, swaying, and rattling and hurling one from side to side in its mad haste to leave Calais and the Occident."

The original Venice-Simplon Orient Express traveled through Zagreb as well as Slavonia on its way to Belgrade. Agatha Christie set the majority of her book, *Murder on the Orient Express,* on a train stuck in a snowdrift between Vinkovci and Brod (the name for Slavonski Brod and Bosanski Brod when they were considered one town).

And this wasn't the only time Agatha Christie came to Croatia. After meeting her archaeologist husband, Max, they took a second honeymoon to Dubrovnik and Split, on the Dalmatian coast.

Brlić Mažuranić, and several nice spots for picnicking. Ask at the **tourist office** (Tourist Information Center Slavonski Brod, Trg pobjede 30, tel. 035/231-939, www.tzgsb.hr) for more information.

Wineries

🄆 **Vinarija Zdjelarević** (tel. 035/427-775, info@zdjelarevic.hr, www.zdjelarevic.hr, 712Kn d., including breakfast) is a bit of a one-stop shop, just 15 minutes west of Slavonski Brod in Brodski Stupnik, with a winery, restaurant, and hotel, all with traditional Slavonian flavor. The place is a must-visit in nice weather, when you can dine overlooking the vineyards on the restaurant's terrace. To get there, exit the highway at "Slavonski Brod Zapad" and follow the signs towards Nova Gradiška/Požega. In the village of Slatinik, follow the road toward Nova Gradiška for six kilometers until you reach the village of Brodski Stupnik.

Accommodations and Food

By far the most charming bed-and-breakfast in the area, the ◖ **Rezidencija Uno** (ul. Štealište braće Radića 6, tel. 035/415-000, rezidencija@uno-brod.hr, www.uno-brod.hr, 568Kn d.) has tasteful antique-filled rooms in a gorgeous Secession-era mansion. The company that owns the hotel also happens to own two of the best places for food and drink in town: the sweet little ◖ **Kavana Mala** (Trg I. B. Mažuranić), literally "small coffeehouse," and **Pizzerija Uno** (Nikole Zrinskog 7, tel. 035/442-107, 9 A.M.–midnight daily, 45Kn), with its dark brick and wood interior and flower-filled summer terrace. If the Rezidencija Uno is booked, another option for overnight is the **Hotel Savus** (Dr. A. Starčevića 2a, tel. 035/405-888, info@savus-hotel.com, www.savus-hotel.com, 1,286Kn d., including breakfast). Right in the center of town, it has a rather gaudy lobby but the rooms are new and comfortable. For cheaper options, contact the **tourist office** (Tourist Information Center Slavonski Brod, Trg pobjede 30, tel. 035/231-939, www.tzgsb.hr) to see about small pensions and private accommodation.

Getting There and Around

Slavonski Brod is one of the largest towns in Slavonia, approximately 200 kilometers east of Zagreb. The city is easily accessed by bus or train. The bus station (Trg hrvatskog proljeća, tel. 035/444-200) has multiple daily connections with Zagreb (3 hours, 110Kn), as well as Osijek (2 hours, 63Kn) and Đakovo (45 minutes, 37Kn). The train (Trg hrvatskog proljeća, tel. 035/441-082) is faster and cheaper; from Zagreb it takes only about 2.5 hours and costs around 100Kn. If driving from Zagreb, simply take the Autocesta in the direction of Slavonski Brod.

ĐAKOVO

Đakovo, 95 kilometers east of Slavonski Brod, is a town of around 30,000 and an important trading center in Slavonia due to its location and history. The city has long been a market town, a place where local farmers and craftsmen met to buy and sell, and Đakovo maintains that feeling even today. The most striking feature of Đakovo, which you'll spot before you even come close to the town, is the giant 275-foot brick **cathedral** (Trg Josipa Jurja Strossmayera 6, tel. 031/802-225, 7 A.M.–noon and 3–7 P.M. daily, free) that seems to dwarf everything by comparison. It was built between 1862 and 1882 by the Bishop Juraj Strossmayer, famed for his mission to unite the Slavs, in the Gothic Revival style.

If you've ever been to Vienna, then you've heard of the Lippizaner horses. Đakovo has one of the few **Lippizaner stud farms** (Ergela Stud Farm, Augusta Šenoe 47, tel. 031/813-286, www.ergela-djakovo.hr, 20Kn), a 10-minute walk from the cathedral. The farm puts on shows for large groups, but individual visitors can still see the horses and a small collection of historical photographs. Call ahead to see what times the horses might be training that day if you'd like to see them in action.

Đakovo is very well connected with Osijek, with over a dozen buses (45 minutes, 30Kn) and half a dozen trains (45 minutes, 28Kn) daily. You can also connect with Zagreb by bus (3.5 hours, 115Kn) or train (3 hours, 94Kn).

OSIJEK

It's worth spending a day in the riverfront town of Osijek, just 20 kilometers from the Serbian border, to walk around its famous fortress, the Tvrđa, a collection of Habsburg-era buildings that sit on the site of a much older Roman stronghold.

Osijek was damaged badly in the war and you'll see some of the scars on buildings today. However, the city has started to regain some of its prosperity of days past.

One of the nicest walks in Osijek is to follow the peaceful walkway **Šetalište Kardinala Frane Šepera** along the riverfront to the **Zimska luka** (winter harbor), where waterfront cafés hug the small marina.

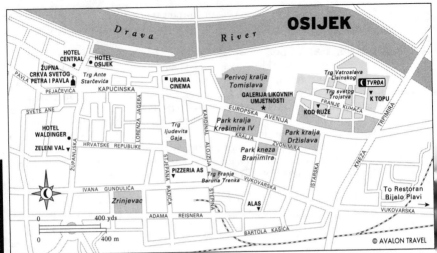

Gornji Grad

Upper Town

Osijek's small Gornji Grad is centered around the **Trg Ante Starčevića,** dominated by the town's brick **Župna crkva svetog Petra i Pavla** (Parish Church of St. Peter and Paul, Trg Ante Starčevića, tel. 031/310-020, www .svpetaripavao.hr, open daily, mass at 7 A.M. and 6:30 P.M. Mon.–Fri., 7 A.M. Sat., 6:30, 8:30, 10, and 11:30 A.M. and 6:30 P.M. Sun., free), built in the 1890s for the growing city. The interior of the church seats 3,000 and is covered in striking frescoes, painted between 1938 and 1942 by Croatian artist Mirko Rački.

The nearby **Europska avenija** starts off with the architecturally interesting, and still in operation, 1912 **Urania Cinema,** just off the beginning of Europska towards the river. The pink facade topped by a mournful mask resembles a giant organ. Back on Europska, you can take a peek at the **Galerija likovnih umjetnosti** (Gallery of Fine Arts, Europska avenija 9, tel. 031/251-280, www .mdc.hr/glu_osijek, 10 A.M.–6 P.M. Tues.–Fri., 10 A.M.–1 P.M. Sat.–Sun., 10Kn), the town's art gallery, with lots of decadent 19th-century portraits by Slavonian painters. From there, Europska becomes a wide tree-lined street,

hugged by glorious art nouveau homes, some decaying, some restored.

Tvrđa

The 17th-century Tvrđa, at the end of Europska's grand portion, is Osijek's most well-known tourist attraction and social hub. The Austro-Hungarian fort is actually a giant complex of buildings, criss-crossed with nice little cobblestoned streets. The area is also Osijek' cultural center and the city is currently renovating more and more buildings for schools the university, and the public.

The heart of the Tvrđa is the **Trg svetog Trojstva,** a huge square punctuated by the **Zavjetni stup** (plague column), a 1729 thank you from those who survived an outbreak that killed a third of the city's population. The cloaked figures at the Baroque pillar's base are saints added in 1784 after several more bouts of plague had attacked the city. The square's **Muzej Slavonij** (Museum of Slavonia, Trg Svetog Trojstva 6, te 031/250-730, 8–11 A.M. and 11:30 A.M.–2 P.M Tues.–Sun., 20Kn) has some interesting exhibi of local history and artifacts.

Entertainment and Events

For nightlife, head to the **Tvrđa,** where Osijek university students and young professiona

© SHANN FOUNTAIN ČULO

the Tvrđa

drink until the wee hours. If you'd prefer to take it easier, there are some nice cafés at the **Zimska Luka** that have great outdoor seating in summer, or take in a movie at **Europa** cinema or the **Urania,** both within walking distance of Gornji Grad.

Hrvatsko narodno kazalište (Croatian National Theater, Županijska 9, tel. 031/220-700) hosts performances of classical music and theater throughout the year.

On the first Saturday of each month, **Trg svetog Trojstva** is overrun with antiques dealers from Croatia as well as neighboring Hungary, Bosnia, and Serbia. You'll get a better deal here than you would at the market's equivalent in Zagreb.

Accommodations

Surprisingly, Osijek has several options for accommodation on the upper end of the scale but little to offer in terms of budget hotels. Travelers watching their wallets should head to the **tourist office** (Županska 2, tel. 031/203-755, www.tzosijek.hr, 7 A.M.–4 P.M. Mon.–Fri., 8 A.M.–noon Sat.), where they can tell you all about renting private rooms. Alternatively, try the **Garni Hotel Ritam** (Kozjačka 76, tel. 031/310-310, www.hotel-ritam.hr, 480Kn d., including breakfast), a small hotel located in the suburbs with clean but very basic rooms.

The **Hotel Central** (Trg Ante Starčevića 6, tel. 031/283-399, www.hotel-central-os .hr, 768Kn d., including breakfast), is located in a pretty old Secession building in Gornji Grad. The rooms aren't as charming as the building but they are fresh and clean and it's hard to beat the location. The nearby **❰ Hotel Waldinger** (Županska 8, tel. 031/250-450, www.waldinger.hr, 931Kn d., including breakfast) has more charming rooms and the same great location at slightly higher prices; the waterfront **Hotel Osijek** (Šamačka 4, tel. 031/230-333, www.hotelosijek.hr, 1,023Kn d., including breakfast), despite its soulless exterior, is considered the nicest hotel in town.

For a slightly quirkier stay, the **Zoo Hotel** (Sjevernodravska obala bb, tel. 031/229-922, zoo-hotel@zoo-hotel.com, www.zoo-hotel .com, 675Kn d., including breakfast), next to Osijek's zoo on the opposite side of the river,

INLAND CROATIA

has modern rooms decorated with zebra- or leopard-print touches and the leafy location is pretty and quiet. (Unless, of course, the animals are restless.)

Food
K Topu (Fakultetska 1, tel. 031/210-904, 10 A.M.–10 P.M. daily, 15Kn) in the Tvrđa is a quick option for a fast sandwich, while **Zeleni Val** (Županijska 22, tel. 031/200-864, 8 A.M.–11 P.M. Mon.–Fri., 10 A.M.–11 P.M. Sat., 11 A.M.–11 P.M. Sun., 30Kn) is the best place in town for the Croatian meat staple *čevapčići*. At **Pizzeria As** (Radićeva 16, tel. 031/212-500, 9 A.M.–11 P.M. Mon.–Sat., 11 A.M.–11 P.M. Sun., 30Kn), order the *Osiječka* pizza topped with Slavonia's famous salami. Going more upmarket, **Restoran Bijelo Plavi** (Martina Divalta 8, tel. 031/571-000, 10 A.M.–11 P.M. daily, 60Kn) cooks up Slavonian and international cuisine, like stuffed veal rolls and pork tenderloin with plum sauce, alongside yummy bread baked fresh daily in the restaurant. **(Kod Ruže** (Kuhačeva 25a, tel. 031/206-066, 9 A.M.–10 P.M.

Mon.–Sat., 75Kn) in the Tvrđa serves up gourmet local dishes (even frog legs are on the menu) in a quaint space loaded with atmosphere and a heavy dose of chic. It claims to be closed on Sunday but you can call because that's not always the case. For the best *fiš paprikaš*, a sort of freshwater fish stew that is a local specialty, try the unassuming restaurant **Alas** (Reisnerova 12a, tel. 031/202-311, 10 A.M.–11 P.M., 60Kn), a bit off the beaten path but worth the trek.

Getting There and Around
Both the bus (Trg Lavoslava Ružičke 2, tel. 031/214-355, www.panturist.hr, 5:30 A.M.– 9 P.M. daily) and train (Trg Lavoslava Ružičke 2, tel. 031/205-155, 5 A.M.–9:30 P.M. daily) stations are close to the center of town, with a 10-to-15-minute walk landing you on the main square. There's a fast InterCity train to Zagreb that takes about three hours and costs approximately 113Kn. Buses take closer to four but the connections are frequent and the trip costs around 125Kn to or from Zagreb. If you have a lot of bags, a tram ride (buy tickets at newspaper kiosks, approx. 8Kn) will take you there faster. The tram's also a great way to zip about town if you're too lazy to walk, though there are only two lines, so you'll be relying mostly on your feet or your rental car. Walking is preferred around the narrow Tvrđa.

(KOPAČKI RIT
On a floodplain created by the Danube and Drava Rivers, Kopački rit (Park prirode Kopački rit, tel. 031/750-855, www.kopacki-rit.com, opening hours vary but generally daily, 60Kn May–Sept. and 45Kn Oct.–Apr.) is a giant nature reserve only 10 kilometers northeast of Osijek. The park spans close to 57,000 acres, with lakes and swampy marshes filled with fish and over 250 species of birds. The forests of the **Tikveš** area of the park are filled with wild boar, deer, and the occasional black stork.

The highlight of Tikveš forest is the lovely **Dvorac,** actually a hunting lodge built by Archduke Franz Ferdinand that later passed into the hands of the Serbian royal family and

© SHANN FOUNTAIN ČULO

Urania Cinema

LAND MINES

The Homeland War may be a piece of history, but land mines left by the conflict continue to do damage around Croatia. An estimated 13 of Croatia's 21 counties are thought to contain land mines, with the area covering close to 1,700 square kilometers.

Croatia ratified the Mine Ban Treaty in 1998 and is working hard to clean up the mines, but the process is slow and expensive, and even after de-mining, some mines can still remain. Since 1991, land mines have hurt thousands of people in Croatia and killed more than 100 since 1998.

Before hiking in rural areas, you should educate yourself to be safe. One of the best sources of information is the **Hrvatski Centar za Razminiranje** (Croatian Mine Action Center, www.hcr.hr). Their website has maps for all regions of Croatia with danger areas marked in red. Also be on the lookout for red signs with the words *Pazi Mina* (Danger Mines) and a skull and crossbones.

Croatia is working on new methods to detect land mines, with a promising study in using the country's tradition of bee-keeping by training bees to sniff out mines. In the meantime, if you'd like to help the country's fight against land mines, visit **Adopt-a-Minefield** (www.landmines.org) to donate toward the cause.

then Tito. Some of the areas have yet to be cleared of land mines, so please watch out for signs warning you to steer clear. An English-language guide and more information are available at the visitors center at the entrance to the park. They can also let you know about boat tours (80Kn), which depart almost daily in warmer months, or help you organize a jeep tour of the park with a local guide.

Accommodations and Food

Within the park toward Tikveš, **Kormoran** (Podunavlje bb, tel. 031/753-099, 11 A.M.– 10 P.M. daily in season, call for winter hours, 75Kn) serves fresh local fish either grilled or as a part of a *paprikaš* stew cooking over glowing coals. The red-and-white-themed house of **Crvendać** (Biljske satnije ZNG RH 5, tel. 031/750-264, pansion@crvendac.com, www .crvendac.com, 298Kn d., including breakfast), literally translated redbird, is clean and happy, and the owners make some great food at reasonable prices. Located in Bilje, only a few kilometers from Osijek, it is an amazingly reasonable option for a night's stay while exploring the area.

Getting There and Around

By car from Osijek, drive to Bilje and turn right at the main intersection. From there, simply follow the signs to the park. Buses leave every half hour to one hour from Osijek to Bilje (20– 30 minutes). At the end of the line, it's about a four-kilometer walk to the visitors center. For those who have bikes, there's a bicycle path of approximately 16 kilometers on the Osijek to Bilje road.

THE BARANJA

At first glance the Baranja is just a lonely stretch of plain, but look closer and you'll uncover some of Slavonia's best finds here. Discovering local wineries is also a great way to get to meet the people, and the hospitable owners of bed-and-breakfasts around the area make visitors feel like they have their own personal guided tour.

Wineries

Baranja has been known for its wines since Roman times. If you have time to visit only one winery in the region, the **Vinarija Josić** (Planina 194, Zmajevac, tel. 098/252-657, www.josic.hr, call for hours) should top your list. The family makes award-winning wines in a brick wine cellar that dates from 1935. The bottles make nice souvenirs as well, not only for the great red or white wine inside, but for the labels, decorated with endangered bird species from nearby Kopački rit. The **Kolar wine cellar** (Maršala Tita 141, Suza, tel. 031/733-184, call for hours) also has a nice restaurant; at **Čočić** (Ružina 20, Zmajevac, tel. 091/120-0569, call for hours) the *vinski podrum*—a brick-lined room of wooden vats—is the perfect place to sample local wines. Last but not least on your list of stops: the **Gerštmajer wine cellar** (Šandora Petefija 31, Zmajevac, tel. 091/351-5586, call for hours), where you can drop by to sample wines or call ahead to arrange a lunch of local specialties.

Accommodations and Food

❰ **Baranjska kuća** (Kolodvorska 99, Karanac, tel. 031/720-180, www.baranjskakuca.odmor .org, 11 A.M.–10 P.M. Tues.–Sun., 40Kn) offers great meals with local wine. Its authentic setting even includes a small ethnographic museum. Just down the road, the ❰ **Sklepić house** (Kolodvorska 58, Karanac, tel. 031/720-303, denis.sklepic@inet.hr, 320Kn d., including breakfast) is possibly one of the nicest experiences in the region. The 1910-era village house is pleasingly authentic, the stay includes a lovely breakfast, and the owner can arrange for typical Slavonian horse-drawn carriage rides as well as tours of Kopački rit and the wine roads of the Baranja.

Getting There and Around

The region is about 30 kilometers north of Osijek. Follow the A7 to Beli Manastir and then follow the signs for the villages, located to the east of the highway. Public transportation is infrequent. You'll really need a car to get around the region.

VUKOVAR

Once a happy and prosperous multicultural community, the city of Vukovar was heavily damaged during the Homeland War. Today Vukovar is only beginning to recover, though the Croat and Serb populations remain divided, and while there's not a lot of sightseeing, there are plenty of reasons to visit.

For one, the city is a great jumping-off point for touring the wine country just outside of town but more importantly, it's great to show support for Vukovar's economy and get to know the people who are welcoming and friendly despite the recent suffering and the lingering wounds of war.

For more information you can contact the **tourist office** (J. J. Strossmayera 15, tel. 032/442-889, www.turizamvukovar.hr). The local agency **Danubium Tours** (Trg Republike Hrvatske 1, tel. 032/445-455, danubium tours@vu.t-com.hr, www.danubiumtours.hr) can arrange for private rooms, as well as very reasonable bike trips, walking tours, and trips through the local wine region, all including excellent lunch stops.

Sights

The **Gradski Muzej** (Town Museum, Županijska 2—actually located on Strossmayera near the market, tel. 032/441-270, 7 A.M.–3 P.M. Mon.–Sat., 10Kn) is housed in the early 18th-century **Dvorac Eltz** (Eltz Castle). Many of the town's permanent exhibitions were seized by the Serbs, with some being officially transported to Serbia and others disappearing altogether. However, an agreement in 2001 has helped many items return to the museum and the city is in the process of restoring the Dvorac Eltz, which was badly damaged in the Homeland War, to its former glory.

As Strossmayera crosses the river it becomes Dr. Franje Tuđmana, which leads through Vukovar's old town. One of the prettiest buildings here is the Grand Hotel. Built in 1897, it was Vukovar's finest hotel until it was sold in 1919 to the Worker's Union and renamed **Radnički Dom** (House of Workers). It was here that the Yugoslav Communist Party was founded in 1920.

Many of the buildings in Vukovar's **stari grad** (Old Town, along and around the street Dr. Franje Tuđmana) were built in the Baroque period, with lovely arched arcades on the ground floors. Most were badly damaged in the war, though some have been restored and some left with the reminders of the violence that disrupted the peaceful city streets.

THE SIEGE OF VUKOVAR

On September 14, 1991, the Croatian National Guard cut off the JNA (Yugoslav People's Army) barracks, leaving them without electricity, food, water, or phone lines. Serb paramilitaries responded by launching a fierce attack, killing civilians as they went, and forcing some 2,000 refugees into the center of Vukovar. During the next two weeks 15 to 80 wounded civilians were brought to the Vukovar hospital each day.

This clearly marked a new phase in the war. On October 4 the JNA attacked – this time fiercely, with air attacks, artillery, and mortar, dropping two bombs on the packed hospital. Most of the hospital was operating out of the basement by this time, protecting most of the patients but making it hard to find room for the 92 additional wounded that poured in that day.

October hardly begun, most people moved into public bomb shelters protected by the Croatian National Guard. The Serb forces were experiencing morale issues as they weren't able to bring down the small and comparatively unarmed town. The group was suffering from a lack of organization, so a new general took over the Vukovar "operation" and launched another serious attack on November 3, advancing to within just a few hundred yards of the town center.

Vukovar felt betrayed by the leadership in Zagreb, who they felt had sold them out by agreeing to an internationally brokered cease-fire. Tuđman reportedly offered no help, worried more about diplomacy than about Vukovar.

Finally on November 18 the town fell, with Serb forces throwing the patients and hospital personnel onto trucks, killing them, and depositing them in a mass grave at Ovčara. Two thousand Croatian civilians and soldiers died defending Vukovar and another two thousand (mostly men who were bussed out of town that late fall day) remain missing.

Southeast of the old town, the 18th-century **Franjevački samostan** (Franciscan monastery, Samostanska 2) was Vukovar's oldest preserved Baroque monument prior to its almost total destruction in 1991. However, Zagreb county contributed to its wonderful and almost exact reconstruction.

Vukovar has several war monuments, but one of the most striking is the **cross** at the mouth of the Vuka and Danube Rivers, in memoriam of the lives lost defending the country. An inscribed Glagolitic text translates, "He who dies justly, shall live forever."

Accommodations and Food

The recently built **Hotel Lav** (Strossmayera 17, tel. 032/445-100, info@hotel-lav.hr, www .hotel-lav.hr, 881Kn d., including breakfast) is a point of pride for Vukovar's residents, marking a new chapter in the life of the city. Its rooms are sleek though perhaps a little bland. But what the rooms lack in personality, the magnificent Danube views make up for. Try the **Restoran Tena** (Dvanaest redarstvenika 33, tel. 032/425-629, 45Kn) for good-quality local cuisine.

Getting There and Around

Vukovar is 35 kilometers southeast of Osijek. By car from Zagreb, take the highway direction Slavonski Brod, exiting at Vinkovci where you'll follow the signs for Vukovar. The drive from Zagreb takes about seven hours. The bus station (Autobusni kolodvor, Olajnica bb, tel. 032/441-829) has multiple daily connections with Osijek (45 minutes, 50Kn) as well as Zagreb and Slavonski Brod. The train (Željeznički kolodvor, Priljevo 2, tel. 032/430-340) is perhaps the nicest way to travel; from Zagreb it takes around 3.5 hours on an intercity ticket and costs 115Kn, and from Osijek it takes two hours and costs 25Kn.

AROUND VUKOVAR
◖ Ilok Wineries

The town of Ilok is a largely undiscovered little

gem with a charming, if small, medieval old town. It's famous for its wines, particularly the gold-tinged Traminac served at the coronation of Queen Elizabeth II. If you're in the mood for wine tasting, start with the 17th-century cellars of **Iločki Podrumi** (Iločki Cellars, Šetalište o. M. Barbarića 4, tel. 032/590-088, www.ilocki-podrumi .hr, call for hours). The winemaker also has a nice ◖ **restaurant** (Šetalište o. M. Barbarića 5, tel. 032/590-126, 11 A.M.–11 P.M. daily, 75Kn) in the restored **Odescalchi castle** and plans to open up a hotel of sorts in the next couple of years.

It's also worth checking out local producers **Julius Stipetić** (S Radića 16, tel. 032/591-068, call for hours) and **Ivan Čobankovic** (V Nazora 59, tel. 032/593-382, call for hours), offering a selection of solid white and red wines.

The **Ilok tourist office** (Trg Nikole Iločkog 2, tel. 032/590-020, info@turizamilok.hr, www.turizamilok.hr) can provide you with maps and info on the local wine routes if you'd like to explore more vineyards and wine producers. An interesting souvenir is a bottle of wine from Ilok's **high school,** founded in 1899 to teach winegrowing, a tradition it continues today.

If you'd like to stick around a while, try the **Hotel Dunav Ilok** (Julija Benešića 62, tel. 032/596-500, www.hoteldunavilok.com, 500Kn d., including breakfast), a small family hotel furnished with antiques. If you're in town at the end of September, the town hosts a **wine harvest festival** with cultural performances and lots of yummy wine tastings.

Karlovac Region

The region around Karlovac is an easy stop-off on your way to the coast. Whether you're headed to Istria, the Kvarner Gulf, Dalmatia, or the Plitvice Lakes, you'll have to pass through Karlovac, and it's a nice place to have lunch and a quick look around before continuing on your way. Driving to Istria or the Kvarner Gulf, you'll pass through the Gorski Kotar, a region that gets few tourists but has lots of activities for fans of adventure and other obscure attractions, like the Museum of Frogs in the village of Lokve.

While the Lonjsko polje isn't quite on the route to anywhere, fans of nature will want to make a detour to see the nature park and its interesting wildlife, particularly the large community of storks that nest there every year.

KARLOVAC

If you're driving from Zagreb to the Dalmatian coast, you'll pass the exit for Karlovac on the highway. It's actually a worthwhile stop, if only for a couple of hours, to see the pretty center of town and maybe have a riverside coffee.

Situated on a delta between four rivers—the Korana, Kupa, Mrežnica, and Dobra—Karlovac was built in the 16th century by the Austrians to help defend their territories from the Turks, explaining the city's neat grid of streets, wide compared with other Croatian old towns. The town once had walls in the shape of a six-pointed star; they were demolished in the 19th century.

Karlovac became an important trade city on the route to the coast in the 18th and 19th centuries. Even as a part of former Yugoslavia, Karlovac was relatively prosperous, with a good base of industries in the area. The city was badly damaged in the Homeland War, when it was on the defensive front lines. It's finally recovering and has restored a significant amount of the charming center.

Sights

A good starting point for exploring the town is the main square, **Trg bana Jelačića.** Its wide expanse is surrounded by refined Baroque buildings, some of which have been restored. In the square's center is a **plague column,** built after an outbreak in 1691. From the square, you can see the steeple of the **Crkva presvetog Trojstva** (Holy Trinity Church).

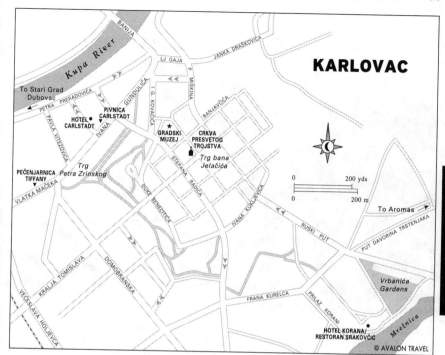

The church is the oldest building in Karlovac, built as a part of the Franciscan monastery in the 17th century. Its interior is gilt and Baroque like so many church interiors, but its lower ceilings, which make it more intimate, add to its appeal.

On nearby **Strossmayerov trg** is the **Gradski muzej** (Town Museum, Strossmayerov trg 7, tel. 047/615-980, www.mdc.hr/karlovac, 8 A.M.–3 P.M. Tues.–Fri., 10 A.M.–noon Sat.–Sun., 10Kn), a nice permanent exhibition of town history presented in the 17th-century palace of Vuk Frankopan, a general who came from a powerful noble family.

If the weather's nice, a stroll through the **Vrbanić gardens** on the banks of the Korana River is a nice way to stretch your legs. Be sure to stop at the **Hotel Korana's restaurant** for a light lunch or snack on the riverside terrace.

Just out of town overlooking the Kupa River is the medieval fortress **Dubovac,** owned in the 15th and 16th centuries by the Frankopans and the Zrinskis. It's about a 30-minute hike up (take Ulica Vladka Mačeka west and uphill to the left) to see a small exhibition and a superb view of all of Karlovac.

A short drive south of town on the road to Plitvice is the **Muzejska zbirka naoružanja Domovinskog rata** (Museum of Arms from the Homeland War, dawn–dusk daily, free), an exhibition of tanks and weaponry used during the conflict, when the front lines were here in Turanj. The collection is displayed around the ruins of four buildings, once Hapsburg army barracks.

Sports and Recreation

There are some great cycling routes in the area of Karlovac. For maps and more information, contact the **tourist office** (Turistička Zajednica Grada Karlovca, Petra Zrinskog 3, tel. 047/615-115).

© SHANN FOUNTAIN CULO

view of Crkva presvetog Trojstva from the main square

Accommodations

The **Hotel Carlstadt** (A. Vraniczanya 1, tel. 047/611-111, carlstadt@ka.t-com.hr, www .carlstadt.hr, 448Kn d., including breakfast) has basic rooms and is located smack in the center of town, while the [**Hotel Korana** (Perivoj J. Vrbanića 8, tel. 047/609-090, info@ hotelkorana.hr, www.hotelkorana.hr, 850Kn d., including breakfast) is a more luxurious option, nestled on the banks of the Korana River in a shady park. The **tourist office** (Turistička Zajednica Grada Karlovca, Petra Zrinskog 3, www.karlovac-touristinfo.hr, tel. 047/615-115) can also point you in the direction of private rooms and apartments for an overnight stay; if you'd like to rough it there's a nice campsite, **Slapić** (Mrežnički Brig bb, tel. 047/854-700, 30Kn per person plus 25Kn for tent site), about 15 kilometers southwest of town.

Food

In the city center, **Pečenjarnica Tiffany** (Vladka Mačeka 6/1, tel. 047/614-666, 7 A.M.–10 P.M. Mon.–Sat., 1–11 P.M. Sun., 35Kn) has sandwiches, grilled dishes, and pizzas in a very casual setting. **Pivnica Carlstadt** (Vranyczanyeva 2, tel. 047/601-900, 11 A.M.–11 P.M. daily, 35Kn) is a conveniently located pub with lots of grilled meats, pizzas, pastas, risottos, and more. Join the young fashionable crowd at **Aromas** (Put Davorina Trstenjaka 1, tel. 047/804-011, 7 A.M.–midnight Mon.–Sat., 9 A.M.–midnight Sun., 45Kn), near the arboretum at the edge of town. The space is trendy but the menu is a laid-back mix of grill, Italian, and Mexican dishes. **Lovački Rog** (Pojatno bb, tel. 047/637-675, www.lovacki-rog.hr, 10 A.M.–11 P.M. daily, 75Kn) on the road to Plitvice specializes in venison and local fish dishes and its outdoor terrace is great in nicer weather. It's really worth the splurge for a meal at the Hotel Korana's [**Restoran Srakovčić** (Perivoj J. Vrbanića 8, tel. 047/609-090, info@hotel korana.hr, www.hotelkorana.hr, 8 A.M.–11 P.M. daily, 65Kn), particularly if it's warm enough to sit outside on the riverside veranda. The restaurant brings a touch of gourmet flair to standard Croatian dishes with the occasional departure from the norm like the quail-egg starter. At the very least, linger over a coffee and a slice of cake.

Getting There and Around

Karlovac is approximately 50 kilometers southwest of Zagreb. The city's bus station (Autobusni kolodvor, Prilaz Vjećeslava Holjevca 2, tel. 047/614-729) is on one of the main thoroughfares a short walk from the center. There are six connections with Zagreb on weekdays, four on Saturdays, and three on Sundays. Tickets cost approximately 36Kn each way. The train station (Vilima Reinera 3, tel. 047/646-244) is just 1.5 kilometers north on the same street (though it has a different name). There are multiple connections daily and a one-way ticket costs around 35Kn. Generally, the bus has been the fastest mode of transport, reaching Zagreb in about one hour. However, road construction might make the train a faster option, particularly if you are traveling during rush hour. By car from Zagreb, simply take the Autocesta A1, direction Karlovac, about one hour's journey southwest.

Karlovac is a great place to stop off on a longer journey, with great connections to the Plitvice Lakes, Zadar, Split, and Rijeka.

ŽUMBERAK

Filled with densely forested hills and the weekend homes of Zagreb city-dwellers, the Žumberak has some of the best easy hikes around and is convenient for a day-trip from Zagreb. Starting about 30 kilometers west of the capital, you can reach the area by connecting in Samobor (Slani Dol, about 6 km from Samobor, is a good entrance point). Though Samobor's not technically part of the Žumberak, its **tourist office** (Trg Kralja Tomislava 1, tel. 01/336-0044, www.tz-samobor .hr, 8 A.M.–7 P.M. Mon.–Fri., 9 A.M.–7 P.M. Sat., 10 A.M.–7 P.M. Sun.) is the place to go to find out more about hiking in the area. It's easy to get around the region by car, though the bus company **Samoborček** (tel. 01/333-5170, www.samoborcek.hr) has good connections within the region.

Ozalj

The wonderful **castle** (no phone, 8 A.M.–3 P.M. Mon.–Fri., posted hours not always observed, 10Kn) on the banks of the Kupa River is a nice stop, particularly if you can find someone to open up the doors. Inside is a great exhibition depicting Croatia's history in English, a harder thing to find than you might think. Below the castle is another tiny pretty building, that looks like a mini-castle on the edge of the river. It was actually a working hydroelectric plant built in 1908. The **tourist office** (Kurilovac 1, tel. 047/731-196, www.ozalj-tz.hr) should be able to help you with more details. In nearby Vivodina, north of Ozalj, the restaurant **Frian** can hook you up with a good meal (Vivodina 3, tel. 047/753-111, call for hours).

Pribić

If you're in the area, and particularly if you love old buildings, it's worth a visit to the hauntingly beautiful **Crkva svetog Blagovijesta** (Church of the Annunciation). The neo-Byzantine Greek Catholic church and monastery is now abandoned and rarely open to the public, but its architecture, an interesting mix of Orthodox and art nouveau, is stunning in itself.

Northern Žumberak

Filled with great **hiking** (contact the Samobor tourist office, Trg Kralja Tomislava 5, tel. 01/336-0044, www.tz-samobor.hr, 8 A.M.–7 P.M. Mon.–Fri., 9 A.M.–7 P.M. Sat., 10 A.M.–7 P.M. Sun.), the northern Žumberak has a couple of super *seoski turizam* hotels and restaurants. Try the 19th-century **Kurija Medven** (Medvenova Draga 13, tel. 01/627-0347, 469Kn d., including breakfast) for cozy authentic rooms and cuisine.

A short drive outside of Samobor in the border town of Bregana is **Eko-Selo Žumberak** (Koretići 13, tel. 01/338-7472, www.eko-selo .hr, 391Kn d., including breakfast), a hamlet of wood and stone cottages in a bucolic setting next to a rushing brook. The rooms are basic, but clean, and it's the perfect spot if you love riding (the Eko-Selo also runs a horse ranch) and other outdoor pleasures.

GORSKI KOTAR

Entering this mountainous and thickly forested region, you might think you fell asleep and ended up in a valley in Austria. Even in the summer the air here is noticeably cooler and in the winter the area is often covered in a blanket of white. If you like adventure sports or great food you'll certainly want to visit the area, conveniently located on the road from Zagreb to Rijeka. It's a great stopping-off point before heading to Istria, virtually overlooked by tourists, and full of adrenaline-fueled pursuits.

It is important to note that parts of the Gorski Kotar are impassable in winter, so this is a trip best made in spring, summer, and fall. The area really shines in summer, when its noticeably cooler temperatures and lack of tourists make it a welcome respite after some time on the busy coast.

Ogulin

The town of Ogulin, 58 kilometers southwest of Karlovac, has an early 16th-century castle with a small but disappointing museum. However, Ogulin is a great starting point to explore **Klek mountain.** Make your way by car or bus to the nearby village of Bijelsko, seven kilometers west of Ogulin, to start your two-hour round-trip journey on foot. Klek is not the highest of the mountains in the area—it stands a bit less than 1,200 meters—but it is certainly the most impressive in the Gorski Kotar region. The sheer rock jutting above the green forested hills has long been the source of local legends involving witches, as well as a princess supposedly locked inside the ominous-looking rock. There's a hut on the mountain that serves refreshments on the weekends and the views at the top are worth the climb if you're the sporting type. Note, though, that this steep hike is not for those with a fear of heights.

Bjelolasica

Bjelolasica, 27 kilometers west of Ogulin, is well known for its **Olimpijski centar** (Olympic Center, tel. 047/562-118, www.bjelolasica .hr), where professional athletes train. The ski season generally runs from mid-December through mid-February, though the season can be on and off even during its short run. Even outside the ski season there's plenty of sporting activities at Bjelolasica. Hiking, climbing, rafting, tennis, caving, fishing, and volleyball are just a few sports on the center's long list of offerings. Call ahead if you'd like to attend ski school (for adults and children) or one of the center's organized climbs or treks. Ski-equipment rentals can be arranged upon arrival. The center offers several levels of accommodation starting at 200Kn for bed and breakfast during the ski season.

Risnjak National Park

If you're looking for hiking, Risnjak National Park (www.risnjak.hr) has better trails than Bjelolasica. It's only a short bus ride from the town of Delnice, the main transportation hub for the area, 60 kilometers west of Karlovac. Pick up maps and information at the **Nacionalni park Risnjak motel** (tel. 051/836-133) in Crni Lug before heading to the park entrance two kilometers out of town. The park offers a good network of trails of varying difficulty, from a relatively easy nature walk, the Poučna staza Leska, to a steep hike up the Veliki Risnjak mountain, not for the faint of heart.

◖ Fužine

Fužine, 132 kilometers southwest of Karlovac, is one of the prettiest towns in the Gorski Kotar, with a nice lake and an interesting cave, the **Špilja Vrelo.** The town is a great jumping-off point for active vacations, with most accommodations helping you arrange fishing, rock climbing, and rafting trips. Most of all, the town has some great homemade specialties to sample. Have a slice of the local *štrudla šumsko voće* (blackberry strudel) and pick up some honey and a bottle of Goranski Jaeger for the trip home.

If you have a warm spot in your heart for amphibians, check out the nearby village of Lokve and its **Muzej Žaba** (Museum of Frogs, Šetalište Golubinjak 50, tel. 051/831-278, www.muzej-zaba.hr, call ahead to arrange visit, donations accepted). The quirky, small

JASENOVAC IN WORLD WAR II

The concentration camp at Jasenovac was set up in the summer of 1941 in a small village south of Zagreb. The camp was one of several in Croatia, though the atrocities committed at Jasenovac caused it to secure an even more sinister place in history.

Jasenovac held Croatian political prisoners (some of whom were thrown in for offenses as small as having been on the guest list for the Serbian king's wedding), though it mainly served as a death camp for Serbs, Jews, and gypsies. The respected archbishop of Zagreb during World War II, Alojzije Stepinac, compared Jasenovac to the mark of Cain, a sin that would sully Croatia forever.

Certainly it has caused the nation loads of shame, though the usual response has been to downplay or cover up what happened. Franjo Tuđman was a prime example, estimating the death toll at only 40,000 and even callously suggesting that the victims of Jasenovac and World War II fatalities (including the pro-Nazi Ustaše) be buried in a common grave with a memorial. Yugoslav historians had the tendency to inflate the numbers to one million. Though it's hard to reach a precise figure, Yale professor and surprisingly unbiased Croatian historian Ivo Banac puts the figure at about 120,000.

Whatever the number, the facts are shocking and deplorable. One of the camp's former leaders, Dinko Šakić, was finally extradited from Argentina in 1998 and sentenced to 20 years in prison. It was too little, too late. Perhaps future Croatian politicians will bring the reality of this tragic past to light to help teach a lesson for the future and to memorialize precious lives lost.

INLAND CROATIA

museum has a simple display of frog photos, live local frogs, and frog paraphernalia. It's not impressive, but still a must-see for those who like to dip into a bit of local culture and support the small community. Lokve even has a yearly frog festival in May, called Žabarska noć (Frog Night), serving frog specialties and filled with songs and small-town charm.

Bitoraj (Sveti križ 1, tel. 051/830-005, info@bitoraj.hr, www.bitoraj.hr, 654Kn d., including breakfast) is one of the nicest places to stay in the Gorski Kotar, and historical too, as it was once the hunting lodge of Josip Broz Tito, leader of Yugoslavia for over three decades. **Konoba Volta** (Doktora Franje Račkog 8, tel. 051/830-830, 6 A.M.–10 P.M. Mon.–Fri., 7 A.M.–11 P.M. Sat.–Sun., 40Kn) is great for heartwarming local meals, or for something a little more upscale try the restaurant at Bitoraj, which specializes in local game.

If you'd like to get the feeling of living in the mountains, rent the charming **Kuća Sobol** (Vučnik 27, tel. 051/812-371, www.sobol.hr, 994Kn, accommodates up to 6 people), located in Butterfly Valley near Fužine where a purported 500 species of butterflies can be found.

Tight on cash? Check with the **tourist office** (tel. 051/835-163, info@tz-fuzine.hr, www.tz-fuzine.hr), which rents cheaper mountain houses in the surrounding countryside as well as private rooms in town. The tourist office can also help arrange excursions to the cave and other activities in the area.

Getting There and Around

The Gorski Kotar region is southwest of Zagreb and west of Karlovac. The Karlovac–Rijeka highway passes right through the best of the region, including Fužine, while the Karlovac–Split highway touches the southern edge, with good access to Ogulin. Each town is around one hour and 45 minutes away from Zagreb by car.

If you'd prefer to travel via rail, the train makes stops at Ogulin (1 hour 30 minutes, 53Kn) and Fužine (2 hours 45 minutes, 78Kn). Ogulin's train station is about a 10-minute walk to the center of town.

Delnice, 60 kilometers west of Karlovac, is the main transportation hub for the area, with buses connecting pretty much everywhere in the Gorski Kotar region. Buses going from Zagreb to Istria stop in Delnice (Delnice bus station, tel. 051/812-060), taking almost three hours and costing around 110Kn. Buses run from Zagreb to Ogulin (2 hours 45 minutes, 100Kn—making the train a much better option); to Fužine you'd need to connect in Delnice (30 minutes, 27Kn).

SISAK

Though Sisak was founded in Roman times, you can still see remnants of a **2nd-century tower** on Trg bana Jelačića. There's little to interest tourists here except a small **Gradski muzej** (Town Museum, Kralja Tomislava 10, tel. 044/811-811, www.muzej-sisak.hr, 10 A.M.–6 P.M. Tues.–Fri., 9 A.M.–noon Sat.–Sun., 15Kn) and a 16th-century **Stari Grad** (Old Town castle, inquire at museum for more information) a few kilometers south of town. Worth a mention is the excellent **Cocktail** (Dr. A. Starčevića 27, tel. 044/549-137, www.cocktail.hr, 10 A.M.–11 P.M. daily, 60Kn) restaurant, a small modern space that offers local dishes as well as a few Italian favorites.

Sisak is 50 kilometers south of Zagreb. The train to Sisak takes about one hour and costs 28Kn, with over half a dozen daily connections on weekdays, slightly less on weekends. The bus takes around one hour as well but is slightly more expensive.

◖ LONJSKO POLJE

Though most well known for the **Lonjsko polje Nature Park** (tel. 044/715-115, www.pp-lonjsko-polje.hr, 25Kn), the region is also filled with storybook wooden houses, most of which date from the 19th and early 20th centuries. **Čigoč,** 30 kilometers southeast of Sisak, is a traditional village of wooden houses within the park; it's also designated as the European Village of the Stork, with a stork's nest on almost every roof. If you'd like to see the storks, try to visit between the end of March and the end of August—though a few make their home here year-round, too lazy to migrate after feedings by the locals. There's even a **stork ceremony** on the last Saturday in June that brings a load of tourists to town. A **park information point** (Čigoć 26, tel. 044/715-115, 8 A.M.–4 P.M. daily) sells tickets to the park, and the village has a small visitors center and a private **Ethnographic Museum** (open when the owners are home, donation requested), which are most likely to be open on summer weekends. The **Stara Hiža** (Čigoć 44, tel. 044/715-321, 70Kn) restaurant in town can be depended on for a drink, though if you want to eat you should call in advance. The owner and his wife also provide overnight stays and can help arrange a boat trip around the area.

The floodplain is filled with wildlife, including Posavina horses, furry Turopolje swimming pigs, and numerous birds. If you'd like to arrange a tour of the park, call the park manager at 044/672-082.

Staying in the nature park is an experience in itself. Jakša and Zlata ◖ **Ravlić** offer rooms in their ivy-covered 200-year-old timber house in Mužilovčica (Mužilovčica 72, tel. 044/710-151, 341Kn d., including breakfast). With its fairytale charm and cozy antique-filled rooms, you may want to move in. But if you just want to eat some of their great home cooking, you'll need to call ahead and let them know.

ISTRIA

Home to sunlit rolling hills, miles of vineyards, and charming stone cottages, and lined with crystal clear, cool water and rocky shores. . . . If you have to pick only one region of Croatia to visit, Istria seems to wrap up the best and present it in a neat, easy-to-travel little package. Travelers flock to the coast for picturesque port towns littered with remnants of the Roman and Byzantine periods, and former fishing villages turned tourist meccas. However, the interior of the peninsula is beginning to hold its own, with travelers realizing it rivals Tuscany or Provence—with cuisine to match. Culinary travelers can discover the region's local black and white truffles, homemade olive oil, and wine roads. This hinterland paradise is also dotted with medieval hilltop towns to explore, from Motovun's backdrop

for an impressive international summer film festival to Grožnjan's artsy core.

Though the Istrian beaches aren't quite as stunning as their Dalmatian neighbors to the south, they're often easier to access, with flat, fine pebbled paths accommodating a bicycle or a stroller. It's just one example of how Istria's tourism is far more developed than in Dalmatia, making Istria easy to travel and navigate. The region has clearly marked roads for sampling wine and olive oil, and information and brochures at every turn. There's almost always some cultural or culinary festival going on and an impressive selection of hotels and restaurants to choose from.

There are other advantages to Istria, too. As Croatia attracts more and more visitors, especially to its coastal regions, many towns are

HIGHLIGHTS

◖ **Amfiteatar:** Pula's Roman amphitheater is one of the best preserved. The city is also the site of a great winemaking museum and hosts a who's who of international stars during the city's summer festivals (page 104).

◖ **Veli Brijun:** Once the playground of European aristocracy and Josip Broz Tito, this nature park and popular day-trip destination is starting to experience a rebirth as a luxe destination for celebrities and politicos (page 111).

◖ **Zlatni Rt:** A forested nature park on the edge of the picturesque town of Rovinj, Zlatni Rt is full of beaches, all easily accessible on foot (page 114).

◖ **Eufrazijeva basilica:** This 6th-century Byzantine church, filled with sparkling mosaics and a big dose of history, is hidden on a side street in Poreč's ancient center (page 118).

◖ **Novigrad:** A small seaside town with some outstanding food, this fairly laid-back town is also a great location from which to explore some of Istria's best wine country, just a short drive away (page 122).

◖ **Grožnjan:** Participants in this hilltop village's young musicians' summer school give heartwarming performances all summer long. And the views aren't half bad either (page 129).

◖ **Hum:** Whether its claim of being the smallest town in the world is true or not, Hum is a

delight, with pretty views, good food, and mistletoe liquor to pick up as a signature souvenir (page 130).

LOOK FOR ◖ TO FIND RECOMMENDED SIGHTS, ACTIVITIES, DINING, AND LODGING.

having a hard time hanging on to what makes them unique. But if you're looking for something besides your typical fish restaurant with its tourist-oriented menu, or a boutique hotel that doesn't try too hard, or a yachting community without the bling, Istria is where you'll find it. Overall, it's refined yet full of laid-back character (except when it comes to truffles, which they tend to get overly excited about, but that's another story).

The Italian influence in the area is strong and adds another dimension to traveling in Istria. Many of the street signs are marked in

Italian as well as Croatian. You'll find this region has long been discovered by European travelers, but there are still enough hidden locales (like secluded villa accommodation o restaurants serving only one party of guests a a time) and rocky coves to escape to.

The worst of Istria is that to see it in its glory you absolutely must rent a car. The best of Istri is that packed within such a small peninsula you've got everything—a giant Roman amphitheater where you can catch a concert, win and olive oil roads, beaches, water sports, tin character-filled villages, superb restaurants

ISTRIA

Golfo di Trieste

ITALY

Trieste

Pivka

Divača

SLOVENIA

Ilirska Bistrica

Piran

Portorož

Koper

7

208

DEGRASSI

MORENO CORONICA

Umag

300

Buje

GIANFRANCO KOZLOVIĆ/ MARINO MARKEŽIĆ

201

CROATIA

3

HOTEL SAN ROCCO

Krasica

GROŽNJAN

Oprtalj

Buzet

Roč

44

DAMIR ORNELA

Brtonigla

301

Livade

44

HUMSKA KONOBA

A9

POLETTI/ RADOVAN

Motovun

LIVIO BENVENUTI

HUM

Lupoglav

Opatija

NOVIGRAD

EUFRAZIJEVA BASILICA

21

IVICA MATOŠEVIĆ

A8

Poreč

302

ZLATNA RIBICA

GIORDANO PERŠURIĆ

48

Pazin

Gračišće

21

Limski Kanal

A8

Žminj

64

Porozina

Rovinj

303

ZLATNI RT

GIANNINO'S

STANCIJA MENEGHETTI

Labin

Rabac

Bale

A9

21

Adriatic

Vodnjan

VODNJANKA

Kvarner Gulf

Cres

VELI BRIJUN

Fažana

Brijuni

66

Brijuni Islands

AMFITEATAR

Pula

RESTORAN MILAN

VALSABBION

Medulin

Sea

0   5 mi

0   5 km

© AVALON TRAVEL

ISTRIA

and solid museums—making it easy for a week to fly by before you know it.

PLANNING YOUR TIME

It's tempting to want to just move to Istria and savor each little corner slowly (and if you feel that way the real estate offices in every village will make it clear you're not the first) but Istria is very doable with two nights on the coast and one overnight in the interior to get a good overview. The best thing about Istria in terms of time is that everything is very close, and you can traverse the distance between the two farthest points in less than two hours. But you'll need a car to do it quickly or thoroughly, whatever your preference may be.

If you have a car, you can really choose to stay in any town; you'll usually get better deals in the interior than on the coast, where the majority of tourists book hotels. If you're traveling by bus you may want to stick to the bigger towns if you're pressed for time, since connections to some of the villages are scarce or even nonexistent. Biking is possible, though you'd want to take lots of safety precautions since the roads are still relatively narrow and sans bike lanes. Additionally, the biking culture is not well established, so drivers aren't really expecting to encounter cyclists as they come around a turn.

Try to squeeze in the region's highlights or tailor your trip to specific interests, such as food, wine, or sacred art. If you have a week you can see the peninsula at leisure and traverse the best villages and towns without a problem.

Summer is the busiest time of year, with prices and the number of fellow travelers peaking in August when it seems like every Italian in Italy has driven over the border. However, summer is also the time when Istria holds the most festivals and some excellent concerts with international opera and pop stars holding court in the larger coastal towns.

Fall and spring are the prettiest times, with far fewer tourists and asparagus harvests (spring), truffle hunting season (fall), and the grape harvest (fall) to make Istria even more interesting. Winter is doable and you will have most places to yourself, but also be aware that some restaurants and hotels close between November and the beginning of March.

Labin

The peaceful hilltop town of Labin is actually one of the region's most political cities. Labin belonged to the Byzantines, Lombards, Franks, Italy, and the Germanic marquisate—all before the 15th century. The Venetian Republic ruled the town from 1420 till 1797 and left the most indelible mark upon the town, whose medieval core will remind you of walking through Venice without the canals. After the fall of Venice, it was ruled by the French, the Austrians, and the Italians, and finally became a part of Croatia after World War II.

Its downhill suburb, the 20th-century Podlabin (literally, beneath Labin), was the country's coal-mining capital, and a center of pro-worker and pro-Tito sentiment. Driving into town you may notice the Tito spelled on the mountaintop with stones or the ax-and-sickle stencils on a wall in the old town.

Today, coal mining has died out and the city has become an artists' haven, attracting a mound of tourists from nearby **Rabac** (a seaside resort town a few kilometers east of Labin) in the summer months. From June to August, Labin welcomes the hordes with its **Art Republika festival,** bringing dozens of performing and visual artists to the city streets.

Since there's little in the way of accommodation in Labin proper, lose the crowds by getting there in the early morning to wander the cobblestone streets—though you'll need to stick around until 10 if you want to pop in to the city's galleries and sights. If you're staying in Rabac, you can drive to Labin, or go green and hike the marked walking trail between the two towns. It's a very doable seven kilometers or so (about 45 minutes)—or you can take the bus.

SIGHTS

Start your tour of Labin at the old town's **Titov trg** (Tito's Square); the 16th-century town **loggia** was the spot of town meetings and peasant dances in centuries past. Climb the cobblestone path to the 14th-century **Crkva rođenja blažene djevice Marije** (Church of the Birth of the Blessed Virgin Mary). The simple stone front hides an elegant interior, worth a peek if mass is in session (11 A.M. Sun.).

Just up the street is the bright reddish Palazzo Lazarini, now the **Narodni muzej Labin** (Labin National Museum, 1.maja 6, tel. 052/852-477, tulio-vorano@pu.htnet .hr, 10 A.M.–1 P.M. and 6–8 P.M. Mon.–Sat., 10 A.M.–1 P.M. Sun., 15Kn), housing a small ethnographic collection, paintings, and Roman relics. The most distinguishing feature of the museum is its small re-creation of a coal mine in the basement, probably the closest most of us will get to experiencing the feel of working underground. Just across the street from the museum, a modern facade tips you off to the **Gradska galerija** (City Gallery, Titov trg 11, Ulica 1.maja 5, tel. 052/852-464, 10 A.M.–3 P.M. Mon.–Fri., plus 8 P.M.–midnight Wed.–Thurs., 10 A.M.–1 P.M. Sat., free), housing revolving contemporary (mostly local) art exhibitions.

At the top of 1.maja street, the **Fortica** (fortress) has a nice view of Rabac, the peaks of Velebit, and the Island of Cres. From here, walk down Giuseppine Martinuzzi to the **Crkvica Gospe od Karmene** (Chapel of Our Lady of Carmel), today the **Gallery Alvona** (Giuseppina Martinuzzi 15, tel. 098/183-0901, 10 A.M.–1 P.M. daily, free), which houses some well-known contemporary artists, particularly during the summer season.

The last stop in Labin, before wandering through some of the city's other galleries, is the birthplace of Matija Vlačić Illyricus, a prominent Protestant theologian and friend of Martin Luther. The **Matija Vlačić Illyricus Memorijalna zbirka** (Memorial Collection of Matija Vlačić Ilirik, Giusepinna Martinuzzi 7, tel. 052/852-477, open sporadically or on request, 10Kn) holds interesting memorabilia, but more curious is the celebration of Protestantism in heavily Catholic Croatia.

BEACHES

Labin is, of course, inland, but nearby Rabac has lots of beaches, the best of which is **Maslinica.** Though it shares its shores with tourist developments, the beach is public. It's not a hidden beach, and is usually crowded with tourists in season, but it does have a pebbly (read: won't kill your bare feet) shore and lots of services, from cafés and snack bars to personal-watercraft rental and mini-golf. Rabac bills itself as the "pearl of the Adriatic." However, loads of oiled bodies and plastic sand pails can't help but sully the marketing angle. If you're looking for luxe or a quiet, natural escape, it's best to head elsewhere in Istria.

ENTERTAINMENT AND EVENTS

While you'll find a sprinkling of bars and cafés near Titov trg and lots of performances during the summer **Art Republika festival** (www.unitedfestival.com) that runs in July and August, you need to head out of town to find more edgy or more raucous nightlife. If it's edgy you're after, head to Podlabin's **Lamparna Cultural Centre** (Rudarska 1, tel. 052/855-289, call for event program), in an abandoned coal-mine building (actually the place the miners stopped to pick up their lamps before going underground, hence the name), where interesting exhibitions and concerts are held. Rabac is the place for the typical touristy beachside discos and clubs, which get a bit better during the **Rabac Summer Festival** (www.rabac festival.com), a long weekend of DJs and bands that add a bit of spin to the otherwise manufactured club scene; it's typically in late July or early August.

ACCOMMODATIONS

If you're determined to stay in Labin proper, check with **Veritas travel agency** (Sv.

Katarine 4, tel. 052/852-758, www.istra-veritas.hr), which has a couple of private accommodations in the old town and dozens in the surrounding area. Most likely, you'll probably find yourself staying a short ways out of town. If you're without a car, you'll find Rabac to be the most convenient: there are multiple bus connections to Labin, or it's about a 45-minute walk between the towns.

Campers can pitch a tent at the woodsy beachfront **Oliva** campsite (P.P.2, tel. 052/872-258, www.maslinicarabac.com, 71Kn campsite without electricity) in Rabac.

The **Palača Lazzarini** (Kort, Sv. Martin, tel. 052/856-006, www.sv-martin.com, 391Kn d.) is 10 kilometers from Labin (best for those who have a car, though the hotel does rent bikes). The cozy apartments, located in an 18th-century summer palace, are a great respite during the busy tourist season.

Another peaceful option for those with transportation is the **Villa Calussovo** (Ripenda, Kras 18, tel. 052/851-188, www.villa-calussovo.com, 597Kn d., including breakfast), a big

yellow country house set on six acres of bucolic bliss. Only four kilometers from the beach, the hotel has comfortable rooms and a good restaurant.

In Rabac, the waterfront **Apartmani Adoral** (Obala M. Tita 2a, tel. 052/535-840, www.adoral-apartmani.com, 804Kn d.) are luxe, modern flats with great sea views, but little place to lay your towel on the rocks out front. If a beach resort is more your style, try the renovated **Valamar Bellevue Hotel and Residence** (Rabac bb, tel. 052/465-200, www.valamar.com, 889Kn d.), with pools and a playground for the kids. Set away from the tourist hustle and bustle, all of the suites at **Villa Annette** (Raška 24, tel. 052/884-222, www.villaannette.hr, 1,200Kn d., including breakfast) have magnificent sea views. Though the hotel is not beachfront, it does have a nice pool for lounging in warmer months, a good restaurant (ask for room service since the restaurant is low on ambience), and super-helpful service. If you're really into the foodie thing, you can even book slow-food or wine-tasting theme weekends at the hotel.

walking up to the Palazzo Lazarini, now the Labin National Museum

FOOD

In Labin, the centrally located **Velo Kafe** (Titov trg 12, tel. 052/852-745, 11 A.M.–11 P.M. daily, 45Kn) has good pasta dishes and a nice terrace for prime people-watching. For seafood, head to Rabac, where the bland atmosphere at **Noštromo** (Obala maršala Tita 7, tel. 052/872-601, www .nostromo.hr, 7 A.M.–11 P.M. daily late Apr.– Oct., call for winter hours, 80Kn) is lifted by the superb views of the bay on the open-air terrace. The restaurant serves up solid fish, shrimp, and salads, perfect for a scorching day. The restaurant at **Villa Annette** (Raška 24, tel. 052/884-222, www.villaannette.hr, 90Kn) serves lots of Istrian and Mediterranean dishes—tender steaks with truffle or asparagus sauce, octopus salad, pastas—at the modern (though rather plain) restaurant. However, poolside dining in the summer months is really quite special.

INFORMATION AND SERVICES

The main **tourist office** (Aldo Negri 20, tel. 052/855-560, tzg.labin@pu.htnet.hr, www .rabac-labin.com) will supply you with tourist brochures and maps for both Labin and Rabac. In season, there's an additional outpost at Titov trg 10.

You can stock up on English books and local literature as well as get a strong dose of cappuccino at Papa Re Café and Bookstore in the old town of Labin.

GETTING THERE AND AROUND

Buses from Pula (1 hour) and Rijeka (1.25 hours), as well as local routes, stop at the bus station (tel. 052/855-220) in Podlabin. One-way tickets from Rijeka and Pula cost about 50Kn and travel multiple times daily. From the bus station, it's a 15-to-20-minute walk uphill into the old town.

Between Rabac and Labin, more than a dozen buses run daily, costing around 15Kn each way.

If you're driving to Labin, take care where you park and make sure you pay the appropriate amount to avoid a ticket. Some parking spots, especially those near the entrance to the old town, have a time limit.

ISTRIA

© SHANN FOUNTAIN ČULO

view of the water in Rabac, a seaside resort town near Labin

AROUND LABIN

Die-hard art fans or those looking to escapes the tourists might want to make an outing to the open-air **Park skulptura** (Sculpture Park, tel. 052/852-464, dawn–dusk daily) in Dubrova, with more than 70 stone sculptures by contemporary artists who have participated in the Mediteranski kiparski simpozij (Mediterranean Sculpture Symposium). Dubrova also hosts an interesting festival, the **Labinske konti,** on the last Saturday in July, featuring folk songs and dances as well as typical local instruments.

The picturesque perch of **Plomin** is somewhat sullied by the giant smokestack of the thermal power plant in the valley below, but its 11th-century **Crkva Sveti Juraj** (church of St. George), home of an early Glagolitic inscription, and the sleepy ancient streets are a nice escape from the hustle of Labin and Rabac in the high season. The tavern **Dorina** (Plomin 54, tel. 052/863-023, www.dorina-plomin.com, 7 A.M.–midnight daily, 50Kn) is a decent place to stop and have a bite.

Another interesting destination, about five kilometers west of Labin, **Raša** is an industrial town built by Mussolini in 1936. Its **Crkva svete Barbare** (St. Barbara's Church, open periodically, free) was designed to resemble a coal cart and lantern.

Pula

Pula is a love-it-or-hate-it sort of city. A busy port town surrounded by communist-style high-rises, the city has a rough-around-the-edges quality that, depending on your personality or your mood, can come as a shock or a welcome change after Istria's mostly slow, charming little villages. Of course, discovering its tender side among the salty remnants of the Eastern Bloc period can be very rewarding.

No matter what your impressions of Pula, though, you can't ignore its impressive sights. Pula's past can be traced back to prehistoric times, but it's the Romans (who left the huge amphitheater) and the Hapsburg era (when the city was the Austro-Hungarians' main, and really only significant, port) that left the strongest marks on the city.

It's best to see Pula in a day and then move on, at the very least to the beaches only a short drive away. The city also has a couple of superb restaurants, possibly some of Istria's best, and summer brings an impressive roster of international opera and pop stars to perform in the town's amphitheater.

SIGHTS
◖ Amfiteatar
Amphitheater
The crowning jewel of Pula tourist stops,

this Roman amphitheater (Flavijevska, tel. 052/219-028, 8 A.M.–7 P.M. daily in summer, 9 A.M.–5 P.M. daily in winter, 20Kn) is the world's sixth-largest Roman arena, and one of the best-preserved. Dating from the reign of Emperor Augustus in the 1st century B.C., the arena was reconstructed over the years until the version you see today was erected by Vespasianus. The arena survives thanks to local architect and Venetian senator Gabriele Emo (who is remembered in an inscription on the second tower), who convinced Venice not to move the arena piece by piece across the Adriatic in the 16th century. Originally built to seat over 20,000 spectators, the amphitheater was built of limestone, which was plundered by locals in the centuries following the fall of Rome (the last time was in the 18th century, when the arena's stone was used in the city's cathedral).

Today the arena seats 5,000 for concerts and events. The underground rooms are also worth a peek, particularly if you're fond of winemaking. The display will tell you all about Roman viticulture.

Zlatna vrata
Golden Gate
South of the amphitheater on the Via Sergia, the soaring Zlatna vrata or the "Triumphal

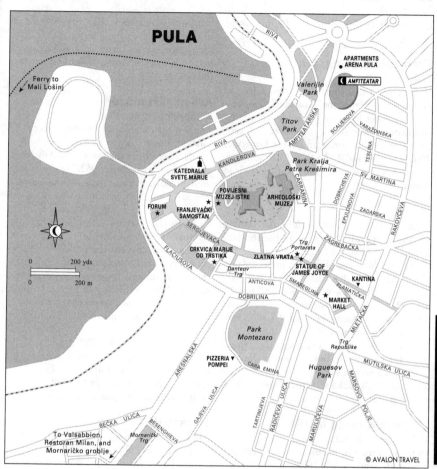

Arch of Sergia" still reminds visitors of an important Roman family, called Sergia, who built the monument to themselves around 27 B.C. The Corinthian arch is impressive, its huge ancient stone bulk standing solitary in the street, but the best thing about it is that it leads you into the ancient, and probably prettiest, parts of the city.

Crkvica Marije od Trstika
Chapel of St. Mary of Formosa

Near the Zlatna vrata on Maksimilijanova is the little Crkvica Marije od Trstika, a sweet 6th-century chapel that was once part of a large Benedictine abbey. It was once covered in Byzantine mosaics, today on display in the Archaeological Museum. A short walk north from the chapel will bring you to a stunning 2nd-century **floor mosaic** in a rather strange location for ancient relics, behind an apartment building. The large mosaic is protected by a metal fence, but free to view and always open since it sits outdoors. The mosaic depicts the punishment of Dirce, tied to the horns of an angry bull by the twins Amphion and Zethos, and was uncovered (and miraculously unharmed) by Allied bombs during World War II.

Franjevački samostan
Franciscan Monastery

If you haven't had your fill of stone relics yet (and the museum at the Temple of Augustus, your next stop, has some of the city's best), the nice little museum beside the austere 13th-century Franjevački samostan (Balde Lupetine, 10 A.M.–1 P.M. and 4–7 P.M. daily in summer, 10Kn) has a few more, some dating back to Roman times.

Forum

Built between 2 B.C. and A.D. 14, the **Temple of Augustus** dominates Pula's Forum, still a major hub of activity in the old town. The Roman temple is one of the best-preserved outside of Italy, though it had to be painstakingly reconstructed after a WWII bomb all but destroyed it. Today it houses a wonderful display (9 A.M.–8 P.M. Mon.–Fri. and 9 A.M.–3 P.M. Sat.–Sun. in summer, 10Kn) of Roman stone and bronze sculptures. Long ago, the Temple of Diana mirrored it, but today only the back wall of that temple survives. The wall became a part of the **Gradska vijećnica** (town hall) in the 13th century.

Katedrala svete Marije
Cathedral of St. Mary

Not far from the Forum, the 5th-century Katedrala svete Marije (Flavijevska, 7 A.M.–noon and 4–6 P.M. daily, free) is worth a peek. Though some parts were tacked on after various fires, many original elements survive, including some nice pieces of 5th- and 6th-century mosaics in front of the main altar.

Povijesni muzej Istre
Historical Museum of Istria

The Povijesni muzej Istre (Gradinski uspon 6, tel. 052/211-566, 8 A.M.–8 P.M. daily in summer, 9 A.M.–5 P.M. daily in winter, 10Kn) is not really worth a visit for its exhibits (unless you're into displays of maritime history, postcards, and uniforms) but for the *kaštel* (castle

fortress) that houses it. Built in 1630 for the Venetians by a French military architect, it has a four-pronged star shape that provides a great perch for enjoying some of the best views in the city.

Arheološki muzej
Archaeological Museum

The blink-or-you'll-miss-them remains of Pula's smallest Roman theater (it had three, back in the day) are in the shadow of the Arheološki muzej (Carrarina 3, tel. 052/218-603, www.mdc.hr/pula, 9 A.M.–8 P.M. Mon.–Sat. and 10 A.M.–3 P.M. Sun. in summer, 9 A.M.–2 P.M. Mon.–Fri. in winter, 10Kn), housed in a pretty building that was once the German Royal Gymnasium, or high school. The museum isn't the most modern, but the exhibits are pretty good if you like Roman relics and remnants of classical buildings. Displays also cover other periods, from prehistory to medieval times, with an assortment of weaponry, fossils, and such. Information is provided in English.

Statue of James Joyce

Perhaps more of a photo op than anything else, the statue of author James Joyce, Pula's most famous expat, is seated in front of the Uliks coffee bar, ready for you to order a round.

Market Hall

Markets are always a great place to get a taste of city life, but Pula's *tržnica* (Narodni trg bb, 7 A.M.–1 P.M. daily) is something of an architectural delight as well. Built in 1903, the giant iron-and-glass structure is similar to Paris's famous Les Halles. Take an hour to browse the lively fish stalls and have a coffee in the glass art nouveau space.

Mornaričko groblje
Naval Cemetery

Located on the edge of the leafy Stoja district, the Mornaričko groblje (Arsenalska, dawn–dusk, free) is a pretty Hapsburg-era graveyard, where more than 150,000 Austro-Hungarian military personnel are buried. It's actually quite park-like, with towering cypresses and peaceful sculptures. From here you can head off to lunch or some of the beaches in Stoja.

BEACHES
In Town

If you just want to take a seaside stroll, or if you're not too picky about your beach, you can hop one of the dozens of daily buses to **Stoja** (#1 or #4, 11Kn), just 3.5 kilometers from the city center. From here there's a great promenade from Stoja to **Valkane** (a mostly run-down concrete beach area) and **Valsaline**, which has some decent spots to lay down your towel; Valkane and Valsaline are four kilometers and five kilometers from the center, respectively.

South of Valsaline, you'll find **Punta Verudela** (take bus #2A or #3A, dozens of connections daily, 11Kn), six kilometers from the center, to be the pick of locals when it comes to taking a dip, though the beaches get packed on a nice day.

Premantura

Ten kilometers south of Pula, the small town of Premantura (bus #26 from Pula, at least 5 connections on weekends, 10 on weekdays, more in summer, 15Kn) is a must-visit for windsurfing aficionados, even beginners. **Stupica** beach is the best place for catching a gust if the infamous *bura* happens to be blowing. **Windsurfing Centar Premantura** (tel. 091/512-3646, bivancic@yahoo.com, www.windsurfing.hr, contact for more info) rents equipment (120Kn for 2 hours) and gives daily courses (from 190Kn) during the summer from a hut on the beach at Autocamp Medulin.

Cape Kamenjak

Located at the southern tip of Istria (bus #25 from Pula, at least 7 on weekends, 14 on weekdays, more in summer, 15Kn), the long narrow peninsula of Kamenjak is home to some of Istria's best beaches. The whole area is a nature preserve (you'll pay around 20Kn to get in) and is covered with dirt paths perfect for hiking or biking and also for finding hidden coves and deserted beaches (watch for strong currents when swimming, though). The Safari Bar is the only place to get a snack or a drink, so you might want to pack a picnic lunch.

Other Beaches

From the village of Marlera, southeast of Medulin, you can take a boat to **Levan Island,** which has a restaurant and sandy beach. Ask a local how to get to the **beaches below the Svetica Hill** (accessible by boat or gravel road—check the insurance policy on the rental car), basically a set of miniature coves perfect for stealing a little privacy; they're to the east of Medulin below Svetica.

ENTERTAINMENT AND EVENTS
Nightlife

Though the center of the city is low on hotels and restaurants, nightlife is a different story. Cruise the streets around the arena and you're bound to run across bars and cafés hopping with people. However, most of them close fairly early, so if you want to dance till dawn, head to **Aruba** (Šijanska cesta 1, no phone) or the marina-side **Club Uljanik** (Dobrilina 2, tel. 098/285-969, www.clubuljanik.hr) for DJs and alcohol. Or head to Premantura and Medulin for a serious summer party scene.

Festivals

Pula is full of festivals, from an **International Theater Festival** (the first five days in May) to the **7.Future Nature** (July), a trance culture festival. The two most well-known events, however, are the **Histria Festival** (July–Aug., www.histriafestival.com), which brings some very-big-name stars to the amphitheater such as Norah Jones, José Carreras, Andrea Bocelli, and Russia's famed Bolshoi Ballet, and the **Pula Film Festival** (July, www.pulafilmfestival.hr), during which Croatian films are screened at the arena.

ACCOMMODATIONS

Though there are more options in town than those listed here, it's hard to recommend many at the moment due to the fact that most are dirty, smelly, or otherwise in poor shape. If you're determined to stay in the center, the one good (read: clean) option is the **Apartments Arena Pula** (Flavijevska 2, tel. 052/516-207, www.pula-apartments.com, 398Kn d.) for nice service, a central location, and basic creature comforts.

In Stoja, the family-owned and -operated **Hotel Milan** (Stoja 4, tel. 052/300-200, www.milan1967.hr, 850Kn d., including breakfast) dates from 1967 but from the sleek, modern building you'd never know it. The leafy, quiet location is a 10-minute bus ride from the center of town and a short walk from the sea.

In the Pješčana Uvala yachting district, **【 Valsabbion** (Pješčana Uvala IX/26, tel. 052/218-033, www.valsabbion.hr, closed Jan., 1,279Kn d., including breakfast) is certainly Pula's chicest hotel. From its much-lauded lobby restaurant to the lush rooms and waterfront yacht-filled location, this is where the beautiful people go.

If you're not afraid of a 30-minute bike ride or you have your own car, the beach areas south of town have a couple of great options for travelers. For those on a budget, you can rent your own lighthouse room in the **Porer lighthouse** (via Adriatica Agency, Heinzelova 62a, Zagreb, tel. 01/610-2000, www.adriatica.net, 107Kn d.) or stay the night at **Camping Puntižela** (tel. 052/465-010, camping@valamar.com, www.camping-adriatic.com, 121Kn hostel bed, including breakfast), where you can pitch a seaside tent or share a room with fellow travelers at the camp's hostel.

The **Oliveto guesthouse** (Funtana 1, Medulin, tel. 091/920-8705, www.oliveto.hr, 426Kn d.) has some of the most charming rooms in the area, with good value for money and convenient access to beaches. The care put into the decor of the small pension shows in the service as well.

FOOD

In town, try the **Pizzeria Pompei** (Clerisseaunova 3, tel. 052/218-218, 7 A.M.–11 P.M. daily, 35Kn) for good pizza and salads or **Kantina** (Flanatička 16, tel. 052/214-054, 9 A.M.–midnight daily, 50Kn), a local favorite

for pastas and daily specials in a brick-lined basement space.

Out in Stoja, **Gostionica Gina** (Stoja 23, tel. 052/387-943, 11 A.M.–11 P.M. daily, 55Kn) is known for its giant portions of fish or meat dishes at reasonable prices. **【 Restoran Milan** (Stoja 4, tel. 052/300-200, www.milan1967.hr, 11 A.M.–midnight daily in summer, 11 A.M.–midnight Mon.–Sat. in winter, 90Kn) is one of the area's best, where superb-quality fish is displayed on cracked ice and the desserts alone are worth the trip.

Farther south there are even more choices, and they're all good. **Restoran Fantasia** (Palisina 29, tel. 052/506-306, www.fantasia-pula.hr, 11 A.M.–11 P.M. Mon.–Sat. and 6–11 P.M. Sun. in summer, 11 A.M.–11 P.M. Mon.–Sat. in winter, 80Kn) doesn't look like much from the outside but the food (a balanced menu of fish, Istrian-style meat dishes, and a smattering of omelets and risottos) makes up for what the place lacks in atmosphere. **Restoran Vela Nera** (Pješčana uvala, tel. 052/219-209, www.velanera.hr, 8 A.M.–midnight daily, 90Kn) has a pretty oceanfront location and boasts its knowledge of wine as an added bonus to the delicious seafood dishes. If your version of food-as-art goes beyond taste to aesthetics as well, the fancy presentation at **【 Valsabbion** (Pješčana Uvala IX/26, tel. 052/218-033, www.valsabbion.hr, closed Jan., 100Kn) will easily rival anything you've had at chic eateries back home. Even better: The food, creatively using the best of local ingredients like truffles, crabs, wild asparagus, and local herbs, lives up to its looks.

INFORMATION AND SERVICES

Lots of information, from brochures to information about tours and excursions, can be found at the Pula **tourist office** (Forum 3, tel. 052/219-197, www.pulainfo.hr, 8 A.M.–8 P.M. Mon.–Sat. and 9 A.M.–8 P.M. Sun. in summer, call for winter hours) on the Forum.

English books and newspapers are available at Algoritam (Prolaz kod kazališta 1, tel. 052/393-987, www.algoritam.hr, 9 A.M.–9 P.M. Mon.–Fri., 9 A.M.–2 P.M. Sat.).

FESTIVALS FOR FOODIES

Istria is loaded with festivals that lean gourmet. Learn all about the local cuisine and culture by catching one during your stay.

- **Oleum Olivarum** (March), Krasica, and **Smotra maslinovog ulja** (Olive Oil Exhibition, April), Vodnjan: Lectures, exhibitions, and tastings plus competitions for the best local olive oil.

- **Vinistra** (April or May), Poreč: A festival of all things culinary, local products like grappa, olive oil, cheese, and prosciutto are on display culminating in a judged ranking of Istrian wines.

- **Fažanska škola soljenja sardela** (Fažana School of Sardine Salting, May), Fažana: One day of presentations and workshops in sardine salting with various local advice on the right combination of salt, oil, and spices. Even if you're not in the mood to learn, you can still judge by tasting the recipes.

- **Dan Vina** (Wine Day, end of May): Cellars all over Istria open their doors 10 A.M.–6 P.M. for tastings. Plan your itinerary by picking up a map of participating wineries from the Istrian Tourist Board.

- **Fešta istarske malvazije** (Istrian Malvasia Festival, end of May or early June), Brtonigla: The festival celebrates the most famous indigenous wine, with tastings, gourmet presentations, and entertainment.

- **Ribarske fešte** (Fisherman's festivals, varying dates throughout the summer), Medulin, Savudrija, Novigrad, Umag, Vrsar, Funtana, and Fažana: Local mariners entertain the crowds with song and feed them grilled fish and seafood, with sides of wine, cheese, and olives.

- **Maneštrijada** (Maneštra Festival, bi- or triannually), Gračišće: The main square comes alive to prepare the area's typical stew, *maneštra*, a pasta-based dish that varies according to the season's ingredients.

- **Subotina uz divovsku fritadu s tartufima** (Subotina with giant truffle omelet, September), Buzet: A giant omelet made of over 2,000 eggs in a 2.5-meter-wide pan kicks off Buzet's traditional festival filled with crafts, folk groups, and food. You can follow special food- or wine-based "trails," stuffing yourself with the best the region has to offer.

- **Fešta mladega vina** (Festival of New Wine, October), Svetvinčenat: A tasting of the Istrian Beaujolais in a beautiful old Venetian palace.

Need to connect with someone back home? The central post office (Danteov trg 4, tel. 052/215-955, 7 A.M.–8 P.M. Mon.–Fri., 7 A.M.–2 P.M. Sat.) can help you send a postcard back home or make a phone call, while the centrally located Cyber Café (Flanatička 14, tel. 052/215-345, 8 A.M.–10 P.M. daily, 20Kn per hour) is a good place to check your email.

Most aches and pains can be solved at the all-night pharmacy (Giardini 15, tel. 052/222-551, 24 hours). For something more serious, Pula's hospital (Zagrebačka 30, tel. 052/214-433) should be able to help.

Luggage can be stored at the bus station (Istarska 3, tel. 052/219-074, 5 A.M.–10 P.M. daily, around 2Kn per hour) or the train station (Kolodvorska 5, tel. 052/541-733, 9 A.M.–4 P.M. Mon.–Sat., around 15Kn per day).

GETTING THERE AND AROUND

Pula's airport (tel. 052/530-105, www.airport-pula.com) is Istria's main hub. The airport is only six kilometers from the center, but for some unknown reason, there is no bus service from the airport. You'll have to take a cab, which usually runs around 200Kn. As Pula airport's website notes, most likely in a

ISTRIA

tongue-in-cheek fashion, "Pula taxi drivers are honest but please check the price of your journey before engaging."

Pula has good train and bus connections. The train station (Kolodvorska 5, tel. 052/541-733) is about a 10-minute walk from the center of town, while the central bus station (Istarska 3, tel. 052/219-074) is only about five minutes away. There's another bus station (Trg Istarske Brigade, tel. 052/502-997) slightly north of the amphitheater that serves mostly local routes, with connections to the beaches and small towns near Pula.

There are several daily trains to Zagreb (7 hours, 131Kn) and at least one to Ljubljana (4 hours, 130Kn).

There are several daily buses connecting Pula with Rijeka (2.25 hours, 84Kn) or Zagreb (5 hours, around 215Kn depending on the time of departure).

Pula is 292 kilometers southwest of Zagreb. From Zagreb, take the highway toward Rijeka and then go through the Učka tunnel, at which point you'll follow the signs to Pula.

If driving to Pula is pretty simple (there's a sign pointing you to the city from most everywhere in Istria), parking is likely to be a wholly different matter. There are few parking spots and most require tricky parallel parking maneuvers. Best to drop off the car at the hotel and continue your sightseeing using public transportation.

Local buses (www.pulapromet.hr) can get you around Pula from stops all over the city. You can buy tickets at newspaper kiosks for 6Kn or onboard for 10Kn to most places around town. Prices are slightly higher to the beaches around Medulin.

AROUND PULA
Vodnjan

Vodnjan, home to the **Vodnjan mummies,** is 11 kilometers north of Pula (hop on a #22 city bus in Pula, takes about 30 minutes, 7 or more buses on weekends and 16 or more weekdays, 15Kn). The mummified bodies of six saints who have never decomposed—due to preservation or miracles, your call—are housed in the **Crkva svetog Blaža** (Church of St. Blaise, tel. 052/511-420, 9 A.M.–7 P.M. Mon.–Sat. and 2–7 P.M. Sun. in summer, call ahead for a winter visit, 35Kn). There are about 14 other churches in or around town, though perhaps more interesting are the some 3,000 kažuni, or stone huts, in the surrounding countryside.

The **Smotra maslinovog ulja** (Olive Oil Exhibition, April) is worth a trip for anyone who enjoys olive oil. The exhibition's highlight is a judging of olive oils by local producers. Snatch a few bottles of the winning oils for the flight back home.

A must-stop for lunch or dinner is the superb family restaurant ◖ **Vodnjanka** (Istarska bb, tel. 052/511-435, 11 A.M.–11 P.M. Mon.–Sat. and 6 P.M.–midnight Sun. in summer, 11 A.M.–11 P.M. Mon.–Sat. in winter, closed Jan., 75Kn), famous for its Istrian sausages, prosciutto, and escargot.

Bale

Bale, northwest of Vodnjan, is a charming village dating from 983. Wander the perfect meandering streets or peek in some of the churches, but don't miss two very interesting (and two very different) places to stay. On the uber-luxe end is the ◖ **Stancija Meneghetti** (Bale, tel. 091/243-1600, www.meneghetti .info, €9,800 per week, sleeps 10, includes three meals daily), a villa complete with pool and private chef, and on the conservation side is the **Eia Eco Art Village** (San Zuian 13, tel. 098/916-0650, www.eia.hr, 50Kn per person), which hosts visitors for next to nothing in its peaceful and ecofriendly space (exhibit A: showering with collected rainwater).

Brijuni Islands

A small archipelago of islands off the Istrian coast, the Brijuni Islands were once an aristocratic playground created by Austrian industrialist Paul Kupelweiser, later a hunting retreat of Yugoslavian leader Josip Broz Tito, and today are a national park. If you want to see the islands, you can either book a day trip through the **Brijuni National Park office** (tel. 052/525-882, www.brijuni.hr, 8 A.M.–10 P.M. daily in July and Aug., 8 A.M.–8 P.M. daily in June and Sept., and 8 A.M.–3 P.M. Mon.–Sat. Oct.–Apr., 4-hour tour 160Kn) or book a hotel or excursion (such as golf or diving) through the harborside office in Fažana. Booking a hotel room or villa offers you the most freedom around Brijuni since day-trippers are generally herded in a neat little jaunt around the island.

◖ VELI BRIJUN

Veli Brijun, the largest of the islands, and one of only a couple of the 14 islands open to the public, holds the majority of the sights. The rough-around-the-edges island contains some stunning scenery, refined villas, wild animals, and even dinosaur footprints. In short, it's the perfect setting for a science fiction movie. Day-trippers to Veli Brijun will take a small tourist train that runs through the **safari park,** which was once stocked with game for Tito's hunting fetishes. You might spot some elephants and zebras as well as animals native to the Istrian landscape. Animals that have died are now on display in the island's Natural History Museum. The train also passes the **Bijela vila** (White Villa), Tito's haunt and overnight destination of many a well-known guest, and stops at the ruins of a Byzantine fortress. If you're on the day tour, you'll probably also see a 15th-century church and the exhibition **Tito on Brijuni** (Tito na Brijunima, 8 A.M.–8 P.M. daily in July and Aug., 8 A.M.–7 P.M. in June and Sept., 8 A.M.–6 P.M. daily in May and Oct., included with excursion to the island), with a fascinating set of photographs of the Yugoslav leader with high-level politicos from 60 countries as well as a smattering of Hollywood stars.

BRIJUNI'S LUXE PAST

Though most people associate Brijuni with Tito, it was Austrian industrialist Paul Kupelwieser who brought the islands to life. Once the retreat of wealthy Romans, the islands had deteriorated to malaria-ridden wastelands when Kupelwieser bought them in 1893. Within just a few years he brought in a Nobel Prize-winner to get rid of the malaria and built a harbor and hotel with a heated seawater swimming pool. Four to five connections with the mainland a day brought in Europe's elite, including the Archduke Franz Ferdinand, the Duke of Spoleto, and Kaiser Wilhelm II.

The resort was popular with the polo circuit but it never did turn a profit. In 1930, Paul Kupelwieser's son committed suicide on the islands. After World War II, Tito took it over and built the Bijela Vila (White Villa) where he entertained stars attending the Pula Film Festival, like Elizabeth Taylor, Richard Burton, and Gina Lollobrigida, and heads of state like Queen Elizabeth II.

Today, a touch of past glamour is beginning to return to the islands. There's a 22-hole environmentally friendly golf course and the yearly Brioni Polo Classic has brought the tradition of polo back to Brijuni. Brioni planned on building a resort on the island, but for the moment plans have apparently been put on hold. Still, the islands have become a secret of the yachting set, welcoming a new crop of stars and politicos to Brijuni's shores.

ISTRIA

If you're staying on Veli Brijun, you're free to explore further. Rent a golf cart or a bicycle to scoot around the island (rentals available from the sports center near the Neptun-Istra hotel, carts around 500Kn half day, bicycles around 120Kn full day), perhaps visiting some of the Roman ruins and Kupelwieser's grave. There's also a **golf course** (greens fees 200Kn for the day, 180Kn if you're staying on the island, 100Kn for a set of clubs for the day) if you'd like to keep your swing from getting rusty.

OTHER ISLANDS

The office also runs trips to **Mali Brijun,** with an old Austro-Hungarian fort as part of the tour. Other than that, Mali Brijun's only other attraction is the quiet pebbly shores—quite impressive, particularly if you fancy yourself a bit of a Robinson Crusoe. **Sveti Jerolim** and **Kotež** are also open for swimming and fish picnic excursions. Boats are allowed to moor on Mali Brijun and Sveti Jerolim only with previous permission and the payment of a fee to the park office. Small boats are allowed freely and without payment on Kozada.

ACCOMMODATIONS AND FOOD

There are two hotels on the island, the expensive and unimpressive **Neptun-Istra** (tel. 052/525-807, 1,030Kn d., including breakfast) and **Karmen** (tel. 052/525-807, 900Kn d., including breakfast). The hotels also have restaurants and cafés where you can get a bit of nourishment. The Neptun-Istra is the nicer of the two,

but either one will do if you make sure to get one of the rooms with terraces facing the sea (a feature of the majority of rooms in both hotels). Or, splurge by renting one of the **villas** (www.brijuni.hr, 1,065Kn to 12,787Kn per night), starting at semi-reasonable prices and skyrocketing to astronomical rates. Standard villas offer plenty of privacy while the luxury villas come with your own personal maid and a private beach, a celebrity-esque touch apropos to the island's past.

GETTING THERE AND AROUND

Your departure point for Brijuni will be the town of Fažana, about a 10-minute drive north from Pula. If you're relying on public transport take bus #21 (at least 7 connections on weekends, 15 on weekdays, more in summer, 15Kn) from Pula. The Brijuni National Park office on Fažana's small harbor sells trips to the island (eight daily May–Oct., one daily rest of the year except Jan. when the park is closed). You can also book a trip through your hotel (usually around 250Kn including transportation to Fažana and lunch), though tours booked at unofficial spots in the Pula harbor may not give you as much for your money as going directly through the park's office.

Rovinj

Rovinj is one of Istria's most charming coastal towns. This also means it's one of its busiest. The town's almost untouched medieval core is sunny, sometimes quite hilly, and filled with bars, cafés, and galleries for poking around. The shady beaches just out of town or across the water are some of the best in Istria, too, making Rovinj a great all-around stop.

Rovinj was once an island; during the 18th century the strait between Rovinj and the mainland was filled in, creating a profitable little port city. Rovinj is still quite profitable, not only from the tourist trade, but from the town's tobacco factory, **Tvornica Duhan Rovinj,** which has made the town's inhabitants

some of the wealthiest in Croatia. That prosperity and popularity translates into a wide offering of hotels and restaurants to service the artsy sun-washed stone enclave.

SIGHTS
Trg maršala Tita
Marshal Tito Square

The harborside Trg maršala Tita is Rovinj's main square and a great starting point for touring the old town. You can branch out onto any of the surrounding streets for some atmospheric wandering or follow the narrow little street called Grisia up to the Crkva svete Eufemije (St. Euphemia's Church). As you're

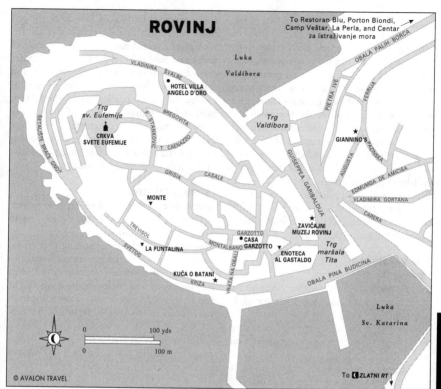

climbing up Grisia, take some time to pop in the art **galleries** and shops selling local crafts and colorful paintings; the street is also home to its fair share of touristy knickknacks.

Zavičajni muzej Rovinj
Rovinj Heritage Museum

On the northern end of the Trg Maršala Tita, the Zavičajni muzej Rovinj (Trg Maršala Tita 11, tel. 052/816-720, www.muzej-rovinj.com, 9 A.M.–noon and 7–10 P.M. Tues.–Sun. in summer, 9 A.M.–1 P.M. Tues.–Sat. in winter, 15Kn) is housed in a Baroque palace next to the **Balbi Arch,** the town's gate back in medieval times. The museum is most proud of its impressive Old Masters collection (with lots from the Italian school), but the place really hits its niche with the displays of Croatian contemporary painting and local artists.

Crkva svete Eufemije
St. Euphemia's Church

Towering over Rovinj's old town at the end of Grisia, the Crkva svete Eufemije (10 A.M.–2 P.M. and 3–6 P.M. daily, free) is named for the town's patron saint, a Christian martyr from the era of Diocletian, who fed her to the lions in 304. The building dates from the 18th century, though its facade was added later. The most interesting parts are the statue of St. Euphemia, who turns atop her perch to show the direction of the wind, and her 6th-century stone coffin behind the altar.

Kuća o batani
Batana House

The Kuća o batani (Obala P Budicin 2, tel. 052/805-266, www.batana.org, 10 A.M.–3 P.M. and 5–10 P.M. daily June–Sept., 10 A.M.–1 P.M.

and 3–5 P.M. daily Mar.–May and Oct.–Dec., closed Jan.–Feb., 15Kn) is a miniature (just over 1,000 square feet) "ecomuseum" devoted to the local *batana* boat. The name of the boat likely derives from the Italian *battere,* meaning to strike or hit, an onomatopoeic reference to the sound made when the waves hit the wooden watercraft. Some form of the flat-bottomed boat has been in use since the 14th century, though the true heyday of the *batana* was in the 1960s, when motors were added and almost every local family had one for fishing or for excursions to the islands around Rovinj. The well-presented displays are even supplied with a soundtrack, the *bitinada* (regional fishermen's songs). The museum also sells a nice cookbook full of regional dishes that makes a tasteful souvenir.

Trg Valdibora
Valdibor Square
Rovinj's **market** (Trg Valdibora, 7 A.M.–4 P.M. daily, best vendors leave just after noon), located on Trg Valdibora north of the Trg maršala Tita, is a nice little spot for some shopping. Vendors sell fruits and vegetables along with good souvenir items like homemade oils and honeys as well as herb-scented soaps. It's also the place to pick up beach towels and postcards to send back home.

Centar za istraživanje mora
Marine Biological Institute
The Centar za istraživanje mora (Obala Giordano Paliaga 5, http://more.cim.irb.hr, 9 A.M.–9 P.M. daily June–Sept., 10 A.M.–4 P.M. in Apr., May, and Oct., 15Kn), a 10-minute seaside walk to the east along the Obala Palih Boraca out of the old town center, has a small selection of local sealife in its aquarium. The most interesting tidbit about the aquarium is its long history, opening in 1891 in the same salmon-colored Austro-Hungarian building that houses it today.

BEACHES
C Zlatni Rt
Golden Cape
Just a kilometer south of Rovinj's harbor, most easily accessed by foot or bike from the old town, you'll find the nature park of Zlatni Rt, with great forested paths leading to dozens of rocky and pebbly beaches. These beaches are convenient, easily accessible by foot, bike, and even stroller. The park extends for seven kilometers; the busiest beaches are on the western side, and the shores at the tip of the Skaraba Cape are much less frequented. Though the beaches aren't officially nudist, don't be surprised if you run across a few nude sunbathers in the little coves along the way.

Islands Offshore
Crveni Otok, literally red island (also known as Otok Sv. Andrija), is a tiny escape just 15 minutes by boat from Rovinj (20Kn), with approximately two boats departing every hour from the harbor in the summer. Though it's not completely undiscovered, the island, with its pinewoods and rocky capes, is worth the trip if you want to while away a day at the wellness center in the **Hotel Istria** (Sv. Andrea, tel. 052/802-500, www.maistra.hr, 1,294Kn d., including breakfast), a nice place to book a massage. Another island, **Sveta Katarina,** can also be reached by water taxi or a ferry (around 20Kn) from the harbor at Rovinj; the ride is under 10 minutes.

Both islands have convenient places for lunch and refreshments. Neither are deserted, but if you're willing to tote your beach bag a bit you should be able to find at least a semi-private space to lay your towel.

ENTERTAINMENT AND EVENTS
Rovinj is no Ibiza, but you'll find some good bars around the southern side of the peninsula like **Zanzibar** (Obala Pina Budicina, tel. 052/813-206, 11 A.M.–1 A.M. daily), great for cocktails, occasional DJs, and people-watching. For just a drink or coffee, the harbor-side bars **Caffé Cinema** (Trg Brodogradili 16, no phone, 7 A.M.–midnight daily) and **Viecia Batana** (Trg Maršala Tita, tel. 091/539-9172, 7 A.M.–1 A.M. daily) are popular, bustling spots with a hip edge. The latter also is

a good place for a light breakfast of pastries and coffee. The **Monvi Centar Rovinj** (Luja Adamovića, tel. 052/545-117, www.monvi center.com, 11 A.M.–4 A.M. daily in summer, call for schedule in winter) has a nice group of discos and bars with some good DJs and live performances as well. To get there, head south of the marina near the package hotels.

Throughout the summer Rovinj's events calendar is packed with concerts, lantern-lit *batana* parades, and traditional Istrian days loaded with typical crafts, foods, and costumes. Also interesting are summer's twice-monthly fishermen festivals, with grilled fish and the a cappella *bitinadas*. August brings a one-day Grisia art festival, named after the street in the old town, where anyone can participate (including tourists) as long as they register the piece at the town museum.

ACCOMMODATIONS

Rovinj has dozens of package-type hotels in its environs; the center offers several good boutique options, heavy on charm. For those who want to rough it, try the beachfront campsite **Porton Biondi** (Aleja Porton Biondi 1, tel. 052/813-557, www.portonbiondi.hr, from 47Kn per person), one kilometer east of town, and the more tourist-friendly **Camp Veštar** (Veštar bb, tel. 052/829-150, www.maistra .hr, from 156Kn per person), which has a bar, pool, and boat and bike rentals only six kilometers east of town. Camp Veštar is right on a nice pebble beach and even has dog showers for campers' furry friends.

There's no shortage of private apartments in the suburbs of Rovinj, but the **Boš-ko apartments** (A. Motovunjanina 14, tel. 052/830-329, www.bos-ko.com, 362Kn d.) are some of the best due to the friendly owners who can regale you with tales and tips to enhance your stay. The apartments are very clean and sunny and most have terraces. In town, the low ceilings and basic interior of the **Apartments Venema** (Augusto Ferry 35, tel. 098/218-904, www.apartmani-rovinj.com, 500Kn d.) don't match the atmosphere of the building itself, but it's hard to beat the location, not far from

Sv. Eufemija. Don't let the narrow-alley location of the **Hotel Villa Angelo d' Oro** (Via Švalba 38-42, tel. 052/840-502, www.rovinj .at, 878Kn d., including breakfast) fool you. It's had more than its share of press, though sometimes the service fails to live up to the luxe reputation. However, it's the only old-town hotel with its own wellness center. **Porta Antica apartments** (three locations in the old town, tel. 052/812-548, www.portaantica.com, 995Kn) are lovely antique-filled spaces, some with seaview balconies right in the heart of the old town; nearby boutique hotel **◖ Casa Garzotto** (Via Garzotto 8, tel. 098/616-168, www.casa-garzotto.com, 995Kn d., including breakfast) gives consistent great service and has very charming rooms, though walking-weary travelers should be warned of the stairs you'll need to climb to get to your room.

Out of town, a complete overhaul of hotel **Monte Mulini** (Šetalište uvale Lone, tel. 052/800-230, www.maistra.hr, 1,422Kn d., including breakfast) has turned the former Tito-era relic into the most upscale of the Maistra Group's hotels. The resort, complete with shady swimming pools, a beach, and a spa, opened in late 2008. Another hotel from the group, the Lone, is planned to debut in 2010.

FOOD

The no-frills **Toni** (Driovier 3, tel. 052/815-303, noon–3 P.M. and 6–11 P.M. Mon.–Tues. and Thurs.–Sun., 45Kn) has a nice range of seafood and pasta at budget-friendly prices and a convenient old town location. **Trattoria Dream** (Joakima Rakovca 18, tel. 052/830-613, 11:30 A.M.–10 P.M. daily, 65Kn) is a bit more flair than substance. Still, the trendy restaurant on a side street has lots of tasty seafood as well as good pastas and dishes that could pass as vegetarian. But since Rovinj is on the sea, it's worth the splurge to try out some of Rovinj's better restaurants. **Monte** (Montelbano 75, tel. 052/830-203, www.monte.hr, 6:30–11:30 P.M. daily in summer, closed mid-Oct.–mid-Apr., 100Kn) is often lauded by guidebooks and hotels (you won't be the only tourists, but the food is good), with quality seafood dishes and a nice location near Sv. Eufemija. At first glance the prices at ◖ **Giannino's** (Augusto Ferri 38, tel. 052/813-402, 11:30 A.M.–3 P.M. and 6–11 P.M. daily, 100Kn) might seem a little high for a *gostionica* (bistro), but the food will change your mind. This place is very popular with visiting Italians and local businessmen. Giannino's has haute seafood dishes(think sole with truffles or grilled lobster) in a slightly shabby atmosphere with real soul (though it has been said the dishes for regulars are often prepared with more care).

If you're looking for a romantic meal, try a fireside dinner in the old town's **Enoteca Al Gastaldo** (Iza Kasarne 14, tel. 052/814-109, 11 A.M.–3 P.M. and 6–11 P.M. daily, no credit cards, 90Kn), specializing in seafood but serving excellent oven-baked meat dishes as well, or the cliff-top **La Puntulina** (Sv. Križa 38, tel. 052/813-186, noon–3 P.M. and 6 P.M.–midnight daily, no credit cards, 90Kn), with solid Italian-Istrian cuisine and a knockout downstairs waterside cocktail bar and terrace.

Restoran Blu (Val de Lesso 9, tel. 052/811-265, www.blu.hr, 10 A.M.–11 P.M. daily, closed mid-Nov.–Feb., 120Kn) is a bit out of the center, but the seaside view alone makes the short drive worthwhile. The atmosphere is laid-back chic and the seasonal menu makes the best use of local fresh specialties with a creative flair, like Istrian sashimi and sea bass with caviar in saffron sauce. **La Perla** (E.Bullessicha 2, tel. 052/811-801, www.laperla.hr, 11 A.M.–midnight in summer, noon–10 P.M. in winter, closed Wed., 100Kn), out of the center in the suburbs, offers a range of seafood and meat dishes that aren't creative or surprising but always top quality. The setting is decidedly local, though the restaurant's reputation draws its share of tourists as well.

INFORMATION AND SERVICES

Rovinj's **tourist office** (Pina Budačina 12, tel. 052/811-566, www.tzgrovinj.hr, 8 A.M.–9 P.M. daily mid-June–mid-Sept., 8 A.M.–3 P.M. Mon.–Sat. rest of the year) is located near Trg maršala Tita to provide you with lots of maps, brochures, and information on bike and boat rentals and scuba diving. You can hop on the Internet at **A-Mar** (Karera 26, tel. 052/841-211, 9 A.M.–11 P.M. daily in summer, call for hours in winter) or **Planet** (Sv. Križa 1, tel. 052/840-494, www.planetrovinj.com, 10 A.M.–9 P.M. daily in summer, call for hours in winter), which also offers drinks and a small travel agency.

GETTING THERE AND AROUND

If you're taking the bus, the station (Trg na lokvi 6, tel. 052/811-453, note the hectagon-shaped 13th-century Romanesque church next door) is only a five-minute walk from the center of town with good connections to Zagreb (approx. 5.5 hours, 220Kn) and Pula (40 minutes, 34Kn). The nearest train station is in Kananfar, 20 kilometers east of Rovinj; there's bus service to Rovinj. A ticket to Zagreb on the train from Kananfar takes approximately six hours and costs around 125Kn. If you're driving, be aware that you'll need to park somewhere and leave your car; parking is scarce and cars are not allowed inside the old town. For taxis, dial 052/811-100.

If you'd like to connect via boat, Venezia Lines (tel. 052/422-896, www.venezialines .com, €70) runs day trips to Venice including a guided tour. The trip takes a total of about nine hours.

AROUND ROVINJ
Limski Kanal

A Mediterranean fjord cutting a sparkling blue line into Istria between Rovinj and Poreč, the Limski Kanal was once the haunt of pirates attacking Venetian ships. Today the Limski Kanal is the perfect spot for a boat trip as well as for visiting **Romuald's Cave,** where St. Romuald lived for two years, and for sampling local oysters and mussels. Romuald's Cave, a 105-meter-long cave in a hillside, was a solitary refuge for the 11th-century saint. Guided tours (arranged through Natura Histrica, Obala A Rismondo 2, Rovinj, tel. 052/830-582, www .natura-histrica.hr, 10–30Kn) are the only way

© SHANN FOUNTAIN ČULO

view of the village of Vrsar, near the Limski Kanal

to see the cave. Tours of the fjord are easily booked through tourist offices in Rovinj, Poreč, or from the harbor in Vrsar. Trips can last a couple of hours or a whole day including a fish picnic, and cost 100–250Kn per person. If you're looking to form your own opinion of the region's famous oysters and mussels, everyone will point you toward the restaurants **Fjord** (Limski kanal bb, tel. 052/448-222, noon–11 P.M. daily, closed mid-Jan.–mid-Feb., 80Kn) and **Viking**

(Lim bb, tel. 052/448-223, 11 A.M.–4:30 P.M. and 6:30–11 P.M. daily, 85Kn).

Wineries

Slightly inland from Vrsar, head to the wineries of **Ivica Matošević** (Krunčići 2, Sv. Lovreč, tel. 052/448-558, www.matosevic .com), a young winemaker and the director of Vinistra, who produces top-rate Malvazija and a good Sauvignon Blanc.

Poreč

Poreč is a charming seaside town, once a Roman colony, with traces of Romanesque, Venetian, and—more interesting—Byzantine architecture. Called Parenzo in Italian and Parentium in Latin, Poreč was an important Roman town, with the largest Roman temple on the Adriatic's east coast. The Byzantine emperor Justinian I also found the city important, building the stunning Eufrazijeva basilica in town, though historians have failed to explain

why he found the city so alluring. Remaining under the Venetian Republic for 500 years, Poreč was a trade and military port, and the Austro-Hungarians established it as a capital of the Istrian region.

In modern times it's a major tourist destination, its outer edges filled with large package hotels. The town's most famous attraction is the 6th-century basilica, though the town has several places of interest to tourists. During

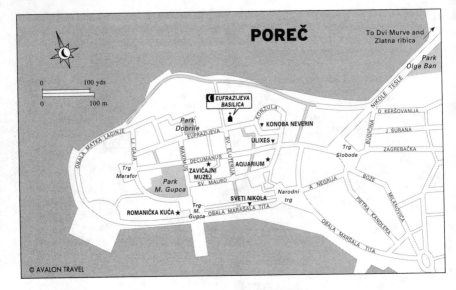

most of the year, it's really a don't-miss stop, though summer makes it one of Istria's most-packed cities as the dozens of hotels and tourist complexes nearby dump thousands into the little place. When the place is really overrun with tourists, visitors often miss the charm and remnants of grandeur that make it special. The upside of visiting in summer is getting to enjoy all of the events taking place, particularly the classical music concerts performed in the stunning basilica.

The best thing about Poreč is the location. Even in the high season, you can dip into town for sightseeing or events and then escape to a town slightly inland or the more upscale Novigrad to the north to get away from the throngs. It's also near the beginning of some nice wine roads, ripe with producers of Istria's outstanding Malvazija.

SIGHTS
◖ Eufrazijeva basilica
Basilica of Euphrasius

If you have time to see only one thing in Poreč, it should be the 6th-century Eufrazijeva basilica (Sv. Eleuterija, tel. 052/431-635, church 7:30 A.M.–8 P.M. daily, tower and museum

10 A.M.–5 P.M. daily, church free, tower 10Kn, museum 10Kn). Unlike most grand churches, its position is almost hidden, in the center of town though slightly off the main thoroughfare on Sveta Eleuterija. The complex was built around 553, during the Justinian period, by the Bishop Euphrasius, whose signature and likeness can be seen in multiple locations. Visitors enter through a stone portal, completed in 1902 and topped with an ancient mosaic depicting Jesus and inscribed in Latin, "I am the gate. Who enters through me, will be saved." The rest of the church is quite well preserved, with one of the few additions being the 13th-century baldachin, or canopy, above the altar, so well integrated that it looks original as well. The still-sparkling Byzantine mosaics were created by artisans shipped in from Constantinople and Ravenna and are by far the most arresting feature of the sight. The mosaics depict biblical stories and saints, as well as a number of female saints.

Euphrasius even put himself and his family in the apse. To the far left is his brother Cladius, a small boy depicting Cladius's son, and Euphrasius, holding a scale model of the basilica in his hands.

If you have plenty of energy, make the hike up the bell tower of the octagon-shaped **Baptisterijum** (Bapistry, 10 A.M.–5 P.M. daily, 10Kn), also part of the original complex, for the best views in town. The **Biskupska palača** (Bishop's Palace, included with ticket to Bapistry) was built much later, in the 17th century, and has a small display of mosaics and Baroque sacral art in its museum.

Aquarium Poreč

You'll see signs for the aquarium (F. Glavinica 4, tel. 052/428-720, www.aquarium-porec .com, 10 A.M.–5 P.M. daily, till 11 P.M. in summer, 25Kn) everywhere, and it's hard not to be wonder what all the fuss is about. One local said you'd see as many fish in the *ribarnica* (fishmonger's)—though he may have been a little harsh, you won't miss anything if you skip this small sampling of local fish in tanks.

Zavičajni muzej
District Museum

Housed in an 18th-century Baroque palace, the Zavičajni muzej (Dekumanska 9, tel. 052/431-585, www.poup.hr, 10 A.M.–1 P.M. Mon.–Sat., 10Kn) is the oldest museum in Istria, dating from 1884. The permanent collection is a nice mix of Roman and Greek stone monuments and pottery as well as a nice display of 17th-century Baroque portraits and art objects.

Romanička kuća
Romanesque House

At the end of Dekumanska you'll find the sweet little stone Romanička kuća (10 A.M.–noon and 8–10 P.M. daily in summer, free) with an interesting wooden wraparound balcony. Built in the 13th century, today its ground floor houses art exhibitions.

Trg Marafor
Marafor Square

At the very end of the peninsula, Trg Marafor is the location of the old Roman forum. The square's name likely derives from the words Mars and Forum, since the large square, rivaling the size of the squares in Pula and Salona,

centered around a 1st-century temple to Mars. The sides of the square were home to small temples of Neptune and Diana. Today, some carved stone remnants are all that's left of the temples of Mars and Neptune, and nothing remains of the temple of Diana.

BEACHES

Poreč's profusion of hotels and tourist complexes doesn't help its beach scene. The most popular is the **Gradsko kupalište,** an unappealing mass of concrete slab. **Sveti Nikola island** (taxi boats 7 A.M.–11 P.M., 12Kn) is prettier, with lots of trees and paved and pebble beaches, though these can also get packed in the summer. If you want to make the trip, there's a boat at the harbor that can take you there every half hour during the summer in less than 10 minutes. Another option is the Zelena Laguna tourist resort, six kilometers from the center of town, with more concrete-slab bathing options. To get there you can either walk the pedestrian path or take the small tourist train leaving regularly from Trg Slobode (May–Sept.).

WINERIES

Giordano Peršurić (Istarske divizije 27, Poreč, tel. 052/431-586, djordano.persuric@iptpo .hr, call for hours) produces the only sparkling wine in Istria—a surprisingly good one too, known as Misal.

ENTERTAINMENT AND EVENTS

Though Poreč's claim to fame might be its basilica, the **Vinistra** (April or May) festival comes in a close second. The most-respected wine fair in Croatia, Vinistra is marked by a competition of Istrian wines, though travelers will likely appreciate the wide variety of culinary offerings during the fair. Local cheeses, olive oils, and other products complement the guests of honor, the local wines.

The best entertainment in Poreč in summer is the weekly **concerts** (June–Aug., check with the tourist office for details, tickets around 30Kn) in the atrium of the

ISTRIA

ISTRIAN WINE

Though the history of wine in Istria dates back to Roman times, much of the area's production suffered during the World Wars and the era of Tito. However, the past 15 years have seen a rebirth of viticulture on the small, sunny peninsula. Istrian vineyards produce a number of wines, but only two are indigenous – the red earthy Teran, and Malvazija, a smooth, slightly sweet white that traces its popularity back to 13th-century Venice.

Istria holds several festivals revolving around wine, but if you can only make one, try to attend the Vinistra Festival in Poreč for four days in late April or early May. Dozens of tastings, judging, and exhibits of local olive oil and cheese make for some tasty testing of the Istrian culinary landscape. At the end of May you can catch Dan Vina, or Day of Wine, when dozens of local vineyards hold an open house from morning till evening, perfect for some serious wine-cruising. And Malvazija fans will appreciate Brtonigla's Malvazija Festival in early June.

There are dozens of wine routes for those who'd like to savor the vintages as they see the countryside. Since many wineries' production is small, lots of excellent wines never make it past the border, so this is your chance to discover what Istria has to offer. For more information about Istrian wine roads, check out www.istra.hr.

basilica (classical) and behind the Zavičajni muzej (jazz). In August the town hosts a great **Street Art Festival** (www.street-art-festival .com) with music, visual arts, and even a bit of acrobatics.

ACCOMMODATIONS

Honestly, Poreč is not the best value for money when it comes to accommodation. A much better value would be to stay in Novigrad or slightly inland at Brtonigla. However, if you really want to stay in town, there are lots of options.

You can search online for private accommodation under 500Kn via the **Istrian Tourist Board** (www.istra.hr). If you can afford to spend a little more, try the two-star **Hotel Jadran** (Obala Maršala Tita, tel. 052/465-000, www.valamar.com, 533Kn d., including breakfast), whose central Riva (waterfront promenade) location almost makes up for the small and somewhat dated rooms. Just down from the Jadran is the **Hotel Neptun** (Obala Maršala Tita, tel. 052/465-000, www.valamar.com, 711Kn d., including breakfast), slightly better and slightly more expensive than its neighbor. Out on Sveti Nikola island, the **Isabella Castle** (Otok Sv. Nikola, tel. 052/465-100, www.valamar

.com, 750Kn d., including breakfast) looks more impressive from the outside than the inside, where rooms are in want of a refresher course. However, the island location is nice and you have access to two pools for taking a dip, but you have to take a boat to get to Poreč. A 15-minute walk from the center of town is the **Valamar Diamant Hotel** (Naselje Brulo 1, tel. 052/465-000, www .valamar.com, 1,205Kn d., including breakfast), a big tourist complex that was renovated in 2007. The hotel has beaches, indoor and outdoor pools, a spa, and a fitness center. Also on the upper end of the hotel chain is the relatively new **Hotel Hostin** (Rade Končara 4, tel. 052/408-800, www.hostin.hr, 920Kn d., including breakfast), which offers great value for money, a pool, a small wellness center, and a nearby beach.

FOOD

The best deal in town is tucked into the wall of a house in the old town. **Konoba Neverin** (Eufrazijeva 8, tel. 098/473-448, 11 A.M.–11 P.M. in summer, call for winter hours, 30Kn) looks like a fast-food fish place, but the service and food (calamari, fresh sardines, salad) are excellent at unbeatable prices. In the center, **Sveti Nikola** (Obala Maršala Tita 23, tel

© SHANN FOUNTAIN ČULO

coffee alfresco in the center of Poreč

052/423-018, www.svnikola.com, noon–midnight daily, closed Jan.–Feb., 110Kn) serves artful truffle-laced dishes in a swank space. Fans of carpaccio will find fish and beef varieties with creative twists like the addition of parmesan or truffles. Though it looks like a tourist trap, **Ulixes** (Decumanus 2, tel. 052/451-132, noon–midnight daily, 90Kn) has surprisingly great food and friendly service in a cozy stone courtyard just off a busy pedestrian street. A short walk out of the center will land you at what looks like a private house on the waterfront; it's actually 🕻 **Zlatna ribica** (N Tesle 21, http://bebakali.googlepages.com/home, tel. 052/452-272, noon–3 P.M. and 7–11 P.M. daily, 110Kn), with a great water-view terrace and traditional seafood dishes. On the Poreč–Novigrad road signs will help guide you to **Dvi Murve** (Grožnjanska 17, tel. 052/434-115, www.dvimurve.hr, noon–11 P.M. daily, closed Jan., 120Kn), usually considered the town's best, though Zlatna ribica is also a contender. Out of season it's filled with local business types and people celebrating special occasions. In season, you'll find a lot more tourists like yourself. Call ahead to order the sea bass baked in a salt crust, one of the restaurant's specialties.

INFORMATION AND SERVICES

The helpful **tourist office** (Zagrebačka 9, tel. 052/451-293, www.istria-porec.com, 8 A.M.–10 P.M. Mon.–Sat. and 9 A.M.–1 P.M. and 5–9 P.M. Sun. July–Aug., 8 A.M.–8 P.M. Mon.–Sat. and 9 A.M.–1 P.M. and 5–8 P.M. Sun. Sept.–Oct. and mid-Apr.–June, 8 A.M.–4 P.M. Mon.–Sat. Nov.–mid-Apr.) can provide brochures, maps, and listings of local accommodation and private rooms as well as help with details about concerts and events. International information, with operators who speak English, can be reached by dialing 902.

GETTING THERE AND AROUND

Poreč's bus station (Rade Končara 1, tel. 052/432-153) has good connections to Pula (around 10 buses daily, 1 hour 10 minutes, 50Kn) and Rovinj (around 5 buses daily, mostly in the mornings, 50 minutes, 37Kn); it also connects to Zagreb (4 hours, 196Kn). Driving to Poreč is easy—just follow the signs from Rovinj or Pazin, in the interior. Parking is another matter. You'll likely circle a while to find a space—just mind the parking fees and maximum times.

AROUND POREČ
◖ Novigrad

Novigrad, 17 kilometers north of Poreč, is a precious little town right on the seafront and a much better choice for accommodation than Poreč. Driving out of Poreč, simply follow the signs for Novigrad or take one of eight buses daily to Novigrad's bus station (Murvi bb, about an eight-minute walk to the town center). The town itself has a couple of sights, a nice parish church and a small museum, but it's not so great for wandering about since the tiny streets are open to cars. Check out the **Museum Lapidarium** (Veliki trg 8A, tel. 052/726-582, www.muzej-lapidarium.hr, 10 A.M.–1 P.M. and 6–10 P.M. Tues.–Sun. in summer, 10 A.M.–1 P.M. and 5–7 P.M. Tues.–Sun. in winter, 10Kn) for Roman relics, and the excellent **Gallery Rigo** (Velika ulica 5, tel. 052/757-790, www.galerija-rigo.hr, call for hours, free) for great expos of contemporary Croatian art. For sunbathing, the beaches north of town are much better than anything Poreč has to offer.

Torci 18 (Torci 34, tel. 052/757-799, www.torci18.hr, 427Kn d., including breakfast) is a family-run pension with clean rooms and a great restaurant stocked by homegrown specialties and wines. Other family-run hotels include **Cittar** (Prolaz Venecija 1, tel. 052/757-737, www.cittar.hr, 880Kn d., including breakfast), smack in the old town, and the newer **Hotel Villa Cittar** (tel. 052/758-780, www.cittar.hr, 1,010Kn d., including breakfast), a 2008 addition to Novigrad with more upscale rooms than its sister property and an indoor pool for year-round swimming. The most luxurious place in town is the **Hotel Nautica** (Sv. Antona 15, tel. 052/600-400, www.nauticahotels.com, 1,450Kn d., including breakfast),

seaside view off the road between Poreč and Novigrad

© SHANN FOUNTAIN CULO

slightly removed from town on a marina populated with moored yachts.

You'll find lots of places to eat in town, from the laid-back pizzeria **Vecchio mulino** (Mlinska 8, tel. 052/726-300, 10 A.M.–late, 45Kn) to the more gourmet ☾ **Damir i Ornela** (Zidine 5, tel. 052/758-134, cittanova@inet .hr, noon–3 P.M. and 6–11:30 P.M. Tues.–Sun., call ahead for reservations, 90Kn), offering great local takes on sushi, grilled seafood, and a standout kiwi flan. Book at least a day in advance. If you have a craving for a cocktail and a stogie, check out the nearby **Cubano** bar, which keeps a decent stock of Cuban cigars.

There are a couple of fun bars in town like hip **Cocktail Bar Code** (Gradska Vrata 20A, no phone, 3 P.M.–midnight, until 2 A.M. Fri.– Sat.) and **Vitriol** (Ribarnička 6, tel. 052/758-270, 8 A.M.–midnight daily), also a great place for a coffee or pre-dinner cocktail on the seaside terrace.

Brtonigla

The neat little village of Brtonigla, about six kilometers northeast of Novigrad, charms travelers from the start. Surrounded by meticulous vineyards, the center of the small, sun-washed stone nucleus is presided over by a picturesque church and the town's hotel and restaurant, which are likely responsible for the discovery of the town by foreigners. The ☾ **Hotel San Rocco** (Srednja ulica 2, Brtonigla, tel. 052/725-000, www.san-rocco.hr, 1,208Kn d., including breakfast) is highly recommended for its small but cozy rooms, nice pool area, and superior restaurant (which has been awarded two stars from Gault Millau) serving sheep's cheese, organic fruits and vegetables, and regional specialties.

Malvazija is arguably Istria's best wine, a gentle white that goes with nearly everything. The **Fešta istarske malvazije** (Istrian Malvasia Festival, end of May or early June) in Brtonigla is a don't-miss for fans of the variety. Highlighting local growers, it's a great time to sample a few producers and choose which ones to add to your suitcase.

Since there's only one bus a day from Novigrad to Brtonigla (45 minutes, 32Kn), it's best to drive to this small town. On the road between Poreč and Novigrad, look for the road to Buje, and after turning, follow the signs to Brtonigla. You can also call a cab from Novigrad (tel. 052/757-224).

Wineries

Take a trip to Višnjan, 12 kilometers east of Poreč (you'll need a car—head north from Poreč toward Novigrad and then follow the signs for Višnjan), to visit two of Istria's best winemakers. **Poletti** (Markovac 14, Višnjan, tel. 052/449-251, www.vina-poletti.com) has won awards for his Malvazija, but his most interesting wine is a Muškat ruža, a variety that used to be native to the area and Poletti is now reviving. **Radovan** (Radovani 14, Višnjan, tel. 052/462-166, vina.radovan@pu.t-com.hr, call for hours) is another young winemaker, equally impressive in reds and whites, particularly his Malvazija, Chardonnay, Cabernet Sauvignon, and Teran.

Fans of food and wine, particularly those who stayed in Brtonigla, should drive to Momjan (head northwest of Buje and follow signs for Momjan; it's about a 30-to-40-minute drive). **Gianfranco Kozlović** (Valle 78, Momjan, tel. 052/779-177, info@kozlovic .hr, www.kozlovic.hr, call for hours) was one of the pioneers of the Istrian wine revolution of the early 1990s. His wines are solid, though the old winemakers consider him a bit of a rebel for bringing new techniques and equipment, like stainless steel vats, to a very old trade. The excellent restaurant of winemaker **Marino Markežić** (Kremenje 96B, Kremenje, tel. 052/779-047, mmarkezic@inet.hr, www .konoba-marino-kremenje.hr, noon–10 P.M. Wed.–Mon., closed Jan. and last two weeks of June), in the nearby village of Kremenje, specializes in truffle-based dishes. Make sure to try his Muscat and elegant gray Pinot while you're there.

Though it's a bit of a drive north of Poreč and Novigrad, the northwestern corner of the Istrian peninsula is home to two excellent wineries (and conveniently located close

ISTRIA

to the Slovenian border if you're headed that way). The best winery in Istria, perhaps, is **Moreno Coronica** (Koreniki 86, Umag, tel. 052/730-196, atc@coronica.com, www .coronica.com, call for hours), a small wine-maker with the highest-quality wines. His Malvazija is outstanding, winning numerous awards, but you should also try his aged Teran, from which he is trying to create a world-class red. **Degrassi** (Bašanija bb, Savudrija, tel. 052/759-250, moreno.degrassi@pu.t-com .hr, call for hours) produces what are arguably Istria's best red wines, but his whites aren't bad either. He was also among the founders of the new Istrian wine movement, along with Gianfranco Kozlović and Ivica Matošević.

Istrian Interior

Though the coastal towns get the bulk of the tourist trade, the beautiful interior of Istria, not unlike Tuscany or Provence, is becoming more hip. Some towns like Motovun have become a bit too popular, but the advantage to the increased tourism is a wave of new restaurants and small hotels to meet demand. Of course, if you really want to get away from it all, visit the region in spring or fall, or try out towns like Pazin or Beram, rarely treaded even by the most enthusiastic of tourist groups.

No matter when you come, the highlight of interior Istria is its gastronomic offerings. To enjoy the serious vineyards producing high-quality wines and the restaurants that serve lots of creative versions of truffles, local cured ham, and asparagus in season, it's best to forget about the diet while you're visiting.

PAZIN

Though Pazin is a somewhat provincial town without a lot of atmosphere, the "capital" of Istria does have a few interesting stops and the added bonus of being off the tourist path. The main attraction is the city's *kaštel* (castle stronghold), which dates back to the late 10th century. Today it is the home of the **Etnografski muzej Istre** (Ethnographic Museum of Istria, Trg Istarskog razvoda 1275. br. 1, tel. 052/622-220, www.emi.hr, 10 A.M.–6 P.M. Tues.–Sun., 15Kn), with a good showing of Istrian costumes and housekeeping tools. From here, make the short walk down the street to the bridge, the perfect place from which to admire the **Pazin cave,** which inspired both Dante

and Jules Verne, whose Mathis Sandor character escapes from the castle by swimming in the underground waterway to the shore.

Six kilometers northwest out of town in the village of Beram, the **Crkvica Majka Bojža na škriljinah** (Chapel of Our Lady on the Rocks, free though a donation would be very kind) in the Beram graveyard is a must-see if you're in the area. You can obtain the keys to the unassuming little church from either Mrs. Marija Gortan (house no. 33, tel. 052/622-444) or Mrs. Sonja Šestan (house no. 38, tel. 052/622-903) or by asking the **tourist office** in Pazin (Ulica Franine i Jurine 14, tel. 052/622-460, call for hours) to arrange a visit for you. The 15th-century chapel (the loggia was added in the 18th century) is decorated with outstanding frescoes created by Vincent of Kastav in 1474. The *Adoration of the Kings* is the largest, but the *Dance of Death* is by far the most famous, with its eerie skeletons parading with mortals right above the entrance. There's a tavern in town, **Vela Vrata** (Beram 41, tel. 091/781-4995, 4–11 P.M. daily, 45Kn), where you can order up some *fuži* (a type of local homemade pasta) and a glass of local wine.

There are two super *agroturizam* hotels in the area around Pazin. First up is **House Ivela** (Pariži 109 A, tel. 052/686-271, www.house ivela.netfirms.com, 3,200Kn a week), about 10 kilometers southwest of Pazin on the road to Kanfanar. If you think the charming cottage and perfectly decorated rooms look like they jumped out of an interiors magazine, you're right: The fairytale house was featured in a local edition of *Elle Décor*. The owners also offer painting courses for the artistically inclined. **Agroturizam Ograde** (Lindarski katun 60, tel. 052/693-035, agroturizam-ograde@ pu.t-com.hr, www.agroturizam-ograde.hr, from 142Kn d.), about 10 kilometers south of Pazin, has a typical little stone house for rent or a double apartment with friendly owners and super meals. Even if you're not overnighting here, it's a great place to have a meal—call ahead for hours.

You can get to Pazin by train from Pula (1 hour 10 minutes) or Rijeka (1 hour), both around 40Kn, arriving at the train station (Stareh Kostanji 1, tel. 052/624-310), about a 10-minute walk to the center of town. By bus (tel. 052/624-364) there are connections with Pula (2 or 3 daily, 1 hour, 40Kn) and Rijeka (6 or more weekdays, 2 on weekends, 1 hour, 49Kn). There are also multiple daily connections to Poreč (45 minutes, 33Kn), Rovinj (weekdays only, 1 hour, 36Kn), and Zagreb (4 hours, 172Kn). Going to Beram or the agrotourism hotels, you'll really need your own car.

GRAČIŠĆE

The 12th-century village of Gračišće is a quiet little place with some impressive cut-stone Venetian homes, including the **Palace Salomon,** lining the main square. The church **Majka Božža na Placu** (St. Mary's-on-the-square) has some nice 15th-century frescoes. If the church is locked, you can ask at the parish office (tel. 052/687-115) or peek through the windows for a view. Perhaps more interesting than the frescoes are the nails stuck in the church walls: Local legend said that if women hammered them into the wall it would help them become pregnant.

Gračišće is also worth a visit for the **Pješačka staza sv. Šimuna,** an 11.5-kilometer walking trail around town. It takes about 2.5–3 hours; you'll pass a peaceful waterfall, the nests of birds who like to feast on bees, and the small stone cottage–filled village of Lovrići.

Gračišće's **Maneštrijada** (Maneštra Festival) brings out dozens of chefs vying for the title of best *maneštra,* a pasta-based stew that varies with the seasons. If you're lucky enough to be in town during a festival (held at least twice a year), head to the main square to sample what's on offer.

ISTRIA

ISTRIAN TRUFFLES

Most people are familiar with truffles – those ugly, bumpy tubers that fetch hundreds of dollars at market. Istria is full of them, both the black and white varieties (though the white is more common). The white variety, or *tuber magnatum,* is particularly precious, selling for €2,000–4,000 per kilogram.

They thrive in the grayish clay soil of Istria's interior, particularly in the area around Motovun, near the roots of the majestic oak, most common near Livade and Buzet. The hunting season runs from the last days of summer to the end of January, when lots of old men and their highly trained hounds can be found around Motovun forest, sniffing for black or white gold.

Istria does all sorts of things with its truffles, from shaving them on pasta to cooking them with meats to putting them into cheese. The white truffles are quite strong in flavor, and are best used to complement plain foods like pasta. Though Istria has its moments with truffles, it can sometimes get a little too tuber-happy, overusing the truffle and falling far short of culinary genius. Look for the *Izvorni Tartuf* or *Tartufo Vero* sign in restaurants, which indicate the use of real truffles and not just essence of truffle.

In October the town of Livade spends weekends debating over the biggest and best truffles as well as auctioning off a few and holding cooking classes on how to use them. It's here that Istria really got on the truffle map in 1999, when Zigante found a truffle that entered in the *Guinness Book of World Records* as the largest truffle in the world.

Motovun, a medieval town known for its film festival

Konoba Marino (Gračišće 75, tel. 052/687-081, marino.buljan@pu.t-com.hr, 50Kn) has some good meat and pasta dishes and has some rooms to offer as well if you'd like to stay in town.

Six kilometers southeast of Pazin, Gračišće is best reached by car, though there are at least two connections by bus from Pazin on weekdays (20 minutes, 21Kn).

MOTOVUN

Istria is filled with picturesque hilltop towns; seen from below, Motovun seems to win top honors, its stone buildings winding their way up the slopes like a well-placed dollop of whipped cream on top of the vineyard-filled valleys below. A small well-preserved medieval town, Motovun was mostly Italian speaking until the mid-20th century, by which point the majority of townspeople had left seeking better opportunities. Motovun has since been repopulated by artists and people seeking a bit of Istrian charm. It used to be somewhat of an undiscovered gem; then the town made the most of its wonderful film festival and marketed itself as a must-see for every visitor to Istria. The reality is not quite as shiny though, with crowded streets, not really that much to see, and mostly sub-par restaurants. If you can make it to Grožnjan feel free to skip Motovun, but if you do give in to peer pressure try to go early in the morning or later in the evening to miss the groups that pour out of the tour-bus circuit.

Sights

The **Crkva svetog Stjepana** (St. Stephen's Church, open most days, free) on the town's main square is a relatively plain yellow Baroque structure, with a somewhat incongruent Romanesque-Gothic bell tower tacked onto its side. Inside, you'll find a pretty Venetian painting of the Last Supper above the altar. Passing the large municipal building, climb up to a path that encircles the old town walls. From here you have some great views of the valleys and vineyards below. For more information and free brochures, contact the Motovun **tourist office** (Trg Andrea Antico 1, tel. 052/681-758).

© SHANN FOUNTAIN CULO

view from Motovun of the surrounding Istrian countryside

Wineries

If you're in Motovun and you're a fan of the grape, make time to stop at **Livio Benvenuti** (Kaldir 7, Motovun, tel. 098/421-189, info@ benvenutivina.com, www.benvenutivina.com, call for hours). The young winemaker has already won multiple awards for his outstanding Malvazija.

Entertainment and Events

The **Motovun Film Festival** (July, www .motovunfilmfestival.com) has only been going on since 1999, but already the festival is the most prestigious in Croatia. It gathers a good group of European actors and directors (and the occasional Hollywood B-lister) as well as fans of cinema and party-circuit types who come for the glamour-by-osmosis. It's a much more accessible film festival for those who've always dreamed of rubbing shoulders with the artsy set and the open-screenings are both laid-back and elegant at the same time. If you'd like to be a part of the action, book well in advance to score a room.

Accommodations and Food

Montona Tours (Kanal 10, tel. 052/681-970, www.montonatours.com) has a good selection of private rooms and villas in and around Motovun for rent. Otherwise, the best in-town options are the **Bella Vista** (tel. 052/681-724, www.apartmani-motovun .com, 585Kn d.), with two apartments in an atmospheric stone townhouse, and the **Hotel Kaštel** (Trg Andrea Antico 7, tel. 052/681-607, www.hotel-kastel-motovun.hr, 590Kn d., including breakfast), its jaunty facade disguising somewhat less jaunty but clean rooms in a couldn't-be-better old-town location. The hotel also recently opened a small wellness center. The Hotel Kaštel also has a restaurant (8 A.M.–10 P.M. daily, 80Kn) featuring hard-to-find Boškarin beef, a type of indigenous cattle that can only be served by permit (which the restaurant has).

For food in town, try **Konoba Mondo** (Barbacan 1, tel. 052/681-791, hours vary, call ahead, no credit cards, 75Kn).

A six-kilometer drive southeast away from Motovun, **Agroturizam Štefanić** (Štefanići 55, tel. 052/689-026, www.agroturizam-stefanic.hr, call ahead, 90Kn) makes all dishes with ingredients that come straight from their farm. It's a great choice for traditional staples, fresh cheese, and roasted meats.

Getting There and Around

You can catch a bus to Motovun from Pazin (at least 2 connections on weekends, more in summer, 45 minutes, around 25Kn) all year. The bus from Pula to Buzet stops in Motovun as well. The station is at the bottom of the hill in Kanal, the more modern part of town. If you're driving, there are a few parking spaces up near the old town (usually there are a couple available early mornings and out of season). Otherwise, you'll have to park at the lot in Kanal and hike up for about half an hour. If you're lazy, proceed to Grožnjan.

OPRTALJ

If you're coming from Motovun, you'll come to a large crossroads (large for the Istrian interior, anyway). Go left for Buje or the beach, right for Buzet, or straight for Oprtalj. Driving to Oprtalj, you'll pass through the village of

Livade, less than a kilometer from the crossroads, worth a stop for lunch or stocking up on truffle souvenirs at the **Zigante Tartufi restaurant** (Livade 7, tel. 052/664-302, www .zigantetartufi.com, noon–11 P.M. daily in summer, noon–10 P.M. daily in winter, 95Kn) and shop in town. From here you'll head up to Oprtalj—it's only a few kilometers, but due to the winding narrow roads, with plenty of pretty scenery to gawk at, the trip will take about 20 minutes.

Oprtalj is quickly being transformed into a proper little tourist town. On the upside, there are plenty of nice spots for refreshment, and many of the homes have been lovingly restored. On the downside are those darn tourist buses, but if you can manage to visit when none of them are parked in the lot coming into town, you'll feel like you have the place to yourself. The town has three interesting churches, dating from the 15th and 16th centuries with some attractive frescoes (though the churches are often closed), and a nice town loggia and lapidarium. However, the best part of Oprtalj is

Oprtalj, one of Istria's prettiest hilltop villages

simply taking in the view beside the town loggia, with sunny rolling hills and stone houses, and strolling around one of Istria's prettiest hilltop villages.

The **Café Volta,** at the entrance to the town gates across from the loggia, has some nice rooms (tel. 052/644-216, klaudio.ipsa@pu .t-com.hr, 220Kn d.), and the **Ravnica Cultural Centre** (Ravnica 8, tel. 052/664-026, www.ravnica.org, 356Kn) has one apartment available for rent in the owners' wonderful gallery/studio/artists' colony just out of town. In addition to Zigante's place down in Livade, Oprtalj's **Konoba Oprtalj** (M. Laginje 11, tel. 052/644-130, noon–10 P.M. Tues.–Sun., 55Kn) has hearty meat and pasta dishes in a cozy atmosphere.

You'll need a car to reach Oprtalj. Otherwise, try booking a tour or day trip from one of the tourist offices on the coast.

◖ GROŽNJAN

The postcard-perfect streets of this quaint medieval hilltop town were all but abandoned when artists started setting up their studios here in the 1960s. Currently, there are close to 30 galleries and ateliers in Grožnjan. Even the street signs are artistic, made of hand-painted ceramic instead of the ho-hum metal in most towns. Summer brings more tourists, but for the moment it's still not swamped even at the height of the season, and most of the artists are in town as well as the **Jeunesse Musicales International Cultural Centre** (Umberta Gorjana 2, tel. 052/776-106). A training ground for young musicians, the center puts on a **student concert** almost every night in season (Musical Summer, www.hgm.hr). Out of season, Grožnjan is still lovely, with views that can easily rival those of Motovun and a much less touristy feel.

Sights

The 18th-century parish **Župna crkva Sv. Vida i Modesta** (Church of Sts. Vitus and Modestus) is not all that impressive if you've seen others in Croatia. However, the large expanse of courtyard next to its bell tower is a

---

KAŽUNI: ISTRIA'S STONE SHELTERS

Dotted throughout the rural landscape of Istria are small circular stone structures with cone-like roofs. You'll also find more modern versions in urbanized areas, used as kiosks or tourist info points. Indigenous to local architecture, the *kažuni* were originally built as shelters for those out tending the fields and vineyards. Though you could be bold and hunker down in one yourself for the night, there's always the chance an upset shepherd could disturb your rest. If you'd like to stay in a modernized version of the huts, there's the quirky **Leader** (Lupoglav 8, tel. 052/685-300, www.istraleader.com, 320Kn d.), a complex of stone *kažuni* east of Hum, each with its own door, fireplace, and air-conditioning. There's also a basic pool and tennis courts for would-be shepherds that can't quite give up their conveniences.

ISTRIA

---

nice place to sit and reflect. The town's 16th-century **Crkvica Sv. Kuzmana i Domjana** (Church of Sts. Cosmas and Damian) has some colorful frescoes, though their provenance is much more recent, having been painted in 1989 by Croatian artist Ivan Lovrenčić. A couple of galleries worth checking out are the **Fonticus Gallery** (Trg Lože 3, tel. 052/776-357, hours vary), the town's largest, and **Pharos** (Gorjana 8, tel. 091/767-9818, 10 A.M.–8 P.M. daily in spring and summer), with a range of furniture and small paintings.

The **tourist office** (Umberta Gorjana 3, Grožnjan, tel. 052/776-131, www.groznjan-grisignana.hr) is a useful place to stop for more information.

Accommodations and Food

You can stay and eat at the family-run **Pintur** (Mate Gorjana 9, tel. 052/776-397, ivan .cerneka@pu.t-com.hr, 345Kn d.), whose restaurant serves typical Istrian fare like *fuži* and local wines, or try the Grožnjan outpost of the **Zigante** chain (U. Gorjan 5, tel. 052/776-099, www.zigantetartufi.com, 10 A.M.–11 P.M. daily in summer, 10 A.M.–8 P.M. daily in winter, 50Kn) for a light snack of cheese, truffles, bread, and wine. You can also grab a meal at **Bastia** (1 Svibanja 1, tel. 052/776-370, 8 A.M.–2 A.M. daily mid-June–Aug., 9 A.M.–10 P.M. out of season, closed mid-Jan.–Feb., no credit cards, 60Kn), with local dishes, a small bar, and an unofficial place to ask about private rooms.

Getting There and Around
Getting to Grožnjan is difficult without a car. If you'd like to try, take the bus from Buzet to Buje (or Buje to Buzet, 3 or more a day, 30 minutes, 33Kn) and ask the driver to drop you off at the nearby village of Bijele Zemlje, from where you must hike a couple of miles uphill.

◖ HUM
Conveniently located on the way into or out of Istria, the little village of Hum claims it's the smallest town in the world, with less than 20 full-time residents. Whether it is or not remains to be seen, but it would be a shame to miss the tiny little walled village and all of the gems it has to offer.

Passing through a large gate, you'll likely hear the laughter and footsteps of patrons of the Humska Konoba above. But once you pass the *konoba,* the town becomes quiet, even deserted, depending on the time of year you happen to visit. The **Crkva blažene djevice Marije** (Church of the Blessed Virgin Mary), the village's main feature, is rarely open, but there is a woman in town who has the key if you absolutely must see inside. Ask at the *konoba,* which also holds the key to the **Crkvica svetog Jeronima** (Chapel of St. Hieronymous), a Romanesque chapel in the cemetery, worth a peek inside to admire the ancient frescoes. Hum has two gift shops that are a good spot for buying the town's own specialty, a mistletoe liquor used since the Middle Ages for killing

Crkva blažene djevice Marije, in Hum

off a variety of ailments. In June the village i host to almost forgotten Istrian music at the **vijulini sopu muškardini** festival.

Any time of the year the ◖ **Humsk Konoba** (Hum 2, tel. 052/660-005, ww .hum.hr, 11 A.M.–11 P.M. daily, 60Kn) is no only the local source for tourist informatior but it's a favorite with locals for the cozy Istria food and the great views of the green valley from its terrace. While you're in the area th small restaurant **Kotlić** (Kotli 3, no phon 2–10 P.M. daily on weekends, 50Kn) is a nic place to stop on the banks of a rushing stream Just park before crossing the river and wal over the bridge on foot, since its sturdiness quite suspect.

You'll need a rental car to get to Hum. N too terribly far from the Učka tunnel (whic connects Kvarner and Istria), less than 10 kilo meters from the village of Roč, you'll see sigr directing you toward Hum.

KVARNER GULF

The Kvarner region is geographically defined as its gulf and the surrounding three sides of steep mountain ranges. Historically, the area was all but cut off from the rest of Croatia by its terrain. The isolation certainly has given Kvarner a culture all its own, different from Istria to its west, Lika to the east, and Dalmatia to the south. Lying at the northern end of Croatia's spectacular coast, the Kvarner Gulf starts things off with worth-the-trip places like laid-back-with-an-edge Rijeka, the luxe Opatija Riviera (historic summer home of wealthy Austro-Hungarians and, in modern times, the richest man in Croatia), and the beautiful islands off the coast. Although these destinations will satisfy beach lovers, many also offer something more. Islands such as Rab, Lošinj, and Pag are rich cultural locales, with festivals and handicrafts in addition to the beaches made for lounging. There are places for those looking for a nonstop club scene, for history (the Greeks, Romans, and Venetians all left their mark), for sports like scuba diving and hiking, and for natural beauty and wildlife, with a sanctuary for griffons on the island of Cres and a dolphin preserve at Veli Lošinj.

There's plenty for foodies and a few gems for wine lovers, though Kvarner is by no means as heavily into wine as other locations in Croatia and Slovenia. Gourmet cuisine is a different story. Food lovers shouldn't miss the area around Opatija and Lovran, where several of Croatia's top restaurants serve up award-winning cuisine, much of it with a view thrown in for extra value.

Most of the islands are connected by

© LIANE MATRISCH/DREAMSTIME.COM

HIGHLIGHTS

◖ **Opatija:** Only a couple of hours from Zagreb and situated near the entrance to Istria on the Kvarner Gulf, Opatija was once a playground for the Austro-Hungarian elite. Today it's regaining some of its aura, with boutique hotels and world-class restaurants along its riviera, particularly in the former fishing village of Volosko (page 140).

◖ **Cres:** The relatively undeveloped island of Cres is home to step-back-in-time fishing villages and the town of Beli, home to the Caput Insulae Eco Centre, a refuge for a colony of griffon vultures, indigenous to the island. Take time to wander through the sanctuary's knobby, twisted forests and try to catch a glimpse of one of the endangered birds (page 151).

◖ **Veli Lošinj:** This laid-back town on the island of Lošinj has a faded-glory vibe, a dolphin preserve, and a wonderful restaurant a walk away in Rovenska. Spend some time peeking through the garden gates of the captains' villas and strolling the waterfront promenade (page 157).

◖ **Susak:** Though it gets its share of daytrippers, mornings and evenings in Susak are almost devoid of tourists. Hike the island's 11-kilometer trail, stopping for a dip at a beach surrounded by the clay cliffs, a geographical feature distinct in the Adriatic's mostly rocky archipelagos (page 158).

◖ **Rab Town:** The medieval core of Rab Town is charming any time of year, but even more so during the annual Rab Fiera, a celebration of olden crafts and trades. The rest of the year it's a nice place to wander around, stopping for an ice cream or a souvenir and walking along the old city walls (page 159).

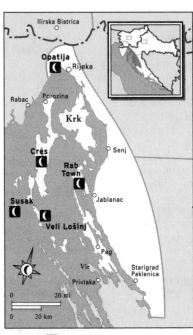

LOOK FOR ◖ TO FIND RECOMMENDED SIGHTS, ACTIVITIES, DINING, AND LODGING.

ferries and catamarans in the summer, making it easy to wind your way through them. Pag, which technically belongs to Northern Dalmatia, has been included in Kvarner because of the number of connections with the gulf and its islands.

PLANNING YOUR TIME

The relative ease with which you can fit a lot into a short period of time is one of the features that makes Kvarner so special. From liberal port-city life in quirky Rijeka to a sheep farm on Pag or party-hopping wit the masses on Krk, you should always be er tertained. Most European tourists come t one spot and camp out for the week, park ing their towels on the beach during the da and going out for dinner at night, possibl squeezing in a tiny bit of sightseeing. But th fact that there's not too much to see in an one place makes it easy to see most, if no all, of Kvarner. You can get a great overvie of the place in a week, spending one or tw nights around Rijeka or Opatija and the

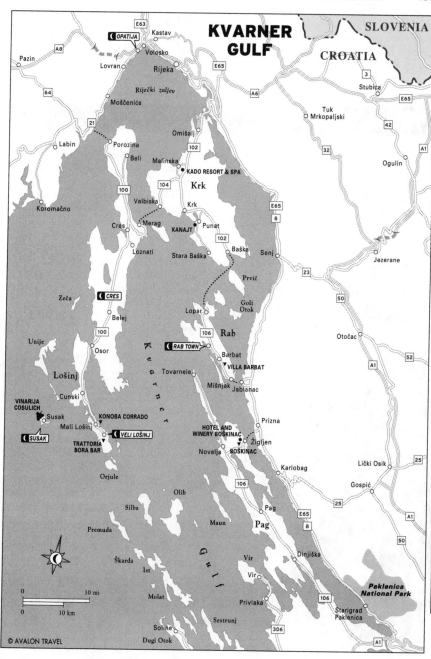

KVARNER GULF

SLOVENIA

CROATIA

E63 Kastav
☾ OPATIJA
Volosko
A8
Pazin
Lovran Rijeka
Riječki zaljev E65
Moščeniče
A6
Stubica
E65
Tuk
Mrkopaljski
21
3
42
Labin Porozina
Omišalj
Beli
102
32
A1
Malinska
104
KADO RESORT & SPA Ogulin
Krk
Kotomačno
100 Valbiska
Krk
E65
Cres Merag
8
KANAJT Punat
Loznati
102
Stara Baška Baška
Senj
Prvić
Jezerane
23
Zeča
☾ CRES Goli
Otok
50
Belej Lopar
Unije
106 Rab
Osor
Otočac
☾ RAB TOWN
52
Barbat A1
Lošinj VILLA BARBAT
Tovarnele
Cunski Mišnjak
Jablanac
VINARIJA
COSULICH Susak KONOBA CORRADO
Prizna
Mali Lošinj ☾ VELI LOŠINJ
☾ SUSAK HOTEL AND
WINERY BOŠKINAC
TRATTORIA Žigljen Lički Osik 25
BORA BAR Novalja BOŠKINAC
Orjule Karlobag
Gospić
Olib
106
Silba
Pag 25
Maun
E65 A1
Pag
8
Premuda
50
Škarda Vir
Ist Dinjiška
Molat Vir
Paklenica
National Park
Privlaka
106
Soline Sestrunj Starigrad
Paklenica
Dugi Otok 306 A1

Kvarner

Gulf

0   10 mi
0   10 km

© AVALON TRAVEL

KVARNER GULF

heading to the islands for a few days. Two weeks and you can see everything at leisure, even spending an entire couple of days soaking up the sun.

If you're just skirting the region on your way to Istria (the Učka tunnel, entrance to Istria, is just northwest of Rijeka), still make time for a quick visit to Rijeka or at least a leisurely lunch at one of the excellent restaurants around Opatija.

Rijeka

Most tourists view Rijeka only as a destination point for getting somewhere else. And it's true that the port city of 150,000 has lots of ferry connections and is close to the airport for making a quick entrance and exit. But the town has a personality all its own, with a heavy dose of hip and a very open mind—probably owing to the fact that it is the country's largest port, which has opened it up to new ideas for centuries.

The city was originally settled by the Romans and ruled by the Hapsburgs, though it's the Hungarians who had the most influence on Rijeka. Coming to power in the late 18th century, they quickly established it as their harbor and built a whole mass of infrastructure to support it. During the first half of the 20th century Rijeka was a center of turmoil, with locals fighting for a united Slav nation, falling to Italian control, then German, then as a part of Yugoslavia, and finally to its current status as Croatia's third-largest city. Though industry suffered at one point, the construction of a highway connecting Rijeka and Zagreb in about a two-hour journey has brought new life to the city's economy and a giant project to grow the port within the next decade promises even more.

The city tower is the entrance gate to Rijeka's Stari Grad.

SIGHTS
Riva

Unlike in many of Croatia's coastal cities, Rijeka's waterfront promenade, locally dubbed the Riva, is not the center of social life in town. But it's still worth a stroll down the street to get a peek at the city's largest showing of 19th-century buildings, which remained after the city was heavily bombed in World War II.

Korzo

One block inland from the Riva, you'll find Korzo, a pedestrian-only street lined with cafés and shops. This is the heart of Rijeka and definitely the place to stop for a coffee and some people-watching. Here you'll find a small gallery of the larger Museum of Contemporary and Modern Art called the **Mali Salon** (Korzo 24, tel. 051/333-548, www.mmsu.hr, 10 A.M.–1 P.M. and 6–9 P.M. daily in summer, price depends on exhibit) with revolving exhibitions of 20th-century and present-day artwork. On the Korzo you'll also find the **Gradski toranj** (City Tower), a medieval gate topped with a frothy Baroque city coat-of-arms and a useful clock. It was located on the water until the 18th century, when landfills extended the city's area and relegated the tower to an interior position.

Stari Grad
Old Town

The entrance to Stari Grad is the Gradski toranj on the Korzo. Despite its charming name, the area is largely unimpressive save for a couple of landmarks and museums, the most stunning of which is **Crkva svetog Vida** (St. Vitus's Church, Trg Grivica 11, tel. 051/330-897, 9 A.M.–noon and 5–7 P.M. daily, free). On the way up to the church, notice the simple Roman arch, which once served as the entrance to the city's Praetorium, or local headquarters of the Roman military. Construction of the church began in 1638, took more than a century, and bled the city's resources. It is still not completed, as some surfaces of the church were never covered in stone. The exterior is rare among Croatian churches, with a vast rotunda

fashioned after the Santa Maria della Salute in Venice. The interior is straight-up Baroque, the marble ostentation incongruous with the altar's centerpiece, a 13th-century Gothic crucifix. Placed above the main altar, it was saved from an older church that stood on the site. Legend has it that in 1296 a certain Petar Lončarić, angered over a gambling loss, threw a stone at the crucifix and it bled.

Near the church you'll find something entirely different. The **Club Peek&Poke** (Ivana Grohovca 2, tel. 091/780-5709, www.peek poke.hr, 5–8 P.M. Mon.–Fri., 10 A.M.–2 P.M. Sat., 10Kn) sounds much more adult than it actually is. This family-friendly computer museum displays working models of really old computers. It's a fun stop for a bit of nostalgia or to show your kids what it was like back in the day (circa 1989, for instance).

Muzejski trg
Museum Square

Positioned northwest of St. Vitus's Church (if you're walking from the church, walk north and turn left on Žrtava fašizma), Muzejski trg is home to three of Rijeka's most important museums. The largest of these is the **Povijesni i pomorski muzej hrvatskog primorja** (History and Maritime Museum of the Croatian Littoral, Muzejski trg 1, www.ppmhp.hr, 9 A.M.–2 P.M. Tues.–Fri., 9 A.M.–2 P.M. Sat., 10Kn), with an extensive collection of local maritime history, including ship's instruments, model ships, logs, and old postcards. The museum also has a decent showing of archaeological artifacts as well as small displays of subjects as diverse as poetry, weaponry, and ethnography. The ornate 19th-century building that houses the museum, the **Guvernerova palača** (Governor's Palace), has its own history as well. It's here that Gabriele d'Annunzio, an Italian right-winger who declared Rijeka as part of Italy in 1919, clashed with Italian military and supporters of Rijeka's independence, forcing d'Annunzio and his *arditi* (a faction that claimed his right to lead the city) to leave. As a matter of fact, it's worth the visit just to admire the palace's grand rooms.

KVARNER GULF

Just outside the museum is the **lapidarium** (same hours as the museum, included in ticket price), housing various tombstones and a row of stone heads known as Adamić's Witnesses, paid for by a local 18th-century merchant to ridicule those who accused him of a crime he didn't commit.

On the western side of Muzejski trg is the **Muzej grada Rijeke** (Rijeka City Museum, Muzejski trg 1, tel. 051/336-711, www.muzej-rijeka.hr, 10 A.M.–1 P.M. and 5–8 P.M. Mon.–Fri., 10 A.M.–1 P.M. Sat., 20Kn), housed in a block-like building supposedly inspired by Mondrian where a small permanent collection (photographs, weaponry, jewelry) and changing temporary exhibitions chronicle the city's history.

Slightly northeast of Museum Square, the **Prirodoslovni muzej** (Natural History Museum, Lorenzov prolaz 1, www.prirodoslovni .com, 9 A.M.–7 P.M. Mon.–Sat., 9 A.M.–3 P.M. Sun., 10Kn) is a well-presented museum with a nice little collection of flora and fauna from the region including an aquarium and pint-sized botanical garden.

Trg Republike Hrvatske
Republic of Croatia Square

South of Muzejski trg, down Frana Supila, is the University Library at Trg Republike Hrvatske. A former 19th-century girls' school, the building now houses the **Izložba glagoljice** (Glagolitic Script Exhibition, Dolac 1, tel. 051/336-129, evgenia.arh@svkri.hr, contact in advance to arrange a visit) for those interested in learning more about the area's medieval common language. The top floor of the library is occupied by the **Muzej moderne i suvremene umjetnosti** (Museum of Contemporary and Modern Art, Dolac 1, tel. 051/492-611, www .mmsu.hr, 10 A.M.–1 P.M. and 5–8 P.M. Tues.–Sun., price depends on exhibition), which has some excellent exhibitions of contemporary art by Croatian as well as foreign artists.

Teatro Fenice

West from Trg Republike Hrvatske along Dolac you'll come across the postmodernist Teatro Fenice (tel. 051/335-225, www.rijekakino.hr, call for a schedule of events or film showings), built in 1913. Once used to stage performances and shows, the building became a cinema after World War II. Today it's used for both purposes, hosting concerts and presentations as well as screening films. Even though the facade is sorely in need of repair, fans of art nouveau architecture will appreciate its beauty.

Trsat

East of the city center, quite a walk from Rijeka's old-town tourist attractions, lies Trsat, a suburb of Rijeka. Long a pilgrimage site for locals, the importance of Trsat dates back to the 13th century, when legend has it that the house of Mary and Joseph rested here for three years during its journey from Nazareth to Loreto, in Italy. The devoted (or the active) will want to climb the 538 steps of the **Trsatske Stube** (Trsat stairs), started in 1531 by the Uskok commander Petar Kružić and added to over the years, to reach the Franciscan monastery. Those with less time or less endurance can take bus #1 from the Riva (every 15 minutes, 15.50Kn).

The **Crkva gospel trsatske** (Church of Our Lady of Trsat, open most days, free) is said to be built on the spot where the house of Mary and Joseph rested. The church and the **Franjevački samostan** (Franciscan monastery) were built, added to, and rebuilt over the years and today represent several architectural styles, including Gothic, Renaissance, Baroque, and Biedermeyer. Our Lady of Trsat was built in the 15th century, only to be almost completely reconstructed in the early 19th century. The altar is topped by an image of the Virgin Mary from 1367. Definitely worth a visit in the complex is the moving **Kapela zavjetnih darova** (Votive Chapel, open most days, free) where candlelight paintings and tapestries given by people whose prayers were answered.

If you drove into Rijeka on the highway from Zagreb, you likely passed **Trsatsk gradina** (Trsat Castle, Petra Zrinskog bb, tel. 051/217-714, 9 A.M.–midnight dail

Apr.–Nov., 9 A.M.–3 P.M. daily Dec., Feb., and Mar., 15Kn for guided tour) as you came into town. Just across from the monastery, the decaying castle holds an amazing position on the rocks above Rijeka. On a clear day there's a magnificent view of the Kvarner Gulf. Parts of the castle date from Roman times, when a lookout tower occupied the spot; then the powerful Frankopan family built a castle here in medieval times. Trsatska gradina was given a final overhaul by Laval Nugent, an Austrian count, who made it his final home and added several romanticist touches, like a Classicist mausoleum in the castle's main courtyard. In the summer, the castle is often the location for open-air concerts. Find yourself in need of lunch? Stop at **Trsatika,** which offers filling, reasonable meals with a great view as well.

Hrvatsko narodno kazalište
Croatian National Theater

A bit out of the way on the Mrtvi Kanal (on the far eastern end of the Riva, dubbed Ivana Zajca Street), the grand Austro-Hungarian Hrvatsko narodno kazalište (Uljarska 1, tel. 051/355-900, www.hnk-zajc.hr, open for performances, box office 9:30 A.M.–12:30 P.M. Mon.–Sat. and one hour before performances), built in 1885, is fronted by two sculptural compositions by Venetian sculptor Benvenutti. Nearby, the town's **market** (open mornings daily) is housed in three striking pavilions, the first two built in 1880 of iron and large panels of glass, heralding a new age of architecture. Unfortunately the original interiors of the older pavilions have been all but destroyed, but the third pavilion, built in 1920 and home to the city's **fish market,** is home to some pleasing stone decorations, mostly centered around sealife, as well as the original open roof and gallery construction.

BEACHES

Though Rijeka's not famous for its beaches, there are a few places to take a dip (and you're likely to find fewer tourists than at Opatija's more popular beaches). The only in-town location is the suburb of **Pećine** (bus #2, 8 minutes, 15.50Kn). The beaches are pretty clean, though they are rocky. Architecture buffs will appreciate the grand Austro-Hungarian-era villas in the area. Traveling even further east, try Kostrena's **Žurkovo cove** (bus #10, 15–20 minutes, 21Kn).

ENTERTAINMENT AND EVENTS
Nightlife

Students looking to start their night at a bar should try slightly shabby **Rozi** (Pavla Ritera Vitezovića 11, tel. 051/338-423, 7 A.M.–10 P.M. Mon.–Sat.) for laid-back snacks and drinks. Students as well as the post-grad crowd will like **Charlie Bar** (Trg Ivana Koblera bb, tel. 095/906-2736, 7 A.M.–1 A.M. Mon.–Wed., 7 A.M.–2 A.M. Thurs.–Sat.), a pub-type place with super outdoor seating in the warmer months.

The pub **Češka pivnica** (Titov trg 6, tel. 098/928-1800, 10 A.M.–midnight Mon.–Sat.) is a well-loved local favorite for the great beers on tap and the hearty Czech-style bar menu.

Karolina (Gat Karoline Riječke bb, tel. 051/330-909, 7 A.M.–1 A.M. Sun.–Wed., 7 A.M.–2 A.M. Thurs., 7 A.M.–4 A.M. Fri.–Sat.) is a beautiful glass-filled space right on the gulf with a super view as well as a nice list of champagnes, wines, and cocktails. Late at night it turns into a dance club with loud DJ tunes.

Hemingway (Korzo 28, tel. 051/211-696, www.hemingway.hr, 7 A.M.–1 A.M. Sun.–Thurs., 7 A.M.–6 A.M. Fri.–Sat.) delivers fashionable design, good music, and drinks and cigars—just what Croatians have come to expect from this local chain of upscale lounge bars. In a pretty Austro-Hungarian building, this spot has been a watering hole for generations, formerly known as the Filodrammatica.

For those who want to stick to one venue all night, three of Rijeka's most popular bars morph into clubs when the clock hits midnight on weekends. Try **Dva Lava** (Ante Starčevića 8, tel. 051/332-390, 8 A.M.–11 P.M. Sun.–Wed., 7 A.M.–4 A.M. Thurs.–Sat.), a dual-story black and white and shiny space serving cocktails and cigars accompanied by DJ-mixed tunes. Positioned at the beginning of the Korzo, **El Rio** (Jadranski trg 4c, tel. 051/214-428, www.el-rio.hr, 9 A.M.–1 A.M. Sun.–Wed., 7 A.M.–5 A.M. Thurs.–Sat.) has been a staple on Rijeka's nightlife scene for quite a while. Pulsing music, DJs, occasional karaoke, and a diverse crowd mix in this large space. **Phanas** (Ivana Zajca 9, tel. 051/312-377, www.phanas .hr, 8 A.M.–1 A.M. Sun.–Wed., 7 A.M.–2 A.M. Thurs., 7 A.M.–4 A.M. Fri.–Sat.) is a bit more laid-back, in a nautically themed pub-type space with some decent rock or dance music.

Concerts and Theaters

Hrvatsko narodno kazalište (Croatian National Theater, tel. 051/337-114, www .hnk-zajc.hr, box office 9:30 A.M.–12:30 P.M. Mon.–Sat. and one hour before performances) hosts opera, classical concerts, and occasional theater performances in Croatian and Italian. Children will enjoy the **Gradsko kazalište lutaka** (B. Polića 6, tel. 051/325-688, www .gkl-rijeka.hr), a small puppet theater with nice plays for the younger set.

If you'd like to catch a movie (remember, most films in Croatia are shown in their original language with subtitles), the historical **Teatro Fenice** (Dolac 13, tel. 051/335-225, www.rijekakino.hr) is right in the center of town. Slightly out of the center, Rijeka's Tower Center shopping mall houses a big multiplex, **Cinestar** (Ul.Janka Polića Kamova 81a in Tower Center, tel. 060/323-233, www .blitz-cinestar.hr), for the latest Hollywood blockbusters.

Carnival

Rijeka's carnival season is by far its most famous event. Starting the Sunday before Lent, the city organizes dozens of performances, presentations, and concerts leading up to the carnival parade, led by lots of people in hideous masks meant to scare away evil spirits. The carnival has a long tradition in the area, though Rijeka's version, begun in 1982, is a fairly recent addition to the world carnival scene. Today it draws more than 10,000 people to town for the colorful celebrations. You can find out more information (though for the moment most of it is in Croatian) at www .ri-karneval.com.hr, or contact the tourist office (Korzo 33a, tel. 051/335-882, tic@ri.t-com .hr, www.tz-rijeka.hr).

ACCOMMODATIONS

Budget accommodation in Rijeka doesn't get much cheaper than the **Omladinski Hostel Rijeka** (Šetalište XIII divizije 23, tel. 051/406-420, www.hfhs.hr, from 126Kn per person, including breakfast), opened in 2006 and located in Pećine (bus #2, 15.50Kn). Housed in a sunny historic villa, the hostel itself lacks character, but it's conveniently located near a bus stop and about a 10-minute walk from the center of town. Private rooms are available and breakfast is included, though they tend to serve it on the early side—around 8 A.M.

Apartments Villa Nora (Podkoludricu 4, tel. 099/215-8511, www.villanora.info, 710Kn d.) are about four kilometers from Rijeka's city center, but have a beautiful position right on Kvarner Gulf in an old villa. The rooms aren't quite as atmospheric as the villa itself, but they are clean, comfortable, and air-conditioned and have satellite television and Internet access. You can take a dip right in front of the hotel, and there's also a nearby gym and fitness complex.

Located in a modern 1920s-era "skyscraper," the 14-story **Hotel Neboder** (Strossmayerova 1, tel. 051/373-538, www.jadran-hoteli.hr, 539Kn d., including breakfast) has recently been renovated top to bottom. Rooms are on the small side but if you ask for a sea-facing room with a balcony, you might not even notice.

The **Jadran Hotel** (Šetalište XIII divizije 46, tel. 051/216-600, www.jadran-hoteli.hr, 773Kn d., including breakfast), fully renovated in 2005, is on the water's edge in Pećine, about two kilometers east from Rijeka's center (bus #2, 15.50Kn). Though it's certainly within walking distance of town, the route is a bit perilous, so plan on taking a bus or a cab. The exterior is rather nondescript, but a sea-view room with a balcony and magnificent vistas across the gulf to Cres more than makes up for the bland architecture.

Considered the swankiest hotel in Rijeka, the **Grand Hotel Bonavia** (Dolac 4, tel. 051/357-100, www.bonavia.hr, 1,134Kn d., including breakfast) is a nondescript glass block from the outside but the rooms inside are well designed. The hotel, just a short walk from the Riva, has a very good breakfast; its nice restaurant, the Bonavia Classic, is located next to lots of shops and cafés.

FOOD

For reliable fast food near the Korzo, **Hamby** (Ante Starčevića 11, E-2, tel. 051/330-653, 24 hours daily, 18Kn) should do the trick day and night. It's not fancy, but has a good selection of hot and cold sandwiches, burgers, soy burgers, and pizza slices.

For a quick, cheap, and hot lunch, try **La Grotta** (Šime Ljubića 8, tel. 091/722-7228, 8 A.M.–5 P.M. daily, 60Kn), decorated like an underground cave and offering decent fish stews, goulashes, and grilled meats and fish.

Though **Konoba Tarsa** (Josipa Kulfaneka 10, tel. 051/452-089, www.konoba-tarsa.net, 11:30 A.M.–midnight daily, 95Kn) is a bit large to officially be called a *konoba,* it's popular with locals for the warm atmosphere and hearty dishes, from seafood platters and black risotto to grilled meats and rib-sticking stews.

Located near Korzo, **Pizzeria Delfino** (Trg Jurja Klovića, tel. 051/336-736, www.delfino .hr, 11 A.M.–11 P.M. Mon.–Sat., 11 A.M.– 10 P.M. Sun., 40Kn), which also has an older, frequented location in nearby Lovran, is legendary in the area. It's a solid choice for pizzas, pastas, and salads.

If the walk up to Trsat has your tummy growling, grab a table at **Trsatika** (Šetalište J Rakovca 33, tel. 051/217-455, 11 A.M.–11 P.M. Thurs.–Tues., 75Kn), preferably one on the terrace that offers a great view. The menu is average—plenty of grilled meats and pizzas—but the location is stunning as well as convenient.

For seafood, one of the most reasonable spots in town is **Na kantunu** (Demetrova 2, tel. 051/313-271, 8 A.M.–10 P.M. Mon.–Sat.,

70Kn), a bit low on atmosphere but high in quality fish dishes and a great wine list. Romantic dinners are best had at local seafood legend **Zlatna Školjka** (Kružna 12a, tel. 051/213-782, 11 A.M.–11 P.M. Mon.–Sat., 125Kn), just off Korzo in the heart of town. It has a reputation for excellent seafood meals served in an eclectic and charming setting.

Trendy types will like **Indigo Bar** (Stara vrata 3, Koblerov trg, tel. 051/315-174, 8 A.M.–4 A.M. Fri.–Sat., 85Kn), with its wild decor, hip vibe, and updated versions of Mediterranean and Croatian dishes. The downside is that it's only open weekends. For Croatian tapas (think bite-sized seafood-stuffed raviolis or fresh squid) there's the **Tapas Bar** (Pavla Rittera Vitezovića 5, tel. 051/315-313, 10 A.M.–11 P.M. Mon.–Sat., 30Kn per portion, 130Kn for three portions and dessert), which also has a good wine selection.

Often hailed as Rijeka's finest restaurant, **Municipium** (Trg Riječke rezolucije 5, tel. 051/213-000, 10 A.M.–11 P.M. Mon.–Sat., 160Kn) offers a wide variety of Croatian dishes, with a heavy emphasis on fish and the occasional flair for the creative—shrimp crepes, anyone?—all served in one of Rijeka's most beautiful historic buildings, though the decor is nothing special.

INFORMATION AND SERVICES

For more information on rooms and apartments, tours, and maps you can contact the local **tourist office** (Korzo 33a, tel. 051/335-882, tic@ ri.t-com.hr, www.tz-rijeka.hr) or get on the Internet at **Inter Club Cont** (Šetalište A. Kačića Miošića 1, tel. 051/371-630, www.interclub-cont .com, 7 A.M.–10 P.M. daily, 3Kn for 15 minutes). If they're closed, there's a handy touch-screen info point outside the Korzo tourist office.

You'll find a post office (Korzo 13, 7 A.M.–9 P.M. Mon.–Fri., 7 A.M.–2 P.M. Sat.) conveniently located on the Korzo.

An all-night pharmacy is conveniently located on the Korzo (Korzo 22, tel. 051/211-036, 24 hours) and a hospital (Krešimirova 42, tel. 051/658-111) near the train station can take care of more serious ailments.

KVARNER GULF

Rijeka's train station (Krešimirova 5, tel. 060/333-4444 or 051/211-638) has a left-luggage office open 24 hours and charging 15Kn per day.

GETTING THERE AND AROUND

Getting to Rijeka is quite easy, with excellent bus, ferry, and train connections from Croatia's major cities letting passengers off a walkable distance from the city center. In the summer some discount airlines offer connections to Rijeka's small airport (tel. 051/842-040, www.rijeka-airport.hr), actually located on Krk. Take the Autorolej bus, meeting most planes, for the slightly less than an hour ride (30Kn). Otherwise you'll be forking over upwards of 300Kn for a ride into town in a cab (tel. 051/332-893).

There are also boat connections from Rijeka to Cres, Mali Lošinj, Rab, and Novalja as well as the Dalmatian ports of Hvar, Korčula, and Dubrovnik. The Riva-located office of Jadrolinija (Riva 16, tel. 051/211-444, www.jadrolinija.hr, 7 A.M.–6 P.M. Mon.–Fri., 8 A.M.–2:30 P.M. Sat., noon–3 P.M. Sun.) can let you know more about times and ticket prices. Ferries from Rijeka are a great option for connecting to Kvarner islands (prices to islands like Cres, Rab, and Mali Lošinj run around 30–40Kn). Ferries to Split (12.5 hours overnight, around 90Kn per person for a 2-bunk berth including breakfast) are quite long, though the price can't be beat for an overnight with breakfast along the coast.

Though the trip by train is much longer than the bus, it is a bit cheaper, making it a good option for those with more time than money. Rijeka's train station (Krešimirova 5, tel. 060/333-4444 or 051/211-638) is about a 10-minute walk west from the city center; it offers connections to major hubs like Zagreb (4 hours, 96Kn) and Pula (2 hours with transfer, 59Kn).

Rijeka's main bus station (Žabica 1, tel. 060/302-010, www.autotrans.hr), where intercity connections arrive and depart, is a 5-to-10-minute walk west of the center on Trg Žabica. Frequent connections are available to towns such as Pula (8 or more buses daily, 2 hours, 84Kn), Zagreb (over a dozen buses daily, 2.5 hours, 144Kn) and Split (four or more buses daily, 7.5 hours, 285Kn).

Around town you can easily walk or take a city bus to Trsat (#1, 5 minutes, 15.50Kn) or the beaches at Pećine (#2, 8 minutes, 15.50Kn) from the Riva. Bus #32 travels to Opatija (30 minutes, 26Kn).

Opatija Riviera

Though the attractive Opatija Riviera (Opatijska rivijera) tends to attract an older crowd, that's not to say there's nothing for the hip and trendy (unless you're looking for a hopping nightlife scene, in which case look elsewhere). The line of coast, hugged mostly by grand old villas built by Vienna's elite in the 19th century, has some excellent boutique hotels and more than its fair share of superb restaurants to keep those chasing the finer things in life entertained for at least a couple of days. The downsides are that some of the most charming parts, like Lovran, are notoriously unwalkable (few sidewalks and busy roads) and almost unparkable.

◖ OPATIJA

An Austro-Hungarian gem on the coast, Opatija is not the place to go if you want to party till dawn, but if you'd like a spot on the coast that isn't packed with a zillion tube-topped youngsters, the genteel charm of the city should win you over.

Sights

The standout of Opatija, the 12-kilometer-long **Šetalište Franza Josefa,** or **Lungomare,** running north toward Lovran, is a wonderful wide seafront promenade, perfect for leisurely strolls. Shaded by trees, you can take in

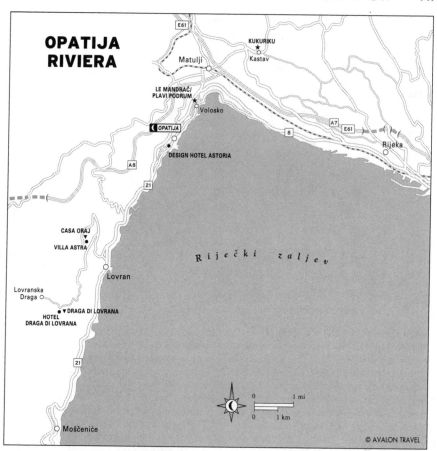

the rocky beaches and the opulent old villas—some painstakingly restored, some decaying in neglect. The most famous of these villas is the **Villa Angiolina,** not only one of the city's finest, but also its first. Built by merchant Higinio von Scarpa in 1844 in honor of his late wife, the grand home and its stunning gardens are periodically open for concerts and performances. Ask at the **tourist office** (Obala m. Tita 101, tel. 051/371-310, www.opatija-tourism .hr, 8 A.M.–9 P.M. Mon.–Sat. and 6–9 P.M. Sun. June–Sept., 8 A.M.–3 P.M. Mon.–Fri. and 8 A.M.–2 P.M. Sat. Oct.–May) for more details.

The pretty **Juraj Šporer Art Pavilion** (tel.

051/272-225, prices and opening times vary with exhibitions) has revolving art exhibitions, mostly contemporary.

If the Lungomare seems too tame, the nearby **Park prirode Učka** (Učka Nature Park, tel. 051/293-753, park.prirode.ucka@inet.hr, www.pp-ucka.hr) has dozens of hiking trails on the mountain that separates Kvarner from Istria. The tourist office can provide detailed maps and guides of the various routes.

Beaches

If you're looking for a swim or just some beachside lounging, you'll need to head slightly south

Opatija, once a playground for the Austro-Hungarian elite

towards Lovran for the best spots. **Ičići** is only about a three-kilometer walk on the Lungomare from the center of Opatija. You could also hop a bus to **Medveja** (bus #32, 25 minutes), which has some nice shingle beaches and an outpost of the locally famous Hemingway franchise to wet your whistle in between swims. If you're a fan of windsurfing, head to Preluk Bay in Volosko, one of the best spots for early-morning windsurfing in the summer and early fall. For information on equipment rental and courses, contact Opatija's tourist office (Obala m. Tita 101, tel. 051/271-310, www.opatija-tourism .hr, 8 A.M.–9 P.M. Mon.–Sat. and 6–9 P.M. Sun. June–Sept., 8 A.M.–3 P.M. Mon.–Fri. and 8 A.M.–2 P.M. Sat. Oct.–May).

Accommodations

For those who don't mind roughing it, there's a great **campsite** (Liburnijska 46, tel. 051/704-836, info@rivijera-opatija.hr, www .rivijera-opatija.hr, 36Kn per person) in Ičići, conveniently located near the beach.

Villa Dubrava (Maršala Tita 188/4, tel. 051/202-680, villa.dubrava@ri.t-com.hr,

www.thalassotherapia-opatija.hr, 355Kn d.) is a pretty great value considering you get to stay in an old Austro-Hungarian villa with a seawater pool, next door to a thalassotherapy center (for those who haven't been brushing up on their spa terminology lately, that basically means sea-based health and beauty treatments) The rooms at **Villa Palme** (Ulica Vrutki br. 8 tel. 051/711-305, www.villa-palme.com, 745Kr d.) won't win any design awards, but the hotel' great pool with a sea view makes up for the lac of punchy interiors.

A villa-hotel with its own rocky beach, th **Hotel Miramar** (Ive Kaline 11, tel. 051/280 000, www.hotel-mirar.info, 710Kn d.) has nic rooms, all air-conditioned and with their ow balcony or terrace. The hotel also has a smal spa facility and a parking garage, a huge boos for travelers with a rental car trying to find space in already-packed Opatija.

The renovated **C Design Hotel Astori** (Obala Maršala Tita 174, tel. 051/706-35(www.hotel-astoria.hr, 922Kn d.) is located i a turn-of-the-20th-century villa decorated wit a sleek modern touch. You'll also find all th conveniences of this century, like powerful air-conditioning and high-speed Internet access.

A second luxury option for those who'd like a bit more history with their hotel, the **Hotel Mozart** (Obala Maršala Tita 138, tel. 051/718-260, www.hotel-mozart.hr, 993Kn d.) is decorated in art nouveau style, fitting the old Austro-Hungarian building it's housed in. The small hotel, only 26 rooms, has a charming deco piano bar and balconies with outstanding water views.

Food

Opatija and the surrounding area are a goldmine for foodies, with dozens of tasty but pricey restaurants servicing tourists and locals alike. You'll find more variety and quality here than in most cities, even tourist meccas like Dubrovnik, particularly in the former fishing village of Volosko, which boasts some of Croatia's finest restaurants.

For coffee and desserts in the center of Opatija, **Café Wagner** (Obala maršala Tita 109, tel. 051/202-071, 7 A.M.–midnight daily) is not exactly hip, but worth a stop. Its interior and service invoke the feel of Viennese-style cafés that were the norm on the Riviera over a century ago. Go for the desserts, the chocolates, the coffee, and a hint of nostalgia.

For moderately priced meals **Gostionica Kaneta** (Nova cesta 64, tel. 051/712-222, 7 A.M.–midnight daily, 80Kn) is a good place for meat and potatoes or pasta dishes in a warm, local atmosphere. In Ičići, **Mali Raj** (Obala Maršala Tita 191, tel. 051/704-074, noon–midnight daily, 90Kn) serves up nice fish dishes alongside a few good steaks. The name of the restaurant means little paradise, which is not too exaggerated a description for the waterside shady terrace. You can walk to or from dinner on the Lungomare, either working up an appetite or working off the calories you consumed.

It's truly worth the detour to the charming village of Kastav, above Rijeka, for lots of atmosphere and an excellent meal at the cozy ◖ **Kukuriku** (Trg Matka Laginje 1A, tel. 051/691-417, www.kukuriku.hr, 1 P.M.–midnight daily, closed Mon. Sept.–Easter, 100Kn). Roosters are everywhere (the restaurant's name means cock-a-doodle-doo), though the menu is heavy on grilled meats and local flavor.

A trip to Opatija wouldn't quite be complete without splashing on some seafood or more gourmet cuisine, something the tiny area is famous for. Volosko, a suburb of Opatija, is brimming with choices. **Amfora** (Črnikovica 4, tel. 051/701-222, www.restaurant-amfora.com, noon–midnight daily, 115Kn) is an old-school staple, with decor that has seen better days. However, the sea view is stunning and the fish is great quality. This is the place to order standards like grilled fish, mussels, and shrimp. Much more chic and the destination for those hoping for creative cuisine, ◖ **Le Mandrać** (Obala Frana Supila 10, tel. 051/701-357, www.lemandrac.com, 11 A.M.–midnight daily, 145Kn) is home to chef Deniz Zembo's mouthwatering creations like octopus carpaccio and black polenta with cuttlefish and shrimp in a lemon and olive oil emulsion. The dishes get even more inventive, though the decor's decidedly local, at ◖ **Plavi Podrum** (Obala Frana Supila 4, tel. 051/701-223, dkramari@inet.hr, noon–midnight daily, 160Kn), winner of multiple "world's best" and fancy French awards. Dishes like St. Jacques shells on a reduction of apples and monkfish with truffles and coffee powder, or desserts such as cake with a hint of port wine and tobacco, will leave even the most cynical gourmets adjusting their belts to make room for just a little more.

Information and Services

Opatija's **tourist office** (Obala m. Tita 101, tel. 051/271-310, www.opatija-tourism.hr, 8 A.M.–9 P.M. Mon.–Sat. and 6–9 P.M. Sun. June–Sept., 8 A.M.–3 P.M. Mon.–Fri. and 8 A.M.–2 P.M. Sat. Oct.–May) can help out with information, brochures, and maps. Rent boats from one of two agencies in the Hotel Admiral (Obala m. Tita 139, tel. 051/271-533).

Getting There and Around

If you're driving to Opatija from Rijeka, just

hop on the main coastal road heading west and don't stop for about 15 kilometers. Otherwise, take bus #32 from Rijeka, about a 30-minute trip that will set you back around 26Kn. Even if you have a car, parking around Opatija is difficult. It's best to leave your car and continue on foot (lots of places are accessible via the Lungomare) or take a taxi (more expensive but possibly worth it to avoid the frustration of locating the hillside restaurants and dealing with tricky parking).

Water taxis (30–50Kn) are a cheaper and more atmospheric option for getting to the beaches and Lovran. They have notoriously unreliable schedules but can be picked up at the harbors of the hotels Millennium (Obala m. Tita 109) and Admiral (Obala m. Tita 139).

LOVRAN

Once a playground of rich Austro-Hungarians with the massive villas to prove it, Lovran is once again attracting Europe's well-heeled. The crowd is slightly younger than Opatija, but no less refined. The tiny harbor is ringed by massive villas, many of which have been turned into boutique hotels and private retreats. There's not too much in the way of actual sights, though you might want to attempt the picturesque climb through Lovran's older section (starting behind the main street, Maršala Tita) to the **Crkva svetog Jurja** (St. George's Church), a 14th-century church with pretty frescoes if you happen to find it open.

Beaches

Beaches in Lovran are fairly nonexistent. The best bets are the beaches at **Medveja** (3 kilometers away, bus #32, 5 minutes) or back at **Ičići**. If you're staying at one of the villas along the waterfront, you'll likely have access to the water via some stairs.

Accommodations

Some of the best hotels in Lovran are owned by one small firm, which has tastefully converted a few of the area's old villas and farmhouses into refined accommodation. Among these properties, the standouts are likely **Villa**

Hotel Draga di Lovrana, located high above Lovran

Astra (Viktora Cara Emina 11, tel. 051/294-589, www.lovranske-vile.com, 1,915Kn d., including breakfast), a 1905 waterfront villa with a pool and a great restaurant. The company's (**Casa Oraj** (Tuliševica 64, tel. 051/294-604, www.lovranske-vile.com, 2,128Kn for house, sleeps eight) is perched on a hilltop high above the sea, about a 10-minute drive from Lovran. The authentic century-old property is filled with antiques and lots of peace and quiet in its sprawling gardens.

Villa Eugenia (Maršala Tita 34, tel. 051/294-800, www.eto.hr, 1,368Kn d.) is another nice choice in Lovran, with attractive fresh rooms, a whirlpool tub, a billiards table, and a decent list of spa treatments and massages. Balconies have a nice view of the sea below. The **Hotel Park** (Maršala Tita 60, tel. 051/706-200, www.hotelparklovran.hr, 1,064Kn d.) is located in a bright blue building with smallish but sleek rooms many of which have balconies. High above Lovran, with an amazing view and even better salt-touched breezes, (**Hotel Draga di Lovrana** (Lovranska Draga 1, tel. 051/294-166, www.dragadilovrana.hr, 851Kn d., including breakfast) offers pretty rooms in a quiet location with an excellent restaurant. Though bus #36 travels between Lovranska Draga and Lovran, it's easier to take a taxi or a car to shuttle you to the beach or to Opatija since the roads are steep and curvy.

If you can't afford the luxury villas, your best bets are private apartments in the area. Two reliable options are the **Pansion Stanger** (M. Tita 128, tel. 051/291-154, www.pansion-stanger.com, 468Kn d., including breakfast) with attractive sea-view rooms and friendly owners, or **Apartments Rukavina** (Medveja 11B, tel. 051/291-159, mira.rukavina@ri.t-com.hr, 490Kn d.), very basic but clean, warm, and cozy and located near some good beaches at Medveja.

Food

Najade (Maršala Tita 69, tel. 051/291-866, 11 A.M.–midnight daily, 95Kn) has been a staple on the Lovran restaurant scene since 1990. Within its homey stone walls, diners chow down on fresh fish and grilled meats.

Though you'll need a car or cab to get there, some of the best food and vistas are north of town. (**Draga di Lovrana** (Lovranska Draga 1, tel. 051/294-166, www.dragadilovrana.hr, noon–midnight daily, 100Kn) has two choices for a good meal: the highly acclaimed restaurant and the more laid-back taverna, both with views of the Kvarner Gulf and the surrounding mountains that alone are worth the trip. The restaurant offers top-notch seafood and international cuisine, while the taverna has simple but filling dishes like minestrone or scrambled eggs with asparagus in season, and a good wine list.

For something heartier, climb towards Učka Nature Park, where **Dopolavoro** (Učka 9, Ičići, tel. 051/299-641, noon–11 P.M. Tues.–Sun., 95Kn) doles out meat dishes enhanced by wild mushrooms and fresh vegetables in season. A great choice if you fancy game like wild boar, deer, and bear.

Information and Services

Lovran has a small **tourist office** (Obala m. Tita 63, tel. 051/291-740, www.tz-lovran.hr, 8 A.M.–2 P.M. and 5–8 P.M. Mon.–Sat. and 8 A.M.–2 P.M. Sun. June–Sept., 8 A.M.–2 P.M. Mon.–Sat. Oct.–May) with maps, brochures, and local information.

Getting There and Around

If you don't have a car, buses are the easiest way to get to and from Lovran. Take bus #32 to Opatija (15 minutes, around 20Kn) and Rijeka (45 minutes, 26Kn). Lovran is west of Opatija along the coastal road.

KVARNER GULF

Kvarner Islands

Far less publicized than the Dalmatian Islands, the Kvarner Islands have their own beauty, turquoise waters, and cultural finds. Many of the islands, such as Rab and Krk, are easier to access from the mainland, though these islands are also the most developed for tourists, which translates into lots of hotels and restaurants but also lots of fellow sun worshippers when it comes time to hit the beaches. Cres and Susak are decidedly more untouched and are great destinations if you're looking for natural attractions and peace and quiet. Partiers will find their groove on Krk and in the 24-hour club hub of Novalja on Pag. Like pretty much all of Croatia, Kvarner has something for every personality and mood. As for the seasons, many of the restaurants and hotels close in the winter, though not quite to the extent of the islands in Dalmatia. If you do visit in winter, you're sure to get a sense of the local culture and people with nary a tourist to compete with for attention.

KRK

Krk is the largest of Croatia's islands and it is extremely popular with tourists, mostly Croatians and Europeans who flood the large package hotels and beaches. The most popular spots are the sandy beaches at Baška, packed to capacity in August, and Krk Town. Quieter spots like Vrbnik and Malinska have some great boutique hotels and little restaurants. Krk has been a tourist destination since the mid-19th century, though the island's history dates back to Roman times, when Caesar purportedly camped at the military outpost located here.

For all the tourists and souvenir shops that go along with them, there are still lots of cultural and gastronomic traditions, particularly Vrbnička Žlahtina, a white wine from Vrbnik, and a local version of the bagpipe, the *mijeh,* fashioned from a goat's stomach. You'll find the most colorful traditions on display during the **Smotra folklore otoka Krka** (Krk Folklore Festival), held in July or August in a different town on the island each year.

Krk Town

The heart of Krk Town is a beautiful little walled city, filled with narrow alleyways, though many are now inhabited by shops selling T-shirts and bric-a-brac. The town walls have protected Krk since pre-Roman times, and the oldest tower at Trg Kamplin was built in the 12th century.

SIGHTS

Don't-miss sights in Krk include the **Trg bana Jelačića** (Ban Jelačić Square), where the 13th-century **guard tower** is enhanced by a recycled Roman gravestone depicting the deceased, who now overlook all the action on the town's main square; a tower at the adjoining Vela placa (at Trg bana Jelačića's western end) sports a 16th-century 24-hour clock.

The Romanesque **Katedrala Uznesenja** (Cathedral of the Assumption, Trg sv. Kvirina, 9:30 A.M.–1 P.M. and 5–7 P.M. daily, free) was built in the early 13th century, though its bell tower was added between the 16th and 18th centuries. Inside the church you'll see more recycling of Roman ruins (this time it's columns) as well as some Renaissance Venetian paintings on the church's altars. Next to the cathedral you'll find the **Crkva svetog Kvirina** (St. Quirinus's Church), which houses a **Izložbena zbirka sakralne umjetnosti** (Collection of Sacral Art, tel. 051/221-341, 9:30 A.M.–1 P.M. daily Apr.–Oct., 15Kn) filled with sacred objects spanning the 14th to 18th centuries. The star of the collection is a paneled golden altarpiece centering on the Virgin.

East of the cathedral hugging the waterfront walls is the **Kaštel** (fortress). The round tower belonged to the Frankopan family, who ruled Krk from the 12th to the late 15th century.

To escape all the touristy action, head north of J.J. Strossmayera, where quiet streets are

BEST OF THE KVARNER ISLANDS

DAY 1

Start your tour in **Vrbnik** on the island of **Krk,** spending the day on the beach and having lunch and a glass of homemade wine at **Nada's.** Spend the afternoon lounging by the pool (and maybe getting a massage) at the **Kado Resort and Spa,** where you'll spend the night.

DAY 2

Connect to **Cres** in the morning. Head to the village of Beli, visiting the **Caput Insulae Eco Centre** and hopefully catching a glimpse of a local griffon on your walk through the fairy-tale forests. Eat dinner and sleep at the simple, cozy **Gostionica Beli.**

DAY 3

This morning continue to **Mali Lošinj** to walk around town and peruse the art at the **Umjetničke zbirke.** Have lunch at the locally famous **Konoba Corrado.** In the afternoon walk the promenade to the even more charming **Veli Lošinj,** where you can admire the grand villas and stop in at a couple of the town's tourist attractions and shops. Have dinner at the sophisticated but unpretentious **Trattoria Bora Bar** before turning in at the **Vila Tamaris,** overlooking the water.

DAY 4

Head out on a **dolphin-viewing boat excursion** or make a day trip to the island of **Susak** for some quiet relaxation, bike riding, and a leisurely seafood lunch, before returning to the mainland via Mali Lošinj.

ENTERTAINMENT AND EVENTS

At night head to a bar for some people-watching or catch a **concert** (check with the tourist office for details) in the summer. After hours, **Jungle** (Stjepana Radića, tel. 051/221-503, 9 P.M.–5 A.M. daily May–Sept.) and **Casa di Padrone** (Šetalište sv Bernardina, tel. 091/229-4602, 8 A.M.–midnight daily late Apr.–Sept.) keeps the music spinning and the crowd dancing.

ACCOMMODATIONS AND FOOD

If you'd like to stay in Krk Town, there are several options. At the bottom of the budget ladder is the **Hostel Krk** (Dr. Dinka Vitezica 32, tel. 051/220-212, info@hostel-krk.hr, www .hostel-krk.hr, 120Kn per person), a member of Hostelling International conveniently located in the old town. The hostel offers dorm rooms and private doubles as well as parking.

Hotel Bor (Šetalište Dražica 5, tel. 051/220-200, www.hotelbor.hr, 553Kn d., including breakfast) is only an eight-minute walk east from the center of town and a minute away from a rocky beach. The rooms are basic but clean and have televisions.

The most luxe choice in Krk Town is the recently renovated **Hotel Marina** (Obala Hrvatske mornarice bb, tel. 051/221-128, www .hotelikrk.hr, 1,135Kn d., including breakfast). The circa 1925 hotel underwent an overhaul in 2008 that created a sleek space right on the seafront. In addition to air-conditioning, satellite TV, and Internet access, every room has a sea view.

For food, don't expect to be blown away in this heavily touristed area. If you don't have the time or energy to explore around the island, try **Konoba Nono** (Krčkih iseljenika 8, tel. 051/222-221, nono@nono-krk.com, 11 A.M.–midnight daily, closed Nov.–late Mar., 90Kn). Krk specialties rule the menu, like *šurlice,* a type of pasta, and lamb and seafood dishes. **Frankopan** (Trg Svetog Kvirna 1, tel. 051/221-437, 10 A.M.–11 P.M. daily, closed Nov.–Dec., 100Kn) serves seafood, grilled meats, and even pizzas to a mostly tourist crowd. In good weather, the outdoor dining in the shadow of the cathedral is lovely, but tons of guests

punctuated by the occasional cat or elderly woman standing in her doorway. Follow Dr. Dinka Vitezića to the 11th-century **Crkva majke božje od zdravlja** (Church of Our Lady of Health, open sporadically, free), which made use of old Roman relics in its construction.

translates to slow service in season. **Corsaro** (Obala Hrvatske mornarice 2, tel. 051/220-084, 11 A.M.–2 A.M. daily, no credit cards, 100Kn) serves decent seafood and local specialties on the harbor with a fairly roomy terrace offering nice views.

INFORMATION AND SERVICES
The **Krk Island tourist office** (Trg sv Kvirina 1, tel. 051/220-226, 9 A.M.–9 P.M. daily in summer, call for winter hours) and the **Krk Town tourist office** (Vela Placa 1, tel. 051/221-414, 9 A.M.–9 P.M. daily in summer, 8 A.M.–3 P.M. Mon.–Fri. rest of the year) offer plenty of helpful information.

You can hop on the Internet at **Krk Sistemi** (Šetalište sv Bernadina 3, tel. 051/222-999, www.krksistemi.hr, 15Kn for 30 minutes).

GETTING THERE AND AROUND
The airport on the tip of Krk also serves Rijeka. Unfortunately, public transportation is not a convenient option from the airport (you'd have to go to Rijeka and then get a bus to Krk Town). Even for those watching their pennies, a taxi is well worth the splurge, around 250Kn.

Getting to Krk by bus is quite easy with good connections from Rijeka (around 10 a day, 1.5 hours, 51Kn) and Zagreb (at least two a day, 5 hours, 181Kn). The bus is also the way to get from town to town on the island, with good connections to Baška and Malinska. The bus station (Obala Hrvatske Mornarice, tel. 051/679-051) in Krk Town is less than a five-minute walk west of the town center.

Northern Krk
If you're looking for something a little more sophisticated, head to northern Krk, where wine and food go hand in hand with a couple of good choices for accommodation. First up is **Vrbnik**, known for its local white wine. You can get a taste at **Nada's** (Glavica 22, tel. 051/857-065, www.nada-vrbnik.hr, noon–11 P.M. daily in summer, noon–11 P.M. Fri.–Sun. spring and fall, closed Nov.–end of Feb., 95Kn), a famous restaurant with local Croatians and tourists alike. The

decor is far from fancy, but it has soul. Home-cured hams hang from the ceiling and diners cram the outdoor benches to savor the great seafood. Don't miss the restaurant's sea bass in salt or lamb stew if it's available, washed down with a prerequisite glass of the restaurant's Vrbnička Žlahtina, made from the owner's grapes.

The most popular beaches in Vrbnik are **Zgribnica,** protected from winds by the cliffs that surround it, and **Potovosce,** a pebble beach with a small bar and restrooms. **Risika** is about six kilometers away but has a nice sandy beach on Sv. Marko Bay. If you're looking for something more private, just pick a little rocky cove and claim it as your own.

Slightly northwest in Dobrinj, **Villa Rustica** (Sv. Ivan Dobrinjski 42, tel. 051/868-110, www.villa-rustica.com, 10,638Kn a week, sleeps four) has sprawling gardens, a pool, and lots of country charm just a short walk away from a good beach.

In Malinska, on the western coast, the ◖ **Kado Resort and Spa** (Brzac 85, tel. 051/862-082, www.apartmani-krk.net, 1,631Kn sleeps up to four, including breakfast) has several beautiful apartments as well as a hot tub, two pools (one for children), a sauna, and a nice little list of massages and spa treatments.

There are two restaurants nearby, both serving hearty portions of fish stew and pasta dishes. The seaside **Portić** (Portić 10, noon–midnight daily Apr–Sept., no credit cards, 75Kn) is very popular, as is the rustic **Konoba Bracera** (Kvarnerska 1, tel. 051/858-700, www.bracera.hr, 10 A.M.–11 P.M. daily, closed Jan., 50Kn).

Malinska has some nice beaches to the west of the town's marina. If you want even more privacy, walk or drive west to Porat, where lots of rocky coves provide calm and quiet.

Punat
Punat is a mostly touristy town, with a small gem of an islet only 800 meters out in the water and a good restaurant. The only must-do in town is to take a water taxi to **Košljun** where a 15th-century **Franjevački samostan** (Franciscan monastery, tel. 051/854-017

9:30 A.M.–6 P.M. Mon.–Sat. May–Sept., call about winter hours and special events such as concerts, 15Kn) takes center stage. There are some pretty works of art in the monastery's church (fans of naive art should look out for Ivan Lacković's drawings) and there's a quirky little museum (with exhibits like a pickled two-headed lamb), but the real draws are the quiet sprawling gardens of the monastery, perfect for a leisurely stroll. The whole excursion takes about two hours and the water taxi will set you back about 12Kn in each direction.

In Punat, there's an acceptable **hostel** (Novi Put 8, tel. 051/854-037, www.hfhs.hr, open June–end of Sept., from 85Kn) in the center of town. The **Hotel Kanajt** (Kanajt 5, tel. 051/654-340, www.kanajt.hr, 151Kn d., including breakfast) has rooms with unexciting standard hotel furniture, but the location directly in front of a marina is what makes it special. Lots of seafaring types get their bearings at the Hotel Kanajt.

Even better is the hotel's super restaurant, ◖ **Kanajt** (Kanajt 5, tel. 051/654-340, www .kanajt.hr, 7 A.M.–1 P.M. and 5–11 P.M. daily, 90Kn), which serves a variety of seafood and meats, the best of which are prepared *ispod peka* (oven baked), including octopus, lamb, and veal.

Punat has some good spots for beginning windsurfers depending on which way the wind is blowing. Nudists will appreciate the beach at Konobe naturist camp, also known as **Acapulca,** a huge beach with tennis and volleyball, clothing optional.

You can get more information about activities and beaches in town from the Punat **tourist office** (Obala 72, tel. 051/854-860, www.tzpunat.hr, 8 A.M.–3 P.M. Mon.–Fri., often longer hours in summer). You can also find out the schedule and destinations of the small tourist train that ferries travelers to some of the busier beaches. The town also has a convenient medical clinic for tourists (Pod Topol 2, 2:30–9 P.M. Mon., Wed., Fri., 7 A.M.–1 P.M. Thurs., 9 A.M.–noon and 6–8:30 P.M. Sat.–Sun.) near the bus station from May through September.

The bus station (tel. 051/222-111), a 10-minute walk to the southeast of the center, connects with both Krk Town (15 minutes) and Baška (30–40 minutes).

Stara Baška

Stara Baška, 12 kilometers south of Punat, is a small fishing village hugging a rocky cliff, parts of which are beautiful and parts of which have been taken over by garish villas. Its most striking feature is the beaches. If you're coming by car, you'll need to park above the beach and walk down a very steep path to reach the pretty coves. It's not to be attempted by the out-of-shape or unsteady, but if you do go pack a picnic basket—you won't want to climb back up for a drink. There's a nice restaurant in town, **Nadia** (Stara Baška 253, tel. 051/844-663, novice .mladenovic@ri.t-com.hr, call for hours, 100Kn), serving lots of fresh fish specialties. Buses are infrequent to Stara Baška, so it's best reached by car.

Baška

At the height of the season, in July and August, you might think the only sights in Baška are the thousands of bodies fighting for attention and space along the beach. But just a 2.5-kilometer walk northwest along the road to Krk Town, the village of **Jurandvor** holds an important spot in Croatian culture as the site where the **Baščanska ploča** (Baška tablet) was discovered. Dating from the 11th century, this oldest known text of Glagolitic script was found at the village's 9th-century **Crkva svete Lucije** (St. Lucy's Church, approx. 10 A.M.–3 P.M. and 5–9 P.M. in summer, check with tourist office in Baška about current hours as they are prone to change, 10Kn). A replica of the tablet is on display (the real tablet is in Zagreb).

The most famous sight in Baška, though, is its **Vela Plaža,** or Great Beach, a mix of tiny pebbles and sand that stretches for about 1,800 meters. In the hottest summer months, its four thousand spaces can be almost filled to capacity. What makes Vela Plaža so nice? Situated right in the center of town, it's easy to get to;

BAŠĆANSKA PLOČA (BAŠKA TABLET)

Anyone who has dealt with real estate in Croatia will probably see the humor in the Bašćanska Ploča, the oldest proof of Croatian literacy and essentially an early land title for a church. It was found in the church it served to protect, Sv. Lucija in Jurandvor near Baška. The abbot writes that the land was given by King Zvonimir to the church and that anyone who refuted it should be "cursed by the twelve apostles and four evangelists and St. Lucy" – perhaps not a bad clause to add to modern-day contracts.

Humor aside, the tablet dates from about 1100 and is one of the most important archaeological finds for Croatian history. The tablet, which weighs nearly 800 kilograms, was written in Croatian Glagolitic script. This alphabet, approved by the Catholic Church (who normally opposed languages other than Latin), was used for translating the gospels into Slavic languages. Priests along the Adriatic were quick to adopt it.

The Glagolitic script persisted until the 18th century, when Austrian and Venetian ruling forces heavily discouraged it. They finally banned its use in official documents in 1818 and it had died out by the late 19th century.

Today the famous Bašćanska Ploča rests in the Academy of Arts and Sciences in Zagreb. Much smaller, but generally quite heavy, knock-offs can be found as souvenirs in shops across Croatia.

---

rimmed with bars, restaurants, and cafés; and relatively shallow, making it great for kids.

Renovated in 2003, the **Hotel Zvonimir** (Emilia Geistlicha 34, tel. 051/656-810, www.hotelibaska.hr, 1,135Kn d., including breakfast) has clean, comfortable rooms and a seaside location. The **Atrium Residence Baška** (tel. 051/656-890, www.hotelibaska.hr, 1,127Kn d., including breakfast) is right on the beach. With fresh and sleek interior design and all the modern conveniences like high-speed Internet access, it became the new crown jewel of local hotels when it opened in 2008.

Baška is well connected by bus from Krk Town (at least four buses daily, 45 minutes, 27Kn). The **tourist office** (Kralja Zvonimira 114, tel. 051/856-817, www.tz-baska.hr, 8 A.M.–3 P.M. Mon.–Fri.) can help with brochures and maps, including a good hiking map of the area.

Sports and Recreation

Squatina Diving (Zarok 88A, Baška, tel. 051/856-034, www.squatinadiving.com, Apr.–Oct.) offers introductory diving courses and trips for certified divers.

Pretty much anywhere you see a larger marina, there are likely boats for rent or water taxis for hire. It's a great way to get off the beaten path and discover your own little private paradise.

You can find hiking maps and more information on outdoor activities at Krk's tourist offices. The **Baška tourist office** (Kralja Zvonimira 114, tel. 051/856-817, www.tz-baska.hr) has an extensive supply of maps and brochures. The **Krk Town tourist office** (Vela Placa 1, tel. 051/221-414, www.tz-krk.hr, 9 A.M.–9 P.M. daily in summer, 8 A.M.–3 P.M. Mon.–Fri. rest of year) can also provide you with lots of ideas for active day trips and brochures of hiking paths in the area.

Getting There and Around

EasyJet (www.easyjet.com) usually offers at least weekly direct flights to Krk from the UK during the summer. If you do fly into Krk's airport (tel. 051/842-132, www.rijeka-airport.hr), called Rijeka Airport since it also serves that town, you'll need to take a taxi (which should run around 250–300Kn to Krk Town) since the bus will route you to Rijeka before depositing you back on Krk. Check with airport information about taxis.

There are many daily buses connecting Rijeka with the island, usually stopping in

Baška, home to Krk's most popular beaches

Krk Town and Malinska before a final stop at Baška. There are around 10 connections a day from Rijeka (1.5 hours, 51Kn) and at least two a day from Zagreb (5 hours, 181Kn).

Krk is well connected with ferries, particularly in the summer, when you can hop a boat to Cres (from Valbiska, 30 minutes), Rab (from Baška, 1 hour), or Crikvenica (from Šilo, 20 minutes, only in summer) on the shore.

CRES

Cres is one of Croatia's largest islands and surprisingly one of its most unspoiled. The 80-kilometer-long island has a shady northern section known as Tramuntana, where you'll find the Caput Insulae Eco Centre, a nature preserve and environmental organization working to protect the griffon vultures that are native to the island. It's in the north that you'll also find the lovely fishing village of Cres Town. In the south there's Osor, the oldest city on the island, with a history full of Roman artifacts. Looking on the map you'll notice a large lake, Lake Vrana. Since Cres and neighboring Lošinj are dependent on the freshwater

lake for water, the lake is strictly off-limits to the public. But there's still plenty of beauty and culture to explore, including summer musical performances in Osor and in the almost abandoned village of Lubenice.

Cres Town

Nestled next to a small medieval harbor, the quaint fishing village of Cres Town has a maze of picturesque streets perfect for getting lost in for a couple of hours.

SIGHTS

Start your tour at the main square, **Trg F. Petrića.** The waterfront square is bordered by a simple town loggia, dating from the 16th century. Cres Town has several pretty churches, though the late-Gothic **Crkva Sveta Marija Snježne** (Church of St. Mary of the Snow, Pod Urom, 9 A.M.–6:30 P.M. daily, free) is certainly one to keep on your don't-miss list. The 15th-century simple stone building (the bell tower was added in the 18th century) is decorated with a few striking reliefs. Though the painting on the main altar dates from the 19th century,

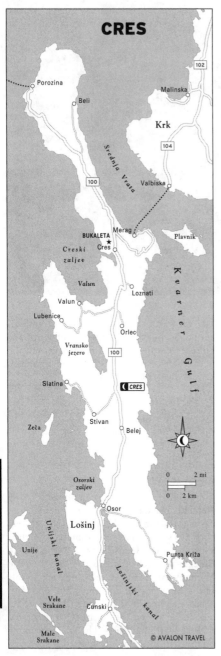

there are a couple of 15th-century works lik
the painting *St. Sebastian with the Saints* b
Alviseo Vivarini and a wooden mournin
scene. Nearby, the **Crkva Sv. Izidora** (Churc
of St. Isidor, check with tourist office for hour
free) is worth a quick stop as well. Built in th
12th century, it is said to be Cres Town's origi
nal parish church. Inside the church you'll fin
several 15th-century wooden sculptures.

Outside the remains of the souther
town walls you'll find an early 14th-centur
Franjevački samostan (Franciscan mon
astery, open for mass on Sun.) with a prett
cloister, housing a small graveyard holdin
the city's most important families and a we
adorned with the oldest known coat of arm
of the town. The monastery also has a sma
museum (tel. 051/571-217, by appt. only, dc
nation necessary) with a few old portraits an
paintings, some dating to the 15th century.

On the northwestern side of town you'
find a circular 16th-century Venetian **defens
tower,** the last one remaining from the town
old defense system.

ACCOMMODATIONS

There aren't a lot of options for hotel ac
commodation on Cres. The **tourist offic**
(Cons 10, tel. 051/571-535, www.tzg-cres.h
8 A.M.–8 P.M. Mon.–Sat. and 9 A.M.–1 P.M
Sun. in summer, 8 A.M.–3 P.M. Mon.–Fri. i
winter) should be able to help arrange pr
vate rooms and apartments. **Camp Kovačin**
(Melin 1/20, tel. 051/573-150, www.camp
kovacine.com) offers campsites, mobile hom
(454Kn d.), and air-conditioned rooms (596K
d., including breakfast) in a nice beachfro
location only a short walk north from Cr
Town. Cres Town has only one hotel, the tw
star concrete **Hotel Kimen** (Melin I 16, te
051/571-322, www.hotel-kimen.com, ope
Easter–Oct., 596Kn d., including breakfa
in the main house). The rooms in the hote
glavna zgrada (main building) have been up
dated, though rooms in its *depandansa* (pe
sion) are still due for a renovation. The new
rooms are quite nice, with sleek bathroom
air-conditioning, and satellite television.

the charming fishing village of Cres Town

FOOD

Cres may be lacking in accommodation options, but eating is an entirely different story—there are dozens of good restaurants and *konobas.* Try **Konoba Bonaca** (Creskog statua 13, tel. 051/572-215, 7 A.M.–2 A.M. daily in summer, 7 A.M.–11 P.M. daily in winter, 75Kn), conveniently tied to the town's fish market, assuring a superb selection. The most famous staple on the Cres restaurant scene is the unassuming **Belona** (Šetalište 23. travnja 24, tel. 051/571-203, 9 A.M.–midnight daily in summer, 9 A.M.–10 P.M. daily in winter, 85Kn). Housed in a small tavern just outside the town walls, Belona's has been serving seafood since before World War II, when the *osteria* took its name from a beautiful and witty barmaid who worked there. Today the barmaid is gone, but the excellent food, like seafood risotto and oven-baked sea bass in summer and sauerkraut with garlic sausages in autumn, keeps diners coming back. **Bukaleta** (Loznati bb, tel. 051/571-606, www.mali-losinj.com/bukaleta, noon–midnight daily Apr.–Oct., 90Kn) is about a 10-minute drive southeast to the tiny

hilltop village of Loznati. The restaurant is famous for its lamb, prepared in all sorts of ways: baked, roasted, stewed, etc. Lambs on the islands are known to be tastier, marinated from birth by the herbs they graze on, and Bukaleta is something of an expert at preparing them. The family's homemade olive oil is a special treat as well.

INFORMATION AND SERVICES

Cres Town's **tourist office** (Cons 10, tel. 051/571-535, www.tzg-cres.hr, 8 A.M.–8 P.M. Mon.–Sat. and 9 A.M.–1 P.M. Sun. in summer, 8 A.M.–3 P.M. Mon.–Fri. in winter) has lots of helpful information as well as brochures and maps.

GETTING THERE AND AROUND

If you're coming straight from the mainland, at least two buses (more in summer) link Cres Town with Rijeka (2 hours, 102Kn). Taking the ferry from Krk you'll land in Merag, connected by at least two buses a day with Cres Town (20 minutes, 23Kn). You can also hop a bus to the island of Mali Lošinj (2 a day, more in summer, 1.25 hours, 47Kn) or to Osor on Cres (up to 7 a day in summer, 2 during winter and weekends, 45 minutes, 33Kn).

Beli

The small town of Beli is one of the oldest villages on Cres. Located 15 kilometers north of Cres Town, Beli has two Romanesque churches, one with several interesting Glagolitic inscriptions and the other, St. Marija, with a small museum. However, the most-frequented tourist attraction is the **Caput Insulae Eco Centre** (Beli 4, tel. 051/840-525, www.caput-insulae .com or www.supovi.hr, 9 a.m.–7 p.m. daily, 20Kn), a park created for the protection of the local griffon vultures. The center has a small display on the griffons and a sanctuary for sick birds. The best part of the park is the seven eco-paths, hiking trails that wind through forests full of twisty knobby trees, abandoned villages, and a series of meditation labyrinths created by the center. There's a pretty good chance of spotting a griffon or two on your walk, too. The center also offers several one-day and multiday educational programs for children and adults. Environmentalists might consider volunteering and staying at the center (tel. 091/335-7124, €155 for one week with food in the high season).

The three-star **Pansion Tramontana** (tel. 051/840-519, www.diving-beli.com, 340Kn d., including breakfast) has long been a source of clean, comfortable rooms in Beli. The owners also own a diving company and can arrange for super diving excursions and nature walks around the area. The hotel has a good restaurant where you can fill up on local specialties whether you're staying there or not. **Gostionica Beli** (tel. 051/840-515, hrzic05@ yahoo.com, www.cres-beli.tk, 213Kn d.) has super meals of local lamb and fresh seafood. The restaurant recently opened a small guesthouse with antique-furnished apartments and cozy rooms for rent.

There is at least one daily bus to Beli from Cres Town on weekdays (30 minutes, 20Kn), leaving in the morning and returning in the early evening.

Osor

Though the port village of Osor seems pretty quaint these days, it has a much grander past. The oldest town on the island, Osor was known as Apsoros in Roman times and was an important port in the Adriatic. Only a few meters from the island of Lošinj, Osor rises above the narrow channel likely dug by the Illyrian Liburni tribe before the Romans arrived. Today a small bridge connects the two islands. There is a small **Arheološki muzej** (Archaeological Museum, 10 a.m.–noon and 7–9 p.m. daily, 10Kn) in the town hall with some interesting Roman finds and a scale model of the town as it was in medieval times. If it's open, the **Biskupska palača** (Bishop's Palace) houses a lapidarium of finds from local churches.

Osor has a really pretty campsite, **Bijar** (Osor 76, tel. 051/237-027, www.jazon.hr, 110Kn daily per person), right by the water. **Apartments Mikulec** (Osor 37, tel. 091/564-0111, www.apartmanimikulec.com, 240Kn d. per night) are a short walk to the beach and offer clean and comfortable rooms and small apartments with private baths. There are several restaurants in town. Try **Konoba Bonifačić** (Osor 64, tel. 051/237-413, 10 a.m.–11 p.m. daily, 85Kn) for good seafood and a peaceful atmosphere.

Osor also holds **musical evenings** during July and August, with many performances of local Croatian musicians and composers held in the Crkva Uznesenja (Church of the Assumption of the Virgin Mary). The tourist office in Mali Lošinj (Riva Lošinjskih Kapetana 29, tel. 051/231-547, www.tz-malilosinj.hr, 8 a.m.–8 p.m. Mon.–Sat. and 9 a.m.–1 p.m. Sun. June–Sept., 8 a.m.–1 p.m. Mon.–Fri. Oct.–May) should have more details.

Buses conveniently connect Osor with Mali Lošinj (at least two daily, 30 minutes, 27Kn) and Cres Town (up to 7 a day in summer, 2 during winter and weekends, 45 minutes, 33Kn).

Around Cres

The beautiful village of **Lubenice,** a stone town 378 meters above the water, holds **Lubeničke**

glazbene večeri, classical music concerts on the main square, on Fridays in July and August. Tickets cost around 50Kn with transportation from Cres Town; you can buy tickets in Cres Town at **Autotrans** (tel. 051/572-050, www .autotrans.hr). Another great secret of Lubenice is its beach, located at the foot of the town, called **Sveti Ivan** (St. John). It's a 45-minute walk down (quite steep, so be careful and make sure you're wearing shoes with treads) and about an hour's climb back up, but if you like beautiful beaches, with clear water ideal for snorkeling (you can see the fish from above the water as well), it's worth the hike. If the day has made you hungry, fill up on local wine and cheese at **Lubenička loza** (Lubenice bb, tel. 051/840-427, 9 A.M.–10 P.M. daily, closed Oct.–end of Apr., 80Kn). You can also stay overnight in Lubenice, thanks to the **Ekopark Pernat Project** (tel. 091/383-5058, kristijan .kowalsky@gmail.com, www.ekoparkpernat .org, 240Kn for a cottage for two), which is restoring the local church and its garden and often organizes classes and workshops for visitors. There are only a few buses a week to Lubenice so you'll need a car to get the most out of your visit.

Valun, 13 kilometers southwest of Cres Town, is another destination for beach lovers, with two nice pebble beaches, the best of which is **Mali Valun** beach, surrounded by mountains and normally quite secluded. If you happen to come on a busy day, rent a kayak at the harbor and find your own spot of paradise. Valun is also served only sporadically by buses, so it's best to have a car to enjoy it fully.

Getting There and Around

Hourly ferries connect Cres with the villages of Brestova (Istria, 30 minutes) and Valbiska (Krk, 30 minutes). There's also a summer-only daily catamaran from Rijeka (1 hour and 20 minutes). The bus station (Zazid 4, tel. 051/571-810) links Cres Town with Mali Lošinj (2 a day, more in summer, 1.25 hours, 47Kn) and Rijeka (2 hours, 102Kn). You'll also find at least a couple of buses linking Cres Town with Osor (up to 7 a day in summer,

2 during winter and weekends, 45 minutes, 33Kn), though connections can be scarce in the off-season months.

LOŠINJ

Just across the small bridge from quiet Cres, the island of Lošinj is far more developed and busy. In fact, Mali Lošinj is the largest town on the Croatian islands, though it didn't grow that large on tourism alone—the shipbuilding industry was responsible for its development in the 18th and 19th centuries.

At one time Veli Lošinj (which means big Lošinj) was bigger than Mali (which means small). Today the situation is reversed, with Mali Lošinj catering to the bulk of the tourist trade. There's lots to see and do on the island, though not so much that you can't relax. After viewing the dolphin colony that lives offshore and visiting a couple of small museums, it's easy to fill up your time strolling the waterfront promenade and gawking at the pastel-colored houses of wealthy captains and merchants of long ago, preening over the water.

Lošinj is connected with Italy via ferries, which makes it possible to continue on a European journey from the island. It also means that thousands of Italians flood the hotels in Lošinj each summer to experience the island's charms. If you happen to be around in September, when the place is significantly quieter, don't miss the island's **Fishermen's festival.**

Mali Lošinj

Though there's not much to see in Mali Lošinj in terms of actual tourist attractions, the town itself is quite pretty, with steep winding streets and a busy Riva (harborfront walkway) filled to the brim in summer with bronzed limbs stretching out at the café tables. The **Umjetničke zbirke** (Art Collections, Vladimira Gortana 35, tel. 051/231-173, 10 A.M.–1 P.M. and 7–10 P.M. daily in summer, 10 A.M.–noon and 7–9 P.M. daily in winter, 20Kn) displays a nice selection of paintings, mostly 17th- and 18th-century Italian pieces and a decent showing of modern Croatian art as well.

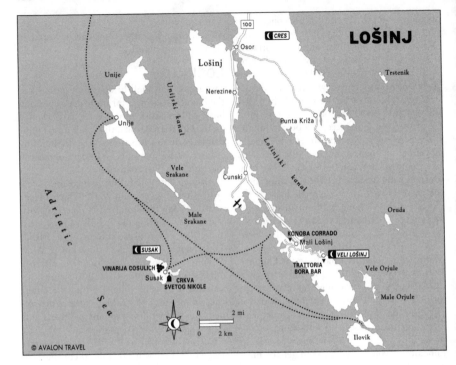

If you're searching for a beach, the **Sunčana uvala** beach in front of the Hotel Aurora is one of the best in Mali Lošinj. With relatively small pebbles and a forested space with a playground, sports facilities, and restaurants, the wind-protected cove is a good all-around choice for beaches. Just north of town, **Čikat Bay** is another nice choice, with a beachfront promenade separating the pebbly shores and a handful of Austro-Hungarian villas. The area has cafés and a few places where you can rent snorkeling gear. The nicest walk on the island is the four-kilometer-long **promenade** south of town connecting Mali and Veli Lošinj, winding its way through forests and coves with plenty of pretty views in between.

ACCOMMODATIONS

Suites Mare Mare (Riva Losinjskih Kapetana 36, tel. 051/232-010, www.mare-mare.com, 998Kn d., including breakfast) are right on the harbor in a charming red building with gleaming white shutters. The rooms are comfortable with a hint of luxe, and the sea-view terrace with a whirlpool tub and massages on offer possibly knocks the hotel up a star.

The **Hotel Aurora** (Sunčana uvala bb, tel. 051/231-324, www.losinj-hotels.com, 1,200Kn d., including breakfast and lunch) has gotten a new coat of paint and a thorough redo of its rooms and exterior areas. Though the architecture is still early concrete block, the service is less than stellar, and the parking situation could be better, it's hard to beat the location—right on one of the best beaches on the island. The hotel also has loads of facilities, from tennis and volleyball courts to a pool and bowling alley.

Renovated in 2004, the **Hotel Apoksiomen** (Riva Lošinjskih kapetana I, tel. 051/520-820, www.apoksiomen.com, 1,170Kn d., including breakfast) is one of Mali Lošinj's better hotels, a

© INA VAN HATEREN/DREAMSTIME.COM

Mali Lošinj, the largest town on the Croatian islands

small boutique establishment right on the town's harbor promenade. The hotel has a nice little terrace restaurant with great views and the rooms all display art by Croatian painters. The **Villa Hygeia** (Čikat 14, tel. 051/232-022, www.hygeia .com.hr, 1,348Kn d.), opened in 2007, is located in a turn-of-the-20th-century villa overlooking the sea. Each apartment has a living room and kitchen area as well as a private terrace.

Budget travelers should check out **Camping Poljana** (Poljana bb, tel. 051/231 726, www .poljana.hr, 248Kn d. for a bungalow), which not only has campsites, but air-conditioned bungalows and small mobile homes as well. The beachfront location isn't bad either.

FOOD

For food, the small island has a surprising number of good options. On the budget end, **Draga** (Braće Vidulić 77, tel. 051/231-132, 11 A.M.–late in summer, 30Kn) is a good option for pizzas and other quick dishes. **Konoba Cigale** (Čikat bb, tel. 051/238-583, www.diver .hr, 9 A.M.–midnight daily June–end of Oct.,

95Kn) and **Konoba Privlaka** (Privlaka 15, tel. 051/231706, 85Kn) are both good choices for grilled meat and fish dishes. The crown jewel of the island's restaurant scene is ◖ **Konoba Corrado** (Svete Marije 1, tel. 051/232-487, 11 A.M.–11 P.M. daily, 110Kn), somewhat legendary for its superb seafood and pretty garden location in the heart of the old town.

INFORMATION AND SERVICES

Mali Lošinj has a **tourist office** (Riva Lošinjskih Kapetana 29, tel. 051/231-547, www.tz-malilosinj.hr, 8 A.M.–8 P.M. Mon.–Sat. and 9 A.M.–1 P.M. Sun. June–Sept., 8 A.M.–1 P.M. Mon.–Fri. Oct.–May) with lots of information. Their website has downloadable brochures on private accommodation, restaurants, and events.

◖ Veli Lošinj

Veli Lošinj is the smaller but grander of the two towns on the island, with dozens of towering villas with pretty walled gardens. Peek through the *portuni* (garden gates) and get a glimpse of what life was like for the upper class of the island (mostly shipowners and captains) many years ago. Other highlights of the island are the large **Crkva svetog Antuna** (St. Anthony's Church, Trg Sveti Antun, open for Sun. mass, free), with its 15th-century painting, *Madonna with Saints,* by early Renaissance painter Bartolomeo Vivarini, and in a 15th-century Venetian tower a small **museum** (tel. 051/231-173, 10 A.M.–noon and 7–9 P.M. daily spring–mid-Sept., 10Kn) displaying paintings and artifacts of the island as well as a Roman statue discovered off the coast in 1999.

Veli Lošinj is home to the **Blue World Institute of Marine Research and Conservation** (Kaštel 24, tel. 051/604-666, www.blue-world.org, call for hours or to arrange a visit, free), housing an interesting display of Adriatic marine life with a special focus on the institute's Adriatic Dolphin Project, studying the indigenous bottlenose dolphins. In addition to providing touch-screen info points, a documentary film with English subtitles, and a children's section, the center informs visitors how they can help protect the dolphins. For example, learn the safe distance to maintain between the dolphins and your boat and how you can become an eco-volunteer.

If you'd like to **see the dolphins,** two local operators (Fran, tel. 098/627-012, and Happy Boat, tel. 091/792-1035) host dolphin-viewing trips. The best time to go is in autumn or spring when the weather is good and the tourist boats are light. If you're hoping to spot them below the surface, contact the **Lošinj Diving Center** (tel. 051/232-155, www.losinj-diving.com) for info on trips, renting gear, and crash courses.

ACCOMMODATIONS

For private accommodation and apartments on the island, the **Palma Travel Agency** (V. Nazora 2, tel. 051/236-179, www.losinj.com) can arrange for an overnight in a number of residences including stone houses and decaying grand villas. The **Grbica Residence** (tel. 051/236-186, www.grbica.hr, 567Kn d., including breakfast) has 24 rooms, a nice pool, and a restaurant. Rooms could use an update, but the hotel is clean and the staff is friendly. The **Pansion Veli Lošinj** (Slavojna bb, tel. 051/236-166, pansion_veli_losinj@hi.t-com .hr, 425Kn d., including breakfast) is a bit simpler affair without the air-conditioning, but the friendly service and the price are excellent. The **Vila Tamaris** (tel. 051/867-900, vila.tamaris@ email.t-com.hr, 710Kn d., including breakfast) is a nice little boutique hotel with small but pretty rooms and a great location right on the waterfront in an old building.

FOOD

The promenade that stretches from Mali Lošinj continues beyond Veli Lošinj to the quaint fishing village of Rovenska, where you'll find the island's only natural sandy beach and a gem of a restaurant, the ◖ **Trattoria Bora Bar** (Rovenska 3, tel. 051/867-544, www.borabar .com, 9 A.M.–2 A.M. daily Apr.–Nov., 100Kn), which serves up creative dishes like tuna carpaccio with celery root and truffles alongside local sausages. The Italian-born chef Marco Sasso owned a restaurant in the United States

before falling in love with Croatia's islands and opening the trendy restaurant, which has Wi-Fi and houses a book exchange for literature-thirsty travelers.

If you have a car, a short drive will land you at another excellent restaurant, **Artatore** (Artatore 132, tel. 051/232-932, 10 A.M.–midnight daily mid-Mar.–mid-Nov., 120Kn) in Artatore Bay. Known for its Kvarner specialties, the restaurant typically serves up dishes like lobster in *buzara* sauce, lamb with gnocchi, and many types of risottos.

Getting There and Around

Summer connections to the island are the best, with a daily catamaran between Mali Lošinj and Rijeka (1 hour and 20 minutes) and Pula (2.5–3 hours) and a car ferry from Zadar (7 hours). You can also connect directly to Venice (www.venezialines.com, 4 hours, €70).

Buses link Mali Lošinj with Cres Town (2 a day, more in summer, 1.25 hours, 47Kn) and Osor (at least 2 daily, 30 minutes, 27Kn).

If you don't feel like walking the promenade between Mali Lošinj and Veli Lošinj, close to 10 buses a day make the 10-minute trip for around 15Kn.

◖ SUSAK

Ten miles southwest of Lošinj, Susak is a delightful (mostly) overlooked island with a completely different composition than the other Kvarner Islands, hence the clay ocher-colored cliffs. The islanders have a culture uniquely their own and their own dialect. Only 150 people call the four-square-kilometer island home year-round. You'll find more natives in the United States, where 2,500 people claim roots from the small island.

The settlement of Susak is the only village on the island, and it is divided into two parts: **Gornje selo** (Upper Village), the oldest part of town, and **Donje selo** (Lower Village). In the Gornje selo you'll find the 1770 **Crkva svetog Nikole** (St. Nicholas's Church), built on the remains of an 11th-century Benedictine monastery; if it's open you're free to go in.

There's a great **11-kilometer track** around

the island that takes about three hours to walk. You can stop off for a swim wherever you feel like it. Make sure to take some water and perhaps a snack for the journey.

The beaches on the northwest side of the island, near the village, are quite shallow and two bays, **Spiaža** and **Bok,** also have wonderful natural sandy bases. Bok Bay is traditionally clothing optional. The southwest side of the island is a better choice for those looking for absolute privacy, though it's exposed to a lot more wind and getting to a flat rock surface in one of the coves is not for the unbalanced.

Wineries

Susak has some nice wines, particulalry Pleskunac, a nice red, and Trojišćina, a rosé. To have a taste try **Vinarija Cosulich** (tel. 051/239-070, call for hours), the cellars of an Italian winemaker who bought up vineyards on the island in the 1990s.

Accommodations and Food

The only accommodation in Susak is through private rooms and apartments. You can get a list from the **Mali Lošinj tourist office** (Riva Lošinjskih Kapetana 29, tel. 051/231-547, www.tz-malilosinj.hr, 8 A.M.–8 P.M. Mon.–Sat. and 9 A.M.–1 P.M. Sun. June–Sept., 8 A.M.–1 P.M. Mon.–Fri. Oct.–May) or from the quirky website www.susak.org. **Apartmani Grgac** (Podgorska 125, tel. 01/339-0358, www .apartmani-grgac-susak.com, info@apartmani-grgac-susak.com, prices by agreement) offers attractive, clean apartments and rooms, surrounded by stone walls a short walk to the seafront. You can eat and sleep at the **Buffet Palma** (Susak 127, tel. 051/239-068, 8 A.M.–midnight daily May–Sept., call for prices), which serves up local fish dishes and clean, basic rooms. Susak's small harbor has a few more *konobas* and pizzerias for lunch or dinner. If you would like to buy some bread for the day, keep in mind that all purchases must be pre-ordered through the local store.

Getting There and Around

Susak gets its share of day-trippers from the multiple ferries run by Jadrolinija that deposit tourists on the island during peak season. The ferry connects with Mali Lošinj (2.5 hours, 50Kn). On Susak you'll have to get around on foot or rent bikes from the Sunbird Agency (8 hours for 75Kn, ask about longer periods) near the Hotel Bellevue in Mali Lošinj or the ASL Travel Agency (Obala m. Tita 17, tel. 051/236-257) in Veli Lošinj.

RAB

Rab was originally settled by the Illyrians, but the Greeks and the Romans also staked a claim here. The island was then ruled by the Venetians, who used the island as a place for refugees of the plagues to come and start a new life in the 15th century. The island started to make a name for itself in tourism in the late 19th century, most notably for its naturist (aka nude) beaches that even drew a king of England.

Today the highlight of Rab for history buffs and charm seekers is its small fortified Rab Town, filled with the cobblestone alleyways and tiny squares prerequisite to a proper Adriatic island town. The island also has some excellent beaches, filled in the summers by Europeans coming from the north for a bit of sun and surf.

◖ Rab Town

If you're looking for a place with medieval charm and twisting, narrow alleys, Rab Town is the perfect fit.

SIGHTS

Positioned on a narrow peninsula jutting out into the sea, the picturesque walled city is punctuated by four church towers. If you're interested in visiting these towers, start with the largest at the **Crkva svete Marije Velike** (Church of St. Mary the Great, tel. 051/724-195, 10 A.M.–1 P.M. and 7:30–9:30 P.M. daily in summer, free), built in the 12th century, with many additions and renovations parlaying a bit of Renaissance flair on the Romanesque church. A cathedral until 1828, it's still known locally as

GOLI OTOK: A YUGOSLAVIAN ALCATRAZ

Goli Otok means naked island and its geography certainly confirms the name – arid, no trees, lots of rocks. However, it's been said that the landscape is not how the island got its name. Instead, the name came about because the island used to be a popular spot for naturists to bathe.

But Goli Otok's fame comes from its history as a prison, the Alcatraz of Yugoslavia, from 1949 to 1988. Instead of housing hardened criminals, though, it held political prisoners. These prisoners were ostensibly former Nazi loyalists or those that sided with Stalin when Tito decided to sever ties with the Soviet Union. However, many people, perhaps betrayed by a jealous neighbor, were thrown in for offenses that would seem small to those used to freedom of speech.

Life on Goli Otok was full of hard labor in the island's quarry, and new prisoners were tortured, beaten, forced to dunk their heads in bodily waste, and more. Not many people talk about their life on Goli Otok – so horrific were the conditions that most choose only to forget.

In the 1950s the island started housing fewer political prisoners and more regular criminals. The hardships also lessened, with prisoners having a music room and football team.

Slightly north of Goli Otok is Grgur, another island that functioned as a women's prison. The existence of Goli Otok was not officially admitted until after Tito's death and the island was abandoned in 1989.

If you'd like to visit the island, you'll see many advertisements for excursions from the island of Rab.

---

the Katedrala. To the west of the church is the **Veli zvonik** (Great Bell Tower, Ivana Rabljanina, 10 A.M.–1 P.M. and 7:30–10 P.M. daily in summer, 5Kn), worth the climb for some stunning views.

The nearby 11th-century **Crkva svetog Andrije** (Church of St. Andrew, Ivana Rabljanina) has the oldest bell tower, dating from 1181. The third tower is located at the **Crkva svete Justine** (Church of St. Justine, Gornja ulica, open daily, ask at tourist office for hours, often 7:30–9 P.M. June–Sept., 10Kn), which also houses a small collection of paintings and sacral art. The star attraction here is the box made of precious metal that holds the skull of St. Christopher. The casket, made in the 12th century, is filled with reliefs depicting St. Christopher's beheading.

At the **Bazilika svetog Ivana Evanđeliste** (Church and Convent of St. John the Baptist, Gornja Ulica), the 12th-century tower is all that remains among the ruins of the Benedictine cloister, said to date from the 6th century. It's worth walking the **town walls** for some nice views of town. At the highest part of the walls, **Crkva Sveti Kristofor** (St. Christopher's

Church, 9 A.M.–noon and 7:30–9 P.M. daily in summer, ask tourist office about off-season hours, donation required) has a small lapidarium next door. It's here that Rab Town's peninsula joins with the mainland, becoming the **Komrčar,** a peaceful park with wide paths winding through the forested hills and depositing locals and tourists alike at the city's beaches.

The **Šetalište Fra Odorika Badurine** is a waterfront walkway reached on foot through Komrčar Park, with some shaded areas and pretty, clean water for taking a dip if you don't mind the concrete beneath your towel.

If you'd like to find a more secluded beach out of town, rent a boat at the western end of the old-town harbor or **Kristofor** (Palit bb, tel. 051/725-543, www.kristofor.hr, around 350Kn per day). You'll want to bring supplies, though, unless you don't plan to stay very long.

ENTERTAINMENT AND EVENTS
In the summer months you'll find lots more to do on Rab, with galleries opening their doors to the public until late in the evening and a few festivals and events. Among these are **Rab Classical Music Evenings,** held every

Sveti Križ, where Rab Classical Music Evenings are held in summer

Wednesday at 9 P.M. in Sveti Križ (Church of the Holy Cross, Gornja ulica) from June to September. The annual **Rab Fiera** (end of July) showcases medieval costumes, handicrafts, and culture in a colorful festival that transforms Rab Town's cobblestoned streets.

ACCOMMODATIONS

The waterfront **Tamaris Pension** (Palit 285, tel. 051/724-925, www.tamaris-rab.com, 596Kn d., including breakfast) is located near Rab Town on the edge of Komrčar Park. The rooms are fairly basic but clean and comfortable, with balconies overlooking the park or the sea and a good restaurant with nice fish dishes.

Though the **Residence Astoria** (Dinka Dokule 2, tel. 051/774-844, www.astoria-rab .com, 698Kn d.) is located in a nicely restored Venetian palazzo, don't expect the rooms to have authentic touches save for the occasional exposed stone walls. Still, the hotel-standard decor is perfectly adequate and the location within the old town walls is excellent.

The finest accommodation in Rab Town is the ❰ **Hotel Arbiana** (Obala Petra Krešimira 12, tel. 051/775-900, www.arbianahotel.com, 1,205Kn d., including breakfast), a boutique hotel set in an old villa right on the waterfront. The hotel has a peaceful walled garden area where you can dine in good weather. The rooms are full of luxurious details and the service is excellent. The only drawback (or an extra charming detail, depending on how you look at it) is its proximity to the church bells.

FOOD

Even though Rab is a busy tourist destination, you'll still manage to find some good food any season of the year. Budget-watchers can start with a *konoba,* like the very reasonable and centrally located but quite small **Konoba Kaldanac** (Biskupa Draga bb, tel. 098/212-008, 10 A.M.–11 P.M. Mon.–Sat., 80Kn) serving a nice variety of fish dishes. The rustic **Konoba Rab** (Kneza Branimira 3, tel. 051/725-666, 10 A.M.–midnight Mon.–Thurs., 5–11 P.M. Fri.–Sun., closed Nov.–mid-Feb., 100Kn) specializes in lamb, though seafood and other meat entrées are also on offer. Call one day ahead to order the delectable *janjetina ispod peka* (brick oven–baked lamb). A cozy stone-walled courtyard is the setting for **Paradiso** (Stjepana Radića 1, tel. 051/771-109, www .makek-paradiso.hr, 8 A.M.–midnight daily, 75Kn), a restaurant with its own wine cellar and shop serving simple dishes and a variety of pizzas alongside 130 wines. The candlelit terrace of the **Astoria restaurant** (Trg Municipium Arbae 7, tel. 051/774-844, www .astoria-rab.com, noon–3 P.M. and 6–11 P.M. daily May–Nov., 120Kn) in the Residence Astoria overlooks Rab's main square and delivers traditional dishes, like grilled meats and seafood, as well as an excellent fish soup.

Quite possibly the prettiest place to dine in town is the ❰ **San Marino restaurant** (Obala Petra Krešimira 12, tel. 051/775-900, www .arbianahotel.com, 125Kn) at the Hotel Arbiana. The interior conjures up an Austro-Hungarian fin de siècle vibe but it's the magical

LEAVE THE BATHING SUIT AT HOME

Rab has an interesting history of naturism, or nudist-friendly beaches. Old articles mention the practice on Rab as early as 1907, though it got its biggest start when Viennese Richard Erhman, then president of a naturist union, opened an official nude beach on the island in 1934. But it was Edward VIII, who visited with Wallace Simpson in August 1936, who made Rab famous. Stopping on the island during their scandalous yachting trip down the Adriatic, Edward and Wallace had a dip sans clothing at Kandarola Cove, on the Frkanj Peninsula west of Rab Town.

Kandarola Cove is still the most popular and well-known nude beach on the island. It is also one of two official nude beaches, the other being Ciganka in Lopar. Still, there are plenty of other unofficial spots for naturists around Rab. If you're interested in pursuing the naturist lifestyle with fewer spectators, try other coves along the Frkanj Peninsula or the nearby island of Dolin.

courtyard, surrounded by stone buildings and ancient twisty trees, that really makes the place something special. The restaurant's food is traditional with gourmet touches, like *zubatac* (a type of fish) in a potato and radicchio crust or *pršut* (prosciutto) with porcini, ginger, and red pepper. Pricey, but worth the splurge.

Around Rab

There's honestly not much to see in terms of tourist stops beyond Rab Town. Other parts of the island have been primarily developed with Central European tourists in mind. Most anywhere you go you'll find signs for *apartmani* and restaurants with multilingual menus. The real draw outside of Rab Town is the beaches, usually packed with tourists.

The most popular beach is the two-kilometer-long **Rajska plaža** (Paradise Beach)

in **Lopar,** on the northern tip of the island. Though its position near the San Marino hotel complex and a huge camping spot means it's hardly private, the sandy shores, clear shallow water (extending some 500 meters before it reaches your waist), and a pine forest edging the beach, if you need a bit of shade, make it one of the island's best. The beach also has cafés and bars, and sports activities like volleyball courts and table tennis. Lopar has 22 beaches and three of them are nudist. The prettiest, even worth a trip for non-naturists if you don't mind sharing the sands with un-clothed loungers, is **Sahara,** so named for its sandy shores and out-of-the-way location; a 30-minute walk over the hill or a short boat ride from Lopar's harbor (the better choice) mean there's less activity than Rajska plaža with pretty views, rock edging the cove, and shallow, clear water.

Hotel Epario (Lopar 456A, tel. 051/777-500, www.epario.net, 705Kn d., including breakfast) in Lopar was built in 2007 and has 25 basic but fresh double rooms with air-conditioning, satellite TV, and balconies, but it's not on the beach. **Camping San Marino** (Lopar bb, tel. 051/775-133, tent camping 150Kn for 2 people) has an idyllic location along the Rajska plaža and lots of facilities including showers, bathrooms, tennis court, mini-golf, a playground, a small market, and more.

Getting to Lopar is simple, with close to 10 daily buses making stops at the San Marino beach and in Lopar proper. A small tourist office (tel. 051/775-508, www.lopar.com) can help with information and brochures.

A few kilometers south of Rab Town, beer-swilling partying types will want to check out **Pudarica,** two kilometers from the village of **Barbat.** The beach shack–style club on the edge of the beach, **Santos,** packs in tourists and locals on its poolside dance floor.

The **Villa Hotel Barbat** (Barbat 362, tel. 051/721-858, www.hotel-barbat.com, 698Kn d.) is situated in an old stone villa, rendered practically unrecognizable through modern renovations. The rooms are decent, though decidedly more three-star than their four-star billing. Their restaurant,  **Villa Barbat** (Barbat 362, tel. 051/721-858, www.hotel-barbat.com, noon–late in summer, call for winter hours, 95Kn) is a wonderful spot for a seafood lunch or dinner on the attractive stone terrace. **Aco's** (Barbat 458, tel. 051/721-527, www.aco-rab.hr, 11 A.M.–11 P.M. daily, closed mid-Oct.–end of Mar., 90Kn) in Barbat serves up tasty local dishes like octopus and potatoes baked in a clay oven and *rapska torta,* Rab cake, for dessert. In addition to dining on the restaurant's waterfront terrace, you can arrange for a boat trip with fish picnic or a fishing trip in one of their boats.

Over a dozen buses daily link Barbat with Rab Town, less than a 10-minute journey.

Getting There and Around

If you're driving to Rab from the mainland, you'll need to connect with the car ferry at Jablanac (look for signs off the Magistrala) to the southern tip of Rab, about eight kilometers from Rab Town. Lines for the ferries can get quite long in summer—try to hit them

when the least people are coming or going (i.e., weekday, early-morning, and late-evening connections).

There is a summer ferry to Baška on Krk Island (links with Lopar, 1 hour, 45Kn), and the summer-only catamaran links Rijeka and Novalja on Pag with Rab (2 hours to Rijeka, 40Kn). There are multiple daily buses from Rijeka (2.5 hours, 121Kn) and Zagreb (5 hours, 230Kn) to the island. The Autotrans line (www.autotrans.hr) runs most of the bus connections.

PAG

Though the island is famous for its cheese, its lamb, and its lace, most tourists descend on the arid island of Pag for partying at the 24-hour club scene near Novalja. But there's much more to see, including ancient limestone Pag Town, an excellent winery, and sampling some of the local cuisine. The cheese (called *paški sir*) and the lamb owe their distinct and delicious flavor to the herbs that grow wild on the island. The sheep graze on sage, tinged with the salt

KVARNER GULF

© LIANE MATRISCH/DREAMSTIME.COM

the island of Pag, viewed from the mainland

from the nearby sea, soaking all their products with a delicate aroma. Pag lace makes a great souvenir, often sold directly in front of a lacemakers house, who has carried on the tradition of generations before her.

Pag Town

Pag Town is full of old stone buildings, but few with much historical or architectural interest besides those on the main square, **Trg kralja Petra Krešimira IV**. It's home to two 15th-century buildings by famous Dalmatian architect Juraj Dalmatinac. The **Kneževdvor** (Duke's Palace) served as the seat of island government until 1905 and the **Zborna crkva** (Parish Church, Trg Kralja Krešimira IV, tel. 051/611-576, 9 A.M.–noon and 5–7 P.M. June–Sept., Sunday mass only Oct.–May, free), diagonally across the square, was built in a grand scale in order with cathedrals of the day, however the church never got to fulfill its purpose. Particular to the church are the reliefs of local women in traditional headdress surrounding the Virgin Mary above the entrance. The interior is mostly from the 18th century, when the church was refitted in grand Baroque style.

On nearby Zvonomirova is the **Kula skrivanat** (Town's Tower), a 15th-century fortification with an arched gate in its center. It's the only remaining tower of Pag's original nine.

Summer in Pag brings in two additional stops. First up is the **Crkva Sveti Jurja** (St. George's Church, Trg Sveti Jurja, 7:30–10 P.M. daily June–Sept.), which is full of art exhibits, and the must-see **Lace Museum** (Kralja Dmitra Zvonimira, 8–11 P.M. daily June–Sept., free), which shows off Pag's tradition of lace-making.

Pag Town has a decent if unimpressive pebbly *gradska plaža* (town beach) across the causeway from the center on the western side of the bay.

ENTERTAINMENT AND EVENTS

Pag's **carnival** runs the first Saturday after the Epiphany to the first day of Lent. Filled with typical masked parties and a smattering of folklore, the party culminates with the burning of a cloth dummy named Marko, blamed for all the bad in the town during the year. The town holds a second one-day carnival for tourists during the summer. Typically held on the last Saturday in July, the event highlights a lot more culture, including the traditional *tanac* dance, costumed performers, and a parade.

ACCOMMODATIONS AND FOOD

There are dozens of apartments and rooms available for rent on Pag. Many turn out to be a great option for budget-conscious travelers. If you're interested, try **Agencija Perla** (Josipa Bana Jelačića 21, tel. 023/600-003 in summer and tel. 023/612-077 in winter, www.perla-pag.hr) or **Mediteran** (Vladimira Nazora 12, tel. 023/611-238, www.mediteran-pag.com) for private accommodation.

The **Hotel Plaža** (Marka Marulića 14, tel. 023/600-855, www.plaza-croatia.com, 865Kn d., including breakfast) is one of Pag's nicer hotels, out of the center (across the bay and slightly north) but right on the beach. Rooms at the small hotel aren't anything out of the ordinary (and have quite small televisions) but they are clean and simple, and the facilities—a small waterfront pool and a wellness center—might even warrant the hotel's purported four stars.

The **Hotel Pagus** (A. Starcevica 1, tel. 023/611-310, www.coning-turizam.hr, 935Kn d., including breakfast) may well be your best option in Pag. The large waterfront hotel, slightly north of the old town, was completely renovated in 2007 and sports indoor and outdoor pools and a more than 10,000-square-foot spa and wellness center. Best of all, it's only a few minutes' walk to the center of Pag Town, where you can stroll the old streets, have a coffee, or browse the shops.

For food, try the centrally located **Konoba Bile** (Jurija Dalmatinca 35, tel. 023/611-127, 50Kn) for a hearty snack of Pag cheese, *pršut*, and olives topped off with a glass of local wine. More substantial fare can be found at the excellent **Na Tale** (Stjepana Radića 4, tel. 023/611-194, www.ljubica.hr, 8 A.M.–midnight daily, closed Christmas–mid-Jan., 100Kn), located at the edge of the town walls. Serving grilled fish, octopus lasagna, and top regional wines, the restaurant is possibly Pag's best and has a shady courtyard to boot.

INFORMATION AND SERVICES

Pag's **tourist office** (Katine, tel. 023/611-286, www.pag-tourism.hr, 8 A.M.–10 P.M. daily June–Sept., 8 A.M.–3 P.M. Mon.–Fri. Oct.–May) can help out with brochures, maps, and hiking routes.

Novalja

Novalja, north of Pag Town, enjoys its reputation as a party destination, packing in young tourists to the local discos and DJ bars. For those not into the party scene, Novalja still has a couple of gems. The only real tourist sight in town is the small **Gradski muzej** (Town Museum, Ul. kralja Zvonimira 27, tel. 053/661-160, gmnovalja@email.t-com.hr, 9 A.M.–1 P.M. and 6–10 P.M. in summer, 10Kn), showing exhibits on local life, culture, and history as well as highlighting finds from a 1st-century Roman ship just off the coast. Licensed divers can explore the site, now protected by a giant iron cage, free of charge.

Pag's most popular beaches are centered around Novalja, with something for almost every type of tourist. Novalja's **Zrće** beach is round-the-clock party central with poolside lounging and beach volleyball during the day and DJ-fueled dancing by night. The clubs there offer a free shuttle from Novalja's waterfront, so it's easy to get there even without a car.

Just north of Novalja in Stara Novalja is the sandy **Trincel** beach, often overcrowded but packed with services and restaurants.

Nudists will find a portion of **Straško** beach reserved just for them. Families will appreciate the other parts of the two-kilometer stretch, bordered by pine forests plus cafés and snack stands for hungry swimmers.

ENTERTAINMENT AND EVENTS

Partygoers will appreciate the summer's full schedule of live concerts and DJs, with activities focused in Zrće beach. You can reach clubs **Papaya, Aquarius,** and **Kalypso,** which operate 24 hours a day in season, by hopping on a free shuttle on Novalja's seafront, usually in front of the **Cocomo** bar.

ACCOMMODATIONS AND FOOD

Budget travelers should check out the beach-front **Kamp Straško** (tel. 053/661-226, www .turno.hr, 777Kn for a mobile home) with camping spots and mobile homes that can sleep up to four people. The hotels in Novalja are largely overpriced. If you're determined to stay in town, try renting a room or apartment through a local agency like **SunTurist** (Kranjčevićeva bb, tel. 053/661-226, www .sunturist.com).

The nicest hotels are outside of Novalja. The lovely **Hotel Luna** (Jakišnica bb, tel. 053/654-700, www.luna-hotel.hr, 1,078Kn d., including breakfast) is a 20-minute drive to the north, in a beautiful location with sleek modern rooms, indoor and outdoor pools, and a sauna. Closer to Novalja, on a hillside just far enough away from town for peace and quiet, you'll find the **Hotel and Winery Boškinac** (Novaljsko polje bb, tel. 053/663-500, www.boskinac .com, 1,420Kn d., including breakfast), a statuesque tile-roof villa with cozy rooms and a terrace perfect for relaxing with a glass of wine from their vineyards.

The hotel's restaurant **Boškinac** (Novaljsko polje bb, tel. 053/663-500, www .boskinac.com, open for lunch and dinner Tues.–Sun., closed Jan.–mid-Feb., reservations required, 120Kn) is also one of the best in the area with traditional dishes made with ultra-fresh ingredients and access to the large wine cellar, stocked with house and international varieties. For a filling meal in the heart of Novalja, try **Konoba Starac i More** (Brače Radić bb, tel. 053/662-423, 10 A.M.–11 P.M. daily, 80Kn). The seafood restaurant has a nice enclosed terrace, a relaxed atmosphere, and a mostly local clientele.

Around Pag

The eastern side of the island has several pretty beaches, though some may say the landscape is more lunar than beachlike. **Ručica,** two kilometers from the village of Metajna, is one of the nicest, and even has a small restaurant on the hillside above that signals lunch and dinner with the ringing of a bell. You'll need a car to enjoy a day here.

Sv. Duh, located on the eastern side of the island about 10 kilometers from Novalja, is a good choice if you're looking for sand. Half of the beach is used by nudists and the beach charges a small entrance fee (around 5Kn).

Getting There and Around

If you're driving to Pag, you can either cross the bridge (almost 30 kilometers north of the village of Posedarje) just off the Magistrala, connecting you with the southern end of the island, or take the hourly ferry from Prizna (look for signs off the Magistrala) to Pag's northern tip, close to Novalja.

Those without a car can rely on buses connecting Rijeka and Zadar that stop on the island of Pag. Rijeka to Pag Town takes about four hours and costs around 150Kn, while Zagreb to Pag Town takes around six hours and costs approximately 250Kn. These buses are the island's only form of public transportation connecting Novalja and Pag Town, though there are almost 10 daily in the summer and they cost around 35Kn.

A catamaran run by Jadrolinija (daily in summer, three times a week from Oct.–May, www.jadrolinija.hr) connects Novalja with Rijeka (3 hours, 60Kn) and Rab Town (1 hour, 45Kn).

NORTHERN DALMATIA

Northern Dalmatia does not have the block-buster destinations of its southern counterpart, but its charming coastal towns are full of Roman-Veneto architecture and make great departure points for discovering private retreats and fishing excursions. It is a bit harder to find a good beach in this area, but they do exist, especially on some of the uninhabited islands just off the coast. The real standouts of Northern Dalmatia are Zadar, with lots of Roman relics and a culture all its own, and the Kornati Islands, a small wild archipelago with national park status. As for overlooked highlights, Šibenik's old town is a must-see that's also a good place to get out of the way of many of the summer's tourists. There's also tiny but lovely Trogir, full of fine well-preserved structures from the Middle Ages, though it fills to capacity with holidaying Europeans in the summer months, making it a bit harder to see the charm.

And cities aren't the only gems of the region. Natural beauty abounds in the area's national parks, in the karst landscape of Paklenica, the stunning Plitvice Lakes, the limestone cliffs of the Kornati, and the beautiful Krka, a rushing river punctuated by waterfalls. Though technically inland, the Plitvice Lakes, one of Croatia's busiest tourist destinations, make a great stop-off on your way to or from the coast or as a day trip from the Northern Dalmatian coastal towns.

Good food is not at all hard to find here, with dozens of seafood restaurants and places serving spit-roasted lamb, one dish with which the region holds lots of expertise.

© SHANN FOUNTAIN ČULO

HIGHLIGHTS

◖ The Forum: Zadar's Roman forum is the central attraction in a town filled with Roman ruins, loads of local culture, and a not-quite-discovered vibe. The giant square is littered with ancient columns and surrounded by worth-a-visit churches and museums (page 170).

◖ Dugi Otok: A great choice for beach bums, this island's Telašćica Bay nature park is filled with spots for swimming and sunning (page 178).

◖ Donja jezera in Plitvice Lakes National Park: The pooling and cascading lakes in Plitvice are bordered by well-marked paths and lush forests. The Donja jezera, closest to the main entrance, are highlighted by the park's biggest waterfalls and are a must-see on the way to or from the coast (page 182).

◖ Kornati Islands: Made up of a string of scruffy islands, this national park is filled with wildlife, deserted stone houses, and a veritable flotilla of top-quality fish restaurants (page 183).

◖ Katedrala svetog Jakova: Juraj Dalmatinac's stunning cathedral overlooking the water in Šibenik is just the beginning of the often unnoticed town's sun-washed medieval core (page 186).

◖ Krka National Park: Whether you only scratch the surface by visiting the stepped rushing falls at Skradinski Buk or continue on

to the park's fairy-tale Byzantine monastery, the beauty of the place makes it obvious why this is one of the region's most-visited destinations (page 190).

LOOK FOR ◖ TO FIND RECOMMENDED SIGHTS, ACTIVITIES, DINING, AND LODGING.

PLANNING YOUR TIME

If you have only two to three nights, try to fit in Zadar, a trip to the Kornati Islands, and perhaps a stop at Jurlinovi Dvori for a taste of traditional Dalmatia and at the famous restaurant Torcida near Šibenik for some *janjetina* (lamb)—this will give you a nice overview of the region. If you have another day or two, spend the night in Šibenik's old town, squeezing in a quick tour around town and a ferry to one of the islands just off the coast for a bit of relaxing. Trogir is close to Split, even closer to Split's airport, making it convenient to spend half a day in transit.

Not surprisingly, the coastal towns and islands are the busiest in July and August. Despite potential crowds around tourist attractions and shops in Zadar and Trogir, you won't find yourself overwhelmed on some of the off-the-coast islands, where you can keep walking until you get to a patch of undiscovered pebble shore. However, the best times to visit are May, June, and September, when the limestone is warm with the sun, but not so warm you're immediately running for the shade. The tourist numbers are dramatically lower in these months, though

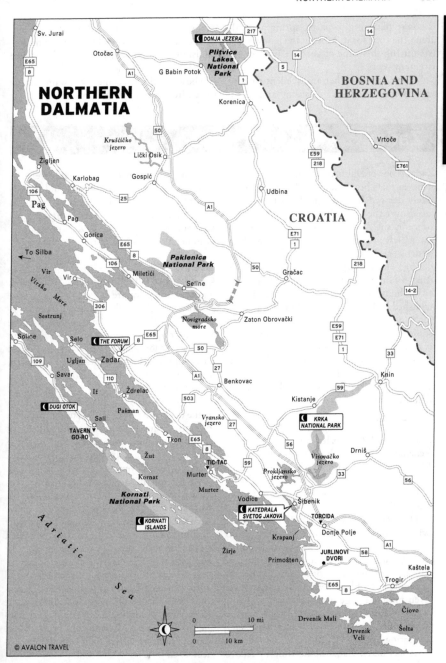

© AVALON TRAVEL

if you're planning to party, spring and fall aren't the time for it. Most of the fellow tourists during this time of year are in their retirement years.

Winter can be either an excellent time to visit (some days turn out sunny and warm enough for only a light coat) or an awful one (if the infamous *bura* is blowing). Some establishments, particularly on the islands, are closed during the winter months. However, it can be a nice time to come if you want to have the entire region to yourself.

Zadar

Zadar is one of Dalmatia's larger cities, though it never feels big. The town has real soul—likely derived from all the hardships it has faced over the years. It was bombed over 70 times by the Allies in World War II (reasons for which are still quite unclear) and held under siege during the Homeland War. Zadar has lots of architecture—from the Roman to Austro-Hungarian municipal buildings. The city is home to Croatia's oldest university, established by Dominican monks in 1396, making it quite a vibrant town when school is in session. When it's not, the number of students is replaced and tripled by tourists who pile in from the beach resorts nearby. Still, one has the feeling that the place is not quite discovered and it maintains its own vibe, independent of summering travelers.

HISTORY

Zadar (called Zara in Italian) was long under Venetian rule and the Italian influence in town has always been strong. The city was even given to Italy in 1921 before being returned to Croatia as a part of Tito's Yugoslavia in the late 1940s.

Damage from World War II was replaced with a crop of modern structures, giving the old town an organic feel as mid-century apartment blocks share a wall with Austro-Hungarian buildings, with discarded Roman columns not a block away. The city received even more damage when Serbian paramilitaries and the JNA (Yugoslav People's Army) surrounded the city in 1991, not completely retreating until 1995.

It has taken Zadar some time to recover economically from the siege. However, the fishing industries, the ferry port, and the appeal of the old-town core, with its museums and Roman architecture, are bringing kuna and tourists back in droves as Zadar once again becomes a destination for those in the know.

SIGHTS
◖ The Forum

Zadar's main square is referred to as the Forum, though it looks a bit more like a junkyard for old Roman columns (only one of the Forum's original columns remains standing). You'll find a lot of the pieces recycled inside the **Crkva svetog Donata** (St. Donat's Church, Zeleni trg, 9 A.M.–10 P.M. daily in summer, 10Kn), today only a tourist stop and musical venue (due to the excellent acoustics). Built at the beginning of the 9th century, the stark Byzantine church was built with remnants of columns, plaques, and other stone pieces the Romans left behind. In July and August the St. Donat Musical Evenings are held inside.

At the northern end of the Forum, steps away from St. Donat's Church, you'll find the **Katedrala svete Stošije** (Cathedral of St. Anastasia, Trg Sv. Stošije, 8 A.M.–6 P.M. daily in summer, 8 A.M.–12:30 P.M. daily in winter, free), a late Romanesque church from the 12th and 13th centuries that displays some magnificent stonework. The interior has some beautiful 13th-century frescoes as well as the 9th-century sarcophagus of St. Anastasia. For some super views of town you can climb up the 56-meter 19th-century **bell tower** (9 A.M.–8 P.M. daily in summer, 10Kn) built by English architect T. G. Jackson.

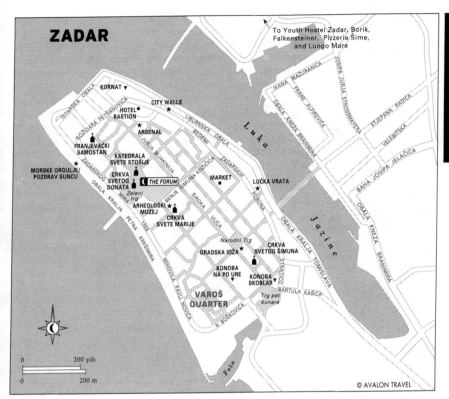

Trg Opatice Čike
Nun Čika Square

Across from St. Donat's Church, the Trg Opatice Čike connects to the southern side of the Forum. Here you'll find the **Arheološki muzej** (Archaeological Museum, Trg Opatice Čike 1, tel. 023/254-626, www.amzd.hr, 9 A.M.–2 P.M. and 5–9 P.M. daily Apr.–Sept., 9 A.M.–2 P.M. daily Oct.–Mar., 10Kn), whose plain building offers a stark modern contrast to the ancient relics around it. Inside, over 100,000 pieces from the prehistoric to the Romans to medieval times can be found on the museum's three floors, including a model of the Forum as it once was.

Next to the Arheološki muzej is the 11th-century **Crkva svete Marije** (St. Mary's Church, Trg Opatice Čike, tel. 023/250-496, 8 A.M.–noon and 5–8 P.M. daily, free) with a 16th-century facade, bombed during Allied raids on Zadar. The church is nice (and a mishmash of styles, from original recycled Roman columns to ornate Baroque balconies added in the 19th century), but the real finds are in the church's museum. the exhibit **Zlato i srebro Zadra** (Gold and Silver of Zadar, Trg Opatice Čike, tel. 023/250-496, 10 A.M.–12:30 P.M. and 6–7:30 P.M. Mon.–Fri. and 10 A.M.–noon Sat. in summer, call for winter hours, 20Kn) is treasure trove of sacral art, caskets, icons, and Byzantine crafts housed in the *samostan* (convent) next door to the church.

Franjevački samostan
Franciscan Monastery

Zadar's Franjevački samostan (Zadarskog mira, tel. 023/250-468, 7:30 A.M.–noon and 4:30–6 P.M. daily, free) is said to have been

Crkva svetog Donata, in Zadar's main square

founded by St. Francis in 1219. Thought to be the oldest Gothic church in Dalmatia, it has an interior that is mostly Renaissance. There's not much to see here beyond a few graves, though the well at the center of the courtyard garden is rather poignant given it was one of the few sources of drinking water for the city during the Homeland War of the early 1990s.

Morske orgulje
Sea Organ

Built in 2005, the Morske orgulje, located on the Obala kralja Petra Krešimira IV, is the inventive idea of local architect Nikola Bašić. The organ looks like a set of giant steps; the power of the waves forces interesting organic sounds out of the openings between the stairs. At night you can watch a stunning light show, **Pozdrav Suncu** (The Greeting to the Sun), also by Bašić, where a 22-meter circle soaks up sun in its solar panels during the day and starts to emit a glowing amalgam of colors at night.

City Walls

From the sea organ you can walk along the 16th-century city walls down the Liburnska obala to the southeastern **Lučka vrata** (Port Gate), fashioned from a Roman triumphal arch into a Renaissance grand entrance topped with the Lion of Venice. There's a wonderful morning **market** (7 A.M.–1 P.M. daily, tourist stalls stay open later) near here on Krnarutića, where you can buy fresh produce and bread for a makeshift picnic lunch as well as a smattering of touristy souvenirs.

Narodni trg
National Square

Past the market on Krnarutića, make a right onto Jurja Barakovića towards Narodni trg, now more of a main square than the larger Forum, which once held center stage. Here you'll find a 16th-century **Gradska straža** (Guard House) with a big clock tower and the **Gradska loža** (Town Loggia, tel. 023/211-174, 9 A.M.–noon and 6–9 P.M. Mon–Fri., 9 A.M.–1 P.M. Sat., 5Kn), now an art gallery and concert venue for the town. Admission to the gallery also gets you into the **Narodni Muzej** (National Museum, Poljana Pape

Aleksandra III, tel. 023/251-851, 8 A.M.–noon and 6–9 P.M. Mon.–Fri. and 9 A.M.–1 P.M. Sat. in summer, 9 A.M.–noon and 5–8 P.M. Mon.–Fri. and 9 A.M.–1 P.M. Sat. in winter, 5Kn). The well-presented museum, located closer back toward the Port Gate (follow Široka to Poljana Pape Aleksandra III and turn right), has a display chronicling Zadar's history, paintings and relics from nearby towns, and scale models of Zadar through the centuries.

Crkva svetog Šimuna
St. Simeon's Church
Most people come to the 17th-century Crkva svetog Šimuna (Trg Šime Budinića, tel. 023/211-705, 8 A.M.–noon and 4–7 P.M. daily in summer, 8 A.M.–noon daily in winter, free) to see the opulent casket of St. Simeon. Fashioned out of some 550 pounds of silver, supported by four equally ornate bronze angels, it holds the body of St. Simeon, one of Zadar's patron saints. There are various legends surrounding the body and its casket. The body supposedly came to Zadar when a merchant shipping it from the Holy Land to Venice fell ill and died here. The identity of the body was said to be revealed to local priests in a dream. The casket, commissioned by Elizabeth, Queen of Hungary, in the late 14th century, some centuries after the death of St. Simeon in the 5th century, has a legend of its own. The story goes that she had the casket built in remorse after she stole one of the saint's fingers and it began to decompose. Once the digit was returned to its proper place, the decay miraculously stopped.

Trg pet bunara
Square of Five Wells
Trg pet bunara was once Zadar's main source of drinking water. These days it's frequented by young locals looking for a bit of recreation—summer brings frequent concerts and performances to the square. Here you'll find the **Kapetanova kula** (Captain's Tower, 10 A.M.–1 P.M. and 5–8 P.M. Mon.–Fri. and 10 A.M.–1 P.M. Sat. in summer, 10Kn), a five-sided tower built by the Venetians to defend the city against the Turks. Currently it's being used as an exhibition space for Croatian artists.

Nearby you'll find the **Kopnena vrata** (Land Gate), lined with eerie-looking cattle skulls, supposedly to scare off attackers.

Varoš Quarter
On the way back toward the Forum from Trg pet bunara, the Varoš quarter is one of Zadar's prettiest neighborhoods, filled with winding streets and little shops. The winding **Stomorica street** is packed with cafés for an afternoon coffee.

BEACHES
There's not a lot to choose from in terms of beaches in Zadar proper. Some tourists and locals swim offshore where the Sea Organ is located, but most head to **Borik,** a package-hotel mecca a short drive away (take bus #5 from Zadar, about 10 minutes). Better yet, take a ferry excursion to one of the **islands** in Zadar's archipelago.

ENTERTAINMENT AND EVENTS
Nightlife
Low-key evenings can be found in the bars and cafés around the Stomorica in the Varoš quarter, worthy of a little pub crawl. Another option is the **Arsenal** (Trg Tri bunara 1, tel. 023/253-833, www.arsenalzadar.com, 7 A.M.–3 A.M. daily in summer, call for winter hours), which bills itself as a multipurpose arts venue. Located in a renovated 18th-century warehouse, the expansive space with soaring ceilings is the perfect place for sipping wine or a cocktail, browsing the small gallery, or listening to a local band of jazz or *klapa* singers. Arsenal also has small shops selling clothing, crafts, and local wines.

For something livelier, head to the crazy, buzz-worthy bars The Garden and Barbarella's. **The Garden** (Liburnska obala 6, tel. 023/364-739, www.thegardenzadar.com, 10 A.M.–1 A.M. daily in summer) is a British-owned club bringing in live bands and well-respected DJs to an outdoor space that's bustling both day and night. Choose from cocktails, tapas, and a solid beer list. The owners of The Garden opened **Barbarella's** (Punta Radman put 8, Petrčane, tel. 023/364-739, www.thegardenzadar.com) in 2008. The seaside location is more of an upscale young beach bar than a lounge club like The Garden.

Festivals and Events

The highlight of Zadar's summer season is the **St. Donat's Musical Evenings** (July and Aug., www.donat-festival.com) with outstanding classical concerts from international performers. Even better is the location, in the St. Donat's Church. **Zadarsko kazališno ljeto** (Zadar Theatrical Summer, late June, July, and Aug.), a mostly Croatian group of performers, and **Zadar snova** (Zadar Dreams, July and Aug.) stage theater and dance performances all over the city's historic core during the summer season.

ACCOMMODATIONS

For students and those stretching their kuna as far as possible, the **Youth Hostel Zadar** (Obala Kneza Trpimira 76, tel. 023/331-145, www.hihostels.com, beds from 78Kn), a member of Hostelling International, offers clean rooms near a beach about five kilometers north from Zadar's ancient center. If you'd like to rent a room or apartment in or around Zadar (there are even a handful in the old town), try **Marlin Tours** (Jeretova 2, tel. 023/305-920, www.marlin-tours.hr) or **Jaderatours** (Poljana Pape Aleksandra III 5/1, tel. 023/250-350, www.jaderatours.hr).

Mare Nostrum (Sveti Petar, tel. 023/391-420, www.marenostrum-hr.com, 611Kn d., including breakfast) is very simple and no frills, but a great location smack on a nice pebbly beach between Zadar and Biograd elevates it a bit.

Though you'll need to have a rental car to get the most out of a stay at the **Aparthotel Lekaviski** (Draznikova 15, tel. 023/265-888, hotel@lekavski.de, www.lekavski.de, 426Kn d.), the basic hotel has magnificent service catering to your every need. From here it's a

20-minute drive south into Zadar but just a short walk to a good beach, and the hotel can whip up excellent meals.

The outside looks like any old restaurant, but the **Hotel Niko** (Obala Kneza Domagoja 9, tel. 023/337-880, www.hotel-niko.hr, 1,306Kn d., including breakfast), located in Puntamika, a suburb north of Zadar, is a great place to stay with cozy rooms upgraded from the standard of most Croatian family hotels. It's only a few meters from the sea and it takes about 20 minutes to get into the heart of Zadar from the bus stop in front.

Though saying **Falkensteiner Club Funimation Borik** (Majstora Radovana 7, tel. 023/206-636, www.falkensteiner.com, 1,564Kn d., including three meals and use of facilities) is a bit of a mouthful, the all-inclusive hotel about 10 minutes from Zadar by car is perfect for families, with sleek rooms and family suites, a huge kids' club, playground, and mini–water park. Guests without kids can enjoy the hotel's spa services and consider booking a room in the quieter and more luxe **C Adriana wing** (1,846Kn d. all inclusive).

Built on the remains of a medieval fortress, the **C Hotel Bastion** (Bedemi zadarskih pobuna 13, tel. 023/494-950, www.hotel-bastion.hr, 1,400Kn d., including breakfast) opened in 2007. The boutique hotel is pleasant bordering on luxurious, with a waterside terrace restaurant and a small cellar-like spa. Located steps from the Sea Organ and other sights in Zadar's old town, it's convenient, pretty, and the best value in Zadar proper.

FOOD

If you're watching your kuna, try **Konoba Na Po Ure** (Špire Brusine 8, tel. 023/312-004, 9:30 A.M.–1 A.M. daily, 40Kn). Usually packed with locals and rustic ambience, the *konoba* has one of the most wallet-friendly menus (from their specialty shark to fish and grilled meats) in town. For less than 10 dollars (give or take depending on the exchange rate) you can get a full meal at **Ljepotica** (Obala kneza Branimira, tel. 023/311-288, 7 A.M.–midnight daily, no credit cards, 40Kn) near

© SHANN FOUNTAIN ČULO

outdoor market in Zadar

the footbridge. Choose from the daily specials (don't miss the *pašticada*, a typical Dalmatian beef dish, if it's on the menu) and enjoy a reasonably priced glass of wine. Another reliable option is **Konoba Skoblar** (Trg Petra Zoranića 4, tel. 023/213-236, 7 A.M.–midnight Mon.–Sat., 7:30 A.M.–10 P.M. Sun., 65Kn), where you can have a light snack or *marenda* of octopus salad with the regulars or go for the heartier black risotto or the *konoba*'s famous *kalelarga* cheesecake.

Had enough fish? Then head to **Pizzeria Šime** (Matije Gupca 15, tel. 023/334-848, noon–midnight daily, no credit cards, 50Kn) in Borik—nearby if you're at the Falkensteiner, not so near if you're not. The restaurant has a giant terrace and a good selection of tasty pizzas.

For more alfresco dining, **Lungo Mare** (Obala kneza Trpimira 23, tel. 023/331-533, 10:30 A.M.–midnight daily, 85Kn) has a stunning view of the sea, particularly if you're lucky enough to catch the sunset. It's a 15-minute walk north from Zadar (particularly convenient if you're staying at the Youth Hostel

Zadar), but the vistas and the food and the extensive wine list make it worth the jaunt. **Kornat** (Liburnska obala 6, tel. 023/254-501, 11 A.M.–11 P.M. daily, 90Kn) is a refined place without the attitude. The wine list is excellent and the menu is peppered with gourmet features like truffles and monkfish. Don't miss the restaurant's fish stew, *na gregadu*.

On the chic and trendy side of Zadar's gastronomic offerings are two restaurants with the same owner. The first, **Dva Ribara** (Blaža Jurjeva 1, tel. 023/213-445, 10 A.M.–11 P.M. daily, 95Kn), means two fishermen, but the menu is actually stronger on the meat side of things. In the heart of town, it has a minimalist interior that contrasts nicely with the ancient surroundings. Ask for a glass of the house wine, much cheaper than the wines listed in the *vinska karta*. Dva Ribara's swankier sister, **◖ Foša** (Kralja Dmitra Zvonimira 2, tel. 023/314-421, noon–midnight daily, 140Kn), could well belong in a much more cosmopolitan city. A staple on the restaurant scene for many years, it has had a complete overhaul that transformed the seafood restaurant into a sleek glass, wood, and chrome space with a wonderful terrace next to the city walls on a small harbor. The menu begins with a choice of 10 different kinds of olive oil, treated like wine, and goes on to include elegant versions of traditional Dalmatian cuisine, like grilled white fish with *blitva* and a few sophisticated touches like octopus carpaccio and filet mignon with truffles.

INFORMATION AND SERVICES

You can find more information, maps, advice, and free brochures from Zadar's **tourist office** (Narodni Trg, tel. 023/316-166, www .tzzadar.hr, 8 A.M.–noon daily July–Aug., 8 A.M.–8 P.M. daily June–Sept., 8 A.M.–3 P.M. Mon–Fri. Oct.–May). Surf the Internet and have something to drink at **Arsenal** (Trg Tri bunara 1, tel. 023/253-833, www.arsenalzadar .com, 7 A.M.–3 A.M. daily). Zadar's main post office (Kralja S Držislava 1, tel. 023/316-552, 7:30 A.M.–9 P.M. Mon.–Fri., 7:30 A.M.–8 P.M. Sat.) can help you send a postcard back home.

There are three spots in town for left luggage. Try the bus station (Ante Starčevića 1, tel. 023/211-555, www.liburnija-zadar.hr, 6 A.M.–10 P.M. Mon.–Fri., 15Kn per day), the train station (Ante Starčevića 4, tel. 052/212-555, www.hznet.hr, 24 hours daily, 15Kn per day), or the Jadrolinija ferry dock (Liburnska obala 7, tel. 023/254-800, www.jadrolinija.hr, 7 A.M.–8 P.M. Mon.–Fri., 15Kn per day).

GETTING THERE AND AROUND

Zadar's airport (tel. 023/313-311, www.zadar-airport.hr) is about a 10-minute drive east from town. Croatia Airlines runs buses (25Kn) into town that coincide with their flights. If you're flying with another carrier, you can wait for the next bus or take a taxi (tel. 023/251-400, 180–220Kn).

Zadar is a large ferry port with connections to Pula (5 hours), Ancona in Italy (7 hours), and multiple points in the Zadar archipelago. Jadrolinija (Liburnska obala 7, tel. 023/254-800, www.jadrolinija.hr) runs almost all of the ferry connections.

The bus station (Ante Starčevića 1, tel. 023/211-555, www.liburnija-zadar.hr, ticket office 6 A.M.–10 P.M. daily) and train station (Ante Starčevića 4, tel. 052/212-555, www .hznet.hr, ticket office 7:30 A.M.–9 P.M. daily) are located next to each other about a 15-minute walk southeast from the old town center. You could also take local bus #5 or hop a cab (about 75Kn). Buses tend to be faster than trains for getting to Zagreb or Split. Bus connections are plentiful: Zagreb (almost two dozen daily in summer, 5 hours, 220Kn), Rijeka (6 daily in summer, 5 hours), Split (8 daily in summer, 3 hours, 120Kn) and Dubrovnik (7 daily in summer, 8 hours, 275Kn). You can also take a fast train to or from Zagreb (2 daily, 7 hours, 160Kn), though the advantage of the bus is that it's quicker and stops at Plitvice (though getting on again is slightly more difficult).

Around town, you can take the rowing boats located between the shores Liburnska obala and Obala kneza Trpirmia. Just show up and they'll shuttle you back and forth for about 7Kn. Buses to Borik are marked Puntamika. Buses to the harbor next to the old town are marked Poluotok. Bus tickets run 6Kn each way if bought from a newspaper kiosk and 10Kn if purchased onboard.

Islands Around Zadar

If you're looking for a bit of lounging seaside, some of Northern Dalmatia's most beautiful coastline is only a short ferry ride away. The islands of the Zadar archipelago are some of the least touristed in Croatia, leaving you with lots of unspoiled beauty to enjoy. Most of the islands are an easy day trip during the summer, when daily ferries connect them with Zadar's harbor. In winter it might be necessary to make an overnight trip in order to visit these wild islands.

UGLJAN

So close to Zadar it's almost a part of the city, the relatively undeveloped island of Ugljan fills up on the weekends as locals head to its shores. The island has two marinas for boaters. The **Olive Island Marina** (tel. 023/335-809, www.olive islandmarina.com) is planning to develop a resort on the island, while the ecofriendly **Preko Marina** (tel. 023/286-169, www.marinapreko.com) is close to Preko's ferry port where buses haul travelers out to the island's villages. Hourly ferries from Zadar take about 30 minutes and cost around 20Kn.

Beaches near the ferry dock get very crowded. Ask the **tourist office** (tel. 023/286-8388, tzpreko@preko.hr, www.preko.hr) in Preko about renting a bike to explore the less-developed western side of the island, or find a water taxi to take you out to the islet of **Galevac**, just offshore, for some of the best swimming. Galevac has a 15th-century monastery and nice beaches backed by thick woods to provide a bit of shade.

Your best option for accommodation on Ugljan is a private room or apartment, booked by visiting the local tourist office on Preko's main square or via their website. The **Konoba Barbara** (Put Jerolimovih 4, tel. 023/286-129, noon–midnight daily, closed Nov.–Mar., 60Kn) is one good option for grilled fish dishes and salads.

PAŠMAN

The sleepy little island of Pašman has some friendly fishing villages and a 12th-century fortress that's now a monastery, in the village of Ugrinći. For swimming, try the coast south of **Tkon**, the busiest town on the island. There you'll discover plenty of sandy shores near the Sovinje nudist resort. If you'd rather your fellow bathers stay clothed, the pebbled beaches of Lučina, on the northern side of the island near Pašman Village, are another option.

If you're inclined to stay overnight try the campsite on the island, **Lučina** (tel. 023/260-173, www.lucina.hr, 80Kn), or book a private room through the **tourist office** (tel. 023/260-155, www.pasman.hr). There are a couple of friendly, clean pensions in town, such as the **Apartmani Lanterna** (Pašman Village, Obala bb, tel. 023/260-179, www.lanterna.hr, 390Kn d.) or the **Vila Kruna** (Kraj 122a, tel. 023/285-410, www.vila-kruna.com, 425Kn d.). The Lanterna also has a good restaurant with fresh fish, most of which is cooked in a stone oven.

You'll get to Pašman by taking the ferry from Zadar to Ugljan and then hopping a bus (almost 10 daily in summer, 25 minutes). The bus first stops in Pašman Village and ends at Tkon, the island's official center.

IŽ

Iž is a tiny, slightly unkempt-in-a-good-way island with two main villages, Veli Iž and Mali Iž. There's not much to do here besides swim, eat, and hike the paths cutting through the slightly wild olive trees. Also near Zadar and serviced by a daily car ferry (which lets off in Bršanj, not the best village if you don't have a car) or the weekly ferries (which let out in the much more developed Veli Iž), the island is relatively undeveloped, leaving private rooms and apartments the best options for accommodation. Try the **Apartmani Švorinić Venka** (tel. 023/278-160, www.svorinic-venka.com, 355Kn d.), which has clean basic rooms, some with sea views, in Mali Iž, or the **Apartmani Strgačić** (tel. 023/319-484, www.apartmani-strgacic.hr, 285Kn d.) in Veli Iž, which also organizes fishing expeditions.

The **Hotel Korinjak** (tel. 023/277-064, www.korinjak.hr, 3,906Kn d. per week, including all meals) is a typical relic of the Tito days, a big concrete block in a good location with basic rooms and basic service. Rooms are only rented on a weekly basis.

There's a smattering of restaurants down by the harbor where you can get a good meal or a strong coffee.

◖ DUGI OTOK

With a name that literally means long island and at 50 kilometers in length and 4.5 kilometers in width, Dugi Otok is the largest of the islands forming the Zadar archipelago. Dugi Otok is arguably its prettiest as well, with a quirky geography forming dozens of indented coves and cliff-backed coastline. The biggest draw for the island is the **Telašćica Bay** nature park (Ulica Danijela Grbin bb, Sali, tel. 023/377-096, www.telascica.hr, 30Kn), where you'll find some nice swimming and a saltwater lake, **Jezero mira**. The park is just a few kilometers out of the village of Sali, a great distance for a bike ride if you don't have a car (and perhaps even if you do).

If you're looking for something a little less quiet, try the sandy **Sahuran beach** just south of Veli Rat.

The best accommodation on the island is in private rooms and apartments, which can be booked through the island's **tourist office** (Obala Perta Lorinija bb, tel. 023/377-094, tz-sali@zd.t-com.hr, www.dugiotok.hr, 8 A.M.–9 P.M. daily July–Aug., 8 A.M.–3 P.M. Mon.–Fri. Sept.–May) located in the village of Sali. The **Hotel Maxim** (tel. 023/291-291, www.hoteli-bozava.hr, 1,165Kn d., including breakfast and dinner) is another option for an overnight. Reconstructed and decked out with a slightly garish facade, the hotel has a nice swimming pool and is located directly on the sea. For a nice tavern atmosphere and good local fish specialties, try **Kod Sipe** (Sali 174, tel. 023/377-137, 10 A.M.–midnight in summer, call for winter hours, 80Kn) or ◖ **Tavern Go-Ro** (Uvala Telašćica, tel. 098/853-434, 10 A.M.–midnight, closed Oct.–Apr., 70Kn)

in Telašćica Bay, with a beautiful view and fish stew and lamb *ispod peka* (call three hours in advance to order lamb).

Taking a day trip to Dugi Otok is really only a possibility in summer (June–Aug.), since ferry connections from Zadar (1.5 hours) get rather sporadic the rest of the year. There are at least two ferries daily in summer (check with the Jadrolinija office in Zadar's harbor) letting off at points like Brbinj, Božava, and Sali. Buses between the towns are few and infrequent, so if you're traveling without a car, try to get a ferry that docks in Sali, the best entry point to the Telašćica Bay park, or Zaglav, where a bus to Sali meets the ferry.

SILBA

This car-free island, the northernmost island of the Zadar archipelago, is filled with lots of peaceful coves and beaches, perfect for bikers and families. The peaceful part is somewhat altered in summer when the year-round population of several hundred is augmented by lots of tourists and locals that descend on the elegant little Silba, lined with patrician merchants' houses and courtyard gardens from its seafaring days. Beaches to the west of Silba Town are definitely the prettiest and offer some spectacular sunsets. The island's **tourist office** (tel. 023/370-010, www.silba.net, 8 A.M.–noon Mon.–Sat. July–Aug., call for off-season hours) has a list of private rooms and apartments. For nourishment try **Konoba Mul** (Port mul, tel. 023/370-351, 11 A.M.–11 P.M. daily July–Aug., call for hours at other times, 75Kn), serving good fish dishes and salads in pleasant surroundings next to the bobbing boats in the little harbor.

There are several boat connections daily with Silba in the summer months. Zadar has the most, though note that the catamarans (1.75 hours) are the fastest. The car ferries can take around 3.5 hours since they have other stops to make. It's also possible to connect with Pula (6 connections weekly in summer), Rijeka (1 connection weekly in summer), and Lošinj (6 connections weekly in summer). Contact Jadrolinija (www.jadrolinija.hr) about current schedules and prices.

Paklenica National Park

Paklenica National Park, founded in 1949, is the best place for trekking through the craggy karst landscape of Northern Dalmatia. Just a couple of kilometers from beaches and package-holiday hotels, nature lovers can lose themselves (hopefully not literally, though) in the park's gorges, peaks, and caves. The park also offers wonderful opportunities for rock-climbing fans and the less-active traveler can still take advantage of the rocky wilderness on an off-road safari.

The small town of **Starigrad Paklenica** is the best base for seeing the park and as a center for accommodation and food. Buses connecting Rijeka and Zadar usually stop in Starigrad Paklenica (note that many locals will refer to it simply as Starigrad, but it's best to add the Paklenica to keep it from getting mistaken for another Starigrad near Senj). The park is about two kilometers north of the town.

At the entrance to the park, you can buy tickets at the ticket booth (40Kn in high season for a one-day entrance, additional 15Kn for entrance to the Manita Peć cave) and pick up a free map of the park's trails, or visit the **park office** (Dr. F. Tuđmana 14a, tel. 023/369-202, www.paklenica.hr, call for hours particularly in autumn–spring) in Starigrad Paklenica before setting out. The office sells detailed maps and can help you plan your trip.

SPORTS AND RECREATION
Hiking and Tours

Paklenica is filled with some 150 kilometers of mapped hiking routes. Most routes will take at least two hours round-trip, though you can wind your way through the park for a few days if you like. Just after you leave the ticket booth, you'll see the **Paklenički mlinovi** (Paklenica Mills, 8 A.M.–7 P.M. daily in summer, by arrangement with the park office out of season). The seven corn- and grain-grinding mills were in use up until the 1960s, serving the area and even the outlying islands. Today there are demonstrations of the water-driven mills, as long as the water flow is heavy enough to operate them.

Continuing up the main trail, following the Velika Paklenica gorge, you'll find a series of underground **tunnels** built by the Yugoslav government to shelter high-level officials in the event of an emergency. At the time of this writing, the tunnels are closed due to construction, but the park plans to open them in the future for events and exhibitions.

Serious hikers will not be put off by the challenging climb to reach the **Manita Peć cave.** The cave must be visited with a park **guide** (guided tours 10 A.M.–1 P.M. Sat. in April, 10 A.M.–1 P.M. Wed. and Sat. in May, 10 A.M.–1 P.M. Mon., Wed., and Sat. in June and Oct., 10 A.M.–1 P.M. daily July–Sept., by arrangement other months of the year, 15Kn). The trip will take about 1.5 hours one-way to see the 175-meter-long cave filled with lots of dripping stalactites and stalagmites.

The mountain has a small rest stop for

BURA WINDS

You'll hear it talked about all over Croatia's Adriatic coast. The *bura* is a cold – sometimes bitterly so – northerly or northeasterly wind that can chill you even on a sunny winter's day on the islands. That's not to say the *bura* can't blow any time of year, but it's that extra cold, gusting wind in winter that really seems to get talked about. The Velebit mountain range is the hardest hit by the *bura;* Kvarner is second in line. The *bura* can come out of nowhere. One moment it's calm and clear and a few hours later winds (in the range of 200 kilometers per hour) are whipping against sailboats and bridges, making all forms of transportation hazardous.

However, the *bura* actually contributes to a lot of the character of the coastal regions. Most of the towns are built densely with narrow streets to counteract the winds. And it's the winds that cure the area's top-quality *pršut* as well.

climbing on limestone rock in Paklenica National Park

snacks and drinks, the **Forest Hut Lugarnica** (10:30 A.M.–4:30 P.M. daily June–Sept., 10:30 A.M.–4:30 P.M. weekends Apr.–May and Oct.), about a two-hour walk from the parking lot depending on which path you take.

For those who don't want to go it alone, the park offers half-day and full-day guided tours as well as specialized tours for bird-watchers. The tours can be arranged in advance through the park office.

There are several options for those who don't want to trek for hours at a time but want to see the beauty of the Velebit Mountains. The tourist office in Starigrad Paklenica can hook you up with agencies providing **boat trips** up the Zrmanja River and the owner of the Hotel Rajna organizes **photo safaris** (tel. 023/369-130, www.hotel-rajna.com) through the Velebit in four-wheel-drive vehicles.

Climbing

Paklenica National Park is a great spot for rock climbers, with some 400 routes, both single-pitch and multi-pitch, available. The park also

hosts an international competition, **Mammut Big Wall Speed Climbing,** every late April/early May. The park office also sells a detailed climbing guide. It's often best to forget about climbing in the winter months when strong *bura* winds might just blow you off the cliff.

ACCOMMODATIONS

Most accommodation will be found in the village of Starigrad Paklenica, though the park has its own **Camp National Park** (Dr. F. Tuđmana 14a, tel. 023/369-202, www.paklenica.hr, from 40Kn per person), located on a stretch of pebbly beach next to the main park office in Starigrad Paklenica. Due to the small size of the camp, reservations are not possible. The Paklenica National Park does not allow camping within its borders, but for those hoping for a longer trek it does offer the **Paklenica Mountain Hut** (tel. 023/213-792 or check at the park office for reservations, 70Kn per person) with a common sleeping room, a kitchen, and a dining hall. You will need to bring your own sleeping bag and supplies.

For slightly cushier digs, the friendly family

Hotel Rajna (Ul. Dr. F. Tuđmana 105, tel. 023/369-130, www.hotel-rajna.com, 340Kn d., including breakfast) is quite a comfy two-star hotel with most basic creature comforts. If you're traveling with friends or want to splurge a bit, the owner also has a charming **(stone cottage Varoš** (tel. 023/369-130, www.hotel-rajna.com, cottage rental 1,986Kn per night, sleeps 15) a 15-minute walk to Paklenica National Park. The 1850-era building is furnished tastefully and traditionally.

FOOD

The restaurant at the **Hotel Rajna** (Jadranska cesta 105, tel. 023/359-121, 6:30 A.M.–11 P.M. daily, closed first two weeks in Jan., 85Kn) has good grilled fish and meats and fish stew. However, the real treat in Starigrad Paklenica is **(4 Ferala** (Joze Dokoze 20, tel. 023/369-304, www.hotel-vicko.hr, 7 A.M.–11 P.M. daily, 95Kn) in the Vičko Hotel, specializing in Dalmatian traditional dishes from roast lamb to mussels in a garlic and wine sauce.

GETTING THERE AND AROUND

Paklenica National Park is located about 200 kilometers south of Rijeka and 45 kilometers north of Zadar on the coastal road. If you're driving, head to Starigrad Paklenica and then follow the signs to the entrance of Paklenica Park (brown signs labeled N.P. Paklenica), about two kilometers north of Starigrad Paklenica. Parking is available at the entrance to the park; there's another lot past the info point, which is the better option.

Buses between Rijeka and Zadar will often stop at Starigrad Paklenica to pick up passengers (unless they're full, which can happen often in the summer); they'll drop you off if you ask. From Zagreb, the best bet is to take a bus to Zadar and connect with Starigrad Paklenica (1.25 hours, 28Kn). There is no public transportation to Paklenica National Park; those without a car will have to walk the two kilometers from Starigrad Paklenica to the park.

Plitvice Lakes National Park

One of Croatia's biggest tourist attractions, the 16 lakes comprising Plitvice Lakes National Park are some of Croatia's most stunning scenery. Though the park is technically inland, travelers most often stop off on their way to or from the coast or via excursions offered from coastal towns.

Plitvice has long been a tourist destination; in the late 19th century visitors started to arrive to admire the natural wonders. The park was under Serb control from 1991 to 1995, with forces using the hotels as barracks. It didn't take long to repair the damage to the buildings and flood the area with travelers once again.

The color of the lakes can be turquoise blue or deep green and the park is filled with giant trees and lots of wildlife. Formed by thousands of years of calcium carbonate deposits, the lakes are held by a natural travertine dam

that grows at least a little each year. The lakes were declared a national park by Yugoslavia in 1949. A UNESCO World Heritage site since 1979, with close to one million tourists seeing the lakes every year, the park is definitely worth a visit. It's also easy to visit, with dozens of paths, lots of information, and an organized system of shuttle buses and boats that's included in the entrance fee.

SIGHTS

Plitvice Lakes National Park (tel. 053/751-015, www.np-plitvice-jezera.hr, 8 A.M.–7 P.M. daily May–Sept., dawn–dusk Oct.–Apr., 110Kn Apr.–Oct., 70Kn Nov.–Mar.) has two entrances from the old Zagreb–Split road. Both entrances have helpful information centers, though Entrance 2 (closest to area accommodation) is often closed in winter. As you walk along the paths and bridges keep an eye out for wildlife, particularly birds (there are over 100 varieties).

◖ Donja jezera
Lower Lakes

Entrance 1 (Ulaz jedan) on the northern end of the park is considered the main entry point. It's here that you're closest to the most-touristed spot, tall Veliki Slap (Big Waterfall). It's about a 10-minute walk to Veliki Slap; paths from there can take you to other waterfalls or to the shuttle boat toward Entrance 2.

The lower lakes include Kaluđerovac Lake, Gavanovac Lake, and Milanovac Lake, small lakes punctuated by waterfalls and a couple of caves (near Kaluđerovac Lake). These feed into the large Kozjak Lake, the largest of Plitvice's bodies of water and the border between the lower and upper lakes.

At the top of Kozjak you'll have the option of taking a shuttle (included in your entrance fee) to Entrance 2, at the southern end of Kozjak, or to continue along the footpath on the eastern shore.

Gornja jezera
Upper Lakes

Reached by trekking about five kilometers from Entrance 1 or by Entrance 2 (Ulaz dva) to its south, the upper lakes are some of Plitvice's most beautiful and also not quite as busy. Near the park's hotels you'll find Gradinsko Lake and then Galovac Lake, where the water descends like stairs, dropping into a series of sparkling blue pools. Galovac is followed by Okrugljak Lake, where waterfalls take center stage, and then Ciginovac Lake and Prošćansko Lake. If all the uphill walking is just too much, a good idea is to take the shuttle from Entrance 2 to Okrugljak Lake and then walk down.

ACCOMMODATIONS AND FOOD

A good choice for budget travelers, **Camp Korana** (tel. 053/751-888, www.np-plitvicka-jezera.hr, 227Kn d. for bungalow, including breakfast) has spots for tents as well as small private bungalows (actually huts), with communal bathrooms. The main downside to the camp is that it's about six kilometers from the park entrance. Try to grab a spot at the simple **Villa Mukinja** (Mukinje 47, tel. 01/652-1857, www.plitvice-lakes.com, 425Kn d., including breakfast and dinner); it's the place to stay in Plitvice. It's a 10-minute walk to the park, and the price includes a good breakfast and dinner, basic but clean rooms, and wireless Internet access. The small hotel doesn't have air-conditioning, which is normally not a problem since the area cools down considerably at night, but that might be a consideration during a heat wave. The **Plitvice Hotel** (tel. 053/751-100, www.np-plitvicka-jezera.hr, 700Kn d., including breakfast) has an excellent location, just a five-minute walk to the park; its communist-era time warp can be an experience in itself. Don't stay for the rooms or the sub-par food (run elsewhere for dinner) but for the convenience.

There are several restaurants around Entrance 2, though the best is across from Entrance 1, the **Lička kuća** (Entrance 1, tel. 053/751-024, 11 A.M.–11 P.M. daily Apr.–Oct., 85Kn), with lots of regional specialties and traditional hearty food like spicy sausage stew. The place is touristy but it's also very good. Even better is to buy some bread and fresh tomatoes from the supermarket and local **homemade cheese** from the usually present vendors. The rounds are typically sold whole but if you ask for half *(pola)* you'll probably strike a deal. The cheese has a slightly nutty, smoky flavor that hits just the right chord on a crisp night.

GETTING THERE AND AROUND

Plitvice is located about 90 kilometers south of Karlovac and 160 kilometers northeast of Zadar. If you're driving to Plitvice, just follow the signs from the highway or the old coastal road. Arriving by bus is fairly easy—most buses going from Zagreb (2.5 hours) to Split (3.5 hours) or other Dalmatian cities will stop here as they pass by; they'll drop you off if you ask, stopping in front of either of the two entrances. Getting back on a bus can be trickier since there's not much in the way of schedules and they won't stop if they're full. As a result, if you don't have a car, it's probably best to book a Plitvice excursion trip (around 350Kn), advertised widely at travel agencies all along the coast.

Murter and the Kornati Islands

If you've ever wondered what it would be like to live on a deserted island, you can probably find a spot in the Kornati archipelago, a largely wild national park, to answer any lingering questions. The town of Murter is the gateway to the islands and also a spot for accommodation before embarking on your journey.

MURTER

There's nothing much to say about Murter except that it's the handiest point of departure for the Kornati archipelago. Since Kornati doesn't have a lot in the way of accommodation, you're more likely to have luck here, planning your trip from the **Kornati National Park office** (Butina 2, tel. 022/435-740, www.kornati .hr, 8 A.M.–3 P.M. Mon.–Fri. June–Sept., call for hours in winter), which sells permits for diving and fishing as well as maps, or from local agencies where you can rent a boat or book an excursion. The agency **KornatTurist** (Hrvatskih vladara 2, tel. 022/435-854, www .kornatturist.hr) can also help you arrange private rooms and accommodation on the island. **Eseker Tours** (Majnova bb, tel. 022/435-669, www.esekertours.hr) rents all sorts of things like bikes (60Kn a day), scooters (45Kn an hour), boats (from 300Kn/day for a simple fishing boat to 2,900Kn/day for an extra-fancy motorboat), and personal watercraft (75Kn for 10 minutes).

For dining try ◖ **Tic-Tac** (Vlade Hrokešina 5, tel. 022/435-230, noon–11 P.M. daily, closed Oct.–Apr., reservations recommended, 85Kn), on a small street not far from the main square. The decor is simple but the menu is nothing less than gourmet. Dishes like tuna carpaccio, cuttlefish in black sauce with polenta, and gnocchi with fish roe and prawns are surprisingly sophisticated for such an unassuming little place.

Getting to Murter is easiest from Šibenik or Vodice. Buses (7–10 a day) connect to the island, conveniently disembarking at Murter's main square. There are also several ferries connecting from Šibenik and Zadar (check with Jadrolinija, www.jadrolinija.hr, for times and prices).

◖ KORNATI ISLANDS

The Kornati Islands stretch out south of Zadar's coast. The archipelago was declared a national park in 1980 and remains one of the most stunning land- and seascapes in Croatia. Though the islands were once covered with oak trees, those were burned to make way for sheep pastures. Instead of taking away the beauty of the islands, it might have made them prettier. The bright-white slightly scruffy karst rock formations are a beautiful contrast with the clear blue waters, which are home to lots of local fish such as bream, eel, sea scorpion, and cuttlefish. The waters around the islands, particularly the eastern edges if the sea is not too rough, are a wonderful place to snorkel or scuba dive.

There's proof of Illyrian and Roman settlements on the islands, though the islands were mostly uninhabited, owned by Zadar's aristocracy until the 19th century. After that, locals from the islands of Murter used them to raise sheep. Sheep aren't tended on the islands today, but you'll see some wild ancestors (though significantly less since some 1,300 died during the drought of 2007), as well as a number of abandoned stone cottages (mostly dating from the early to mid-20th century), occasionally inhabited in summer by their owners from Murter, who defected long ago. Other than the sheep, there's not a lot of wildlife save for the occasion lizard, snake, or bird.

The islands are immensely popular with yachters, so though there's not a lot of accommodation, there are multiple places to choose from for an amazing seafood lunch or dinner. If you'd like to stay on Kornati, you can rent one of the abandoned stone cottages through an agency in Murter, who will leave you there for several days with a stash of supplies, in case you ever wanted to see for yourself what it's like on one of those reality shows.

Food

Whether it's thanks to the number of yachts and fancy sailboats that cruise around Kornati, occasionally mooring in the coves and harbors, or simply a local sensibility for good food—or some of each—the fact remains that Kornati is a treasure trove of excellent restaurants. There are at least 17 restaurants in the uninhabited island chain, almost one for every nautical mile. Not fancy restaurants, mind you—you're likely to sit on plastic chairs. But you'll have an awesome view and cuisine that would satisfy even the toughest food critic. Best of all, you can tie your boat up right in front, eat to your heart's content, and then keep on sailing. One note: The restaurants don't really have menus (they basically fix whatever they've caught). Figure on paying somewhere between 80Kn and 120Kn for a main dish, much more for lobster.

Katina Island: Mare's (Vela Proversa, tel. 098/273-873, www.restaurant-mare.com, 10 A.M.–midnight daily, no credit cards) has been a fixture on Kornati since the 1950s; the family who owns it has been on the island since the 19th century. The family still tends a grove of olive trees, producing sweet organic oil, and they grow the vegetables served alongside the main dishes. If it's available, try the *Brudet od ljutice i janjetina s krumpirom* (shallot soup and lamb with potatoes).

Strižnja Bay, Kornat Island: The menu at **Darko's** (Uvala Strižnja, no phone, 8 A.M.–midnight daily, closed Oct.–Mar., no credit cards) is quite simple—you'll get whatever it is that Darko caught that day, baked or broiled,

alongside fish soup and octopus salad. In fact, the owner makes it a principle to never serve less than the best quality, so if you want lamb here, you'd better come in the spring when it's at its most tender.

Vrulje, Kornat Island: Ante's (Uvala Vrulje, tel. 022/435-025, 10 A.M.–midnight daily, no credit cards) is a back-to-basics restaurant run by a true fisherman. The octopus *(hobotnica)* à la Veneziana, a thick tomato-based stew with more than a hint of red wine, is highly recommended.

Opat Cove, Kornat Island: A stone house with green shutters nestled on a rocky, barren hill is the location for **Opat** (Uvala Opat, Luke 47, tel. 022/435-061, 9 A.M.–midnight daily), a family restaurant known for its brick oven-baked seafood, like scorpionfish with potatoes. Some of the dishes seem highly creative, like fish soaked in milk before cooking then seasoned with mustard and fennel, or the sea-egg risotto, though the atmosphere is totally laid-back.

Vela Smokvica Island: Located in a deep blue cove, **Piccolo** (Obala Smokvica Vela, tel. 022/435-106, 7 A.M.–midnight daily, closed Oct.–Apr., no credit cards) is one of the islands' most popular restaurants. It's a family-run business: The wife cooks what the husband catches. Dine on lots of fresh grilled seafood, or fish stew seasoned with paprika.

Getting There and Around

There are no ferries to Kornati. If you'd like to visit you have two choices: Travel on your own boat (you'll need an international captain's license) or take an organized tour of the islands. Tours can be booked through the many agencies in Murter, such as **KornatTurist** (Hrvatskih vladara 2, tel. 022/435-854, www.kornatturist.hr), or by signing up with one of the clipboard-wielding young people along Murter's harbor. Most of the excursions include a tour, a swim, and lunch for around 250Kn per person. If you'd like to explore the island with more freedom and you don't have a captain's license, inquire in Murter at the **Kornati National Park office** (Butina 2, tel. 022/435-740, www.kornati.hr, 8 A.M.–3 P.M. Mon.–Fri. June–Sept., call for hours in winter).

Šibenik

One of the most overlooked towns in the country, Šibenik has a wonderful old town, not too packed with tourists even at the height of the season and with some great finds in accommodation. An important location in Venice's fight to hold off the Turks, the town flourished in the Middle Ages, and in modern times as well, when a big aluminum plant kept the locals employed. However, the war in the 1990s changed all of that, with the plant drying up (now a decaying relic along the Magistrala) and the city falling on hard times.

Most Croatians would probably wrinkle their noses if you mention Šibenik, since it's never really been thought of as a tourist destination. There are no resorts to speak of, no real beaches. So why would you go?

The old town center, for one, is totally charming and almost perfectly preserved, yet it doesn't have any of the made-for-tourists feel that many other cities with lots of original buildings have. Though you won't find any mega-resorts, the center is packed with character-filled apartments where you can live like

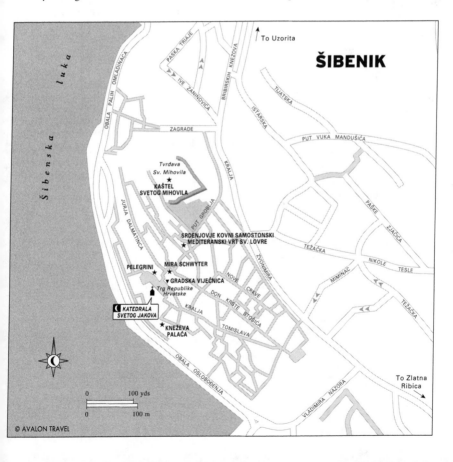

© AVALON TRAVEL

a local during your vacation, heading down to one of the town's best cafés for breakfast and a coffee with the other regulars. And who needs a town beach when you can walk down to the ferry dock and hop a boat for a 20-minute or one-hour ride to an island almost devoid of cars, with wild, natural beaches, way less crowded than any near the resorts.

Basically, if you know how to work Šibenik you'll love it, particularly if you're a contrarian who likes to stay away from tourist-laden spots.

SIGHTS
◖ Katedrala svetog Jakova
St. Jacob's Cathedral

Outshining all of the town's pretty architecture and churches, the 15th-century Katedrala svetog Jakova (Trg Republike Hrvatske, tel. 022/214-899, 9:30 A.M.–8 P.M. Mon.–Sat. and 1–8 P.M. Sun. July–Aug., 9 A.M.–6:30 P.M. Mon.–Sat. and 1–6 P.M. Sun. Sept.–May, free) glows over Šibenik's old-town waterfront. The church was built by local architect Juraj

© SHANN FOUNTAIN ČULO

Katedrala svetog Jakova

JURAJ DALMATINAC, FAMED ARCHITECT

Dalmatia's most famous stone mason and architect, Juraj Dalmatinac, put his stamp on churches and buildings up and down Croatia's coast. He was born in Dalmatia around the year 1400, and studied his trade in Venice, where he had an atelier and contributed to carvings on the Doge's Palace. In Italy he was known as Giorgio da Sebenico (or George of Šibenik); he returned to Dalmatia with his first big commission for the Šibenik cathedral. He settled down here, building a house in town, but due to lack of funding the cathedral project often stalled, and he spent the time working on other projects up and down the coast. His touch is found on several palaces in Split as well as an altar in the Split cathedral, the Minčeta Fortress in Dubrovnik, and a loggia in Ancona, Italy, among others. He died in 1473, the Šibenik cathedral still unfinished. A statue of Dalmatinac by Meštrović stands across from the cathedral, looking over the water.

Dalmatinac, among others, since it took over 100 years to complete. The inside is luxurious, with lots of gilt and a soaring ceiling topped by an octagonal dome. The most interesting features, however, are on the Gothic and Renaissance facade. The building is encircled by 71 stone heads—according to legend the faces of those townspeople who didn't pony up for the construction, making the addition of the dog head all the more humorous. The top of the dome itself is beautiful, with a gilt-topped cupola and four somber statues guarding the town and sea below, but it's hard to catch a glimpse of them unless you climb the steps next to the loggia (above Trg Republike Hrvatske) and look back from the top.

Kneževa palača
Duke's Palace

To the south of St. Jacob's Cathedral down a

small alleyway, you'll come to the 15th-century Kneževa palača. Inside, the **Muzej grada Šibenika** (City Museum, Gradska vrata 3, tel. 022/213-880, www.muzej-sibenik.hr) has exhibits on a variety of historical periods and persons such as architect Juraj Dalmatinac. The museum's permanent collection, however, was in storage at the time of writing, while the space undergoes renovations. It's due to reopen in 2009.

Trg Republike Hrvatske
Republic of Croatia Square

The large square to the eastern side of St. Jacob's Cathedral is the Trg Republike Hrvatske, flanked by the town hall and its 16th-century **loggia**, today home to a café. To the north of the cathedral you'll find the delightful **Bunari Museum** (Palih omladinica 2, tel. 022/485-055, 8 A.M.–midnight daily May–Sept., 15Kn), located in a 15th-century water-storage facility. Today visitors can walk through a display of Šibenik's past; younger guests will get the most out of the multimedia exhibit. There's also a small café with revolving art exhibits.

Srdenjovje kovni samostanski mediteranski vrt Sv. Lovre
Medieval Mediterranean Garden of St. Lawrence's Monastery

Opened in 2007, the Srdenjovje kovni samostanski mediteranski vrt Sv. Lovre (Strme stube 1, tel. 022/212-515, www.spg.hr, 8 A.M.–11 P.M. in summer, call for winter hours, 15Kn) re-creates a medieval garden, heavy on herbs and indigenous plants. A must for gardeners, it's also the perfect place to have a coffee or a drink among the fragrant lavender and thyme on your way to or from the city's old fortress.

Kaštel svetog Mihovila
St. Michael's Fortress

From pretty much anywhere in the old town you can climb up to the northeast to find Kaštel svetog Mihovila (approx. 9 A.M.–dusk, 10Kn), a crumbling Venetian fortress most noteworthy for its peaceful views out over the bay. Considering the medieval town plan, one of the most straightforward ways to get there is to follow the Strme Stube to the Medieval Mediterranean Garden and keep climbing, following the signs marked Kaštel.

Etnoland

Though it bills itself as Croatia's first theme park, Etnoland (Postolarsko 6, Drniš, tel. 099/220-0205, www.dalmati.com, daily mid-Mar.–mid-Nov., call to reserve a tour, from 30Kn without lunch) is actually more of a historical village. In Drniš, a short drive from Šibenik, visitors leave behind modern times in the parking lot as they embark on a journey through traditional Dalmatian life, learning about celebrations, customs, and crafts, and seeing mock-ups of houses from a century ago. Though you can wander through the park alone, most guests book a tour that lasts 3.5 hours and includes a traditional Dalmatian

---

TWO DAYS IN ŠIBENIK

DAY 1

Arriving in the afternoon, visit the **cathedral** and perhaps a museum before making a beeline for the **Medieval Mediterranean Garden of St. Lawrence's Monastery** for a coffee among the fragrant herbs. Head to **Pelegrini** for dinner, preferably in the courtyard, making sure to order a starter of cheese, *pršut*, and local olives along with a glass of wine.

DAY 2

After a night in your old-town apartment, start the morning at Pelegrini again, this time snagging a table around 9 A.M. on the stairs overlooking the cathedral and the water. Linger with coffee until your ferry leaves for **Zlarin** or **Prvić**. Spend the day soaking up the sun and salt-tinged breeze before returning to Šibenik in the evening. Have dinner on the vine-surrounded terrace of **Uzorita** to top off a perfect day.

lunch. The park opened in 2007, and is well thought out if a bit touristy. The Jurlinovi dvori on the hills of nearby Primošten are more authentic in feel.

BEACHES

Šibenik itself has nothing in the way of beaches, but there are plenty of nearby spots for sun and surf, making the city an easy point of departure. A few beaches are accessible by car, though unless you're with the kids there's little to recommend them. The Solaris hotel complex (drive south of town on the Magistrala and look for the signs or take bus #6) has a sandy beach, a new bar area constructed of authentic stone huts, and plenty of video games and bouncy castles for the little ones. However, the best beaches are a short water taxi or ferry ride away. First up and closest to Šibenik's center is the tiny island of **Zlarin,** known for its coral jewelry; it's about 20 minutes across the water to reach Zlarin. There's an excellent *konoba* at the end of the marina's dock and two shops specializing in expensive (or overpriced, given your view) coral jewelry; they fill to capacity as soon as every ferry lands. Otherwise the island is super quiet, with a small pebbly beach to the left of the marina if you're facing the island and concrete bathing areas further on. Keep walking around to find a really wild and beautiful stretch of deserted beach, not so good for swimming given the winds and the rocks, but perfect for wading and lounging in solitude.

Another choice of island excursions is the slightly farther afield **Prvić** (45-minute ferry journey from Šibenik), a car-free island covered with pines and herbs sprouting out of rocky stretches. The best beach on the island is at **Šepurine.** If you'd like to stay overnight unlike the hordes of day-tripping tourists, the simple but lovely **Hotel Maestral** (tel. 022/448-300, www.hotelmaestral.com, 298Kn d., including breakfast), located in an old stone house in Prvić Luka, is a great spot.

Šibenik's harbor is the spot to catch the (usually) twice-daily ferries to the islands. Check with the Jadrolinija office at the harbor for schedules and prices, since even the schedule posted outside the office is not always correct.

ENTERTAINMENT AND EVENTS
Nightlife

Though Šibenik's not known for its partying scene, the club **Inside** (Bioci, no phone,

the island of Zlarin, known for its coral jewelry

7 A.M.–midnight Mon.–Wed., 7 A.M.–4 A.M. Fri.–Sat., 7 A.M.–1 A.M. Sun.) has lots of space for dancing and clubbing in a converted military building on the road to Split. The view's not much to speak of but the crowd is more local than what you'll find at most bars up and down the coast. Back in town try the bars on the seafront in the old town for a post-dinner drink.

Festivals and Events

If you're looking for a bit of Dalmatian flavor in Šibenik, Thursday evenings in July and August bring out local *klapa* groups (contact the tourist office at Obala Dr. Franje Tuđmana 5, tel. 022/214-411, www.sibenik-tourism.hr, for more details). The end of August is heralded by two days of varied musical performances during the **Večeri Dalmatinske Šansone** (Dalmatian Chanson Evenings, www.sansona-sibenik.com), though the city's biggest event is the **Međunarodni Dječji Festival** (International Children's Festival, www.mdf-si .org), held for two weeks from the end of June to the beginning of July every year since 1958. The town hosts dozens of performances, art exhibitions, and hands-on educational exhibits, all revolving around children.

Shoppers will appreciate the weekly **antiques fair** (around the Crkve Svetog Frane, http://sibenik.antikviteti.net, 8 A.M.–3 P.M. Sat.), which operates additional days in the summer.

ACCOMMODATIONS

Šibenik is surrounded by several hotels and apartments that are, for the most part, overpriced and under-performing. If you're on a tight budget, check with the **Cromovens agency** (Trg Republike Hrvatske 4, tel. 022/212-515, www.cromovens.hr), on the Trg Republike Hrvatske near St. Jacob's Cathedral, about private rooms and apartments. Just be sure to check their distance from public transportation, as most are not located within walking distance of the old town (or anything else, for that matter).

The best options are apartments in Šibenik's ancient core. ◖ **Ms. Mira Schwyter** (tel.

091/211-0962, mira.schwyter@si.t-com.hr, www.bedandbreakfastdalmatia.com, 690Kn d., including breakfast at Pelegrini) rents out two beautiful apartments, located in a historic 15th-century building that had a previous life as a café and art gallery. Paintings still hang on the wall available for purchase as pricey souvenirs, alongside photos of famous actors and local musicians, all guests of the former café. Each apartment has antique furniture, stone walls, air-conditioning, and a small kitchen and bath. Second on the list of apartments are the **Konoba** (Andrije Kacića 8, tel. 091/198-8989, www.bbdalmatia.com, 533Kn d.) owned by a lovely Dutch family and decorated simply but tastefully. One of the apartments has a wonderful balcony with a view over the old town's roof tops, though it does lack air-conditioning.

FOOD

In the heart of the old town try **Konoba Dalmatino** (Fra Nikole Ružića 1, tel. 091/542-4808, generally open 11 A.M.–10 P.M. daily in summer, call for winter hours, 75Kn), nestled in a narrow alleyway with a handful of outdoor tables serving good cheese, salads, and fish dishes alongside the potable house wine—not the finest but homemade by the restaurant's owner, who often doubles as a waiter. **Gradska Vijećnica** (Trg Republike Hrvatske 3, tel. 022/213-605, 9 A.M.–midnight daily, 50Kn) is located on the main square in the old Venetian town hall. It's usually not all that busy, but don't let that scare you away. The food is decent, the prices good, and the location excellent. However, the best table in town has to be at ◖ **Pelegrini** (Jurja Dalmatinca 1, tel. 022/213-701, www.pelegrini.hr, 8 A.M.–midnight daily, 90Kn), set just across from the gorgeous St. Jacob's Cathedral. In good weather you can dine at the few outdoor tables overlooking the water (ideal for a superb breakfast) or in the open-air courtyard just beyond the restaurant (open only at night in season). In the winter dine inside the restaurant's pretty stone-clad space. Anytime of year, the excellent menu, from fried eggs and bacon in the morning to afternoon snacks of olive, cheese, and salted anchovies to mains of roast, risotto, and seafood ravioli, never fails to satisfy.

A 20-minute walk northeast (or take bus #3) from the old town in the suburb of Šubičevac, **Uzorita** (Bana Jelačića 58, tel. 022/213-660, 11 A.M.–1 A.M. daily, 90Kn) has been serving diners since 1898. There's a wonderful terrace surrounded by vines and stone buildings. Fish is the specialty of the house, particularly the mussels.

If you have a car or you're willing to foot the bill for a water taxi (actually a nice way to spend a few minutes), **Zlatna Ribica** (Krapanjskih Spužvara 46, tel. 022/350-695, www.zlatna-ribica.hr, 11 A.M.–11 P.M. daily, 100Kn) in the seaside village of Brodarica, a few kilometers south of Šibenik on the Magistrala (drive, hop a water taxi, or take bus #7), is considered one of the area's finest. The decor is quite average but the fish is always fresh and the view to the tiny island of Krapanj is very nice. The restaurant also rents rooms.

INFORMATION AND SERVICES

The **Šibenik tourist office** (Obala Dr. Franje Tuđmana 5, tel. 022/214-411, www .sibenik-tourism.hr) has some information on the area, though the travel agencies on the Trg Republike Hrvatske, **Atlas** (tel. 022/330-232) and **Cromovens** (tel. 022/212-515, www.cromovens.hr), may be more useful at hooking you up with private rooms and excursions in the region. If you order a drink or snack at **Cafe Castello** (Božidara Petranovića 8, tel. 022/226-385, www.castello.hr), you can at least check your email in the 15 minutes of free Internet access that you get with any purchase.

GETTING THERE AND AROUND

Šibenik's bus station (Draga 14, tel. 060/368-368) is close to the ferry terminal and a short five-minute walk south from the old town. The bus heads frequently to Split (close to two dozen daily, 2 hours, 60Kn), Zadar (close to four dozen a day, 1.5 hours), Dubrovnik (several daily in summer, 6 hours), Rijeka (around a dozen a day in summer, 6 hours), and Zagreb (over a dozen daily in summer, 6.5 hours, 235Kn). Tickets on city buses cost around 10Kn. Bus schedules can be found online at www.atpsi.hr.

Šibenik also has a train station with a couple of daily connections to Zagreb (6.5 hours, 150Kn) and Split (2 hours, 43Kn).

Ferries in town only travel to nearby islands and have no major connections to places like Split.

By car, you can connect with Split (south) or Zadar (north) by simply following the Magistrala or getting back on the highway (a little quicker but less scenic).

AROUND ŠIBENIK
◀ Krka National Park

The Krka National Park (80Kn June–Sept., 65Kn Mar.–May and Oct., 25Kn Jan.–Feb. and Nov.–Dec.) follows the rushing Krka River between Knin and Skradin, the latter of which is located only a 15-minute drive northeast from Šibenik. The entrance at the village of Skradin is where you can pick up boat tours (Mar.–Nov., 70Kn) run by the national park, while at the Lozovac entrance a shuttle bus goes down to the river. Local buses connect Šibenik with Skradin (around 8 connections on weekends, 2 or 3 on weekends, 30 minutes) and the excursion is an easy day trip from Šibenik. Keep in mind that if you want to go further up the river from Visovac to the Krka monastery (additional 70Kn Mar.–Nov.)as described here, you should depart early in the morning—the tour takes around four hours round-trip and schedules make it into a whole-day affair. If you'd like to do the longer tour, it's a good idea to stop by the **Krka National Park office** in Šibenik (Trg Ivana Pavla II 5, tel. 022/217-720, www.npkrka.hr) for more information, or book a package tour through one of the travel agencies in Šibenik.

Boat tours departing from Skradin first stop in the village of Skradinski Buk, where a series of small waterfalls rush over the craggy outcroppings of limestone. One of

ACQUIRING A TASTE FOR *JANJETINA*

Janjetina, or lamb, is a sacred food to many Croatians, particularly those along the coast. Consumed on special occasions and de rigueur at Easter, the best lamb is found in ramshackle roadside establishments on the way to the beach.

Janjetina can be a bit of an acquired taste. In my case, it just seemed sort of, well, fatty, I guess, and not very flavorful. When they served it I felt like I was in a medieval court, with the pieces of meat seemingly hacked off at random and piled on a platter and people digging in without forks or knives.

Word got around about me not being a fan of lamb and suddenly friends and family had made it their mission to introduce me to this food of foods. We were invited to every *roštilj* (cookout) for miles around, with a plate of lamb coming to me first, to see if this would be the one that would succeed in the collective mission to convert me.

Approximately 14 years after I'd first tried *janjetina,* we were spending the week in Šibenik, and after having consumed fish for five days straight my husband mentioned to our friend Mickey that he'd like some *janjetina.* And between Šibenik and Split there is only one real place to go for *janjetina:* Torcida.

Torcida (Donje Polje 42, tel. 022/565-748, www.restoran-torcida.hr, 8 A.M.–11 P.M. daily, 80Kn) is also the name of Split's soccer fan club, so chances were pretty good it would be excellent since Dalmatians do not take anything relating to their soccer lightly.

Torcida is in the middle of nowhere, way up the hill from the coast. Once you think you have certainly passed it and are hopelessly lost, keep going until you see about four dozen cars parked in the arid landscape. Torcida tries to be more than a cinder-block establishment with granite-tile floors. But sophisticated it is not.

Out back is a veritable factory of lamb-on-a-spit, with a dozen spits spinning a dozen lambs.

Inside, the tables are packed with families, young and old, most wearing some Italian designer or other, pulling meat off the bones with their teeth, wiping their hands every once in a while on a napkin, taking toothpicks from the handy container in the middle of the table.

The waitress came out to take our order, no menu or pad and pen in sight – because what else would we order anyway? Our table ordered a bottle of white wine, a bottle of mineral water (you mix the two together to make *gemišt*), and lamb.

It was summer and the restaurant was hot. A sign on the front door boasts that it is *klimatazirano* (air-conditioned), but with 500 bodies squished table to table inside, the air-conditioning unit is on the losing end. We refreshed with a couple of glasses of *gemišt* and the waitress came with a basket of bread, a plate of tomatoes and spring onions, and a platter of lamb, still warm from the fire.

Everyone started with forks and knives, but five bites in we were all using fingers to pull and turn and get the sweet meat into our mouths any way possible.

"This is not lamb," I said.

"Ah, but it is," Mickey smiled. "The best lambs are from Dalmatia. And you should see the ones from the islands!"

In Dalmatia, and on islands like Pag, the sheep and lambs feed on little aromatic herbs that grow between the rocks.

"It's like marinating them from birth," Mickey explained.

Whatever it is, that was all I needed to convert. Torcida was what I was looking for. Like my favorite barbecue restaurants back home, it has no pretensions. The decor is nothing special – except, perhaps, for the large framed painting of the Mona Lisa smoking a joint. I faded into a food-induced coma. And I wondered: Just what herbs are those lambs feeding on after all?

the falls spills into a nice pool where you can swim, though you certainly won't be the only one taking a dip. Here you'll also find some peaceful hiking trails through the forests and over the river. From here you can catch the bus to Lozovac or continue further upriver on a boat, visiting the fairy tale–like Franciscan monastery on the tiny island of Visovac, Roški slap, another set of waterfalls, and finally the Krka monastery, a Byzantine-style Serbian Orthodox church and monastery filled with icons and art dating as far back as the 14th century.

You can arrange for private accommodation through Skradin's **tourist office** (Obala bana Šubića 1, tel. 022/771-306, www.skradin .hr) or you can upgrade and stay at the **Hotel Skradinski Buk** (Burinovac bb, tel. 022/771-771, www.skradinskibuk.hr, 540Kn d., including breakfast), where the rooms are on the bland side, but the value for money is better than most hotels in the area. There are several good restaurants around the village of Skradinski Buk. Try the **Konoba Bonaca** (Rokovača 5, tel. 022/771-444, noon–3 P.M. and 5 P.M.–midnight daily, closed Oct.–Apr., 70Kn) or **(** **Zlatne Školjke** (Grgura Ninskog 9, tel. 022/771-022, www.zlatne-skoljke.com, noon–11 P.M. daily, closed mid-Jan.–mid-Feb., 90Kn) for good seafood and local wines.

Krapanj Island

If you're a good swimmer, you could technically swim from the coast in Brodarica (a few kilometers south of Šibenik, take bus #7 or hop a water taxi) and reach the shores of tiny Krapanj Island, just several hundred meters offshore. Its claim to fame is as the smallest inhabited island in Croatia, but it's really known for its sponge diving, the trade that kept it alive for decades. Today sponge diving has largely died out, but the 15th-century **Franjevački samostan** (Franciscan monastery) has a simple **museum** (9 A.M.–noon and 5–7 P.M. Mon.–Sat. June–Sept., 15Kn) following the history of sponge divers on the island. It gets packed in July and August with day-trippers (take a taxi boat from Šibenik or Brodarica), but if you're lucky enough to visit in the off-season it's a sleepy island with its own personality.

Southeast of Šibenik

Thirteen kilometers southeast of Šibenik (take the Magistrala toward Split though you'll soon turn off on the road for Vrpolje) is legendary restaurant **(** **Torcida** (Donje Polje 42, tel. 022/565-748, www.restoran-torcida.hr, 8 A.M.–11 P.M. daily, 80Kn), famous for its *janjetina*, or spit-roasted lamb. On weekends you'll find it hard to get a table here; it's enormously popular with the local population. It's definitely worth the detour for a taste of true Dalmatia.

Primošten

Once a hopping party town before the Croatian in-crowd moved to Hvar, Primošten has some good restaurants and bars they left behind. The old town is precious, a little island connected by a thin stretch of land to the mainland, and worth a quick walk around before heading out of the now mostly lower-end tourist trade.

SIGHTS

Though there's nothing specific to see in Primošten proper, it's nice to walk around the cobblestone-paved old town before heading up into the hills to the wonderful **Jurlinovi dvori complex** (Draga bb, tel. 022/574-106, info@ jurlinovidvori.org, www.jurlinovidvori.org, call to reserve a visit, if you can't get anyone who speaks English have a local tourist office or your hotel call for you) in the preserved village of Draga. Stone houses are clustered around a central courtyard, and each small home is part of the museum, showcasing a traditional Dalmatian kitchen, living room, cellar, sleeping quarters, and a domestic chapel. One home also holds a collection of sacral objects.

Nearby is a 13th-century Romanesque chapel, the church of St. George. The whole place has a laid-back air, preserving history and showing it off to tourists without being gimmicky. It's also one of the few places in Dalmatia where you can get a look at the history and culture of the people.

WINERIES

Wine lovers and foodies will find a couple of gems in town. The local Babić wine has a specific salty taste, certainly worth a try, and lobster prepared in the local style is a must-try at one of the better restaurants in town. Check with the tourist office for excursions and tours of the local wine trails, through the rocky villages of Burnji in the hills above Primošten.

BEACHES

There's a big beach fronting the cafés and tacky souvenir shops along the street connecting the parking lot and the old town. It's usually quite crowded, though the convenience to a coffee is not bad. Better beaches can be found by walking along the promenade to the north of town.

ACCOMMODATIONS AND FOOD

Book private rooms from **Agency Nik** (Trg Stjepana Radića 1, tel. 022/571-200, www .nik.hr). Another option is the Tito-era package hotel **Zora** (Raduča bb, tel. 022/581-022, www.azaleahotels.com, 1,060Kn d., including breakfast), with an ugly unpromising exterior

but clean, basic rooms a 10-minute scenic walk to the old town. Guests rave about the idyllic location, which must make up for the lack of character and updates to the property. However, the price in-season makes private accommodation a better bet.

An absolute must-eat is the charming step-back-in-time **(Jurlinovi dvori** (Draga bb, tel. 022/574-106, info@jurlinovidvori.org, www .jurlinovidvori.org, call to arrange a meal, if you can't get anyone who speaks English have a local tourist office or your hotel call for you), with excellent local cuisine, warm hospitality, and a one-of-a-kind experience in the hills above Primošten. Back in town you'll find lots of *konoba*-style restaurants and pizzerias. For a really great view and filling food, try **Restoran Babilon** (Težačka 15, tel. 022/570-769, noon–2 P.M. and 6–8 P.M., closed Oct.–Apr., 85Kn) and its charming open-air dining.

GETTING THERE AND AROUND

Take buses #14, #15, or #16 from Šibenik during weekdays (on weekends take the #16, at least once daily, 30 minutes) to get to Primošten. If you're driving, it's about 20 kilometers south of Šibenik. You'll exit right off the Magistrala (well, it's more of a turn than an exit). Once you're in town there are at least two small lots where you can pay to park (around 10Kn an hour in summer). From the lot, walk south along the waterfront to reach the old town area.

Trogir

A postcard-perfect prosperous fishing village with a lively Riva for strolling after dark, Trogir also has some charming architecture. Beaches are just across the bridge on the island of Čiovo, though the best ones are found by boat, on some of the almost uninhabited islands offshore. Trogir fills up in the height of summer, making it hard to walk, let alone enjoy the full beauty of the place. Its proximity to Split and Split's airport however, make it a worthwhile stopping-off point if you're in transit.

SIGHTS
Kopnena vrata
Land Gate

When you enter Trogir, passing the little market on the right and crossing the small bridge, you'll see the big 17th-century Kopnena vrata. The guy on the top is the town's Sveti Ivan (St. John), a local 12th-century bishop locals claim was blessed with miracle-working

powers. Following the road leading through the gate, you'll arrive at the **Gradski muzej** (Town Museum, Gradska vrata 4, tel. 021/881-406, Mon.–Sat. 9 A.M.–1 P.M. and 5–10 P.M. July–Aug., 9 A.M.–noon and 5–8 P.M. June–Sept., 9 A.M.–2 P.M. Oct.–May, 10Kn). Inside is a small display of photographs, documents, local costumes, and a few pieces of artwork and archaeology. It's only a small view of Trogir's past, though the courtyard is charming and the museum sometimes has *klapa* concerts during the summer, making it a worthwhile stop.

Katedrala svetog Lovrijenca
St. Lawrence's Cathedral

On Trg Ivana Pavla II, arguably Trogir's nicest square, are the must-see early 13th-century (though it wasn't completely finished until the 15th century) Katedrala svetog Lovrijenca (tel. 021/881-426, 9 A.M.–7 P.M. Mon.–Sat. and mass on Sun., 9 A.M.–noon in winter, hours are

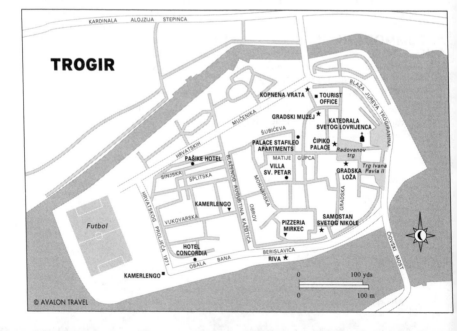

not always observed, free) and its much later addition, the Venetian bell tower seen peeking above Trogir's red tiled roofs. If the tower's open you can climb the almost 50 meters to the top for about 10Kn and get some nice views of Trogir. The most stunning feature of the church is the western portal, where wonderful reliefs by the 13th-century stone carver Radovan compete for attention in a busy amalgam of reality and fantasy. The interior of the church depicts scenes from the life of Sveti Ivan of Trogir. Opening off the north of the interior, the **Kapela svetog Ivana Trogirskog** (St. John of Trogir's Chapel) has an impressive ceiling populated by angels carved by apprentices of the renowned Dalmatinac. Beyond the chapel you'll find a small *riznica* (treasury, 9 A.M.–7 P.M. Mon.–Sat., 10Kn) with a smattering of gilt and carvings.

Čipiko Palace

Just across from the cathedral on Trg Ivana Pavla II is the Čipiko Palace, a decaying Venetian-style home that's pretty to admire from the outside, but with nothing to see on the inside. It's significant to the city since it was home of the Čipiko family, a family of nobles important to Trogir in the Renaissance. The family dabbled in seafaring military life and literary pursuits, as well as funding some of the cathedral's stash of art and sculpture.

Gradska loža
Town Loggia

You'll also find the Gradska loža on the Trg Ivana Pavla II. Though the loggia was restored in the late 1800s, many of its ornate reliefs date back to the Middle Ages. The one that doesn't was actually carved by Meštrović, of the Bishop Petar Berislavić, on the loggia's south wall. Next door in a former bishop's palace is the **Pinakoteka** (tel. 021/881-426, 9 A.M.–8 P.M. Mon.–Sat. and 3–7 P.M. Sun. June–Sept., call for winter hours, 20Kn), which houses an attractive collection of Trogir's sacral art, including a 15th-century altarpiece by local painter Blaž Jurjev of the Madonna and Child with the saints.

Čiovo Island, with beaches just across the bridge from Trogir's old town

FINDING YOUR OWN PRIVATE PARADISE

If you really want to find a stretch of deserted beach, it's not that hard to do in Croatia, with hundreds of uninhabited islands just off the coast. The first thing to do is to ask the locals, though keep in mind that another person's idea of paradise may be very different from your own. If you're used to navigating a boat, rent one from the marina and set out to find your own spot, either mooring offshore or parking one of those inflatable types right on the beach. Not confident with taking to the high seas? Rent a water taxi with a captain who can take you there, perhaps even negotiating a fish picnic in the deal. Of course, you'll see lots of advertisements for these fish picnics, but unless you want to share them with 20 other hungry tourists, it's better to hire your own private boat. If all else fails, walk. Usually just beyond the beach where everyone is packed in is a beach where everyone isn't. It's probably harder to get to, just short of requiring rock-climbing skills (at least remember to wear a pair of thick-soled shoes), but you're usually rewarded for your efforts.

Because a private beach usually means a remote one, make sure you don't go so far that you get lost, and bring plenty of supplies, because if you're hungry or thirsty, even paradise doesn't seem so great.

© SHANN FOUNTAIN ĆULO

Finding a private beach is not that hard to do in Croatia.

Samostan svetog Nikole
Convent of St. Nicholas

South of Trg Ivana Pavla II, the Samostan svetog Nikole (tel. 021/881-631, 10 A.M.–noon and 4–6:30 P.M. in summer, contact tourist office for out-of-season hours, 15Kn) is worth the trip for its Greek relief of Kairos from the 3rd century and for its treasure-chest haul of icons and art from the 13th to 17th centuries. Most touching are the hope chests carried by young girls entering the convent.

Riva

Following along the water is the wide café-and-yacht-lined Riva, which fills with tourists and locals on summer evenings. At the far end you'll see the 15th-century **Kamerlengo** (9 A.M.–7 P.M. daily in summer, 10Kn), a medieval fortress that has nice views from the top and hosts open-air movies and concerts during the hottest months.

BEACHES

The best beaches directly around Trogir are on **Čiovo Island,** just across the bridge from the old town. Turning to the left after the bridge you'll see a few convenient, but usually crowded, beaches. The best are found by driving until the road turns to gravel and continuing further (all the way until the old quarry if you like) and finding a stretch of beach backed by a few trees for some quiet lounging. If you see a couple of kids charging an entrance fee, feel free to hand them a few kuna. If you don't have a car, hire a boat and captain for the day (try friendly local Mario Oštrić at tel. 095/806-0382 or 091/530-1802) to take you on a private fish picnic to one of the uninhabited, or barely inhabited, islands offshore. Looking for something a bit longer or luxurious? Mario's dad is the cook on the **Gullet Andi** (tel. 091/188-7136, ante.slamic@st.t-com.hr, www.gulets-andi.com, contact for prices and schedules), a beautiful wooden sailboat shuttling passengers on seven-day cruises around the Dalmatian islands, departing from Trogir.

ENTERTAINMENT AND EVENTS

Though Trogir's not really a party town, there's a decent selection of spots to drink and dance. Quieter sorts should try the bars in **Radovanov trg**, the square behind the cathedral. Those looking for something louder should hit the cafés along the Riva, often hosting live bands in the summer, or the local favorite **Martinino** (Hrvatskih Mučenika 2, no phone, 8 A.M.–1 A.M. daily) near the Land Gate.

In summer the city of Trogir plays host to a number of music groups, from pop to classical to folk, during its **Trogirsko kulturno ljeto** (Trogir Cultural Summer, July–Aug.). Check with the tourist office to see what's playing.

ACCOMMODATIONS

If you plan on roughing it, **Camp Seget** (Hrvatskih žrtava 121, tel. 021/880-394, www.kamp-seget.hr, 120Kn) is located two kilometers north from Trogir. The camp has space for tents and RVs plus a handful of hostel-type rooms. For private rooms, try **Travel Agency Portal** (Obala bana Berislavića 3, tel. 021/885-016, www.portal-trogir.com), with a decent selection of old town accommodation as well as beachfront rooms, apartments, and villas. It's advisable to book ahead for the best spots.

The **Palace Domus Maritima** (Put Cumbrijana 10, tel. 091/513-7802, www.domus-maritima.com, 604Kn d.) is located in a 400-year-old stone building just across the bridge from the old town on the island of Čiovo,

making it about a three-minute walk into town. The hotel has a rough-around-the-edges elegance. The comfortably furnished rooms have exposed stone walls and slightly garish (and often nude) original art serving as decor. There is a decent restaurant on the premises and you can arrange for art workshops in advance. The best thing about the **Hotel Concordia** (Obala Bana Berislavića 22, tel. 021/885-400, www.concordia-hotel.net, 680Kn d., including breakfast) is its location, right on the harborfront promenade of old Trogir. The position on the Riva, which pulses with thousands of tourists on summer nights, makes it convenient but certainly not the quietest location in town. The furnishings in the small rooms are very plain, though their 1960s vibe almost makes them swank, and the hotel can help arrange free parking nearby.

The ◖ **Pašike Hotel** (Sinjska bb, tel. 021/885-185, www.hotelpasike.com, 800Kn d., including breakfast) is located down a narrow little street in Trogir's medieval core, furnished with wonderful antiques in a bit of an organic fashion.

The **Palace Stafileo apartments** (Budislaviceva 6, tel. 091/731-7607, www.trogironline.com/stafileo, 426Kn d.) offers excellent value for money. The rooms in the 15th-century center-of-town palace don't have a lot of character, but they have satellite television, air-conditioning, and small kitchens.

◖ **Villa Sv. Petar** (Ivana Duknovica 14, tel. 021/884-359, www.villa-svpetar.com, 820Kn d.) is another convenient option set in a stone building in the heart of the old town. The furnishings are fairly simple but the service is great. Ask for a room with exposed stone walls for the most authentic charm.

FOOD

For a casual meal, try **Pizzeria Mirkec** (Budislaviceva 15, tel. 021/883-042, open 11 A.M.–midnight daily in summer, call for off-season hours, 60Kn) for good pizzas and pasta dishes, served outside on the bustling Riva-front (with a great show of people-watching during dinner) in the summer or inside the tiny upstairs dining room in winter. **Škrapa** (Hrvatskih Mučenika 9, tel. 021/885-313, noon–11 P.M. daily in summer, noon–11 P.M. Mon.–Sat. in winter, 65Kn) has a good selection of simple local dishes at friendly prices. You can dine indoors or out at the cozy little *konoba*. **Kamerlengo** (Vukovarska 2, tel. 021/884-772, www.kamerlengo.hr, 9 A.M.–midnight daily, 90Kn) is a reliable choice for grilled fish in the center of the old town, though the most interesting place to eat in town is probably **Čelica** (otok Čiovo-Lučica, tel. 021/882-3440, 11 A.M.–midnight daily in summer, 4–11 P.M. daily in winter, no credit cards, 85Kn), located on a defunct wooden car ferry just across the little bridge on the island of Čiovo. It's not overpriced and the dishes, mostly seafood, are good quality.

INFORMATION AND SERVICES

Trogir's **tourist office** (Ivana Pavla II broj 1, tel. 021/881-412, 8 A.M.–9 P.M. daily June–Sept., 8 A.M.–2 P.M. Mon.–Fri. Oct.–May) can provide maps, brochures, and information on private accommodation. The bus station has a left-luggage office (9 A.M.–10 P.M. daily, 15Kn a day).

GETTING THERE AND AROUND

It's easy to get to Trogir from Split's airport. Take bus #37, which runs every 20 minutes and takes about 20 minutes. Trogir's small bus station (tel. 021/881-405), across from the market, has multiple connections with Split daily (buses leave every 20 minutes, about 1.5 hours due to all the stops). There's also a ferry for Split, which takes an hour and runs four times a day in the summer. Check with the tourist office for more information on schedules. It's easy to walk around Trogir's main town and possible but a bit risky (due to traffic) to stroll to some of the first beaches on Čiovo Island. To get to the best beaches you'll need to have a car or hire a boat.

AROUND TROGIR
Kaštela

Hugging the shoreline between Trogir and Split is a series of villages referred to as Kaštela. There's some pretty architecture here as each village is formed around a castle built centuries ago to protect crops and property. Today the villages are decidedly more local than most towns on the Dalmatian coast, even in the height of summer. The prettiest village is **Kaštel Gomilica,** though **Kaštel Kambelovac** has a good, reasonable restaurant in the **Baletna Škola** (Ante Starčevića, tel. 021/220-208, 8 A.M.–midnight daily, 80Kn), located in a former ballet school that looks more like a rustic fisherman's house. The villages are great for walking from bar to bar in the evenings along the waterfront promenade starting in **Kaštel Štafilić** and ending in **Kaštel Stari.** Bus #37 to Split makes stops at each village.

Drvenik Mali and Drvenik Veli

A daily morning ferry connects Trogir with Drvenik Veli and Drvenik Mali Islands (connections tend to be in the early morning and then evening since the ferry services people who live on the islands but work in Trogir). The best beach is on Drvenik Veli at **Krknjaši Bay,** a stretch of pebbly beach and clear water backed by a simple seafood restaurant of outstandingly high quality, **Krknjaši** (Uvala Krknjaši, tel. 021/893-073, 11 A.M.–11 P.M. in summer, 70Kn), open only in the summer. The family's fish soup is highly recommended.

The beach is about a 45-minute walk from the ferry stop, though, so give yourself time to make the boat's early-evening departure, around 6 P.M. Drvenik Veli is also a nice place to hike through the rural roads and olive trees. Drvenik Mali is the smaller and wilder of the two islands, with some excellent beaches (the sandy one at **Vela Rina** is likely the best), though you won't find any restaurants or cafés nor much in the way of shade, so pack a picnic and a small umbrella.

SOUTHERN DALMATIA

As you get deeper into Croatia's Dalmatian coast you realize you're going somewhere quite singular—it's here that you'll find some of the most stunning coastline and picturesque islands of the Adriatic. Cities like Hvar have graced the pages of dozens of magazines and newspaper articles while islands like the beautiful Mljet are significantly less hyped. Split has plenty of historic interest and also serves as a port gateway to most of Croatia's islands. The Makarska Riviera is usually packed with European tourists at its large package hotels, Korčula is a must-see for fans of Dubrovnik, and islands like Vis are perfect for getting away from it all.

The Adriatic's clear blue waters are the main draw here, whether your preferences tend toward island hopping, sunbathing, diving, or dining in restaurants with views worth traveling halfway around the world for. However, all the region's advantages have translated into loads of travelers. There are still out-of-the-way spots to get away from all the tourists, particularly the islands of Mljet, Lastovo, and Vis—but it's worth braving the crowds to get a look at the birthplace of Marco Polo, the pirate stronghold of Omiš, or a riverside meal on the Cetina Gorge, or making a compromise, like the hidden-away-but-popular Senko's, a restaurant located in a tiny hamlet on the shore of the island of Vis.

PLANNING YOUR TIME

To get a really thorough overview of Southern Dalmatia, with time to do some prerequisite lounging on the beach and lingering over a

SOUTHERN DALMATIA

HIGHLIGHTS

◖ Diocletian's Palace: The palace is impressive not only for its Roman relics, immense size, and art treasures, but also for the fact that it isn't some relic with a rope around it, but a vital part of Split's center. Small apartments, restaurants, bars, shops, and even a couple of hotels occupy the space once held by the despot ruler (page 204).

◖ Galerija Ivana Meštrovića: The family home of Croatia's most famous artist not only houses hundreds of his impressive sculptures and drawings, but the jaunt out to its location on the pine-covered Marjan Peninsula is a great way to spend a couple of hours during a visit to Split (page 206).

◖ Hvar: Hvar's been rated, overrated, and underrated, but what remains is an island with a celebrity-packed nightlife, top-end hotels and restaurants, and a few things you might not have

expected. From wineries to small villages and a restaurant without electricity, there's plenty besides the sleek yachting life (page 218).

◖ Vis: A former military base opened to the public in 1989, the tourism trade didn't really even start on Vis until after 2000. It's still the destination for those that want to break from the crowds and step back in time (page 224).

◖ Korčula: Brimming with culture within the walls of Korčula Town (often called a mini-Dubrovnik), the island is also known for its sandy beaches near the village of Lumbarda (page 228).

◖ Mljet: Mljet is a small paradise with two saltwater lakes at its center, one topped with a 12th-century monastery. The island's relative lack of development makes it a great spot for biking (page 232).

LOOK FOR ◖ TO FIND RECOMMENDED SIGHTS, ACTIVITIES, DINING, AND LODGING.

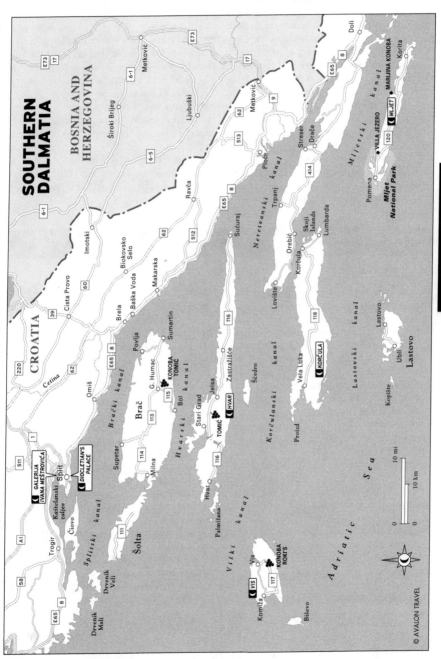

SOUTHERN DALMATIA

SOUTHERN DALMATIA

BOSNIA AND HERZEGOVINA

CROATIA

Doli

Korita

MLJET

MARIJINA KONOBA

120 VILLA JEZERO

Mljet National Park

Pomena

Mljetski kanal

Streser

Drače

Plode

Trpanj

Neretvanski kanal

Lumbarda

Skoji Islands

Orebić

Korčula

Lovište

KORČULA

Vela Luka

Korčulanski kanal

Proizd

Šćedro

Lastovski kanal

Lastovo

Ubli

Lastovo

Kopište

Metković

Ploče

Šućuraj

Zastražišće

Jelsa

HVAR

TOMIĆ

KONOBA TOMIĆ

G. Humac

Bol

Hvarski kanal

Stari Grad

Sumartin

Povlja

Brač

Supetar

Milna

Brački kanal

Omiš

Cetina

Split

DIOCLETIAN'S PALACE

GALERIJA IVANA MEŠTROVIĆA

Kaštelanski zaljev

Čiovo

Trogir

Drvenik Veli

Drvenik Mali

Splitski kanal

Šolta

Palmižana

Hvar

Viški kanal

Vis

VIS

KONOBA ROKI'S

Komiža

Biševo

Adriatic Sea

Metković

Ljubuški

Široki Brijeg

Imotski

Cista Provo

Ravča

Biokovsko Selo

Makarska

Baška Voda

Brela

Široki

E73   17

6-1

6-5

220

39

62

60

1

511

A1

58

E65   8

E73

17

513

62

9

8

E65

8

414

116

118

120

8

512

116

111

114

113

115

117

0   10 mi

0   10 km

N

© AVALON TRAVEL

long lunch, you'll need about two weeks. Start your tour in Split, convenient because it's pretty much the departure point for all the islands. Then start an island-hopping tour that fits in as much as you feel comfortable with—doing an island every 48 hours should allow you to visit several while still having time for lounging by the sea. That said, you can take more time in any one place, discovering its nooks and crannies even further until you know exactly which cove is your favorite.

Whatever you choose keep in mind that Split is a must-see (particularly given its convenience) and the other islands should be chosen based on your interests and tastes and not how many times you've read about it in a magazine. All of the islands are stunning and each has its own personality. While it is true you won't find a manicure and a massage or high-thread-count sheets on all of them (if that's your style head straight to Hvar), you will find excellent restaurants, friendly people, and film-worthy sunset views in each and every port.

And don't forget how close you are to Bosnia-Herzegovina when in Southern Dalmatia—it's a great chance to take a day (or even longer) to see another country.

Split

Croatia's second-largest city, home to close to 250,000 people, Split is big and busy, traffic-clogged and even a bit seedy in certain sections. But it's also full of loud and fun people, tons of historic monuments and buildings—a once grand palace at times refined, at times decrepit, surrounded by a network of concrete multistory apartment buildings; half-completed buildings beside garish villas; and a large port ferrying travelers out to the islands.

Whatever your impressions, Split is a don't-miss on your itinerary and one of the most authentic cities on the Dalmatian coast, even in the height of summer. It's a city where the locals still outweigh the tourists and you'll never feel catered to. If you're in town in winter, Split's carnival is a really good one, though not the largest in Croatia. And on May 7 the city celebrates Sveti Duje, the town's patron saint; the whole town takes to the streets to preen and parade. Catch this organic Split while you still can. The city is making big steps to clean up its bustling side—with plans for moving the bus and train stations and replacing worn benches and paving—though it's hard to believe a lot of the city's character won't be lost in the process.

HISTORY

The general consensus has been that Split sprang up around Diocletian's Palace (neighboring Salona was a giant city for its day), built between 295 and 305. But archaeological finds are telling a different story—it seems Romans had settled the area at least as far back as the 2nd century.

After Diocletian died, the palace had various owners, until it became a refuge for citizens of Salona fleeing the Slavs in the 7th century. They moved in and over a thousand years later, people are still living among the palace walls, hanging their laundry out of the windows.

Like most of Dalmatia, Split was ruled by the Venetians from the 15th century, suffered repeated attacks from the Ottoman Empire, and then moved under Austrian rule, when the city became a more important port and factory (mainly shipbuilding) base. The city has really grown due to an influx of immigrants (first from the hills in the hinterland who came to escape extreme poverty after World War II) and then from refugees fleeing neighboring Bosnia-Herzegovina, which received much of the brunt of the Homeland War.

Split is also the home of many of Croatia's biggest stars and athletes—from Wimbledon

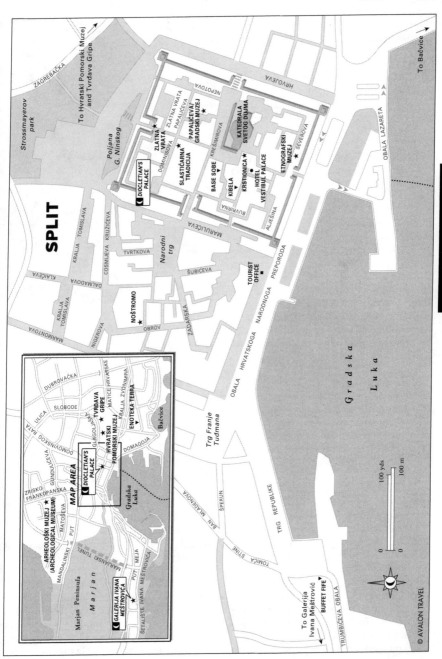

SPLIT

SOUTHERN DALMATIA

© AVALON TRAVEL

winner Ivanisević to soccer players to many of Croatia's biggest singers and musicians.

SIGHTS
◖ Diocletian's Palace

By far the most important of Split's buildings and relics, Diocletian's Palace is almost more of a quarter or a walled city within a city than an actual structure. Declared a UNESCO World Heritage site back in 1979, the late Roman palace itself was reconstructed and built upon many times, so much so that much of the original building remains. The palace is very much in daily use—at least two hotels and dozens of apartments are located within its walls. It was once considered one of the city's worst places to live, but some of the apartments are finding new life with foreigners who pay thousands per square meter to live in a piece of history or as shopfronts catering to the ever-increasing tourist trade. Start your tour at the **Riva** (its lesser-known official name is the Obala hrvatskog naradnog preporoda), Split's center of social activity. From here, you'll pass through the **Porta Aenea** (Brass Gate), which once served as the emperor's access to the sea. To the left of the gate are the *podrumi* (cellars, 8 A.M.–8 P.M. daily in summer, 8 A.M.–noon and 4–7 P.M. in winter, 10Kn) of the palace. These underground chambers serve as a map for reconstructing what the palace was once like above (as the basement exactly mirrored the ground floor), prior to all the renovations. These substructures served for housing people during the Middle Ages, but much older relics have been found, such as a frieze from a 2nd-century temple (likely here before the palace).

On the basement's northern end, you'll find steps leading up to the **Peristil** (Peristyle), today a large square and intersection of the old town's main streets. Surrounded by huge columns and arches, the Peristil was meant for large crowds of Diocletian's adoring subjects to bow before him as he came out through the vestibule from his apartments. In modern times, the square has been a social and sometimes political center in Split. In the late 1960s

Diocletian's Palace

© HOLGER METTE/DREAMSTIME.COM

students painted the floor of the Peristil red, a move that angered authorities who labeled it vandalism. In 1998, on the 30th anniversary of the Red Peristil, a black circle was painted on the stones, an artistic statement against the government at the time. Today, the Peristil is often used as a concert venue, for both classical and rock performances.

Katedrala svetog Dujma
Cathedral of St. Domnius

To the east of the Peristil, at the foot of what is today's church belfry, you'll find two lions and a black granite sphinx-like figure to the right. Around 3,500 years old, the sphinx supposedly once had a twin. The building that is today's cathedral was once Diocletian's mausoleum. Octagonal from the outside, the mausoleum is round on the inside, with red granite Corinthian columns. Converted into a Christian church at the beginning of the 5th century, the building became the Katedrala svetog Dujma (7 A.M.–noon and 5–7 P.M. Mon.–Sat., 10Kn) in the 7th century,

EMPEROR DIOCLETIAN

Though he died with the fancy name Gaius Aurelius Valerius Diocletianus, Diocletian was born Diocles, the son of slaves, around A.D. 237. It's possible he was even born in Salona, near Split.

He never did receive much of an education, barely learning to read and write, but his prowess in the Roman military proved to make his fortune. In 284, when the emperor Carus was killed by a bolt of lightning (or by more human means), Diocletian was proclaimed emperor after Numerian, son of Carus, mysteriously died.

Diocletian's first goal was to bring the army under control, which he did, though he became increasingly more like a despot than a Roman emperor. Subjects were required to refer to him as Dominus Noster, or Lord and Master, and he identified himself with Jupiter.

He did, however, split the division of power to some extent by creating a tetrarchy, dividing territories among hand-picked leaders. The tetrarchy worked well at first, until Diocletian retired in 305 – an unheard-of move for an emperor. He had planned for the line of succession to move down the tetrarchy, but the division of power didn't sit so well with the new government. Diocletian died, possibly by his own hand, in Split.

dedicated to one of Diocletian's victims, the bishop of Salona. Huge 13th-century walnut doors depicting the life of Christ serve as the entry to the cathedral. The belfry (same hours as the cathedral, 5Kn), started in the 14th century though it wasn't finished until 1908, is a must-climb if you're willing to trade the effort for some great views of the city. The interior of the cathedral is a heady gilded and marble mix of reliefs, saints, and altars. The most impressive of the altars is the **Altar of St. Anastasius,** where the bones of Domnius are held in a sarcophagus looked over by the stunning and graphic *Flagellation of Christ* by famous stonemason Juraj Dalmatinac. To the

right of the delicately wood-carved choir stalls you'll find the treasury, a display of sacral art. Don't leave without looking closely around the dome for the frieze with two medallions thought to be portraits of Diocletian and his wife Prisca. It's believed that Diocletian's body was here for almost two centuries before it disappeared.

Krstionica
Baptistry

Though it's now known as the Krstionica (7 A.M.–noon and 5–7 P.M. Mon.–Sat., 5Kn), this converted building was once the temple of Jupiter in Roman times, likely around the 5th century. Located slightly northwest of the cathedral, it's one of the best-preserved Roman temples in Europe. With an impressive barrel-shaped coffered ceiling covered in reliefs, it's certainly worth a peek. The ceiling, original to the temple, is covered in motifs of flowers and heads that seem to be either laughing or screaming, depending on your interpretation. Turned into a Christian bapistry, the temple also has a simple statue of St. John the Baptist by Meštrović and a cross-shaped baptismal font, decorated with a carving of a Croatian king, probably Krešimir IV or Zvonimir, dating from around the 11th century. The carving was once part of an altar partition in the cathedral and was incorporated into the baptismal font, likely around the 13th century.

Etnografski muzej
Ethnographic Museum

The Etnografski muzej (Severova 1, tel. 021/344-161, www.etnografski-muzej-split .hr, 9 A.M.–9 P.M. Mon.–Fri. and 9 A.M.–1 P.M. Sat. in summer, 9 A.M.–3 P.M. Mon.–Wed. and Fri., 9 A.M.–7 P.M. Thurs., and 9 A.M.–1 P.M. Sat. in winter, 10Kn) was founded in 1910. The stone-enclosed space is filled with various regional costumes and a nice presentation of local trades. The streets past here are best traversed during the day, as it's one of the poorest and shadiest parts of town, long a meeting place for underground transactions.

Papalićeva Palača
Papalić Palace

The 15th-century late-Gothic Papalićeva Palača was built by Juraj Dalmatinac for a local aristocrat. Within the palace is Split's **Gradski muzej** (City Museum, Papalićeva 1, tel. 021/360-171, www.mgst.net, 9 A.M.–9 P.M. Tues.–Fri., 9 A.M.–4 P.M. Sat.–Mon., 10Kn), where Split's history is told in manuscripts, photographs, and artwork. The exhibit also displays fragments of sculptures, old buildings, and a homage to the first Croatian poet, Marko Marulić, who was a friend of the Papalić family and frequent guest at the palace.

Porta Aurea
Golden Gate

On the northern end of the palace complex, you'll reach the Porta Aurea (also called Zlatna vrata), the grandest of the four gates into the palace. The gate is surprisingly intact, save for some missing statues that once filled the empty niches and the columns that surrounded them. It's thought that the pedestals at the top of the wall once held statues of the four tetrarchs (Diocletian, Maximian, Galerius, and Constantius Chlorus). Next to the gate on the outside of the palace you'll find the menacing **statue of Grgur Ninski,** a 10th-century bishop, sculpted by Ivan Meštrović. Unveiled in 1929, the work was meant to commemorate Ninski's fight for the use of Croatian instead of Latin, making it a bit of a national statement. Also next to the Golden Gate, you'll find the miniscule 6th-century **Crkvica Sv. Martina** (Church of St. Martin), once a passage for watchmen guarding the gate and turned into a Christian church in the 9th century. Standing only a little over 1.5 meters wide and 10 meters long, it's likely one of the smallest Catholic churches in the world.

Arheološki muzej
Archaeological Museum

Located just north of the town center, Split's Arheološki muzej (Zrinsko–Frankopanska 25, tel. 021/329-340, www.mdc.hr/split-arheoloski, 9 A.M.–2 P.M. and 4–8 P.M. Mon.–Sat., 20Kn) is the oldest museum in Croatia, founded in 1820. Many artifacts were found in nearby Salona, with thousands of pieces of carved stone, a nice selection of Greek and Roman ceramic and glass, and a courtyard filled with sarcophagi and statues. There are also relics from the Illyrian and medieval periods.

Marjan Peninsula

West of the old town, accessed by walking up Senjska, you'll find the old quarter of **Veli Varoš,** a must-see for those who'd like to get off the beaten path and see a bit of the soul of Split. Here you'll find the **Vidilica** (Nazorov prolaz 1, tel. 021/589-550) café and restaurant, behind which you'll find a small 16th-century Jewish graveyard. From here you're entering the Marjan Peninsula, filled with lush forests and winding paved paths perfect for strolls or bike rides. The green peninsula was actually built in the mid-19th century, when locals started planting pine trees here, and in 1903 even formed an early eco-society called the Marjan Society, which is still responsible for the peninsula's well-being.

The highest point on the peninsula is **Telegrin,** rising some 175 meters above the Adriatic and offering excellent views. Marjan is also home to the 13th-century **Sveti Nikola** (St. Nicholas's Chapel) and the modest **Sveti Jere** (St. Hieronymous's Chapel) backed against a cliff.

It's a 20-minute walk from the center to the **Muzej hrvatskih arheološki spomenika** (Museum of Croatian Archaeological Monuments, Šetalište Ivana Meštrovića 18, tel. 021/323-901, www.mhas-split.hr, 10 A.M.–1 P.M. and 5–8 P.M. Mon.–Fri., 10 A.M.–1 P.M. Sat., 30Kn), founded in 1893, though the current location was opened in 1976. The displays focus on Split's medieval history and the 3,000 pieces on display range from weaponry to jewelry and from tools to sculpture.

◾ Galerija Ivana Meštrovića
Ivan Meštrović Gallery

A short jaunt further down the street will land you at the Galerija Ivana Meštrovića (Šetalište

Ivana Meštrovića 46, tel. 021/340-800, www
.mdc.hr/mestrovic, 9 A.M.–7 P.M. Tues.–Sun.
in summer, 9 A.M.–4 P.M. Tues.–Sat. and
10 A.M.–3 P.M. Sun. in winter, 30Kn). The
huge palace was built by Meštrović, Croatia's
most famous sculptor, between 1931 and
1939 as a family home. Though it took him
eight years to build, he lived in it less than
ten years, from 1932 and 1941, and donated
the home to the people in the early 1950s as
a gallery of his work. Today the mammoth
house displays some 190 sculptures and over
500 drawings from the artist. Near the gallery you'll find the **Kaštelet** (Šetalište Ivana
Meštrovića 46, tel. 021/358-185, www.mdc
.hr/mestrovic, same hours as gallery, free with
gallery admission), originally built as the
16th-century summer home of a local noble
family and later used as a quarantine home
and a tannery, among other things. Restored
by Meštrović in 1939 to be used as a gallery
for his 28 wooden reliefs depicting the life of
Christ, it serves its intended purpose today
resulting in a powerfully moving display no
matter what your spiritual inclinations. The
museums are definitely worth a visit even if
you've never heard of Meštrović.

Bačvice

Officially the city's beach since 1919, Bačvice
is not nearly as pretty as some of the island
beaches but it will do if you're up for a swim.
Given Croatia's Blue Flag Award for cleanli-
ness, the beach is usually crowded with locals,
and received a much-needed injection of life
in the form of a modern pavilion housing a
handful of popular cafés and restaurants. If
you notice a bunch of men in Speedos throwing themselves at a small rubber ball, don't be
alarmed. It's just *picigin,* a local game with no
winners or losers, just a lot of fun.

Tvrđava Gripe
Gripe Fortress
On the northeastern side of town you'll find the
Tvrđava Gripe, built in the 17th century to defend the city against the Turks. One of the fortress's former barracks is home to the **Hrvatski**

pomorski muzej (Croatian Maritime Museum,
Glagoljaška 18, tel. 021/347-788, www.hpms
.hr, 9 A.M.–2 P.M. and 5:30–8:30 P.M., 10Kn)
with an interesting display of commercial and
military seafaring in the area. Costumes, statues, model ships, and old flags are a sample of
what you'll find.

ENTERTAINMENT AND EVENTS
Nightlife
Coffee sipping and club hopping are a way
of life for Splićani, young and old. Close to
the Riva you'll find the eccentric and artsy
Academia Ghetto Club (Dosud 10, tel.
021/346-879, 10 A.M.–1 A.M. daily) and a
more local version, **Po Bota** (Subićeva 2, tel.
098/215-379, 6 P.M.–1 A.M. Mon.–Sat.) close
to the Trg braće Radića. It's a smoky, bohe-
mian spot with surprisingly good beer on tap.
There are plenty of other bars along the Riva
and around, but when they close at one in the
morning, head to Bačvice Beach, where **Tropic
Club Equador** (no phone, 10 A.M.–2 A.M. daily)
packs in bodies on the dance floor, or down
the Marjan Peninsula to **Obojena Svetlost**
(Šetalište Ivana Meštrovića 35, tel. 021/358-
280, noon–3 A.M. daily) with cushy lounging
under the palm trees, cuing at the pool table,
and dancing in summer to DJ-spun tunes.

Festivals and Events
The best festival in Split is its **Splitsko ljeto**
(Split Summer Festival, mid-July–mid-Aug.,
www.splitsko-ljeto.hr), when theater, classical
music, and opera converge on the city; many
performances are held in the Peristil.

SHOPPING
There are several spots for wines, oils, and
other local gourmet products. Try **Oleoteka
Uje** (Marulićeva 1, tel. 021/342-719, www.uje
.hr, 10 A.M.–10 P.M. Mon.–Sat., 10 A.M.–5 P.M.
Sun.) for a huge selection of olive oils as well as
pampering soaps and other Dalmatian goodies.
Perhaps one of the best take-homes from Split
is a jersey from the local soccer team, Hajduk.
The nicest ones can be found at **Cro Fan Shop**

(Trogirska 10, tel. 021/343-096, www.cro-fan-shop.com, 10 A.M.–9 P.M. Mon.–Sat.). **Studio Naranča** (Majstora Jurja 5, tel. 021/344-118, 9 A.M.–8 P.M. Mon.–Fri., 9 A.M.–1 P.M. Sat.) is a small gallery showcasing the work of graphic designer Pavo Majić and his wife as well as other Croatian artists and artisans. English books and newspapers can be purchased at **Algoritam** (Bajamontijeva 2, tel. 021/348-030, www.algoritam.hr, 8 A.M.–8:30 P.M. Mon.–Fri., 8 A.M.–1 P.M. Sat.).

SPORTS AND RECREATION
Spectator Sports
There's only one real word you need to know around Split: **Hajduk** (www.hnkhajduk.hr). The local football (soccer) club is more like a religion than a sport. Local fans, who refer to themselves as *torcida,* can be whipped into a frenzy over a victory against their biggest rival, Zagreb's Dinamo. If you'd like to experience the excitement, you can purchase tickets at the office at **Poljud Stadium.**

ACCOMMODATIONS
The **Kamena Lodge** (Don P. Perosa 20, tel. 021/269-910, www.kamenalodge.co.uk, 177Kn d.) is an excellent budget accommodation run by a friendly couple from London. Located in a traditional stone house just outside of Split's center, the hotel has a pool and a minibus service that runs several times daily to the heart of town.

Villa Stina (Na Toc 6, tel. 091/752-5980, www.villa-stina.com, 700Kn d.), a short walk to the beach and the bus and railway stations, has exposed stone walls, comfortably furnished rooms, and plenty of modern creature comforts like satellite television and air-conditioning.

The **Garden Cottages and Apartments Old City** (Solurat 22, tel. 098/171-1730, www.croatiasplitapartments.com, 350Kn d.) are wonderful rooms (with en suite bath) and cottages located a five-minute walk from Diocletian's Palace. The furnishings are rather basic but the surroundings are peaceful and authentic. Make sure to book the apartments and rooms at the Solurat address—the company has a few apartments at a beach location farther away.

Located within the walls of Diocletian's Palace, **(Base Sobe** (Kraj Svetog Ivana 3, tel. 098/234-855, www.base-rooms.com, 496Kn d.) may be the best deal in Split. You can't get more central and the rooms are way better quality than you'd expect for the money.

Five minutes from Diocletian's Palace, **Villa Varoš** (Miljenka Smoje 1, tel. 021/483-469, www.villavaros.hr, 485Kn d.) is a family-owned hotel in a pretty little neighborhood of Split. The simple rooms are extremely clean and tidy and the hotel owns a nearby restaurant where you can grab a reasonable breakfast.

Hotel Slavija (Buvanina 2, tel. 021/323-840, www.hotelslavija.com, 790Kn d., including breakfast) is the oldest hotel in Split, founded at the turn of the 20th century in a 17th-century building in the center of Diocletian's Palace. The history, however, can be traced even further back—there's a preserved Roman spa in the basement of the hotel. The rooms are bland but clean and have air-conditioning and cable TV. Try to avoid the rooms over the narrow alley, where partying-related noise carries on until the wee hours.

The Atrium (Domovinskog rata 49A, tel. 021/200-000, www.hotel-atrium.hr, 1,135Kn d.) is a modern, minimalistic hotel located about a 10-minute walk from the core of ancient Split. If you're tired of old-world charm and exposed stone walls, this might be the place for you. The hotel also has a top-floor spa and pool for a bit of post-sightseeing pampering.

The **Hotel Peristil** (Poljana kraljice Jelene 5, tel. 021/329-070, www.hotelperistil.com, 1,150Kn d.) is a bit on the pricey side for a three-star, relying on its location within Diocletian's Palace to bring in the tourists. The standouts of the hotel are the friendly service and the flat-screen televisions.

The chicest spot in the old town, the **(Hotel Vestibul Palace** (Iza Vestibula 4, tel. 021/329-329, www.vestibulpalace.com, 1,180Kn d.) could have stepped out of an interiors magazine, getting the mix of minimalist modern and ancient architecture just right.

The hotel is small (only seven rooms) and pricey, but then again, how often do you stay in a 1,700-year-old palace?

If you're looking for full service, including restaurant, spa, and a place to moor your yacht, try **Le Meridien Grand Hotel Lav** (Grljevačka 2A, tel. 021/500-500, www.lemeridien.com/split, 1,890Kn d., including breakfast), about six kilometers from Split in the suburb of Podstrana. One of Croatia's few five-star hotels, it pulls out all the stops—an infinity pool, champagne bar, a spa with truffle- and gold-based treatments, foodie-quality restaurants, and of course the marina for dozens of shiny yachts.

FOOD

For a quick snack or dessert, **(Slastičarna Tradicija** (Bosanska 2, tel. 021/361-070, 8 A.M.–11 P.M. Mon.–Sat.) has been doling out cakes and ice creams for over 70 years. Just before Easter, you'll see dozens of locals lining up outside the small bakery, down the alleyway, for *pinca,* a type of bread prerequisite on Easter morning. Best of all, the shop has a special case of "historic" cakes and cookies, like *mandolat* (a cookie made with almonds) and *kotonjada* (quince jelly), once ubiquitous around the area and today rare outside of local homes. Vegans and vegetarians will appreciate **Makrovega** (Leština 2, tel. 021/394-440, www.makrovega.hr, 9 A.M.–7 P.M. Mon.–Fri., 9 A.M.–5 P.M. Sat., no credit cards, 55Kn). The small place has macrobiotic and vegetarian options, with a menu that includes a great selection of soups, salads, mains like burritos and lasagna, and some quite tempting desserts. **Kibela** (Kraj svetog Ivana 3, tel. 021/346-205, 7 A.M.–11 P.M. daily, 80Kn) has been a steady presence on Split's restaurant scene for a quarter of a century, located in an old-quarter alleyway so narrow locals refer to it as "let me pass." Though you won't find it devoid of tourists, the place is a staple for locals as well, particularly for *marenda* and the typical but not stereotypical cuisine the restaurant serves—such as roast spare ribs and hearty bean stew. However, you'll also find a smattering of fish here as well.

If you go to only one *konoba* in Split, though, head to **Buffet Fife** (Trumbićeva obala 11, tel. 021/345-223, 11 A.M.–10 P.M. daily, 60Kn), in the Varoš quarter. It's a simple restaurant that doesn't seem like anything special at first glance, but the food they serve is legendary in Split (just ask a local). It's not fancy by any means—don't look for any truffles here. But if you're looking for daily fisherman's food, a mean *pašticada* on Sundays, and a heavy dose of Split local flavor (particularly in the winter), it doesn't get much better.

Slightly out of the center behind Bačvice Beach, **Enoteka Terra** (Prilaz braće Kaliterna 6, tel. 021/314-800, www.vinoteka.hr, 10 A.M.–midnight Mon.–Sat., 11 A.M.–midnight Sun., 80Kn) has a small but excellent restaurant and a great **wine shop** (8 A.M.–8 P.M. Mon.–Fri., 9 A.M.–1:30 P.M. Sat.) selling a huge selection of Dalmatian and Istrian wines. Terra's *konoba* is a cozy affair—exposed stone walls surround the candlelit tables in the basement of an old building. One of the best restaurants in Split, **(Noštromo** (Kraj Sv Marije 10, tel. 091/405-6666, www.restoran-nostromo.hr, 11 A.M.–11 P.M. daily, no credit cards, 90Kn) and its chef have won multiple national distinctions for their mastery of Dalmatian staples like grilled fish, risottos, and fish soup. The food doesn't come cheap and can't be paid for with a credit card, so hit up the ATM before you come—it's worth the splurge.

INFORMATION AND SERVICES

For information and a few free maps, visit Split's **tourist office** (Peristil bb, tel. 021/345-606, www.visitsplit.com, 9 A.M.–8 P.M. Mon.–Sat. and 9 A.M.–1 P.M. Sun. in summer, 9 A.M.–5 P.M.) on the Peristil.

English books and guides can be purchased at Algoritam (Bajamontijeva 2, tel. 021/348-030, www.algoritam.hr, 8 A.M.–8 P.M. Mon.–Fri., 8 A.M.–1 P.M. Sat.). The main post office (Kralja Tomislava 9, 7 A.M.–8 P.M. Mon.–Sat., 8 A.M.–1 P.M. Sun.) offers mail and telephone services as well as money exchange.

Clean your clothes at a coin-operated

laundry (a rarity in Croatia) (Šperun 1, tel. 021/315-888, 8 A.M.–8 P.M.), only 45Kn for wash and dry, or splurge for their turn-key service (less ironing) for 75Kn per load.

Drop your luggage at Split's bus station (Obala Kneza Domagoja 12, tel. 060/327-327, www.ak-split.hr, 6 A.M.–10 P.M. daily, 3Kn per hour).

GETTING THERE AND AROUND

Split's airport (tel. 021/203-555, www.split-airport.hr) is located 20 kilometers north of town near Trogir. Croatia Airlines runs a reasonable bus (tel. 021/203-119, 30Kn) service to Split. Call the office to check for departure times (they meet all Croatia Airlines flights). You can also take a taxi (try Radio Taxi, 970, or Taxi Riva, tel. 021/347-777). You could hop on a local bus, too, but honestly it's not worth the time or hassle, so we won't explain the hoops you'd need to jump through to get from the airport to Split's center. Wait on the Croatia Airlines bus (only 10Kn more) or splurge on a cab (an alarming 250Kn trip) instead.

Long-distance bus connections are frequent, since Split is one of the main transportation hubs for Dalmatia. The station (Obala Kneza Domagoja 12, tel. 060/327-327, www.ak-split.hr) is located next to the ferry terminal on Split's harbor. There are good connections with Zagreb (over two dozen daily, 8 hours), Dubrovnik (about 12 daily, 5 hours), and Rijeka (about 6 daily, 8 hours). If you're traveling by bus to Dubrovnik, remember you'll need your passport—a portion of the journey goes through Bosnia.

The train (especially fast ones, labeled *brzi*) is a great option for getting to and from Split. Fast trains to Zagreb (about 3 daily, 160Kn) take about six hours, while trains to Šibenik (about 5 connections daily, 2 hours, 45Kn) and Zadar (3–4 connections daily, 4.5 hours, 90Kn) are also convenient. The station

(Zlodrina poljana 20, tel. 021/338-525, www.hznet.hr) is a short walk to the harbor or the main bus station.

Split's ferry terminal is a short walk from the Riva and it can take you for day trips to Hvar (1.5 hours) and Brač or a longer trip (around 2 hours) to Vis. Catamarans and hydrofoils, which have the quickest journey times (one hour to Hvar), can be picked up from the Riva. At the marina end of the Riva are kiosks for Jadrolinija (Gat Sveti Duje bb, tel. 021/338-333, www.jadrolinija.hr) and Split Tours (tel. 021/352-533, www.splittours.hr), which also books trips to Ancona in Italy.

Around Split you can rely on walking to get you most anywhere you want to go. Hikes out to the Marjan Peninsula can be circumvented by taking a local bus (#12 from the Trg Republike). A bus ticket will set you back about 10Kn, payable to the driver, or pick one up at newspaper kiosks.

AROUND SPLIT

Largely part of a neighboring suburb of Split, Solin, the ruins of **Salona** (tel. 021/211-538, 9 A.M.–7 P.M. Mon.–Fri., 10 A.M.–7 P.M. Sat., and 4–7 P.M. Sun. June–Sept., 8 A.M.–3 P.M. Mon.–Fri. Oct.–May, 20Kn) are all that's left of a giant city for its time (some 60,000 inhabitants), established around the 2nd century B.C., and an important center of early Christianity. Though many of the prettier statues and pieces were excavated in the 19th century and taken to museums, the remains of the amphitheater, the aqueduct, the bishop's complex, and the Forum are still worth a peek for fans of the Roman period. You can get more information from the **Tourist Board of Solin** (tel. 021/210-048, www.solin-info.com).

You can get to Solin from Split by driving north on the Magistrala toward Trogir or by taking city bus #1. The main information booth and ticket center is just behind the parking lot for Salona.

Omiš

A pretty town at the mouth of the Cetina river gorge, Omiš is most famous for having been a pirate stronghold against mighty Venice in the 13th century. The city is quite stunning: Craggy rocks give way to narrow streets and old stone houses, and finally to the crystal-blue waters of the Adriatic.

SIGHTS

The best sights here are the remains of medieval fortresses built by the nobles of Kačić and Bribir, which harbored the pirates who moored their ships slightly up river. **Mirabela** (8 A.M.–noon and 4:30–8:30 P.M., 10Kn) is the most accessible—just follow the many stairs behind the parish church to climb the tower for a nice view. Further up, the **Fortica** (dawn–dusk, free) is a bit of a hike, about 1.5 hours, for vistas and great photo opportunities.

Omiš has a wonderful *klapa* festival (www.fdk.hr), founded in 1967 and now attracting some 80 groups. The deep a cappella rhythms were once mocked but are now being reclaimed as an integral part of Dalmatian culture. If you'd like to find out more about *klapa* in English, try the website www.klapa-trogir.com.

ACCOMMODATIONS

Private rooms and apartments can be booked through **Active Holidays** (Knezova kačića bb, tel. 021/861-829, www.activeholidays-croatia.com) in Omiš.

There's only one downside to the **Hotel Villa Dvor** (Mosorska 13, tel. 021/863-444, www.hotel-villadvor.hr, 800Kn d., including breakfast): You'll need to climb about 100 stairs to reach the pretty hotel from the parking lot (staff will help you with your bags). If you can get past the climb, the views over stone ruins, the canyon, and the sea are spectacular. The rooms are nicely furnished, though they tend to run on the small side.

the city of Omiš, famed as a medieval pirate stronghold

SOUTHERN DALMATIA

THE PIRATES OF OMIŠ

The geography of Omiš – large flat rocks that overlook the mouth of the Cetina Gorge on one side and the sea on the other – is to thank or to blame for the pirates that once hung out here. It offered perfect protection for their fleet of light and fast ships that preyed on those who happened to sail by. The Venetians and the Kingdom of Naples, who generally thought they ruled the Adriatic Sea, thought of the city of Omiš as a pirate town. The people of Omiš generally thought they were only extracting tolls from those who were using their part of the sea.

In defense of the Venetians and the Kingdom of Naples, the pirates, ruled by the Kačić Dukes, were quite violent and they weren't altogether fair, even attacking ships heading on crusades, which outraged the Pope and brought Pope Honorius III's fleet into battle with the pirates in 1221. The Kačić won that battle, but a later fight in 1228 pretty much ended their approximately century-long reign of terror.

Hotel Plaža (Trg kralja Tomislava 6, tel. 021/755-260, www.hotelplaza.hr, 936Kn d., including breakfast and dinner) opened in 2007 and has been so popular that during the summer it is difficult to book a room for less than a week. Right on a stretch of sandy beach in town, the hotel is tastefully decorated and has a small spa, and the terrace turns into an ice skating rink in the winter.

FOOD

It's worth the climb to have dinner on the terrace of (**Villa Dvor's restaurant** (Mosorska 13, tel. 021/863-444, www.hotel-villadvor.hr). Overlooking the Cetina Gorge and the sea, it's particularly beautiful in twilight—you may not even notice the food, good renditions of local Poljica specialties, focusing on meats and vegetables with a few creative takes on traditional fish dishes. One of the best restaurants in the region, the (**Kaštil Slanica** (tel. 021/862-073, www.radmanove-mlinice.hr) serves excellent local fare (and mouthwatering bread cooked *ispod peka*) with gorgeous river views.

INFORMATION AND SERVICES

The Omiš **tourist office** (Trg kneza Miroslava, tel. 021/861-350, www.tz-omis.hr) can provide you with lots more information, from festival info to rafting excursions.

GETTING THERE AND AROUND

Omiš is about 25 kilometers south of Split. From Split, take bus #60 from the Lazareti bus stop on the Riva or an inter-city bus to Omiš. If you're driving, just follow the Magistrala south from Split.

CETINA GORGE

The Cetina Gorge is full of stunning karst rock formations, dotted with deep-green scraggly forest, and cut through by bright-blue water. You'll find some of the gorge's prettiest scenery just upstream from Omiš. In the summer, boat trips a few kilometers up the gorge are widely advertised at the harbor for very reasonable prices. You can also drive along the gorge, all the way to Zadvarje about a half an hour or so on, where a **vodopad** (waterfall, follow the signs) culminates a nice scenic drive.

Sports and Recreation

One of the best ways to see the gorge is to go on a rafting trip on the Cetina. The trip is pretty mild unless there's been a lot of rain recently. Try **Active Holidays** (Knezova kačića bb, tel. 021/861-829, www.activeholidays-croatia .com) or **Adria Tourist** (Duce, Rogac 1/10, tel. 021/734-016, www.rafting-pinta.com) for booking a trip, which lasts 3–4 hours.

Food

The **Restoran Radmanove Mlinice** (Kanjom cetine, tel. 021/862-073, www.radmanove-mlinice.com, 8 A.M.–midnight daily, closed Nov.–Mar., 85Kn) sits in a peaceful location on the Cetina River about six kilometers from Omiš. Many boat trips end up here anyway, but don't let its tourist popularity throw you off. It's perfect for cooling off on a hot summer's day and for tucking in to fresh trout and frog's legs on the shady terrace.

Makarska Riviera

Packed with tourists in the summer, particularly from neighboring Bosnia, it can be hard to find a spot for your towel on the Makarska Riviera's great pebbly beaches. For the most part, it's a jumble of package hotels, kids looking for a party, and families interested in relaxing by the sea. The area is popular with tourists and day-trippers from neighboring Bosnia as well as Germans and Hungarians spending a couple of weeks in the sun. It is possible to use it as a comfortable overnight stop and offers a handful of hotels and good restaurants. There are also some outstanding beaches, particularly in Brela, though they are best savored outside the busiest months of July and August.

BRELA

South of Split and north of Makarska, Brela is set on a six-kilometer stretch of pebbly beach, rimmed by olive and fig trees. The sea slopes gently here, making it great for young children and hesitant swimmers.

Beaches

Punta Rata is Brela's most popular beach, a long white-pebbled line backed by lots of facilities including restaurants, lifeguards (generally 8 A.M.–8 P.M. in summer), and changing areas. The 400-meter **Berulija** beach has a few more secluded spots, since the coastline dips into three different coves. If you're looking for a romantic beach, **Vrulja** is a hidden cove slightly north of town. The best approach is by boat. You can rent a small one at Brela's marina. Don't be surprised to find a few skinny dippers in the quieter stretches of beach.

Accommodations and Food

The chain of Blue Sun Hotels is the best choice for accommodation in Brela. The **Berulia** (Frankopanska 22, tel. 021/603-190, brela@bluesunhotels.com, www.bluesun hotels.com, 355Kn d., including breakfast) is probably the best value for money. Basic but comfy rooms in the stark modern building overlook a sparkling pool and a gentle slope to the beach. The **Soline** (Trg Gospe od Karmela 1, tel. 021/603-190, brela@ bluesunhotels.com, www.bluesunhotels .com, 640Kn d.), positioned at the upper end of the chain, has swish rooms with wood floors and a giant spa as well as indoor and outdoor pools.

Indoors or out, dining at the **Ivandića Dvori** (Banje 1, tel. 021/618-407, 5 P.M.–1 A.M. daily, 90Kn) is a lovely experience. Sitting on a stone-floored terrace overlooking the water or beside a roaring fire inside in the winter, you can choose from a good variety of grilled fish and meat dishes.

Information and Services

You can pick up information from Brela's **tourist office** (Alojzija Stepinca bb, tel. 021/618-455, www.brela.hr, posted hours are 8 A.M.–9 P.M. daily in summer, 8 A.M.–3 P.M. Mon.–Fri. in winter, but don't stress if you find the door locked).

Getting There and Around

Getting to Brela by car is easy—just follow the Magistrala. By bus it's somewhat more difficult. Buses from Split regularly run to Makarska, though you should alert your driver you want to be dropped off near Brela. If you're trying to catch the bus here, you may need to flag it down to stop, though in the high season you likely won't be the only one waving.

A SIDE TRIP TO BOSNIA-HERZEGOVINA

Just across the border from the Southern Dalmatia coast is Bosnia-Herzegovina (BiH). It would seem wrong to write about Croatia without mentioning **Herzegovina,** where most of the residents are actually Croats. It's right across the border from Dalmatia and you don't even need to bother with changing money, as the locals are happy to accept Croatian kuna. The Catholic pilgrimage site of **Medugorje** is here in the heart of Herzegovina.

Going further into **Bosnia,** you'll find the stunning capital, **Sarajevo,** and **Mostar,** with its dramatic old bridge and lots of Ottoman-influenced touches. If you have time, they're definitely worth the visit, though plan for at least a couple nights. There are still relatively few tourists even during the summer.

If you'd like to visit for a day or longer, you can pass border patrol without a visa if you're a U.S., European Union, Australia, or New Zealand citizen. There are trains from Ploče to Mostar (2 hours) and Sarajevo (4 hours), and buses leave Zagreb, Split, and Dubrovnik daily for Bosnia-Herzegovina's main cities (Dubrovnik to Mostar, 3 hours; Dubrovnik to Sarajevo, 6 hours; Split to Sarajevo, 7 hours; Zagreb to Sarajevo, 9 hours).

Bosnia-Herzegovina is safe except for the large amount of land mines still lying in the fields, so it's best not to go hiking or trekking without a local guide. If you'd like to see the country in more detail or see remote parts of the country without worrying about land mines, contact the excellent ecofriendly tourist agency **GreenVisions** (Radnička bb, Sarajevo, tel. 387-33/717-290, sarajevo@greenvisions.ba, www.greenvisions.ba/gv), a friendly company specializing in guided trips through Bosnia-Herzegovina.

BAŠKA VODA

Low on charm factor but filled with lots of services for tourists (think mid-range hotels, souvenir shops, and loads of postcards), Baška Voda is best as an overnight (or 24 hours) on your way elsewhere.

Accommodations and Food

Rooms at the **Hotel Villa Bacchus** (Obala sv. Nikole 89, tel. 021/695-190, www.hotel-bacchus.hr, 495Kn d.) all have nice mountain or sea views and access to an indoor pool.

Hotel Horizont (Stjepana Radića 2, tel. 021/604-555, www.hoteli-baskavoda.hr, 1,007Kn d., including breakfast) was renovated when the Russian owners took over and now offers fresh but basic rooms, indoor and outdoor pools, and over-the-top spa facilities.

There are plenty of pizza and seafood restaurants along the waterfront, with something for everyone, though without anything likely to impress aspiring gourmets.

Information and Services

The town has a small **tourist office** (Obala svetog Nikole 31, tel. 021/620-713, www.baskavoda.hr, 8 A.M.–9 P.M. daily in summer, call for winter hours) that can help you with advice about the area.

Getting There and Around

There's no proper bus station in town, so some buses traveling from Split to Makarska will drop you conveniently near the water, while others will drop you off on the Magistrala. If it's the latter, you've got about a 15-minute walk into town. Driving, of course, is simple. Just follow the Magistrala south from Split.

MAKARSKA

There's really not anything to see in Makarska besides the beach. It's usually packed in summer, leading the town to have a bustling nightlife.

Makarska's main **beach** is slightly to the west of the center of town, rimmed by loads of package hotels. For fewer crowds rent a boat from the marina or hike from the Riva

SANJA BALJKAS/DREAMSTIME.COM

Makarska's waterfront

towards the east, where you'll find signed paths leading to **Nugal,** about three kilometers on, where it's much quieter and the scenery is spectacular.

Accommodations and Food

Rooms at the **Dalmacija** (Kralja Petra Krešimira IV bb, tel. 021/615-777, 794Kn d., including breakfast) are extremely simple despite recent renovations, but the hotel is relatively convenient and has swimming pools, a restaurant, and a decent array of facilities.

Though the **Mlinice Boarding House** (Put Mlinica bb, tel. 021/615-889, mlinice@st.htnet.hr, www.makarska-croatia.com/mlinice, 320Kn d., including breakfast) is not on the beach, it's only a two-kilometer (about 30-minute) walk downhill to town. The rooms facing the sea have stunning views and the value for money is quite good for the area. The boarding house also houses a good restaurant if you don't feel like going out again after a long day sunning on the beach.

Restoran Jež (Petra Krešimira IV 90, tel. 021/611-741, 11 A.M.–midnight daily, closed Jan.), literally Hedgehog Restaurant, has long been considered one of Makarska's top spots for fish dishes, seafood appetizers, and a solid wine list.

Information and Services

The town has a helpful **tourist office** (Obala kralja Tomislava bb, tel. 021/612-002, www.makarska.com, 8 A.M.–9 P.M. daily in summer, 9 A.M.–3 P.M. Mon.–Fri. in winter).

Getting There and Around

Makarska's bus station (Ante Starčevića 30, tel. 021/612-333) is only a few minutes' walk to the water. From here you can catch one of several daily buses to Dubrovnik (3 hours) or Split (1.5 hours). Driving to Makarska, just take the Magistrala south from Split.

Southern Dalmatian Islands

BRAČ

Brač is Croatia's third-largest island, and arguably one of its most popular. Stemming from the bustling beach life of towns like Bol and Supetar and fueled by its proximity to the mainland (only one hour), Brač sees thousands of tourists every summer. If you're seeking peace and quiet, though, it's easily found in the semi-abandoned interior. Neglected vineyards are the only remnants of the once large winemaking trade on the island. Many plants succumbed to disease in the early 20th century, forcing winemakers to abandon their fields and their livelihood.

Supetar

Given that Supetar has a fairly small old town, there aren't a lot of visit-worthy sights in town. The best historic sight in Supetar is actually the **town cemetery,** a peaceful cypress-lined park beyond the town's beaches. The impressive sculptures that decorate the graves and mausoleums were carved by two of Croatia's leading 19th- and early 20th-century sculptors, Ivan Rendić and Toma Rosandić.

Supetar is the main tourist center of the island, though, with plenty to keep beachgoers and young families busy. Stretching to the west of Supetar are lots of pebbly beaches with clear water perfect for snorkeling.

The best beach can be found by driving to **Lovrečina Bay,** with a nice beach and the remains of an old basilica.

Campers can check out **Autocamp Supetar** (Ul. Malašnica bb, tel. 021/630-088, 80Kn per person), situated on a beach a couple of kilometers out of town. **Pansion Palute** (Put Pašika 16, tel. 021/631-730, palute@st.htnet.hr, 380Kn d.) is a small family hotel with clean, cozy rooms and air-conditioning.

Aparthotel Bračka Perla (Put Vele Luke, tel. 021/755-530, www.perlacroatia.com, 1,631Kn d.) has eight suites and three rooms, all decorated in bright colors and modern furnishings. At this upmarket stone hotel the pool area is enveloped by comfy wicker loungers. Inside, a fireplace makes for homey dining in cooler weather. The **Villa Adriatica** (Put Vele luke 31, tel. 021/343-806, www.villaadriatica .com, 993Kn d., including breakfast) is a 24-room boutique hotel with plain but fresh rooms and a much more luxe garden and pool area. Nearby the beach, the hotel also has a restaurant and small wellness center.

Even if you've come straight off the beach, **Punta** (Punta 1, tel. 021/631-507, www .vilapunta.com, 8:30 A.M.–midnight daily, closed Dec.–Mar., 85Kn) is the sort of place you can plop down for a relaxed lunch. Food is

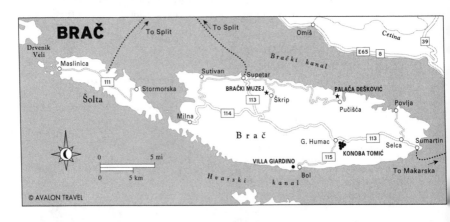

the typical grilled meats and fish, though there are a couple of options for vegetarians as well, and the location is great—a quiet spot a short walk away from the hustle and bustle of busy Supetar. Even quieter is **Restoran Gumonca** (Mirca, tel. 021/630-237, noon–midnight daily, no credit cards, 75Kn), located in the peaceful village of Mirca three kilometers from Supetar.

Vinotoka (Jobova 6, tel. 021/630-969, noon–midnight daily, 90Kn) is a family restaurant in Supetar. In addition to the seafood dishes, be sure to sample some of the owners' homemade olive oil and wines.

Bol

The popular resort town of Bol has two sightworthy stops. The first is the **Branislav Dešković Gallery** (Porat b. pomoraca bb, tel. 021/635-270, call for hours and prices, which vary according to exhibit), a modest museum that manages to include some of the biggest names in 20th-century Croatian art. Bol is also home to a 15th-century **Dominikanski samostan** (Dominican monastery, 10 A.M.– noon and 5–8 P.M. Mon.–Sat. in summer, mass only rest of year, 15Kn) that looks out over the town. Inside you'll find some Greek artifacts and a tender painting by Tintoretto, the *Madonna with Child*. The gardens here are also worth a peek.

But the biggest draws to Bol are the beaches, most notably **Zlatni Rat** (Golden Horn), a long stretch of tiny-pebble beach known for windsurfing and a partying crowd. To get there, just follow the path west of the center. It's about a 20-minute walk; once there you'll find cafés and basic services. If you're interested in a full-body tan visit the more remote **Pakleni naturist beach** (clothing optional) on the western end of Zlatni Rat.

Among package-hotel destinations, the **Hotel Borak** (Zlatni Rat d.d., tel. 021/635-210, www.bluesunhotels.com, 1,060Kn d., including breakfast) is a good choice, located steps from Zlatni Rat with large outdoor pools, tennis courts, and children's activities, though rooms are still stuck in a 1980s hotel time warp.

The **tourist office** (Bol harbor, tel. 021/635-638, www.bol.hr) has free maps as well as a brochure outlining private accommodation around the town, probably the right choice for budget travelers.

Possibly the best value for money in Bol, the ◖ **Villa Giardino** (Novi put 2, tel. 021/635-900, www.dalmacija.net/bol/villagiardino, no credit cards, 700Kn d.) truly lives up to its villa status. Tastefully furnished antiquefilled rooms, a genteel garden, and ceiling fans (though it has air-conditioning too) deck out the old home where Emperor Franz Joseph once laid his head (in room no. 4).

Overhauled in 2008, the **Hotel Kaštil** (Frane Radića 1, tel. 021/635-995, www.kastil.hr, 740Kn d., including breakfast) has a convenient waterfront location in an old building. Most of the plainly furnished but brand-new rooms have sea views. The building also houses two hotel-owned restaurants and a bustling bar, which make for plenty of late-night noise.

A homey, rustic atmosphere describes **Konoba Gust** (Radićeva 14, tel. 021/635-911, www.konobagust-bol.com, noon–2 A.M. daily, closed Nov.–late Mar., no credit cards, 90Kn), known for its *gregada* (fish stew), *pašticada* (beef stew), and surprisingly upscale offering of regional wines.

Savor fish hot off the grill at **Konoba Mlin** (Ante Starčevića 11, tel. 021/635-376, 5 P.M.– midnight daily, closed Nov.–Apr., 75Kn), a 19th-century mill a short way from the marina. Its cozy terraces are the perfect spot to enjoy a leisurely meal.

Definitely one of Bol's pricier establishments, **Ribarska kućica** (Ante Starčevića, tel. 021/635-033, www.ribarska-kucica.com, 10 A.M.–midnight daily, closed Nov.–May, no credit cards, 135Kn) delivers your money's worth on seaside terraces with amazing views of the blue water and craggy coastline of the island. And the food—fish carpaccio, frogfish with smoked ham, steaks—is sophisticated and well prepared.

Around Brač

A short drive from Supetar (or take one of the three daily buses) you'll find the village of **Škrip,** an ancient village that's home to the **Brački muzej** (Museum of Brač, check with the tourist office in Supetar for hours and prices, tel. 021/630-551, www.supetar.hr). The small museum has an interesting collection of Roman artifacts and a small Roman mausoleum outside, where locals claim one of Diocletian's relatives is buried.

If you're traveling with friends, **Limunovo Drvo** (Bunta, Sutivan, tel. 44-1225/865-591 (UK), www.croatiancottage.co.uk, £800 per week in high season, accommodates up to 11), whose name translates to lemon tree, is a charming rental villa in the village of Sutivan.

The most luxe hotel on Brač, the 15th-century **◖ Palača Dešković** (Pučišća, tel. 021/778-240, www.palaca-deskovic.com, 1,702Kn d., including breakfast) has all the amenities you'd expect from a fine boutique hotel, plus a library and games room, a good restaurant, an art gallery and studio, and parking spaces for cars or yachts.

Wineries

◖ Konoba Tomić (Gornji Humac, tel. 021/647-228, www.konobatomic.com, 5 P.M.– midnight daily, closed Nov.–Apr., no credit cards, 95Kn) is a family-run restaurant and winery, located in their 800-year-old farmhouse in the village of Humac. The family sells their wines all over Croatia as well as in the restaurant, which also offers lots of homegrown, homemade, and fresh-from-the-sea delicacies, like wind-cured *pršut* and octopus cooked *ispod peka*. If you're lucky enough to visit in the autumn, you can see the family making wine.

Getting There and Around

Brač is most often accessed via ferries from the Split mainland (1 hour); they dock at Supetar. Jadrolinija (tel. 021/631-357, www.jadrolinija .hr) and Split Tours (tel. 021/352-481, www .splittours.hr) run close to two dozen ferries a day in the high season. There's also a catamaran (run by Jadrolinija) linking Split with Bol and a small airport (tel. 021/631-370, www .airport-brac.hr) a few miles from Bol that connects to Zagreb.

Around the island, buses (station is east of the harbor, tel. 021/631-122) link Supetar with Bol, Milna, and Sumartin.

◖ HVAR

If you're looking for a quiet Dalmatian experience, Hvar Town is not what you're searching for. But that said, Hvar has advantages that brought the tourists, and the services those tourists have demanded have increased the town's advantages. It's one of the few places in Dalmatia where you'll find multiple chic bars, hotels, and restaurants, loads of yachts, and the occasional celebrity sighting. The island is fairly young, drawing foreigners and locals alike, though more and more Croatians are being priced out of their own playground. Year after year newspaper articles decry the outrageous prices of burgers, beer, and a simple coffee, which in Hvar's summer season can easily run 30Kn.

However, there are a few spots to escape the crazy prices and crowds so that you can have the best of both worlds, choosing where you want to go and when depending on your mood.

Hvar Town

Most of the year, Hvar Town is a quiet fishing village with about 3,000 residents. But by the time July swings around, tourists are descending on the place at a rate of about 30,000 a day. This translates into packed bars and restaurants and lots of jockeying to be noticed by seriously fashion-coordinated young people. But before you worry about the nightlife, there are a few things to see during the daylight hours as well.

Hvar Town was sacked by the Turks in the late 16th century, and the island capital was rebuilt by the Venetians in the early 17th century. Its hub is the the **Trg sv Stjepana,** known as the **Pjaca** (pronounced like piazza). The square's namesake is the church at the eastern end, the **Katedrala sveti Stjepan**

(St. Stephen's Cathedral, open most mornings and for mass), with its very Venetian-style belfry, though its inspiration actually came from Korčula's cathedral. The interior, which has no set opening hours, shelters a pretty Venetian painting of the Madonna and Child from the early 13th century. Next to the church you'll find the *riznica* (Bishop's Treasury, 9 A.M.–noon and 5–7 P.M. in summer, 10 A.M.–noon in winter, 15Kn), displaying a colorful array of liturgical vestments and sacral art.

The square is flanked on its southern side by the Arsenal, built in the early 16th century. A **theater** (10 A.M.–noon and 5–11 P.M. June–Sept., 10 A.M.–noon rest of year, 20Kn including admission to the gallery) was built in the Arsenal in 1612. It was one of the first theaters of its day open to the general public; the present interior dates from the 19th century. Next door is the **Arsenal Gallery of Modern Art** (tel. 021/741-009, 10 A.M.–noon and 7–11 P.M. June–Sept., 10 A.M.–noon rest of year, 20Kn including admission to the theater), which displays works by contemporary local artists.

The northern end of the old town within the city walls is referred to as the **Groda.** Here you'll find the **Crkva svetog Duha** (Church of the Holy Spirit), whose facade was decorated with fragments from other Hvar churches and the **Crkva svetog Kozme i Damjana** (Church of Sts. Cosmos and Damian), the oldest church in town. Its pretty carved Baroque roof is well

worth a look. Many of the houses in the Groda were built between the 14th and 17th centuries, though two stand out from the rest: the shell of the never-completed **Užičić Palace** (often mistakenly referred to as the Hektorović Palace) and the **Leporini Palace** (identifiable by the rabbit carving on its facade). Both palaces are located on Matije Ivanića.

From Groda, follow Ivanića until you arrive at a winding path, which leads to the **Fortica** (Fortress, 8 A.M.–midnight June–Sept., 9 A.M.–dusk Oct.–May, 10Kn). The Fortica is often referred to by locals as the Španjola, since the Spanish helped the Venetians construct it in the 16th century. On a clear day there's a great view from here all the way to Vis.

ENTERTAINMENT

Hvar Town's best-known bar is certainly **Carpe Diem** (Riva, tel. 021/742-369, www.carpe-diem-hvar.com, 9 A.M.–3 A.M. daily in summer, 9 A.M.–midnight daily in winter), a frequent haunt of the beautiful, the wealthy, and the famous (at least a few seem to get snapped here every summer). You'll need to reserve a table in the morning if you want to hang here at night. A younger crowd piles into **Veneranda** (east of Hvar's near the Hotel Delfin, no phone, 10 P.M.–5 A.M. daily in summer), a spring-break sort of place with a swimming pool and gyrating house dancers. In the summer there's a steep cover charge (100Kn) due to the place's popularity.

Mellower evenings can be had at the **Pršuta**

HVAR OFF THE BEATEN PATH

Hvar can get quite crowded in the peak season, and if you were looking for sleepy fishing villages and almost-secluded rocky beaches, sometimes the throngs can really to get to you. Try the following spots on Hvar for a taste of peace and quiet away from all the buzz along Hvar Town's streets.

- The island of **Palmižana** just off the coast of Hvar Town is not completely quiet – it's host to fashion shows and art exhibits in season – but it's full of lush forests and gardens, created at the turn of the 20th century by Eugen Meneghello, who also opened up his namesake hotel, today with 14 romantic bungalows and a great restaurant.

- **Jelsa** and **Stari Grad** are both less touristed, yet no less interesting, than Hvar Town. And why not explore the tiny villages,

like the remote port of **Sućuraj** or charming **Sveta Nedelja,** if you have a car and really want to get away? Hire a moped or car from **Luka Rent** on Hvar Town's harbor.

- You'll need to walk for close to an hour to get from the center of Hvar Town to **Robinson** on Mekičevića Bay, but it's well worth the trek. The restaurant has no water or electricity but it's a great place to eat (all organic, fresh-catch, and homegrown products) and bathe in the bay out front.

- It's not undiscovered but it's totally unpretentious – **Kamanjo's** restaurant on Milna Bay is a small affair. Make sure to try some of their homemade brandies, signature pastas, and other Italian-influenced dishes, like beef risotto with saffron.

Tri Wine Bar (Petra Hektorovića, Groda, tel. 098/969-6193, 6 P.M.–2:30 A.M. daily in summer, call for winter hours), with over 50 open bottles behind the bar for a wide selection of wines by the glass. It's the perfect place to try local wines.

ACCOMMODATIONS

Only five minutes' walk to the beach or to the center of Hvar Town, **House Gordana** (Glavica bb, tel. 021/742-182, www.house-gordana-hvar.com, 355Kn d.) is a bit like staying at a friendly grandmother's house, and the price is right as well. Also a short walk from town or the shore, **Apartments Ana Dujmovic** (Zastup bb, tel. 021/742-010, www.hvar-croatia.com/dujmovic, 567Kn d.) are bright and sunny, many with balconies. The 14th-century **Villa Nora** (Petra Hektorovića, tel. 021/742-498, www.hvar.netfirms.com, 1,450Kn d., including breakfast) has all the modern conveniences like Internet and air-conditioning in a central location.

Hotel Riva (Riva, tel. 021/750-100, www.suncanihvar.com, 2,482Kn d., including breakfast) is one of Hvar's best (or at least one of the first upscale hotels), set in a century-old stone building right on the busy Riva. Minimalist rooms are accented with bright red and oversized photos of legendary screen stars. Though the hotel is too small to have a pool or spa, it does have a good restaurant and a super terrace for watching the shiny yachts pass by.

The boutique **Hotel Park** (Hvar Town, tel. 021/718-337, www.hotelparkhvar.com, 1,773Kn d., including breakfast) opened in 2007. The 14 airy apartments and one room have pretty sea views, Internet, and plasma televisions.

The **(** **Adriana Hotel** (Fabrika bb, tel. 021/750-200, www.suncanihvar.com, 2,837Kn d., including breakfast) is currently the only Croatian hotel included in the venerable Leading Small Hotels of the World. For the not-so-budget price you get a location overlooking the marina and the old city center, with indoor and outdoor pools, a spa, and a swank rooftop lounge. In 2008 the Sunčani Hvar chain (which runs the Adriana) unveiled their latest luxe hotel, the **Amfora Grand Beach Resort** (Majerovica bb, tel. 021/750-300, www.suncanihvar.com, 2,269Kn d.,

Hvar Town, a quiet fishing village most of the year — and anything but quiet in peak season

including breakfast), with a cascading pool, private 1930s stone cabanas for relaxing, and light, sleek rooms.

FOOD

A good value on the ever-pricier island of Hvar, **Luna** (Petra Hektorovića, tel. 021/741-400, noon–midnight daily in summer, noon–3 P.M. and 6 P.M.–midnight April and Sept., 85Kn) serves up dishes such as seafood pasta and meat with dumplings and mushroom sauce in the cheery dining room or on the superb rooftop terrace.

In Groda, **Macondo** (Petra Hektorovića, Groda, tel. 021/742-850, noon–2 P.M. and 6:30 P.M.–midnight Mon.–Sat., 6:30 P.M.–midnight Sun., closed Nov.–Mar., 130Kn) packs in tourists in season, making getting a table a bit of a challenge. The reason for the cozy place's popularity? The fresh daily catches served, as well as the great selection of cakes and desserts for dine-in or takeout.

The nearby **Konobo Menego** (Petra Hektorovića, Groda, tel. 021/742-036, www .menego.hr, 11:30 A.M.–2 P.M. and 5 P.M.–midnight daily, closed Dec.–Mar., 120Kn) has a traditional interior and a slightly out-of-the-box menu. Serving up tapa-size portions of local dishes, this restaurant has a big following. One of Hvar's trendier restaurants, **Yakša** (Petra Hektorovića, Groda, tel. 021/717-202, www.yaksahvar.com, 10 A.M.–4 P.M. and 7 P.M.–1 A.M. daily in summer, noon–2 P.M. and 7 P.M.–1 A.M. daily in winter, closed Dec.–Jan., 150Kn) is only 20 meters from the cathedral and serves up brunch (from omelets to American pancakes) and lunch and dinner (starters like young cheese over baked eggplants on tomato-lentil confit and mains like lobster and fries or honey chicken breast with green chile *sambal*). The ambience is nice too—in a cozy underground Gothic space with minimalist furniture or on an open-air patio. The restaurant also plans to offer accommodation in the near future.

On the less-touristed route, **Restoran Luviji** (tel. 021/741-646, 10 A.M.–2 P.M. and 7 P.M.–midnight daily, closed Oct.–May, 85Kn) serves the usual fish alongside out-of-this-world bread and some very good homemade wines, cultivated on Hvar and the Pakleni Islands.

If you'd like to dine away from Hvar's busiest

sections, head to **Zorače** (Uvala Zorače, tel. 021/745-638, 11 A.M.–11 P.M. daily in summer), six kilometers away on a quiet stretch of beach. The menu is predictable, the decor traditional, and the view from the cliff-top terrace completely out of this world. Another option is the out-of-the-fray **Robinson** (Mekičevića Bay, tel. 091/383-5160, www.robinson-hvar .hr, 11 A.M.–sunset daily June–Sept., no credit cards, 85Kn), an hour's walk from Hvar Town. There's no water, and no electricity, but plenty of local, organic food and grilled seafood, plus a nice bay where you can take a dip before or after lunch.

Two kilometers southeast of Hvar Town is Milna Bay, with lovely beaches and the totally unpretentious **Kamanjo's** (Uvala Milna hvarska, tel. 021/745-010, noon–midnight in summer, call for winter hours, 100Kn). The owners' philosophy is that it is difficult to cook well for a large crowd, so he keeps things small. Make sure to try some of their homemade brandies (from chamomile, rose petals, oranges, and artichokes), the restaurant's signature pastas, and other Italian-influenced dishes like beef risotto with saffron.

INFORMATION AND SERVICES

The Hvar Town **tourist office** (Trg sv Stjepana bb, tel. 021/741-059, www.tzhvar .hr, 8 A.M.–1 P.M. and 5–9 P.M. Mon.–Sat. and 9 A.M.–noon Sun. June–Sept., 8 A.M.–2 P.M. Mon.–Sat. Oct.–May) is located on the corner of the Pjaca.

Palmižana

A short water taxi ride away from Hvar Town, the over-100-year-old **Pansion Meneghello** (Palmižana, Sv. Klement, Pakleni Islands, tel. 021/717-270, www.palmizana.hr, closed Nov.–Mar., 461Kn d.) on Palmižana is like a vacation within a vacation. The quiet island is worlds away from the constant buzz of nearby Hvar and the gorgeous rooms and suites, decorated with a mix of antiques, modern art, and well-placed pops of color, have a style best defined as peaceful, laid-back luxe. The family-run hotel hosts special events during the summer,

often involving themed art exhibitions. If you don't want to stay overnight, you can still come for lunch and a swim.

Stari Grad

Stari Grad is the point of entry for many ferries coming from Split, but there's plenty to see in this town that gets a lot less tourist traffic than the island's capital. It's also home to a growing art scene. Aficionados will enjoy cruising the narrow alleys looking for galleries and artists during the summer months. The most popular sight in Stari Grad is the **Tvrdalj** (tel. 021/765-068, 10 A.M.–1 P.M. and 6–8 P.M. daily June–Sept., 10Kn), the summer home of Hvar's 16th-century poet Petar Hektorović. Though the home is largely unimpressive, bits of the preserved gardens, a pretty fish pond, and dozens of inscriptions on the walls—all the work of Hektorović—make for a restful, contemplative meander. There's a 15th-century Dominican monastery nearby with a small **museum** (10 A.M.–noon and 4–7:30 P.M. Mon.–Sat. in summer, 10Kn) where you'll find some Greek tombstones, Hektorović artifacts, and a Tintoretto.

There are plenty of beaches in Stari Grad, though the best ones are on the southern side of the Riva towards Borić.

The Stari Grad **tourist office** (Nova Riva 2, tel. 021/765-763, www.stari-grad-faros.hr, 8 A.M.–9 P.M. daily June–Sept., 8 A.M.–2 P.M. Mon.–Fri. Oct.–May) can help hook you up with private accommodation, generally a much better option than the overpriced concrete resorts in the area. When you need to grab a bite, Stari Grad has two excellent options. The first, **Antika Restaurant and Café Bar** (Donja Kola, tel. 021/765-479, noon–3 P.M. and 6 P.M.–1 A.M. daily, closed Dec.–Jan., 80Kn), located in a 16th-century building, is a funky little spot with a very different menu from most small-town Dalmatian establishments. Try the steak with green pepper sauce. In the heart of the old town, **C Jurin Podrum** (Donja kola 8, tel. 021/765-804, noon–2:30 P.M. and 6 P.M.–midnight daily in summer, 110Kn) has been famous with

Europe's elite since it opened in the 1930s (Edward VIII and Wallace Simpson dined here the year of his abdication). The restaurant offers dishes from a simple starter of new goat cheese topped with grilled vegetables to an unexpected spaghetti with octopus and zucchini, a featured dish on the menu.

Jelsa

Though Jelsa sees more and more tourists every year, it's nothing like Hvar Town. Take an hour or so to wander the old alleyways, admiring the stone buildings and the 16th-century **Crkva svetog Ivana** (Church of St. John). Though the beaches in Jelsa tend to get a bit crowded, the local **Mina** beach, next to the Hotel Mina, is good for kids. Just 1.5 kilometers away you'll find **Grebišce beach** with a small bar and restaurant, or take a water taxi from the Jelsa harbor to nudist **Zečevo** island or the usually not nudist **Glavica Peninsula**.

The **Hvar Hostel** (Jelsa bb, tel. 098/978-4143, www.hvar-hostel.com, 285Kn d.), formerly Pension Huljić, has much nicer rooms than you'd expect, plus a peaceful garden and a location that's walking distance to practically everything you need (beach, bus station, and restaurants, to name a few). A charming little family-run hotel conveniently located near the bus station, the **Pansion Murvica** (Sv Roko, Jelsa, tel. 021/761-405, www.murvica.net, no credit cards, 350Kn d., including breakfast) offers clean rooms and a good restaurant. **Huljić** (Banski Dolac, tel. 021/761-409, noon–3 P.M. and 7 P.M.–midnight daily, closed late Oct.–mid-April, no credit cards, 95Kn) serves plenty of dishes that are a departure from the ever-present grilled fish, plus tastings of the owners' own red and white wines. Eight kilometers southeast from town, ◖ **Humac** (Humac, tel. 091/523-9463, noon–10 P.M. daily in summer, no credit cards, 90Kn) is a restaurant in a practically deserted village. All the dishes are cooked on the fire—there's no electricity in town—and romantic candlelight is provided.

If you're looking for something a bit more hopping, head to **Chuara** (Riva, tel. 091/575-5114, www.chuara-jelsa.hr, 9 A.M.–1 P.M. and 5 P.M.–5 A.M. daily in summer), for swish cocktails and DJ tunes.

Jelsa has a **tourist office** (Riva bb, tel. 021/761-918, www.tzjelsa.hr).

Sveta Nedelja

On the southern side of the island, almost due south of Stari Grad (though it's better connected to Jelsa), is the village of Sveta Nedelja, a must for wine lovers. You can overnight at the basic **Vila Irming** (Sveta Nedelja, tel. 021/745-768, www.irming.hr, closed Nov.–Apr., no credit cards, 425Kn d.) in the fishing village of Sveta Nedelja. It's not a fancy sort of place but there are nice beaches (paved and pebbled) a short walk away and you can take a water taxi pretty much anywhere on the island from the local marina (ask the staff to help you arrange transport).

As for wineries, be sure to hit up **Zlatan Plenković** (Sveta Nedelja, tel. 021/745-725, www.zlatanotok.hr, call for information about tours) and sample some of his Grand Cru wine, made from Plavac Mali grapes. The Grand Cru is most similar to an excellent Barolo, but with its own flair. He also has a guesthouse where you can stay and a restaurant, **Bilo Idro** (Sveta Nedelja, tel. 021/745-725, www.zlatanotok.hr, 9 A.M.–1 A.M. daily mid-May–mid-Oct.), which serves his wines plus great seafood in a waterfront location.

Svirče

A worthwhile excursion from either Jelsa or Vrboska, this small interior village is not only a way to get off the beaten path, but is also home to the **Tomić** (tel. 021/768-160, www.bastijana.hr, contact for hours and visits) winery. They produce a variety of wines and brandies, but it's most famous for its dessert *prosecco* called Hectorovich, after Hvar's most famous poet.

Vrboska

Vrboska is a quiet little town and a great location for beachgoers. The village has two interesting churches: the **Crkva svete Marije** (St. Mary's Church, 10 A.M.–noon and 6–7 P.M. Mon.–Sat., free), whose floor is largely made up of tombstones, and the Baroque **Crkva svetog**

Lovre (St. Lawrence's Church, 10 A.M.–noon Mon.–Sat., free) with a couple of pretty Italian paintings inside.

The most popular beach is **Glavica,** about one kilometer from Vrboska. If you have a car you can park at the Soline parking lot. **Soline** is the main beach here, drawing sun worshippers from many parts of the island. Walking 5–15 minutes from the parking lot to the north, you'll hit the nudist beaches, with big flat rocks perfect for roasting in your birthday suit, or continue to the romantic coves of Maslinica and Palinica.

Right in Vrboska, family-run **Villa Darinka** (tel. 021/774-188, no email or website, closed Nov.–Mar., 355Kn d.) has comfortable rooms with sea-facing balconies and neat-as-a-pin decor. For sustenance, try the **Restoran Gardelin** (tel. 021/774-280, www.gmp-art-studio.com/Gardelin, daily in summer, call for exact hours, 85Kn) for grilled fish, stewed fish, and baked fish.

Sućuraj

On the far eastern side of the island, the fishing village of Sućuraj is one of Hvar's quieter towns. A great place for beach lovers, the town is surrounded by lounging options. A short walk from the center of town you'll find sandy Cesminica to the south or pebbly Bilina to the north. You can rent a boat or hop in a water taxi from the small harbor to the sandy bays of Mlaska (north) or Perna (south).

Getting There and Around

Stari Grad is the main port serving ferries from Split (around 7 daily in the high season, 1.5 hours), Rijeka (13 hours, stops in Split), and Dubrovnik (7.5 hours, stops in Korčula). You can link to Makarska via the ferry at Sućuraj (only viable if you have your own car on the ferry, since there are no buses to speak of out of the small village).

If you're traveling without a car, the best way to get to town is the hydrofoil from Split (Jadrolinija, tel. 021/631-357, www.jadrolinija.hr), which takes less than an hour into Hvar Town, the center of all the action. There's also a catamaran (at least one daily in summer) linking Brač (from Bol) to the town of Jelsa on Hvar.

Buses are waiting for the larger ferries and link Hvar Town and Stari Grad (30 minutes). Buses from Stari Grad also connect with Vrboska and Jelsa (each 30 minutes). Keep in mind that buses on the island can be highly unpredictable.

You can rent mopeds and cars from Luka Rent (on Hvar Town's harbor, tel. 021/742-946) or Pelegrini Tours (Riva bb, Hvar Town, tel. 021/742-250, www.pelegrini-hvar.hr). Mopeds cost around 300Kn per day. The agencies are also good sources for boat and bicycle rentals.

⬤ VIS

A military base under Tito for some 40 years, Vis is a relatively new addition to the Croatian tourist trade. The island has long been filled with farmers and fishermen, who both know a thing or two about good food, making Vis somewhat of an unassuming gourmet destination. Though you'll still find your share of tourists in July and August, it's much quieter than many of the surrounding islands and coastline.

Vis Town

Located on the northeast side of Vis, Vis Town is the largest village on the island. Though it's popular with yachters—the main marina is located here—its history is more agricultural, with much of the produce and wines grown in the hills outside of town having supplied trade for the little port. These days you'll find top-quality restaurants and a handful of fun bars with a seafaring edge.

SIGHTS

There's not too much to see here, but the **Arheološki muzej** (Archaeological Museum, tel. 021/711-729, 10 A.M.–1 P.M. and 5–8 P.M. Tues.–Sun. in summer, 20Kn), located in the **Baterija,** an old Austrian fortress, has a nice collection of objects from Vis's Greek past. In Kut, the yachting section of town, the old patrician palaces, **Crkva svetog Ciprijana** (St. Cyprian's church), and a **British naval cemetery** are

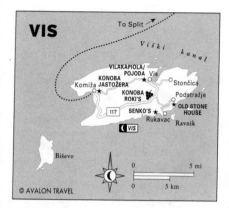

located in Vis's first (circa 1911) hotel, serves lunch and dinner as well. Tuck into French toast with syrup, pancakes with fresh oranges and lemon jam, or a bowl of orange soup for brunch, washed down with a strong cup of espresso.

The artsy **Kantun** (Biskupa Mihe Pusića 17, tel. 021/711-306, 6 P.M.–midnight daily, no credit cards, 90Kn) mixes traditional and modern in the decor as well as the menu. It's a solid choice for dinner with a phenomenal smoked tuna carpaccio, a variety of well-prepared pasta dishes, and some good-quality meat and fish as well.

One of the few pizza places with a good wine list, **Karijola** (Šetalište Viskog Boja 4, tel. 021/711-433, noon–late night daily July–Aug., 5–11 P.M. June and Sept., 70Kn) serves up super oven-baked pizza on a terrace with a pretty view.

Vila Kapiola (V. Nazora 32, tel. 021/711-755, 5 P.M.–midnight daily in season, reservations recommended, 110Kn) is one of Vis's best, nestled in a secret garden beside an old Italian villa under the shade of palm trees. The menu is local and the quality superb, with dishes like smoked fish soup and a selection of great local wines. **Pojoda** (Don Cvjetka Marasovića 8, tel. 021/711-575, noon–3 P.M. and 5 P.M.–midnight in summer, 4–11 P.M. in winter, 120Kn) is one of Croatia's most famous fish restaurants. Located in an old house complete with cloistered garden, the restaurant is beautiful—but the creations of

the main attractions. The cemetery is about a 20-minute walk from Kut, but just beyond it you'll find a wonderful gem of a beach at **Grandovac.** A 20-minute walk northwest of Vis Town's ferry landing you'll find a few crumbling graves at the **Helenističko groblje** (Ancient Greek Cemetery, afternoons daily in summer, free) and what's left of a few old Roman baths with some attractive mosaics.

ACCOMMODATIONS
Hotel Paula (Petra Hektorovića 2, tel. 021/711-362, www.hotelpaula.com, 690Kn d.) is a 35-room hotel in Kut, within Vis's old section. The stone building, with a peaceful courtyard and a good fish restaurant, houses simple but comfortable rooms with air-conditioning and satellite television.

You could also look into booking a room or apartment through one of the agencies in town. Try **Navigator** (Šetalište stare Isse 1, tel. 021/717-786, www.navigator.hr), which also rents cars and scooters.

FOOD
You can certainly eat well—very well, in fact—in Vis Town, though if you're looking for the absolute best, you'll need to check out other villages around the island. An excellent place to start your day is **Doručak kod Tihane** (Obala Sv. Jurja 5, tel. 021/718-472, www.restoranti hana.com, 9 A.M.–1 P.M. and 6 P.M.–midnight daily, 70Kn), though the charming restaurant,

HIKING SAFELY ON VIS

Though there wasn't a war on Vis, there are potential land mines left over from the old military base. If you're going to hike, make sure to follow the rules. Watch for signs with a skull and/or crossbones that say *Pazi Mina.* It's also not a bad idea to check with the tourist office in Vis Town before doing any hiking or trekking in the wilderness.

SOUTHERN DALMATIA

© 123RF.COM

the fishing village Komiža, on the western end of Vis

chef-owner Zoran Brajčić are the star attractions. Brajčić infuses the native Dalmatian cuisine with his Slavonian roots; dishes like the *manistra na brudet,* a bean and pasta soup, and the grilled belted bonito, treated to a spice rub and weighted down for 10 hours before cooking, provide diners with a stunning gourmet performance. *Hib,* a traditional biscuit made from ground dried figs, is a sweet ending to the evening.

INFORMATION AND SERVICES

Vis's **tourist office** (Šetalište stare Isse 5, tel. 021/717-017, www.tz-vis.hr, 9 A.M.–1 P.M. and 6–9 P.M. Mon.–Sat. in summer, 9 A.M.–1 P.M. Mon.–Fri. in winter) can help with maps, brochures, and information on hiking in the area.

Komiža

On the western end of Vis, ten kilometers from Vis Town, Komiža is a fishing village extraordinaire, slightly stubbly, laid-back, rather quiet, and washed with sun, much like many of the older fishermen in town. You'll find the

13th-century Venetian **Kaštel** (Castle Fort) by the sea, where the **Ribarski muzej** (Fishing Museum, 9 A.M.–noon and 6–10 P.M. daily, 10Kn) will help you get more in touch with the local culture and historical livelihood. There are great views from the Kaštel's 16th-century tower as well.

The most interesting of the town's churches is the **Gospa Gusarica** (Our Lady of the Pirates) near the Biševo Hotel, so named for the legend that claims a painting of the Virgin stolen by pirates made its way back to shore after a shipwreck.

Once a lobster storage facility, 【 **Konoba Jastožera** (Gundulićeva 6, tel. 021/713-859, www.jastozera.com, 5 P.M.–midnight daily, closed late Oct.–mid-Apr., 300Kn) still wrestles fresh lobster out of an underwater cage for your dinner. Tables are placed on planks above the water and the sound of the sea lapping below is a great accompaniment to the food, which has been enjoyed by a number of celebrities (their photos line the walls). Lobster is the feature of the menu—lobster spaghetti, lobster cream soup, and several preparations of main-course lobster. Shrimp, mussels, and a smattering of meat dishes round out the offerings.

The simple and beautiful apartments at **Villa Nonna** (Ribarska 50, tel. 098/380-046, www .villa-nonna.com, no credit cards, 496Kn d.) are an excellent value—pleasingly furnished and only a minute's walk to the marina. If rooms here are booked ask the owners for recommendations around town.

Approximately half a dozen buses connect Komiža and Vis Town daily, taking about 25 minutes.

Stončiča

Rent a boat or take a water taxi to Stončiča, about six kilometers from Vis Town. The beaches in this sandy bay are heavenly and there's a lighthouse and a restaurant. Set in a romantic cove, (**Stončica** (Stončica 1, tel. 021/711-669, lists summer hours as "always" and winter hours "by agreement," 100Kn) is a family restaurant serving their own home-grown and daily-catch specialties. The menu varies according to what's fresh, but you'll always find grilled fish and vegetables. Dive into the *pašticada nona* when available and sample the homemade spicy lamb salami (*kulen*) and dark red prosecco while sitting under the shade of palm trees and meandering vines.

Though (**Senko's** (Mola trovna, tel. 098/352-5803, noon–midnight daily, no credit cards, 110Kn) is no longer undiscovered, it's still an experience. Located in a cove on the southern side of Vis, between Stončica and Stupišće, is chef-owner Senko Karuza's laid-back restaurant, filled with wooden tables and benches on a stone terrace overlooking the water. The fruits and vegetables come from Senko's organic garden. The menu is whatever's available and whatever he feels like making, and all of it is good, from smoked fish soup with rosemary and smoked eel soup to fish or bean and pasta stew to grilled fish and shrimp, flavored with wild herbs and washed down with some of Senko's wine. It's a must to make a reservation in season.

Rukavac and Biševo

In Rukavac village, 10 kilometers south of Vis Town on the southern side of the island, you'll find **Srebrena plaža** (Silver Beach), another piece of paradise just across from the islet of **Biševo,** home to the legendary **Modra špilja** (Blue Cave, 30Kn), reached only from the sea. The only way to describe the grotto is as an other-worldly mix of bright blue that seems like it's lit from below, covered by a canopy of dark rock. However you see it, it's been a major tourist attraction since the 1880s. If you'd like to visit the cave, take a trip from either the Komiža or Vis Town harbors (the excursions are heavily advertised) or take a taxi boat.

Natural Holiday (Salbunara Bay, tel. 098/173-1673, www.bisevo.org, no credit cards, approximately 3,350Kn weekly depending on requested excursions and meals) is part hotel, part lifestyle concept. It's a totally green village of huts powered along by solar panels and the wind, with mosquito netting and ergonomic beds. It's not luxurious, but it is peaceful. Lay back in one of their hammocks while waiting on dinner, prepared by the owners, of organic vegetables and fresh fish.

You'll need to book early to snatch one of the rooms at (**Old Stone House** (Rukavac, tel. 098/131-4179 or 44-1834/814-533 (UK), www.weareactive.com, 5,950Kn per week includes activities, daily breakfast, four lunches, and three dinners) in the miniscule village of Rukavac. The home is super stylish and best of all includes an invigorating customized activity program that can consist of mountain biking, kayaking, hiking, and a spot of yoga.

Rukavac is easily reached from Vis Town on a good asphalt road. You can also take a taxi boat.

Wineries

Eleven kilometers east of Komiža or seven kilometers south of Vis Town, **Konoba Roki's** (Plisko Polje 17, tel. 021/714-004, noon–late daily April–Oct., no credit cards, 120Kn) is a winery and restaurant a short drive from Vis Town by cab or car (the restaurant will pick up parties of four or more from Vis Town). Not only is the food good but it's fun to sample the red and white wines produced by the owners.

Getting There and Around

Vis is served by at least one daily car ferry from Split year-round (2 hours 20 minutes, 45Kn). In the summer, there are one or two more catamarans from Split (1 hour 15 minutes, 60Kn).

Komiža is connected with Vis Town by a bus that runs according to ferry schedules. In the summer it's quite reliable, but out of the high season you may need to wait (bring a book).

To get around the island, it's not a bad idea to rent a small car or scooter. Agencies such as Navigator (Šetalište stare Isse 1, tel. 021/717-786, www.navigator.hr) and Ionios (Obala Svetog Jurja 36, tel. 021/711-532) rent transportation options around the island—Navigator offers cars and scooters, and Ionios offers scooters and bicycles.

◖ KORČULA

Korčula, a small island with a much grander past, is filled with small museums, pretty festivals, and tiny sun-washed villages. There are plenty of pebbly beaches lapped by the calm Adriatic waters and the island is home to some quality white wines and top olive oils, famous for their rich flavor, from the town of Vela Luka. Korčula was settled by the Greeks in the 6th century B.C., when it was known as Black Corfu. The island was relatively unimportant until the Venetians came in the 10th century, using it as an important naval base. Korčula thrived from the 13th to the 15th centuries, though an outbreak of plague in 1571 brought an end to the island's importance. Korčula began to find life again as a tourist destination in the 1920s and by the 1970s the island was burgeoning with hotels and restaurants to serve the summer visitors.

One of the highlights of Korčula is its colorful **festivals.** The Moreška sword dancers that perform throughout the summer for visitors, the processions held during Easter week, and the reenactment of the 1298 Battle Korčula (early Sept.) all lend a bit of local flavor to

Korčula Harbor

© SHANN FOUNTAIN CULO

a stay on the island. Contact the Korčula **tourist office** (Obala Franje Tuđmana, tel. 020/715-701, www.korcula.net, 8 A.M.–3 P.M. and 4–10 P.M. Mon.–Sat. and 8 A.M.–1:30 P.M. Sun. June–Oct., 8 A.M.–2 P.M. Mon.–Sat. Nov.–May) for more information on times and locations of events.

Korčula Town

Often compared with Dubrovnik, Korčula Town reminds visitors of a smaller version of the seaside walled city. But at a closer glance you'll find the Venetians, who built the small city, did a much better job of planning than the planners of Dubrovnik. Streets are laid out to make use of summer winds and to keep out the bitter northeasterly *bura.* Still, the Venetians seem to get lost in the limelight created by the town's most famous citizen, Marco Polo, likely (though not proven) born here in 1254. You'll see his name used in everything from pizzas to hotels to desserts.

SIGHTS

While the claim that Marco Polo was from Korčula is not unreasonable, the idea that the

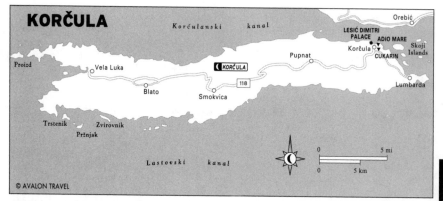

circa-17th-century house touted as the **House of Marco Polo** (Ulica DePolo, 9 A.M.–9 P.M. daily in summer, 15Kn) was actually his house is a very big stretch. Plans have been underway for years now to turn the house into a museum, but you can still only climb to the top of the tower for some nice views over the water.

Heading south towards the small space known as the main square, called the **Trg Sv. Marka** or the **Pjaceta,** you'll find the **Gradski muzej** (Town Museum, Trg Sv. Marka bb, tel. 020/711-420, 10 A.M.–9 P.M. Mon.–Sat. in summer, call for winter hours, 15Kn), housed in a 16th-century Venetian palace. The star exhibits are a 4th-century Greek tablet, the earliest proof of civilization on the island, and a mock-up of a peasant kitchen.

Across from the museum is the **Katedrala svetog Marka** (St. Mark's Cathedral, Trg Sv. Marka bb, tel. 020/711-049, 9 A.M.–2 P.M. and 5–7 P.M. daily, April–Oct., 15Kn). The imposing building is considered one of the most beautiful Croatian churches. Inside, look for the two works by Tintoretto, particularly the restored 1550 painting of St. Mark between St. Bartholomew and St. Jerome, and the frothy stone canopy carved by local stonemason Marko Andrijić in the late 15th century. Next door you'll find the *riznica* (treasury, tel. 020/711-049, 9 A.M.–2 P.M. and 5–7 P.M. daily Apr.–Oct., call for winter hours, 15Kn), filled with a wonderful but modest art collection of Dalmatian and Italian Renaissance painters.

West of the old town, fans of more modern works will appreciate the **Galerija Maksimiljana Vanke** (Memorial Collection of Maksimiljan Vanka, Put Sv. Nikole, 9 A.M.–noon and 6–9 P.M. daily July–Aug., 5Kn), with paintings from art nouveau painter Maksimiljan Vanka as well as occasional exhibits by other Croatian artists.

ACCOMMODATIONS

A minute's walk from the ferry stop, rooms at **Roberta's Guesthouse** (Put Sv. Nikole 24, tel. 020/711-247, robertamk@hotmail.com, 290Kn d., including breakfast) are cozy and the hostess, Roberta, is a delight. Try to book the room with the small waterfront balcony.

The **Royal Apartments** (Trg Petra Segedina 4, tel. 098/184-0444, open June–Oct., no credit cards, 690Kn d.) aren't fancy but they're clean, the owner is very kind and helpful, and the location (slightly west of the old town on a small waterfront square) is wonderful. The renovated **Hotel Marko Polo** (Šetalište Frana Kršinića, tel. 020/726-100, www.htp-korcula.hr, 965Kn d., including breakfast) has sleek and trendy though incredibly small rooms. The hotel has indoor and outdoor pools and access to a pebbly beach about one kilometer from the bus station. Though the property has received an overhaul, unfortunately the service has not. Opening in spring 2009, the (**Lesić Dimitri Palace** (Don Pavla Poše 1-6, tel. 020/715-560, www.lesic-dimitri.com) promises to be the gem of Korčula hotels. The small luxury retreat (with just six mega-suites) nestled within the walls of an 18th-century bishop's palace in the center of town also plans to include a spa and restaurant.

FOOD

The island offers a plethora of seafood restaurants, but the pastry shop ◖ **Cukarin** (Hrvatske bratske zajednice bb, tel. 020/711-055, 8:30 A.M.–noon and 6–9 P.M. daily) is the island's true culinary gem. Make sure to try the Marko Polo *bombica,* a chocolate-encased cream delight, or the walnut-filled *klašun,* and take home a bottle of one of the dessert wines made from the local *grk* grape. Dine alfresco on the square next to the Town Hall at **Gradski Podrum** (Trg Antuna Kaporova, tel. 020/711-222, 11 A.M.–2 P.M. and 6–10:30 P.M. daily, closed Nov.–Mar., 85Kn). The menu offers something for everyone, from pasta and salads to meat and fish. Even though **Kanavelić** (Ulica Franje Tuđmana 1904, tel. 020/711-800, 6 P.M.–1 A.M. daily, closed Dec.–Apr., 90Kn) is popular with the tourist trade, it has a nice ambience (high ceilings, a courtyard with fruit trees) and the food is good, particularly the fish stew served over a steaming mound of polenta. The outdoor terraces of the rustic **Konoba Belin** (Zrnovo Prvo Selo, tel. 091/503-9258, www.konobabelin.com, 10 A.M.–midnight daily in season, no credit cards, 100Kn), some two kilometers away from town in Zrnovo Prvo Selo (First Village Zrnovo), are the best part of the busy restaurant. The food is solid, too, with wind-cured ham and cheese appetizers, seafood risotto, and grilled fish.

◖ **Adio Mare** (Sv. Roka 2, tel. 020/711-253, 5 P.M.–midnight daily in summer, call for winter hours, 135Kn) is a staple on the Korčula restaurant scene and generally declared one of the island's best. It's imperative to book a dinner reservation in season to snag a table at this seafood restaurant just steps from the main square.

Call in advance to order *peka* at **Ranč Maha** (Zrnovo–Pupnat Road, tel. 098/494-389, 1–11 P.M. daily in summer, call for hours in winter, no credit cards, 95Kn), a family farm in the hills above town where hikers and tourists converge to eat the clay oven–baked meat and seafood washed down with some seriously strong homemade herbal grappa. In winter a crackling fire makes dining here even better.

Lumbarda

The village of Lumbarda, six kilometers from Korčula Town, is best known for its sandy beaches. A short drive south of the village will bring you to Sveti Križ (Holy Cross Church) set amongst vineyards, where you'll veer left to **Bilin Zal**, a fairly quiet beach with rocky sections. For lunch there's a good little *konoba* here in the ruins of an old summer residence. Keep driving southeast to reach **Vela Pržina,** facing the Italian coast, about 15 minutes away. Pržina is a long beach, but quite popular as well, and gets filled early.

If you don't mind sharing the garden with the occasional goat, stay at the farmhouse **Pansion Marinka** (Lumbarda, tel. 098/344-712, marinka.milina-bire@du.htnet.hr, www.korcula.net/firme/private/lumbarda/bire_marinka.htm, no credit cards, 230Kn d., including breakfast), a grandmotherly bed-and-breakfast with kind owners who are happy to regale you with stories of the island if you ask. The rooms are basic but cozy and sampling some of the farm's products, particularly the olive oil, is a real treat. One and a half kilometers from Lumbarda the **Apartments Val** (Uvala Račišće bb, tel. 020/712-430, www.korcula-val.com, 290Kn d.) are situated on a quiet bay. Each apartment has a sea-facing terrace and satellite TV and the hosts can rent bicycles and a small boat for cruising around the island. The casual, quiet restaurant **More** (Lumbarda, tel. 020/712-068, lunch and dinner daily in summer, call for hours in winter, 110Kn) has a shady vine-enveloped terrace. The specialty of the chef is the melt-in-your-mouth lobster accompanied by pasta in tomato sauce.

Vela Luka

A 20-minute walk from town is the **Vela Špila cave** (tel. 020/813-602, www.vela-spila.hr, hours vary, 10Kn), a limestone cave inhabited by various people since 18,000 B.C. Archaeological finds from the site can be found in Vela Luka's small **Gradski muzej** (Town Museum, ask at tourist office for hours, 10Kn). The **tourist office** in town (Ulica 41 br. 11, tel. 021/813-619, www.tzvelaluka.hr, 8 A.M.–9 P.M. Mon.–Sat. June–Sept., 8 A.M.–3 P.M. Mon.–Sat. winter) can direct you to private rooms, good restaurants, and where to buy some of the town's famous olive oils. You'll find two small islands just off the coast of Vela Luka. Taxi boats can take you to **Proizd** (20 minutes, 35Kn) or **Ošjak** (30 minutes, 60Kn), where pretty pebbly beaches and small restaurants are the perfect spot to get away—don't be shocked by the nudists.

Getting There and Around

The island's two major ferry ports (Korčula Town and Vela Luka) have good connections to the mainland. Jadrolinija (www.jadrolinija.hr) runs the majority of the ferries, with a daily car ferry (in summer, check with Jadrolinija for winter connections) connecting both ports with Split (around 3 hours, 50Kn), often making a stop in Hvar as well. There's also a ferry connecting Korčula Town with Dubrovnik (3 hours). Catamarans link Dubrovnik and Korčula Town (4 weekly, 2.5 hours) as well as Split (daily, 2.25 hours). Both trips cost around 60Kn.

Korčula has excellent connections with the Pelješac Peninsula, with connections from Orebić on the mainland and Korčula Town in only 15 minutes. There's at least one daily car ferry and one passenger ferry on summer weekdays.

Buses regularly connect Korčula Town with Lumbarda and Vela Luka (6 on weekdays, less weekends, 1 hour, 35Kn). Water taxis are another good way to jump between Korčula Town and Lumbarda.

There's a daily bus to Dubrovnik (twice daily in summer, once daily in winter, 3 hours, 95Kn), but since it often fills up in summer it's a good idea to make a reservation in advance.

SKOJI ISLANDS

To really get away, rent a small boat on Korčula (you can try Rent a Djir, Obala Hrvatskih mornara, tel. 020/711-908, www.korcula-rent.com, which also rents cars and scooters) and navigate your way to the Skoji Islands, a group of 19 small islands just off the coast of Lumbarda. The two largest islands, Badija and Vrnik, have places for a light lunch as well as beaches. The other, uninhabited islands are just the place to find your own stretch of pebbly perfection.

LASTOVO

The island of Lastovo was chosen by settlers as a safe harbor from the constant raids of Uskok, Turkish, and Genoese pirates. Built in the crater of a former volcano, the town is almost invisible from the tall cliffs that surround it. In 2006, the island was declared a national park and it's a great place to see Dalmatia as it once was. It's served by only one ferry from Split a day, and the narrow alleyways of the old village are relatively uncrowded, especially out of high season. In between chilling out, you can visit the 15th-century **Crkva svetog Kuzme i Damjana** (Church of Sts. Cosmos and Damian) or hike up to the 19th-century fort for some stellar views, and then try to find a **water taxi** (ask at the tourist office or the marina) to take you to the small island of **Šaplun** for even more waterfront peace and quiet.

Festivals

The island of Lastovo is famous for its **Poklad festival,** a winter carnival centering around a giant effigy of a Turk (from the medieval era when the island suffered constant pressure from the invading Ottomans) that is carried around town and treated quite poorly before being lifted by rope above the town and burned. It's loud, it's a little strange (lots of drunken shouting involved), and it's totally interesting—one of those festivals completely unaware of any tourists who might have ventured to the island in winter to see it. As with Mardi Gras, the biggest celebration is on the Tuesday before Ash Wednesday. Contact the Lastovo **tourist office** (in Ubli on the main square, tel. 020/801-018, www.lastovo-tz.net, 8 A.M.–noon Mon.–Fri.) for more information.

SOUTHERN DALMATIA

Accommodations and Food

The **Vila Antica** (Sv. Kuzme i Damjana 3, tel. 098/447-311, www.vila-antica.com, 600Kn d.) in Lastovo village is a pretty old stone house, simply but tastefully outfitted, that's walking distance to the bus station, restaurants, and the beach, accessed via a shady path. The local diving center also runs a small hotel, the **Ladesta** (Uvala Pasadur, tel. 020/802-100, www.diving-paradise.net, 275Kn d.), near the port of Ubli. The circa-1837 **Struga Lighthouse** (Skrivena luka 110, tel. 01/245-2909, www.adriatica.net, 298Kn d.) has several simply furnished apartments run by the lighthouse keepers, who also cook filling meals for guests. From here you can explore Lastovo's villages and festivals.

If you ever wanted to live like Robinson Crusoe, **Mrčara Island** (tel. 021/384-279 or 099/212-0853, branko.pavelin@st.t-com.hr, www.adriatic-lastovo.vze.com, 922Kn d.), just off the coast of Lastovo, is the place to go. Six rooms in a stone house and three little cabins (a nice word for shacks) offer back-to-basics accommodation and facilities. Read: There's no electricity and washing and cooking are done with rainwater. In return you get some of the most beautiful nature and a fun, friendly atmosphere with like-minded guests.

The **Konoba Augusta Insula** (Zaklopatica Bay, tel. 020/801-167, www.augustainsula.com, 100Kn) serves up lobster spaghetti and a good white wine, made by the owners, on a waterfront terrace.

Getting There and Around

A daily car ferry connects the island with Split via Hvar Town and Vela Luka on Korčula. The ferry takes about three hours from Split (about 60Kn) and docks at the village of Ubli on Lastovo. Taxis wait here to ferry you to various spots around the island.

◖ MLJET

There's not so much in terms of sights on Mljet besides the natural beauty of one of Dalmatia's most unspoiled islands. Just across from Dubrovnik, this heavily forested national park has a unique feature—two sparkling saltwater lakes. The largest lake has its own island, on which stands a 12th-century Benedictine monastery.

Sights and Recreation

The **Mljet National Park** is the biggest draw on Mljet, covering one third of the island. The crown jewels are the saltwater Veliko and Malo jezero (Big and Small Lake). Veliko jezero has a small island within the lake, topped by the Benedictine Svete Marije (St. Mary's), a church and 12th-century monastery. Other than that the biggest attractions of the island are sport and relaxation. **Biking** the island is the best way to get around (rent bikes from the Polače harbor, the Hotel Odisej, or the park's ticket office, all around 90Kn daily), though you can also rent a canoe or kayak (try Adriatic Kayak Tours, www.adriatickayaktours.com) or go windsurfing or diving (arranged through the Hotel Odisej). The **diving** is interesting since a 3rd-century Roman

---

LIGHTHOUSE ACCOMMODATIONS ON THE CROATIAN COAST

Some lighthouses on the Croatian coast are a bit out of the way, while others are totally remote, but all of them offer cheap, interesting accommodation on islands all over Croatia. One of the more famous lighthouses is on Palagruža, an island whose rocky shores are rumored to be the resting place of Greek hero Diomedes; the island's sunlit coves are fringed by the Adriatic's most startlingly blue waters. Many of the lighthouses are the ultimate in secluded escapes, with lots of flora and fauna to discover and abundant marine life, perfect for divers and snorkelers. It's imperative to bring your own provisions, though you may be able to arrange for meals or at least fresh fish from the lighthouse keeper. Check out **Adriatica.net** for more information and reservations for lighthouses on the coast.

shipwreck and a sunken WWII German torpedo boat are right off the coast.

Accommodations

At the mouth of Veliko Jezero, the **Srsen Apartments** (Soline bb, tel. 020/744-032, sandra.srsen@du.t-com.hr, 375Kn d.) have pretty water views and a large communal terrace. In the heart of Mljet National Park you'll find the beautiful 🌒 **Villa Jezero** (Njivice 2, tel. 020/744-019, www.jezero.tk, 496Kn d., including breakfast), a huge old limestone building that has served guests since 1934. The rooms are simple and the meals are lovingly prepared by the owners by arrangement. This is out-of-the-way peace at its best. To get there you'll take the national park bus to the owners' boat (ask when you get on the bus), which will take you across the lake; call to arrange pickup. It's plain, and it's a 1970s communist relic, but the **Hotel Odisej** (Pomena, tel. 020/744-022, www.hotelodisej.hr, 795Kn d., including breakfast) does meet basic requirements for shelter. Actually it's not all that bad. Some rooms have nice waterfront balconies and the staff is a pretty friendly bunch.

Food

🌒 **Marijina Konoba** (Prožura, tel. 020/746-113, 8 A.M.–midnight in summer, call for winter hours, 95Kn) in Prožura is the definition of a family restaurant. The owners grow or catch everything on the menu, as well as prepare the food and serve the guests. Boats can be tied to the moorings in front. On the shaded terrace overlooking the bay the restaurant serves homemade cheese marinated in oil and brick oven–baked lobster with potatoes along with a selection of wines from their well-stocked cellar.

Though there are plenty of tourist-oriented restaurants preying on visitors to St. Mary's Island, **Melita** (St. Mary's Island, tel. 020/744-145, 10 A.M.–midnight daily, closed Oct.–Apr., no credit cards, 120Kn) is the real deal, located inside the monastery near the church. It's not cheap but the location is prime and the food is good. In Bavino Polje you'll find the bar **Komarac** (Sršenovići 44, no phone, 8:45 A.M.–midnight daily, no credit cards, 70Kn), a mosquito-themed bar with an eccentric vibe, perfect for a laid-back drink. Next door is **Triton** (Sršenovići 43, tel. 020/745-131, 10 A.M.–midnight daily, closed Nov.–Mar., no credit cards, 95Kn), an amiable place specializing in walnut liqueur and goat. If you're not a fan, they have seafood and other meats as well.

Getting There and Around

You can visit Mljet as a day trip from Dubrovnik, taking the passengers-only Nona Ana catamaran (Atlantagent, Obala Stjepana Radića 26, Dubrovnik, tel. 020/313-355, www.atlantagent.com, 70Kn) from Gruž in the morning, usually around 9 A.M. or 10 A.M. The boat stops at Sobra and Polače before heading back from Gruž in mid- to late afternoon. You'll have to stay overnight if you take the Jadrolinija car ferry, also departing from Gruž harbor, leaving in the afternoon and returning the following morning. It docks in Sobra, a 20-minute drive away from the national park.

Buses meet ferries in Sobra and connect to Polače and Pomena (both take over an hour), but they're not always reliable, particularly outside the busiest months of July and August. To get around and explore the island, it's really helpful to have a car. Mini Brum (tel. 020/745-260 or 098/285-566) rents cars from several locations on Mljet. Renting a bike is another option. Try the Polače harbor, the Hotel Odisej, or the park's ticket office, all charging around 90Kn daily.

DUBROVNIK

Ragusa. Dubrovnik. No matter what the city's been called over the centuries, it has never failed to inspire. Within Dubrovnik's ancient stone walls lies a tangle of creamy stone structures and quiet little alleyways filled with stunning relics of its past. The city's rich history has created a vibrant cultural and musical scene, with concerts and galleries hiding in the most unexpected places. However, at the height of the summer season, Dubrovnik's glorious past draws thousands of visitors, with large cruise ships docking to release their masses—perhaps not a part of the trip you envisioned.

Of course there are plenty of reasons the tourists continue to pile into town. Chief among them is the sheer beauty of the city, which can be both grand and quaint, melancholy and sun-drenched-happy, depending on the view or the fall of the shadows. The city has impressed generations of holidaymakers, though sadly Dubrovnik's self-confidence often turns into an air of coldness and over-importance, a bit like other once-grand seaside provincial towns. Look past the occasional attitude to the magnificent buildings and island-peppered sea beyond.

Of course, some of the attitude is deserved. Dubrovnik is the crown jewel of Croatia and accounts for a huge bulk of the country's tourist trade—it's the city everyone's heard of. The upsides to all this bustle are the many fine hotels and shops and the breadth of tourist amenities you're likely to find. Of course, it's hard to see the upside when you're jam-packed with fellow travelers or left waiting for a table. When the Stradun gets too crowded, escape to less-visited

© DREAMSTIME.COM

HIGHLIGHTS

Gradske zidine: There's not a better way to get an eyeful of the white city and start a tour around the old core of Dubrovnik than a walk along the 15th-century walls (page 238).

Stradun: Though it's impossible to miss the Stradun, it's easy to miss its beauty when you're moving along in a river of travelers. Stop for a coffee at one of the cafés to soak in the atmosphere on Dubrovnik's main artery (page 238).

War Photo Limited: This moving gallery hosts a permanent exhibition of photographs from Croatia's 1990s Homeland War, as well as work from other regions of the world by renowned photojournalists (page 240).

Pustijerna: Dubrovnik's oldest quarter, with many medieval buildings that survived the 1667 earthquake, is also home to the stunning Crkva Sv. Ignacija (page 243).

Lokrum: One place to get away from the biggest crowds, thisforested island is a nice spot for a swim or a hike (page 245).

Trsteno: Fans of formal gardens or those in search of an escape should head to these Renaissance gardens, full of herbs, fruit trees, and languid statues that have inspired many a local poet and writer (page 254).

Pelješac Peninsula: Wine lovers and foodies shouldn't miss this excursion near Dubrovnik for oysters, seafood, and a wine crawl (page 256).

LOOK FOR **(** TO FIND RECOMMENDED SIGHTS, ACTIVITIES, DINING, AND LODGING.

sights around Dubrovnik, like Trsteno— former summer home of Dubrovnik's nobility, the sparsely populated Elafiti Islands, or a winery on the Pelješac Peninsula.

HISTORY

Dubrovnik was originally a small island, inhabited by the Illyrians and the Romans. Its name, historically Ragusa, was first mentioned in 667. At that time it was a refuge for people fleeing invaders that came after the demise of the Roman empire. A Slav settlement sprung up across the channel, called Dubrava. The narrow waterway was filled in between the 10th and 11th centuries, the two cities merged, and the city spread all the way to the foot of Mount Srd.

During the 9th and 10th centuries Dubrovnik was under the control of the Byzantine Empire, which helped protect the port city from invaders. In the 11th century, however, Dubrovnik flipped from Byzantine to Venetian control (in 1000), back to Byzantine (1018), and to the Normans (1081). By the 12th century, Dubrovnik was becoming a powerful and important city-state, signing trade

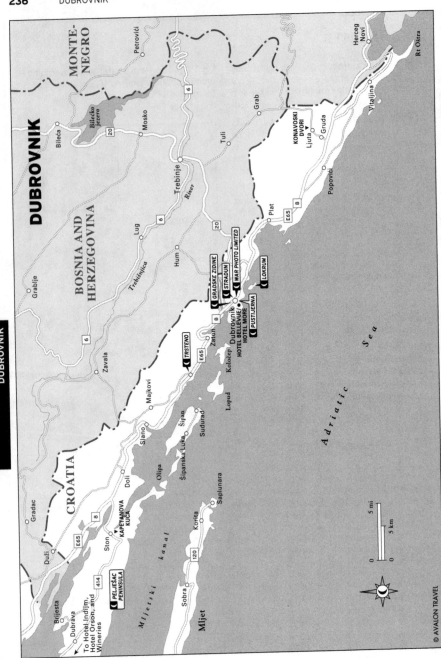

DUBROVNIK

© AVALON TRAVEL

agreements and treaties. In 1189 Dubrovnik, Ragusa's Croatian name, was used for the first time in a trade agreement (though Ragusa was used regularly to refer to the city until the early 20th century).

Dubrovnik's freedom was short-lived, however. Venice once again brought the city under its control in 1232, forcing strict trading restrictions and taxes that severely diminished Dubrovnik's position as an important port. It wasn't until the 13th century, when an armistice from Croatian-Hungarian king Louis I in 1358 made Dubrovnik an independent city-state, the Ragusan Republic. Louis I placed no restrictions on Dubrovnik's trade, even allowing them to do business with Venice and Serbia, often at odds with the Croatian-Hungarian nation.

The prosperity of Dubrovnik changed the city, with the last of its wooden houses being demolished in the early 15th century and the town reconstructed completely out of white stone. Palaces, fountains, towers, a public school, and a shipyard were all built during the town's golden era.

The time of prosperity was brought to an abrupt halt when an earthquake struck in 1667, destroying buildings, killing around 4,000 people (over half the city's population at the time), and pulverizing many pieces of art. The city recovered due to its trade, but its glory days were over. It continued to suffer blows to its position (war with Venice, an unfortunate trade agreement with France, a defeat of the navy by Napoleon's forces) until its status as city-state was taken away by Napoleon's Marshall Marmont in 1808. Six years later Dubrovnik became a part of the Kingdom of Dalmatia, under Austrian rule.

Still, the legend of Dubrovnik continued to permeate among visitors, who raved about the city and began to come in droves by the late 19th and early 20th centuries. It continued to be a frequented destination for visitors throughout its time as a part of Yugoslavia. Though the war left its scars, it was quick to recover tourists based on its legendary reputation and the grand scale of the city that continues to seduce.

PLANNING YOUR TIME

Ideally, you'll have at least three full days in Dubrovnik. Spend the first day with all the other tourists visiting the must-see city sights and the second day relaxing on Lokrum or one of the Elafiti Islands. Spend the third day on a wine crawl on the Pelješac Peninsula, a long but doable day trip from the city. Four full days should be enough to thoroughly see Dubrovnik and its surroundings, leaving you time to scoot to some of the Southern Dalmatian islands like Mljet or Korčula, both with easy connections to the area.

If you don't like waiting for a table in restaurants, try to go outside of the peak lunch and dinner hours (12:30–2 P.M. and 7–9 P.M.). The same goes for tourist sites, as a good portion of the tourists are brought into town from the cruise ships between 9 A.M. and 6 P.M. If some of the places you want to see have wider operating hours, try to slate your visits then, when the bulk of the tourists have gone home.

There's not really any time of year when Dubrovnik is devoid of tourists, though the least will be visiting in the dead of winter (when the vicious *bura* is known to blow) and the most will be in town in July and August. Though the peak season can get a little wild, you do have the advantage of the excellent **Dubrovnik Summer Festival,** packed with classical concerts and theater performances, a must for culture buffs.

ORIENTATION

Dubrovnik stretches its boundaries for over five kilometers along the coast, though the three most important sections for tourists are the Old Town (within the famous city walls) in the center, Lapad to its west, and Ploče to its east. The Old Town is pedestrian-only and likely to occupy the bulk of your visit to Dubrovnik. It's peppered with sightseeing stops, shops, services, restaurants, and even a few places for accommodation. The city is dissected by the all-important Stradun (also referred to as Placa), a wide street running east–west. At the western end of the

Stradun, you'll find the Pile Gate, outside of which buses pick up and drop off and taxis wait for their next fare.

Since many of the city's hotels are located in Lapad and Danče (west of the city but not as far as Lapad), you may find yourself around the Pile Gate often, hopping the #6 bus for the 30-minute ride to Lapad. It's also in this western section where you'll find the majority of the city's better beaches.

The eastern neighborhood of Ploče, once Dubrovnik's cattle market, is a residential suburb with a handful of accommodations and a few more sightseeing stops worth your time.

Sights

Though you can easily get a good overview of Dubrovnik in a day, there's enough here to fill up a few days, lazily wandering through the town's museums and galleries. Make sure to start with the Old Town sights, the best of the bunch.

OLD TOWN
◖ Gradske zidine
City Walls

Taking a walk along Dubrovnik's Gradske zidine (entrance inside the Pile Gate to the left, 9 A.M.–7 P.M. daily in summer, 9 A.M.–3 P.M. daily in winter, backpacks discouraged and prohibited in some sections due to winds, 30Kn) is absolutely the best way to start your tour of the Old Town. Running for about two kilometers, the walk around will take you 1–1.5 hours depending on your speed and the size of the crowds.

Built and tweaked from the mid-15th century until the great earthquake in 1667, the walls feature the rounded **Minčeta fortress** (built in response to the invention of gunpowder) in the northwest, the **Revelin** in the east, **Sveti Ivan** (St. John) by the harbor, and the beautiful **Bokar** (worked on by stone masons Michelozzi and Dalmatinac) in the southwest. The best views are likely from the walls that face the sea, looking towards the red-tiled roofs on one side and the sea on the other. The **Pile Gate,** where most travelers enter into the old core of Dubrovnik, is topped by a somber statue of the town's protector, St. Blasius, welcoming you to town.

◖ Stradun
This is possibly the most important spot in Dubrovnik to explain, given the confusion

---

TWO DAYS IN DUBROVNIK

DAY 1
Head into town early for a coffee on the **Stradun** before it gets too busy and then head out for a tour of Dubrovnik, starting with a walk around the **city walls.** Visit some **galleries** or stop for a quick peek at the **Sponza Palace** and the **Rector's Palace** before breaking for lunch at **Buffet Škola** for one of the city's most famous sandwiches. Continue your tour, saving the **Franciscan monastery** for later in the day when the crowds have tapered off. After refreshing back at your hotel, head to the **Sunset Lounge** for a cocktail and a perfect sunset view over the water. Have dinner at **Proto** and cap off the night with an ice cream along the Stradun.

DAY 2
Today head to the **market** on Gundulićeva poljana for provisions for a beach picnic. From the Old Town's harbor, catch a water taxi to **Lokrum** where you can while away the day lounging on the beach and strolling the shady paths. Splurge on dinner at the phenomenal **Gil's** restaurant under a starlit sky.

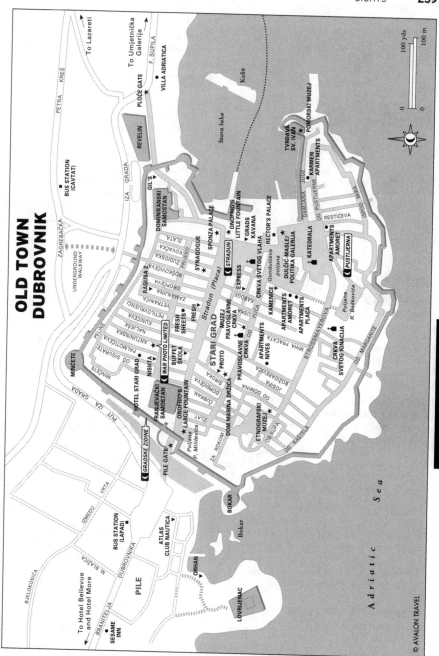

OLD TOWN DUBROVNIK

DUBROVNIK

To Hotel Bellevue
and Hotel More

SESAME
INN

BRANITELJA

BJELOKOSIĆA

M. BLAŽIĆA

IZMEĐU

VRTA

PILE

DUBROVNIKA

BUS STATION
(LAPAD)

ATLAS
CLUB NAUTICA

ORHAN

LOVRIJENAC

Bokar

Adriatic   *Sea*

BOKAR

PILE GATE

GRADSKE ZIDINE

HOTEL STARI GRAD

FRANJEVAČKI
SAMOSTAN

ONOFRIO'S
LARGE FOUNTAIN

Poljana
P. Miličevića

ZA ROKOM

ČUBRANOVIĆEVA

ZLATARIĆEVA

DOM MARINA DRŽIĆA

ETNOGRAFSKI
MUZEJ

OD RUPA

OD KAŠTELA

OD MARGARITE

OD DOMINA

JOSIPA BOŽIDAREVIĆA

MIHA PRACATA

STROSSMAYEROVA

R. Boškovića

Poljana

CRKVA
SVETOG IGNACIJA

APARTMENTS
NIVES

APARTMENTS
AMORET

APARTMENTS
PLAČA

KAMENICE

KABOGE

CRKVA SVETOG VLAHA

Gundulićeva
poljana

DULČIĆ-MASLE/
PULITIKA GALERIJA

RECTOR'S PALACE

GRADS
KAVANA

KATEDRALA

APARTMENTS
AMORET

PUSTIJERNA

RESTIĆEVA

JUDE

ISPOD MIRA

DAMJANA

OD PUSTIJERNE

KARMEN
APARTMENTS

POMORSKI MUZEJ

TVRĐAVA
SV. IVAN

Kaše

Stara luka

ONOFRIO'S
LITTLE FOUNTAIN

STRADUN

EXPRESS

OD PUČA

PRAVOSLAVNE
CRKVA

APARTMENTS
AMORET

PRAVOSLAVNE
CRKVA

MUZEJ

PROTO

Stradun (Placa)

STARI GRAD

FRESH
SHEET'S

FRESH

BUFFET
ŠKOLA

WAR PHOTO LIMITED

NISHTA

OD SIGURATE

MINČETE

MINČETE

PUT IZA GRADA

PELINE

NALJEŠK

NATJUNINSKA

PALMOTIĆEVA

PETILOVRIJENCI

KNEŽEVA

VETRANIĆA

ZAMANJINA

BOŠKOVIĆEVA

ŽUDIOSKA

KOVAČKA

PRIJEKO

ZLATA...

RAGUSA 2

DROPČEVA

SIROKA

DRŽIĆEVA

SYNAGOGUE

SPONZA PALACE

DOMINIKANSKI
SAMOSTAN

GIL'S

REVELIN

PLOČE GATE

VILLA ADRIATICA

To Umjetnička
Galerija

F. SUPILA

PETRA KREŠ

BUS STATION
(CAVTAT)

ZAGREBAČKA

IZA GRADA

UNDERGROUND
WALKWAY

0   100 yds
0   100 m

© AVALON TRAVEL

© REINER KAUFMANN/DREAMSTIME.COM

the Stradun, the Old Town's main street

410, www.malabraca.hr, 9 A.M.–6 P.M. daily, 25Kn) is among the city's most popular tourist attractions. The Baroque look of the building was a later addition, making up for severe damage suffered in the earthquake and fire of 1667. One of the only surviving pieces of the original late-15th-century church is the portal, the fire having also destroyed paintings by Caravaggio, Titian, and many others. The cloisters and the monastery's courtyard are perhaps the most beautiful features of the complex, packed with fragrant orange trees. Don't miss the **Old Pharmacy** in the alley between the monastery and the Church of Our Savior. The 700-year-old pharmacy is still frequented by locals today, prescriptions in hand. To battle less of a crowd, try to visit the monastery at the end of the day.

◖ War Photo Limited

A small but moving gallery run by New Zealand war photographer Wade Goddard, War Photo Limited (Antuninska 6, tel. 020/322-166, www.warphotoltd.com, 9 A.M.–9 P.M. daily June–Sept., 10 A.M.–4 P.M. Tues.–Sat. and 10 A.M.–2 P.M. Sun. May and Oct., 30Kn) showcases work by some of the world's

its name can cause the average tourist—some people call it **Placa** and some use its colloquial name, Stradun. Running from the Pile Gate to the Ploče, the Stradun (or Placa, according to street signs) is the meeting and strutting spot for all of Dubrovnik. It also divides the city into the southern side, Ragusa (derived from the Greek *Laus,* for rock), inhabited by the Illyrians in the 4th century, and Dubrava, on the north, settled several centuries later by the Slavs. The Stradun, which used to be a marshy channel, was filled in the 12th century. In 1438 Onofrio designed a fountain for either end of Dubrovnik's main street. Croatian writer Slobodan Prosperov Novak described the Stradun: "Ragusans see their homes as places where they die of boredom—while Stradun is the place where they live."

Franjevački samostan
Franciscan Monastery

One of highlights of old Dubrovnik, the Franjevački samostan (Placa 2, tel. 020/321-

THE SIEGE OF DUBROVNIK

The attack on Dubrovnik by Serb forces came out of nowhere for Dubrovnik's citizens. Not really seen as an important port and with hardly any Serb residents to speak of, Dubrovnik was attacked more to hurt Croatian morale than for any strategic purposes. The people of Dubrovnik were bombed and shot at from November 1991 until May 1992, with the Old Town sustaining plenty of damage. The fortresses of the city walls once again became practical structures as locals hid inside them for shelter and safety. The brave people of Dubrovnik held out and the siege ended in July of 1992, when the Croatian army secured a path to the beautiful city.

top war photojournalists. Permanent displays chronicle the 1990s Homeland War and revolving exhibits bring home to the viewer the grimness of struggles in places such as Africa and Palestine.

Žudioska
Jew's Street

The small Žudioska is home to a tiny but significant **synagogue** (Žudioska 5, tel. 020/321-028, 10 A.M.–8 P.M. daily in summer, 9 A.M.–noon Mon.–Fri. in winter, 10Kn) dating from the 14th century. The Jewish community who founded the synagogue was composed of refugees from the Spanish Inquisition—one of the oldest communities of Sephardic Jews in the Balkans. Inside the synagogue are a Torah, religious texts, and a Moorish carpet all brought by the people fleeing persecution.

Unfortunately, they did not totally escape persecution here either. The people of Dubrovnik regularly ridiculed the Jews, barred them from drinking from all but one fountain, and mocked them in local festivals.

Palača Sponza
Sponza Palace

At the end of the Stradun is the busy Trg Luža (Luža Square). Here you'll find the *gradski zvonik* (town bell tower) built in the 15th century. Most notable among the buildings on the square is the Sponza Palace (Luža, tel. 020/321-032, 9 A.M.–2 P.M. daily, free), a customs house built in 1520. Today the palace is home to the **Državni arhiv u Dubrovniku** (Dubrovnik State Archives, tel. 020/321-032, www.dad.hr, 8 A.M.–3 P.M. Mon.–Fri., 8 A.M.–1 P.M. Sat., 15Kn), containing records back to the first half of the 11th century, with some on revolving display for the public. It also houses a permanent exhibit, the **Spomen soba poginulim dubrovački braniteljima** (Memorial Room of the Defenders of Dubrovnik, 10 A.M.–10 P.M. Mon.–Fri., 8 A.M.–1 P.M. Sat., free) displaying pictures and portraits of those who died during the siege of Dubrovnik.

SVETI VLAHO (ST. BLASIUS)

Sveti Vlaho has been the protector of Dubrovnik since the 11th century. Legend has it that a local religious authority had a vision of the saint that saved them from attack by the Venetians. As you're touring around Dubrovnik keep an eye out for St. Blasius, usually portrayed with a long beard, a tall bishop's hat, and a raised hand with one finger extended as if to make a point. St. Blasius Day is celebrated every February 3 in Dubrovnik, with processions carrying the reliquaries containing his head and a few other body parts.

Crkva svetog Vlaha
St. Blasius's Church

Across from the Sponza Palace, the present Crkva svetog Vlaha (Luža 3, tel. 020/323-462, open to the public morning and evening daily, free) stands on the spot of an earlier Romanesque structure destroyed in the earthquake of 1667. The church you see today, a mass of creamy stone carved with statues, was finished in 1714. Don't miss the sculpture of St. Blasius with a model of Dubrovnik in his hand, a survivor from the previous, and much older, church.

Orlando's Column

In the middle of Luža Square you'll see a relatively unimpressive column carved with a statue of a knight and supporting a flag. Known as Orlando's Column (Orlando was a legendary medieval knight), the monument is much more important to the city than it looks. Considered the most important symbol of freedom for the city, it first had a flag hoisted above it in 1419, celebrating Dubrovnik's position as an independent city-state; it was lowered in 1808 when Napoleon's army marched into town. The statue was blown over by a strong wind in 1825 (even Orlando was no match for the *bura*) and put in storage for some 50 years. When he was returned, he no longer faced east

DUBROVNIK

THE CULT OF ORLANDO

A knight who died in the 8th century, Roland (also known as Orlando) became a superstar of his day when he was immortalized and given legendary qualities in the medieval epic poem *Chanson de Roland* (Song of Roland).

His admirers, mainly northern Europeans, formed a cult, but the fever reached Dubrovnik when Sigismund, the Hungarian and Czech king who would later rule Germany as well, visited the city of Dubrovnik. Orlando was promptly adopted by Dubrovnik as having fought a battle with a Saracen corsair named Spuzente ("bad breath"), even though the battle actually took place long after Roland's death.

explosions (the palace was also used for storing munitions) rendered the old building almost useless. The new palace is a grand affair, with lots of stone carvings and columns along the facade (Dalmatinac, a famous 15th-century stone mason and architect, was among the many craftsmen who worked on the building), the most interesting of which is a relief of Greco-Roman god Asclepius sitting in his pharmacy. The funny part of the story is that locals confused his birthplace Epidaurus (in Greece) with the nearby city of the same name (today Cavtat) and made him its protector.

Inside the palace, the **Gradski muzej** (City Museum, Pred Dvorom 1, tel. 020/321-437, 9 A.M.–6 P.M. daily June–Sept., 9 A.M.–1 P.M. Mon.–Sat. Oct.–May, 35Kn) is largely unimpressive. Sparsely furnished rooms and lots of Baroque (mostly anonymous) paintings decorate the rooms where the rector and other political figures once sat.

against the Turks, but north, towards the ruling body that oppressed Dubrovnik's freedom (the Austrians). Today it flies a flag that reads *libertas* (freedom).

Onofrio's Little Fountain

Near Luža Square is Onofrio's Little Fountain, a much smaller work than the giant domed fountain at the other end of the Stradun. The 15th-century fountain is delicate, with decorations of cherubs and frolicking dolphins.

Knežev dvor
Rector's Palace

Though the building is called the Knežev dvor, it was actually more of a government building than a palace for a ruler. The rector wasn't much of a ruler anyway—the title was more honorary than one of real power, as he was given only a one-month term (ineligible for the two years following) and a few apartments in the palace for his living quarters. The palace also held a dungeon that must have made sleeping in the place a bit difficult due to prisoner noise.

The current palace was constructed in the 15th century after a couple of gunpowder

courtyard of the Knežev dvor

Galerija Dulčić-Masle-Pulitika
Dulčić-Masle-Pulitika Gallery

Close to the Rector's Palace in a refined Baroque townhouse, the Galerija Dulčić-Masle-Pulitika (Poljana Marina Držića 1, tel. 020/323-172, www.ugdubrovnik.hr, 10 A.M.–8 P.M. Tues.–Sun., 30Kn) is worth visiting for the views over the cathedral as much as it is for the art inside. The 1st floor displays works by the three Dubrovnik artists for whom the gallery is named, while the 2nd floor is home to works by Cavtat artist Vlaho Bukovac and Croatia's famed Ivan Meštrović. By the way, don't throw away your ticket: You'll be able to use it at Umjetnička Galerija in Dubrovnik's Lazareti, saving you about 30Kn.

Katedrala
Cathedral

Although its dome is one of Dubrovnik's post-card views, the Katedrala (Poljana Marina Držića, tel. 020/323-459, 9 A.M.–5:30 P.M. Mon.–Sat., 11 A.M.–5:30 P.M. Sun. as well as mass, 10Kn for treasury) has an interior that is more ho-hum than exciting. The original church, purportedly built by Richard the Lionhearted in the 12th century in return for the kindness he was shown after a shipwreck, was destroyed in the 1667 earthquake. Excavations following a 1979 earthquake uncovered another, possibly Byzantine, church from the 7th or 8th century under the cathedral. The Baroque structure you see today (built between 1672 and 1713) does have a visit-worthy *riznica* (treasury) that houses several oddities, including the arm, head, and lower leg of St. Blaise in a golden Byzantine 11th-century box and a diaper purportedly belonging to baby Jesus.

Tvrđava Sv. Ivan
St. John's Fortress

Near the cathedral, Tvrđava Sv. Ivan is where you'll find a definitely skippable aquarium and the lovely **Pomorski muzej** (Maritime Museum, Tvrđava Sv. Ivan, tel. 020/323-904, 9 A.M.–6 P.M. daily in summer, 9 A.M.–1 P.M. daily in winter, 35Kn), one of Dubrovnik's most important museums. Following the history of the city's seafaring, it has everything from model ships to medicine chests to the blueprints for building the Gruž harbor. Given the importance of the sea to the development of Dubrovnik, it's hard to pass up this stop.

◖ Pustijerna

The Pustijerna is one of Dubrovnik's most ancient quarters, with many buildings dating from before the earthquake of 1667. The neighborhood is quite medieval in feel. Here you'll find the Jesuit **Crkva Sv. Ignacija** (St. Ignatius's Church, Ruđera Boškovića 6, tel. 020/323-500, 7 A.M.–8 P.M. daily, free), a giant Baroque church built in the first half of the 18th century and modeled on the church of Gesù in Rome. The grand staircase leading to it was also inspired by the eternal city, modeled on the Spanish Steps. The steps and the square are often used for performances during the Dubrovnik Summer Festival.

Descending the wide stairway you'll run into **Gundulićeva poljana** (Gundulić Square) where the morning market is held, watched

DUBROVNIK

IVAN GUNDULIĆ, POET AND PLAYWRIGHT

Born in 1589 to a wealthy and affluent Dubrovnik family, Gundulić began writing plays around 1615; they were performed in front of the Rector's Palace. But Gundulić was not only a playwright and poet. Having studied law, he held numerous political positions in Dubrovnik including judge and senator, though he died too early to be appointed rector, a position given only to men age 50 or older.

The first verse of his most well-known pastoral play, *Dubrava*, serves as an unofficial motto for Dubrovnik: *"O lijepa, o draga, o slatka slobodo"* ("Oh beautiful, oh beloved, oh sweet freedom").

Ivan Gundulić died in 1638 in Dubrovnik of a high fever.

over by a statue of Croatia's well-loved poet Ivan Gundulić. The reliefs around the statue reflect scenes from one of his most famous works, *Osman,* an epic about the Poles' victory over the Turks.

Od Puča

From Gundulićeva poljana take Od Puča, a street that runs parallel with the Stradun, west to the **Muzej pravoslavne crkve** (Orthodox Church Museum, Od Puča 8, tel. 020/323-283, 9 A.M.–2 P.M. Mon.–Sat., 10Kn). The museum houses a number of delicate icons of Byzantine and Cretan origin. Next door is the Orthodox Church, built in the 19th century.

Close to Od Puča, look for **Iza Roka** (Behind Roc), where you'll come across the Crkva Svetog Roka (Church of St. Roc), not very important but quite interesting for an **inscription** written on the eastern wall of the facade. A grumpy neighbor was obviously tired of some young boys breaking his window during their games and wrote in Latin, "Go in peace, and remember that you will die, you who now are playing ball." Maybe no one had told him about defamation of property?

Nearby is the **Dom Marina Držića** (House of Marin Držić, Široka 7, tel. 020/323-242, 10 A.M.–6 P.M. Tues.–Sun., 35Kn), a Gothic townhome where the slightly eccentric playwright was born in the 16th century. He was constantly at odds with local authorities, as the Dubrovnik of his day didn't think much of his plays and comedies—the only paper regarding Marin Držić in the state archives is a paper regarding a loan. There's not much to see here, but if you happen to catch one of his comedies at the Dubrovnik Summer Festival, where the writer is honored posthumously, and want to know more about him, this is the place to go.

Etnografski muzej Rupe
Rupe Ethnographic Museum

Supposedly the reason to come to the Etnografski muzej Rupe (Od Rupa, tel. 020/412-545, 9 A.M.–6 P.M. daily in summer, 9 A.M.–2 P.M. Mon.–Fri. in winter, 35Kn) is to admire the costumes and relics related to life in the rural areas around Dubrovnik. However, you'll find a stronger reason might be the sweeping views of mountains, sea, and red-tiled roofs from the top-floor display. The building was once the city's granary, a very important location during its heyday when individuals were issued tickets allotting them a certain amount of grain. It's here where they picked up the grain stored in *rupe* (holes), hence the name.

Dominikanski samostan
Dominican Monastery

The somewhat plain exterior of the 14th-century Dominican monastery (Sv. Dominika 4, tel. 020/321-423, 9 A.M.–6 P.M. daily in summer, 9 A.M.–3 P.M. daily in winter, 20Kn) hides an interior decorated with a delicate Gothic and Renaissance cloister and an outstanding collection of paintings by local artists. Included in the exhibit are a painting of Dubrovnik before the great quake and *The Miracle of St. Dominic* by turn-of-the-20th-century Cavtat artist Vlaho Bukovac, as well as works by Titian and Veneziano.

Dubrovnik's Dominican monastery, founded in 1315

CONVENTS IN DUBROVNIK

Dubrovnik's old convents often go unnoticed by the average visitor, though the city was home to eight nunneries before the great earthquake of 1667. Today only two are somewhat preserved – that of St. Catherine (today a music school) and the Clarist convent near Onofrio's large fountain.

Many women were put inside the convents by their elders, aristocrats bent on preserving the purity of their family line. With hardly anyone for them to marry, their parents thought it better to enter a convent than sully the blood with a commoner. The plan backfired – by the late 17th century, the town was already promoting common families to the rank of nobles to make up for the disappearing aristocracy.

Life inside the nunnery was not much better than a prison. A law passed in 1433 required the convents to be surrounded by thick walls without windows and sleeping quarters were locked at night.

One nun, Agnes Beneša, set fire to her convent, possibly to try to escape, in 1620. She was walled up in the Rector's Palace dungeon as a punishment but still managed to wiggle through a hole left for confession and find her way to freedom.

EAST OF THE CITY WALLS
Revelin Fortress

The Revelin Fortress took almost a century to complete, with work ramped up and quickly finished in 1539 due to threats from the Ottoman Empire. Now the Revelin is a concert venue during the Dubrovnik Summer Festival and also houses a café and nightclub. Near the Revelin is the **Ploče Gate,** the eastern entrance to town, which welcomed most of the tradesmen to town in its day. Like the Pile Gate, it's guarded over by a statue of St. Blaise.

Lazareti

Dating from the late 16th century, the buildings of the Lazareti are today part of the modern suburb of Ploče. Most of the neighborhood, which used to be a large market for cattle as well as produce, has been destroyed and paved over. But the Lazareti, built to inspect the health and goods of foreigners before they entered the city, remain untouched. The purpose of the row of gated buildings was not only to protect the health of Dubrovnik's citizens, but also to keep the city from becoming raucous at night and to ferry the tradesmen into town in an orderly fashion.

Today the buildings house the **Art Radionica Lazareti** (Art Workshop Lazareti, 10 A.M.–5 P.M. daily), which displays contemporary art in its Otok gallery, as well as being home to other studios and hosting the occasional concert or party.

Umjetnička Galerija
Dubrovnik Art Gallery

Near the Lazareti you'll find the Umjetnička Galerija (Frana Supila 23, tel. 020/426-590, www.ugdubrovnik.hr, 10 A.M.–6 P.M. Tues.–Sun., 30Kn or show your ticket from the Dulčić-Masle-Pulitika Gallery) in a grand 1930s mansion. There's often an excellent contemporary exhibition on and the gallery brings in a big name from the art world most summers.

OFF THE COAST
◖ Lokrum

Purportedly the island where King Richard the Lionhearted was shipwrecked while returning from a crusade (in 1192 likely due to a late-fall *bura*), the forested island of Lokrum (boats leave the Old Town port, Stara Luka, every 30 minutes in summer, around 50Kn one-way) lies one kilometer off the coast of Dubrovnik. The island was once home to a Benedictine monastery, but it was an Austrian who really shaped the place. In the mid-19th century Archduke Maximilian

DUBROVNIK

ESCAPING THE CROWDS IN DUBROVNIK

In June and July when masses of tourists descend on Dubrovnik from the hotels and from the giant cruise ships that dock in her harbors, the crowds can get to be a little much. There are, of course, out-of-the-way spots around Dubrovnik (head to **Trsteno**) or just off the coast, like the **Elafiti islands** or **Šipan** (home to over 30 churches, at least six of which date from pre-Roman times), **Koločep** (only 30 minutes by ferry with lots of secluded beaches), and **Lopud** (with plenty of sightseeing and beaches).

On a summer Sunday, head to the village of **Čilipi** (near the airport), where colorful folk performances draw large crowds – but not as large as those strolling the Stradun.

The best tip for escaping the crowds is to visit the Old Town in the **early morning** and the **late evening**, when the critical mass has returned to their cruise ships or their package hotels and you're left to walk around without worrying if you're going to unknowingly whack someone with your backpack.

Ferdinand von Habsburg, brother of Emperor Franz Joseph of Austria, built a summer home on the island as well as a **Botanički vrt** (Botanical Garden), still open to the public free of charge. This is a great place for a swim—there's a nice little lake at the southwest corner of the island—as well as for strolling along the paths that lead to a **napoleonsko utvrđenje** (Napoleonic fort).

BEACHES

The city beach at **Banje,** near the Ploče Gate, is a decent place for a swim, though a much better spot, the beach at **Sveti Jakov,** is a 20-minute walk along the Vlaha Bukovca past Villa Dubrovnik and down a long stairway (remember you'll have to hike back up). It's usually not too crowded and has a superb view of a golden-dipped Dubrovnik at sunset. Remember that hotel beaches are either private or accessed per day for a fee. In return you get to use the beach and the pool, if the hotel has one.

The beach at **Dance,** west of the Old Town, is rocky but quite clean and the **Betina špilja** (accessed via water taxi) is a cave with a nice pebbly beach, though it doesn't have any services or cafés. **Lapad,** west of the Old Town (take bus #6 from the Pile Gate), is also filled with beaches, though it's probably nicer to hop a water taxi to **Lokrum.**

Entertainment, Shopping, and Recreation

ENTERTAINMENT AND EVENTS
Nightlife

If you're capping off a perfect day or beginning a just-as-perfect evening, try the **Sunset Lounge** (Hotel Dubrovnik Palace, Masarykov put 20, tel. 020/430-000, www.dubrovnikpalace.hr, noon–1 A.M. daily) in the Hotel Dubrovnik, a bar that certainly deserves its name. Giant windows allow the sea and surrounding islands to spill into the trendy space serving cocktails, reasonable wines, pricey snacks, and Moet et Chandon for special occasions.

Troubador (Bunićeva poljana 2, tel. 020/323-476, 9 A.M.–3 A.M. daily in summer, 5–11 P.M. daily in winter, no credit cards) is the place to go for summer jazz concerts on the terrace overlooking the cathedral and a too prominently advertised Internet hot spot.

Though there's a slight cheese factor at the hip and trendy **East West beach club** (Banje Beach, Frana Supila, tel. 020/412-220, www.ewdubrovnik.com, 5 P.M.–3 A.M. daily) it's hard to beat the convenience (five minutes' walk from the Old Town), the size, the good drinks menu, and some catchy DJ music

Lazareti (Lazareti complex, Frana Supila 8, tel. 020/324-633, www.lazareti.du-hr.net, 9 P.M.–4 A.M. when events are scheduled, no credit cards) has more of an edge. Set in the old quarantine barracks of Lazareti, the club hosts live concerts and good DJs throughout the year. Check with the tourist office for a local events guide if the website hasn't been updated recently.

Festivals and Events

The crown jewel of the city's events is the **Dubrovnik Summer Festival** (tel. 020/412-288, info@dubrovnik-festival.hr, www.dubrovnik-festival.hr, 30–200Kn) in July and August, when classical music and plays are performed in eye-catching venues all over town. The festival usually includes a spot of opera and a bit of Shakespeare in addition to the concerts and theater performances of local playwrights like Marin Držić. Dubrovnik usually manages to draw a couple of big international names and these tickets sell out months in advance, some as soon as the schedule comes out in April. If you haven't had that much time to plan, once you get to town you can usually pick up tickets for other performances from festival info booths on the Stradun and at the Pile Gate. During July and August you'll also find a healthy schedule of pop and jazz performances around the Old Town.

The **Libertas Film Festival** (late Aug.–early Sept., www.libertasfilmfestival.com), screening both art films and interesting documentaries, is another Dubrovnik event worth a peek if you're in town at the time.

If you're looking for classical music the rest of the year, try the **Dubrovnik Symphony Orchestra** (tel. 020/417-101, www.dso.hr), which performs in the Revelin Fortress.

SHOPPING

You can shop for books, English magazines and newspapers, and a good selection of books on local topics and history at **Algoritam** (Stradun 8, tel. 020/322-044, www.algoritam.hr, 9 A.M.–8:30 P.M. Mon.–Fri., 9 A.M.–3 P.M. Sat., 10 A.M.–1 P.M. Sun.).

Dubrovnik has more than a few places to buy fun jewelry. The largest is **Đardin** (Miha Pracata 8, entrance on Od Puča, tel. 020/324-744, 9:30 A.M.–6 P.M. Mon.–Fri., 9:30 A.M.–12:30 P.M. Sat.), with masses of necklaces and jewels throughout the many rooms and courtyards of a grand old building. **Ivana Bačura** (Zatarska 3, tel. 091/543-1321, www.ivanabacura.com, 9:30 A.M.–6:30 P.M. Mon.–Fri., 9:30 A.M.–12:30 P.M. Sat.) designs unique silver pieces with contemporary flair. On the high end, **Trinity** (Palmotićeva 2, tel. 020/322-350, www.trinity.hr, 9 A.M.–8 P.M. daily) offers creative designs using precious and semiprecious stones as well as local licensed coral.

If you don't have a lot of time, try **Dubrovačka kuća** (Od sv Dominika, tel. 020/322-092, 9 A.M.–9:30 P.M. Mon.–Sat. and 9 A.M.–7:30 P.M. Sun. in summer, call for winter hours), a one-stop shop selling gourmet souvenirs (liquors, wines, and olive oils), books, posters, and handmade items through its partnership with the Museum of Arts and Crafts in Zagreb.

SPORTS AND RECREATION

To see another side of Dubrovnik it doesn't hurt to unleash your athletic side. Even beginners can take to the seas in a kayak, with a tour to the island of Lokrum through **Adriatic Kayak Tours** (Zrinsko-Frankopanska 6, tel. 020/312-770, www.adriatickayaktours.com). The firm also offers white-water rafting in nearby Montenegro and mountain biking in the Konavle. Scuba divers can check out **Blue Planet Diving** (Masarykov put 20, tel. 091/899-973, www.blueplanet-diving.com) in the Hotel Dubrovnik Palace and **Navis Underwater Explorers** (Copacabana Beach, tel. 020/356-501, www.navisdubrovnik.com) for trips and courses for all levels and interests. For the slightly lower-key adventure-seeker, **Villa Neretva** (Krvavac 2, Metković, tel. 020/672-200. www.restaurant-villa-neretva.hr) offers photo safaris and nature schools in the Neretva River delta, ending with an excellent meal at the family-run restaurant offering equally adventurous dishes of eel and frog.

Accommodations

Dubrovnik is not the cheapest place to find accommodation, especially in the summer months. It also books up early, so it's wise to reserve your room in advance. If you do find yourself in a bind, try one of the agencies that rent private rooms such as **Gulliver** (Obala Stjepana Radića 32, tel. 020/313-313, www.gulliver.hr) across from the ferries or **Atlas** (Svetog Đurđa 1, tel. 020/442-565, www.atlas-croatia.com) near the Pile Gate. Try to avoid people hawking rooms at the ferry terminal and the bus stations, as you'll generally find them way off the beaten track and they often turn out to be giant rip-offs.

INSIDE THE CITY WALLS
Under 700Kn
Fresh Sheets (Vetranićeva 4, tel. 091/896-7509, www.igotfresh.com, 178Kn per person, including breakfast) is clean and friendly, plus it offers free Internet and a convivial travelers' bar. There's also a selection of attractive apartments in the 650Kn to 1,100Kn range if you're traveling as a group. The **Apartments Amoret** (Restićeva 2, tel. 020/324-005, www.dubrovnik-amoret.com, from 640Kn d.) are located in the heart of the Old Town, steps from the Stradun in a 16th-century building. Furnished tastefully with a bit of antique flair, they also have satellite TV, air-conditioning, and wireless Internet. The **Apartments Placa** (Gundulićeva Poljana 5, tel. 091/721-9202, tonci.korculanin@du.htnet.hr, www.dubrovnik-online.com/apartments_placa, from 640Kn d.) front Gundulić Square, the sight of a morning market where you can buy fresh fruits and vegetables for the day. The rooms are bright and sunny with small kitchenettes.

700-1,400Kn
Within the city walls, one street over from the Rector's Palace and next to the hosts' swinging jazz café where Jimi Hendrix once jammed, the **Karmen Apartments** (Bandureva 1, tel. 020/323-433, www.karmendu.tk, 710–1,032Kn) are well decorated and filled with charm. **Apartments Nives** (Nikole Božidarevića 7, tel. 020/323-181, www.dubrovnik-palace.com, 748Kn d.) is another choice, with two small apartments and a tiny room with beamed ceilings, some antiques, and good hospitality.

Over 1,400Kn
The **Hotel Stari Grad** (Od Sigurate 4, tel. 020/322-244, www.hotelstarigrad.com, 1,495Kn d., including breakfast) is in the heart of Old Town. The small rooms and baths are furnished with antiques and the rooftop terrace is a great spot for breakfast or a coffee. However, the number of stairs to get up to bed will not be appreciated by those who've let their fitness slide.

OUTSIDE THE CITY WALLS
Under 700Kn
Slightly west of town in Lapad (hop on bus #6 from the Pile Gate), the **Orka Apartments** (Lapadska obala 11, tel. 020/356-800, www.orkaapartments.com, 425Kn d.) were built in 2007 and offer clean, no-nonsense accommodation a short trip from Dubrovnik. It's only a 10-minute walk to the **Simply Angelic Apartments** (Ploče, tel. 091/911-6901, nena28@vip.hr, www.dubrovnik-online.com/simply_angelic, 496Kn d.), east of the Old Town, which have great views over the sea to the island of Lokrum. The rooms are basic but nice and they are located near a small supermarket, café, and a beach, though those with walking difficulties or knee troubles should beware of the stairs one has to climb to reach the apartments.

700-1,400Kn
Only 150 meters west from the Pile Gate, the three comfy rooms at the **Sesame Inn** (Don Frana Bulica 5, tel. 020/412-910, www.sesame.hr, 1,025Kn d., including breakfast) are also close to a nice beach at Dance and the inn has a

good restaurant as well. Outside the Ploče Gate to the east you'll find the **(Villa Adriatica** (Frana Supila 4, tel. 020/411-962, miroslav .tomsic@du.htnet.hr, www.dubrovnik-online .com/villa_adriatica, 710Kn d.), an early 19th-century family home with one apartment and four rooms. The rooms are sunny and bright, furnished with antiques, and the home has a delightful garden with lemon trees. The **Hotel Zagreb** (Šetalište Kralja Zvonimira 27, tel. 020/438-930, www.hotels-sumratin.com, 995Kn d., including breakfast) in Lapad, west of the Old Town, is located in a sunny refurbished villa with a palm- and cypress-filled garden. The rooms are solidly three-star and the trek to Dubrovnik and the beach is fairly short. Nearby, the small rooms at the **Hotel Lapad** (Lapadska obala 37, tel. 020/432-922, www.hotel-lapad.hr, 1,050Kn d., including breakfast) have been renovated in a minimalist, modern style. The hotel has a small pool area overlooking the sea but no direct access to the beach. Hop on bus #6 at the bus stop across the street for a quick delivery to Dubrovnik's town gates.

The new **Hotel Uvala** (Masarykov put 6, tel. 020/433-580, www.hotelimaestral.com, 1,139Kn d., including breakfast) offers some of the best value for money in Dubrovnik for those who want a hotel with all the trimmings. A few kilometers west of the Old Town in a peaceful location, its features include indoor and outdoor pools, a spa, a macrobiotic restaurant, and wireless Internet access. An equally good use of funds is the **Importanne Resort** (Kardinala Alojzija Stepinca 31, tel. 020/440-100, www.importanneresort.com, 1,139Kn d., including breakfast), an overhaul of four hotels into one property that was reopened in 2007. The hotel has a great beach, two seawater pools, and sports facilities, though it is a 10-minute drive to the city walls.

Over 1,400Kn

The **(Hotel More** (Kardinala Stepinca 33, tel. 020/494-200, www.hotel-more.hr, 1,780Kn d., including breakfast) is close to Lapad, west of the Old Town; the area has lots of restaurants and cafés. The 34-room hotel has a small pool area and a beach at the water's edge. It's about a 20-minute bus ride to the gates of Dubrovnik. Much closer to town is the **Hilton Imperial Dubrovnik** (Marijana Blažića 2, tel. 020/320-320, www.hilton.com, 2,137Kn d., including breakfast), just a quick walk to the Pile Gate. The concierge at the hotel is outstanding and can help you with recommendations, advice, and day trips to the islands. Make sure to ask for a sea-view room, as some actually face a wall. The location of the **(Hotel Bellevue** (Pera Čingrije 7, tel. 020/330-000, www.hotel-bellevue.hr, 2,280Kn d., including breakfast), practically part of a cliff face overlooking the Adriatic, is stunning, as are the well-designed public and private spaces. The hotel has a small beach below and an indoor pool. It's located west of the walls in Danče, so it's a 30-to-40-minute panoramic walk to the Old Town—though with the hotel's chic restaurant and stellar views you may not go out for dinner after all.

DUBROVNIK

Food

Eating in Dubrovnik is rarely cheap and often not as good as what you'll find in other parts of Croatia, particularly in the high season. That said, here are a few best bets that will at least leave you satisfied and possibly even impress you.

CAFÉS AND DESSERTS

The **GradsKavana** (Luža 2, tel. 020/321-414, www.mea-culpa.hr, 8 A.M.–2 A.M. daily in summer, 8 A.M.–11 P.M. daily in winter) offers coffee and cake in a grand Austro-Hungarian space mixed with modern simplicity. Try the café's famous macaroni cake. Another spot for sweets and caffeine is **Dolce Vita** (Nalješkovićeva 1a, tel. 020/321-666, 9 A.M.–midnight daily), located just off the Stradun, with cakes, ice cream, and some decent muffins if you're feeling homesick.

FINE DINING

Ragusa 2 (Zamenjina 12, tel. 020/321-203, www.ragusa2.com, 8 A.M.–midnight daily, 130Kn) has operated in Dubrovnik's city walls for over 35 years. The cozy space has lots of Mediterranean dishes and a selection of 150 wines. Not quite as touristy as some of Dubrovnik's restaurants, Ragusa 2 was honored in a local poll of favorite Croatian restaurants in 2007. Though you'll have to hike up some steps to get there, **Levanat** (Šetalište Niki i Meda Pucića, tel. 020/435-352, 10:30 A.M.–midnight daily, closed Nov.–Feb., 130Kn) near Lapad has nice tables outside or in. Dishes are quite creative, such as the surprisingly good shrimp with honey and sage. Certainly the most fashionable restaurant in town, **Vapor** (Pera Čingrije 7, tel. 020/330-000, noon–3 P.M. and 6–10 P.M. daily, 180Kn) at the Bellevue has a knockout interior by designer Renata Štrok and an amazing view plus sophisticated spins on Mediterranean cuisine. Tops on the list of Dubrovnik's restaurants is **◖ Gil's** (Sv Dominika, tel. 020/322-222, www.gils dubrovnik.com, noon–midnight daily, 450Kn for three courses), a must-book table. From the

In Dubrovnik, you'll find everything from fine dining to traditional specialties like *palačinke* (crepes).

ROMANTIC DINING OUTSIDE OF DUBROVNIK

For fewer tourists or just for a change of pace, heading out of Dubrovnik for lunch or dinner can be refreshing to both mind and wallet.

◖ **Gverović-Orsan** (Stilkovića 43, tel. 020/891-267, www.gverovic-orsan.hr, noon-midnight Mon.-Sat., closed Jan.-Feb., 100Kn), in the fishing village of Zaton Mali, is popular with low-key foodies. Black risotto is the house specialty, while marinated fish carpaccio and the salad of local *motar* (a plant that grows wild near the sea) are not to be missed. You can also take a swim while you're waiting for your meal from the beach in front. Zaton Mali is seven kilometers northwest of Dubrovnik going toward Split on the main coastal road.

In the village of Zaton Veliki, 10 kilometers northwest of Dubrovnik, you'll find the water-front **Konoba Ankora** (Zaton bb, tel. 020/891-031, 9 A.M.-midnight daily in summer, 95Kn), perfect for a seafood meal at sunset.

Owned by the same group as respected Dubrovnik restaurants Proto and Atlas Club Nautika, ◖ **Konavoski Dvori** (Ljuta, Konavle, tel. 020/791-039, www.esculap-teo.hr, noon-midnight daily, 100Kn) is set in a peaceful location next to a rushing brook. Marinated cheese, fresh trout, and meats baked under an iron bell are the specialties of the house. Konavoski Dvori is located in Konavle, 21 kilometers southeast of Dubrovnik going toward Montenegro. If you're driving to Konavle, take the road to Montenegro and when you reach Gruda, take the road for the village of Ljuta, where the restaurant is located.

contemporary cuisine (black ravioli with lobster sauce, sushi rolls in foie gras) to the stellar view (overlooking the old harbor) to the wine cellar (with 6,000 bottles), a meal at Gil's is actually worth the money. After dinner head to the terrace lounge bar to kick back with some hip tunes.

QUICK BITES

Quick, filling, and cheap in the center of the Old Town, **Express** (Marojice Kaboge 1, tel. 020/323-994, 10 A.M.-10 P.M. daily, 25Kn) is the place to go for stews and hearty pasta dishes suitable for a backpacking budget. Nestled in a small space off the Stradun, ◖ **Buffet Škola** (Antuninska 1, tel. 020/321-096, 8 A.M.-2 A.M. daily in summer, call for winter hours, 40Kn) is famous for its sandwiches on fresh-baked bread and smoked ham and cheese snack plates. **Kamenice** (Gundulićeva poljana 8, tel. 020/323-682, 7 A.M.-midnight daily, 35Kn) is located in one of the most tourist-heavy areas of town beside the market. While it might not get high marks on decor or service, the mussels, oysters, and seafood dishes (all generously sized) are some of the best values in town.

Expect to wait 10 to 20 minutes for a table. The **Oliva Pizzeria** (Lučarica 5, tel. 020/324-594, 35Kn) near St. Blaise's serves pasta, salads, and pizza by the slice for only 10Kn. **Fresh** (Vetranićeva 4, tel. 091/896-7509, www.igotfresh.com, 9 A.M.-2 A.M. daily in summer, call for winter hours, 30Kn) offers wrap sandwiches (even a breakfast wrap) and healthy smoothies at tremendously reasonable prices.

SEAFOOD

Proto (Široka 1, tel. 020/323-234, 11 A.M.-11 P.M. daily, 120Kn) has a good Old Town location and a nice terrace, where you should try and reserve a table in summer. The menu is mostly fish with lots of local offerings and even snails. The wine list is solid, too. Proto's big brother, the **Atlas Club Nautika** (Brsalje 3, tel. 020/442-526, noon-midnight daily, closed mid-Dec.-mid-Jan., 600Kn for a five-course meal) holds Dubrovnik's prime position for a restaurant, right next to the Pile Gate with two large terraces overlooking the sea. The best tables are numbers in the thirties on the Penatur terrace or try numbers 56 or 57 on the Lovrijenac terrace. The food here is fancy, like the shrimp soup with black truffles, though it doesn't quite live up to the hype. The view, however, does. Thrifty types might want to opt for a light lunch here instead.

TRADITIONAL

Walk outside the city walls for about 10 minutes, heading west out of the Pile Gate, and you'll find **Tovjerna Sesame** (Dante Alighieria bb, tel. 020/412-910, www.sesame.hr, 8 A.M.–midnight daily, 85Kn). The cozy restaurant serves breakfast as well as reasonable lunches and dinner with dishes like seafood risotto and orange-and-almond crepes for dessert. In the seaside suburb of Lapad, **Blidinje** (Lapadska obala 21, tel. 020/358-794, 9 A.M.–midnight daily, 80Kn) opened in the summer of 2006 with a great location overlooking the Gruž harbor. The meats *ispod peka* are super and should

be ordered two to three hours in advance. For walk-ins there are still lots of grilled meats, pastas, and nice pizzas. A short walk from the Pile Gate, the terrace at **Orhan** (Od Tabakarije 1, tel. 020/414-183, www.restaurant-orhan.com, 11 A.M.–midnight daily, 95Kn) is something of an experience itself, nestled between two medieval fortresses overlooking the water. The food is good and reasonable with everything from pasta to seafood to steak on the menu.

VEGETARIAN

Nishta (Prijeko 30, tel. 098/186-7440, www.nishtarestaurant.com, 9 A.M.–midnight Mon.–Sat., 3 P.M.–midnight Sun., 60Kn) offers lots of tasty vegan options right in the Old Town. The vibe is international with a menu offering curries, spring rolls, and wraps. Nishta also doles out non-dairy shakes from its smoothie bar.

Information and Services

TOURS AND TOURIST INFORMATION

Your first stop for information should be the slightly out-of-the-way branch of the Dubrovnik **tourist office** (Ante Starčićeva 7, tel. 020/427-591, www.tzdubrovnik.hr, 8 A.M.–8 P.M. daily in summer, 9 A.M.–4 P.M. Mon.–Fri. and 9 A.M.–1 P.M. Sat. in winter). A short walk from the Pile Gate, the office has much friendlier employees than their colleagues on the Stradun. Stop by to pick up maps, brochures, advice, and free monthly guides to what's on. The tourist office here also has Internet access so you can check your email.

If you'd like a guide to help you navigate the city, **Dubrovnik Walks** (www.dubrovnikwalks.com, May–Oct., 1.5 hours, 90–140Kn) offers two guided walking tours in English (each with two departures daily) between May and the end of October. There's no need to reserve a spot; just show up at the appointed time and

place, provided on a convenient map on the website (currently in front of the club Fuego outside the Pile Gate).

COMMUNICATION

Get online at **Net Café** (Prijeko 21, tel. 020/321-025, 9 A.M.–1 A.M. daily in summer, 9 A.M.–11 P.M. daily in winter, 18Kn/1 hour), conveniently located near the Stradun. Snail mail is most easily sent from the main post office (corner of Široka and Od Puča, 9 A.M.–6 P.M. Mon.–Sat.).

OTHER SERVICES

Left luggage can be deposited at the bus station (Put Republike 29, tel. 060/305-070, 5:30 A.M.–9 P.M. daily, 20Kn daily). Two pharmacies, Gruž (Obala Pape Ivana Pavla 9, tel. 020/418-990) and Kod Zvonika (Placa 2, tel. 020/321-133), take turns as the city's designated all-night pharmacy.

Getting There and Around

GETTING THERE
Air

If you're flying into Dubrovnik's airport (tel. 020/773-333, www.airport-dubrovnik.hr), you'll need to find a way to get the 20 or so kilometers from its location southeast in Čilipi to your hotel. Incoming flights operated by Croatia Airlines and British Airways are met by a shuttle bus (30 minutes, 30Kn), which stops near the Pile Gate and at the main bus station near the ferry terminal. On the way back, they leave from the main bus station 1.5 hours before departures. Taxis (dial 970) from the airport will run you in the 300–350Kn range depending on the location of your hotel. You can also arrange for pickup through your accommodation, usually offered for a fare comparable to or slightly less than the taxis.

Bus

By bus (Put Republike 29, tel. 060/305-070, www.libertasdubrovnik.hr, 5:30 A.M.–10:30 P.M. daily) there are almost hourly connections with Split (4.5 hours) and around six connections daily with Zagreb (11 hours); you'll need your passport since a portion of each journey goes through Bosnia. If you're headed to Montenegro, have your passport handy and take a bus that leaves at least once daily. The bay of Kotor, for example, is about a 2.5-hour journey.

From the main bus station, it's about a 30-minute walk to the Old Town, or hop on bus #1A or #3, which will take you to the Pile Gate.

Car

If you're driving to Dubrovnik, keep in mind that you'll have to pass through Bosnia, so keep your passport and papers handy. Dubrovnik is about a 3.5-hour drive (216 km) south of Split and about a seven-hour drive (580 km) south of Zagreb.

Boat

Ferries (harbor tel. 020/418-989) run from the main terminal in Gruž (for Rijeka, Zadar, Split, Montenegro, and the islands) while smaller catamarans and water taxis in the old harbor near the Ploče Gate will take you to Lokrum and Cavtat. In the summers, there are usually two ferries a day to popular destinations like Hvar and Split and multiple connections to Lokrum, Cavtat, and the Elafiti Islands (most islands around 30 minutes, around 25Kn). Winters bring less frequent connections. Check with **Jadroagent** (Obala Stepjana Radića 32, tel. 020/419-000, www.jadro linija.hr) about tickets, schedules, and prices.

GETTING AROUND
Bus

Around town the city buses (www.libertas dubrovnik.hr) can get you where you need to go. Buy tickets from the newsstands (8Kn) or the driver (10Kn) or pick up a daily pass (25Kn) from the Libertas bus kiosk just outside the Pile Gate. Many of the city's hotels and apartments are located in the western suburb of Lapad. Hop on bus #6 from the Pile Gate to get there.

Taxi

Taxis are usually a slow way of getting around town (the bus is often quicker). Look for one outside the Pile Gate (or call 970); it's 25Kn to start plus 8Kn per kilometer.

Car

You don't really need a car in Dubrovnik—traffic is awful, parking is scarce, and the Old Town, where most of the stuff you'll want to visit is located, is completely pedestrian. That said, Dubrovnik has all the major rent-a-car companies like Budget (Obala Stejana Radića 24, tel. 020/418-998, www.budget .hr) and Hertz (Frana Supila 9, tel. 020/425-000, www.hertz.hr) as well as the fun Rent-A-Smart (Kralja Tomislava 7, tel. 01/487-6172, www.rentasmart.com.hr) located in Lapad.

Boat

Water taxis can be a useful way for getting to some of the area's more hidden beaches and an atmospheric mode of transport as well. Pick them up at the Stara Luka (Old Port).

DUBROVNIK

Around Dubrovnik

◖ TRSTENO

If you're a fan of gardens, you can't miss Trsteno (8 A.M.–8 P.M. daily in summer, 8 A.M.–5 P.M. daily in winter, 15Kn), about 15 kilometers northwest from Dubrovnik. The Gučetić family built the villa and beautiful gardens at Trsteno in the early 16th century. The entrance to the noble landscape is between two ancient plane trees. Filled with Renaissance gardens of lavender and rosemary, fruit trees, and languid statues surrounded by creeping bougainvillea, Trsteno is the ideal place to unwind and enjoy nature. From the end of the garden's palace ruins (which aren't ruins at all, but actually a bit of 19th-century folly architecture) you can grab a nice view of the sea and then go down the stairs to a small stretch of beach for a bit of seaside lounging.

To get there by car, hop on the Magistrala, direction north, and follow the signs. Buses headed to and from Split pick up and drop off here (contact Libertas, www.libertasdubrovnik.com, tel. 0800-1910); the ride is about 40–45 minutes.

CAVTAT

On the Magistrala 20 kilometers to the south of Dubrovnik, Cavtat has a long history intertwined with Dubrovnik. Settled by the Greeks in the 3rd century B.C., the city (then called Epidaurus) was actually a forerunner of Dubrovnik. Attacks by the Slavs in the 7th century forced the people to flee to Dubrovnik (at that time across a channel of water) and abandon the city. Cavtat was later an important fishing village, birthplace of many sea captains and the region's famed painter, Vlaho Bukovac. In the 20th century Cavtat became a tourist destination, with loads of concrete tourist hotels ruining the original beauty of the quiet seaside town. Cavtat is one of the few cities in the Konavle (the area south of Dubrovnik) that was not destroyed in the Homeland War. Its charming old town is worth a visit if you have the time or are looking for somewhere slightly quieter than Dubrovnik.

There are several interesting sightseeing stops in the palm tree–laden old town. A must for book lovers, the **Zbirka Baltazar Bogišić** (Baltazar Bogišić Collection, 9:30 A.M.–1 P.M. Mon.–Sat., 15Kn) displays a collection bequeathed by local scholar Baltazar Bogišić, a great lover of Slavic literature who died in 1908. There are over 20,000 books and manuscripts as well as a wonderful painting by Vlaho Bukovac that depicts the city's carnival—still celebrated in a grand tradition today—with some 80 locals portrayed in their finest costumes around the turn of the 20th century. There's more Vlaho Bukovac at the **Crkva svetog Nikole** (St. Nicholas's Church), with a painting above the main altar, and at the **Vlaho Bukovac Gallery** (Bukovčeva 5, 9 A.M.–1 P.M. and 4–8 P.M. Tues.–Sat., 20Kn), a former residence of the artist that exhibits his portraits (from which he made his living), frescoes he painted on the walls as a teenager, and other paintings, including one with his interpretation of the afterlife. The **Račićev mauzolej** (Račić Mausoleum, 10 A.M.–noon and 5–7 P.M. Mon.–Sat., 5Kn) in the Groblje svetog Roka (St. Roc Cemetery) is another must-see in town. Located at the highest point in the old town behind the **Samostan snježne Gospe** (Monastery of Our Lady of the Snow), the opulent gravesite, built in the 1920s, is one of Ivan Meštrović's finest works. The white stone building guarded by two austere yet tender angels is made even more beautiful by its position among towering cypresses overlooking the sea.

If you find yourself in need of sustenance, try the **Taverna Galija** (Vuličevićeva 1, tel. 020/478-566, www.galija.hr, 110Kn), with a stone terrace and stone-walled interior near the monastery. The menu has something for everyone, from steaming risottos to steak to grilled fish dishes.

Catch one of over a dozen buses that depart Dubrovnik daily for Cavtat (take bus #10), or take a boat from the Stara Luka (Old Port) in Dubrovnik (50Kn). Buses and boats take about 45 minutes.

ELAFITI ISLANDS

The Elafiti (or Elaphite) Islands are a nice escape from the summer hordes of Dubrovnik (though don't expect to find them completely void of tourists, there are just fewer of them). A short ferry ride away from Dubrovnik (from 20 minutes to over an hour depending on which one you choose; check with Jadrolinija, www .jadrolinija.hr, for times and prices), the islands are mostly car-free and full of great beaches for lounging.

Koločep

It takes only 20–30 minutes to reach Koločep, a small green island filled with pines and forests. Historically, the island was known for its coral, though today it's mostly known for being a peaceful spot for a swim. There's a nice sandy beach in **Donje Čelo,** a village at the north end of the island.

Lopud

The boat to Lopud takes a little under an hour and lets off at the island's only village, also named Lopud. Despite the lack of villages, the

island is (and always was) the most developed of the Elafiti. Today you'll still see some of the **former sea captains' Gothic homes** around town. West of the harbor and up a set of steps you'll find the remains of the villa belonging to Miho Pracat, a 16th-century sea merchant, who was supposedly the richest man in Dubrovnik at the time. He was also one of the kindest, leaving a giant amount of money to the poor of Dubrovnik. The city thanked him by placing his likeness in a prominent location in the Rector's Palace.

Near the ruins of Pracat's villa you'll find the **Perivoj Đorđić-Mayner** (Đorđić-Mayner Park), a peaceful park, and finally the ruins of a **Tvrđava** (fortress, follow the signs), from whose superb viewpoint you can admire the surroundings.

Locals and tourists alike will agree that **Uvala Šunj,** a sandy beach 20 minutes' walk south of the village, is Lopud's best beach. Near the beach is the **Gospa od Šunja** (Our Lady of Šunj, tel. 020/759-038, open sporadically, free). If the 12th-century church is open, make sure to take a peek at the rather

Lopud, the most developed of the Elafiti Islands

disturbing painting of a large snake swallowing a young child.

Lopud has a good selection of seafood restaurants along the Obala Iva Kuljevana, the town's main street, as well as snack bars on the Šunj beach.

Šipan

While Lopud is the most developed, Šipan is the largest; it's a little over an hour away from Dubrovnik. The island is home to dozens of churches, including several that date from before the 9th century. The first ferry stop is Suđurađ (or Sudjuradj), a village predominated by the giant walled villa of the 16th-century seafaring family Stjepović. Parts of the villa have been restored but are currently only open to tour groups.

If you want to see something the groups likely won't, hike up toward the **Crkva velike Gospe** (Church of Our Lady, two kilometers up), which looks like a fortress, on the hill above town. On the way you'll come across some ruins, once the **Biskupovo** (Bishop's House). Inside is a fresco depicting Michelangelo, who was a friend of the bishop of Dubrovnik Lodovico Beccadelli. Old letters prove that Beccadelli begged his friend to visit him on Šipan, but Michelangelo RSVPed no.

From Suđurađ you can either walk to the village of **Šipanska Luka** on a seven-kilometer road (there are few to no cars on the island so it's quite doable) or get off at the second ferry stop, which debarks at Šipanska Luka. There are some more beautiful sea captains' villas from the 15th and 16th centuries, though the real draw here is the beaches, located on both sides of the harbor (the further you walk, the prettier they get).

You can rent bikes in Šipanska Luka from the **Hotel Šipan** (Šipanska Luka 160, tel. 020/758-000, www.hotel-sipan.hr, 900Kn d., including breakfast, closed Oct.–Apr.). The hotel's restaurant, **Pjat** (tel. 020/758-130, 11 A.M.–midnight daily, 95Kn), offers fusion dishes served on the terrace. There are a couple of other good restaurants in town, such as tourist-oriented (read: English menu) **Tauris**

(Šipanska Luka, tel. 020/758-088, www.sipan .info, 8 A.M.–midnight daily, closed Nov.–mid-Apr.) that serves decidedly quality local specialties: fresh fish, fish stew, fish pâté, olive oil, and refreshing salads.

◖ PELJEŠAC PENINSULA

Lying just to the north of Dubrovnik, the Pelješac Peninsula stretches its verdant arm into the sea toward the island of Korčula. It's actually quite remote and a nice respite after all the busyness of Dubrovnik. The peninsula is also a great stop for food and wine lovers, with some of Croatia's best wines being produced in its vineyards. Even from Dubrovnik or Korčula it's possible to fit in a day trip of winery-hopping.

Orebić

A small town that relied heavily on its trading alliance with nearby Dubrovnik for several centuries, Orebić is now home to lots of hotels catering to those who come to enjoy the nice shingle beaches on its shores.

But before you put on your bathing suit, take a peek at the **Franjevački samostan** (Franciscan monastery, 9 A.M.–noon and 5–7 P.M. Mon.–Sat., 5–7 P.M. Sun., 10Kn), about a half-hour walk up the hill out of town. Filled with attractive icons and paintings, most given by sailors in gratitude for safe journeys or rescues, the monastery also has a lovely view of the surroundings from its terrace.

If you're looking for a sandy beach, head 20 minutes east from the ferry terminal to **Trstenica,** great for kids and with plenty of cafés and konobas for refreshment.

The **Hotel Orsan** (Kralja Petra Krešimira IV 119, tel. 020/797-800, orebic-htp@du.t-com .hr, 263Kn d., including breakfast) is not fancy, the rooms are quite outdated, and the food's not that great. The upsides? You can walk to town via a waterfront promenade, lounge by the pool, sun on the beach right in front of the hotel, and enjoy the pretty sea views for relatively little money.

For something a bit more chic, try the small boutique **Hotel Indijan** (Škvar 2, tel. 020/714-

555, www.hotelindijan.com, 997Kn d., including breakfast). The modern hotel has a beach right outside, an indoor/outdoor pool, and a solid restaurant if you don't feel like eating out.

For meals try the **Pelješki dvori** (Obala Pomorca 36, tel. 020/713-329, 10 A.M.–midnight daily, closed Nov.–Dec., 95Kn) for decent, though slightly touristy, meats and seafood. The quirkier **Taverna Mlinica** (Obala Pomorca, tel. 020/713-886, call for hours, 190Kn) is more of a local place with specialties like baked octopus and lamb, though the character doesn't come cheap.

Orebić is about a two-hour drive northwest of Dubrovnik. There are several daily buses from Dubrovnik to Orebić (1.5–2 hours), usually continuing on to Korčula. Orebić is also connected by several daily (in summer, less in winter) ferries to the island of Korčula, which take only about 15 minutes.

Ston and Mali Ston

The walled city of Ston, important to the protection of Dubrovnik for centuries, has a pre-Romanesque church just west of town, the **Crkva svetog Mihovila** (St. Michael's Church), that's nice to see. However, the real draw of the area is enjoying a meal of the oysters that come from the beds in nearby Mali Ston (the towns are less than a kilometer apart).

The small family-run hotel **Ostrea** (Mali Ston, tel. 020/754-555, www.ostrea.hr, 710Kn d., including breakfast) is right on the water, with attractively furnished rooms; it's conveniently located right next to the best restaurant in town, Kapetanova kuća, owned by the same family.

Don't leave without trying ◖ **Kapetanova kuća** (Mali Ston, tel. 020/754-555, www .ostrea.hr, 9 A.M.–midnight daily, 170Kn) for excellent food including Ston oysters and even octopus burgers. The interior is nice (with the prerequisite stone walls, convivial atmosphere, and neat table settings), but it's the harborside terrace, with a lulling view of the bobbing boats, that might make you drag out your meal as long as possible.

With restaurants in both Split and Zagreb,

the town of Ston, on the Pelješac Peninsula

Bota Šare (Kroz polje 5, tel. 020/754-482, www.bota-sare.hr, 9 A.M.–11 P.M. daily, 100Kn) is known as a reliable source of good seafood. The cozy stone interior in Mali Ston is a plus as well.

Ston and Mali Ston are 60 kilometers northwest of Dubrovnik. Buses traveling from Dubrovnik to Orebić pass through Ston and Mali Ston. They take about 1.5 hours. If you're driving from Dubrovnik, take highway 8 toward Split and take road 414 toward Ston and Mali Ston (it's unlikely you'll notice 414 so it's better to look out for signs for Ston or Orebić). The drive should take about 1.5 hours.

Wineries

Home to some of Croatia's best wineries, the Pelješac Peninsula is the perfect place for a wine crawl through the steep grape-laden vineyards. The peninsula is home to a variety of whites and reds but it's best known for its rich Dingač, a reliable wine that can veer into world-class territory depending on the maker and the year. There are dozens of wineries in the area but it's worthwhile to call out a few of the best. First up

is the **Grgić winery** (Trstenik 78, tel. 020/748-090, grgic-vina@du.htnet.hr, 10 A.M.–5 P.M. Mon.–Sat.) in Trstenik, about 15 kilometers east of Orebić, actually the Croatian branch of American Grgich Hills Winery in Napa Valley, California. Mr. Grgić returned to his homeland in the 1990s to start a vineyard that has quickly gained a serious reputation, particularly for its Plavac Mali.

In the village of Potomje, about 10 kilometers east of Orebić, visit **Niko Bura** (tel. 020/742-204, call for hours) for his Dingač Bura and Postup wines as well as **Vedran Kiridzija** (Potemje 40, tel. 020/742-312, call for hours) and **Goran Miličić** (tel. 020/742-031, call for hours) to sample their Dingač varieties.

The area has a marked **wine road** (Pelješki vinski put, Kuna 8, tel. 020/742-139, vinskiput@net.hr), calling out wineries and gastro stops in a neat little package. If you want to go it on your own, try **Dalmatinska kuća** (Borak, tel. 020/748-017, noon–midnight daily, closed Nov.–Mar., 90Kn) for local specialties and a glass of the owner's wine while dining on the restaurant's terrace.

LJUBLJANA

With a cultural menu to rival much larger capitals, a funky nightlife, and a strong sense of self (despite being squeezed in the middle of various ruling empires throughout history), Ljubljana is a European capital minute in size but big on character. The city is charming precisely because it is small. You can get intimate with Ljubljana, see the sights, and still have time left to discover a few gems of your own.

Most impressive about Ljubljana may be the tremendous mark made on its streetscapes and buildings by the country's most famous architect, Jože Plečnik. Whether you admire his style, heavily influenced by the classicists, or not, it's impossible not to admire the sheer amount of work he undertook during his lifetime and his vision for a grand city, even if it is

quite small. Ljubljana is also full of good restaurants, lots of clubs and bars for evenings out, and plenty of stops to interest younger visitors. Though it's several hundred thousand residents smaller than Zagreb to the south (Ljubljana has close to 270,000 in the metro area), it's more developed, hitting just the right chord between East and West.

Ljubljana hasn't been overrun by tourists . . . yet. It's still overlooked by lots of visitors, like Germans and Austrians traveling down to Dalmatia who just drive straight through. You can easily see the city in one day and still have time to explore it further or get out into the countryside for a day trip. Travelers that take the time to wander the Old Town, eat in the restaurants, and browse the antiques markets and tiny galleries will find a warm, friendly

© J. SKOK/SLOVENIAN TOURIST BOARD

HIGHLIGHTS

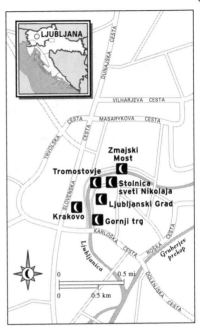

◖ Tromostovje: Also known as the Triple Bridge, this is a trademark of the city, built by architect Jože Plečnik (page 262).

◖ Zmajski Most: Stopping for a photo op on this bridge, famous for its iconic dragons, is a must (page 264).

◖ Stolnica sveti Nikolaja: The city's cathedral has all the things you've come to expect in European churches: frescoes, gilt, and sculptures. It also has some unexpected features, like fabulous bronze doors (page 265).

◖ Ljubljanski Grad: The views from this hilltop castle complex make it worth the hike (page 265).

◖ Gornji trg: The one-stop shop of the Old Town, this picturesque square and its extension, Levstikov trg, are home to some of the city's most beautiful facades and churches (page 266).

◖ Krakovo: A laid-back fishermen's settlement turned into a quarter for artists on a pension, Krakovo is filled with peasant-style homes, a few Roman ruins, and lots of character (page 268).

LOOK FOR ◖ TO FIND RECOMMENDED SIGHTS, ACTIVITIES, DINING, AND LODGING.

town, slightly quirky, always confident in the treasure that is Ljubljana.

HISTORY

The Romans came to the area in the 1st century A.D. and called the city Emona; an invasion by Attila the Hun in the 5th century destroyed most of the Roman structures. The city lay fairly barren until the 12th century, when a new settlement was built below the castle by Carniolan aristocracy. In the 14th century the Hapsburgs took over and didn't let go, except during a brief reign by Napoleon when Ljubljana was capital of the Illyrian provinces between 1809 and 1813.

The age of rail travel transformed Ljubljana, making it a major center of culture and tourism. An earthquake in 1895 damaged the city's buildings, many beyond repair, but made room for an even grander city, marked by over-the-top Secessionist buildings.

Ljubljana, once a stop on the Orient Express, flourished until World War II. Even after inclusion in Tito's Yugoslavia, the city grew substantially as people from rural villages moved into town for factory jobs, changing the landscape of modern Ljubljana, whose suburbs are marked by huge apartment buildings.

It's always been a prosperous city, relishing in its location between East and West, accepted by both sides as one of their own and capitalizing on that singularity. As the capital of the first former Yugoslav republic to enter the European Union (in 2004), Ljubljana is poised to use its position to even more advantage.

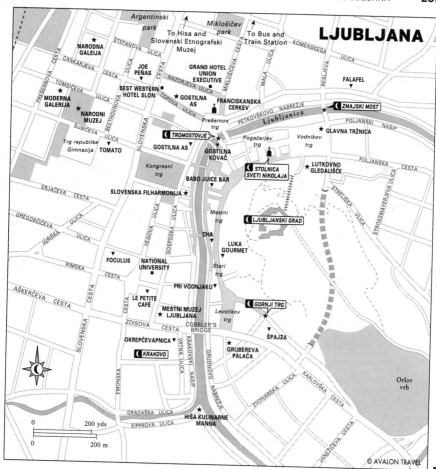

LJUBLJANA

Argentinski park

To Hisa and Slovenski Etnografski Muzej

Miklošičev park

To Bus and Train Station

KOMENSKEGA ULICA

NARODNA GALERIJA

STEFANOVA ULICA

CANKARJEVA CESTA

TOMŠIČEVA ULICA

PREŠERNOVA CESTA

JOE PEÑAS

NAZORJEVA ULICA

ČOPOVA ULICA

GRAND HOTEL UNION EXECUTIVE

MIKLOŠIČEVA CESTA

MALA ULICA

RESLJEVA ULICA

FALAFEL

BEST WESTERN HOTEL SLON

GOSTILNA AS

FRANCISKANSKA CERKEV

PETKOVŠKOVO NABREŽJE

ZMAJSKI MOST

MODERNA GALERIJA

BEETHOVNOVA ULICA

NARODNI MUZEJ

Prešernov trg

Ljubljanica

POLJANSKI NASIP

GLAVNA TRŽNICA

SUBIČEVA ULICA

Trg republike Gimnazija

TOMATO

SLOVENSKA CESTA

GOSTILNA AS

TROMOSTOVJE

GOSTILNA KOVAČ

Pogačarjev trg

Vodnikov trg

POLJANSKA CESTA

ERJAČEVA CESTA

Kongresni trg

BABO JUICE BAR

SLOVENSKA FILHARMONIJA

STOLNICA SVETI NIKOLAJA

LUTKOVNO GLEDALIŠČE

STROSSMAYERJEVA ULICA

STRELIŠKA ULICA

GREGORČIČEVA ULICA

VEGOVA ULICA

GOSPOSKA ULICA

Mestni trg

LJUBLJANSKI GRAD

IGRIŠKA ULICA

RIMSKA CESTA

CHA

LUKA GOURMET

AŠKERČEVA CESTA

FOCULUS

NATIONAL UNIVERSITY

Stari trg

PRI VODNJAKU

SLOVENSKA CESTA

LE PETITE CAFÉ

MESTNI MUZEJ LJUBLJANA

Levstikov trg

GORNJI TRG

ZOISOVA CESTA

COBBLER'S BRIDGE

KRAKOVSKI NASIP

OKREPČEVAPNICA

KRAKOVO

VRTNA ULICA

GRUDNOVO NABREŽJE

GRUBEREVA PALAČA

ŠPAJZA

EMONSKA

ZVONARSKA ULICA

KARLOVŠKA CESTA

Orlov vrh

GRADAŠKA ULICA

EIPPROVA ULICA

HIŠA KULINARNE MANNA

JANEŽIČEVA CESTA

0   200 yds

0   200 m

© AVALON TRAVEL

LJUBLJANA

PLANNING YOUR TIME

If you have two or three days to spend in Ljubljana, you won't regret it. That said, the city is very small and easily doable on foot, and it's possible to pack in the highlights in one full day.

A quick tour should hit Prešernov Trg, Ljubljanski Grad, and the Old Town (Mestni trg, Stari trg, and Gornji trg), with a stop at the Zmajski Most for a photograph. Top off the day with a good dinner and at least one coffee and cake. If you have another day, fit in some

of Ljubljana's excellent museums, galleries, and a bit of shopping. With a third day, spend some time in Tivoli Gardens and hopefully a visit to the charming quarter of Krakovo.

The city is beautiful all throughout the year, though summer is probably the most fun, with warm evenings and long days perfect for strolling along the river and sipping a wine at an outdoor café. December is also nice, with the festive decorations and holiday market making the already gingerbread-vibe city an excellent holiday getaway.

ORIENTATION

The Ljubljanica River divides the city into two distinct sides. To the east, you'll find Ljubljana's most ancient core, with the castle, cathedral, and medieval squares taking center stage in most tourists' itineraries. The west is the more modern side, though you'll still find a fair share of Austro-Hungarian architecture; a lot of the city's museums and galleries, as well as the University of Ljubljana, make their home on the western side. The two sides are linked by four bridges, three of which are architecturally interesting (the Zmajski Most, Tromostovje, and Čevljarski Most).

Further west you'll find the beautiful green spaces of Tivoli Gardens, while walking south along the left bank of the Ljubljanica River will land you in the Krakovo district.

Sights

PREŠERNOV TRG
Prešeren Square

This is the place where all of Ljubljana seems to literally meet, from the intersecting city streets to the groups of students on the stairs leading up to the rose-colored **Franciskanska cerkev** (Franciscan Church of the Annunciation, Prešernov trg 4, 8 A.M.–6 P.M. daily, free), Prešernov trg's most striking feature. Inside the mid-17th-century church is an ornate Baroque altar by Francesco Robba, an 18th-century Italian sculptor who spent most of his life in Ljubljana. There are several services daily (7, 8, 9, 10, and 11:15 A.M. and 4, 7, and 9 P.M.).

Also on the square is **Centromerkur** (Trubarjeva 1, tel. 01/426-3170), Ljubljana's oldest department store. Though it's not the best place for shopping, the art nouveau building is worth a look for fans of the style, from the impressive wrought-iron entrance topped with a statue of Mercury to the winding staircases within.

But it's the statue in the square, a monument to Prešeren, that's caused the most fuss in Ljubljana's past. The classical nude by Ivan Zajcs and Maks Fabiani was once seen as scandalous for being placed so close to a church.

◖ Tromostovje
Triple Bridge

Inspired by the bridges of Venice, the Tromostovje is a Plečnik design that has become a city trademark. The Ljubljana-transforming architect added two delicate arched bridges on the sides of the original single bridge, creating a unique and practical effect. The central bridge, once called the Hospital Bridge, was built in 1842. Traffic was creating many problems for the busy thoroughfare, so in 1929 Plečnik had the ingenious idea to build the parallel bridges for pedestrians to prevent the original bridge from being destroyed and to route traffic in a

THE GREAT POET FRANCE PREŠEREN

France Prešeren is widely considered to be the greatest Slovenian poet of all time and the force that shaped the country's subsequent literature. He was born in 1800 in Vrba; his parents recognized his intelligence and sent him to elementary school in Ribnica at the age of eight. He attended high school in Ljubljana and university in Vienna, where he studied law.

Prešeren had a tragic life, losing (or actually never winning over) his one true love, never marrying the mother of his three children, losing close friends to death, and battling alcoholism. Still, all of this intense emotional upheaval helped create his beautiful, tender poetry.

The great Romanticist poet of Slovenia, Prešeren's image can be found on the Slovenian two-euro coin and Ljubljana's busy Prešernov trg.

PLEČNIK'S LJUBLJANA

It's rare to have a city almost entirely designed (or at least renovated) by one architect. Though that may be an overstatement, there's no doubt about the strong impression Plečnik left on Ljubljana.

An 1895 earthquake left the city badly damaged and left open a door for Ljubljana to recreate and modernize itself, and it was Jože Plečnik who led the way.

Born in Ljubljana in 1872, Plečnik studied with the famous Viennese architect Otto Wagner, working in his office during the 1890s. He completed several structures in Vienna before moving on to Prague, where the Czech president appointed him the chief architect in charge of renovating Prague Castle.

Plečnik returned to Ljubljana in 1921, transforming the city during the 1920s and '30s. He renovated churches and the municipal cemetery, Žale, and built new bridges, waterfronts, buildings, monuments, and parks.

Jože Plečnik died in Ljubljana in 1957.

DISCOVERING THE ARCHITECT IN A DAY

Start your tour in the Trnovo neighborhood at **Plečnik's house** (Karunova 4, tel. 01/280-1600, www.aml.si, reserve a tour in advance by phone, €4). Today the surprisingly sparse space, preserved as he left it upon his death, gives you a sense of the architect and the man. Cross the **Trnovo Bridge,** with its interesting pyramids mimicking the spires of the Church of St. John the Baptist and the trees growing along the bridge, also a Plečnik idea.

Continue toward the city center on Emonska cesta, stopping at its intersection with Mirje, where even a set of old **Roman walls** were not left untouched by the architect.

The most striking of his additions is the large pyramid over one of the openings in the wall.

Back on Emonska, you'll pass the **Faculty of Architecture,** where he taught from 1945 to 1947, and a **monument** to the Illyrians he designed on Trg Francoske Revolucije.

The nearby **Križanke theater** was not only designed by Plečnik (when he was in his eighties, no less), it was also the site of a couple of jokes on the communists who commissioned him to create it. In one of the complex's courtyards he put in a vast amount of lighting, so much that some people questioned the idea. His excuse? The communists needed enlightening. He also placed columns decorated with the hammer and sickle directly opposite a statue of Christ in the main courtyard. Plečnik was a devout Catholic and likely this was his own way of injecting a snub at the Yugoslavian regime.

From here, double back to **Vegova cesta,** a beautiful street planned by the architect. Heading past **Kongresni trg,** which was also touched by Plečnik's skilled hand, though many features have been paved over with asphalt, to the west of the square you'll find a staircase leading to the beautiful tree-lined river **promenade.** From the river, you can see the rear facade of the **Philharmonica,** another Plečnik creation.

Walking along the river, you should hit the **Tromostovje,** or Triple Bridge. It was Plečnik who had the brilliant idea of adding two pedestrian bridges alongside the motor bridge, along with some handsome street lamps. From here, it's off to the **market,** where even the banality of buying bread did not escape his elegant and symmetrical touch.

LJUBLJANA DRAGON

© J. SKOK/SLOVENIAN TOURIST BOARD

the Ljubljana dragon, a symbol of the city

Dragons don't really figure into much of the architecture around Slovenia and neighboring Croatia, yet the mythical creature holds an important spot in Ljubljana culture. The origins of the Ljubljana dragon are tied closely with Greek legends. The hero who stole the Golden Fleece, Jason, was running away from the king he took it from and was forced to head up the Danube River. From there he and his men sailed to the Sava and then to the Ljubljanica River. On their journey they came across a big lake and marsh, where Jason supposedly fought and killed a vicious monster. The monster, the Ljubljana dragon, remained local folklore and was adopted as a part of Ljubljana's coat of arms and as mascot of the city.

more efficient manner. The balustrade-lined Tromostovje, along with the Zmajski Most, is considered a symbol of the city by locals.

EAST OF PREŠERNOV TRG
Hiša Eksperimentov
House of Experiments

If you're traveling with the kids, check out Hiša Eksperimentov (Trubarjeva 39, tel. 01/300-6888, www.h-e.si, 11 A.M.–7 P.M. Sat.–Sun., €5), a small museum with plenty of hands-on displays teaching scientific principles. Exhibits include a giant bubble maker and a piano that plays music according to weight.

Slovenski Etnografski muzej
Slovene Ethnographic Museum

Though it's a bit out of the way (across the river to the northeast), the Etnografski muzej (Metelkova 2, tel. 01/300-8700, www.etno-muzej.si, 10 A.M.–6 P.M. Tues.–Sun., €4.50) has a good overview of Slovenian cultural history with a look at everything from costumes to folk music. The museum has careful translations in English, making it a more worthwhile stop.

VODNIKOV TRG
Vodnik Square

This attractive square, built at the very end of the 19th century after the earthquake, is home to Ljubljana's central market, filled with colorful stands of fruits and vegetables from Monday through Saturday.

◖ Zmajski Most
Dragon Bridge

It's impossible to miss Zmajski Most, located near Vodnikov trg. It was the first modern bridge to cross the Ljubljanica, and traffic still uses it today. Built in 1901 by Dalmatian architect Jurij Zaninović, it was originally dedicated to Emperor Franz Joseph, but the menacing green dragon statues were just too iconic for the name to catch on. Legend has it that if a virgin walks across the bridge, one of the dragons will wave its tail. A wonderful example of art nouveau architecture, the bridge is mainly important as a symbol of Ljubljana.

Glavna tržnica
Main Market

A trip to the Glavna tržnica (Mon.–Sat. mornings) is a nice break from museums and monuments. However, it's also an essential stop for fans of Plečnik—he designed the market, filled with his signature columns, that stretches

the city's main market

through Pogačarjev trg and Vodnikov trg next to the Cathedral of St. Nicholas.

◖ Stolnica sveti Nikolaja
Cathedral of St. Nicholas

A 1701 Baroque cathedral built on the site of an earlier 13th-century church of the same name, the grand Stolnica sveti Nikolaja (Dolničarjeva 1, tel. 01/234-2690, www.lj-stolnica.rkc.si, 6 A.M.–noon and 3–7 P.M. daily, free) was designed by Italian architect Andrea Pozzo. Inside, there are some pretty frescoes by Quaglio (18th century) and Langus (19th century). Perhaps the biggest don't-miss here, though, are the impressive and solemn **bronze doors,** added in 1996 by artist Tone Demšar to commemorate the Pope's visit and the 1,250th year of Christianity in Slovenia.

Lutkovno Gledališče
Puppet Theater

It's fun to catch a show at the Lutkovno Gledališče (Krekov trg 2, tel. 01/300-0970, www.lgl.si, ticket office 4–6 P.M. Mon.–Fri., 10 A.M.–noon Sat.). If you can't make a show,

catch the puppets that pop out of the **clock** above the theater at the top of every hour 8 A.M.–8 P.M.

◖ LJUBLJANSKI GRAD
Ljubljana Castle

The hill that Ljubljanski Grad (Studentovska ulica, reached via Vodnikov trg, tel. 01/432-7216, 9 A.M.–11 P.M. daily Apr.–Oct., 10 A.M.–7 P.M. daily Nov.–Mar., tours at 10 A.M. and 4 P.M. June–mid-Sept., €5) sits on has always been home to forts, first occupied by the Celts, then the Illyrians, and later the Romans. The earliest part of the current structure, however, dates from the early 16th century. The highlights of the castle are the 15th-century **Kapela sv. Jurija** (St. George's Chapel), decorated with 60 colorful coats of arms from the 18th century, and the 19th-century **Lookout Tower,** where you can get a super view of Ljubljana and the Julian Alps. The castle complex has a decent gift shop and a **café** (9 A.M.–11 P.M. daily in summer, 10 A.M.–9 P.M. daily in winter) for a caffeine fix. After your tour, make sure to take time to hike around some of the leafy peaceful paths at the castle's base; the paths were designed by Plečnik in the 1930s.

OLD TOWN

The old core of Ljubljana has a storybook quality, with meticulous Baroque and medieval buildings filled with locals shopping in the small boutiques and stopping for a coffee in the area's many cafés.

Mestna hiša
Town Hall

Built in the 15th century, the imposing Mestna hiša assumed its current appearance during an 18th-century renovation. The best feature of the building is its beautiful Gothic courtyard with a Francisco Robba fountain depicting Narcissus.

Mestni trg
Town Square

It's worth wandering around the small galleries and boutiques on this picturesque cobbled square. The jaunty Baroque facades that line the square replaced the 12th-century square's medieval buildings, most of which were destroyed in the earthquake of 1511. Francesco Robba took his inspiration for **Robbov Vodnjak** (Robba's Fountain, Mestni trg) from fountains he saw while visiting Rome. Built in the 18th century and Robba's final work in Ljubljana before moving to Zagreb, it represents the three rivers of Carniola (Ljubljanica, Sava, and Krka).

From here head down to nearby Ribji trg, the location of Ljubljana's **oldest house** (No. 6), built in 1528.

◖ Gornji trg
Upper Square

Gornji trg is where you'll find the city's **medieval houses** (though the facades are mostly Baroque) and the 17th-century **Cerkev sv. Florijana** (Church of St. Florian, Gornji trg 18, tel. 01/252-1727). The church was built in the late 17th century, though Plečnik left his mark here too when he moved a statue by

Ljubljana's old town

Francesco Robba in front of what was once the main portal.

Flowing out of Gornji trg is **Levstikov trg** (Levstik Square), redesigned in the 20th century (again by Plečnik). It's worth a peek in the Baroque interior of the **Cerkev sv. Jakoba** (Church of St. James, Gornji trg 18, tel. 01/252-1727, services at 8 A.M., 9:15 A.M., 10:30 A.M., and 5 P.M., free), whose 17th-century **Kapela sv. Frančiška Ksaverija** (Chapel of St. Francis Xavier) is probably the prettiest and most ornate church in town. Just across from the church is the rococo **Grubereva Palača** (Gruber Palace, Zvezdarska ulica 1, tel. 01/241-4200), built between 1771 and 1783, which today houses the **Narodni arhiv Slovenije** (National Archives).

Čevljarski Most
Cobblers' Bridge

More of a square than a bridge, this column-lined Plečnik-designed pedestrian bridge divides Gornji trg and Mestni trg, or the old and new sides of town. Though the cobblers' huts that once lined a medieval wooden bridge here are now gone, the name keeps their memory alive.

LEFT BANK

Though it's more modern than the Old Town that skims the base of the castle, Ljubljana's Left Bank is filled with plenty of attractive Austro-Hungarian architecture, as well as many of the city's museums, theaters, and restaurants.

Slovenska Filharmonija
Slovenian Philharmonic Hall

The Slovenska Filharmonija (Kongresni trg 10, tel. 01/241-0800, www.filharmonija.si) is one of the world's older philharmonic orchestras. Originally founded in 1701, its members have included greats such as Haydn, Brahms, and Beethoven. The building was designed by Austrian architect Adolf Wagner and built in 1891. However, even this building did not escape Plečnik's master hand, changing the back facade and adding onto the neo-Renaissance structure.

Moderna galerija
Modern Gallery

The austere, gray home of the Moderna galerija (Tomšičeva 14, tel. 01/241-6800, www.mg-lj.si) is currently closed for extensive renovations. They hope to finish renovation in 2009 to show off the nice collection of contemporary Slovenian art.

Mestni muzej Ljubljana
Ljubljana City Museum

Ljubljana is packed with excellent museums, though the top of your list should be the Mestni muzej Ljubljana (Gosposka 15, tel. 01/241-2500, www.mm-lj.si, 10 A.M.–6 P.M. Tues.–Sun., English guided tours at 1 P.M. Sun., €4), where you can get a quick overview of the city's history, including photographs, documents, and scale models of planned but never completed Plečnik designs.

Narodna galerija
National Gallery

The location of the Narodna galerija (Prešernova 24, tel. 01/241-5418, www.ng-slo.si, 10 A.M.–6 P.M. Tues.–Sun., €5, free Sat. 2–6 P.M.) is worth a visit in itself. The 1896 Czech-designed building is loaded with gilt and over-the-top ceilings, a superb example of the Secessionist era, that lend added grandeur to the fine art housed here. The core of the collection centers on Slovenian art from the 13th to the 20th century, though it also houses a solid collection of European paintings as well. The gallery has a café and a nice shop for souvenirs.

Narodni muzej
National Museum

Though it's the oldest museum in Slovenia, the exhibition at the Narodni muzej (Prešernova 20, tel. 01/241-4400, www.narmuz-lj.si, €3) is relatively small. It features some Roman stone monuments, an Egyptian mummy, bronze artifacts from the Illyrians, and various artifacts, weapons, jewelry, and archaeological finds.

Železniški muzej
Railway Museum

Young and old should enjoy the Železniški

muzej (Parmova 35, tel. 01/291-2641, 10 A.M.–6 P.M. Tues.–Sun., €3). Admire the shiny steam engines, railway memorabilia, uniforms, and even art from Slovenia's history of railroading. You'll also find some decaying trains in the yard outside and a re-creation of a station master's office inside.

Pivovarski muzej
Brewery Museum

Fans of beer or history or both will appreciate the charming Pivovarski muzej (Pivovarniška 2, tel. 01/471-7340, www.pivo-union.si, 8 A.M.–1 P.M. first Tues. of the month, reserve in advance, free). Located in the 150-year-old Union Brewery, the displays consist of the history of brewing in Slovenia, a tour of the brewery, and a beer tasting.

Tobačni muzej
Tobacco Museum

Though it may not be politically correct, the Tobačni muzej (Tobačna 5, tel. 01/477-7344, www.tobacna.si, 10 A.M.–6 P.M. first Wed. and third Thurs. of the month, free) is quite interesting even for non-smokers. Not only do the displays track tobacco's history in Europe since the Middle Ages, but it also shows the importance of the factory for women's emancipation in Slovenia.

TIVOLI PARK

A giant peaceful green space in the middle of the city, Tivoli Park is so big it makes one think previous generations had very high hopes for Ljubljana's growth. A Plečnik-landscaped promenade leads to the **Tivoli Mansion,** where the **Mednarodni Grafični Likovni Center** (International Center for Graphic Arts, Pod Turnom 3, tel. 01/241-3800, www.mglc-lj .si, 11 A.M.–6 P.M. Wed.–Sun., €3.50) resides today. The center is a must for fans of graphic and visual arts, with posters, book designs, and more, most from the second half of the 20th century. Children will like the small zoo, while history fans will like the **Muzej Novejše Zgodovine** (Museum of Modern History, Celovška 23, tel. 01/300-9610, www.muzej-nz.si, 10 A.M.–6 P.M. Tues.–Sun., €3.50), where an excellent display of Slovenian history during the 20th century will leave you feeling like you know the country a little better than before.

◖ KRAKOVO

A pleasant neighborhood to walk around, dating from the 15th century, Krakovo was originally a fishermen's settlement and later home to the Slovenian impressionist painter Rihard Jakopič; the neighborhood still has an organic, almost country feel to it. The **Jakopič Garden** (Mirje 4, tel. 01/241-2506, www.mm-lj.si, dawn–dusk) is home to a few Roman ruins, including a few additions to the ancient walls by Plečnik, but the real draw to Krakovo is its artsy, unpretentious vibe. Wander the enclave of peasant-style homes, many with gardens that supply the town market, and narrow little streets with pleasing flower and vegetable patches, and stop at one of the funky cafés.

Entertainment and Events

NIGHTLIFE
Bars

Ljubljana has a great bar and club scene with something for everyone. Literary and artsy types might want to check out the **KUD France Prešeren** (Karunova 14, tel. 01/283-2288, 11 A.M.–1 A.M. daily), home to a small café and a strong presence on Ljubljana's arts scene since 1919. Something happens here most every night, from readings and performances to concerts and workshops. **Geonatvik** (Kongresni trg 1, tel. 01/252-7027, www.geonatvik.com, 7 A.M.–1 A.M. Mon.–Thurs., 7 A.M.–3 A.M. Fri., 8:30 A.M.–3 A.M. Sat.) is a café/shop selling maps and guides that also hosts the odd travel lecture or live music act, advertised on the chalkboard out front. Relatively undiscovered, the just-out-of-center **Pilon** (Prešernova 15) is aesthetically pleasing, plus it has lots of artsy and style-conscious magazines to peruse if you're bored. The interior of **Boheme** (Mestni trg 19, tel. 01/548-1342) often gets overlooked by patrons, but the shabby elegance lends one to literary musings.

Trendy sorts and fashionistas should check out **Salon** (Trubarjeva 23, tel. 01/439-8764, www.salon.si, 9 A.M.–1 A.M. Mon.–Wed., 9 A.M.–3 A.M. Thurs.–Sat., 3 P.M.–1 A.M. Sun.) where kitsch decor competes with the trendily dressed crowd, downing some quite good cocktails. **Kuriln'ca** (Mestni trg 18) has a more serious interior and is definitely part of the popular crowd. The decor at **Minimal** (Mestni trg 4, tel. 01/426-0138) is supplied by the well-dressed patrons. The bar has a good drinks list and sushi on Wednesday night.

Maček (Krojaška 5, tel. 01/425-3791, 9 A.M.–midnight daily) is in the heart of Ljubljana's hip right bank. A prime people-watching spot, it's a popular place for weekend morning coffee.

A more professional, albeit chic, crowd swill coffee by day and cocktails by night at the attractive **Opera Bar** (Cankarjeva 12, tel. 01/421-0390, www.opera-bar.com, 7 A.M.–12:30 A.M. Mon.–Wed., 7 A.M.–2 A.M. Thurs.–Sat., 10 A.M.–6 P.M. Sun.).

Beer lovers fear not: Ljubljana has dozens of pubs to choose from. Narrowing down the list, try **Zlata Ladjica** (Jurčičev trg 1, tel. 01/241-0696, www.zlataladjica.si, 8 A.M.–1 A.M. Mon.–Sat., 10 A.M.–10 P.M. Sun.), where riverside outdoor seating and great old-town views are the draw, or **Kratochwill** (Kolodvorska 14, tel. 01/433-3114, www.kratochwill.si, 9 A.M.–11 P.M. Mon.–Fri., noon–11 P.M. Sat., noon–10 P.M. Sun.), the city's only microbrewery, for local flavor. If you're feeling homesick, try expat hangouts **Cutty Sark** (Knafljev prehod 1, tel. 01/425-1477, 9 A.M.–1 A.M. Mon.–Sat., noon–1 A.M. Sun.) or **Patrick's** (Prečna 6, tel. 01/230-1768, 10 A.M.–1 A.M. Mon.–Fri., noon–1 A.M. Sat., 5 P.M.–midnight Sun.) for on-tap Guinness and English-speaking companionship. Sports fans will like the gimmicky **Rugby Pub & Lounge** (Židovska Steza 6, tel. 01/426-4062, 8 A.M.–12:30 A.M. Mon.–Thurs., 8 A.M.–1 A.M. Fri., noon–1 A.M. Sat., noon–midnight Sun.) for three floors of big-screen TVs blaring sporting events, lots of beer, and sport-themed decoration.

Students shouldn't miss **Zmavc** (Rimska 21, tel. 01/251-0324, 7:30 A.M.–1 A.M. Mon.–Fri., 10 A.M.–1 A.M. Sat., 6 P.M.–1 A.M. Sun.), a graffiti-covered bar filled with comic-strip walls, raucous fun-loving staff and customers, and a general good vibe. Also worth checking out: **Birdland** (Trubarjeva 50, tel. 01/231-7937, 1 P.M.–midnight Mon.–Fri., 4 P.M.–midnight Sat.–Sun.) for a friendly, laid-back spot with few patrons over 25. Art and philosophy majors will appreciate **NUK café** (Turjaška 1), in the basement of the stunning National University Library, which affords lots of private nooks for deep discussions.

If you're in the mood for something different, Slovenia's capital has lots of theme bars, from the skeleton-filled **Pr Skelet** (Ključavničarska 5, tel. 01/252-7799, 10 A.M.–3 A.M. daily) cocktail bar to Hemingway memorial **Casa del**

LJUBLJANA

Papa (Celovška 54, tel. 01/434-3158, noon–midnight daily), which plays pop music instead of something more atmospheric, but the drinks make up for the faux pas. If you're feeling a bit juvenile, race electric go-karts around a track at the racing-themed **Rollbar** (Hala 18, tel. 01/585-2570, www.indoor-karting.com, 7 A.M.–midnight Mon.–Thurs., 8 A.M.–1:30 A.M. Fri.–Sat., 8 A.M.–11 P.M. Sun.) in the BTC City shopping center.

If all the bars have closed and you want to keep going, join the after party at rowdy Turbo-Folk **Klub 12** (Prušnikova 95, tel. 041/678-577, www.klub-12.com, 7 A.M.–5 A.M. Mon.–Fri., 6 P.M.–5 A.M. Sat.–Sun.) or the faithful **Druga Pomoč** (Šmartinska 3, tel. 01/431-3277, 6 A.M.–3 A.M. daily), serving drinks with a smile to the bleary-eyed hardcore.

Live Music and Dance Clubs

A solid choice for chilling out to a quality jam session, the elegant but low-key **Gajo Jazz Club** (Beethovnova 8, tel. 01/425-3206, www.jazzclubgajo.com, 9 A.M.–1 A.M. Mon.–Fri., 9 A.M.–midnight Sat.–Sun.) hosts local and international acts. For more party atmosphere with your jazz, **Sax Pub** (Eipporva 7, tel. 01/283-1457, 10 A.M.–1 A.M. Tues.–Sat.,

4–10 P.M. Sun., noon–1 A.M. Mon.) has Thursday-night live jazz inside a graffiti-painted riverside cottage.

Students should head to **KMŠ** (Tržaška 2, tel. 01/425-7480, www.klubkms.si, 8 A.M.–5 A.M. Mon.–Fri., 9 P.M.–5 A.M. Sat.), a student-run club located in an old factory. Inside, two floors host a young crowd that fills to capacity on weekends.

Klub K4 (Kersnikova 4, tel. 01/438-0261, www.k4.org, from 11 P.M. Tues.–Sun.) is a Ljubljana club-scene establishment, with a nondescript metal and neon interior and something different every night, ranging from techno to funk to Sunday's pink party for the local gay community.

Aspiring supermodels line up in front of **Global** (Tomšičeva 1, tel. 01/426-9020, www.global.si, 9 A.M.–5 A.M. Mon.–Sat.) to mix with the in crowd and enjoy great views of the city from atop the Nama department store.

On the more extreme side (or at least as extreme as Ljubljana gets) **Metelkovo Mesto** (Metelkova cesta, tel. 01/432-3378, www.metelkova.org, call or visit website for schedule) is a former army barracks that hosts themed events, including punk, dance, and gay/lesbian. It's usually hard to find out what's

TURBO-FOLK

Hundreds of kids stand on tables, arms around each other, loudly belting out the lyrics of a Turbo-Folk song on a Saturday night. It sounds whiny and very – well, Balkan, which is not a word most Croatians or Slovenians like to be associated with.

More importantly, Turbo-Folk is almost strictly Serbian, and for many older Croatians (and Slovenians as well) who still remember the scars of the war, the idea of embracing a part of Serbian culture seems traitorous. The topic has created a lot of debate in Croatia, from radio talk shows to political television interviews with calls for banning the music, which is not played on television or local radio stations.

Locally referred to as *narodnjaci* (closest

translation: folk music), it was described by a journalist from Croatia's *Jutarnji List* newspaper as "a mixture of mutated Balkan melodies, howling vocals, idiotic lyrics and sampled disco and house rhythms." Think of something like country music, with its themes of lost love, adultery, and revenge, mixed with gangsta rap's big cars, big guns, and big money, and you'd have something close to Turbo-Folk.

The controversy is somewhat less in Slovenia, and if you'd like to get a taste, Ljubljana is a safer place to do it than Croatia, where the underground Turbo-Folk scene often gets mixed in with other underground pursuits and unsavory groups under the influence of too much alcohol.

going on ahead of time, so if you can't get anyone on the phone, have a peek to see if it seems like your style.

Packed, sweaty, and loud are a few words you could use to describe **Orto Bar** (Grabloviceva 1, tel. 01/232-1674, 8 P.M.–4 A.M. daily), a lounge swathed in red velvet serving shots and pulsing music from blues to punk.

THE ARTS

Ljubljanski Grad (Ljubljana Castle, Studentovska ulica, tel. 01/232-9994, www .ljubljanafestival.si) hosts musical and theatrical performances throughout the year. **Poletno gledališče Križank** (Križanke Summer Theater, Miklošičeva 28, tel. 01/439-6445, www.ljubljanafestival.si) is an open-air theater located on the site of a former monastery. The entire complex has a sliding roof that makes for outstanding theater and concerts, from classical to pop and jazz, in all sorts of weather. Home to the Slovenian Philharmonic Orchestra, the **Slovenska Filharmonija,** the Philharmonic

Hall (Kongresni trg, tel. 01/241-0800, www .filharmonija.si) is a dependable venue for solid classical performances. The frothy 1882 home of the **Slovensko narodno gledališče** (Slovenian National Opera and Ballet Theater, Zupančičeva 1, tel. 01/425-4840) is a fitting location for Verdi, Mozart, and *Swan Lake*. If you're traveling with kids or you're just a kid at heart, a marionette show at the **Lutkovno Gledališče** (Puppet Theater, Krekov trg 2, tel. 01/300-0970, www.lgl.si, ticket office 4–6 P.M. Mon.–Fri., 10 A.M.–noon Sat.) is a nice way to while away an afternoon.

No need to hunt for a special foreign-language cinema in Slovenia. Most films (with the exception of some children's films) are not dubbed, only subtitled, which means you can easily rub shoulders with the locals and still enjoy the movie. Try the old-school but renovated **Kinoklub Vič** (Trg Mladinskih Delovnih Brigad 6, tel. 01/241-8411, www.kolosej.si) for major releases and the occasional offbeat movie. For art and foreign films (fun if you speak French, less choice if you only speak

Ljubljana Jazz Festival

English), check out **Kinoteka** (Miklošičeva 28, tel. 01/547-1580, www.kinoteka.si). For the standard big multiplex experience, head to BTC City, where **Kolosej** (Šmartinska 152, tel. 01/520-5500, www.kolosej.si) has a big selection of Hollywood blockbusters.

FESTIVALS AND EVENTS

The **Festival Dokumentarnega Filma** (International Festival of Documentary Film, www.fdf.si) screens documentary films from around the world every year in late March or early April. At the beginning of May, the **Wire Walk** (www.pohod.si), whose longest trek is 35 kilometers around the city, memorializes Ljubljana's occupation by the Italians who surrounded the city with barbed wire during World War II.

Museums are free of charge on the International Day of Museums (May 18), the Museum Summer Night (usually June 16), and the Day of Culture (Dec. 3), celebrating the birthday of Prešeren.

The **Ljubljana Festival** (www.ljubljana festival.si), held every summer from sometime in June to sometime in August, is an outstanding arts festival that brings together international chamber and symphony orchestras, visual artists, and even an open-air cinema for dozens of cultural performances. Summer also brings the **Ljubljana Jazz Festival** (www .ljubljanajazz.si), an outstanding event that has been an annual feature for 50 years. **Trnfest** is another summer festival, bringing free concerts and performances to the Trnovo neighborhood the entire month of August.

In December, Christmas spirit fills Ljubljana's streets, with decorations and lots of stalls selling gifts and refreshments in the Old Town.

Shopping and Recreation

SHOPPING
English Books

If you are really interested in the local topography or are looking for detailed city maps, the best store is **Kod in kam** (Trg francoske revolucije 7, tel. 01/200-2732, 9 A.M.–8 P.M. Mon.–Fri., 8 A.M.–1 P.M. Sat.), located near the National University Library. For reprints of classics in English, maps, and dictionaries, head to **Oxford Center** (Kopitarjeva 2, tel. 01/360-3789, 8 A.M.–7 P.M. Mon.–Fri., 8 A.M.–1 P.M. Sat.), which stocks a large supply of titles for locals learning English. The downtown location of **Konzorcij** (Slovenska 29, tel. 01/241-0650, 9 A.M.–7:30 P.M. Mon.– Fri., 9 A.M.–1 P.M. Sat.) has a nice supply of foreign-language titles, including travel, and it has free Wi-Fi. The cheapest deal in town is the underground **Bukvarna** (across from the Ursuline church on Slovenska, 10 A.M.–1 P.M. and 3–6 P.M. Tues. and Thurs.), which stocks used Slovenian books and a good selection of secondhand English books, priced by weight.

Food and Wine

If you'd like to pick up some souvenirs for the gourmets in your life, the wine shop of **Koželj** (Dvorni trg 1, tel. 01/251-3644, www.kozelj. si, 11 A.M.–8 P.M. Mon.–Fri., 10 A.M.–2 P.M. Sat.) is a must on your shopping trip. Around 80 percent of its selection is local and it's a great place to find out all you ever wanted to know about Slovenian winemaking. **Čokoladnica Cukrček** (Mestni trg 11, tel. 01/519-9286, www.cukrcek.si, 9 A.M.–8 P.M. Mon.–Sat., 10 A.M.–7 P.M. Sun.) has hundreds of attractively packaged chocolate confections, hot chocolates, and even chocolates shaped like Ljubljana's signature dragon or one of its most famous poets, Prešeren. You also may want to pop by the **Glavna tržnica** (Main Market, tel. 01/300-1200, Mon.–Sat. mornings) for locally produced honeys and other sundries.

Foodies will also appreciate the stash at **Honey House** (Mestni trg 7, 10 A.M.–6 P.M. Mon.–Fri., 10 A.M.–1 P.M. Sat.), with everything you could imagine produced from honey, including wine and candies. **Piranske soline** (Mestni trg 19, tel. 01/425-0190, 9 A.M.–8 P.M. Mon.–Fri., 9 A.M.–5 P.M. Sat., 10 A.M.–3 P.M. Sun.) sells a range of products from bath salts to cooking salts, all from the famous salt pans of the coastal city of Piran. Don't pass up trying the salted chocolates.

Souvenirs

You can buy lace from Idrija, whose long tradition of lace-making is legendary in Slovenia, at **Idrijska čipka** (Mestni trg 17, tel. 01/425-0051, www.idrija-lace.com, 10 A.M.–1 P.M. and 3–7 P.M. Mon.–Fri.). Though much of it is typical souvenir bric-a-brac, you might find something for your suitcase at **Rustika** (Ljubljana Castle, Studentovska ulica, 9 A.M.–8 P.M. daily in summer, 10 A.M.–7 P.M. daily in winter) inside Ljubljana Castle.

Antiques

The riverside **Sunday market** (Cankarjevo Nabrežje, 8 A.M.–2 P.M. Sun.) near the Cobblers' Bridge is the place to find fun antiques, old postcards, and jewelry to stash in your suitcase. For antiques of a different sort, **Spin Vinyl Rock n Roll Ploščarna** (Gallusovo Nabrežje 13, tel. 01/251-1018, 10 A.M.–7 P.M. Mon.–Fri., 10:30 A.M.–2 P.M. Sat.) is an old-school old-town record shop selling stacks of vinyl from the former Yugoslavia—a fun souvenir for music fans.

Fashion

Though avant-garde knitting might seem like an oxymoron, **Draž** (Gornji trg 9, tel. 01/426-6041, www.drazdraz.com, tel. 01/426-6041, 9 A.M.–1 P.M. and 3–7 P.M. Mon.–Fri., 10 A.M.–1 P.M. Sat.) just might change your mind. The local fashion house designs dresses, skirts, and sweaters that are all runway ready.

Shopping Centers

If you still haven't found quite what you're looking for, **BTC City** (Šmartinska 152, tel. 01/585-1100, www.btc-city.com, 9 A.M.–9 P.M. Mon.–Sat.), a few kilometers northeast of the center, has 400 shops, restaurants, bars, a cinema, a post-office, and even a water park.

SPORTS AND RECREATION
City Tours

Ljubljana offers several excellent tours, including a two-hour **walking tour** (depart from the town hall, check with tourist office for times, €10) of the Old Town and castle complex, one-hour **boat tour** (depart from the Cankarjevo nabrežje dock, check with tourist office for times, €10), and two-hour guided **bike tour** (check with tourist office for times and departure points, May–Oct., €20).

Recreation

The **Pot spominov in tovarništva** (Path of Remembrance and Comradeship, www.pohod.si) is a 35-kilometer circuit commemorating the Italian occupation during World War II, following the perimeter that was enclosed in barbed wire. Today, it's a great trek or cycling path through the city's surroundings, passing some worthwhile stops like Plečnik's re-creation of the municipal graveyard, Žale cemetery, and Fužine castle. Follow the signs marked POT.

Skok Sport Center (Marinovseva 8, tel. 01/512-4402, www.skok-sport.si) offers rafting, kayaking, and cycling, as well as kayaking courses around Ljubljana and beyond. The center also rents bicycles and canoes. If you'd like to take to the skies, **Balonarski Center Barje** (Flandrova 1, tel. 01/512-9220, balon@siolnet) or the tourist office can help arrange balloon flights over the city and countryside.

Spectator Sports

Ljubljana's soccer team plays at **ŽSD Stadium** (Milčinskega ulica 2, tel. 01/438-6470). One of the most popular spectator sports these days is hockey; the Ljubljana team HDD Tilia Olimpija takes to the ice at **Hala Tivoli** (Tivoli Hall, Celovška cesta 25, tel. 01/431-5155). The sports hall is also home to basketball and volleyball games. A great source of tickets in Ljubljana, for both sporting events and concerts, is www.eventim.si.

LJUBLJANA

Accommodations

Ljubljana is quite expensive in terms of accommodation, particularly when it comes to value for money. But there are a few gems, and the city has an impressive range of hostel accommodations, some of which seem more like hotels than the backpacker establishments they claim to be. Hotels and guesthouses can be found in the center of town, in the old town core and around the most-frequented tourist sites, as well as out of center, so be sure to figure in time and transportation costs when deciding between your options.

CENTRAL
Under €50

The **Hostel Simbol Castle** (Gerbičeva ulica 46, tel. 041/720-825, www.simbol.si, €15 per person) is in the city center, walking distance to most tourist stops and the train and bus stations. The **Most Hostel** (Petkovškovo nabrežje 41, tel. 041/632-800, €30 d.) exceeds hostel expectations, with a whirlpool tub and shower, fast free Internet, and friendly staff, all a mere five-minute walk to the Dragon Bridge.

The **Hostel Celica** (Metelkova Ulica 8, tel. 01/230-9700, www.hostelcelica.com, €25 per person) is by far one of the most interesting hostels anywhere. Located in a former military prison, most of the rooms are actually cells, all immaculately clean. The mood here is student-party central, with free Internet; it's very close to the train station and ten minutes' walk to the center of town.

€50-100

The **Bed and Breakfast Petra Varl** (Vodnikov trg 5a, tel. 01/430-3788, petra@varl.si, €60 d., including breakfast) is a charming little bed-and-breakfast, a two-minute stroll from the center, with friendly service from the artist-owner. The room with the terrace is particularly sweet.

Certainly one of the best places to stay in Ljubljana, the **◖ Slamic Bed & Breakfast** (Kersnikova Ulica 1, tel. 01/433-8233, www .slamic.si, €95 d., including breakfast) offers surprisingly luxe rooms, complete with cable TV, free Internet access, and hardwood floors. Located only 10 minutes' walk to either the train and bus stations or the Old Town core, the small hotel also has a popular (and very good) café and sweet shop on the ground floor, perfect for a leisurely breakfast before sightseeing.

If you're interested in **private apartments** in town (a great value for families or for those that like to prepare their own meals), clean and cozy flats are available from www.apartmaji.si.

Over €100

The **Antiq Hotel** (Gornji trg 3, tel. 01/421-3560, www.antiqhotel.si, €144 d., including breakfast) has an excellent location on a pedestrian square in the center of town. The hotel's decor is either homey (lace-trimmed towels and antique furniture) or outdated grandmotherly, depending on your attitude. The only downside for some travelers might be the stairs—the building has no elevator.

With all the amenities of big chain hotels, such as an in-hotel sauna, restaurant, lounge bar, and valet parking, the **Best Western Hotel Slon** (Slovenska cesta 34, tel. 01/470-1100, www.hotelslon.com, €190 d., including breakfast) has swank public spaces in a restored 1930s-era building. The rooms don't have the same character but the hotel is convenient, a short walk to the old town, and has free Internet access in the lobby.

While it's hard to see all five of the stars the **Lev Hotel** (Vošnjakova ulica 1, tel. 01/433-2155, www.hotel-lev.si, €195 d., including breakfast) advertises, its location on the edge of Tivoli Gardens is nice and it's clean and comfortable with free parking, a restaurant, and a bar all on-site.

The **Grand Hotel Union Executive** (Miklošičeva 1, tel. 01/308-1270, www.gh-union.si, €230 d.) has a perfect location in the center of old Ljubljana and a pool for those who'd like to take a dip. The hotel has a stunning art nouveau facade and while the rooms are quite nice, their basic hotel-standard interiors don't live up to the promising entrance.

OUT OF THE CENTER
Under €50

If you happen to be in Ljubljana during the summer, the cheapest accommodations around are the *dijaški dom* (contact the tourist office at the Triple Bridge, €15 d.), or student dorms. All are well connected by bus, with stops located conveniently next to the dorms; they are also walkable, from 10 to 30 minutes from the center. The rooms are simply furnished, with one to three single beds, and it's hard to beat the price.

€50-100

A guesthouse option is **Pri Zabarju** (Viška cesta, tel. 01/428-2462, www.prizabarju.si, €90 d., including breakfast), a cozy place with air-conditioning, parking, a restaurant of the same name, and a sinful cake place all in one convenient location. You'll need to take a bus or taxi to get from this spot, approximately four kilometers west of the core, to the center of things.

Over €100

Despite the fact it's located 2.2 kilometers from the city center, the **AHotel** (Cesta Dveh Cesarjev 34D, tel. 01/429-1892, www.ahotel .si, €125 d., including breakfast) is possibly the best value-for-money hotel in town. With a sleek, trendy lobby and bar, sparkling minimalist rooms, and a good continental breakfast buffet, the AHotel isn't exactly luxe, but it still exceeds expectations. It's located in Trnovo, a very pretty old quarter of town, and is well connected by bus.

The **Austria Trend Hotel** (Dunjaska 154, tel. 01/588-2510, www.austria-trend.at/lju, €222 d.) offers sleek and spacious rooms. The hotel is two kilometers north of town in Bežigrad, connected by shuttle or via bus to the city center.

The uber-modern **Mons Hotel** (Pot za Brdom 55, tel. 01/470-2700, www.hotel.mons .si, €195 d.) is a couple of kilometers west of the center. Be aware that sometimes the service does not live up to the hotel's four stars, and be sure to ask for a room facing the woods rather than the highway. There is a free shuttle to the center, or you can take a taxi.

Food

CENTRAL
Breakfast

The immensely popular ◖ **Le Petite Café** (Trg francoske revolucije 4, tel. 01/251-2575, 7:30 A.M.–11 P.M. Mon.–Fri., 9 A.M.–11 P.M. Sat.–Sun., €8) is a local pick for breakfast staples (eggs, toasted baguettes) in a Provençal-themed café.

Cafés and Desserts

For ice cream, the unassuming **Pixi** (Mestni trg 17, tel. 01/426-8460) has some great homemade flavors and a few desserts. The often overlooked **Pri Vodnjaku** (Stari trg 30, tel. 01/425-0712, 8 A.M.–midnight daily) has super old-school atmosphere in which to sip tea and tuck into dessert. The park-side **Zvezda** (Wolfova 14, tel. 01/420-9090, 7 A.M.–11 P.M. Mon.–Sat., 10 A.M.–8 P.M. Sun.) is far trendier and offers lots of ice cream, coffees, and cakes, while **Babo Juice Bar** (Krojaška 4, tel. 040/533-334, 9 A.M.–9 P.M. daily) has some 50 juice combos. Located smack in the old town, it's the perfect spot to refuel for some more sightseeing.

For real tea, from English to herbal, served in pretty porcelain for flair, try **Cha** (Stari trg 3, tel. 01/252-7010, 9 A.M.–10:30 P.M. Mon.–Fri., 9 A.M.–3 P.M. and 6–10:30 P.M. Sat.).

Fine Dining

Foodies should head straight to the cozy ◖ **Hiša Kulinarke Manna** (Eipprova ul. 1/A, tel. 01/283-5294, www.kulinarika-manna.com, noon–midnight Mon.–Sat., €30) for slow-food specialties like smoked duck breast with horseradish terrine, lamb with herb crust, and the house cake, Manna.

While 【 **Gostilna As** (Čopova 5a, tel. 01/425-8822, www.gostilnaas.si, noon–midnight daily, €25) may not be as trendy as some spots on the city's restaurant scene, it is still the establishment restaurant of Ljubljana's movers and shakers. The food is excellent, the atmosphere warm and local, and the terrace is superb for warm-weather dining.

Špajza (Gornji trg 28, tel. 01/425-3094, noon–11 P.M. Mon.–Sat., €19) has local atmosphere infused with a romantic vibe. Serving typical Slovenian dishes (think horse and venison) prepared with care as well as a good selection of fish, brought in daily from Croatia, the restaurant has a nice outdoor courtyard for fair-weather dining. **Pri Vitezu** (Breg 20, tel. 01/426-6058, noon–11 P.M. Mon.–Sat., €18) is another choice, from the owner of the popular Luka Gourmet. With a focus on seafood from the Adriatic coast, but with plenty of dishes for more beefy palates as well, the food and service live up to the reputation for quality.

International

If you've had enough local flavor for one day and need a Szechuan noodle fix, **nim8min** (Kolodvorska 20, tel. 01/231-2168, 11 A.M.–11 P.M., €4) has delicious, and cheap, hot wok meals served in eight minutes or less.

The name, **Falafel** (Trubarjeva 40, tel. 041/640-166, 10 A.M.–midnight Mon.–Sat., 1–10 P.M. Sun., €4), describes this miniscule spot's menu pretty well. In addition to the Middle Eastern staple, it serves hummus, burgers, and pizza.

Joe Peña's (Cankarjeva 6, tel. 01/421-5800, www.joepenas.si, 10 A.M.–1 A.M. Mon.–Thurs., 10 A.M.–2 A.M. Fri.–Sat., noon–midnight Sun., €9) is quite possibly the best Mexican in the former Yugoslavia. With an impressive array of fajitas, enchiladas, and margaritas, the place can be packed around midday with lunch voucher–wielding students.

Currently (though probably not for long) the only sushi in Ljubljana, **Sushimama** (Wolfova ulica 12, tel. 01/426-9125, 11 A.M.–11 P.M. daily, €12) serves up rolls and sashimi to a trendy, mostly young crowd.

Local Cuisine

It's worth the trouble to find slightly hidden **Operna Klet** (Zupančičeva 2, tel. 01/252-7003, 11 A.M.–11 P.M. Mon.–Fri., 11 A.M.–6 P.M. Sat., €19) for the excellent selection of Adriatic fish, particularly the octopus salad, served in a no-frills but usually packed space.

Pasta and Pizza

Head to the laid-back **Pasta Nona** (Gosposvetska 2, tel. 01/438-2424, 8 A.M.–11 P.M. Mon.–Fri., €8) for big bowls of pasta and tasty salads. Located in the center of the city's business district, it fills to capacity around lunch.

Though the funky restaurant has sometimes less-than-stellar service, **Foculus** (Gregorčičeva 3, tel. 01/251-5643, 10 A.M.–midnight Mon.–Sat., noon–midnight Sun., €7) is a must-visit for fans of pizza, with over 60 varieties, including Turkish, truffle, and seafood.

For breakfast, lunch, or dinner, unassuming 【 **Luka Gourmet** (Stari trg 9, tel. 01/425-0118, www.lunchcafe.net, 9 A.M.–11 P.M. Mon.–Fri., €15) goes beyond just the typical pasta dishes, serving a full menu, mostly Italian inspired, from Caesar salads to truffle steak to Pannacotta. The killer location right on Stari trg combined with the great value-for-money food (order one of the homemade soups) means it may be hard to snag a table, so reservations are recommended.

As Lounge (Čopova 5a, tel. 01/425-8822, www.gostilnaas.si, 9 A.M.–3 A.M. daily, €9) is the more casual offshoot of the pricier Gostilna As. Turning into a popular club spot as the night wears on, it's also the destination for pastas and salads at reasonable prices in a swank setting.

Quick Bites

Ljubljana has a great selection of budget-friendly restaurants aimed at locals on their lunch break and students in need of sustenance. **Paninoteka** (Jurčičev Trg 3, tel. 01/425-0055, 8 A.M.–1 A.M. Mon.–Sat., 9 A.M.–11 P.M. Sun., €4) is the place to go for generous sandwiches made with fresh Italian bread. It's hard to miss the location of **Tramvaj Ekspres Pizzeria** (Trg mladinskih Delovnih Brigad 10, tel. 041/916-407, 10 A.M.–6 P.M. Mon.–Fri., closed mid-July–mid-Aug., €6): two old bright-red trams parked in the center of a city square. Hungry students pack inside to pick up pizza and hot sandwiches.

Tomato (Šubičeva 1, tel. 01/252-7555, www.tomato.si, 7 A.M.–9 P.M. Mon.–Fri., €3) has an extensive menu of breakfast dishes, sandwiches, burgers, and pastas at amazing prices, catering to an exam-cramming crowd. The same students that haunt Tomato by day may be found around **Nobel Burek** (Miklošičeva 30, tel. 01/232-3392, 24 hours, €2) by night. Conveniently located near the bus and train stations, it offers steaming hot *burek* and pizza 24 hours a day.

If you'd prefer to be surrounded by a slightly older, more business-y crowd, try **Restaurant 2000** (Trg Republike 1, tel. 01/476-6925, 7 A.M.–7 P.M. Mon.–Fri., 8 A.M.–5 P.M. Sat., €6) for basic but filling cafeteria food inside Maxi market.

Vegetarian

Technically, the only vegetarian restaurant in town is outside the city center. However, several mainstream restaurants offer a good variety of vegetarian dishes, like **Foculus** (Gregorčičeva 3, tel. 01/251-5643, 10 A.M.–midnight Mon.–Sat., noon–midnight Sun., €7) and **Falafel** (Trubarjeva 40, tel. 041/640-166, 10 A.M.–midnight Mon.–Sat., 1–10 P.M. Sun., €4), both described earlier.

OUT OF THE CENTER
Fine Dining

Though the cuisine is not as haute as the more central Manna, **Gostilna Kaval** (Tacenska 95, tel. 01/512-5596, www.bid.si/kaval, 10 A.M.–11 P.M. Mon.–Fri., noon–11 P.M. Sat.–Sun., €15), about seven kilometers northwest of the center, has some tasty Tuscan-inspired cuisine and a romantic terrace at pretty good prices.

The swank space at **Cubo** (Šmartinska c. 55, tel. 01/521-1515, www.cubo-ljubljana.com, 11 A.M.–11 P.M. Mon.–Fri., noon–11 P.M. Sat., €18), about three kilometers northeast of the center, is as stylish as its food. A Mediterranean-inspired menu and sinful desserts are gobbled up by a chic clientele.

Local Cuisine

Vinske Kleti Slovenija (Dunjaska 18, tel. 01/431-5015, 11 A.M.–11 P.M. Mon.–Fri., 4–11 P.M. Sat., €20) is the country's largest wine shop; the accompanying cellar restaurant is one of the best places to try good Slovenian dishes with one of some 80 local wines. It's about two kilometers north in the Bežigrad neighborhood, not far from the Austria Trend Hotel.

While all its dishes aren't exactly Slovenian, **Gostilna pod Rožnikom** (Cesta na Rožnik 18, tel. 01/251-3436, www.gp-vic.si/roznik .asp, 10 A.M.–11 P.M. Mon.–Fri., noon–11 P.M. Sat.–Sun., €19) has a great selection of regional cuisine, like grilled *ražnjiči* skewers, fried sweet peppers, and Serbian salads. Located in a leafy spot near the city zoo, it also has a huge shady terrace for alfresco dining.

Worth the drive or taxi ride to the edge of town for a special meal, the █ **Gostilna Kovač** (Pot k Savi 9, tel. 01/537-1244, www.kovac-co.si, noon–10 P.M. Mon.–Fri., €38) has been serving traditional Slovenian cuisine since 1849. The interior is romantic, with wood-beamed ceilings and antiques, and there's a nice terrace as well. The restaurant is about five kilometers northeast of the center, just above the Bežigrad neighborhood.

Quick Bites

Though many may find it offensive, **Hot Horse** (Tivoli Park, tel. 01/521-1427, www.hot-horse.si, 10 A.M.–6 A.M. Mon., 9 A.M.–6 A.M. Tues.–Sun., €3) is a local institution, serving late-night horseburgers next to Tivoli Park. They have a veggie burger on the menu too, though it's doubtful that many animal lovers are eating here.

In the Krakovo district, **Okrepčevapnica** (Vrtna 8, tel. 041/843-106, €8) is the place to go to sample grilled-meat specialties straight from Sarajevo. Wash it down with a Turkish coffee, accompanied by a complimentary cigarette. See a slice of Bosnia without putting the stamp in your passport.

Vegetarian

On the northeastern side of Tivoli Park, **Vegedrom** (Vodnikova 35, tel. 01/513-2642, www.vegedrom.com, 9 A.M.–10 P.M. Mon.–Fri., noon–10 P.M. Sat., €7) serves great vegan and vegetarian dishes, many with an Indian twist.

Information and Services

TOURIST AND TRAVEL INFORMATION

The **Tourist Information Center** (Adamič-Lundrovo Nabrežje 2, tel. 01/306-1215, www.ljubljana-tourism.si, 8 A.M.–9 P.M. daily June–Sept., 8 A.M.–7 P.M. daily Oct.–May), next to the Triple Bridge, not only offers maps and guidance, but is also the source for tours of the city. **Walking tours** (€7.50 per adult) depart twice daily (10 A.M. and 6 P.M.) between May and September, and on Friday, Saturday, and Sunday the rest of the year. You'll also find outposts of the tourist office at the bus and train stations (8 A.M.–10 P.M. daily June–Sept., 10 A.M.–7 P.M. Oct.–May) and the airport (11 A.M.–5:30 P.M. Mon.–Fri., 11 A.M.–4:30 P.M. Sat.). The tourist board also offers **bike tours** for groups of three or more from mid-April to the end of October. Tours should be booked ahead with the tourist office.

If your muscles have had more than enough, the tourist office has two more leisurely tours on the menu. **Boat rides** (€7.50 per adult) leave from Ribji trg pier near the Triple Bridge. For something even more panoramic, **hot air balloons** float across the surrounding countryside daily from March to September. Contact the Tourist Information Center for pricing and reservations.

Dial 981 for an **English-speaking operator** who should be able to help you with entertainment and events around Ljubljana.

BANKS AND CURRENCY EXCHANGE

Handling money in Ljubljana is easier than ever since Slovenia adopted the euro. If you need to change money, most any bank (Ljubljanska Banka is the major local bank) can swap your dollars for euros, probably at better rates than the hotels. ATMs all over town should work with your bank card.

INTERNET ACCESS AND COMMUNICATIONS

DrogArt Info Point (Kolodvorska 20, tel. 01/439-7270, www.drogart.org, 10 A.M.–6 P.M. Mon.–Fri., €3 for one hour) is conveniently located directly across from the train station. **Kiberpipa** (Kersnikova 4, www.kiberpipa.org, 10 A.M.–10 P.M. Mon.–Fri., free) has a few online computers and places to plug in a laptop. You can access the Internet 24 hours a day at the **City Hotel Turist** (Dalmatinova 15, tel. 01/234-9130, www.hotelturist.si). It's free, but there's only one station so it has a tendency to be in use. If you're really desperate, the two info points outside of the main **tourist office** on Prešerenov trg allow you to check email and send e-postcards free of charge.

LAUNDRY SERVICES

Chemo Express (Wolfova ulica 12, www.chemoexpress.com, tel. 01/251-4404, €10 for a load) can dry clean or wash your dirty clothes.

EMERGENCY SERVICES

The police can be reached by dialing 113; emergency info (ambulances and fire) is at 112. If your rental car is in distress, call 987 for roadside assistance. Minor medical emergencies

Ljubljana in winter

can be attended to at the Medical Center in Bohoričeva 4 (tel. 01/232-3060) or the Klinični center Ljubljana (Zaloška cesta 2, tel. 01/522-5050). The pharmacy Ljekarna Ljubljana (Prisojna ulica 7, tel. 01/230-6230) is open 24 hours a day, seven days a week.

Getting There and Around

GETTING THERE
Air

There are several carriers that fly into Ljubljana's Brnik airport (tel. 04/206-1981, www.lju-airport.si), 23 kilometers northwest of the center. Adria Airways (Gosposvetska 6, tel. 01/231-3312, www.adria.si) is Slovenia's national carrier, with flights to most major cities in Europe. Air France (www.airfrance.com) flies to Paris every day of the week, while EasyJet (www.easyjet.com) offers daily service to and from London.

From the airport, you can hop a city bus (departure at 10 past the hour Mon.–Fri., less frequent on weekends and holidays) or a taxi (stand in front of the terminal, tel. 04/206-1678, www.skokica.com, around €35 into town). There is also an airport shuttle, which costs around €10 and takes about 30 minutes into the city center. Call 040/887-766 for shuttle information.

Train

Railway travel isn't as glamorous as it once was, but traveling the tracks around Slovenia is reliable and relatively inexpensive. The station is conveniently located near the city center, a 10-to-15-minute trek to the main tourist sights. There are good international connections, and it's also a good way to see some other towns in Slovenia: Maribor (2.5 hours), Kamnik (1 hour), Postojna (1 hour), and Koper (2.5 hours) are all served by the train. Contact the railway station (Trg Osvobodilne fronte 6, tel.

LJUBLJANA

Ljubljana's airport, 23 kilometers from the city center

01/291-3332, potnik.info@slo-zeleznice.si, www.slo-zeleznice.si) for timetables and more information.

Bus

The bus station (Trg Osvobodilne fronte 4, tel. 090-4230 or 01/234-4600, avtobusna.post-aja@ap-ljubljana.si, www.ap-ljubljana.si) has both international and local connections and is a 10-to-15-minute walk to the city center. It is a safe and reliable means of getting around and connects to more locations than the train. You can connect to cities such as Škofja Loka (45 minutes), Lake Bohinj (2 hours), Kranjska Gora (2 hours), and Piran (2.75 hours).

Car

All highways in Slovenia (there are only one and a half anyway) lead to Ljubljana, so it's pretty much impossible to get lost if you're coming from another country. The highway to Zagreb (E70) takes you between the two capitals in about two hours depending on how fast you drive the 120-kilometer distance. Driving around Ljubljana is safe and, given that it's not too big, usually manageable for most every driver.

GETTING AROUND
Bus

City buses (Ljubljanski Potniški Promet, LPP, Trdinova 3 or Slovenska 55, tel. 01/434-3248, www.lpp.si) are a reliable means of getting around town if you're staying in the suburbs. Otherwise you won't really need them since Ljubljana's core is quite small and easily accessible on foot. The 22 bus lines run between 5 A.M. and 10:30 P.M., with a few operating until midnight and beyond. Tickets can be purchased onboard (€1) or from a newsstand or kiosk (look for signs advertising *žetoni*, or tokens, €0.70). A great deal for travelers in Ljubljana is the Ljubljana Card, offering free city transport, admission to museums and galleries, and savings at a number of restaurants, hotels, shops, and even taxi fares all over the city for 72 hours. The Ljubljana Card can be purchased online (www.visitljubljana.si) or from sales outlets around the city (such as the bus and train stations, tourist office, and many hotels) for €12.52.

Car

Major rental agencies such as Avis (www.avis-alpe.si) and Hertz (www.hertz.si) have outlets in Ljubljana. If you're driving around remember that blue zones allow parking for 30 minutes free of charge, while white zones allow you to park one hour with a parking ticket (€0.50, available at newsstands and kiosks).

Taxi

If you'd rather take a taxi, you'll find taxi stands outside the Best Western Slon Hotel, the railway station, close to Mestni trg, and on Prešernov trg (only at night). Each firm has different prices, though holders of the Ljubljana Card get a 20 percent discount from Rumeni Taxi (tel. 041/731-831).

Bicycle

Rent a bike in front of Café Maček (Krojaška 5, tel. 01/425-3791, €13 per day). The tourist office has also started a program to lend bikes from outlets all over the city (in front of the Slovenian Tourist Information Centee, Antiq Hotel, Ljubljana Railway Station, Ljubljana Resort, Grand Hotel Union Garni, Hostel Celica, Zlata ribica, M Hotel) from April through October (8 A.M.–7 P.M., 9 P.M. in July and Aug.) for only €1 (2 hours) or €5 (from two hours to one day). Ljubljana Card holders get four hours of free bicycle hire.

Around Ljubljana

IŠKI VINTGAR

Only 15 kilometers south from Ljubljana, a small rapid river forms a pretty spot for nature fans. A beautiful limestone gorge, filled with rapids and waterfalls and a ten-meter-high solitary rock formation dubbed the Rock Man, the Iški Vintgar gorge is a great place to go for hiking, with lots of trails, including the E6 European Foot Trail. Marked with white and blue signs, the trail will eventually link Italy, Austria, Slovenia, and Croatia.

The bus from Ljubljana takes between 30 minutes and one hour, depending on the number of stops.

RAKITNA

Thirty kilometers southwest from the capital, the small village of Rakitna has a nice Baroque church and the remains of a Roman defensive wall. The real draw here, though, is the sports on offer. In winter, the flat landscape makes for great cross-country skiing on the snowy karst plateau and ice skating on the lake, while in summer you can head there for a bit of swimming in the lake. The tourist association (Turistično društvo Rakitna, Rakitna Tourist Society, tel. 01/365-0082) can direct you to information regarding ski and skate rentals.

The bus from Ljubljana takes one hour.

ZBILJSKO JEZERO

Zbiljsko jezero, only 16 kilometers northwest of the capital, is the perfect day trip from Ljubljana. Here you can escape city hustle and bustle by renting a boat or carriage to tour around the peaceful lake, created in the 1950s. The lakeside village of Zbilje is much older, first mentioned in the 14th century. There's also a great hike following the 18th-century **Kalvarija** (Stations of the Cross), an uphill pilgrimage path dotted with over a dozen shrines.

The bus from Ljubljana takes 30 minutes.

STIČNA

Thirty-five kilometers southeast of Ljubljana, the **Stična Samostan** (Stična Monastery, Stična 17, tel. 01/787-7100, www.rkc.si/sticna, 8 A.M.–noon and 2–5 P.M. Tues.–Sat., 2–5 P.M. Sun., €4.50) only has a few full-time residents, but the cute Baroque church and the Slovenian Religious Museum (Slovenski Verski muzej) are nice for visiting if you have extra time. The Cistercian monastery is one of the oldest in Slovenia, dating from the 12th century, and resembles a castle more than a monastery due to fortifications to ward off the Turks in the 15th century. Especially of note here are the herbal teas, produced by the monks and nuns at the cloister, that claim to heal a variety of ailments. They make an interesting souvenir purchase.

The bus from Ljubljana takes one hour.

LJUBLJANA

INLAND SLOVENIA

The interior of Slovenia boasts snow-capped mountains, ethereal lakes, rushing rivers, and an extensive network of caves, making the region ideal for sports enthusiasts. You can even ease your muscles at the thermal spas in the eastern end of the region after all your adventures. For those interested in more pastoral pursuits, this region is where travelers can truly explore the core of Slovenia and its culture. You can learn more about the country's history, food, and lifestyle in its Roman ruins, herding stations, vineyards, and centuries-old churches and castles. The region is also home to plenty of culture, including the quirky folk carnival celebration called the Kurentovanje, and a mass of vineyards and wine roads well worth sampling.

Less-touristed towns like Maribor and Ptuj are worth a stop and the interior is filled with several decent ski runs and thermal spa centers. The highlight of the interior, though, is certainly Bled, with its fairy-tale lake and the nearby Triglav National Park, encompassing several villages and towns, filled with rushing streams and a vast selection of outdoor adventures for active tourists.

The wine roads of the Bela Krajina are a must for gourmets, while quieter travelers will appreciate Idrija's wonderful manor hotel and lace-making traditions.

Whatever your preference, the interior of Slovenia offers something for everyone, from snowy slopes to rolling hills dotted with vineyards with lots of picturesque castles and churches and interesting museums in between.

© BRANIMIR RITONJA/SLOVENIAN TOURIST BOARD

HIGHLIGHTS

🌙 **Kurentovanje:** Ptuj's colorful carnival celebration, typified by the horned mask of the mythical Kurent, is one of Slovenia's most interesting festivals (page 288).

🌙 **Škofja Loka:** An almost perfectly preserved medieval town with a 6th-century bridge, this village is the heart of rural Slovenia and an easy day trip from Ljubljana (page 294).

🌙 **Velika Planina:** The summer herding of livestock on Velika Planina is a rare experience. Stay in a mountain hut, eat your fill of fresh cheese, and then work it off with an invigorating mountain bike ride (page 295).

🌙 **Bled:** One of the few spots that lives up to, or even surpasses, its postcard shots, the ethereal blue lake of Bled, with a tiny church-topped island, surrounded by mountains, is one of those things you just have to see to believe (page 300).

🌙 **Bovec:** Pick a sport. Almost any outdoor sport. Then head to this alpine town for an adrenaline fix, followed by some serious chill-out in one of Bovec's idyllic hotels (page 307).

LOOK FOR 🌙 TO FIND RECOMMENDED SIGHTS, ACTIVITIES, DINING, AND LODGING.

PLANNING YOUR TIME

If you have only one day, head directly to Bled, likely the best of Slovenia's interior region. From here, your planning will depend on your interests. You could spend two days skiing or pursuing some outdoor activities around Bovec and Bohinj or take a couple of days to slowly wind your way through the Bela Krajina and Dolenjska wine regions. Many locations are possible long day trips from Ljubljana, such as Škofja Loka and Idrija, among others.

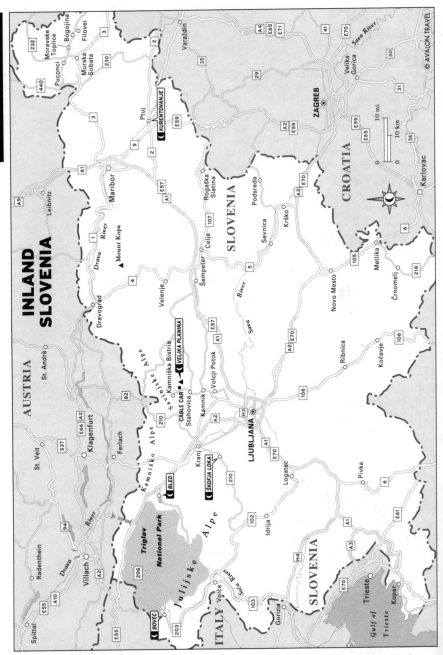

© AVALON TRAVEL

Pohorje Region

This is a flat fertile area at the edge of the Alps, famous for its white wines, covered in thick evergreen forests, and home to one of Slovenia's larger cities, Maribor. Outside of Maribor you'll also find some nice ski slopes, suited to pleasure-seekers more than professionals, but fun all the same—especially if you end your day in one of the area's steaming thermal pools.

MARIBOR

It's Slovenia's second-largest city, but most people see Maribor as primarily a business town, a pass-through on the way to Austria. Even the tourist office advertises a "Maribor in Two Hours" itinerary, hoping to lure people in a little longer.

But actually it's a charming Austro-Hungarian town with a young spirit, supplied by the gaggle of university students in town. And it's on the edge of wine country, serving as a good base to explore the area, with plenty of tastings and decent whites to keep fans of the grape interested.

Sights

Rotovški trg, also referred to as **Glavni trg** (Main Square), is where the hub of Maribor's old town comes to life. Here you'll find the Renaissance-style 16th-century **Rotovž** (Town Hall), where Hitler once stood on the balcony and proclaimed Maribor as part of his territory. The **Alojzijeva cerkev** (Aloysius church, tel. 02/234-6611, mass at 8 A.M. Mon.–Sat. and 10 A.M. Sun., free) is also worth a visit. The 18th-century baroque church has an ornate interior highlighted by pretty landscape paintings of the surrounding region. The center of the square is punctuated with a gilded **Kužno Znamenje** (plague column), built by the locals in the 17th century to thank the Virgin for sparing them in a plague that wiped out a third of the population.

Another must-visit if you're in town is **Lent,** which in Maribor doesn't refer to refraining but to a busy riverside neighborhood. There are lots of bars, restaurants, and shops to peruse as well as **Židovski trg** (Jewish square) and its synagogue, a rather rare find in the former Yugoslavia.

Wineries

Maribor is a particularly interesting stop for wine lovers. In Lent, stop at the **Hiša Stare trte** (The Old Vine House, Vojašniška 8, tel. 02/251-5100, 10 A.M.–6 P.M. Tues.–Sun.) to see the oldest vine in Slovenia, a 400-year-old grape vine still producing today. It's also a nice place to taste regional wines. Then head to the **Vinag Wine Cellar** (Trg svobode 3, tel. 02/220-8119, www.vinag.si) with its 2.5 kilometers of underground tunnels that stretch below the center of the city, holding some 250,000 bottles of wine. Arrange for tours and tastings ahead of time.

In late September Maribor hosts **Festival Stare trte** (Old Wine Festival), with tastings,

© VLADIMIR TOŠ/SLOVENIAN TOURIST BOARD

one of the many vineyards in the Pohorje region

© SMILJAN PUŠENJAK/SLOVENIAN TOURIST BOARD

timber rafting on the Drava River by Maribor

colorful presentations, folk music, dancing, and even a vegetarian day. Contact the Maribor **tourist office** (Partizanska 6a, tel. 02/234-6611, www.maribor-pohorje.si) for more details.

Last but certainly not least are the region's four marked **wine roads**. Detailed information, plus the possibility to book a guided tour, can be found at the Maribor tourist office.

Sports and Recreation

The Maribor area has lots of great sports for adventure enthusiasts. **Športni center Pohorje** (Sports center Pohorje, Pohorska 60, tel. 02/220-8843, info.vzp@sk-branik.si, www.pohorje.org) is a great one-stop shop for bike rentals, ropes courses, skydiving, summer sledding, and more.

Contact the Maribor **tourist office** (Partizanska 6a, tel. 02/234-6611, www.maribor-pohorje.si) about ski passes for the Pohorje, which are also valid for other runs in Slovenia, such as Kranjska Gora.

NK Maribor (Mladenska 29, tel. 02/228-4700, www.nkmaribor.com) is Slovenia's most successful soccer team, playing games at Maribor's **Ljudski vrt** (People's Garden).

Accommodations and Food

Summertime means that most dorm rooms in town are available for rent to visitors. Contact the tourist office for more details.

The **Youth Hostel Hotel Uni** (Volkmerjev prehod 7, tel. 02/250-6700, uni.hotel@termeb .si, €25 per person) is more of a hotel than a hostel, with clean rooms with a work area, bathroom, and Internet access plus an excellent buffet breakfast.

The **Hotel Betnava** (Jadranska cesta 30, tel. 02/333-4100, www.betnava.si, €116 d., including breakfast) is a new hotel on the edge of the city next to a peaceful forest. Modern, clean, and quiet, the room also includes free admission to the wellness center.

The **Hotel Bellevue** (Na Slemenu 35, tel. 02/607-5100, www.termemb.si, €130 d.) is a solid four-star hotel with a great wellness center, featuring thermal baths and saunas.

For a quick lunch, **Mesarstvo, trgovina in okrepčevalnica Bolarič** (Jurčičeva 3, tel. 02/250-5910, 8 A.M.–5 P.M. Mon.–Fri., 7 A.M.–1 P.M. Sat., €4) has good hot pots and breaded, fried meats with basic sides for unbelievably cheap prices. If you'd prefer something a bit more chic without putting a dent in your wallet, try **Aroma hiša kave** (Slovenska ulica 11, tel. 02/250-2179, 7 A.M.–11 P.M. Mon.–Fri., 9 A.M.–11 P.M. Sat., 9 A.M.–10 P.M. Sun., €5), a coffeehouse in the center of the old town, with good coffee, a terrace, and a children's corner to entertain the little ones.

Not one to try the local cuisine? **Tako's Restaurant** (Mesarski prehod 3, tel. 02/252-7150, www.takos.si, 11 A.M.–11 P.M. Mon.–Thurs., 11 A.M.–2 A.M. Fri.–Sat., €7) serves Tex-Mex staples like quesadillas and chicken wings and offers specials on multiple beer purchases.

For traditional Slovenian specialties, the out-of-town **Gostilna Pec** (Sp. Selnica 1, tel. 02/674-0356, www.gostilnapec.si, 11 A.M.–11 P.M. Mon.–Sat., 11 A.M.–8 P.M. Sun., €14) is a quiet, relaxing place with a nice terrace for summer dining.

In town, **☾ Rožmarin** (Gosposka ulica 8, tel. 02/234-3180, www.rozmarin.si, 11 A.M.–10 P.M. Mon.–Thurs., 11 A.M.–11 P.M. Fri.–Sat., wine bar open later, €12) is the place to go for just about everything culinary and wine related. The trendy swank space serves everything from breakfast to dinner in its restaurant, while the minimalist coffeehouse provides good coffee and the wine bar is the perfect place to hang out over a glass of wine. The place even has a wine store for picking up a few bottles for the trip home.

Information and Services

The **tourist office** (Partizanska 6a, tel. 02/234-6611, www.maribor-pohorje.si, 9 A.M.–7 P.M. Mon.–Fri., 9 A.M.–5 P.M. Sat., 9 A.M.–1 P.M. Sun. and holidays) provides maps and offers guided tours around the city.

Getting There and Around

Located about 120 kilometers northeast of Ljubljana, Maribor is a well-connected city. The Avtobusna postaja Maribor (Bus Station Maribor, Mlinska ulica 1, tel. 02/235-0212 or toll-free within Slovenia tel. 080-11-16) provides dozens of links to regional as well as international destinations such as Ljubljana (3

hours) and Ptuj (30 minutes). Since Maribor is Slovenia's second-largest city, the train station (Partizanska cesta 50, tel. 02/292-2164, picmaribor-mednarodnablagajna@slo-zeleznica .si) has excellent connections including multiple daily services to Ptuj (45 minutes), Ljubljana (2.5 hours), Postojna (3.5 hours), and Koper (5 hours). You'll also find international connections daily to cities such as Vienna, Graz, Zagreb, Budapest, and even Venice. The train from Ljubljana to Maribor is a nicer trip than the bus.

PTUJ

Ptuj is a beautiful town on the Drava River. It's overlooked by tourists most of the year, but the town swells for the city's famous Kurentovanje, or Carnival celebration, typified by the wooly horned Kurent costume. A local tradition for centuries, the Kurent is said to drive away winter and welcome spring.

Any time of the year, the town's a nice stop-off, and cruising the wine routes around town is a must for those who enjoy tasting local wines.

Sights

The **Ptuj Grad** (Ptuj castle, Grajska Raven, tel. 02/787-9230, www.pok-muzej-ptuj .si, 9 A.M.–5 P.M. daily mid-Oct.–Apr., 9 A.M.–6 P.M. daily May–June and Sept.–mid-Oct., 9 A.M.–6 P.M. Mon.–Fri. and 9 A.M.–8 P.M. Sat.–Sun. July–Aug., €4) is impossible to miss, occupying a hill in the center of town. Parts of the castle date from as early as the 11th century, though the structure has undergone almost as many additions and renovations as it has owners. Today it is home to a small but nice museum with exhibitions of musical instruments, weaponry, folk art on glass, and perhaps most unique of all, a display of traditional carnival costumes from the town's most well-known event, the Kurentovanje.

Another outpost of the town's regional museum is located in a former **Dominikanski samostan** (Dominican monastery, Muzejski trg 1, tel. 02/787-9230, 9 A.M.–5 P.M. daily mid-Apr.–Nov., €4). It's worth visiting the 13th-century building in and of itself, and

the town of Ptuj, famous for its Kurentovanje festival

this way you get a decent exhibition of small archaeological finds and some Roman statues added to the deal.

Igrišče za golf Ptuj (Ptuj golf course, Mlinska ulica 13, tel. 02/788-9110, www.golf-ptuj.com) is a barely decent golf course for those who want to play a few holes. Be warned that you'll have to prove your skill level on the driving range before being allowed on the greens.

Kurentovanje

Ptuj is most famous for its colorful Kurentovanje festival (www.kurentovanje .net), a don't-miss if you happen to be in the area during the 10 days that lead up to Mardi Gras. There's a procession of men dressed in the horn-masked sheepskin Kurent costume, which looks like something between a devil and a wooly mammoth. The purpose of the costumes is to scare away winter and welcome in spring. The festival has been held every year for half a century, though its origins date back hundreds of years, and today it draws some 100,000 visitors each February. During the day you'll find plenty of theater and musical performances to keep you entertained. At night there are balls and dancing accompanied by lively folk music performances.

Wineries

Even if you're not a huge wine connoisseur, make a visit to **Ptujska klet wine cellars** (Vinarski trg 1, tel. 02/787-9810, www.ptujska-klet.si, tours 9 A.M.–3 P.M. Mon.–Fri.), where daily scheduled tours and tastings will help you sample some of the local whites. The KK Ptuj-Haloze cellars, over 400 years old, are another stop, located in a former monastery. They produce some excellent white wines, particularly Rieslings and late-harvest wines known as *suhi jagodni izbor*. Also contact the **tourist office** (Slovenski trg 5, tel. 02/779-6011, www.ptuj-tourism.si) for more detailed info and maps on two **wine routes** you can take from Ptuj.

One of the best routes around Ptuj is the **Haloze Hills** route, starting near Borl Castle. Between the villages of Podlehnik and Poljčane, stop at **Štatenberg Castle** (Štatenberg 86, 02/803-0216), an 18th-century Baroque

WHAT DID YOU SAY?: SLOVENIAN DIALECTS

Slovenian is one of the most varied languages in the world. With only two million speakers, Slovenian has at least 32 different dialects, which are derived from the seven main dialects – Carinthian (spoken in and in the regions directly bordering Austria), Upper Carniolan, Lower Carniolan (around Ljubljana), Styrian, Pannonia (near Hungary), and Rovte. The speech is so different that it is very likely that residents of one part won't understand residents of other area, even though in written form the difference is relatively small.

While standard Slovene, taught in schools and published in newspapers, is based on the dialect spoken in and around Ljubljana, known as Lower Carniolan, other areas speak a daily language peppered with various vocabulary and accents. This diversity is largely due to the difficult geography of Slovenia, which isolated various regions from each other.

Though the first printed book in Slovenian emerged in the 16th century, modern Slovenes can thank the work of early-19th-century linguist Jernej Kopitar, who published a book about the language, beginning to give it a standard literary form. It is interesting to note that written and spoken Slovenian are very different from one another, since the literary language is based on a form hundreds of years old.

mansion that today is home to a good restaurant that serves superior local wines.

Accommodations and Food

The exterior of the **Hotel Mitra** (Prešernova 6, tel. 02/787-7455, www.hotel-mitra.si, €71 d., including breakfast) is quaint and sweet and it might lead you to have better expectations for the rooms, which are decorated in poor and outdated taste. Still, it's clean, it's in the center of town, and the hotel offers free wireless Internet and parking (though you'll need to ask about the parking at the front desk). The **Grand Hotel Primus** (Pot v. toplice 9, tel. 02/749-4100, www.terme-ptuj.si, €110 d.) opened in late 2007. It's definitely the nicest place in town and comes with a wellness center and thermal baths to take your mind off guidebooks and church visits.

Ribič (Dravska ulica 9, tel. 02/749-0638, 10 A.M.–11 P.M. Tues.–Thurs. and Sun., 10 A.M.–midnight Fri.–Sat., €12) has great freshwater fish and super views from its riverside terrace.

Getting There and Around

Regular buses (station: Osojnikova 11, tel. 02/771-1491) link Ptuj, about 130 kilometers northeast of Ljubljana, with Maribor (30 minutes) and Ljubljana (3.5 hours). You'll need a car to take the wine routes around town. By car from Ljubljana take the highway toward Maribor, exiting at Slovenska Bistrica. There are several trains (station: Osojnikova 2, tel. 02/292-5702) daily from Ptuj to Maribor, taking about 45 minutes. You can also take connect by train to Ljubljana (3 hours).

SLOVENSKE KONJICE

Slovenske Konjice is a beautiful village quite worthy of a laid-back detour. The 12th-century **Žička kartuzija** (Žiče Carthusian monastery, Stare Slemene 24, tel. 03/759-3110, call for hours) is worth a visit to see the living quarters, including dining room and kitchen, of the monks who left the cloister in the 18th century. There's a restaurant on-site for a quick bite and you shouldn't leave without at least visiting the **Viva Sana** herb shop to check out their herbal preparations.

Accommodations and Food

Zlati Gric (Stari trg 29A, tel. 03/758-0350, www.zlati-gric.si, €80 d.) is a winegrowing compound, complete with vineyards, a golf course, a nice restaurant, and apartments in a historic building for staying a relaxing night or two or three.

Getting There and Around

Slovenske Konjice is most easily reached by car. From Ljubljana take the A1 direction Celje/Maribor and take the exit for Slovenske Konjice, a total of about 90 kilometers east of Ljubljana.

MOUNT KOPA AREA

Part of the Pohorje mountain range, the area is full of alpine charm and small villages, some filled with an interesting tourist stop or two.

Fans of history or mining will enjoy experiencing an old mine in the region. Traveling 3.5 kilometers into the mountain, the tourist train at the lead and zinc mine museum in Mežica, **Podzemlje Pece** (Glančnik 6, tel. 02/870-0180, www.podzemljepece.com, tours at 11 A.M. Apr.–June and Sept.–Nov., 11 A.M. and 3 P.M. July–Aug., €7.80), takes you through an interesting look at mining life by expert guides. Cycling enthusiasts can also rent a bike and cycle through the mine.

The small town of **Slovenj Gradec** is worth an hour or two to check out its preserved old town and a couple of its museums and churches, particularly the Cerkev Sv Elizabeta (Church of St. Elizabeth) on Trg Svobode, the 15th-century Cerkev Sv Duha (Church of the Holy Spirit), and the **Likovnih Umetnosti Slovenj Gradec** (Slovenj Gradec Art Gallery, Glavni trg 24, tel. 02/884-1283, www.glu-sg .si, 9 A.M.–6 P.M. Tues.–Fri., 10 A.M.–1 P.M. and 2–5 P.M. Sat.–Sun., €2), a surprisingly good modern art gallery housed in the old town hall. The Slovenj Gradec **tourist office** (Glavni trg 24, tel. 02/881-2116, www.slovenj-gradec .si, 9 A.M.–6 P.M. Mon.–Fri.) is a good source of local information, including information about skiing and hiking in the nearby

Kope ski center, which typically sees snow November–April.

Another worthwhile stop is the village of **Ravne,** which has long been an ironworking center. Today its **Koroški pokrajinski muzej** (Carinthian Museum of Ravne na Koroškem, Na gradu 2, tel. 02/870-64 61, www.kpm.si, 10 A.M.–1 P.M. Tues.–Thurs., €2) displays a bit about the history of ironworking and some interesting modern iron sculptures as well as exhibitions about the development and culture of the Carinthian region. Contact the **tourist office** (Trg Svobode 21, tel. 02/822-1219, www.ravne.si/tic, 8 A.M.–4 P.M. Mon.–Fri., 8 A.M.–noon Sat.) for more details.

Accommodations and Food

The cheapest accommodations around are the alpine huts that provide shelter, a bed, and a bath. Many of the rooms are shared; bring a sleeping bag and be prepared to hike to get to them. These huts can be booked through the Slovenian Tourist Board (www.slovenia.info). The **Gostišče Delalut** (Dobja vas 119, tel. 02/821-8240, €50 d.) in Ravne has a good restaurant serving hearty Slovenian specialties and clean rooms. The **Okrepčevalnica Orada** (Trg svobode 3, tel. 02/823-7098, 11 A.M.–10 P.M. Tues.–Sun., €15) in Slovenj Gradec can offer reasonably priced freshwater fish plates and can arrange for fishing trips.

Getting There and Around

Slovenj Gradec is 110 kilometers northeast of Ljubljana. While you'll need a car to really dig deep into the area, Slovenj Gradec does have excellent bus connections to Ljubljana (2.5 hours). Buses from Slovenj Gradec head to the ski areas regularly in season.

Pomurje Region

Green fields wind along the river Mura in the Pomurje region, one of Slovenia's most agricultural areas. This translates into lots of bucolic scenery and sleepy towns to traverse. To reach some of the smaller towns, it's best to have a car. Another alternative is to travel by bike. Several routes are well marked; they vary in distance from 10 to 50 kilometers. Pick up a map from the Murska Sobota **tourist office** (Slovenska 37, tel. 02/534-1130, 9 A.M.–5 P.M. Mon.–Fri.).

MURSKA SOBOTA

The **castle** in Murska Sobota is a Renaissance-era structure set in the middle of a huge park. It houses a nice regional museum, **Pokrajinski muzej Murska Sobota** (Murska Sobota Regional Museum, Trubarjev drevored 4, tel. 02/521-1155, www.pok-muzej-ms.si, 9 A.M.–5 P.M. Tues.–Fri., 9 A.M.–1 P.M. Sat.–Sun., €3), whose most interesting exhibit is the history of the region's Jewish population, from rural life to their persecution in World War II.

Have lunch at the **Tourist Farm Vinski hram kupljen** (Okoslavci 2a, Sveti Jurij ob Ščavnici, tel. 02/568-9073, no credit cards, call for reservations), in the village of Okoslavci 12 kilometers southwest of Murska Sobota, and sample the farm's homemade jellies, salamis, sausages, and peach and pear brandies. The farm can also arrange guided wine tastings.

Murska Sobota is 182 kilometers northeast of Ljubljana and 41 kilometers east of Maribor. It is connected by bus with Maribor (2 hours) and Ljubljana (4 hours). Trains also connect the town with Ljubljana (3.5 hours), Maribor (1.5 hours), and Ptuj (1 hour).

MORAVSKE TOPLICE AND SELO

The **Hotel Livada Prestige** (Kranjčeva 12, tel. 02/512-2288, www.hotel-livada.si, €83 d.,

The Pomurje region is one of Slovenia's most agricultural areas.

including breakfast) in Moravske Toplice, seven kilometers northeast of Murska Sobota, offers lots of thermal baths, spa treatments, a restaurant, and a golf course for a nice relaxing break. While it's not the five stars it claims, it is good value for the money.

Near Moravske Toplice, the **Rotunda Sv. Nikolaj** (St. Nicholas Chapel, 9 A.M.–5 P.M. daily Apr.–Nov., or ask in the village about the key, €1.70), at the edge of the village of Selo, is a striking example of Romanesque architecture. Likely built in the 13th century, the cylindrical church houses some beautifully preserved paintings, including the *Adoration of the Magi* from the beginning of the 14th century. For more information, contact the Moravske Toplice **tourist office** (tel. 02/538-1520, www.moravske-toplice.com).

BOGOJINA

If you didn't get your fill of architect Jože Plečnik in Ljubljana, his addition to the **Cerkev Gospodovega vnebovzetja** (Church of the Ascension, open daily, free) in Bogojina, about 10 kilometers east of Murska Sobota, is a beautiful combination of 20th-century and more classic architecture. The church incorporates local folk pottery into its decoration, making it all the more interesting. Check with the Moravske Toplice tourist office (tel.

02/538-1520, www.moravske-toplice.com) for specific hours.

FILOVCI

Pomurje is well known for its pottery. The village of Filovci, about 3–4 kilometers east of Bogojina, has several famous potters who will welcome you into their studios. Check with the **tourist office** (Filovci 410, tel. 02/547-1248) for arrangements. Also of interest in nearby Filovski Gaj are the thatched wine cellars, part of the area's typical architecture that is disappearing today.

PUCONCI

Ride through the vineyards of **Radgonske gorice** (Jurkovičeva 5, Puconci, tel. 02/564-8526, www.radgonske-gorice.si, 7 A.M.–5 P.M. Mon.–Sat., call ahead for reservations) on a tourist train and enjoy guided tastings of the wines. The vintners claim to have produced Slovenia's first sparkling wine. Puconci is about five kilometers north of Murska Sobota.

WINE ROAD

The Pormurje region has a wine route, the **Goričko Wine Road,** filled with both cultural and culinary stops. Contact the office of the association of local wine producers (Puconci 79, tel. 02/545-9673, zkstrp.puconci@siol.net) for more details and a printed map.

Savinjska Valley

The green Savinjska Valley is one of Slovenia's most picturesque, yet one of the least-visited areas. Filled with medieval castles, the largest and most famous being the one at Celje, the region has other attractions—from Roman ruins to thermal parks to caves and a mining museum, just to name a few.

CELJE

The town of Celje is most visitors' first stop in the Savinjska Valley. Though the outskirts are filled with factories and block-like structures, the old core is well preserved and charming. The

Stari Grad Celje (Celje Castle, 9 A.M.–9 P.M. daily in summer, 10 A.M.–5 P.M. daily in winter, free), the largest in Slovenia, is an interesting outing. It's close to an hour's hike on foot, though you can take the easy way and hail a cab. The early 13th-century structure has been added to and changed over the years. There's not a lot to see in the castle itself, but there are some nice views. If it's displays you're after, the **Pokrajinski muzej Celje** (Celje Regional Museum, Muzejski trg 1, tel. 03/428-0950, www.pokmuz-ce.si, 10 A.M.–6 P.M. Tues.–Sat. Mar.–Oct., 10 A.M.–6 P.M. Tues.–Fri. and

© B. BAJŽELJ/SLOVENIAN TOURIST BOARD

the Savinjska Valley region – picturesque but little visited

10 A.M.–noon Sat. Nov.–Feb., €3.50) in Celje's Stara Grofija manor house has an impressive collection of artifacts and art from prehistoric to post–World War II.

Accommodations and Food

The **Sobe pod gradom** (Castle View Hostel, tel. 70/220-069, www.elfa-sp.si/hostel, €17 per person) is a good youth hostel in Celje with clean, bright rooms.

You can find lots of casual restaurants and bars in the town of Celje for a bite to eat.

Getting There and Around

Celje is 46 kilometers southwest of Maribor and 73 kilometers northeast of Ljubljana. You can reach Celje by bus or train. There are connections by bus to cities such as Ljubljana (1.5 hours), Maribor (1.5 hours), and Ptuj (2 hours). Trains connect Celje with cities such as Ljubljana (1.5 hours), Ptuj (1 hour), and Maribor (45 minutes) as well as local villages like Velenje (45 minutes) and Rogaška Slatina (45 minutes). A taxi stand can be found on Krekov trg near the train station. If driving from Ljubljana, take the Maribor highway and exit Celje. From Maribor, take the highway direction Ljubljana and exit Celje.

ŠEMPETER

The Celje Regional Museum runs the **Arheološki park Rimska nekropola** (Roman necropolis archaeological park, 10 A.M.–3 P.M. daily Apr. 1–15, 10 A.M.–6 P.M. daily Apr. 16–Sept. 30, 10 A.M.–4 P.M. Sat.–Sun. Oct., €4) in Šempeter, 12 kilometers west of Celje. Containing over 100 Roman tombs, the outdoor museum is one of the best-preserved Roman monuments in Slovenia. Outstanding among the many family gravestones, the eight-meter-high Spectatius tomb, likely dating from the 2nd century, is covered with intricate reliefs including a depiction of the four seasons and a gruesome Medusa head guarding the remains.

The nearby **Pekel Cave** (entry every hour on the hour 9 A.M.–4 P.M. Sat.–Sun. Mar. and Oct., 9 A.M.–5 P.M. daily Apr.–Sept., €6) has the highest underground waterfall in Slovenia.

For more information about the necropolis and Pekel Cave, contact the Šempeter **tourist office** (Ob Rimski nekropoli 2, tel. 03/700-2056, www.td-sempeter.si).

VELENJE

Though the city of Velenje is not the most attractive in Slovenia, history fans and older children (visitors must be seven or older) will enjoy a visit to the **Muzej premogovništva Slovenije** (Coal-Mining Museum of Slovenia, Stari jašek—Koroška cesta, tel. 03/587-0997, www.rlv.si/muzej, 9:30 A.M.–5 P.M. Tues.–Sun., €8.50). An elevator takes visitors 160 meters into the ground to see what it was like to be a coal miner in the early 20th century. The museum also features a guided tour of the mines, a film on the daily life of the miners, and a coal miner's lunch. The museum also accommodates individuals with disabilities, but arrangements should be made in advance for wheelchairs.

Eighteen kilometers northwest of Celje, Velenje is connected by bus to Slovenj Gradec (45 minutes), Celje (45 minutes), and Ljubljana (2 hours) and by train to Celje (50 minutes).

ROGAŠKA SLATINA

The **Grand Hotel Rogaška** (Stritarjeva 1, tel. 03/811-2000, www.terme-rogaska.si, €92 d.) is located in a former Austro-Hungarian palace in the town of Rogaška Slatina. The rooms (the hotel bills itself as four-star but it is a solid three-star by most standards) do not live up to the beauty of the palace, but the setting is spectacular and you can use the hotel's thermal pools and spa.

Rogaška Slatina is about 25 kilometers east of Celje and is connected to Celje by a train that takes about 45 minutes.

PODSREDA

First mentioned in the 13th century, **Grad Podsreda** (Podsreda castle, 10 A.M.–6 P.M. Tues.–Sun. in summer, €2) is a pretty Romanesque fortress, located on a hill above the village of Podsreda, with some small exhibitions of local glasswork and concerts during the summer. It's a nice way to spend an hour if you're in the area. If you find it closed, the keys are kept at the Kozjanski Park office (Podsreda 45, tel. 03/800-7100, kozjanski-park@kp.gov.si).

Podsreda is 20 kilometers south of Rogaška Slatina and about 35 kilometers southeast of Celje.

Savinjske Alps Region

In this region of rolling green hills that give way to rocky alpine peaks, the beauty of nature competes with pretty villages full of churches, castles, and quaint museums for travelers' attention. No matter what the season, you can take to the slopes for a bit of fresh air and sport.

◖ ŠKOFJA LOKA

The must-see of the Savinjske Alps is the medieval village of Škofja Loka. Filled with old buildings and charming squares, the well-preserved town has a fairy-tale quality, special even among Slovenia's picturesque villages.

Start with a tour of the town's castle and small museum. The 13th-century castle, called **Loka Grad** (Grajska pot 13, tel. 04/517-0400, www.loski-muzej.si, 9 A.M.–6 P.M. Tues.–Sun. Apr.–Sept., 10 A.M.–5 P.M. Tues.–Sun. Oct.–Mar., €2.50), houses a few nice displays, most with English descriptions. After visiting the castle, continue wandering around the steep and winding streets, admiring the town's churches (particularly the 15th-century Cerkev Sv Jakob, whose interior was recast by Plečnik) and medieval buildings and crossing the 6th-century Capuchin Bridge. On the last weekend in June the town holds **Venerina pot,** the Path of Venus medieval street fair, definitely worth a visit if you're in the area at the time.

Accommodations and Food

The **Goštišče Kveder** (Kveder Guest House, Spodnja Luša 16, tel. 04/514-1499, www.kveder-sp.si, €40 d., including breakfast) is a farm that offers comfortable but basic rooms and good meals in a peaceful alpine setting. Only one kilometer away from skiing, the bed-and-breakfast can also arrange for horseback riding in the valley.

The **Kašča restaurant** (Spodnji trg 1, tel. 04/512-4300, www.kasca-plevna.com, noon–11 P.M. Mon.–Sat., €11) in the basement of the medieval granary in Škofja Loka has hearty dishes, from Slovenian meat and potato staples to pizzas.

Information and Services

The **tourist office** (Mestni trg 7, tel. 04/512-0268, www.skofjaloka.info) can organize guided tours for groups by arrangement. The town website, www.skofjaloka.si, also provides useful information.

Getting There and Around

Škofja Loka is 21 kilometers northwest of Ljubljana. It's well connected via bus (station: Kapucinski trg 13, tel. 04/517-0300, www.alpetour.si) to Ljubljana (40 minutes) and Kranj (15–20 minutes), and via train (station: Kidriceva cesta 61, tel. 04/294-4174) to Ljubljana (30 minutes), Kranj (10 minutes), and Bled (35 minutes). The train station is a few kilometers from the town center but hourly buses link the station with the town. In town you can easily get around on foot.

VOLČJI POTOK

The **Arboretum Volčji Potok** (Volčji Potok 3, tel. 01/831-2345, www.arboretum-vp.si, 8 A.M.–8 P.M. daily in summer, 8 A.M.–6 P.M. daily in winter, €5) belonged to private owners before World War II; they surrounded their baroque mansion (now destroyed) with sprawling gardens. Today it's a great botanical garden with an outdoor café that's open in good weather. It's about 20 kilometers east of Škofja Loka and about 18 kilometers northeast of Ljubljana. From Ljubljana, take the highway toward Celje and exit Domžale to Radomlje, and then follow the signs for the park.

KAMNIK

The attractive little medieval town of Kamnik is small but beautiful, framed by snow-capped mountains. There's not a lot to see, though it makes a nice stopover for lunch and a look around, or perhaps whiling away a few hours of a lazy day. The town's **Mali Grad** is a little 12th-century castle with a two-story chapel. You can visit the castle anytime, but make arrangements through the **Turistično informacijski center Kamnik** (Tomšičeva 23, tel. 01/831-8250, tic@kamnik-tourism.si, www.kamnik-tourism.si) to visit the interior of the castle and chapel. The town also has an interesting gallery, the **Galerija Miha Maleš** (Miha Maleš Gallery, Glavni trg 2, tel. 01/831-7647, 8 A.M.–1 P.M. and 4–7 P.M. Tues.–Sat., donation appreciated), which has an exhibition of the work of Maleš, a local 20th-century painter, as well as changing temporary exhibitions.

There are several pizzerias and taverns in town, though the **Pivnica Pri Podkvi** (Trg Svobode 1, tel. 041/961-559, €5) offers excellent value for money, particularly its daily menu, offering sturdy meat dishes and local specialties.

Located 25 kilometers north of Ljubljana, Kamnik is well connected by bus and train with Ljubljana. With close to a dozen connections daily, the bus takes 30 minutes to an hour depending on how many stops the bus has on its route, while the train takes close to an hour.

VELIKA PLANINA AND KRVAVEC
◖ Velika Planina

The Velika Planina mountain (www.velikaplanina.si), about 10 kilometers northeast of Kamnik, offers active recreation year-round. In the summer take the cable car (the station is 11 kilometers north of Kamnik) to Velika Planina, and then walk about 30 minutes to the summer **herdsmen's settlements** (just past the Lodging House Zeleni Rob you'll see signs for the herdsmen's settlements on Mala Planina) to see the sheep herdsmen and their livestock, taste fresh milk and cheese, and visit the typical cottages in the area, which is rife with hiking and mountain-biking trails. There's also plenty of warm-weather skiing, perfect for beginners and amateurs. In the winter Velika

Planina has slopes ranging from beginner to moderate difficulty and a free kindergarten program on weekends for the little ones. Ski and snowboarding gear can be rented on the slope and information on hiking and biking trails is available on site as well.

Krvavec

Krvavec mountain (www.rtc-krvavec.si, €28 for a full day), 10 kilometers northwest of Kamnik, has more challenging slopes.

Accommodations and Food

The Velika Planina area has several great accommodation options. If your load is light (because you have to carry your own luggage from the cable car), the **Jarški dom** (tel. 01/832-5571 or 041/621-732, call for reservations and current prices) on Mala Planina is sort of a rural youth hostel with shared rooms and lots of convivial rustic charm. Though the experience is closer to camping than a hotel, it's hard to beat the setting.

The cottages on Velika Planina aren't luxe, but comfortable, and they're perfect for skiing holidays, when you can walk to the lift and, after a long day on the slopes, kick back in a typical cottage, complete with kitchen, television, bath, and cozy bed. They're perfect for families. Some of the nicest are from the **Alpe Jadran agency** (tel. 01/831-7228, pernef@volja.net, www.alpejadran.net).

On Velika Planina, the **Lodging House**

Zeleni Rob (tel. 051/341-406, zeleni.rob@velikaplanina.si, 8 A.M.–8 P.M. in summer, 8 A.M.–8 P.M. Fri.–Sun. out of season, €8) is the place to go for typical alpine meals like bread-loaf bowls of mushroom soup, bean and sauerkraut soup (locally called *jota*), and apple pie for dessert.

Krvavec offers full equipment rental and several accommodation options, though the most interesting is definitely the █ **Igloo Village** (tel. 01/300-3845, info@koren-sports.si, open late Dec.–Mar.), a hotel complex composed of individual igloos for overnights. The package (€89) includes snowshoeing, a cocktail, dinner in the igloo restaurant, a DJ party in the ice bar, overnight in an igloo, and breakfast. If you prefer to sleep in a heated room but want to experience the Igloo Village, the complex also offers snowshoeing and dinner with a cocktail and DJ party in the Ice Bar for €45 per person.

Getting There and Around

Two to three daily bus services connect Kamnik with Velika Planina (15–20 minutes) and Krvavec (about 20 minutes). Bus connections are too infrequent to stay in Kamnik and ski during the day on the mountains, so if you don't have a car, try arranging for accommodation at Velika Planina or Krvavec to cut down on hassle.

There are about three daily buses that run between Kamnik and the cable car station in Kamniška Bistrica. If you're driving, follow the signs to Kamniška Bistrica–Gornji Grad.

Dolenjska and Bela Krajina

Vineyards and castles are only two of the attractions of these southeastern Slovenian regions. The lush, picturesque valleys are perfect for a relaxing trip through the countryside.

DOLENJSKA

A string of rolling green hills hugging the Croatian border, the Dolenjska region is dotted with castles and thermal spas. The most charming of the region's towns is likely Novo

Mesto, an attractive old town surrounded by a bustling modern economy.

Ribnica

Though most of the 12th-century **Ribnica castle** (Škrabcev trg 40, tel. 01/836-9335, call for hours, €2.50), about 40 kilometers south of Ljubljana, was burned in World War II, the remaining arcades and towers house an excellent small museum, with exhibitions of

WINE ROADS OF SLOVENIA

© D. MLADENOVIĆ/SLOVENIAN TOURIST BOARD

Wine roads criss-cross Slovenia, which has 40,000 registered wineries.

Slovenia's main wine-growing regions are Podravje (Pohorje and Pomurje regions, where you'll find the most marked wine routes), Posavje (Bela Krajina and Dolenjska regions), and Primorska (coastal region). Many of the country's 40,000 registered wineries are more hobbies and retirement occupations than anything else. Still, there's plenty of quality to be had and given the small operations of most of the producers, it's likely you've never had the chance to try many of them – the production is just too low to export. Slovenia produces both red and white wines, though the whites are by far the best. Most all of Slovenia is criss-crossed by one wine route or another. One less-traveled spot for wine lovers is the Brda region, bordering Italy, sure to bring lots of discoveries from the small winegrowers along the roads.

the town's well-known woodenware and pottery as well as some archaeological finds. It's not the sort of place to go out of your way to see, but if you're nearby, it makes a nice sightseeing stop.

Novo Mesto

It's easy to spend a half day in the town of Novo Mesto. With several castles and churches that are nice to peek into, the small town also makes a great departure point for exploring the area's wine roads.

A worthwhile stop in town is the **Dolenjski Muzej** (Dolenjska Museum, Muzejska 7, tel. 07/373-1130, www.dolmuzej.com, 8 A.M.–5 P.M. Tues.–Fri., 10 A.M.–5 P.M. Sat., 10 A.M.–1 P.M. Sun. Apr.–Oct.; 8 A.M.–4 P.M. Tues.–Fri., 9 A.M.–noon Sat.–Sun. Nov.–Mar., €3), which displays artifacts from Novo Mesto's long history, dating back to the Bronze Age.

Though there are several good places to eat in town, the most convenient is certainly the **Restavracija Breg** (Cvelbarjeva 9, tel. 07/332-1269, €8), which has a nice terrace for warm-weather dining and specializes in Dolenjska specialties.

Novo Mesto's **tourist office** (Novi trg 6, tel. 07/393-9263, www.novomesto.si, 9 A.M.–7 P.M. Mon.–Fri., 9 A.M.–4 P.M. Sat., 9 A.M.–noon Sun. June–Sept., 9 A.M.–6 P.M. Mon.–Fri., 9 A.M.–2 P.M. Sat. Oct.–May) can provide more information about the region, as well as help arrange for hotel and apartment stays and rent bicycles.

Novo Mesto is well connected by bus (station: Topliška 1, tel. 07/332-1123) to Otočec (15 minutes) and Ljubljana (1 hour). By train (station: Kolodvorska 1, tel. 07/298-2100) you can link with Metlika (1.5 hours) and Ljubljana (2 hours).

Around Novo Mesto

One of the nicest hotels in Slovenia, the ◖ **Hotel Grad Otočec** (Grajska cesta 2, tel. 07/384-8600, www.terme-krka.si, €260 d., including breakfast) is located in a castle on a small island in the Krka River, surrounded by lovely countryside. The hotel has a golf course and tennis center, and also offers information on a variety of walking trails in the area. The restaurant in the castle (6 A.M.–11 P.M. daily) serves good food in a hard-to-beat setting. Otočec is eight kilometers northeast of Novo Mesto, right off the highway to Zagreb. A taxi from Novo Mesto costs around €20. Ask the hotel about transfers from the Ljubljana airport.

The **Terme Hotel at Čatež** (tel. 07/493-6700, www.terme-catez.si, €100 d., including breakfast) is rather dated and not really the four stars it claims to be, but it does have nice indoor and outdoor swimming pools, saunas, and Roman baths (outdoor pools 10 A.M.–6 P.M. Apr. and Oct., 9 A.M.–7 P.M. May and Sept., 8 A.M.–8 P.M. June–Aug., indoor pools 9 A.M.–9 P.M. daily, €11–13). You can buy a daily ticket to enjoy a little water-fueled relaxation. The village of Čatež is 42 kilometers east of Novo Mesto, and there are several daily bus connections (1 hour).

Only a few kilometers from Čatež, on the other side of the highway from Terme Čatež, the ◖ **Golf Hotel Castle Mokrice** (tel.

07/493-6700, www.terme-catez.si, €86 d., including breakfast) is the nicest spot to stay in the area, set amid forested hills with an excellent wine cellar and an 18-hole golf course. The rooms aren't necessarily the most tastefully furnished (ask for one with hardwood floors), but the bathrooms are big and have whirlpool tubs. The **restaurant** at the hotel is well worth the splurge. The cuisine is basic traditional but the setting, amid a grand ballroom with windows overlooking the rolling hills, is really worth a stop-off, if only for a long lunch.

Very basic rooms are available at **Vinoteka Bizeljsko Pri Peču** (Stara vas 58, tel. 07/452-0103, www.klimaexpert.com/vinoteka, €50 d., including breakfast), located north of Čatež on the road from Brežice to Bizeljsko. The Vinoteka also has a nice restaurant (10 A.M.–1 A.M. daily) with a terrace and decent local wines. You'll need a car to get here.

Wine Road

The **Upper Dolenjska Wine Road** is dotted with plenty of cellars, as well as places to buy fruit vinegars and dine on local specialties such as sausages and hearty stews. Contact the Sevnica **tourist office** (Boštanj 80 tel. 07/816-5462, tip@kstm.si, 9 A.M.–7 P.M. Mon.–Fri., 10 A.M.–7 P.M. Sat.) for a detailed map and tips.

BELA KRAJINA

Near the Croatian border lies the region of Bela Krajina. Though the region is miniscule in size, its beautiful landscape, known for the white-barked birch trees that populate the area, and its strong cultural traditions make it stand on its own. Bela Krajina is particularly known for its folk music traditions, celebrated by several festivals. The region is well connected by buses, but the best way to see Bela Krajina is with a rental car or on top of a bicycle. The tourist offices in most towns can help you rent one.

Metlika

If you can get past the communist-era bloc buildings in the outer ring, the well-preserved old town in Metlika is well worth a visit. The **Metliški Grad** (Metlika Castle, Trg Svobod

4, tel. 07/306-3370, 9 A.M.–5 P.M. Mon.–Sat., 9 A.M.–noon Sun., €4) has a small gallery, a viticulture exhibition, and the **Belokranjski muzej** (Bela Krajina Museum), with displays chronicling the area's history from prehistoric times through World War II. Kids will enjoy the **Slovenski gasilski muzej** (Fire Brigade Museum, Trg Svobode 5, tel. 07/305-8697, 9 A.M.–1 P.M. Mon.–Sat., free), highlighting Bela Krajina's fire brigade, the first in Slovenia. The old fire engines, uniforms, and photographs are an interesting step back in time. In May, Metlika hosts the **Vinška vigred festival,** with lots of wine tastings, bottles to buy as souvenirs, and colorful folk performances.

A fun lodging option in the area is the **Turistična kmetija Črnič** (Grabrovec 65, tel. 07/305-0114, €40 d., including breakfast), a farm a few kilometers outside of Metlika, right off a bike trail. The farm not only offers cozy accommodation, but good food and homemade wine.

The Metlika **tourist office** (Mestni trg 1, tel. 07/305-8331, www.metlika-turizem.si, 8 A.M.–3:30 P.M. Mon.–Fri. 9 A.M.–noon Sat.) can provide you with maps of wine routes in the area, marked with cellars, sights of interest, and restaurants along the way. The office also can arrange for bike rental.

About 17 kilometers southeast of Novo Mesto, Metlika is linked by bus and train with Novo Mesto (1 hour) and Ljubljana (2 hours).

Rosalnice

The most interesting architectural features of the region are the **Tri fare** (Three Parishes, free), a complex of three Gothic churches surrounded by a wall in the village of Rosalnice, three kilometers east of Metlika. Lack of records has left the history of the churches somewhat blank. Some think the churches were built by the Knights Templar in the 12th century while others claim they were built in the 14th or 15th centuries. Whatever the true provenance, the churches have been a pilgrimage site for hundreds of years.

For more information, check with the Metlika County office (Mestni trg 14, Metlika, tel. 07/305-8331, www.metlika-turizem.si).

Črnomelj

Larger than charming Metlika, which is 12 kilometers to the northeast, the town of Črnomelj is also somewhat more neglected. However, the city is full of history, including a 12th-century castle and a couple of churches. The best time to visit is during the **Jurjevanje festival** (www.jurjevanje.si), held sometime between late April and late June, featuring folk music and dance performances from all over Slovenia. The oldest folk festival in Slovenia, it's been held every year since 1964.

Around Črnomelj

Near the tiny village of **Rožanec,** five kilometers northwest of Črnomelj, there's a surprisingly well-preserved Roman-era temple to the sun god Mithras. Ask in the village for directions.

Wine Roads

The vineyards of Bela Krajina are responsible for some of Slovenia's best reds and whites. The local wine is Metliška Črnina, which combines four different types of red grapes.

Bela Krajina has several marked wine routes, perfect for biking on a crisp fall or spring day, sampling local wines along the way. Contact the Bela Krajina **tourist board** (tel. 07/305-6530, tic.crnomelj@ric-belakrajina.si, www.ric-belakrajina.si) for maps and information. The Metlika tourist office can also provide maps and information. In Črnomelj, the Črnomaljska Klet information center (Ulica Mirana Jarca 2, tel. 07/306-1100) has local wines for sampling and purchase.

Julian Alps

Possibly Slovenia's most beautiful region and home to the Triglav National Park, the Julian Alps have something for adventure seekers, nature lovers, and everyone in between. It's a region most associated with its vistas—snow-capped mountains cut through by gorges filled with turquoise-blue rushing rivers and covered with evergreen forests. In a word, it's idyllic. You'll find genteel turn-of-the-20th-century hotels around Lake Bled, harking back to a grander time, down the road from back-to-basics pensions in the middle of no-where—both extremes providing spots to just relax and let go. The **Soča River Valley** is one of the best places for active adventures, particularly rafting the rushing streams or just admiring them from a walking path above, while towns like Idrija offer quieter pleasures, from dining in a stately manor hotel to admiring (and perhaps purchasing) some of the town's famous lace.

◖ BLED

With a medieval castle overlooking the bright-blue lake's church-topped island, rimmed with majestic evergreens and surrounded by mountains, Bled should be tops on your must-see list. One of Slovenia's most photographed spots, Bled's castle draws in the tourists, while its surroundings keep them coming back. It's perhaps among the few places in the world that surpasses its postcards.

Pilgrims have been coming to Bled since the 8th century, when the Caranthanians came to worship Živa, the Slavic fertility goddess, on the island spot where the Church of the Assumption stands today.

Bled became a popular tourist spot in the late 1800s. By 1900 Bled had rooms for over a thousand tourists and in the years leading up to World War II the town continued to flourish, adding over a dozen tennis courts and a golf course.

Cerkev Marijinega Vnebovzetja, on an island in the middle of Lake Bled

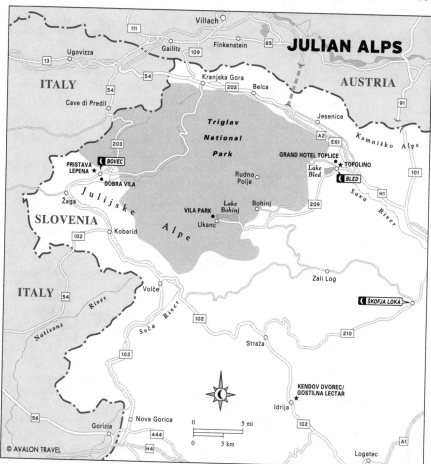

Though Bled suffered throughout World War II, Tito gave it his stamp of approval, building a villa on the lake and constructing new hotels for a new generation of tourists.

Those hotels take some of the shine off of Bled as you drive into town. But once you're past their block-like facades and the lake comes into view, you'll realize why you and so many others have come to this corner of Slovenia.

Sights

The lake itself is Bled's most stunning sight. The natural glacier-formed lake is rimmed by a promenade that's worth the walk before you schlep up to the **castle** (Grajska 25, tel. 04/578-0525, 8 A.M.–8 P.M. daily May–Sept., 9 A.M.–5 P.M. daily Oct.–Apr., €7), some 140 meters above the lake, for a panoramic view and a small exhibition of the history of Bled and the castle. The castle was first mentioned in the early 11th century and there are still some Romanesque remnants to be spotted around the castle. The castle was altered and changed throughout the centuries, including a heavy 20th-century renovation. There's also an herbal gallery, wine cellar (call to arrange a visit), and

THE LEGEND OF LAKE BLED

Once upon a time there was a beautiful princess . . . Or so the story usually goes. In Bled, the story started almost the same. A young aristocratic girl, married to the handsome owner of Bled castle, lived happily high above Bled's splendid lake. One day, her husband was out hunting and was killed by some robbers. Devastated, the young widow took all of her gold and had it fashioned into a bell for the church on the island in the lake, so that every time it rang, it would remind her of her sorrows.

While the bell was being transported to the island, a huge storm came up and the boat that was carrying it sank, along with the heavy bell, which disappeared below the blue water. Distraught, the woman went into a convent in Rome. After she died, the Pope sent another bell to the little church on the island in Lake Bled. Ever since, pilgrims have traveled to the island believing if they touched the bell and prayed to the Virgin Mary, their prayers would be answered. And according to the legend, the bell that sank can still be heard ringing below even today.

reenactments of medieval life by theater groups during the summer and on special occasions.

Thermal springs in the northeastern part of the lake are directed into three pools at the Hotels Toplice, Park, and Golf, which can be accessed for a fee.

Several spots on the lake offer boat rides, including the typical gondola-like **pletna** (in front of the Health Park, Hotel Park, Mlino, and the Rowing Center, tel. 041/427-155, €12). Take one to the **Cerkev Marijinega Vnebovzetja** (Church of the Assumption) on the tiny island in the middle of the lake. Built in the 15th century, the church has been through two earthquakes, responsible for the renovations that formed its current baroque style. All that remains of the former Gothic church are a wooden statue of the Virgin Mary

and a few frescoes. Keep in mind that there are close to 100 steps from the boat dock up to the church.

You can also hop in an Austrian-style **fijaker,** or horse-drawn carriage, to travel around the area, even going as far as the lake at Bohinj. Carriages can be found in front of Festival Hall or call 04/574-1121.

Four kilometers northeast of Bled, the **Vintgar Gorge** winds its way through 1.6 kilometers of stunning beauty. It's well worth the trip to walk the paths and footbridges and just generally marvel at nature.

Sports and Recreation

Bled is full of dozens of sporting activities. The easiest is hiking, with marked walking paths throughout the area. Pick up a trail map at the **tourist office** (Cesta svobode 10, tel. 04/574-1122, www.bled.si). The surrounding rivers make for good rafting and kayaking. Try **Bled Rafting** (Hrastova 2, tel. 041/678-008, www.bled-rafting.si) in Bled and **3glav Adventures** (Ljubljanska 1, tel. 041/686-184, www.3glav-adventures.com) in Bohinj. 3glav Adventures not only offers rafting, but also hiking, diving, parachuting, and paragliding outings.

The **Golf and Country Club Bled** (Kidričeva 10c, tel. 04/537-7711, www.golf.bled.si) has two courses, rents equipment, and provides instruction if you've never even putted before.

Accommodations

The **C Grand Hotel Toplice** (Cesta svobode 12, tel. 04/579-1000, www.hotel-toplice.com, €164 d., including breakfast) is the swankest place in town, harking back to Bled's glory days. Room rates include use of the hotel's thermal and outdoor pools and saunas.

The **Vila Bled** (Cesta svobode 26, tel. 04/579-1500, www.vila-bled.com, €228 d., including breakfast) may have lost some of its luster since Tito lived here, but even if just for the history, this four-star hotel deserves a mention. The rooms are renovated, refreshingly maintaining the villa's 1950s decor.

Garni Hotel Berc (Pod Stražo 13, tel. 04/576-5658, www.berc-sp.si, €65 d., including

© BOBO/SLOVENIAN TOURIST BOARD

Grand Hotel Toplice

breakfast) is just a few minutes' walk to the center of Bled. The hotel has clean wood-lined rooms, friendly service, and a hearty buffet breakfast.

The **Bledec Youth Hostel** (Grajska 17, tel. 04/574-5250, www.mlino.si, €16 per person or €46 for a double room) is a budget option, only ten minutes' walk to Bled Castle.

Food

For dessert and coffee, try the local cream cake on the terrace of the **Park Hotel** (Cesta svobode 15, tel. 04/579-1800, www.hotel-park-bled.com, 9 A.M.–9 P.M. daily).

In the heart of Bled's center, **Bar Union 99** (Ljubljanska cesta 9, tel. 04/578-0119, www.union-bled.com, 8 A.M.–11 P.M. Mon.–Thurs., 8 A.M.–1 A.M. Fri.–Sat., 10 A.M.–10 P.M. Sun., €4) is the perfect spot for a quick sandwich or pizza as well as checking your email—the bar has two computers with Internet connections.

Pension Mlino (Cesta svobode 45, tel. 04/574-1404, www.mlino.si, call for reservations and hours, €10) is a 15-minute walk (along a lakeside footpath) for hearty dishes of grilled meats and a nice outdoor seating area.

After your meal, take a *pletna* out in the lake from the Mlino's dock.

The intimate low-lit interior at ⟨ **Okarina** (Ljubljanska cesta 8, tel. 04/574-1458, 6 P.M.–midnight Mon.–Fri., noon–midnight Sat.–Sun., €20) is perfect for romantic dinners. Local Slovenian dishes like wild boar cutlet or fish stew share the menu with Indian staples like chicken masala and hot naan bread.

Gourmets should try ⟨ **Topolino** (Ljubljanska cesta 26, tel. 04/574-1781, www.topolino-slo.com, noon–11 P.M. Wed.–Mon., €20) for adventurous dishes like homemade spinach gnocchi with smoked goat cheese and fried pumpkin or pear cooked in Teran wine with gorgonzola and walnuts. The restaurant also has a strong wine list, with a nice showing of Slovenian wines.

Though it's a few kilometers southeast of Bled, ⟨ **Gostilna Lectar** (Linhartov trg 2, tel. 04/537-4800, www.lectar.com, noon–11 P.M. Wed.–Mon., €18) in Radovljica started in the 18th century making the colorful gingerbread hearts the region is known for. Today, the restaurant still houses a gingerbread museum where you can buy souvenirs, but the real draw is the excellent food in the old house, filled with rustic cozy charm. While the restaurant serves traditional Slovenian cuisine, the owners take pride in their dishes created especially for vegetarians.

Information and Services

You can get more information on Bled, including maps of walking trails, at the **tourist office** (Cesta svobode 10, tel. 04/574-1122, www.bled.si, 8 A.M.–9 P.M. Mon.–Sat., 9 A.M.–5 P.M. Sun. July–Aug.; 8 A.M.–7 P.M. Mon.–Sat., 11 A.M.–5 P.M. Sun. Mar.–June and Sept.–Oct.; 9 A.M.–6 P.M. Mon.–Sat., noon–4 P.M. Sun. Nov.–Feb.).

Getting There and Around

Buses (station: Cesta svobode 4, tel. 04/574-1114) leave and arrive hourly connecting Ljubljana and Bled (about 1.5 hours). Buses for Bohinj (40 minutes) depart at least a couple of times a day. You can also take a bus to Bled from Idrija and Kobarid, though connections are less frequent. The Bled tourist office should be able to provide you with more details and current schedules, which change with the seasons. The train is not the most practical way to reach Bled, since the station is far from the center of town. Buses connect the train station in Lesce (Zelezniska 12, tel. 04/531-8364) with the center of Bled every 30 minutes and take about 15 minutes. By train you can connect to Ljubljana (1 hour) and Kranj (25 minutes). The Bled Jezero train station (Koldovorska 50, tel. 04/294-2363) offers excellent connections to Bohinj (20 minutes) by an old steam train in the summer months. This station is only 1.5 kilometers out of town.

Bled is 57 kilometers northwest of Ljubljana. If you're coming by car, simply take the E61 highway from Ljubljana.

BOHINJ

While it may not be as fairy-tale beautiful as Bled, Bohinj is a pretty lake in its own right, albeit in a wilder way. It's far less touristy than Bled and there are plenty of secluded spots to get completely away from the pack. Because

Cerkev Sveti Janez, on Lake Bohinj

the lake is part of Triglav National Park, there's very little development. The north shore, for instance, is completely natural and a great place for hiking.

The name Bohinj refers to the lake, since there's no town named as such. Usually when people refer to Bohinj, they think of the town of **Ribčev Laz,** which serves as a sort of area center on the eastern edge of the lake. You can go there to find pretty much anything you need, from a post office to a grocery store. At the opposite end, on the western shore, there's the village of **Ukanc,** with a hotel, campsite, and some shops.

There's not much to really "see" in Bohinj besides the Gothic **Cerkev Sveti Janez** (Church of St. John, 9 A.M.–noon and 5–8 P.M. daily July–Aug., ask at tourist office for off-season hours, donation requested), in Ribčev Laz. The 13th-century church has been restored and altered over the years, explaining the Baroque bell tower and altars, though there are some nice 14th-century frescoes inside. The church is also a great vantage point for views of the lake.

The rest of the lake's activities revolve around getting in touch with nature. Start with a panoramic view of the surrounding Julian Alps, the lake, and a 195-foot waterfall by taking the **cable car** (8 A.M.–6 P.M. daily, until 7 P.M. in summer, €3) up Mt. Vogel. The station is near the village of Ukanc, on the western end of the lake. Another nice way to see the area is the summer **steam train** that travels several weekends from May to October. A round-trip between Bled and Bohinj costs €10 and takes about 40 minutes. Reservations must be made in advance with ABC Rent-a-car in Ljubljana (Ulica Jožeta Jame 16, tel. 01/510-4320, www .europcar.si) or one of their authorized outlets (check with ABC Rent-a-car to find out who qualifies). You can reserve one day before, if they have space.

Sports and Recreation

Once you've had a taste of the surroundings, jump into some sports to really make the most of Bohinj's natural advantages. **Alpinsport** (Ribčev Laz 53, 04/572-3486, www.alpin sport.si, open daily, hours vary with the season) can organize all sorts of outings: Rafting, kayaking, canyoning, spelunking, rock climbing, and skiing are all on the menu. If you prefer to adventure alone, they also rent bikes, canoes, kayaks, and ski equipment.

There is excellent **fly-fishing** in the Bohinj area. **Hotel Pension Stare** (Ukanc 128, tel. 04/574-6400, www.impel-bohinj.si) sells fishing tickets for the lake as well as provides guides and rents equipment for fishing in the lake, river, and streams in the area.

Accommodations

You can find private rooms and apartments throughout the Bohinj area at the **tourist office** (Ribčev Laz 48, tel. 04/574-1122, www.bohinj.si, 8 A.M.–8 P.M. Mon.–Sat., 9 A.M.–7 P.M. Sun. July–Aug.; 8 A.M.–7 P.M. Mon.–Sat., 9 A.M.–3 P.M. Sun. Sept.–June) or pitch a tent at **Camp Zlatorog** (Ukanc 2, tel. 04/572-3482, www.aaturizem.com, €9) on the shores of Lake Bohinj near Ukanc.

The only real disadvantage to the **YH Pod Voglom** (Ribčev Laz 60, tel. 04/572-3461, podvoglom@siol.net, www.hostel-podvoglom .com, €16 per person or doubles from €38) is that it's five kilometers from Ribčev Laz. The advantage, though, is the pretty location and all the activities organized through the hostel's sports center, from kayaking and rafting excursions to skiing. The hostel does have its own restaurants and also rents bikes and kayaks.

Possibly the best deal in Bohinj, the **Hotel Bohinj** (Ribčev Laz 45, tel. 04/572-6000, info@aaturizem.com, www.aaturizam.com, €80 d.) is a fresh hotel with friendly service, spacious rooms, and an incredibly central location. The family-run **Hotel Kristal** (Ribčev Laz 4a, tel. 04/577-8200, www.hotel-kristal-slovenia.com, €120 d., including breakfast) offers pleasant, spacious rooms (many with great views) and a solid restaurant. It's a short walk from the center of things, but that makes it all the more peaceful.

In an even quieter location in the tiny village of Ukanc, the ◖ **Vila Park** (Ukanc 129, tel. 04/572-3300, €62 d.) is full of friendly service and great accommodation, for not too much money. Located beside a turquoise-green stream and outfitted like an alpine hut, it's well worth the splash of cash. Ask for a room with a large balcony overlooking the mountains.

Food

Since most of the guesthouses in the area offer full board, there are relatively few restaurants around town. Anywhere you go, it's hard to go wrong ordering Bohinj trout if you like fish. In Ribčev Laz try **Center Pizzerija** (Ribčev Laz 50, tel. 04/572-3170, noon–10 P.M. daily, €10) for pizza as well as local fish. Just out of Ribčev Laz, **Planšar** (Stara Fužina 179, tel. 04/572-3095, 10 A.M.–8 P.M. Tues.–Sun., until 9 P.M. in summer, €12) is a small restaurant in the equally small village of Stara Fužina, serving superb local cheeses and hot, steaming plates of dumplings and stews. Even farther out of town is **Gostilna Rupa** (Srednja Vas 87, tel. 04/572-3401, 10 A.M.–midnight Tues.–Sun., €15), serving huge portions of meat and sauce-laden dishes in a folksy setting. There's a terrace next to a playground for kids.

Information and Services

The **tourist office** (Ribčev Laz 48, tel. 04/574-1122, www.bohinj.si, 8 A.M.–8 P.M. Mon.–Sat., 9 A.M.–7 P.M. Sun. July–Aug.; 8 A.M.–7 P.M. Mon.–Sat., 9 A.M.–3 P.M. Sun. Sept.–June) is located in Ribčev Laz.

Getting There and Around

The best way to get to Bohinj, about 25 kilometers southwest of Bled, is by car on the road 209 (signs for Bohinj are well marked). There are also buses that connect with Bled (40 minutes) and Ljubljana (2 hours). You'll also find good train connections with Bled (20 minutes), a scenic way to see the area. Contact the tourist offices in Bohinj or in Bled for more information.

KRANJSKA GORA

Kranjska Gora is the country's largest ski resort, with a charming little mountain-town center. Best suited for beginning or laid-back skiing, perfect for families, it also has a lot of warm-weather sports for the sunnier months.

The area has 20 different ski lifts plus lots of cross-country skiing. The **Kranska Gora Recreational Ski Center** (Borovška 103a, tel. 04/580-9400, www.kr-gora.si) is the town's ski lift operator and source for information, rentals, instruction, and more. There's even a kindergarten that serves as a camp/fun center for the kids while the parents tackle more difficult runs.

In the summer the ski center hosts summer sledding and tubing. There's also a bike park, which rents mountain bikes to use on the trails and obstacle courses made for heart-stopping rides. The summer activities are open from May to September.

Accommodations and Food

For budget accommodation, try the **Pr'Tatko Hostel** (Podkoren 72, tel. 031/479-087, www.prtatko.com, €13 per person), located in a turn-of-the-20th-century house, three kilometers from town.

The new **Grand Hotel Prisank** (Borovška cesta 93, tel. 04/588-4820, www.hit.si, €162 d., including breakfast) is a large full-service hotel with use of a nearby pool and spa. Its no-frills comfort and convenience to the center of town (and about 100 meters to the slopes) make it a great place for skiing holidays. The **Larix Hotel** (Borovška cesta 99, tel. 04/588-4100, www.hit.si, €170 d., including breakfast) is older, but its in-house pool and spa are great for recuperating tired leg muscles and it's extremely close to the slopes.

A small family-run hotel, the **Hotel Miklic** (Vitranška 13, tel. 045/881-635, www.hotelmiklic.com, €130 d., including breakfast) has large rooms (a bit on the 1980s side in decor) and a good restaurant for après-ski sustenance. It's a five-minute walk from the hotel to the center of town.

Papa Joe Razor (Borovška cesta 86, 9 A.M.–late daily, €10) is a good source of pizzas and light meals. After dinner, it's Kranjska Gora's party central, turning into more of a disco than a restaurant.

For the very hungry, the traditional **Gostilna pri Martinu** (Borovška cesta 61, tel. 04/582-0300, 10 A.M.–11 P.M. daily, €15) has sausages and meat and potato stews to satiate even the heartiest of appetites.

Getting There and Around

Bus service connecting Kranjska Gora with Bled (about 1.5 hours) and Ljubljana (2.5 hours) is very reliable. In the summer there are also good connections with Bovec (2 hours). Driving to Kranjska Gora from Ljubljana, take the E61 highway. Kranjska Gora is 85 kilometers from Ljubljana and 39 kilometers from Bled. Keep in mind that the road connecting Bovec and Kranjska Gora is often blocked by heavy snowfall in the winter, adding considerable traveling time between the two locations.

◖ BOVEC

The main attraction in Bovec is the **Soča River,** rushing and careening through the forested valley. The river is the best reason for sports enthusiasts to visit, particularly in spring and summer, when it's at its best for rafting and kayaking. Bovec is on the edge of **Triglav National Park,** criss-crossed with hiking and biking trails. The less adventurous should be sufficiently impressed by the river's almost surreal color—a bright blue or green that's rarely seen in nature.

You'll find maps of the surrounding bike and hiking paths at the **tourist office** (Trg Golobarskih Žrtev 8, tel. 05/384-1910, info@bovec.si, www.bovec.si, 9 A.M.–8 P.M. daily July–Aug., 9 A.M.–5 P.M. Mon.–Fri. and 9 A.M.–noon Sat.–Sun. rest of year). For high-quality mountain-bike rentals, try **Outdoor Freaks** (Klanc 9A, tel. 041/553-675, www.freakoutdoor.com).

For rafting and kayaking, **Soča Rafting** (Trg Golobarskih Žrtev 48, tel. 05/389-6200, www.socarafting.si) or **Alpe Šport Vančar** (Trg Golobarskih Žrtev 28, tel. 05/389-6350, www.bovecsport.com) should be able to hook you up with equipment and guides down the river. Alpe Šport Vančar also has canyoning and paragliding for the courageous traveler.

Accommodations and Food

It's hard to believe such a small place is home to two gems of overnight options. ◖ **Dobra Vila** (Mala vas 112, 05/389-6400, www.dobra-vila-bovec.com, €95 d.) is a funky little hotel with upscale theme rooms and super-friendly owners. Most of the rooms don't have bathtubs (just showers) though the rooms have DVD players and the hotel has a few English-language movies on hand for late-night entertainment.

The location of the ◖ **Pristava Lepena** (Lepena 2, tel. 05/388-9900, www.pristava-lepena.com, €66 per person) makes you wonder if you've somehow been beamed up to the local version of heaven. Sitting in the middle of rocky snow-capped mountains, about six kilometers east of Bovec, the unassuming little cottages vary in size and sleep 2–8 people, with discounts for weekly rentals. Each cottage has its own terrace and is pleasantly furnished but not likely to win any design awards. The complex has a pool, a sauna, and a very good restaurant. It is a slice of quiet, perfect relaxation. The Pristava Lepena is a great spot for dinner or lunch, particularly if the weather is good enough that you can sit on the terrace surrounded by the tranquil mountains.

For a quick meal in the center of Bovec, try the **Pizzerija Letni Vrt** (Trg golobarskih žrtev 1, tel. 05/389-6383, www.letni-vrt.com, 11 A.M.–10 P.M. Wed.–Mon., €12) for pizzas and meat and potato dishes.

Getting There and Around

Buses depart from Ljubljana to Bovec regularly, though it's a long trip, upwards of 3.5 hours. Buses also link Bovec with Kobarid (30 minutes). The bus stop is in front of the Pizzerija Letni Vrt. Bovec is about 120 kilometers northwest of Ljubljana. If you're traveling by car, be aware that during winter the Vršič pass is closed, meaning that you can't get to Bovec directly from Kranjska Gora, 35 kilometers to the north.

KOBARID

Kobarid is most famous for its bloody WWI battle between Austrian and German and Italian forces. Today, the quiet little town's **Kobariški muzej** (Kobarid Museum, Gregorčičeva 10, tel. 05/389-0000, www.kobariski-muzej.si, 9 A.M.–6 P.M. Mon.–Fri., 9 A.M.–7 P.M. Sat.–Sun., €4) has an interesting display about the battle, including a short video in English. The **Kobarid Historical Walk** (pick up a map at the Kobarid Museum) is a three-mile trek through multiple markers recounting details of the WWI battle. Even if you're not that into history the well-marked path itself is worth the jaunt, with lots of pretty, peaceful views to enjoy.

Accommodations and Food

Hotel Hvala (Trg svobode 1, tel. 05/389-9300, www.hotel-hvala.si, €51 d.) is a small family-run hotel. The rooms aren't anything special but the service is friendly, the place is very clean, and the restaurant is excellent. If you come for anything come for the freshwater fish, which is somewhat legendary—plenty of Italians cross the border just to eat here.

Information and Services

You can find more information about Kobarid and the surrounding area at the **tourist office** (Gregorčičeva 10, tel. 05/389-9200, www.kobarid.si, 9 A.M.–6 P.M. Mon.–Fri., 9 A.M.–7 P.M. Sat.–Sun.), located in the Kobarid Museum.

Getting There and Around

There are at least two buses from Ljubljana to Kobarid every day, which take about three hours. Several daily connections link Kobarid with Bovec (30 minutes). At least one daily connection makes getting to Idrija (2 hours) possible from the town. The drive northwest from Ljubljana is about 115 kilometers. During the winter, the Vršič pass is closed, obliterating the direct connection with Kranjska Gora and adding time to your journey if you're linking locations in the Julian Alps.

IDRIJA

This town is famous for three things: its mercury mine, its lace, and its fantastic hotel. Most people start at the hotel and then explore the mine and the lace on the side.

Women in Idrija have been making lace for 300 years. A presence in town since 1876, the **Čipkarska šola** (Lace-making School, Prelovčeva 2, tel. 05/373-4570, www.cipkarskasola.si, 10 A.M.–1 P.M. and 3–6 P.M. end of June to end of Aug., €2.50 per person) has a small exhibition of lace by students of the school as well as lace for sale, which makes a lovely souvenir.

The **mercury mine** (Kosovelova 3, tel. 05/377-1142, rudnikzs@siol.net, www.rzs-idrija.si, tours at 10 A.M. and 3 P.M. Mon.–Fri. and 10 A.M., 3 P.M., and 4 P.M. Sat.–Sun. or by arrangement, €6) is worth a visit. The oldest part of the mine, which dates from 1500, and an 18th-century underground chapel are open for visitors to see.

Accommodations and Food

Located in a 14th-century manor, the hotel ◖ **Kendov Dvorec** (Na Griču 2, tel. 05/372-5100, www.kendov-dvorec.com, €150 d.) is the town's main draw. The rooms are decorated with local antiques and Idrian lace and the terrace is superb. A meal in the manor's cozy restaurant is certainly worth the splurge.

Getting There and Around

Idrija is 55 kilometers west of Ljubljana. By car, the trip from Ljubljana takes about an hour. By bus, you can connect with Kobarid (2 hours), Bovec (1.5 hours), and Ljubljana (1.5 hours).

COASTAL SLOVENIA AND THE KARST REGION

Slovenia's tiny coast often gets overlooked by tourists, as well as most Slovenians, who usually head to Dalmatia and Istria for holidays. While not as grand as the Croatian coast, coastal Slovenia offers a fair amount of things to do. For nature lovers, there is a bird sanctuary, and for art lovers, stunning architecture and unique medieval frescoes. Coastline walking paths and winding cobblestone street–filled towns will satisfy those in search of a pretty view. Piran, with its Venetian-influenced atmosphere and architecture, is a favorite stop in this region.

The coast of Slovenia, much like Istria to the south, was ruled by the Venetians. The Italian influence is still strong, from the historic buildings to modern cuisine and even the language. Italian is still spoken as at least a second language by most of the region's natives.

The coast is fully booked during July and August, populated mostly by vacationing Italians.

Slightly inland from the coast is Slovene Istria, full of good wines and good food, particularly the wind-cured karst *pršut* the region is famous for, much like Croatian Istria to the south. The villages are interesting to explore, particularly Hrastovlje, whose church sports a haunting fresco of dancing skeletons celebrating death. Further inland you'll also find a network of stalactite-filled karst caves, from the caves at Postojna, the most famous, to the Škocjan caves, the most stunning. Another interesting detour is the Lipizzaner stud farm, where Vienna's famous team of majestic horses has been bred for centuries.

HIGHLIGHTS

◖ **Hrastovlje:** A simple church and its macabre *Dance of Death* fresco are worth the detour from Koper to this inland village (page 313).

◖ **Piran:** The pride of the Slovenian coast, the small historic town of Piran is beautiful, charming, and relatively unspoiled (page 315).

◖ **Škocjanske Jame:** These caves are smaller than the nearby Postojna Cave but much more impressive. Not just a bunch of stalactites and stalagmites, the caves feature a 300-meter-long gorge cut by a bright-green underground river (page 318).

◖ **Kobilarna Lipica:** The provenance of Vienna's famous Lipizzaner horses, this stud farm puts on performances and even gives lessons (page 319).

LOOK FOR ◖ TO FIND RECOMMENDED SIGHTS, ACTIVITIES, DINING, AND LODGING.

PLANNING YOUR TIME

Fitting in a thorough tour of coastal Slovenia only takes a few nights: two nights in a coastal town, likely Piran, and a day to explore Slovene Istria while on the way to the Škocjanske Jame and the Lipizzaner stud farm. Of course, you could always extend your tour or shorten it, spending one night on your way down from Ljubljana, taking in one of the coast's interior sights and another night on the coast, giving you a decent overview of the tiny region.

Keep in mind that you're just over the border from Italy, making a day trip to Trieste an easy jaunt for the day or even overnight.

The Coast

The small coast of Slovenia is heavily influenced by the countries that border it. Italy has loomed large in the region since it occupied this corner of Slovenia from World War I and into much of World War II. Italian replaced Slovenian in local schools, settlers from Italy were installed in the area, and Italian street signs appeared. Though Slovenian is today the language of choice, you'll still find that many locals speak Italian and the Italian community, descendants of the settlers, is a strong influence. Signs are still printed in both Italian and Slovenian and the Italian vibe is felt in everything from the architecture, which heralds from Venice's powerful past, to the cuisine.

The main cities on the coast are Koper, Izola, Piran, and Portorož. Koper and Izola both have charming old-town cores, though they find it hard to compete with the picturesque Piran. Portorož is unfortunately a town revolving around package-holiday hotels and loads of souvenir shops hawking T-shirts, beach towels, and plastic bric-a-brac.

KOPER

Koper is not the most charming of Slovenian coastal towns. Once an important harbor in the Venetian heyday, the city lost its position when the Austro-Hungarian Empire looked to other coastal towns for shipping. A port town with some great architecture from the 15th and 16th centuries, it's best used as a cheaper source of accommodation than other pricier coastal towns.

Sights

The old Venetian core is pretty, starting with the **Stolnica Marijinega vnebovzetja** (Cathedral of the Assumption, 7 A.M.–noon and 3–7 P.M. daily, free), a Romanesque structure with a Venetian Gothic facade on the town's main square, Titov trg. One of the oldest church bells in Slovenia hangs in its bell tower, dating from 1333.

On the other side of the square is the impressive 15th-century Venetian **Pretorska Palaca** (Praetorian Palace), once home of the town mayor. The looming building is a mishmash of Gothic and Renaissance features, and looks a bit more like a castle than a palace. A free tour of the palace is available by arrangement with the **tourist office** (Titov trg 3, tel. 05/664-6403, tic@koper.si, www.koper-tourism.si, 9 A.M.–8 P.M. Mon.–Sat., 9 A.M.–noon Sun. July–Aug., 9 A.M.–5 P.M. Mon.–Fri., 9 A.M.–noon Sat. Sept.–June).

The **Pokrajinski muzej** (Regional Museum, Kidriceva 19, tel. 05/663-3570, 8 A.M.–1 P.M. Mon.–Sat., €3), in an attractive 16th-century palace, has a few exhibits chronicling Koper's past, as well as a copy of the *Dance of Death* from the village of Hrastovlje.

Wine Road

Check with the Koper **tourist office** (Titov trg 3, tel. 05/664-6403, tic@koper.si, www

Malvazija, a white wine produced in the Koper area

.koper-tourism.si) about the Istrian wine road out of Koper, highlighting some of the area's wineries. Wine lovers will appreciate Slovene Istria's takes on Malvazija and Teran as well as the locally produced Muškat.

Accommodations and Food

The **Koper Hotel** (Pristaniška ulica 3, tel. 05/610-0500, www.terme-catez.si, €60 d.) has dated motel-like rooms, but the position on Koper's waterside promenade is not bad. This hotel is central, with no pool or spa, but guests can use the pool facilities at a sister hotel nearby. The **Hotel Convent** (Jadranska 25, Ankaran, tel. 05/663-7346, www.adria-ankaran.si, €100 d., including breakfast), four kilometers north in Ankaran, is a historic convent that has been renovated. The 24-room hotel's decor isn't what you'd call chic, but its clean freshness, hardwood floors, and beautiful public spaces make the hotel one of the best in the area. Ask for a room overlooking the bay. The **Gostilna "Za gradom"** (Kraljeva ulica 10, tel. 05/628-5504, noon–10 P.M. Tues.–Sat reservations recommended, €20) serves typical Istrian foods like *fuži* as well as lots of fresh fish. The **Ribič Inn** (Veliki trg 3, tel. 05/641-8313, call for hours, €25) has been serving guests for 130 years. The great daily fish is best enjoyed on the sea-view terrace.

Getting There and Around

Koper is 100 kilometers southwest of Ljubljana. Koper's bus station (Kolodvorska 11, tel. 05/639-5269) has lots of connections to other coastal towns such as Izola (15 minutes), Piran (30 minutes), and Portorož (30 minutes). A couple of daily connections (more in summer) link Koper with Ljubljana (2.5 hours), Postojna (1.5 hours), and Celje (4 hours). Train travel is also possible—the station (Kolodvorska 11, tel. 05/639-5263) links Koper with Ljubljana (2.5 hours) and Postojna (1.5 hours)—though connections are far less frequent than the bus.

The Big Red passenger boat (tel. 05/641-8310) runs from June through early September, connecting all the Slovenian ports of call including Piran, Koper, Izola, Portorož, and Ankaran.

◖ HRASTOVLJE

The nearby village of Hrastovlje is a beautiful detour from Koper. The 15th-century **Cerkev sveti Trojice** (Church of the Holy Trinity, generally open 9 A.M.–noon and 1–5 P.M. Wed.–Mon., otherwise ask for key from Rozana Rihter, tel. 031/432-231, free) is pretty in its simplicity and its setting, surrounded by vineyards. However, the most famous feature is the *Dance of Death* painted on the inside of the church walls. The Gothic fresco portrays people from all walks of life (a baby, a king, etc.) dancing with skeletons. Other church frescoes display scenes from the Bible. The location is listed as a UNESCO World Heritage site. There are only a few such death paintings in the region, making its rarity and macabre beauty all the more reason to visit the church.

Hrastovlje is 18 kilometers southeast of Koper. Driving from Koper, you'll take road 10, exiting at Črni Kal. From here follow road 208 toward Buzet in Croatia until you see the signs for Hrastovlje. There's a parking lot not far from the church. Trains also stop near Hrastovlje, but you should check current schedules for connections from Koper. Buses stop some eight kilometers away in Črni Kal.

IZOLA

A relaxed fishing village most of the year, Izola becomes a popular tourist destination in summer, frequented by a young and fairly artsy crowd. There's not too much to specifically do or see (the town's old walls were destroyed in the 19th century), but the old core has some pretty old churches and villas that are nice to gawk at. Most of the old town dates from the 15th and 16th centuries, built by Izola's powerful neighbors across the Adriatic, the Venetians. The **tourist office** (Sončno nabrežje 4, tel. 05/640-1050, tic.izola@izola.si, www.izola .si, 8 A.M.–7 P.M. Mon.–Fri., 8 A.M.–5 P.M. Sat.–Sun. July–Aug., 8 A.M.–7 P.M. Mon.–Fri., 9 A.M.–noon Sat. Sept.–June) has started a summer **Street Museum** program, which provides maps pointing out specific shops, art studios, and coffee shops to visit throughout the town. They eventually hope to add activities and presentations that connect with Izola's maritime traditions.

Accommodations and Food

Located in the nearby village of Korte, five kilometers south of Izola, **Youth Hostel Stara šola** (Korte 74, tel. 05/642-1114, www.hostel-starasola.si, €24 per person) opened in 2006 in a turn-of-the-20th-century schoolhouse. It's conveniently located near Koper, Izola, and Piran and makes a great base, particularly if you have a car.

On the waterfront in Izola's old town is the excellently located three-star **Hotel Marina** (Veliki trg 11, tel. 05/660-4100, www.hotel marina.si, €91 d.). The rooms offer basic decor, television, air-conditioning, and a mini-bar. The hotel grounds feature a nice spa with saunas and massages.

For casual dining in Izola, head to **Pizzerija Gušt** (Drevored 1. maja 5, tel. 041/675-953, 8 A.M.–midnight daily, €12) for pizza and

CIAO, ITALIA: SHORT TRIPS TO ITALY

The Slovenian coast is just over the border from Italy, making a trip to another country a tempting, and easy, possibility. **Trieste** is the closest large city, once the favored destination of Yugoslav citizens on shopping expeditions, looking for brands they couldn't buy in their own country. Fifteen years ago the city was filled with all the name-brand stores, but as many of those stores have opened in independent Slovenia, Croatia, and Bosnia, many of those in Trieste have gone out of business only to be replaced with a variety of Chinese discount stores. While Trieste is not the most charming, it is another country, and is linked by frequent bus and train connections as well

as day trips provided by local travel agency Kompas tours (www.kompas.si).

More attractive is a short trip to **Venice,** linked with Ljubljana by the fast new Casanova train that takes only four hours and travels once daily. From cities on the coast, the *Prince of Venice* (Obala 41, Portorož, tel. 05/617-8000, www.kompas.si) takes passengers on boat rides between Izola and Venice (daily departures Mar.-Oct., 2.5 hours each way), and included is a guided tour of Venice. Tickets can be purchased from Kompas travel agencies all over Slovenia. Venezia Lines (tel. 39-041/520-5473, www.venezialines.com, €89 round-trip ticket) connects Venice with Piran.

Istrian pasta dishes. For some of Izola's seafood, try **Parangal** (Sončno nabrežje 20, tel. 05/641-7440, 10 A.M.–midnight daily, €16), which also has a nice waterfront terrace.

Getting There and Around

Izola is 110 kilometers southwest of Ljubljana and six kilometers west of Koper. Buses connect Izola with Portorož (10 minutes), Koper (15 minutes), and Piran (20 minutes) every hour or so. At least one daily connection links the town with Ljubljana (2.5 hours). One of the best ways to get around is the Big Red passenger boat (tel. 05/641-8310), connecting all the Slovenian ports of call June–early September.

PORTOROŽ

This is Slovenia's busiest, and least attractive, seaside resort. Unless you're looking for the kind of place that attracts spring-breakers stateside (mainly with package hotels, cheap beer, and lots of nightclubs), you can feel free to skip this stop.

If you'd like to see what's under the water around Portorož, **Nemo Divers** (Laguna Bernardin, tel. 05/674-4198, www.nemo-divers .si) can hook you up with courses in scuba diving and waterskiing, as well as diving and waterskiing excursions and pedal boat and jet ski rentals.

Accommodations and Food

Though the **Grand Hotel Bernardin** (Obala 2, tel. 05/695-5104, www.h-bernardin.si, €230 d., including breakfast) is technically in Portorož, it's on the edge of town, making it a leisurely 10-minute walk to the much more charming town of Piran. The hotel is often billed as a five-star. Though the exterior spaces are solid four-star (even by international standards), the rooms are a bit small and dowdy, though immaculately clean. The hotel has restaurants, bars, a casino, a heated indoor swimming pool, and private beach as well as high-speed Internet and the use of a spa.

Getting There and Around

Portorož is 122 kilometers southwest of Ljubljana and six kilometers south of Izola. Buses have frequent connections to towns on the coast, such as Piran (5 minutes), Izola (10 minutes), and Koper (25 minutes). Less-frequent connections serve Postojna (2 hours) and Ljubljana (3 hours). The Big Red passenger boat (tel. 05/641-8310) runs June–early September and connects Piran, Koper, Izola, Portorož, and Ankaran.

It takes less than an hour to walk to Piran from town. You can also rent a bicycle or scooter from Atlas Express (Obala 55, tel. 05/674-6772).

© J. SKOK/SLOVENIAN TOURIST BOARD

Piran, the prettiest town on the Slovenian coast

◖ PIRAN

A medieval walled Venetian town, Piran is the prettiest city on Slovenia's coast. Filled with winding cobblestone streets, Venetian architecture, and a view of the lights of Trieste from the waterfront, Piran is mercifully unsullied by the tacky trappings of many seaside resorts.

Piran's history likely dates to a Greek settlement, before the Romans and the Slavs both inhabited the seaside town. However, it's the Venetians, who owned the town from the 13th to 18th centuries, who left an indelible mark on the architecture and personality of Piran.

Today the city is quickly being restored as old buildings are snatched up by EU citizens looking for vacation homes in the charming enclave.

Sights

The **Stolna Cerkev Sv Jurija** (Church of St. George, 11 A.M.–5 P.M. daily) takes center stage in the little town, peering down from the hilltop. Today it's a mostly baroque church, but the original structure dates from the 12th century.

Fans of classical music will appreciate the **Tartinijeva Hiša** (Tartini's House, Kajuhova 12,

tel. 05/663-3570, 9 A.M.–noon and 6–9 P.M. daily June–Aug., 11 A.M.–noon and 5–6 P.M. Mon.–Fri. Sept.–May, €2), the home of the 18th-century composer Giuseppe Tartini, with displays including his death mask and one of his violins.

The town's **Pomorski muzej Sergej Mašera** (Sergej Mašera Maritime Museum, Cankarjevo nabrežje 3, tel. 05/671-0040, www.pommuz-pi .si, 9 A.M.–noon and 3–6 P.M. Tues.–Sun. Sept.–June, 9 A.M.–noon and 6–9 P.M. Tues.–Sun. July–Aug., €3.50) has an interesting collection of model ships, navigational instruments, sailors' uniforms, and paintings. The museum also skims the surface of Piran's salt mining, from which it made its wealth.

Accommodations

Budget travelers will appreciate the exclusive location of **Youth Hostel and Garni Hotel Val** (Gregorčičeva 38a, tel. 05/673-2555, www .hostel-val.com, €25 per person), in the heart of the old town, even if the rooms are basics-only.

In another super old-town location, the six-room **Hotel Max** (Ulica 9. Korpusa 26, tel. 05/673-3436, €65 d.) has loads of character—just the sort of place you'd expect to stay in a charming seaside town like Piran. The 18th-century building means that rooms are on the small side (and it would have been nice if they'd used furnishings more fitting to the building), but the service is great and the rooms comfortable. Potential guests should be warned of the nearby bell tower, which rings every hour—a possible point of contention for light sleepers.

Food

The Lovrečič family owns two restaurants in Piran, **Pavel 1** (Gregorčičeva 3, tel. 05/674-7101, 11 A.M.–11 P.M. daily, €25) and **Pavel 2** (Kosovelova ulica 1, tel. 05/674-7102, 11 A.M.–11 P.M. daily, €30), known locally for reliable, good seafood and wine. **[Neptun** (Župančičeva 7, tel. 05/673-4111, noon–4 P.M. and 6 P.M.–midnight daily, €20) is a small restaurant specializing in grilled seafood. The ambience is cozy and the menu simple, mainly fish and potatoes, but always the best quality, fresh from the sea. Also try the **Ivo Inn** (Gregorčičeva 31, tel. 05/673-2233, call for hours, €25) with marina-side terrace dining.

Getting There and Around

Piran is 119 kilometers southwest of Ljubljana and three kilometers north of Portorož. The town is well connected by bus to Portorož (5 minutes), Izola (20 minutes), and Koper (30 minutes), with connections almost hourly during the day. There are a couple of daily connections with Postojna (2 hours) and Ljubljana (3 hours). If you're coming by car, parking in Piran can be an issue. The parking lot at Formace near the Grand Hotel Bernardin resort complex is a 15-minute walk, or take the free shuttle bus.

SEČOVLJE SALINA NATURE PARK

If you're interested in delving into the salt-mining tradition, the Sečovlje Salina Nature Park (Seča 115, tel. 05/672-1330, kpss@soline.si, www.kpss.si, 9 A.M.–6 P.M. daily Apr.–Oct., €2.50) features a small museum and a place where you can see salt-making in action. The salt pans date from the 9th century, so the park quite an interesting history. The marshlands park also has walking and biking routes for admiring the indigenous wildlife, such as the some 282 bird species that call the park home.

There is currently no public transport to the park. If you're driving, take the main Lucija-Sečovlje road headed to Croatia and follow the signs for Lera, a couple of kilometers south of Piran. There are two entrances to the park; the more convenient one is at Lera, where you can also rent bikes for just a few euros a day. Another fun way to see the park is to take a boat tour from Solinarka (tel. 031/653-682), which picks up from the Grand Hotel Bernardin resort at 9:45 A.M. and 4:15 P.M. daily from April through October.

The Karst Region

The Karst Region (Kras) is one of Slovenia's toughest, not only geographically, with its wind-swept rocky base, but also historically. The area was filled with partisans who were persecuted by the Nazis, their homes burned and their people thrown into concentration camps.

The area has a rough beauty and is really a don't-miss for gourmets, who should stop to sample the area's famous wind-cured hams and earthy Teran red wine.

The limestone plateau that gives the region its name is littered with caves. The two most impressive are the Postojnska Jama and the Škocjanske Jame. The Postojna cave is the more famous, but it's the smaller Škocjan cave that's really the must-see.

There aren't a lot of options for upscale accommodation in the area. If you're used to room service, it's probably best to stay in Ljubljana or one of the coastal towns and make the Kras a day trip.

THE BRDA REGION: A SLOVENIAN TUSCANY

© D. MLADENOVIĆ/SLOVENIAN TOURIST BOARD

Goriška Brda, one of the main towns of the hilly Brda region

In the far west of Slovenia, the region of Brda is a hilly area reminiscent of Tuscany, and almost throwing distance to Italy. It's also home to some excellent fruity wines and two well-marked wine routes including a few sightseeing stops and spots to eat as well. You can pick up maps from the **Brda tourist office** (Grajska cesta 10, Dobrovo, tel. 05/395-9594, tic@brda.si, www.brda.si).

It's worth pointing out two great wineries in the area. The first, **Kristančič** (Medana 1, tel. 05/395-9533, call for hours), in the village of Medana, is one of the area's largest private vineyards, with about 37 cultivated acres. Kristančič houses most all of its wines in stainless steel barrels, giving the wine a contemporary taste. His specialties are the very modern Manzoni, and the more traditional Tokaj, a white almond-flavored wine, and Cabernet Frank, a rich red best drunk when it's aged three to five years. Another respected local winemaker is the **Simčič family** (Ceglo 3b, tel. 05/395-9200, call for hours), in the village of Ceglo; the majority of their vineyards technically are across the Italian border. Their wines have won multiple regional awards. Don't miss their Sivi Pinot, Chardonnay, and Beli Pinot.

Reaching and exploring the Brda region is easiest by car. If you're driving, the region is south of Kobarid along the Italian-Slovenian border or north of Štanjel on the highway going through Nova Gorica. The main towns are Dobrovo, Šmartno, and Goriška Brda. Bus connections are possible but infrequent.

POSTOJNSKA JAMA
Postojna Cave

Postojnska Jama (tel. 05/700-0100, www.posto jnska-jama.si, visits every hour 9 A.M.–5 P.M. May, June, and Sept., every hour 9 A.M.–6 P.M. July–Aug., 10 A.M., noon, 2 P.M., and 4 P.M. Apr. and Oct., 10 A.M., noon, and 3 P.M. Jan.–Mar. and Nov.–Dec., €19) is a network of 23 kilometers of underground rock formations that are millions of years old. Though the first recorded visit to the caves was in the 13th century, it wasn't until the 19th century when the caves became a staple on the tourist map. The Postojna cave is especially famous for its "human fish," a colorless lizard-type animal that lives for up to 60 years.

The guided tour, which takes a little over an hour, combines a train ride with a bit of walking. Towards the end of the tour, you can also choose to visit the cave's Human Fish Museum, exhibiting a few of the captive animals as well as some related displays, for a couple of extra euros.

Postojna is 45 kilometers south of Ljubljana. Buses from Ljubljana (1 hour) and Koper (1 hour) as well as trains from Ljubljana (1.5 hours) and Koper (1.5 hours) connect with the village of Postojna. The caves are a 1.5-kilometer walk from the village.

☾ ŠKOCJANSKE JAME
Škocjan Caves

At Škocjanske Jame (Škocjan 2, tel. 05/708-2110, www.park-skocjanske-jame.si, visits every hour 10 A.M.–5 P.M. daily June–Sept., 10 A.M., 1 P.M., and 3:30 P.M. daily Apr., May, and Oct., 10 A.M. and 1 P.M. daily plus 3 P.M. Sun. Nov.–Mar., €14), a UNESCO World Heritage site, a 1.5-hour tour takes you through almost art-like stalactites before unveiling the pièce de résistance—a 146-meter-high gorge with a bright-green river rushing below. Certainly some of the world's most beautiful caves, they were discovered in the 2nd century B.C., though it wasn't until the 19th century when scientists began exploring them in earnest.

The tour begins with the Silent Cave, filled with giant stalactites and stalagmites, and continues to the Great Hall, a mammoth space whose ceiling looms 30 meters above. Following is the Murmuring Cave, which feels like you've entered an adventure movie, followed by the Gours, some pretty rock pools, out to the Schmidlova dvorana (Schmidl hall, the last part of the cave), and the exit.

The Škocjan caves are 25 kilometers southwest of Postojna and 75 kilometers southwest of Ljubljana. By car, take the A1 from Ljubljana and exit at Divača. Then follow the brown signs for the caves. If you're relying on public transport, take a train to Divača, where a well-marked three-kilometer path will take you to the cave entrance.

ŠTANJEL

At first glance nearby Štanjel is low on history, much of the village having been damaged in World War II. However, artists have been slowly taking over the town with their studios and the town is the perfect getaway for those who like to get off the tourist track, relaxing with a leisurely lunch or perusing the market, held the third Sunday of every month. The **Štanjel Grad** castle has a gallery of local graphic artist and painter Lojze Spacal. The castle also houses a small bar that sells light snacks and a souvenir shop. You can get more information from the **tourist office** (tel. 05/769-0056, www.komen.si, 11 A.M.–4 P.M. Mon., Wed., and Sat.) located near the castle.

Accommodations and Food

For budget travelers, the **Pliskovica Youth Hostel** (Pliskovica 11, tel. 05/764-0250, www.hostelkras.com, €12 per person), a few kilometers southwest of Štanjel, is an old Karst farm and full of local flavor.

Osmica Kmetija Kosmina (Brje pri Komnu, tel. 05/766-7240, 9 A.M.–1 A.M. daily, €15), about 12 kilometers southeast of Štanjel, is a local, rustic place with huge helpings of the region's famous cuisine—*pršut,* homemade sausages and cheeses, and earthy Teran wine.

Getting There and Around

Štanjel is 100 kilometers southwest of Ljubljana and 24 kilometers northwest of the Škocjan caves. A couple of daily buses connect the village of Divača with Štanjel, taking about 40 minutes.

LIPICA

The town of Lipica was made famous by its horses, the famed Lipizzaners of Austria's Spanish Riding School.

◖ Kobilarna Lipica
Lipica Stud Farm

The Kobilarna Lipica (Lipica 5, tel. 05/739-1708, www.lipica.org, performances 3 P.M. Tues., Fri., and Sun. Apr.–Oct. with additional performances on public holidays, €14–18) was established by the bishop of Trieste and purchased in 1580 by the Austrian archduke Karl II. The Lipizzaner breed is a mixture of indigenous horses with Spanish and Arabian lines. The white horses, which are grey and black at birth and turn white over time, are a majestic breed, whose muscular frame made them a favorite of the Austrian royalty. It's said that the rough karst landscape creates the horses' tough hooves.

If you can, see a display of the Classic Riding School, where the highly trained horses appear to be dancing rather than galloping; it's truly a don't-miss. The horses aren't carted off to Vienna anymore but perform locally for visitors. There are daily pony rides for children and riding classes weekly for novices as well as more experienced riders.

Food

The **Gostilna Gombač** (Lokev 165, tel. 05/767-0466, 11 A.M.–10 P.M. Thurs.–Mon., €20) is a good place for dinner after a visit to the Lipica Stud Farm. The house specialty is roast game.

Getting There and Around

Lipica is 80 kilometers southwest of Ljubljana. There are no buses or trains to Lipica. The closest hub is the village of Sežana; buses and trains take about two hours from Ljubljana.

COASTAL SLOVENIA

BACKGROUND

The Land

CROATIA
Geography

Croatia covers a little more than 55,000 square kilometers. The topography within its borders swings from fairly flat and fertile to rocky mountains and hilly craggy karst to the sea, where islands dot the Adriatic.

The country can be broken down into three major geographical regions. The verdant fields of Slavonia and the Baranja become increasing hilly but just as green as they reach Zagreb and Zagorje in the northwestern part of the country. The coastal regions are isolated by very mountainous and little-developed regions of the Gorski Kotar. The hinterlands of the Adriatic are barely habitable mounds of karst rock. The sea is mostly pebbly, sometimes rocky, and filled with islands that vary from forested to almost barren.

The islands are one of the features that make the country special—it has over 1,200 and most are uninhabited. The coastline, while only 1,777 kilometers in length if measured point to point, has so many coves and indentions that the actual length covers over 4,000 kilometers.

Climate

Inland Croatia and its coast vary greatly. The interior experiences a continental climate with cold, wet winters and increasingly hot

Croatia's varied landscape includes the waterfalls of mountainous Plitvice Lakes National Park.

summers. The coast is hot and dry in the summer and mild, often rainy, in winter.

Winds on the coast have a significant effect on daily life. In the summer the *maestral,* a breeze blowing over the sea, keeps the temperatures down and is responsible for Croatia's image as a great sailing destination. In winter the southeasterly *široko* brings in warm air, sometimes creating cloudy days, but it's the northeasterly *bura* (capable of annoying at any time of year, but most vicious in winter) that never ceases to frustrate locals. Its gusts can knock cars off bridges and make sailing dangerous. The *bura* is also responsible for plenty of cold bursts of air, unwelcomed by any sun-loving Dalmatian.

Environmental Issues

Because Croatia was relatively low on industry in years past, the water and air have remained relatively unpolluted and most of the forest, which covers close to a quarter of the country, is thick and green. However, acid rain and logging are constantly threatening the forests,

eating away at them year by year. And virtually every year Dalmatia's dry climate couples with the wind and a too-soon-discarded cigarette to burn acres and acres of Croatia's forests. It's estimated that the fires have destroyed about 10 percent of the forests in the last two decades.

Overfishing of the Adriatic has been a constant problem, though the Croatian fishing fleet is not entirely to blame as it represents only a small portion of the fishing capacity. The fishing rights are shared with other nations and with an ever-increasing number of poachers using the waters illegally.

Though Croatia has emissions laws, it's obvious that its application is often less than rigorous, provided that the car owner is willing to provide a small payment to the friendly technician at the annual check-up.

Flora and Fauna

Near the eastern border of Croatia you'll find Kopački Rit, a wetlands nature preserve filled with the area's indigenous wildlife including cormorants, herons, lots of fish, wild pigs, and deer. The Lonjsko Polje near the town of Sisak is the place to go to see the hundreds of storks that populate the area.

Heading toward the coast, the mountainous Gorski Kotar is marked by dense forests of maple, beech, fir, and spruce. A number of deer, brown bears, and lynx populate the region.

The Krka National Park is home to a rare sea otter, herons, geese, and ducks as well as several nonpoisonous snake species, like the leopard snake. Paklenica National Park has two poisonous varieties of snakes as well as many large birds like peregrine falcons, hawks, and owls.

On the islands, Cres is important as a refuge for the giant griffon vulture and most all the islands are home to wild herbs that grow out of the rocks. The coast is also known for maquis and lavender as well as juniper, olive, and fig trees, which all flourish in the dry windswept climate of the seaside region.

The Velebit Range boasts the greatest range of plant life, with over 2,500 species, including the endangered edelweiss.

SLOVENIA
Geography
Nestled between the Alps, the Adriatic Sea, and the Pannonian Plain, Slovenia only covers slightly more than 20,000 square kilometers but packs in a substantial variety within the small space. Most of the country is Alpine, with plenty of snow-covered peaks and green valleys. Close to half of the country's population lives in the chilly Alpine area. The coastal region is made up of sunny vine-covered hills and karst rock (home to close to 1,000 caves) while the Pannonian Plain is a fertile region dotted with thermal springs.

Climate
Due to the vast differences in geography, the small country of Slovenia is home to three distinct climates. The Alpine region is bitterly cold and snowy in winter and relatively mild during the summer. Still, you'll need a cozy sweater around the regions of Bled, Bohinj, and the Triglav National Park even at the height of summer. The plains are more continental, with cold and wet winters and warm to hot summers. The coastal climate is sub-Mediterranean, with hot, dry summers and sometimes rainy winters.

Environmental Issues
Slovenia is the third most-forested country in the European Union, with close to 60 percent of its land covered in thick forests. Still, acid rain has become a serious threat to forests along the coast and the Sava River has been polluted by industrial waste.

Flora and Fauna
Due to its diverse geography and climates, Slovenia is home to a wide range of flora and fauna. The interior of the country is dominated by beech and oak trees with pine, fir, and spruce becoming more common as the altitudes reach higher in the Alpine region. You'll find the ever rarer edelweiss and the Alpine ibex, a goatlike wild animal.

Most of Slovenia is Alpine.

Slovenia is also home to marmots, deer, and wild boars, and its rushing rivers and streams are filled with trout. The marble trout, however, is the only indigenous type of trout.

In the eastern section of the country, towards Hungary, you'll find the white stork and a number of migrating birds.

The karst region is best suited to plants that flourish in the Mediterranean climate, particularly olive trees and wild herbs.

History

ANCIENT CIVILIZATION

The first proven inhabitants of Croatia were a type of Neanderthal, the Krapina man, whose bones were discovered in a cave in Zagorje at the turn of the 20th century. A better description might have been Krapina men and women, since over 800 bones were found at the site; they were x-rayed and dated at around 100,000 years old.

But the Zagorje is not the only region to have been settled by ancient peoples. There is evidence of neolithic tribes on Hvar, and in Slavonia the discovery of the famous Vučedol Pigeon, a ritual vessel made of pottery, shows that an early culture lived near Vukovar 4,500 years ago.

The Illyrian people, a group of tribes approximately covering the geography of the former Yugoslavia, were the predominant culture from the first millennium B.C. to the 4th century B.C. They built fortresses and monuments, some of which survive today, with their iron tools and established cities along Croatia's coast and throughout Slovenia. Friezes found in Ljubljana depict early sacrifices, battles, and sporting events.

EARLY HISTORY

The Greeks showed up on the Croatian coast in the 6th century B.C., setting up trading posts like Issa (modern-day Vis) up and down the Adriatic. They often battled with the Illyrians, who proved to be their downfall despite their own waning power. In the 3rd century B.C., the Illyrian King Agron together with the Macedonians battled the Greeks, and Agron's widow, Queen Teuta, attacked their weakened forces again. The Romans then swooped in,

taking control, and by the 2nd century B.C. they had gained the predominant foothold in the region.

Once A.D. rolled around, the Romans held all of Dalmatia and their inland territories stretched all the way to Hungary. The Romans set up cities like Salona, which became the regional capital, and took over the Illyrian Jadera (modern-day Zadar). In Istria Parentium (Poreč) and Polensium (Pula), as evidenced by its large amphitheater, were important centers as well. In Slovenia the major cities were Emona (Ljubljana), Celeia (Celje), and Poetovio (Ptuj).

The Adriatic coast of Croatia became important for Rome not only strategically, but as a source of soldiers who were absorbed into the Roman army. The region produced two emperors for the empire—Diocletian (whose giant palace still stands in Split) and Constantine.

By the 5th century, the Romans' power was slipping and Visigoth, Hun, Lombard, Avars, and finally Slavs started eating away at the empire until Rome's hold on Dalmatia officially ended in the 7th century. Its refugees fled to Spalato (Split) and Ragusa (Dubrovnik) for safety.

The Slavs, from which modern-day Croats and Slovenes descended, were mainly agricultural people until the 7th century, when they came to the region and starting fighting along with the Avars. Some historians believe they were encouraged by the Byzantine Empire to serve as a balance for the Avar tribes, though it seems their loyalties waffled between both groups.

MIDDLE AGES

It was Christianity that held Croatia together in the early Middle Ages. The Franks had fought their way down into Dalmatia by the 9th century, spreading their beliefs with them. The result was a link with the church at Rome that kept Dalmatia tied to the Pannonian provinces even though Dalmatia remained largely controlled by the Byzantine Empire.

In the 7th century tribes in Slovenia were united under Samo's Tribal Union. Though the union disintegrated when the Slav leader Samo died, it made a fairly easy transition to a Slavic principality known as Carantania, which came under Frankish rule.

The 10th-century King Tomislav was the first ruler to officially join the inland and coastal regions of Croatia. He had a lot of things going for him, mainly approval from Rome and the military power to defeat the Hungarians when they attacked in 924. Tomislav ushered in a time of peace and stability for the country, though by the late 11th century the power to keep Croatia independent was waning. Three kings died without an heir, opening the door for Ladislas of Hungary (brother-in-law of one of those kings, Zvonimir) to take over by 1102.

The takeover of Croatia by Hungary changed the economic and political landscape of the country. Since towns like Varaždin and Zagreb were conveniently located on the route between Hungary and the sea, a flourish of activity and prosperity occurred in northern Croatia. This prosperity was mostly felt by the land owners and aristocracy, however, as the feudal system kept most citizens under its thumb.

A huge blow to the area came in 1242 when the Tatars attacked. Though King Bela IV managed to escape and the Tatars were thrown out, the cities attacked suffered substantial damage, with many medieval buildings and monuments lost during the fighting.

On the coast, Dalmatia had been flip-flopping rulers since the 11th century, but as the centuries passed most of the fights were between the Venetians and the Hungarians for control of the seaside provinces. In the end the Venetians won, though not through military might: They bought Dalmatia from a frightened King Ladislas of Naples for 100,000 ducats at the beginning of the 15th century.

Though Venice's rule did result in some beautiful Italian architecture, the period was by and large an unfortunate one for Dalmatia and Istria. The Venetians clear-cut forests for their own use (once they were gone and the soil eroded, trees never grew back), banned trade with anyone other than themselves (driving down prices), and invested precious little in the provinces as a whole. By the end of the 18th century the people were not only poor, but starving, living off whatever they could manage to pluck from the land.

WAR WITH THE OTTOMANS

For inland Croatia, the Ottomans created havoc between the late 15th and late 17th centuries. The Ottomans had already moved into Bosnia by the 1450s and the Croatians knew it was only a matter of time before they advanced further. In 1493, the time had come, though even a strong showing of Hungarian and Croatian forces at Krbavsko polje (near Plitvice) couldn't stop them. Though the coast was now open to periodic raids by the Turks, the worst was suffered inland, as they burned towns in their way, capturing or killing residents.

When the Hungarian king was killed in a battle with the Ottomans, everyone looked to Austria, where Archduke Ferdinand I took over the Hungarian empire and tried to help the Croats. But even he wasn't much help. At the end of the 16th century only land around Zagreb, Karlovac, and Varaždin remained under Austro-Hungarian control; Venice had managed to retain the coast.

The Hapsburgs took advantage of the refugees, known as Vlachs, who had fled Serbia for northern Croatia, by using them to settle the lands south of Zagreb and protect the land from invasion. The tide started to turn in 1571 when the Ottomans were defeated at the Battle of Lepanto. Over the next 120 years, cities seized by the Ottomans gradually returned to Hapsburg control and in 1699 the Treaty of Sremski Karlovci officially erased any claims of the Ottomans on Croatian and Hungarian lands.

NAPOLEON AND THE AUSTRO-HUNGARIAN EMPIRE

The 18th century had managed to maintain the status quo, more or less, in Dalmatia, Istria, and inland Croatia, but Napoleon was about to change the political landscape of Croatia substantially.

When Venice fell to Napoleon in 1797, he gave Dalmatia to the Austrian empire, but by 1808 the entire Croatian coast and Slovenia were under French control, dubbed the Illyrian provinces, and even given a French governor, Marshal Marmont.

The short period under Napoleonic rule was marked by a return of the Slavic language and infrastructure the coastal provinces sorely needed. Napoleon's aim had been to strengthen the provinces—including Slovenians, Croatians, and Serbs—to form an identity separate from their ruling forces.

This idea was somewhat squashed with the Treaty of Vienna in 1815, when the Hapsburg empire laid claim to all of Slovenia and Croatia, putting Croatia under the jurisdiction of Hungary. But the nationalist ideas had taken on much more of a life than the new government would have liked, with the Croatian writer Ljudevit Gaj heralding a new Illyrian movement. The Austrians and the Hungarians thought the pro-Slav sentiment was getting out of hand in the mid-19th century, and even banned the use of the word Illyria.

Croatians saw the 1848 revolution of Hungary against Austria as an opportunity for more independence. The Croatian Sabor bargained that in exchanged for sending the military forces under Ban Josip Jelačić in support of the emperor, Hungary would no longer have control over Croatia and the country would maintain more autonomy. Though Jelačić and his men's efforts did help to end the revolution in Vienna, they did not bring the war with the Hungarians to a victory (in the end it was the Russians who came to Austria's aid). After the threat was gone, Austria reneged on its promises and shut its doors to the idea of more Croatian independence.

The bitterness that resulted was actually one of the undercurrents that formed Yugoslavia. Led by the charismatic Bishop Strossmayer, the Illyrian movement, by then called the National Party, advanced in its ideas that all Slavs are the same, not different. They theorized that the Austrians magnified their differences to keep them weaker.

WORLD WAR I

The beginning of World War I brought a period of uncertainty for Croatians and Slovenians who figured that once again they'd be pawns in a much larger game. They initially supported the Austro-Hungarian Empire, but more and more defeats made the effort look hopeless. Before they waited for larger countries to decide their fate, they brokered a deal for the formation of a Slav state (called the National Council of Slovenes, Croats, and Serbs), with its headquarters in Belgrade. The Croats knew they would have to choose between Italy and Serbia, and Serbia was their preference. Italy quickly pounced upon Istria, claiming it as their territory.

The democracy was short-lived, however. The laws and power fell heavily in favor of Serbia, which was the strongest, both politically and militarily, of the three. Croat Stjepan Radić stood in opposition, pushing for a federal democracy, but the Serbs quickly squashed these hopes; Radić and two Croatian members of parliament were fatally shot in the national parliament in Belgrade in 1928, and King Aleksander declared the country a royal dictatorship.

WORLD WAR II

Killing Radić and instituting a royal dictatorship created several angry groups who fled the country but planned to regain independence by any means. Among these was the Ustaše Movement, led by Ante Pavelić. During Pavelić's exile in Italy, Mussolini recognized an opportunity to reassert Italian interests in Croatia through his organization. Though Pavelić claimed he and his group were protecting Croatian interests, he readily agreed to cede vast territories of Croatia, including ports like Rijeka in Istria and many Croatian islands, in return for Mussolini's support.

Other parties were organizing their own coups, such as the HSS (Croatian Peasants' Party), led by Vlatko Maček, the successor of the unfortunate Radić, and the Communist Party of Yugoslavia (KPJ), heavily supported by Moscow and led by Josip Broz Tito from 1937.

The outbreak of World War II provided the perfect opportunity for the competing political forces to fight it out. Germany invaded Yugoslavia on April 6, 1941. Pavelić and his fascist cronies used the Axis occupation of Yugoslavia as a chance to gain political control and rid themselves of their enemies, who included scores of innocent Serbs, Jews, and Roma as well as Croatian political opponents. Over the next four years, some 150,000 lives (according to the most well-researched estimates, though estimates range from 30,000 to one million) were lost in the concentration camp at Jasenovac.

Tito's National Liberation Partisan groups, which included Croatians, Serbs, Slovenians, and other nationalities, were fighting the Germans and Italians and gained strong support from the Allies, who saw them as the most significant opponent to the fascists. Tito set up Partisan governments wherever he maintained a victory, and when he marched into Belgrade in the fall of 1944 he was declared prime minister. The Ustaše fled Zagreb in 1945 when Germany surrendered, leading the way to a unified southern Slav state—including Slovenia, Croatia, Macedonia, Serbia, Montenegro, and Bosnia and Herzegovina—under Josip Broz Tito.

YUGOSLAVIA UNDER TITO

It quickly became apparent that Yugoslavia was an authoritarian state. Until the 1980s Tito's heavy-handed rule opposed any hint of anti-government sentiment, obliterated political parties, and kept an iron thumb over the Catholic Church. Tito broke with Stalin in 1948, and Yugoslavia gained freedoms that other Eastern Bloc countries didn't have, like the ability to have passports and travel.

Croatian and Slovenian sentiment towards Belgrade was already waning by the 1960s. The two republics were significantly more

JOSIP BROZ TITO

Josip Broz was born in the village of Kumrovec on May 7, 1892, in the Croatian Zagorje. He was one of 15 children, and left school at the age of 12.

He fought in World War I, drafted into the Austro-Hungarian army. While fighting on the Russian front against the Serbs he was captured and thrown in prison. While in prison he learned Russian and began to embrace communist ideals. When Czar Nicholas II abdicated, Tito was released and immediately headed to fight with Lenin's army, for which he was thrown into prison again until the communists took power later that year.

Returning to Croatia in 1920, he joined the Communist Party of Yugoslavia and by the early 1930s he was one of the party's stars. It was during this period he adopted the nickname Tito. One of the many versions of how he got the name is that it came from the phrase "*Ti to!*" meaning "You [do] that!" – an allusion to his brusque manner. During World War II, Tito's Partisans fought against the Germans, the Ustaše, and the royalist Chetniks. The Partisans' success in tying down significant numbers of German forces helped them win Allied support and in 1945 Tito became dictator of Yugoslavia. Tito broke with Stalin in the late 1940s, which allowed the Yugoslav peoples more freedom than any of the Eastern Bloc countries. However, Tito's reign was heavy-handed, and anyone uttering a word against the government or Tito was severely punished.

Tito died in Ljubljana on May 4, 1980, slightly more than a decade before the country he'd ruled fell apart.

prosperous, yet their gains were doled out to the central government in Serbia and the poorer republics. Also, Belgrade kept a heavy number of Serbs in Croatian and Slovenian government and police positions, ostensibly as a program to aid the disadvantaged.

In 1971, Croatians launched a political movement known as the Croatian Spring. The leaders of the movement came from within Tito's Communist Party—high-ranking officials and the intelligentsia made up a great portion of the movement's supporters. The movement was striving for more autonomy for the republic and more personal freedoms. What they got was a swift crackdown by Tito, who jailed dozens and drove many into exile, drastically reducing the influence of the Croatians in the central and regional governments. However, the event was an indication of the underlying currents in Yugoslavian politics, and it pointed to the direction in which the country was headed once Serb dominance eroded through the weakening of the Eastern bloc and the lack of economic progress.

BREAKING FREE

After Tito's death in 1980, the country was still left with his legacy of debts. Inflation skyrocketed and the economy was in a state of severe crisis.

The Slovenians were the first to take the lead toward freedom, moving to multi-party elections and calling for changes to the Yugoslav constitution in favor of more independence. Slovenia's lead was followed by Croatia, which was still reasserting itself after the purges following the Croatian Spring movement.

In January 1990, at the meeting of the Yugoslav League of Communists, the Slovenians called for autonomy for each republic. The Serbs rejected the idea and the Slovenians and Croatians walked out of the room in defiance. The Croatian Democratic Union (HDZ), the first non-communist party in Croatia, was formed in May 1989 under the leadership of Franjo Tuđman. The party was vehemently anti-Yugoslav and called for secession. The not-even-a-year-old party won the elections by a landslide in the spring of 1990. In June 1991, both the Republic of Croatia and the Republic of Slovenia declared themselves independent.

The Serbs in Krajina, in the far east of Croatia, immediately claimed the Krajina as their own and intense fighting broke out—the start of what is known in Croatia as the Homeland War. Slovenia was also engaged in some skirmishes, though for them the war was over in 10 days. For Croatia it was a different story. Over the next three months, Croatia lost a quarter of its territory to Serb forces, Vukovar was sieged and eventually leveled to the ground, and the UN imposed an arms embargo on all of former Yugoslavia, further disadvantaging the severely underarmed Croatia, already in a desperate situation.

The tide began to turn for Croatia in 1992, when the European Commission (forerunner of the EU) formally recognized the country. The UN plan was to maintain the borders of the former federal republics in accordance with the Constitution of Yugoslavia. However, for years the plan went nowhere, as local Serbs supported by Slobodan Milošević and the Serb-controlled Yugoslav Army rejected the implementation of the UN resolutions.

When the attention turned to the atrocities in Bosnia-Herzegovina, Croatia managed to get arms and gradually make headway until they reclaimed Maslenica, near Zadar, and entered Slavonia in 1995.

There were a number of instances in which abandoned Serb homes and villages were burned and horrific attacks on some Serbs who stayed behind were carried out. Croatia had agreed, however, to protect human rights and cooperate with the International War Crimes Tribunal, so following the end of the war in 1995, Croatia eventually agreed to keep their commitments after receiving pressure from the international community. Croatia extradited a number of its citizens accused of war crimes to stand trial.

AFTERMATH OF THE WARS OF INDEPENDENCE

Slovenia had a quick recuperation from their short war and has already entered the European Union and adopted the euro.

Croatia has had a somewhat harder time, hampered by the decisions of Franjo Tuđman, which stifled economic growth and slowed the way for entry into the EU.

The war-torn regions of Karlovac, Maslenica, and especially eastern Slavonia were devastated in the war and economic recovery has been slow. It has taken most Serb refugees some time to reclaim homes and land, though Croatia finally has not only allowed their return but has also rebuilt residences destroyed during the war.

Government and Economy

GOVERNMENT
Croatia
ORGANIZATION

Croatia's constitution was adopted on December 22, 1990, creating a parliamentary democracy. Subsequent changes have weakened the office of presidency so that it is more of a ceremonial position than one with much power.

The executive branch consists of the president and the prime minister. The president is elected by popular vote for a five-year term, while the prime minister is appointed by the majority party in Parliament. The legislative branch is split into the Županijski Dom (House of Districts) and the Zastupnički Dom (House of Representatives), both comprised of officials who are elected by popular vote (with the exception of five members of the House of Districts who are appointed by the president) and serve a four-year term. The judicial branch is made up of the Supreme Court, a body of judges appointed by a council elected by the House of Representatives.

POLITICAL PARTIES

Croatia has 18 political parties, though only three truly vie for top position: the Social Democratic Party (SDP), the Croatian People's Party (HNS), and the Croatian Democratic Union (HDZ). Other significant parties include the Istrian Democratic Party, one of the strongest regional parties; the Croatian Party of Rights (HSP), a far-right-leaning party; and historical parties like the Croatian Peasants' Party (HSS).

Slovenia
ORGANIZATION

Slovenia's constitution was adopted on December 23, 1991, and the country is a parliamentary democracy. The executive branch of the Slovenian government is made up of the president, elected for a five-year term by popular vote, and a prime minister, generally chosen from the majority party in Parliament. The legislative branch is made up of the Državni zbor (National Assembly) with 90 members elected for a four-year term. 88 members are elected by popular vote and 2 members are elected by ethnic minorities.

POLITICAL PARTIES

Slovenia has a multi-party system and over a dozen political parties. The strongest parties tend to be the Slovenian Democratic Party (SDS) and the Liberal Democracy of Slovenia (LDS). However, the country has several special-interest parties for groups such as pensioners, youth, and environmentalists.

ECONOMY
Croatia

During its years as part of Yugoslavia, Croatia enjoyed a position as one of the country's most prosperous and industrious republics. Industries in shipbuilding, aluminum, chemicals, and oil refining thrived. When Croatia became independent in the early 1990s, the country had an excellent opportunity to make use of its industries and attract foreign companies who would invest money in the new country.

Somehow, Tuđman's team managed to sell off factories and industries for paltry sums to friends and cronies who sucked them dry of any cash, stripped their assets, and sold off their real estate holdings. This business model reduced the tax base and left the industry in dust, worthless to any buyer. The rampant corruption significantly limited the amount of foreign investments, in spite of the relatively high level of economic development. Instead, the companies expanding their operations to Eastern Europe largely chose to set up local operations elsewhere in the region, severely stifling Croatia's growth.

Tourism was an important industry for Croatia, particularly in the 1960s and 1970s, though the war in the '90s all but obliterated it for several years. In the early 1990s you could visit Trogir and Split without encountering any other tourists except a few straggling UN personnel. Many tourists were still afraid to return in the late '90s, even though the war had ended in 1995. Around 2000 things started to really take off, with islands like Hvar and destinations like Dubrovnik gracing the pages of more than a few European and American glossies. Tourism reached a peak in 2007, with a decrease in 2008, especially in high-priced destinations like Hvar. Zadar and Zagreb were busier, however, probably a reflection of tourists seeking a less crowded and less expensive city yet to be "discovered."

The average net monthly salary in Croatia is around 5,000Kn; in Zagreb it is somewhat higher, around 6,000Kn monthly. Unemployment is around 14 percent, much lower than in the mid-1990s when it topped 20 percent. Work in construction, brought on by a boom in real estate, has helped move these figures lower and lower.

Slovenia

Slovenia was, along with Croatia, the most successful of the republics in the former Yugoslavia. Exports from Slovenia made up one-third of exports from Yugoslavia. When Slovenia became independent in 1991, it made a swift and easy transition into the European economy. Slovenia became a member of the European Union in 2004 and adopted the euro as its currency in 2007. Unemployment is around 8 percent.

While real GDP grew by 6.8 percent in 2007, the fastest since independence, there was a slowdown in 2008, with figures for the year dropping back to around 5 percent. Inflation has been quite high since Slovenia became a part of the Eurozone and 2008 figures are likely to be around 6 percent. One of the major problems for Slovenia's economy in the future is dealing with an aging population; a low birth rate is doing little to alleviate the country of the issue.

Even though Slovenia is quite green, agriculture makes up very little of the country's GDP. Many products farmed are consumed locally, including the region's wines, since most of the producers are too small to export effectively. Lead and zinc mining, which were once vital to the country's economy, have all but died out. Today, Slovenia is mostly involved in mid- to high-tech manufacturing.

Services make up a large part of the Slovenian economy and tourism is increasingly becoming one of the sector's most important forces. Ljubljana has become a favorite destination of the travel columns for its charm and Prague-without-the-crowds vibe. Bled and Bohinj also draw their share of travelers, while the country's ski slopes attract a mostly local crowd, along with weekenders from neighboring Croatia.

Though the country has done better with foreign investors than neighboring Croatia, the privatization process in Slovenia was often marred by corruption, with more than a few political-insider purchases. Outside investment is still quite low for an EU nation. That said, the country is now working towards a very favorable environment for foreign investment and is doing phenomenally well among the transition countries, largely due to an educated and motivated work force and excellent infrastructure.

People and Culture

CROATIA
Demography

Croatia is home to approximately 4.5 million people. The largest city is its capital, Zagreb, with approximately one million people in the metro area. Split is second with around 180,000 in the city proper and over 200,000 including its suburbs. Rijeka comes in third with around 150,000. The birth rate is extremely low, about 9.6 births for every 1,000 people, translating into a slightly shrinking and aging population.

Though Croats make up close to 90 percent of the population, Serbs make up 4.5 percent, with Bosnians, Italians, Hungarians, and Slovenes making up much of the remaining 5.5 percent. There is little immigration besides a small stream of Chinese who come to work in family businesses or to study.

Religion

Over 80 percent of Croatians are Roman Catholic with Orthodox, Muslim, and atheist making up much of the rest. Catholicism is very important to the national identity and you'll find churches packed on Christmas, Easter, and August 15th (Velika Gospa). However, the churches are much less full on any given Sunday.

Catholicism was not prohibited under Tito's Yugoslavia but it was heavily frowned upon. Schools operated on Christmas day, and if children didn't show up their parents would likely be brought in for questioning. People who held state jobs refrained from going to church since it wasn't at all helpful to one's career nor even, sometimes, job security.

When Croatia claimed its independence in 1991, attending church and defining oneself as Catholic was seen as integral to being a "good Croatian." The church enjoyed lots of power in the government under Tudman, though that has eroded in recent years.

Language

Croatian is a Slavic language, actually classified as either Serbo-Croat or Croato-Serbian by most linguists. The language is spoken in Croatia, Bosnia and Herzegovina, and Serbia, though the vast majority of locals in each country would beg to differ.

Most Croatians speak Croatian as well as at least one other language. On the coast, this language is likely to be Italian. For older people, it's probably German. Most Croatians under 40 speak at least some, if not a lot, of English, largely due to the number of U.S. television shows broadcast locally with subtitles.

The Arts

One of the most underappreciated arts in Croatia is its rich tradition of folk music. Unfortunately, the country doesn't have a lot of places to go and see music performances outside of periodic folk festivals. Bars and clubs rarely play folk music, though a good inland Croatian wedding should always have a *tambura* band.

The *tambura* (also called the *tamburica*) is the most important instrument in Slavonian folk music. The instrument is most similar to a mandolin and was brought to the region by the Ottomans.

On the coast, the dominant folk music is the *klapa,* an a capella group of 4–10 men who sing rather sad songs. A good group can be quite impressive and it's highly recommended to hit a *klapa* festival if you have the chance.

Though Istrian music is not as popular, it is interesting if you happen to come across some at one of the local festivals. The instruments—like the *sopila,* a type of large oboe, and the *mijeh,* a bagpipe made of a goat bladder—are what really make the music unique.

Croatian architecture is quite varied, with lots to see around the country. In Dalmatia you'll find some pre-Romanesque churches—the best example is St. Donat's Church in Zadar, built at the beginning of the 9th century. Romanesque and Gothic styles followed, with Dalmatian sculptor Juraj Dalmatinac (c. 1400–1473) at the forefront of the Gothic style, sculpting reliefs and erecting buildings all over the Dalmatian coast. A good mix of both Renaissance and Gothic styles can be found in Šibenik's 15th-century Katedrala svetog Jakova. Other great examples of Renaissance architecture can be found all along the coast in places such as Hvar and Dubrovnik (the latter was a center for Renaissance architecture, though much of it was destroyed by the great quake in 1667). In northern Croatia the Baroque style was predominant; Varaždin is the town most known for its Baroque architecture, dating from the 17th and 18th centuries. The Secessionist style (the local term for the art nouveau style) became popular in the late 19th century and early 20th century. A beautiful example of Secessionist architecture is the Državni Arhiv in Zagreb, built in 1913.

The most famous Croatian painter is Vlaho Bukovac (1855–1922), a 19th-century artist from Cavtat near Dubrovnik who was a master of light landscapes and realistic paintings. Croatian-born sculptor Ivan Meštrović (1883–1962) has enjoyed international acclaim. Many of his works dug deep into the Croatian national spirit for inspiration. However, the most interesting and unique style of painting is naive painting; the work not only depicted rural peasant life in the first half of the 20th century but also came under fire for its political themes. Ivan Generalić (1914–1992) is the most well-known artist of this genre.

SLOVENIA
Demography
Slightly more than two million people live in Slovenia. Ljubljana, the capital, is the biggest city, with more than 250,000 people. The city is small but quite cosmopolitan given the number of embassies and consulates in town. Maribor is the second largest, with approximately 115,000 residents. Several towns hover around the 50,000 mark, like Kranj and Koper. The birth rate is extremely low, about 9.63 births for every 1,000 people.

Slovenes make up over 80 percent of population. Italians and Hungarians are both considered indigenous minorities and are given a special status in the National Assembly, with one seat each to represent them. There are also people from the former Yugoslav republics; most are refugees who have made Slovenia their new home.

Religion
Close to 60 percent of Slovenians are Roman Catholic. Other groups include Protestants, Orthodox Christians, Muslims, and Jews. Protestantism was quite popular in the 16th century, though today its followers make up only about 1 percent of the population, located mostly in the Murska Sobota region. Jews were driven out in the 15th century and today there is a very small community of only 100 or so. Muslims make up a little over 2 percent of the population and are mostly newcomers to Slovenia, usually escaping the horrors of Bosnia during the war.

The Slovenian constitution declares the separation of church and state and maintains that all religions are equal, though it is clear that the Catholic church has more sway in affairs of the state than minority religions. That said, the church's say in Slovenia is considerably less than in neighboring countries Austria, Hungary, and Croatia. A 1996 visit by the Pope was met with far less fanfare than in Croatia.

Language
Slovenian is a Slavic language. It is similar to Croatian but not enough that speakers from the two countries could closely understand each other (think of speakers of Spanish and Italian having a conversation). People who grew up under the Yugoslav regime speak Serbo-Croatian, but young people under 25 likely speak little or perhaps none at all.

Most Slovenes speak at least two languages. Many Slovenes speak English, as it is widely taught in schools and seen on television. German, Italian, and Hungarian are also popular second languages.

The Arts
Music is an important part of the Slovenian cultural landscape. The small country boasts five orchestras and two opera companies, and

it's also home to a variety of modern bands like the popular rock group Siddharta. However, it's the country's folk music *(ljudska glasba)* that is truly distinctive. Varied and rich, local folk music features not only its own rhythms and tunes, but also its own instruments, such as the *cymbalom,* a string instrument played with sticks, and the *zvegla,* a wooden cross flute.

Slovenia is full of architectural styles, from the pre-Romanesque, Gothic, and Baroque to more modern styles. The most abundant of these styles are likely Baroque (Ljubljana's cathedral is an example) and Secessionist architecture (Ljubljana's Miklošičeva street is teeming with it). One name stands out among all the architects—Jože Plečnik (1872–1957), whose classical and symmetrical style transformed the city of Ljubljana in the early 20th century following the 1895 earthquake.

Slovenia's folk craft tradition is definitely worth a mention; it's been an important part of the culture since medieval times. From delicate Idrija lace to wooden crafts and iron-working, Slovenia is full of quality handiwork.

Visual arts have always been important to Slovenia, with close to 50 art museums throughout the country. Churches are full of examples of Gothic frescoes (Hrastovlje's Dance of Death is one of the most famous), while Baroque sculptures, like Francesco Robba's fountains in Ljubljana, are found in cities throughout Slovenia. In the 19th century, impressionist Rihard Jakopič was the best-known painter, while most of the 20th century was dominated by the Club of Independents, a group of painters who focused on socialist realism, a Soviet-influenced style of strong lines and powerful images. Over the past 30 years, postmodernist style has prevailed with a crop of interesting artists such as sculptor Marjetica Potrč.

Though Slovenia's history of film was rather sparse, since its independence the country has made quite a name for itself. With dozens of movies winning local and regional acclaim, it was director Jan Cvitkovič's *Odgrobadogroba* (Grave Hopping) that was nominated for a Foreign Language Oscar in 2007.

ESSENTIALS

Getting There

CROATIA
Air

There are several international airports in Croatia, though the busiest of these is Zagreb's Pleso Airport (www.zagreb-airport.hr). Many of the coastal airports, like Pula (www.airport-pula.hr), Rijeka (www.rijeka-airport.hr), Zadar (www.zadar-airport.hr), and the island of Brač (www.airport-brac.hr), have a lot more flights available during the summer than in the off-season. Split (www.split-airport.hr) and Dubrovnik (www.airport-dubrovnik.hr) are the largest coastal airports, while Osijek's small airport (www.osijek-airport.hr) is useful for getting to Slavonia without a drive.

All of the airport websites will direct you to flight schedules, lists of airline carriers, car rental companies, and information on buses and shuttles into town.

It is important to know that if you're planning to travel on to Serbia, Bosnia, or Montenegro, there are few or absolutely no direct flights. Your closest connections are in Ljubljana.

There are currently no direct flights from the United States to Croatia. You'll have to connect in a larger European city like London, Frankfurt, Munich, or Vienna. **Croatia Airlines** has the biggest selection of flights, with several daily connections between

Zagreb or Split and Frankfurt or Munich. **British Airways** flies from London to Split and Dubrovnik. There are some great budget-carrier options from the British Isles, like **EasyJet** (www.easyjet.com), **Ryanair** (www.ryanair.com), and **Wizzair** (www.wizzair.com), though most connect to the coast and fly more frequently, or even exclusively, during the summer.

Round-trip tickets from North America, with one connection in a major European capital, run about $1,200. You can save money by being flexible on travel dates (mid-week is usually cheapest) and times (early-morning or late-evening flights tend to be in less demand).

Another option if you're on a tight budget is to get a bargain fare to a major hub like Vienna and then take the train to Croatia. You have a similar option with flights to cities like Venice and then connecting with a ferry to one of the Croatian islands or coastal ports. Of course, you should account for lost time (trains and ferries take up to six hours plus transfers) when deciding if the savings makes sense. On the upside, it's a nice way to fit in a stopover in another European city.

You could get the best of both worlds by connecting to Istria and Dalmatia (and sometimes Zagreb) via low-cost carriers, most of which fly out of smaller airports around London.

For international flights, it's best to arrive two to three hours early. In the summer and early fall, when lines at overcrowded airports can get unruly, err on the three-hour side. Security check-ins in Croatia move along pretty smoothly, though you still may have to take off your shoes (this rule seems to change with the month) and leave the bottled water at home, since Croatia observes the liquids ban. You'll be quicker if you have your sample-size bottles in a plastic zip-top bag, pack your metal jewelry in your carry-on, and wear shoes that are easy to remove. Croatian airports are very particular about batteries in checked luggage. Remove any batteries and put them in your carry-on unless you want to unpack your bags at the check-in counter.

Land

Train travel to Croatia from Austria takes about six hours. Sometimes you'll get a new, fairly modern train, and other times you might get a train that looks like it's been riding the rails since the 1940s. If you're traveling around Europe by train, look into the **Eurail Pass** (www.eurail.com) and **Rail Europe** (www.raileurope.com), though the passes don't currently cover Croatia and Slovenia. If you're traveling frequently by train throughout Europe, it's worthwhile to buy the **Thomas Cook European Timetable** (www.thomascooktimetables.com, approx. $25.50), which has schedules of over 50,000 trains as well as ferry routes.

You can also take the bus to Croatia, but there's always a debate about which method is faster. Technically, the bus is quicker, but it's happened more than a few times, particularly on the routes from Austria and Germany, that the bus will detour to drop off regular passengers at their homes. This happens most often on Fridays, when locals who work in Germany and Austria are on a weekend visit to their families, and it can add another hour or more to your trip.

Driving to Croatia from Austria is quite easy, particularly now that the highway between Ljubljana and Zagreb is close to being completed. If you're going to Istria or Kvarner, simply take the road toward Rijeka instead of Zagreb. From Italy, come through Ancona, where you can also catch a ferry to lots of points on the Dalmatian coast. From the Italian city of Bari, you can get a ferry to Dubrovnik.

Though the European Union has declared vignettes (a sticker allowing you to use a particular country's highway system) illegal, some countries continue to use them, including Slovenia. You can buy the sticker at the border or at a gas station.

Sea

Cruise ships dock regularly in and around Dubrovnik. Ship staff should be able to give you information on getting to your next destination. Ferries are available to Croatia from the Italian coast, with departures from Ancona, Bari, Pescara, Rimini, and Venice. There are several ferry companies, though the most frequent and varied is **Jadrolinija** (www .jadrolinija.hr). You will want to book your ticket in advance if you have a car and are traveling in July and August.

Traditional ferry service from the Italian coast to Split takes about eight or nine hours. If you're traveling without a car, **SNAV** (www .snav.it) has high-speed ferries that take about four and a half hours from Ancona and Pescara to Split.

SLOVENIA
Air

Slovenia's main airport is the small Brnik Airport (www.lju-airport.si), about 23 kilometers from Ljubljana. A number of carriers connect with the airport going to a surprising number of destinations, including Serbia and Bosnia, making Ljubljana better than Zagreb for connecting with other countries in the region.

There are no direct flights from North America to Slovenia; you'll need to connect through a larger European city to get to there. **Adria Airways** (www.adria-airways.com), **Austrian Airlines** (www.aua-si.com), and **Czech Airlines** (www.czechairlines.com) all fly into Ljubljana from major European hubs, while **EasyJet** (www.easyjet.com) is a good source of budget flights from the British Isles into Slovenia.

There are two small airports, in Maribor (www.maribor-airport.si) and Portorož (www .portoroz-airport.si), that might also be worth checking out for other possible routes to the country.

Round-trip tickets from North America, with one connection in a major European capital, run about $1,200. You can save money by being flexible on travel dates (mid-week is usually cheapest) and times (early-morning or late-evening flights tend to be in less demand).

Booking a cheap ticket with a budget airline like **Ryanair** (www.ryanair.com) into Trieste (approximately 100 kilometers) or Klagenfurt

(approximately 80 kilometers) and connecting with Ljubljana via train or bus is another possibility. You'll lose time with this option, so take that into consideration along with cost.

If you'd like to take advantage of a stopover in Venice, there's a high-speed train connecting it with Ljubljana.

Land

You can connect with most any country in Europe, including other former Yugoslav republics, through **Slovenske Železnice** (Slovenian Railways, tel. 01/291-3332, potnik .info@slo-zeleznice.si, www.slo-zeleznice.si). There's a new high-speed train, the Casanova, that connects Venice and Ljubljana in just four hours (about the same as driving on a day without traffic). The Casanova travels once daily. Most of Slovenia's trains are new and modern. If you're traveling around Europe by train, look into the **Eurail Pass** (www.eurail.com) and **Rail Europe** (www .raileurope.com), though keep in mind the passes do not cover Slovenia.

Bus service around Slovenia is reliable and safe. The Ljubljana **Avtobusna postaja** (bus station, Trg Osvobodilne fronte 4, avtobusna .postoja@ap-ljubljana.si, www.ap-ljubljana.si) has connections to Slovenian and international cities. A trip to Zagreb will take about two and a half hours.

Driving in Slovenia is easy and the routes are well marked. You can connect to Slovenia via Villach, Klagenfurt, or Graz in Austria, or Trieste from Italy. An almost completed highway links Zagreb to Ljubljana in under two hours. Slovenia currently requires vignettes for cars traveling around Slovenia. You can buy the windshield sticker at gas stations around the country. It is valid for one year and costs €35.

Sea

During the summer season, ferries run between Venice and Portorož and Piran on the Slovenian coast. If you're interested in taking to the Adriatic Sea, check out **Prince of Venice** (www.kompas-holy.si) and **Venezia Lines** (www.venezialines.com).

Getting Around

CROATIA

Air

Traveling by air in Croatia can save considerable time, particularly the Zagreb to Dubrovnik route, cutting off about eight to ten hours of driving time. **Croatia Airlines** (www.croatia airlines.com) offers a good array of flights, particularly to destinations in Dalmatia. Keep in mind, though, that tickets within Croatia are best booked once you get to Croatia, unless purchased as part of your international flights. Booking these flights locally will cost at least 50 percent less than you would have paid when booking from home.

Train

Hrvatske željeznice (Croatian Railways, www.hznet.hr) trains are fairly reliable, fairly clean if a little old at times, and usually cheaper and more convenient than taking the bus. The railways offer super connections throughout inland Croatia or to destinations on the coast from Zagreb, though many coastal towns are not connected by train. The Zone D Inter-Rail pass (www.raileurope.com) is valid for Croatia and might be worth the money if you plan to do a lot of train travel. Unfortunately, Inter-Rail passes are only available for European citizens.

Be aware that there are two categories of trains: the *putnički* (slow trains, stopping at every village along the way) and IC (inter-city trains). The IC trains are more expensive but save a lot of time. You can buy your tickets at the station before leaving or from the conductor on the train if you're in a real hurry (you'll pay a premium, though). A red *vožnje* (timetable) is posted at every station. *Odlasci* are departures and *dolasci* are arrivals. You can also buy a timetable at larger stations or find out more information on the Croatian Railways website.

Bus

Buses connecting Croatian cities are run by multiple private companies, though the system is quite well organized. Long-distance buses are almost always air-conditioned and quite comfortable, though shorter connections might well be made on old and rather shabby buses. There are multiple connections (sometimes hourly) between Zagreb and other major Croatian cities. Smaller towns may only have one or two connections a day during the week and perhaps none on the weekends.

You'll need to buy your tickets at the counter of the bus station. One thing to keep in mind: You can only buy tickets in advance if you are getting on the bus at its original departure point. If you want to board a bus at a city along its route, you won't be able to buy your ticket until the bus pulls up at the station.

If you're traveling to the coast from Zagreb or vice versa, it's a good idea to buy your ticket a day or two in advance since they tend to sell out during the summer. If you can't find anywhere to buy a ticket, just sit on the bus and wait for the driver, who should be able to sell you one.

Tickets for buses traveling within a town (around Zagreb for instance) can be purchased at newspaper kiosks or on the bus from the driver. Remember to insert your ticket in the machine inside the bus to validate it.

Boat

Ferries to the Croatian islands close to the coast (Rab and Cres, for example) are usually marked from the road (look for signs with a picture of a boat and the word *trajekt*). You don't need a reservation, just drive up and wait in line. If you're going by foot, it's even easier and rarely more than 30Kn for passage.

Ferries running to islands further out run on exact timetables. You'll find most of these ferries' schedules at **Jadrolinija**'s website (www.jadrolinija.com). Faster hydrofoils and catamarans link Split with islands such as Brač, Hvar, and Vis. They're more expensive but also much faster and usually worth the splurge.

Car

Traveling by car in Croatia is almost essential

if you plan on seeing some more out-of-the-way destinations. It's also fairly easy, with the country's network of excellent highways connecting major cities. There are multilane highways between Zagreb and eastern Croatia towards Serbia, Zagreb and Varaždin and on to Hungary, as well as Zagreb and Ljubljana. There's a great highway between Zagreb and Split (with plans to reach Dubrovnik), though it is quite expensive, with tolls running upwards of 200Kn. There's also a highway connecting Zagreb with Rijeka, making the trip to Kvarner only two hours from the capital.

Other roads are often narrow and are not always well maintained. They can also be quite traffic-y, though some, like the coastal road, called the Magistrala, offer great views. It's probably best to avoid driving the Magistrala at night; at all times of day and night remember to watch for pedestrians walking along the narrow and often cliff-hugging road.

You will need your driver's license to drive in Croatia; an international driving license (available from AAA) is recommended. The rental car company will provide you with any additional documents. If a police officer stops you and asks you for your *prijava,* tell him which hotel you are staying at or give the name of the apartment or home owner, as they are supposed to register you. If you are bringing your own car to Croatia, you must have third-party insurance, usually available for purchase at or near the border.

You can buy detailed roadmaps at bookstores, some newsstands, and most gas stations.

Gas stations *(benzinska stanica)* are open at least 7 A.M.–7 P.M. Monday–Saturday. Some stations are closed on Sundays, but every town and major highway should have some 24-hour stations. It's best to try to fill up your tank Monday through Friday since gas station inspections aren't conducted on weekends and holidays, making those the most likely times for employees to stick water in the tank, leaving you stranded a couple hundred kilometers down the road.

If you do break down, you can call **HAK** (www.hak.hr, dial 987), the Croatian Auto Club, for 24-hour emergency roadside assistance. A tire repair shop is called a *vulkanizer* and there are often roadside signs to direct you to the closest one.

RULES OF THE ROAD

Speed limits are posted on roads and range from 40 kph in town to 130 kph on highways. Currently, Croatia allows a 0.05 percent blood alcohol limit for drivers, upped in 2008 from a much-criticized 0 percent limit imposed in 2004 (a local newspaper showed you technically couldn't eat a chocolate-covered cherry and drive); it's worth checking online right before departure, though, to see if any laws have changed, since there have been two changes within a short span of years.

Random breath tests and random stops by police are legal in Croatia. You should not pass a stopped bus (though you'll see lots of locals attempting to do so) nor should you drive on tram lines when the tram line is marked in yellow. A few high-traffic spots in the center of Zagreb allow for cars to share the lane with the trams. Police are allowed to collect fines on the spot, though sometimes it's anyone's guess as to whose pocket the money goes in.

Remember that you are not allowed to make a right turn on red in Croatia. If it's not green, don't go. Punishment for Croatians is the seizure of their driver's license for three months, though police are not allowed to seize foreign driver's licenses. Instead, you'd likely get a hefty fine.

CAR RENTAL

You will need your driver's license, passport, and a credit card to rent a car in Croatia.

Car rental in Croatia is very expensive (around $100 a day for a small car with unlimited mileage, including insurance). You'll find all the major rental agencies (such as **Hertz** (www.hertz.com), **Budget** (www.budget.com), and **Alamo** (www.alamo.com) in Croatia. You can either book online or in an agency in-town or at the airport once you arrive. The largest European rental car agency is **Europcar** (www.europcar.com). You may also want to check out the budget booker **Easy Car** (www.easy car.com) for a cheaper deal.

Under most circumstances cars rented in Croatia can be driven to Slovenia (and vice versa), though you should always check with the rental company before doing so. Sometimes there are additional fees for the privilege to do so.

PARKING

Though driving in Croatia is relatively easy, parking rarely is. Illegally parked vehicles are often towed. Handicapped spaces are usually marked with a sign and/or paint; beware of parking in signless spaces or those with fading paint, difficult to see at night, leaving you an unwelcome surprise in the morning. In many of Croatia's northern and inland towns, regular spaces marked in blue, and handicapped spaces (marked in white or yellow) are more likely to have a sign in front of them than in southern Croatia. In Zagreb and the coast, handicapped spaces are almost always marked with blue paint. Most cities have at least one parking garage.

In Zagreb you can pay for parking with your cell phone—particularly handy if you've picked up a prepaid cell phone. You send your license plate number via a text message (the number you send it to is determined by what zone you're parked in). It is charged to your cell phone immediately (it's either added to your bill or, if you have a prepaid card, deducted from the balance). If you don't have a cell phone, you go up to the nearest machine, insert coins, get a receipt, and put it on your dashboard. More and more locations outside of Zagreb are also adopting the pay by cell phone system.

SLOVENIA
Train

If you're traveling to or from Ljubljana, train travel might be just the ticket. **Slovenske Železnice** (Slovenian Railways, www.slo-zeleznice.si) trains are quite clean and a lot of the fleet is relatively new. However, the rail system has few connections between smaller towns so it often doesn't pay to use the train if you're planning on connecting some smaller destinations. IC (inter-city) trains are the fastest and only a little more expensive than slower trains. If you see a boxed *R* on the timetable next to the train you would like to take, you'll need to make a reservation in order to get on the train. An *R* without a box means that you can reserve a seat, but aren't required to. It's cheapest to buy tickets at the counter, but if you have (or don't need) a reservation, you can also jump on the train and buy your ticket directly from the conductor for a slightly higher price.

Bus

Most cities in Slovenia are connected by bus. Longer, more frequented routes are likely to be serviced by the nicest buses, while buses connecting small towns are almost sure to be somewhat older. Prices are calculated by the distance covered.

The timetables, called *vozni red*, are a bit difficult to decipher. Color-coded tables usually follow the following formula: black (daily), blue (weekdays), green and orange (except Sun.), yellow (school hours), red (Sun. and holidays). If the timetable uses letters, look for letters instead: V (daily), D (weekdays), D+ (except Sun.), N (Sun.), NP (Sun. and holidays), ŠP (school hours).

You can buy tickets at the local *avtobusna postaja* (bus station) or pay when you get on the bus. You can make a seat reservation one day in advance for a small fee.

Car

Driving in Slovenia is much like driving in Croatia, only somewhat tamer. There is a major highway running between Ljubljana and Zagreb and another under construction between Ljubljana and Villach. There's also a smaller highway going to Maribor. Otherwise, plan to take rural roads, which have the advantage of offering some stunning scenery. But since they're only two-lane, expect the occasional traffic snarl.

Currently, you'll need to purchase a vignette (around €30) to use highways in Slovenia if your rental car doesn't already have one. This is available from most any gas station off the highway. You should carry your driver's license and passport when driving, though having an international driving license (available from AAA) is not a bad idea. If you are bringing your own car to Slovenia, you must have third-party insurance, usually available for purchase at or near the border.

Good road maps are available at most every gas station along the highway, though gas stations along rural roads might not have such a wide selection.

If you break down in Slovenia, you can get emergency roadside assistance by calling 1987, the number of **Auto-Moto Zveza Slovenije** (AMZS, Slovenian Auto Club, info.center@ amzs.si, www.amzs.si). Their website is also a useful tool, with lots of information about driving in Slovenia as well as constantly updated traffic conditions.

As in Croatia, pay attention, as many road rules are ignored by overzealous drivers, and take care driving out of the city at night (especially on rural roads)—drinking and driving is a common offense.

RULES OF THE ROAD

Speed limits range between 40kph in work zones and some in-town sections and 130kph on major highways. Slovenians rarely respect these limits, but police can induce a hefty fine if you're caught speeding.

The blood alcohol limit is 0.05 percent. You may not make a right turn on red in Slovenia. It is not permitted to use a cell phone while driving. You may not honk the horn in busy areas unless you need to avoid a traffic accident. Seatbelts are required for all occupants of the car and low-beam headlights must be kept on at all times. During the winter months (November–March) you are also required to carry snow chains.

As in Croatia, police are allowed to stop you for any reason. Police near small towns are particularly known for random checks and for keeping an eye out for speeding violations. Many offenses require immediate payment of the ticket.

CAR RENTAL

You will need your driver's license, passport, and a credit card to rent a car in Slovenia.

You should be able to rent a car for around €50 per day, including insurance. Slovenia has all the major rental agencies, such as **Hertz** (www.hertz.com), **Budget** (www.budget.com), and **Alamo** (www.alamo.com), though rental is very expensive. If you need to book at the last minute, Ljubljana has offices of all the major agencies. The largest European rental car agency is **Europcar** (www.europcar.com). You may also want to check out the budget booker **Easy Car** (www.easycar.com) for a cheaper deal.

Under most circumstances, you can drive your rental car into Croatia, though you should always check with the car rental company before doing so in case there are additional fees or paperwork involved.

PARKING

Slovenia is very small, making it somewhat easier to park compared with Croatia. However, the cities do not have a lot of garages, so you'll need to brush up on your parallel parking skills. Parking is allowed in white zones for up to one hour and in blue zones for up to 30 minutes for free.

Visas and Officialdom

CROATIA
Visas and Passports

You should have no trouble getting through immigration if you have the right paperwork. For U.S., EU, Canadian, Australian, and New Zealand citizens, this simply means a passport; no visa is required for stays up to 90 days. Citizens of other countries will want to check visa regulations for Croatia. Visit the Consular Department of the Croatian Foreign Ministry's website at www.mvp.hr for more information.

You are required to register with the police within 24 hours of your arrival. If you're staying in a hotel, hostel, or camp, or have a room booked through an agency, they should register for you. If you are staying with friends or booked a room yourself, your hosts should technically register you, although the authorities are usually lax on this rule, particularly in touristy areas, as long as the stay is not too long. The worst consequence is throwing you out of the country, though it's more likely they'd advise you to leave and enter again and then register properly.

Croatian Embassies and Consulates

Croatia has embassies and/or consulates in many countries, such as the United States (tel. 202/588-5899, www.croatiaemb.org), the United Kingdom (tel. 0870/005-6709, www.croatia.embassyhomepage.com), Canada (tel. 613/562-7820, www.croatiaemb.net), and Australia (tel. 02/6286-6988, croemb@bigpond.com).

Foreign Embassies in Croatia

Embassies and consulates are your lifeline in case of emergency. If you have lost your passport, have a medical emergency, or run into trouble with the local law, contact your embassy or consulate for help. If you require assistance, contact the following, all in Zagreb: American embassy (Ulica T. Jefferson 2, Buzin, tel. 01/661-2200, www.usembassy.hr); Australian embassy (Centar Kaptol, Nova Ves 11, tel. 01/489-1200, www.auembassy.hr); British embassy (I. Lučića 4, tel. 01/600-9100, www.britishembassy.gov.uk/croatia); Canadian embassy (Prilaz Gjure Deželića 4, tel. 01/484-1200).

Customs

All large items brought into Croatia (such as boats, laptops, etc.) should be declared so that you can take them back out with you when you leave. You are only allowed to bring in 200 cigarettes, one liter of alcohol, and 500 grams of coffee. You can even bring your pets if you have a current proof of vaccination.

In Croatia many purchases over 500Kn are tax-free. Make sure you get the form from the store at time of purchase (they'll need your passport number to fill it out) and you can get a refund after you get home or once you cross the border. You are not allowed to leave the country with more than 2,000Kn in cash. If you purchase a work of art, ask about export approval before purchasing.

You can find out more information at www.carina.hr.

Police

Croatia is quite safe and has a low rate of crime. Your biggest dangers arise from pickpockets and petty theft. Basic safety practices will help minimize risk: Take out a travel insurance policy before you leave home, don't wear flashy jewelry, and keep your bag close under your arm.

It is legal for police to perform random identity-card checks, so it is helpful to have your passport at all times, though you're unlikely to be asked for it. In any case, make a couple of photocopies of your passport's identity page, which will expedite getting a new one from your embassy or consulate. Police in Croatia are friendly. To report a crime you can dial 92 from anywhere in Croatia.

SLOVENIA
Visas and Passports

You should have no trouble getting through immigration if you have the right paperwork. For

U.S., Canadian, Australian, and New Zealand citizens, this simply means a passport; no visa is required for stays up to 90 days. Citizens of the EU, Switzerland, and Croatia can visit for up to 30 days with only a national identity card. However, as visa requirements can change, it's useful to check the Slovenian Ministry of Foreign Affairs website (www.sigov.si/mzz).

Slovenian Embassies and Consulates

Slovenia has embassies and/or consulates in many countries such as the United States (tel. 202/667-5363, www.embassy.org/slovenia), the United Kingdom (tel. 020/7222-5400, www.slovenia.embassyhomepage.com), Canada (tel. 613/565-5781, vot@mzz-dkp.gov.si), and Australia (tel. 02/6243-4830).

Foreign Embassies in Slovenia

Embassies and consulates are your lifeline in case of emergency. If you have lost your passport, have a medical emergency, or run into trouble with the local law, contact your embassy or consulate

for help. If you require assistance, contact the following, all in Ljubljana: American embassy (Prešernova 31, tel. 01/200-5500, www.usembassy.si); Australian consulate (Trg Republike 3/XII, tel. 01/425-4252); British embassy (Trg Republike 3/IV, tel. 01/200-3910, www.british-embassy.si); Canadian consulate (Miklošičeva 19, tel. 01/430-3570).

Customs

EU citizens are not restricted on bringing in alcohol or tobacco for personal use. Non-EU citizens are limited to 200 cigarettes or 50 cigars, 2 liters of wine, and 1 liter of alcohol.

For more information, check out www.carina.gov.si/eng.

Police

Crime is quite low in Slovenia. Theft is the most common complaint, and if you find yourself a victim, you should report the incident to the police. Police in Slovenia are quite friendly and generally speak at least basic English. The emergency number for the police is 113.

Recreation

Croatia and Slovenia are definitely sporting destinations, whether your tastes run to the spectator side of things or you'd prefer to get down and dirty in some adrenaline-boosting adventure sports. Croatia in particular is known for the many athletes the country has produced, including NBA stars, European league soccer players, Olympic medalist skiers, and a Wimbledon champion.

In general, if it's adventure sports you're after, Slovenia is the better choice, with faster rapids, higher slopes, and more rocky traverses to climb. Croatia is your destination for sailing and diving. Both countries have beautiful hiking trails.

HIKING

There's no better way than hiking to see the natural beauty of Croatia and Slovenia or to

commiserate with the locals. Hiking has a long tradition in the region, with serious hikers (often in their sixties and seventies) outfitted in proper hiking attire and walking sticks. Around Zagreb, Mount Medvednica and the hills around Samobor are littered with hiking trails and *planinarski domovi* (mountaineer's huts), where you can stop for a drink and a bite to eat at the top. Other areas to explore are the Gorski Kotar, Učka Nature Park in Kvarner, and Paklenica National Park and Plitvice Lakes National Park in Dalmatia.

In Slovenia, the Julian Alps will keep you in awe of the surrounding mountains and deep-green forests. Keep in mind that many mountaineer's huts are only open on weekends and/or in season, so don't depend on them for shelter or sustenance.

You can get lots more information from

the **Croatian Mountaineering Association** (Hrvatski planinarski savez, tel. 01/482-4142, hps@plsavez.hr, www.plsavez.hr) and the **Alpine Association of Slovenia** (Planinska zveza Slovenije, tel. 01/434-3022, www.pzs.si).

DIVING

Scuba diving in Croatia is some of the best in the Mediterranean. The sea is clean, the water is clear, tides are generally mild, and the stone base of most of the coastline makes for great visibility. There's lots of variety too, with spots for cave diving, reef viewing, and shipwrecks. You'll find plenty of excursions and courses through diving centers throughout the country. Particularly strong areas for diving include Mljet and Vis in the Southern Dalmatian Islands, the pristine Kornati Islands, and shipwrecks around Lošinj in the Kvarner Islands and off the coast of Rovinj in Istria.

The Croatian Port Authorities require you to buy a diving card (around 100Kn) after showing your diving license. Diving cards can be purchased at local diving centers or the *lučka kapetanija* (port captain's office) of marinas and harbors. If you don't have a license, you'll find lots of reasonable certification courses.

For more information contact the **Croatian Diving Federation** (www.diving-hrs.hr) or check out the website **Diving in Croatia** (www.diving.hr).

Diving is also popular in Slovenia, though not so much as in Croatia since there are fewer dive sites. Try **Nemo Divers** (www.nemo-divers.si) in Portorož for diving courses and excursions or **3glav Adventures** (www.3glav-adventures.com) in Bohinj for diving below the surface of Lake Bled. The **Slovenian Diving Federation** (Slovenska Potaljaška Zveza, www.spz.si) is a great source of information for divers and those who would like to take a course. Cave diving is a very interesting sport, but you can only do it with a licensed guide; contact the diving federation for more information.

SKIING

Skiing in Croatia is popular both as a spectator sport (popularized further by Olympic medalist Janica Kostelić) and as an active sport. There are really only two spots for skiing, either Sljeme in the hills above Zagreb or Bjelolasica in the Gorski Kotar. However, don't expect any double black diamonds or superb facilities. It does make a fun day trip or outing, however.

Slovenia is a much better choice for skiing. The most popular slopes are in the Kranjska Gora and Pohorje areas, though there are runs all over the country. While skiing here is no match for the Austrian slopes, it's nice, well organized, and generally very reasonable.

SPECTATOR SPORTS

Soccer, or football as it is commonly known in Europe, is by far the region's favorite spectator sport. National teams occasionally play in Zagreb and Ljubljana, usually vying for qualification in a tournament such as the European or World Cups. You're more likely to catch a local

---

SAILING CROATIA

The absolutely best way to see the Croatian coast, from Istria all the way down to deepest Dalmatia, is via sailboat. The coast and islands are loaded with small marinas, places to berth, and even restaurants with a convenient place to anchor and come in for a bite. You can find remote coves and lots of great scenery.

If you're game, try **Ultra Sailing** (www.ultra-sailing.hr) for charters and courses, from beginners to families to advanced. **Nautika Centar Nava** (www.navaboats.com) is another option for charters, with a selection of yachts for the well-heeled as well. For help with navigating, check out the **Adriatic Navigator** (www.adriatic-navigator.com), which also publishes a guide available at VIP mobile phone stores and certain harbors and marinas in Croatia. Not confident in your seafaring skills? Ask the charter companies about hiring a captain to go along with the boat and leave the navigating to someone else.

game: The biggest are Zagreb's Dinamo or Split's Hajduk. In Slovenia the most successful team is NK Maribor. The season lasts from mid-August to the end of May, with a break in January and February. Tickets are relatively cheap and can be purchased on-site before the game. Only big matches between the big teams (sometimes) and national team games (almost always) require ticket purchases in advance of the actual event.

Basketball is also popular in Croatia. Its small hometown teams like Cibona have produced major NBA names like Tony Kukoč. The Croatian handball team has always been excellent and the country's pride in their success shows. A giant arena just for handball is currently being built on the outskirts of Novi Zagreb. Volleyball and water polo are also popular sports.

Accommodations

There are dozens of places to stay in Croatia and Slovenia and finding a room shouldn't pose any problem. You will want to reserve ahead during the summer on the coast (mostly to get a good room versus an overpriced mediocre one), otherwise you can probably just show up and find a room in all but the most rural locations—which may have no accommodation at all.

Should you find yourself on the coast without a room, head to one of the Tourist Information offices for help in finding a hotel or private room. Realize that the majority of these offices are in no way related to the town's tourist office. They are in fact agencies brokering rooms, many of them far from the sea and quite expensive for those who show up at the last minute. Stick to your guns about price (or location or air-conditioning or television or whatever else is important to you) and they should be able to come up with something. If that fails, along Croatia's Dalmatian coast you'll often see older women and men standing by the road with signs marked *sobe* or *pension*. They'll also be found in bus stations and train stations. Be aware that some of these people may try to rip you off and women traveling alone should avoid them altogether. If you do decide to see what they have on offer, ask to see the room before agreeing to anything and get a commitment for a price first.

In the case of agencies or private rooms, know that you are not obligated to take the room if you don't like what you see. Politely decline and start round two of finding a place to stay for the night.

These private rooms and apartments are probably your best value along the coast, though you'll find the best deals through official tourist offices and reputable agencies like the ones noted throughout this book. Overbuilding means sometimes you can strike a phenomenal deal, getting a basic room for the night for only 10 or 15 euros (70 or 100 kuna). These super-cheap rooms won't be right on the beach, though.

Package hotels are an option for the traveler who wants to check in and not venture much farther than the hotel pool or beach. But they are not always the best deal for the traveler who likes to see what's around the area, since the price includes breakfast and a lunch or dinner (which, by the way, are rarely culinary treats in themselves). Quite a lot of European travelers frequent the package hotels.

If you're traveling in a group, renting an apartment or house is a great way to go. Check out Home Away (www.homeaway.com) for dozens of properties in Croatia and Slovenia, particularly along the coastal regions.

HOTELS

Huge soulless concrete hotels are one of the traces of former Yugoslavia left all over Croatia and Slovenia's tourist destinations. You'll most likely find that the service, staff, and decor date from the same era as well. Though some of these complexes have received upgrades, for the most part it's best to avoid them and look for more charming places to stay.

One thing to keep in mind as you're researching hotels in Croatia and Slovenia is that in reality hotels are typically one star lower than the rating advertised. A true five-star hotel in the region is a rare find (although more are cropping up every year). Most hotels rated five star are in fact four star, four stars really three stars, and so on.

Generally, hotels rated three stars or lower will be overpriced for what you get. It's better to try to find a small boutique hotel, *pension,* or private room or apartment.

On the coast, most hotels offer full-board and half-board add-ons for meals. Usually it's best to forgo these options unless you're staying somewhere extremely rural.

If it's the hotel facilities you're really after (such as pools, bars by the beach, and hot springs), some of the socialist leftovers actually sport nicer surroundings than they do rooms. If you're staying somewhere else, you're generally allowed to come on the resort's property—you'll know it's okay if you don't see any signs restricting it. No one will say anything, as long as you're buying drinks and snacks at one of the outdoor cafés.

Hotels on the coast are the best deal for families who want access to a kiddie club, pools, etc. A few new and newly renovated properties offer good value for money, while the older socialist-era hotels will just make you feel like you've been ripped off.

TERME

Terme (thermal spas) in Croatia and Slovenia are hotels with thermal pools, saunas, and sometimes other facilities like spas and kiddie clubs. Unfortunately, most of these properties are severely in need of renovations, with tired furniture, threadbare carpet, and a depressing ambience.

However, the countries are making a big effort to update them; Slovenia leads with at least four good *terme,* while Croatia currently has only one worth a visit.

If it's just the thermal pools you're after, most of the *terme* have day passes available for purchase so you can use the facilities without staying in the hotel.

PRIVATE ROOMS AND APARTMENTS

Sobe (private rooms) are some of the best values in Croatia and Slovenia, with the added bonus of getting to know the locals who run the place. The owners are usually friendly and very hospitable, willing to help in any way they can.

If you're looking for luxury accommodation, this is rarely the way to go, but you are almost certain to find clean, comfortable rooms and often a tasty continental breakfast. The rooms are ranked by the local tourist board, with the lowest rated having shared bathrooms and the highest often having air-conditioning and television. However, you may want to ask for details since the ratings system sometimes seems a bit skewed.

On the coast of Croatia rooms are available most of the year, though a lot are closed during the winter. In the high season, you'll probably need to book ahead to snatch up the best rooms. There are fewer private rooms in inland Croatia and Slovenia, but they do still exist.

To find a room, check with the local tourist association or look for buildings with a small sign bearing a picture of a bed and the word *sobe* or a homemade sign with *sobe* or *zimmer frei* (German for room available). You can knock on the door or ring the bell at these establishments and see what's on offer.

Apartmani (apartments) get booked a little faster than the rooms and usually have a minimum stay requirement, particularly during the high season. In this category you'll find everything from basic to quite luxurious. A local travel agent or specialty provider should be able to help you book an apartment that meets your expectations.

SEOSKI TURIZAM AND TOURIST FARMS

To really see the traditional side of Croatia and Slovenia, a rural homestay is almost prerequisite. Most of the establishments boast magnificent surroundings, which make up for the typically basic amenities, though some rural homes do have elaborate interiors.

In Croatia, you'll find *seoski turizam* (village tourism) or *agroturizam* (agro-tourism) establishments throughout, particularly in inland Croatia and Istria. You also might want to check out the Istrian Tourism Board's website (www.istra.com) for a good listing of *agroturizam* options.

In Slovenia, check out the **Slovenian Tourist Board** (www.slovenia.info) or **Hiše s tradicijo** (Houses of Tradition, www.hisestradicijo.com) for lots of charming bucolic cottages.

HOSTELS

Hostels in Croatia are decent, though Slovenia's are typically better; all are generally clean and safe, and most welcome all ages. They can be a good deal, depending on the location (though bathrooms might be a bit below standard in terms of water pressure, quality, and availability of toilet paper).

The number of Croatian hostels affiliated with **Hostelling International** (www.hihostels.com) is somewhat limited. In Slovenia there's a relatively better selection. Most hostels are open year-round, though it's wise to book ahead, particularly during the summer months.

Private hostels are a bit harder to gauge. Try a website like www.hostelz.com for reviews from other travelers.

CAMPING

Slovenia and Croatia have dozens of campgrounds (in Croatia *autokamp,* in Slovenia *kamps*), particularly in the coastal regions. Campgrounds are usually open April to October and cost only a few euros (35 to 50 kuna) for a pitch and another few euros per person. Some rent tents for those who don't have them.

Most camps offer electricity, showers, laundry services, and more. Some even rent small cabins or bungalows.

It is illegal to camp in places other than a designated campsite.

Food

It's hard to pin down what constitutes typical Slovenian or Croatian food. The countries' geography and history have created a varied culinary offering, strong on regional dishes, influenced by Austrian, Italian, Hungarian, and even Turkish cuisine. What is almost always certain is that the food will be excellent quality and the portions are likely to be huge, particularly by European standards. Many main meat and potato dishes should suffice for two people, particularly if you add a salad and dip into the bread basket, a must-have on any Croatian and Slovenian table.

TYPICAL FARE

Slovenia and Croatia have some dishes and flavors that overlap, and there are certain items that are typical all over. One staple is *kremšnite,* a custard and pastry dessert claimed by multiple towns in Slovenia and Croatia, though it is suspiciously similar to the Germanic *cremeschnitte. Burek* has its origins in the Ottoman Empire, but that doesn't keep it from being a staple in bakeries throughout Croatia and Slovenia. The ultimate cheap sustenance, perfect after a night of clubbing, the flaky pie can be filled with cheese, potatoes, meat, or even apples. Last but not least there's *pršut* (prosciutto or cured ham). The best *pršut* tends to come from Istria and Dalmatia, where it's said that the strong winter *bura* winds help age the ham. A little *pršut,* cheese, and olives with fresh bread on the side is highly recommended as a starter or light lunch.

Croatia

Croatia's Zagorje region is filled with meat and potato dishes and veal, pork, or turkey prepared *zagrebački* style (stuffed with ham and cheese, then breaded and fried). Other typical dishes for the region are *purica s mlincima,* turkey baked with a decadent type of pasta, and *punjene paprika* or *sarma,* peppers stuffed with rice and meat. *Štrukli* (pastry baked with cheese and cream) is also common, either a salty version as a starter or side dish or a sweet version for dessert.

A trip to Slavonia would be amiss without sampling some of the region's famous pork dishes and its spicy *kulen* (salami). A meal in inland Croatia and Zagorje is frequently preceded by soup, often a clear broth with a few noodles.

Istria is very proud of its truffles and there are few dishes that escape their touch, though often the touch is a bit heavy-handed. You can have pasta, steak, cheese, or even omelets with truffles. Istria is also known for its *fuži,* a type of pasta, and *maneštra,* a thick bean and vegetable soup.

HOW TO GET GOOD FISH

The biggest obstacle between you and an outstanding seafood meal at the coast (particularly in high season) is frozen or day-old fish. It's common for restaurants to serve the sub-par fish to foreigners, who they know they'll never see again anyway, and give the best stuff to the locals.

To avoid this unfortunate but all too common scenario, ask to see the fish that's on offer, as the locals do. A platter of different types of fish will be brought out for you to choose from. Keep in mind that the eyes should be clear and never cloudy, and ask the waiter if he'll lift the gills so you can see their color, which should be a bright red. Dull or deep red means they're old or frozen.

Even if you have no idea what to look for, asking to see the fish should get you a better selection than if you hadn't seen it, and they may even think you know what you're talking about.

Dalmatia is heavy on seafood, often served in a sauce called *buzara,* which has a base of garlic and white wine. Some *buzara* adds tomatoes.

Grilled fish is the most common of the seafood dishes, usually accompanied by a side of *blitva,* a vegetable similar to Swiss chard, cooked in garlic and olive oil with potatoes.

Other excellent seafood dishes are lobster or octopus *ispod peka* (baked in a brick oven) and mussels and oysters. However, don't eat *prstače* (date shells)—it's an endangered species and illegal to sell.

If you'd like something besides seafood, but still typical of Dalmatia, try *pašticada,* beef cooked in a sauce of vinegar, wine, and prunes or tomatoes. *Janjetina,* or lamb, is found at restaurants all over Dalmatia, usually off the coast and up the hills or along the old coastal road. Generally roasted on a spit, it's at its best in the spring and early summer when the lambs aren't too big and the meat is still tender. *Janjetina* is considered a delicacy (despite the basic restaurants it's usually served in) and sometimes a must-eat for those journeying to the coast.

Slovenia

Though regional cuisine varies widely in the small country, there are a few staples that are found most everywhere. Fresh bread is de rigueur at every meal and you'll find a heaping basket of it served alongside your meal. The second staple is soup *(juha),* which begins most every meal, from a barley or bean soup in winter to a lighter fish soup on the coast in summer.

Pork *(svinjina)* is the most favored meat of the country, though you'll find veal *(teletina)* and beef *(govedina)* on almost every menu. *Žganci,* or a porridge of corn or buckwheat, is a common side dish.

In Slovenia's mountainous regions you'll find lots of variations on meat and potatoes, gooey dumplings, and fried doughnuts. You'll also find a fair amount of freshwater trout *(postrv)* and game *(divjačina).* On the coast, it's fish, fish, and a little more fish.

As you edge toward Hungary in the Prekmurje region, you'll find spicy goulashes,

Croatian and Slovenian specialties include *pršut* (cured ham) and *gibanica* (a Slovenian pastry).

while other regions favor heavy potato-and-bean soups. *Prekmurska gibanica,* a pastry with nuts, poppy seeds, apples, raisins, and cheese, is a filling dessert.

But if it's something more exotic you're looking for, Ljubljana is the place to go, with Asian and Italian cuisines as well as twists on the traditional.

FINDING A RESTAURANT

If you'd like to explore beyond this book's recommendations, there are some simple rules you can follow for finding a restaurant in Croatia and Slovenia. An establishment labeled *restoran* (Croatia) or *restavracija* (Slovenia) tends to be more formal, though not always completely atmospheric. Service at these establishments tends to be very good, with professional waiters taking pride in what they do. You may have to flag down the waiter for the bill (*račun* in both Croatian and Slovenian) or mention that you're in a hurry if you want to speed up the process. It is considered rude for waiters in restaurants of this type to rush you through your meal.

A *konoba* (Croatia) or *gostišče* (Slovenia) is one step down in formality, though usually a step up in atmosphere. Frequently cozy, wood-beamed, and decorated with local farm implements, a *konoba* serves its food with warmth. Prices will remain in line with a *restoran* or *restavracija*.

Even less formal is the *gostiona* (Croatia) or *gostilna* (Slovenia). This is the sort of place you'll likely find local business types chowing down for lunch and all but empty in the evenings.

This said, there's a trend to call more upmarket establishments *konoba* or *gostilna,* similar to the way a bistro in Manhattan might bring a three-figure bill. If you're looking for inexpensive but filling food, ask for a place that serves *gablec* (Croatia). It's a colloquial term that refers to a lunch menu (though literally it means a light snack), usually priced for workers on their lunch breaks.

Most restaurants open around 10 or 11 A.M. and close around 11 P.M. As for the day of the week they are closed, it's anyone's guess, though the most likely day is Monday for traditional restaurants or Sunday for those that cater to working types.

Pretty much every town in Croatia and Slovenia has a pizzeria with great pizzas and sometimes pasta dishes. You can also nip into a bakery for a slice of pizza to go, a sandwich, or a slice of *burek*.

Croatians and Slovenians breakfast on the light side, if at all. Most hotels and bed-and-breakfasts will offer at least a continental breakfast. Otherwise, buy a pastry and take it to a café. Since most cafés don't sell food, they won't mind you dunking your doughnut into their coffee.

DRINKING

Croatians and Slovenians adore their coffee, spending lots of time seeing and being seen in cafés all over, at all hours of the day and night. Espresso and *macchiato (kava s mlijekom)* tend to be on the strong side. If you'd like something a little lighter, order a *bijela kava (macchiato* with extra milk) in the capital cities. Out of the capitals, the *bijela* (white) side tends to be a little skimpy. Lots of young people drink Nescafe, in vanilla or chocolate flavors, so don't feel you're alone if the other items on offer are too strong for your tastes. You won't have any trouble locating a café in Croatia and Slovenia, where sometimes it feels like there's one every 20 meters. They're open from the early morning until late at night.

If you'd like something non-caffeinated, make sure to specify whether you want it with gas *(gazirano)* or without gas *(negazirano)*. Also be aware that ordering "juice" will always bring you orange juice. If you'd like apple, make sure to specify.

Croatian and Slovenian beers are lighter than their Germanic counterparts. Karlovačko and Ožujsko are the most common in Croatia, while Velebit, Tomislav, and Osiječko Crno are richer and worth a try. The most frequent Slovenian brand is Laško. Beers tend to be very reasonable, with a huge glass setting you back only a few euros (25 to 30 kuna).

Croatians and Slovenians are very proud

© R KI ADNIK/SLOVENIAN TOURIST BOARD

Croatia and Slovenia both boast a long winemaking history.

of their brandies. Though plum brandy is the most common, you'll also find pear brandy, herb brandy, honey brandy, and walnut brandy. Zadar in Dalmatia is famous for its cherry liqueur, *maraskino*. They are typically taken as an aperitif before a meal.

Croatian and Slovenian wines are high in quality but often are not known to Western travelers. Because most of the producers sell out their stock locally, few bottles make it to supermarket shelves out of the country. Traveling around the countryside is a great way to get to know the locals as well as pick up a few bottles of regional wines. Istria's Malvazija, a light, crisp white, should satisfy pretty much any drinker when it is drunk young. Teran, also indigenous to Istria, is an earthy red with a strong taste best suited to local palates. Other well-known Croatian wines are reds made from Plavac Mali grapes in Dalmatia and the whites of Slavonia, whose reputation is growing. Slovenia is most known for its Beli Pinot and Šipon, both white wines, and for Kraški Teran in the Karst. The country also produces Cviček, similar to a rosé, and some decent sparkling wines.

If you happen to get a low-quality wine in Croatia or Slovenia, do as the locals do and mix it with other beverages. *Bevanda* mixes white or red wine with plain water, *gemišt* mixes white wine and bubbly mineral water, while *bambus* uses coca-cola to take the edge off a bitter red wine.

Tips for Travelers

OPPORTUNITIES FOR STUDY AND EMPLOYMENT

Getting a work permit in Croatia and Slovenia is difficult to impossible. However, there are a few ways to spend more time in the area.

Teaching English or teaching in an international school is probably your best bet, though even these jobs are hard to come by. Many locals have an excellent level of English, so it's rare for schools to want to deal with the paperwork required to recruit a native speaker with no residency or work permit. If you'd like to find such a job, contact local language schools or the international schools in Zagreb and Ljubljana to inquire about positions.

Volunteer work is another option, with most posts revolving around the environment. **Caput Insulae Eco Centre** in Beli, Croatia (www.caput-insulae.com), helps protect endangered griffon vultures on the island of Cres and **Blue World** (www.blue-world.org) monitors dolphins from the island of Lošinj.

There are many language schools in Croatia. A couple to check out are the **APLO** (www.aplo-centar.com) and the **Croatian Heritage Foundation** (www.matis.hr), as well as the all-purpose www.studyabroad.com, which lists dozens of study and work programs for many countries, including Croatia and Slovenia.

ACCESS FOR TRAVELERS WITH DISABILITIES

Options for physically challenged travelers have improved in Croatia and Slovenia, but the facilities are still far from what they should be to properly accommodate wheelchairs and other special needs. The older sections of town are difficult to maneuver, often with narrow cobbled streets, but even more modern parts of town often fail to have wheelchair-friendly curbs. Newer and upper-end hotels, as well as airports, almost always have elevators and bathrooms specially designed for wheelchairs. To avoid frustration, plan in advance as much as possible.

Your first stop should be the website of the **Society for Accessible Travel and Hospitality** (www.sath.org), which has a wonderful section of general travel tips to assist in planning. Then contact the tourist office for the cities you would like to visit to find out about sights and hotels with adapted facilities (it's a good idea to double-check this information with the venues before booking).

TRAVELING WITH CHILDREN

Traveling with kids is easy in Croatia and Slovenia. People in the region love children, and generally, the further south you go, the more they love them. You'll often see children around cafés, walking with their parents in the evening, at weddings and family events, and in restaurants, though less so due to monetary constraints on most young families.

Sightseeing

Monuments and museums are open to children, often with free or discounted entrances. You'll find at least one *igraonica* (play center) in most every city. While there aren't lots of spots specifically for very young children, school-age kids will appreciate sights like Rovinj's museum for the *batana* boat, the mummy at Zagreb's archaeological museum, Ljubljana's excellent children's science museum, and the many medieval castles around the area. Make the trip more interesting by creating a treasure hunt for info tidbits to get the kids more involved at the sights you visit.

Restaurants

Children are welcome in most restaurants in Croatia and Slovenia. Diners are generally happy sharing their meal with children, and turn a blind eye to those that run around freely. You may even find not-too-busy waiters or waitresses entertaining them while you eat.

The only exception might be a very chic modern restaurant where small, squealing kids might draw some dirty looks. Also take into account that during the busy summer season not all restaurant patrons are Croatian and Slovenian, and non-locals may have different expectations of young children.

Most restaurants don't have high chairs or booster seats, so if you really need one, you may want to call ahead to find one that does or bring your own portable one. The U.S. website **One Step Ahead** (www.onestepahead.com) has some great travel gear for little ones.

Croatian children generally eat whatever the adults are eating and no one will mind if you ask for another plate so your kids can share

BUSINESS HOURS

Though we've tried to list as best we can the working hours for various restaurants, tourist offices, sightseeing destinations, and shops, it's wise to remember that hours can be somewhat flexible in Croatia and Slovenia. The general rule is that this flexibility grows the smaller the town and the farther south and toward the coast you go. It's not unheard of for a tourist office to suddenly take a week's vacation or a small museum to lock its doors because it just wasn't busy. Keep a positive attitude and move on to the next place. If you're really going out of your way to visit a particular place, it's advisable to call ahead to see if they will be open.

your dish. Nearly every place can whip up a *tjestinine Bolognese* (pasta with meat sauce) or *Milanese* (tomato sauce without meat), some *pohani piletine* (breaded and fried chicken), or *pomfrit* (french fries) for picky eaters. For food emergencies McDonald's can be found in Ljubljana, Maribor, Zagreb, Osijek, Varaždin, Karlovac, Rijeka, Pula, and Split.

Transport, Accommodations, and Supplies

It's best to take a car, plane, or train when traveling around Croatia and Slovenia with young children—buses can be just too much for wiggly little souls to handle.

Most hotels levy a surcharge for children staying in your room, but are happy to provide a *kinderbet* (crib) and extra sheets and towels. On the coast, large hotels and resorts will likely have kiddie clubs or an *igraonica* where children can enjoy a program just for them.

Pharmacies sell a limited selection of baby food and supplies. You'll find a better selection in grocery stores or *drogerie marts* like the chains DM and Müller.

You're unlikely to find many changing facilities outside of shopping centers, McDonald's, highway gas stations, and airports. For young children it's best to bring some changing pads and change them in a stroller or on the seat of the car.

WOMEN TRAVELING ALONE

Croatia and Slovenia are safe for female travelers and you're unlikely to encounter any real problems. That's not to say you won't be "hit on" by the locals, particularly if you go to a bar or disco—it's probably better to find some traveling companions at your hotel or hostel to go out with.

Rape and violent crime are rare in both countries, but that doesn't mean you should forget about safety. Basic common sense should keep you safe: Be wary of strangers; don't drink too much; try to avoid walking on dark, empty streets alone; and don't flash money or jewelry.

GAY AND LESBIAN TRAVELERS

Attitudes toward the gay community in Croatia are still rather in the dark ages, though the younger generation is more accepting. Kissing and holding hands by couples of the same sex is almost never seen, particularly in smaller towns, where it may even cause a confrontation. The one exception to this rule is Zagreb's annual gay pride parade, a huge step for the homosexual community in Croatia.

There are a few havens for same-sex couples in Zagreb, including some gay bars and alternative bars that attract a laid-back crowd of heterosexual and homosexual patrons. Rijeka is probably Croatia's most liberal town and has lots of bars and clubs open to same-sex couples.

For more information check out the website www.travel.gay.hr, about traveling around Croatia; **Iskorak,** an organization for the advancement of gay and lesbian rights, also has a website (www.iskorak.hr) worth a visit.

Though Slovenia is also fairly conservative when it comes to accepting gay and lesbian culture, the community has made some amazing strides in the recent past, making the country even more tolerant than Croatia. The yearly **Ljubljana Gay and Lesbian Pride Parade** (Parada ponosa, www.ljubljanapride.org) has been running since 2000, and a transvestite band, Sestre, was Slovenia's 2002 entry in Eurovision, a popular song contest.

TRAVEL INSURANCE

Travel insurance can come in handy in case of cancellations, missed flights, or stolen property. Before purchasing insurance, you may want to check your current policies as well as your credit cards to see what is already covered. If you need to purchase additional insurance, your own insurance company is one option, or one of dozens of companies that specialize in trip insurance. Try **Betin** (www.betins.com), **Travel Insured** (www.travel insured.com), or **World Nomads** (www.world nomads.com), which targets the backpacker and budget travel market.

HEALTH AND SAFETY
Health Issues

There are no immunizations required for Croatia or Slovenia, though travelers planning to spend a lot of time hiking or in wooded areas may want to consider being inoculated against tick-borne encephalitis. In lieu of getting a shot, you can also avoid heavily forested areas between the months of April and August, wear long sleeves and long pants and a hat, and use an insect repellent with DEET.

Small medical complaints can probably be solved at the local *ljekarna* (pharmacy). Younger staff will likely speak some English, particularly in Croatia, but you can also bring a small dictionary or use the glossary in this book to help you along.

Pharmacies are generally open 8 A.M.–8 P.M. Monday–Friday and 8 A.M.–2 P.M. Saturday. Neighborhood pharmacies take turns staying open 24 hours. Information should be posted at the door or window of all pharmacies or found in the local newspaper. Zagreb has several 24-hour pharmacies that are open every day of the year. These can be found at Trg bana Jelačića 3, Ilica 301 (this would be an extremely long walk from the main square, so take a cab), Grižanska 4, and Ozaljska 1.

EMERGENCY NUMBERS

CROATIA
- Police: 92
- Fire: 93
- Ambulance: 112
- Roadside assistance: 987
- International operator: 901

SLOVENIA
- Police: 113
- Fire: 112
- Ambulance: 112
- Roadside assistance: 1987
- International operator: 115

For medical emergencies, go directly to the nearest *bolnica* (hospital) or call an ambulance (dial 112 in Croatia and Slovenia). EU citizens are entitled to free health care; others will want to check their countries' agreements with Croatia and Slovenia as well as their health insurance. Doctors in Croatian and Slovenian hospitals are usually wonderful and very well trained. Hospitals, particularly in large cities, are very well equipped with all the necessary machines and instruments, though they are shockingly low on even the most basic creature comforts, with Croatia being far worse than Slovenia.

You may want to check out the website of the **International Society of Travel Medicine** (www.istm.org) for a list of some local clinics. Travel Health Online's website (www.tripprep .com) has some excellent tips and country by country information.

Health Insurance

If your own health insurance doesn't cover you while you're traveling, a traveler's health insurance policy is usually worth the money spent if only for the peace of mind. Realize that in any case, you'll need to cover any costs out-of-pocket and then be reimbursed once you return home. A couple of agencies to check out when shopping for travel health insurance are **Travel Guard** (www.travelguard.com), **STA Travel** (www.statravel.com), and **World Travel Center** (www.worldtravelcenter.com).

CONDUCT AND CUSTOMS
Croatia

Croatians are friendly and outgoing and you shouldn't have trouble striking up a conversation with a local. Croatians rarely split the bill; usually one person covers it with the expectation that the favor will be returned at a later date.

One thing that all Croatians are wonderful about is their hospitality. If you are invited to their home, they will likely stuff you with food and drink. Since Croatians are stingy with their compliments to each other, they love receiving them—don't be shy. Croatians particularly love to hear nice things about their coastline, and since it really is beautiful, you might as well go ahead and say it.

If a Croatian visits your home or apartment and you offer them a drink, they will almost invariably say no, as it is considered polite behavior. Gently insist a couple of times; that failing, bring them the drink anyway, "just in case."

There are a few things that North Americans might consider to be rude that are in fact quite normal behavior in Croatia. Elderly people will tend to try to cut in line, which is generally tolerated, if not entirely fair. Lots of diners will employ toothpicks at the table after a meal.

Some travelers complain of poor service, even at luxury establishments. You're more likely to receive this sort of treatment from older employees, a holdover from the socialist regime. If you do experience it, try to have a sense of humor about it and not let it ruin your vacation.

Most Croatians eat a heavier lunch and a lighter dinner, so if you're in a little-touristed

HOLIDAYS

Croatia and Slovenia have lots of official national holidays. While these are fun for locals, who often link them with the nearest weekend or weekends to take a trip, they're not always the most fun for tourists. Most sights, shops, and businesses will close for the day, though you should be able to find some restaurants open. If you find yourself in town on a holiday, make the best of it by following the locals to the nearest park, hiking trail, or beach.

CROATIA

January 1	New Year's Day
January 6	Epiphany
March or April	Easter Monday
May 1	Labor Day
May	Corpus Christi
June 22	Anti-Fascism Day
June 25	Day of Croatian Statehood
August 5	National Thanksgiving Day
August 15	Assumption
October 8	Independence Day
November 1	All Saints' Day
December 25 and 26	Christmas holidays

SLOVENIA

January 1 and 2	New Year's holidays
February 8	Prešeren Day
March or April	Easter Monday
April 27	Day of Uprising Against the Occupation
May 1 and 2	Labor Day
May	Pentecost
June 25	Slovenia Day
August 15	Assumption
October 31	Reformation Day
November 1	All Saints' Day
December 25	Christmas Day
December 26	Independence Day

area, don't be put off by an empty restaurant in the evening.

Tipping is not common practice, though it is polite to leave a kuna or two after a coffee or leave around 10 percent to waitstaff in a restaurant. If you plan on returning, tipping is almost sure to bring you a higher level of service the next time around.

Smoking is commonplace in Croatia and can be positively suffocating in winter, when packed bars and cafes are overloaded with it. Though required by law to have non-smoking areas, the tiny footprint of most establishments negates their impact.

Slovenia

Slovenians are hardworking, generally very well educated, and somewhat more reserved than the people of other Slavic countries. They consider it polite to shake hands when meeting, particularly for the first time. Close friends will kiss twice, once on each cheek.

If you're invited to dinner or to someone's home in Slovenia, it's nice to bring some flowers or a bottle of wine. Meals are considered an important part of family life and most people, young and old, meet up with their friends in cafés.

It is customary to leave a 10 percent tip in restaurants and bars; also give a small tip to taxi drivers.

Slovenia has finally passed a no-smoking ban in indoor places, making going out fun even in the winter.

Public toilets are generally very clean, but don't be surprised if you need to leave a tip for the bathroom attendant. Sometimes the amount is posted. If it isn't, about €0.20 is acceptable.

WHAT TO TAKE

You can buy almost anything you need in Croatia and Slovenia, but keep in mind it will likely be much more expensive than North America. Still, it's best to pack light, hopefully fitting everything into a not-too-big bag with wheels so you can pull it along behind you as you travel around. Backpacks are probably best left to serious backpackers since they tend to make you a target for thieves by labeling you a "tourist."

Try to pack light items that won't need ironing since some small hotels might not have an iron. Layers are great, especially in some inland areas of Croatia and Slovenia where temperatures can vary vastly from day to night. A small umbrella that can fit in your bag and a light rain jacket are a good idea, especially in fall and winter. Also bring a pair of UVB-blocking sunglasses.

Perhaps most importantly, pack some comfortable rubber-soled shoes, especially for seeing the museums and monuments in the old towns, where cobblestoned streets can turn slippery for flat-soled sandals and may catch even medium-sized heels between their grooves.

Though Croatians and Slovenians dress more formally than the average North American, you won't stand out in smart casual clothes and a pair of rubber-soled shoes, though the sneakers you wear to aerobics class might be out of place. Croatians do dress to impress, so you might want to bring along one or two outfits for more formal dinners or club-hopping to fit in with the crowd. You can leave the jacket and tie at home, though, as a collared shirt is acceptable in even the chicest establishments. (That's not to say you won't see locals sporting jackets and ties, however.)

Do keep in mind that some churches might frown on sleeveless or low-cut tops, so dress accordingly when sightseeing.

A hair dryer is a good idea, particularly if you are staying at smaller hotels or in private rooms. Just make sure it's dual voltage, and don't forget the adapter. If you're bringing electronics like laptops or digital cameras that need recharging, make sure they are also dual voltage before packing them.

Also pack any prescription drugs you'll need for at least the length of your stay, as well as a photocopy of the drug's label or a copy of your prescription just in case you need a refill.

Most importantly, don't forget your passport, a copy of your passport in case it's lost or stolen, and your driver's license if you plan on renting a car. You don't have to have an international driving license, but it's not a bad idea. They're available at AAA offices all over North America. Make sure you have a copy of your credit card numbers and the phone numbers for reporting them lost or stolen.

Information and Services

MONEY
Croatia

Croatian currency is called the *kuna*. Bills are denominated in 5, 10, 20, 50, 100, 200, 500, and 1,000 kuna. Coins are available in 1, 5, 10, 20, and 50 *lipa* (100 lipa make 1 kuna) or 1, 2, and 5 kuna.

If you need to exchange money, go to a *banka* (bank) or *mjenjačnica* (exchange bureau).

If you'd like to check the current rate of exchange, try the website www.xe.com. Banking hours are generally 8 A.M.–5 P.M. Monday–Friday and 8 A.M.–noon Saturday, though banks in larger cities may have extended hours and those in small towns or on the coast will often close Saturdays and sometimes for lunch. Banks in coastal tourist areas may stay open until 9 P.M. during the high season.

Most *mjenjačnice* (exchange bureaus) remain open longer than banks, and major post offices often have currency exchange counters as well. The least value for your dollar, pound, or euro is almost always given at hotels.

These days, travelers checks are more of a burden than a blessing. To travel safely, bring credit cards and keep in a separate place the card numbers and phone number to call if a card is lost or stolen. Croatian establishments almost always accept Visa, MasterCard, and oddly enough, Diners Club, which was the first available credit card in the country, giving it a substantial market share. American Express is making serious headway and most places take it as well. Leave your Discover card at home; only a few places will take it.

Be aware that some places, particularly small stores and businesses in smaller towns, may only take cash. Some stores and restaurants also give discounts, sometimes 10 or 20 percent, for paying with cash.

ATMs provide an easy way to get cash (though your bank is likely to charge you a usage fee for withdrawing money). ATMs are available in bigger cities and sometimes very small towns, though you shouldn't count on it. You should have no trouble using your debit card in one of these machines.

Slovenia

Slovenia adopted the euro in 2006. Bills are denominated in 5, 10, 20, 50, 100, 200, and 500 euros. Coins are available in 1, 2, 5, 10, 20, and 50 cents, plus 1 and 2 euros. Banks in Slovenia are generally open 8:30 A.M.–12:30 P.M. and 2–5 P.M. Monday–Friday. Many banks also open 8:30 A.M.–noon on Saturday. Banks in Ljubljana will often be open the entire day, without stopping for lunch.

Using ATMs is a much easier method of getting cash than constantly exchanging money. Machines accepting Visa, Maestro, Cirrus, and MasterCard are all over the country, though you may have a tough time finding ATMs in small villages. The exchange rate offered by the banks is generally reasonable, though your bank will likely charge you a usage fee for withdrawing money.

If you do need to exchange money, banks, post offices, and exchange offices are your best bets.

Major credit cards such as American Express, Visa, MasterCard, and even Diners Club are accepted at most stores, restaurants, and hotels.

COMMUNICATIONS AND MEDIA
Mail

In Croatia and Slovenia you can buy stamps at the *pošta* (post office), easily recognizable in both countries by a black horn against a yellow background. Most post offices are open 8 A.M.–7 P.M. Monday–Friday and 8 A.M.–noon or 1 P.M. on Saturday. The main post offices in large cities and towns are likely to be open even longer. The Slovenian mail system is a little faster and more reliable than Croatia's (where the city of Zagreb uses a local courier service to deliver monthly utility bills). Still, if you need to ship something really quickly, try FedEx (www.fedex.com) or DHL (www.dhl.com); FedEx often works out to be the cheaper of the two. Packages shipped through any postal service should not be sealed until customs is able to take a look at them (you take the package to the desk at the post office, they have a look, and then seal it).

Telephone

To use a phone booth in Croatia and Slovenia, you'll need a telephone card (*telekarta* in Croatia, *telekartica* in Slovenia), available for sale at post offices and newspaper stands. These cards, offered in units of 25, 50, 100, 200, or 500, can be used for making local, long distance, and even international calls (buy at least a 50 for international calls). If you're calling home and not sure how long you'll be on, it might be a good idea to head to the main post office and ask for a cabin, where you make a call and pay afterward. You'll probably want to avoid direct-calling from your hotel room, though using a phone card shouldn't set you back much.

In Croatia, phone numbers can vary in length, with some numbers having six digits, though most have seven these days. In Slovenia, land-line phone numbers have seven digits, and cell phone numbers have six digits. If you're calling Croatia or Slovenia from abroad, you'd dial the international access code, the country code (385 for Croatia, 386 for Slovenia), the area code (drop the initial zero), and the number. If you're dialing within the country, you'll need the area code (including the initial zero) plus the number. Cell phones are preceded by 098, 095, 091, and 099 in Croatia and 031, 040, 041, and 051 in Slovenia. To call abroad from Croatia or Slovenia, dial 00, the country code (1 for the United States and Canada), the area code, and the number.

CELL PHONES

If you'd like to use your cell phone in Croatia or Slovenia, before leaving home check with your service provider about procedures and costs. One of the cheapest options is to buy local SIM cards for use in GSM phones, so you can make calls within Croatia and Slovenia. If you're staying in Croatia or Slovenia longer than a couple of weeks, it's probably a great investment. Before leaving home make sure your phone won't be locked when you insert the local SIM card. Hint: Getting a phone unlocked in Croatia is relatively cheap and simple if you do get stuck (ask at a cell phone store, which typically advertise various carriers). Three SIM card providers to try in Croatia are T-Com, VIP, and Tele2, fairly new to the game and likely to be the cheapest. In Slovenia try Si.mobil.

Internet Access

Internet cafés are found in most cities and towns around Croatia and Slovenia and fees are reasonable. You might want to bring your passport along in case the café requires registration before using a computer.

Wi-Fi access is unfortunately still in short supply, but more cafés and restaurants are popping up with Wi-Fi every month. At the time of writing, Wi-Fi access can be found in most of Croatia's upmarket hotels, as well as at lounge bar Škola (Bogovićeva 7, tel. 01/482-8196, 10 A.M.–1 A.M. Mon.–Sat., 11 A.M.–1 A.M. Sun.) in Zagreb, most T-Mobile stores around the country, and some cafés. The Zagreb and Dubrovnik airports also offer Wi-Fi access.

In Slovenia, most upmarket hotels, airports, and the Konzorcij bookshop (Slovenska 29) in Ljubljana offer free Wi-Fi. You can also subscribe to Slovenia's wireless network, www .neowlan.net, to gain access to hotspots all over the country. You can top up your credit at newspaper kiosks and post offices.

Also try the website www.hotspot-locations .com for a complete list of unpaid and paid wireless access locations in Croatia, Slovenia, and the rest of the world.

English-Language Press

In Croatia, the English-language press is almost entirely confined to the free *In Your Pocket* (www.inyourpocket.com) guides available for Zagreb, Rijeka, Zadar, Dubrovnik, and Osijek. Otherwise, head to a local kiosk or bookstore for English-language dailies and weeklies.

In Slovenia, *In Your Pocket* offers free guides for Ljubljana and Bled. There are some excellent expat newspapers in Slovenia, like the *Slovenia Times* (www.sloveniatimes.com), an English-language daily that can keep you in the know about virtually everything going on in Slovenia. The quarterly magazine *Ljubljana Life* (www.ljubljanalife.com) is also worth checking out.

Croatian and Slovenian Press

Croatia's main national newspapers are *Vjesnik* (www.vjesnik.com), *Jutarnji List* (www.jutarnji .hr), and *Večernji List* (www.vecernji-list.hr). There's also a free daily, published by *Metro* (www.metro.com.hr).

In Slovenia, the major newspapers are *Delo* (www.delo.si) and *Dnevnik* (www.dnevnik.si).

MAPS AND TOURIST INFORMATION
Maps

If it's a simple city map you're searching for, most tourist offices and sometimes hotels can provide you with one that's suitable for a walk around town. You can also purchase maps at bookstores and almost all gas stations. Gas stations on highways should provide a large range, with detailed road, highway, and sometimes even city maps.

If you'd like to purchase maps before leaving home, look on www.amazon.com.

A quick look at Google Maps (www.maps.google.com) can help you get your bearings, but detailed information isn't always available for Croatia and Slovenia, particularly once you're out of the big cities.

Tourist Offices and Websites

A quick look at some of the main tourism websites for Croatia and Slovenia serves as a great way to fill in any holes, ask questions, or search for tour operators and private rooms. The **Croatian National Tourist Office** (www.croatia.hr) should be your first stop for Croatian tourism info. The **Slovenian Tourist Board** (www.slovenia.info) has a feature where you can reserve all types of accommodation, from hotels to private rooms, online.

WEIGHTS AND MEASURES

Both Croatia and Slovenia use the metric system. You can find a handy conversion chart at the back of this book.

The electrical system is 220 volts. Most newer appliances have dual-voltage capability; if not you'll need a voltage converter. Plugs in Croatia and Slovenia are the typical European variety, two-pinned with round prongs. Plug adapters can sometimes be found for sale in airports or heavily touristed areas, but otherwise you'll spend precious time looking for one, so it's best to pick one up before leaving home.

Croatia and Slovenia are in the Central European time zone, meaning that they are one hour ahead of the United Kingdom, six hours ahead of the East Coast's Eastern Standard time zone, nine hours ahead of the American West Coast, 10 hours behind Australian Central Standard time, and 12 hours behind New Zealand. Croatia and Slovenia use the military or 24-hour clock, especially for bus and ferry schedules, though not in conversation. Starting from midnight (0000) add one hour for each hour of the day: 0100 is 1 A.M., 0700 is 7 A.M., 1200 is noon, 1300 is 1 P.M., and 1400 is 2 P.M.

RESOURCES

Glossary

CROATIAN

bijelo vino white wine
cesta road
crkva church
crno vino red wine
dobro good
donji grad lower town
država country
duplo double
gornji grad upper town
grad town
gradska vijećnica town hall
hladno, hladna, hladan cold
ime name
jama cave
janjetina lamb
jezero lake
kavana coffee shop
ljudi people
most bridge
muzej museum
odlično/super great
otvoreno open
pivo beer
plaža beach
samostan monastery
stari grad old town
svijet world
trg square
ulaz entrance
vino wine
vrata gate
vrijeme weather
vrt garden
vruće hot

zatvoreno closed
život life

SLOVENIAN

belo vino white wine
cerkev church
cesta road
črnina red wine
dobro good
država country
dvojen double
grad castle
hladen cold
ime name
jama cave
jezero lake
ljude people
most bridge
muzej museum
odličen great
odprt open
pivo beer
plaža beach
samostan monastery
svet world
trg square
vhod entrance
vino wine
vrata gate
vreme weather
vroč hot
vrt garden
zaprto closed
življenje life

Croatian Phrasebook

Croatian is not the easiest language to learn, so try using English first since most people under 40 speak at least some English. That said, Croatians are extremely happy when someone at least tries to speak Croatian. It's a sure way to break the ice and bring a smile to their face.

PRONUNCIATION

The great thing about Croatian is that it is almost entirely phonetic. If you can master the pronunciation, you can read almost anything even if you have no idea what it says.

Vowels

a like the "a" in "father": *kada* kah-DAH (when)

e like the "e" in "bed": *med* MEHD (honey)

i like the "ee" in "sheet" or "need": *ime* EE-may (name)

o like the beginning of the English dipthong "ou," making the pronunciation of the o something between that in the words "hot" and "ought" (you can also just imagine saying the letter o and use that pronunciation): *dobro* DO-bro (good)

u like the "oo" in "boot" but shorter – purse your lips: *luk* LOOK (onion)

Consonants

c like the "ts" in "dots": *starac* star-AHTS (old man)

č referred to as a hard accent pronounced with a confident "ch" sound like "church" or "arch": *čist* CHEEST (clean)

ć a soft accent, like the "ch" in "chalk" but softer: *noć* NOCH (night)

đ, dž like the "j" in "jam": *đak* JAHK (pupil)

h like the guttural German *ach*, but softer: *hlad* HLAHD (cold)

j like the "y" in "yellow" or "you": *jutro* YU-tro (morning)

lj like the "lli" in "brilliant": *ljubav* lyoo-BAHV (love)

nj like the "ni" in "lenient": *konjak* KON-yak (cognac)

r should have a slight roll to it, like "rr": *vrlo* VRR-low (very)

š like the "sh" in "mash": *naš* NAHSH (our)

ž like the "s" in "treasure": *žena* ZHEH-na (woman)

BASIC AND COURTEOUS EXPRESSIONS

Hello *Bok*

Good morning *Dobro jutro*

Good afternoon *Dobar dan*

Good evening *Dobro veče*

How are you? *Kako si? Kako ste?*

Very well, thank you. *Dobro sam, hvala.*

Okay, good. *Dobro.*

Not okay, bad. *Loše.*

So-so. *Tako-tako.*

And you? *A Vi?*

Thank you. *Hvala.*

Thank you very much. *Puno Vam hvala.*

You're very kind. *Vrlo ste ljubazni.*

You're welcome. *Nema na čemu.*

Goodbye. *Doviđenja.*

See you later. *Vidimo se kasnije.*

Please. *Molim Vas/Te.*

yes *da*

no *ne*

I don't know *Ne znam.*

Just a moment, please. *Samo trenutak molim Vas.*

Excuse me, please. *Oprostite, molim Vas.*

Pleased to meet you. *Drago mi je što smo se upoznali.*

What is your name? *Kako se zovete?*

Do you speak English? *Govorite li engleski?*

I don't speak Croatian well. *Ne govorim hrvatski baš dobro.*

I don't understand. *Ne razumijem.*

How do you say . . . in Croatian? *Kako se kažete . . . na Hrvatskom?*

My name is . . . *Zovem se . . .*

Would you like . . . *Želite li . . .*

Let's go to . . . *Idemo u . . .*

TERMS OF ADDRESS
I *ja*
you (formal) *Vi*
you (familiar) *Ti*
he/him *ona*
she/her *ona*
we/us *mi*
you (plural) *vi*
they/them *oni*
Mr., sir *gospodin*
Mrs., madam *gospođa*
miss, young lady *gospodična*
wife *supruga*
husband *suprug*
friend *prijatelj*
boyfriend; girlfriend *dečko; djevojka*
son; daughter *sin; kći*
brother; sister *brat; sestra*
father; mother *otac; majka*
grandfather, grandmother *djed; baka*

TRANSPORTATION
Where is . . . ? *Gdje se nalazi . . . ?*
How far is it to . . . ? *Koliko ima do . . . ?*
from . . . to *od . . . do*
Where (which) is the way to . . . ? *Kojim putem do . . . ?*
the bus station *autobusni kolodvor*
the bus stop *autobusna stanica*
Where is this bus going? *Kamo ide ovaj autobus?*
the taxi stand *stajalište taksija*
the train station *željježnička postaja*
the boat *brod*
the airport *zračna luka*
I'd like a ticket to . . . *trebam kartu do . . .*
first (second) class *prvi (drugi) razred*
round-trip to . . . *put oko . . .*
reservation *rezervacija*
Stop here, please. *Molim Vas stanite ovdije.*
the entrance *ulaz*
the exit *izlaz*
the ticket office *prodaja karata*
(very) near; far *(vrlo) blizu; daleko*
to; toward *do; prema*
by; through *kraj, uz; kroz*
from *od*

the right *desno*
the left *lijevo*
straight ahead *ravno naprijed*
in front *ispred*
beside *pokraj*
behind *iza*
corner *ugao*
stoplight *semafor*
a turn *skretanje*
right here *upravo ovdje*
somwhere around here *negdje u blizini*
street; boulevard *ulica*
highway *autoput*
bridge; toll *most; cestarina*
address *adresa*
north; south *sjever; jug*
east; west *istok; zapad*

ACCOMMODATIONS
hotel *hotel*
Is there a room? *Imate li sobu?*
May I (may we) see it? *Mogu li (možemo li) je vidjeti?*
What is the rate? *Koja je cijena?*
Is that your best rate? *Dali je to Vaša najbolja cijena?*
Is there something cheaper? *Ima li što jeftinije?*
a single room *jednokrevetna soba*
a double room *dvokrevetna soba*
double bed *bračni krevet*
with private bath *sa privatnom kupaonicom*
hot water *topla voda*
shower *tuš*
towels *ručnici*
soap *sapun*
toilet paper *toaletni papir*
blanket *deka*
sheets *plahte*
air-conditioned *klimatizirano*
fen *ventilator*
key *ključ*
manager *upravitelj*

FOOD
I'm hungry. *Gladan sam/gladna sam.*
I'm thirsty. *Žedan sam, žedna sam.*

menu *jelovnik, meni*
order *narudžba*
glass *čaša*
fork *vilica*
knife *nož*
spoon *žlica*
napkin *salvete*
breakfast *doručak*
lunch *ručak*
daily lunch special *dnevni meni*
dinner *večera*
the check *račun*
soft drink *bezalkoholno piće*
coffee *kava*
iced coffee *ledena kava*
tea *čaj*
bottled water *voda u boci*
tap water *voda iz slavine*
bottled carbonated water *gazirana mineralna voda u boci*
bottled uncarbonated water *negazirana mineralna voda u boci*
beer *pivo*
wine *vino*
white wine *bijelo vino*
red wine *crno vino*
milk *mlijeko*
juice *sok*
cream *vrhnje*
sugar *sečer*
eggs *jaja*
cheese *sir*
yogurt *jogurt*
almonds *bademi*
walnut/nut *orah*
pastry/pie *fina peciva/pite*
cake *kolač, torta*
bread *kruh*
butter *putar*
salt *sol*
pepper *paprika*
basil *bazilika*
garlic *bijeli luk, češnjak*
salad *salata*
vegetables *povrće*
artichoke *artičoka*
asparagus *šparoga*

avocado *avokado*
carrot *mrkva*
corn *kukuruz*
cucumber *krastavac*
eggplant *patlidan*
lettuce *zelena salata*
mushroom *gljiva, šampinjon*
olive *maslina*
onion *crveni luk*
pea *grašak*
potato *krumpir*
spinach *špinat*
tomato *rajčica, paradajz*
truffle *tartuf*
zucchini *tikvica*
fruit *voće*
apple *jabuka*
banana *banana*
cherry *trešnja*
fig *smokva*
grape *grožde*
lemon *limun*
lime *limeta*
orange *naranča*
peach *breskva*
pear *kruška*
plum *šljiva*
raisins *grožđice*
raspberry *malina*
strawberry *jagoda*
fish *riba*
shellfish *školjke*
anchovies *inčuni*
clam *kamenica*
crab *rak, morski rak*
mussels *dagnje*
octopus *hobotnica*
oysters *ostrige*
salmon *losos*
shrimp *škampi*
tiny squid *mala lignja*
trout *pastrva*
tuna *tunj*
meat *meso*
without meat *bez mesa*
poultry *perad*
chicken *pile/piletina*

duck *patka*
quail *prepelica*
turkey *puran, pura*
pork *svinjetina, svinjsko meso*
bacon; ham *slanina; šunka*
cured ham *pršut*
beef; steak *govedina; odrezak*
lamb *janjetina*
rabbit *zec*
chop *kotlet*
ribs *rebra*
sausage *kobasica*
croquette *kroketi*
fried *prženo*
roasted *pečeno*
barbecue; barbecued *roštilj, sa roštilja*

SHOPPING

money *novac*
money-exchange bureau *mjenjačnica*
I would like to exchange travelers checks. *Želio/željela bih promjeniti putnicke čekove.*
What is the exchange rate? *Koji je tečaj?*
How much is the commission? *Kolika je provizija?*
Do you accept credit cards? *Primate li kreditne kartice?*
How much does it cost? *Koliko košta?*
expensive *skupo*
cheap *jeftino*
more *više*
less *manje*
a little *malo*
too much *previše*

HEALTH

Help me please. *Molim Vas pomožite mi.*
I am ill. *Bolestan/bolesna sam.*
Call a doctor. *Zovite doktora.*
Take me to . . . *Odvedite me do . . .*
hospital *bolnica*
drugstore *ljekarna*
pain *bol*
fever *vručica*
headache *glavobolja*
stomachache *bol u želucu*
burn *opeklina*

cramp *grc*
nausea *mucnina*
vomiting *povračati*
medicine *lijek*
antibiotic *antibiotik*
pill; tablet *pilula; tableta*
aspirin *aspirin*
ointment; cream *mast; krema*
cotton *vata*
sanitary napkins *ženski ulosci*
birth control pills *kontracepcijske pilule*
contraceptive foam *kontracepcijska pjena*
condoms *kondomi; prezervativi*
toothbrush *četkica za zube*
toothpaste *pasta za zube*
dentist *zubar*
toothache *zubobolja*

POST OFFICE AND COMMUNICATIONS

I would like to call . . . *Želio bih/željela bih nazvati . . .*
collect *na račun primatelj poziva*
station to station *od stanice do stanice*
person to person *od osobe do osobe*
credit card *kreditna kartica*
post office *pošta*
general delivery *običnom postom*
letter *pismo*
stamp *markica za pismo*
postcard *razglednica*
air mail *slanje avionom*
registered/certified *registrirano/potvrđenc*
money order *poštanska narudzba*
package; box *paket; kutija*
string; tape *spaga; traka*

AT THE BORDER

border *granica*
custom *carina*
immigration *imigracijski ured*
tourist card *turistička karta*
inspection *inspekcija*
passport *putovnica*
profession *zanimanje*
marital status *bračno stanje*
single *neoženjen/neudata*

married; divorced *oženjen/udat; rastavljen/ rastavljena*
widowed *udovac/udovica*
insurance *osiguranje*
title *naziv*
driver's license *vozačka dozvola*

AT THE GAS STATION

gas station *benzinska stanica*
gasoline *benzin*
unleaded *bezolovni*
full, please *pun, molim Vas*
tire *guma*
air *zrak*
water *voda*
oil (change) *ulje (zamjeniti)*
grease *mast*
My ... doesn't work. *Moj ... ne radi.*
battery *akumulator, baterija*
radiator *radiator*
alternator *alternator*
generator *generator*
tow truck *pauk*
repair shop *automehaničarska radiona*

VERBS

to buy *kupiti*
to eat *jesti*
to climb *penjati se*
to do or make *napraviti*
to go *ići*
to love *voljeti*
to work *raditi*
to want *zeljeti*
to need *trebati*
to read *čitati*
to write *pisati*
to repair *popravljati*
to stop *stati*
to get off (the bus) *sići (sa autobusa)*
to arrive *stići*
to stay (remain) *ostati*
to stay (lodge) *nastaniti se*
to leave *otići*
to look at *gledati*
to look for *tražiti*
to give *dati*
to carry *nositi*

to have *imati*
to come *doći*

NUMBERS

zero *nula*
one *jedan*
two *dva*
three *tri*
four *četri*
five *pet*
six *šest*
seven *sedam*
eight *osam*
nine *devet*
10 *deset*
11 *jedanaest*
12 *dvanaest*
13 *trinaest*
14 *četrnaest*
15 *petnaest*
16 *šesnaest*
17 *sedamnaest*
18 *osamnaest*
19 *devetnaest*
20 *dvadeset*
21 *dvadeset i jedan*
30 *trideset*
40 *četrdeset*
50 *pedeset*
60 *šezdeset*
70 *sedamdeset*
80 *osamdeset*
90 *devedeset*
100 *sto*
101 *sto i jedan*
200 *dvijesto*
500 *petsto*
1,000 *tisuću*
10,000 *deset tisuća*
100,000 *sto tisuća*
1,000,000 *milijun*
one half *pola, polovina*
one third *jedna trećina*
one fourth *jedna četvrtina*

TIME

What time is it? *Koliko je sati?*
It's one o'clock. *Jedan je sat.*

It's three in the afternoon. *Tri su popodne./ Petnaest je sati.*
It's four in the morning. *Četri su ujutru.*
six-thirty *šest i trideset/pola sedam*
a quarter till eleven *petnaest do jedanaest/ deset četrdeset pet*
a quarter past five *pet i petnaest*
morning *jutro*
afternoon *popodne*
night *noć*

DAYS AND MONTHS
Monday *ponedjeljak*
Tuesday *utorak*
Wednesday *srijeda*
Thursday *četvrtak*
Friday *petak*
Saturday *subota*
Sunday *nedjelja*
day *dan*

today *danas*
tomorrow *sutra*
yesterday *jučer*
January *Siječanj*
February *Veljača*
March *Ožujak*
April *Travanj*
May *Svibanj*
June *Lipanj*
July *Srpanj*
August *Kolovoz*
September *Rujan*
October *Listopad*
November *Studeni*
December *Prosinac*
a week *tjedan*
a month *mjesec*
after *iza*
before *prije*

Slovenian Phrasebook

PRONUNCIATION
Slovenian is a mostly phonetic language, though it has many more exceptions than its neighboring Croatian. Here are a few of the most important:

- When *l* is placed at the end of a word or after any other consonant than *j*, it is pronounced as a *w*.
- When *v* is placed at the end of a word, after a vowel, or before a consonant it is pronounced as a *w*.
- When *v* is at the beginning of a word, between consonants, or before two consecutive consonants, it is pronounced as *u*.
- If you come across a word with two vowels or consonants that are the same, like *dd*, pronounce the sound as you normally would, only slightly longer.

Vowels
a like the "a" in "father": *da* DAH (yes)
e like the "e" in "bed": *med* MEHD (honey)

i like the "ee" in "sheet" or "need": *ime* EE-may (name)
o like the beginning of the English dipthong "ou," making the pronunciation of the o something between the words "hot" and "ought" (you can also just imagine saying the letter o and use that pronunciation): *dobro* DO-bro (good)
u like the "oo" in "boot" but shorter – purse your lips: *jutro* YOO-tro (morning)

Consonants
These consonants are pronounced differently than English consonants:
c like the "ts" in "dots": *babica* BAH-bee-tsa (grandmother)
č referred to as a hard accent pronounced with a confident "ch" sound like "church" or "arch": *čist* CHEEST (clean)
j like the "y" in "yellow" or "you": *jutro* YOO-tro (morning)
r should have a slight roll to it, like "rr": *večer* VEH-CHER (evening)

š like the "sh" in "mash": *kakšna* KAHK-shna (what is)

ž like the "s" in "treasure": *žena* ZHEH-na (woman)

BASIC AND COURTEOUS EXPRESSIONS

Hello *Živijo*
Good morning *Dobro jutro*
Good afternoon *Dober dan*
Good evening *Dober večer*
How are you? *Kako si? Kako ste?*
Very well, thank you. *Hvala, dobro.*
Okay, good. *Dobro*
And you? *A Vi?*
Thank you. *Hvala.*
Thank you very much. *Hvala lepa.*
You're welcome. *Ni za kaj.*
Goodbye. *Nasvidenje.*
Please. *Prosim.*
yes *da*
no *ne*
Excuse me *Oprostite.*
Pleased to meet you. *Lepo da sva se spoznala.*
What is your name? *Kako vam je ime?*
Do you speak English? *Govorite li angleško?*
I don't speak Slovenian. *Ne govorim slovensko.*
I don't understand. *Ne razumem.*
How do you say ... in Slovenian? *Kako se kažete ... na Slovensko?*
My name is ... *Ime mi je ...*

TERMS OF ADDRESS

I *jaz*
you (formal) *Vi*
you (familiar) *Ti*
he/him *ona*
she/her *ona*
we/us *mi*
you (plural) *vi*
they/them *oni*
wife *soproga*
husband *soprog*
friend *prijatelj*
son; daughter *sin; hči*
brother; sister *brat; sestra*

father; mother *oče; mati*
grandfather; grandmother *ded; babica*

TRANSPORTATION

Where is ... ? *Kje je ... ?*
How do I get to ... ? *Kako pridem do ... ?*
from ... to *od ... do*
the bus station *avtobusna postaja*
Where is this bus going? *Dje ima ohod avtobus do?*
the taxi *taksi*
the train station *željezniška postaja*
the boat *brod*
the airport *letališče*
reservation *rezervacija*
Stop here, please. *Vstavi tukaj, prosim.*
the entrance *vhod*
the exit *izhod*
the ticket office *prodaja vozovnic*
(very) near; far *(zelo) blizu; daleč*
to *do*
by; through *po; skozi*
from *od*
the right *desno*
the left *levo*
straight ahead *naravnost*
in front *pred*
beside *poleg*
behind *zadaj*
stoplight *semafor*
a turn *zasuk*
here *tukaj*
street; boulevard *ulica*
highway *avtocesta*
bridge; toll *most; cestarina*
address *adresa*
north; south *sever; jug*
east; west *vzhod; zahod*

ACCOMMODATIONS

hotel *hotel*
Is there a room available? *Ali imate prosto sobo?*
May I see the room? *Si lahko ogledam sobo?*
What is the rate? *Kakšna je cene sobe?*
Is there something cheaper? *Imate kakšno cenejšo?*
a single room *enoposteljne sobe*

a double room *dvoposteljne sobe*
with a bath *s kopanicu*
hot water *vroča voda*
with a shower *s prho*
towel *brisača*
soap *milo*
blanket *deka*
sheets *rjuhe*
fan *ventilator*
key *ključ*
manager *direktor*

FOOD
I'm hungry. *Lačen sem.*
I'm thirsty. *Žejen sem, žejna sem.*
menu *jedilnik*
order *naročilo*
glass *kozarec*
fork *vilice*
knife *nož*
spoon *žlica*
napkin *servieta*
breakfast *zajtrk*
lunch *kosilo*
dinner *obed*
the check *račun*
coffee *kava*
tea *čaj*
water *voda*
beer *pivo*
wine *vino*
white wine *belo vino*
red wine *črnina*
milk *mleko*
juice *sok*
sugar *sladkor*
eggs *jajca*
cheese *sir*
yogurt *jogurt*
walnut/nut *oreh*
pastry/pie *pita*
cake *torta*
bread *kruh*
butter *maslo*
salt *sol*
pepper *paprika*
garlic *česen*
salad *solata*

vegetables *zelenjava*
asparagus *beluš*
cucumber *kumara*
eggplant *melencana*
lettuce *solata*
olive *oliva*
pea, bean *grah*
spinach *špinača*
tomato *paradižnik*
fruit *sadje*
apple *jabolko*
banana *banana*
cherry *češnja*
fig *figa*
grape *grozd*
lemon *limona*
orange *pomaranča*
peach *breskev*
pear *hruška*
raspberry *malina*
strawberry *jagoda*
fish *riba*
shellfish *školjke*
crab *rak*
salmon *losos*
trout *postrv*
tuna *tuna*
meat *meso*
without meat *brez mesa*
chicken *piščanec*
duck *raca*
turkey *puran, pura*
pork *svinjina*
ham *šunka*
beef *govedina*
lamb *jagnje*
rabbit *zajec*
fried *pražen*
roasted *pečen*
barbecue *žar*

SHOPPING
money *denar*
money-exchange bureau *menjalnica*
bank *banka*
Can you exchange a travelers check? *Mi lahko vnovčite potovalni ček?*

What is the exchange rate? *Kakšno je menjalno razmerje?*
Do you accept credit cards? *Ali spejemate kreditne kartice?*
How much does it cost? *Koliko stane?*
expensive *drago*
cheap *poceni*
more *bolj*
less *manj*
a little *malo*
too much *preveč*

HEALTH
I need help. *Potrebujem pomoč.*
I am ill. *Bolen sem.*
Call a doctor. *Zovite zdravnika.*
hospital *bolnica*
drugstore *lekarna*
pain *bolečina*
headache *glavobol*
burn *opeklina*
medicine *zdravilo*
antibiotic *antibiotik*
pill; tablet *tableta*
aspirin *aspirin*
ointment; cream *mazilo*
tampons *tamponi*
toothbrush *zobna ščetka*
toothpaste *zobna krema*
dentist *zobozdravnik*
tooth *zoba*

POST OFFICE AND COMMUNICATIONS
credit card *kreditna kartica*
post office *pošta*
letter *pismo*
stamps *znamke*
postcard *dopisnica*
air mail *zračna pošta*
string; tape *vrvica; trak*

AT THE BORDER
border *meja*
custom *carina*
immigration *imigracija*
inspection *inspekcija*

passport *potni list*
profession *poklic*
single *samski/samska*
married *poročen/poročena*
insurance *zavorovanje*
title *naslov*
driver's license *vozniško dovoljenje*

AT THE GAS STATION
gas station *bencinska črpalka*
gasoline *bencin*
unleaded *neosvinčen bencin*
full, please *poln, molim Vas*
tire *guma*
air *zrak*
water *voda*
oil (change) *olje (zamenjati)*
grease *mast*
My ... doesn't work. *Moj ... ne radi.*
battery *akumulator, baterija*
radiator *hladilnik*
alternator *alternator*
repair shop *servis*

VERBS
to buy *kupiti*
to eat *jesti*
to climb *prelaziti*
to do or make *narediti*
to go *iti*
I go *grem*
to love *ljubiti*
to work *delati*
to want *hoteti*
to read *čitati*
to write *pisati*
to repair *popravati*
to stop *ustaviti*
to arrive *priti*
to stay (remain) *ostati*
to leave *oditi*
to look at *gledati*
to look for *iskati*
to give *dati*
to carry *nesti*
to have *imeti*

NUMBERS

zero *nula*
one *ena*
two *dva*
three *tri*
four *štiri*
five *pet*
six *šest*
seven *sedem*
eight *osem*
nine *devet*
10 *deset*
11 *enajst*
12 *dvanajst*
13 *trinajst*
14 *štirinajst*
15 *petnajst*
16 *šesnajst*
17 *sedemnajst*
18 *osemnajst*
19 *devetnajst*
20 *dvajset*
21 *enaidvajset*
30 *trideset*
40 *štirideset*
50 *petdeset*
60 *šestdeset*
70 *sedemdeset*
80 *osemdeset*
90 *devedeset*
100 *sto*
101 *stoena*
200 *dvesto*
500 *petsto*
1,000 *tisoč*
10,000 *deset tisoč*
100,000 *sto tisoč*
1,000,000 *milijon*
one half *pol*

TIME

What time is it? *Koliko je ura?*
It's one o'clock in the afternoon. *Ena polpodne.*
It's two in the morning. *Dve zjutraj.*
two-thirty *pol treh*
a quarter till one *ob tri četrt na eno*
a quarter past twelve *ob četrt čez dvanajst*
morning *jutro*
afternoon *popoldan*
night *noč*

DAYS AND MONTHS

Monday *ponedeljek*
Tuesday *torek*
Wednesday *sreda*
Thursday *četrtek*
Friday *petek*
Saturday *sobota*
Sunday *nedjelja*
day *dan*
today *danes*
tomorrow *jutri*
yesterday *včeraj*
January *Januar*
February *Februar*
March *Marec*
April *April*
May *Maj*
June *Junij*
July *Julij*
August *Avgust*
September *September*
October *Oktober*
November *November*
December *December*
a week *teden*
a month *mesec*
later *kasneje*
before *pred*

Suggested Reading

ARTS AND LITERATURE

Bogataj, Janez. *Handicrafts of Slovenia: Encounters with Contemporary Craftsmen.* Rokus, 2002. This beautiful tome with hundreds of color photos looks at Slovenia's traditional and modern-day crafts, from woodworking to ceramics, musical instruments, and more.

Drakulić, Slavenka. *As if I Was Not There.* Abacus, 1999. A quite disturbing novel about a Bosnian woman in a Serbian prison camp, it's still one of the best by controversial author Drakulić. Her criticisms of her homeland in books like *Café Europa* and *How We Survived Communism and Even Laughed* have caused her much negative press in Croatia, but both books are worthwhile reads, though they can ring bitter from time to time.

Erlande-Brandenburg, Alain. *Cathedrals and Castles: Building in the Middle Ages.* Harry N. Abrams, 1995. An interesting look into how castles, cathedrals, and even city walls were designed and built. With plenty of pictures and diagrams, it's a must for architecture and history buffs as a companion to sightseeing in Croatia and Slovenia—or any European country, for that matter.

Jergović, Miljenko. *Sarajevo Marlboro.* Archipelago Books, 2004. Though this book of short stories focuses on the conflict in Bosnia, the author now lives in Zagreb and writes for a popular weekly magazine. The book is one of the best, yet saddest, you'll ever read on the war. The horrific is kept in check by a lot of dry humor, which endears the people of Sarajevo to the reader even more for their amazing strength in the face of tragedy.

Krleža, Miroslav. *On the Edge of Reason.* New Directions Publishing Corporation, 1995. This 1938 novel from one of Croatia's most respected writers blasts conformity by outlining the struggles his hero endures due to an unexpected and against-the-grain observation about a powerful businessman.

Ugrešić, Dubravka. *The Museum of Unconditional Surrender.* New Directions Publishing Corporation, 2002. A deeply moving and touching book, profiling various fictional characters in vignettes that reflect on many topics, from political to emotional, but ultimately hopeful.

HISTORY AND POLITICS

Banac, Ivo. *The National Question in Yugoslavia: Origins, History, and Politics.* Cornell University Press, 1988. Examining the period just before the formation of Yugoslavia after World War I till the Vidovdan Constitution of 1921, Banac writes a scholarly and thoughtful account of the problems and underlying ideas that were never properly solved, ultimately leading to the conflict in the 1990s. One of the best books of its kind.

Benderley, Jill. *Independent Slovenia: Origins, Movements, Prospects.* Palgrave Macmillan, 1996. A decent introduction to Slovenia's recent history, politics, economy, and a bit of culture, this book of essays written by various Slovenian scholars offers a look into the country from a local perspective.

Bracewell, Catherine Wendy. *The Uskoks of Senj: Piracy, Banditry, and Holy War in the Sixteenth-Century Adriatic.* Cornell University Press, 1992. Tracing the history and battles of the Uskoks, this well-researched book is a great look at the pirates who ruled the Adriatic in the 16th and 17th centuries.

Glenny, Misha. *The Balkans: Nationalism, War, and The Great Powers, 1804–1999.* Penguin, 2001. Tackling the very big issue of "the Balkans," Ms. Glenny wisely starts at the beginning of the 19th century, finally disputing the idea that the conflict was based on "ancient hatreds." Her arguments are sound, never prejudiced to any side, and the book is very well written, making its lengthy 742 pages go quite quickly.

Harris, Robin. *Dubrovnik: A History.* Saqi Books, 2003. Beginning her account in the 7th century, Harris weaves together the complex history of Dubrovnik along with its arts, architecture, and economic success and struggles in one easy-to-read volume. Highly recommended for fans of Dubrovnik and of history in general.

Little, Alan, and Laura Silber. *Yugoslavia: Death of a Nation.* Penguin, 1996. The authors, correspondents for the BBC and the *Financial Times,* write a gripping first-hand account of the breakup of the former Yugoslavia. Their positions as journalists gave them access to behind-the-scenes interviews with key figures in the conflict. Another excellent book that dismisses arguments that the conflict was born of ethnic hatreds, the book is a great lesson on the region in the 1980s and 1990s.

Tanner, Marcus. *Croatia: A Nation Forged in War.* Yale University Press, 1997. Written by a Balkan correspondent for London's *Independent* newspaper, Mr. Tanner witnessed the breakup of the Balkans first-hand. His grizzly accounts, factual and unbiased reporting, and excellent writing make for a must-read primer on the Balkan conflict.

TRAVEL AND IMPRESSIONS

Eames, Andrew. *The 8:55 to Baghdad: From London to Iraq on the Trail of Agatha Christie and the Orient Express.* Overlook TP, 2006. Though the title might seem irrelevant to Slovenia and Croatia, the book includes a section where the author tracks down locals who met Ms. Christie during her journeys and also visits the Croatian location of the inspiration for her book, *Murder on the Orient Express,* based on the real-life blizzard that snowed in the famous train for more than a week. Mr. Eames is a keen observer and his musings on Croatia and Slovenia are not to be missed.

Fortis, Abbé Alberto. *Travels into Dalmatia.* Cossimo Classics, 2007. A travelogue published in the 18th century, this book chronicles the journey of the Italian Fortis into a hitherto little-traveled land. His observations on the customs and culture of Dalmatia during this time are historically fascinating.

Novak, Slobodan Prosperov. *Dubrovnik Revisited.* VBZ, 2005. Well-known Croatian writer and former Yale professor Slobodan Prosperov Novak writes a lovely guide to Dubrovnik, seen through tender and witty eyes. Like a class with your favorite college professor, the book points out interesting tidbits and weaves literature, culture, art, and a few laughs through your tour of Dubrovnik's most well-known (and sometimes overlooked) sights. Look out for Novak's *Hvar Revisited,* sure to be a wonderful companion to the author's birthplace and summer home. If you can't find these books before you leave, you'll surely be able to pick them up at English bookstores in Croatia.

West, Rebecca. *Black Lamb and Grey Falcon.* Penguin Classics, 2007. If you buy only one book on the region, Ms. West's excellent travel book from her trip through Yugoslavia in the 1930s is a good choice—it's stunning how accurate some of her observations remain today. She's been criticized for generalizing the former Yugoslavia, but her detail on the local scenery, characters, and history as well as the underlying tension of the time makes for an absorbing read.

Internet Resources

TRAVEL INFORMATION

Croatian National Tourist Board
www.htz.hr

The official site of Croatian tourism, this should fill in all the details you need. Listing destinations and points of interest small and large, accommodation in dozens of cities and villages, and activities around the country, the site also offers an excellent events calendar. A simple search will turn up all sorts of festivals, from Istria's prized Vinistra to more obscure events.

Slovenian Tourist Board
www.slovenia.info

Slovenia's Tourist Board provides a website with pages and pages of information for travelers. Accommodation, events, and sights are definitely listed, but you'll also find information on wine and other themed trails, sportfishing, and shopping. The site seems to have something for even the tiniest, most remote spot in the country. An excellent resource to check out before you go.

Burger Landmarks
www.burger.si

If you want to have a better look at the sights you'll be visiting, this website offers 360-degree panoramas of many sights and landmarks around Slovenia and Croatia.

Find Croatia
www.find-croatia.com

Though the site's not very flashy, each section, whether it's about a city or island or ferry connections, is constantly updated with the latest news stories and information.

Five Stars Croatia
www.fivestars.hr

Initially just for the Zagreb area, Five Stars has expanded to include the Adriatic coast as well.

Browse this easy-to-navigate site to find restaurants, hotels, marinas, and more. Though the site does receive money for advertisements and listings for most of the locations, it does tend to list the best of the best, especially those favored by the local expat community. The site is in English.

Gastronaut
www.gastronaut.hr

Though this site is in Croatian, a few clicks should still get you to a very comprehensive list of restaurants by town. The site's yearly ranking of the top 100 restaurants in Croatia is a reliable to way to find a good to excellent place to eat in the country.

Mali Podrum
www.mali-podrum.com

This site is devoted to Croatian wines, in English, Croatian, and German. Though the events section is in need of an update, you'll find a list of hundreds of wineries, links to some with an online presence, and basic information on Croatian wines.

Kulinarika
www.kulinarika.net/english

The English version of this local Slovenian site lists restaurants divided by region. It also lists recipes, if you'd like to recreate something you ate once you get back home.

TRIP PRACTICALITIES

U.S. State Department
www.state.gov

The U.S. government provides lots of quick facts and practical info for travelers including visa requirements, advice on immunizations, what to do if your passport is lost or stolen, and much more.

CURRENT AFFAIRS

Slovenia Times
www.sloveniatimes.com

This excellent daily news source has articles about current events in Slovenia as well as plenty of information on happenings and things of interest around the country, particularly Ljubljana. If you'd like to talk politics with the locals, a week or so of reading will have you sounding like a native.

Southeast European Times
www.setimes.com

The Southeast European Times site has news in English for countries throughout Southeastern Europe, including Croatia.

Index

A

accommodations: 232, 343-345; *see also specific place*

agroturizam hotels: 345

air travel: 13, 333-334, 335, 336

Alojzijeva cerkev (Aloysius church): 285

Amfiteatar (Roman amphitheater): 23, 104

ancient history: 323

Animafest: World Festival of Animated Films: 44

animals: 321, 322

Anindol: 60

antiques: 44, 189, 273

Aquarium Poreč: 119

aquariums: 119, 136

Archaeological Museum (Arheološki muzej), Cres: 154

Archaeological Museum (Arheološki muzej), Pula: 106

Archaeological Museum (Arheološki muzej), Split: 206

Archaeological Museum (Arheološki muzej), Vis: 224

Archaeological Museum (Arheološki muzej), Zadar: 171

Archaeological Museum (Arheološki muzej), Zagreb: 39

archaeological sites: Amfiteatar (Roman amphitheater) 104; Arheološki park Rimska nekropola (Roman necropolis archaeological park) 293; Crkvica Majka Bojža na škrijinah (Chapel of Our Lady on the Rocks) 124; Crkvica Marije od Trstika (Chapel of St. Mary of Formosa) 105; Eufrazijeva basilica (Basilica of Euphrasius) 118; Krapina 69; Omiš 211; Osor 151; Temple of Augustus 106

Archbishop's Palace: 32

architecture: Ban Jelačić Square (Trg bana Jelačića), Zagreb 30; Basilica of Euphrasius (Eufrazijeva basilica) 118; Cathedral of the Assumption of the Blessed Virgin Mary (Katedrala Marijina Uznesenja) 32; Crkva svetog Marka (St. Mark's Church) 34; Croatian 330-331; Croatian National Theater (Hrvatsko Narodno Kazalište), Zagreb 36-37; Dalmantinac, Juraj 185; Državni arhiv (State Archives) 38; Kaštela 198; Lonjsko polje 96; Market Hall 106; Mirogoj 41; Plečnik, Jože 263; Rijeka villas 137; Rosalnice 299; Rotunda Sv. Nikolaj 292; Sea Organ (Morske orgulje) 172; Šipan 256; Sisak 96; St. Jacob's Cathedral (Katedrala svetog Jakova) 186; St. Vitus' Church (Crkva svetog Vida) 135; Trakošćan 70; Veliki Tabor 69; Villa Angiolina 141; Zrinjevac 39; *see also* castles

Arheološki muzej (Archaeological Museum), Cres: 154

Arheološki muzej (Archaeological Museum), Pula: 106

Arheološki muzej (Archaeological Museum), Split: 206

Arheološki muzej (Archaeological Museum), Vis: 224

Arheološki muzej (Archaeological Museum), Zadar: 171

Arheološki muzej (Archaeological Museum), Zagreb: 39

Arheološki park Rimska nekropola (Roman necropolis archaeological park): 293

Arsenal Gallery of Modern Art: 219

art: Croatian 330; naive movement 35, 78; Slovenian 331-332; *see also specific place*

Art Collections (Umjetničke zbirke): 155

Art Pavilion (Umjetnički paviljon): 39

Art Republika festival: 100, 101

Austro-Hungarian Empire: 325

B

backpacking: 179

Bačvice: 207

Balbi Arch: 113

Bale: 110

ballooning, hot-air: 273

Ban Jelačić Square (Trg bana Jelačića), Krk: 146

Ban Jelačić Square (Trg bana Jelačića), Zagreb: 30-31

Ban Jelačić statue: 31

Banski dvor: 35

Baptistry (Krstionica), Split: 205

Baranja, the: 21, 87-88

Baranska kuća: 21, 88

Bašćanska ploča (Baška tablet): 39, 150

Bašić, Nikola: 172

Basilica of Euphrasius (Eufrazijeva basilica): 118

Baška: 149

Baška tablet (Bašćanska ploča): 39, 150

Baška Voda: 214

basketball: 49
Batana House (Kuća o batani): 23, 113
Baterija: 224
Bazilika svetog Ivana Evandeliste (Church and
    Convent of St. John the Baptist): 160
beaches: Baška 149; Bol 217; Brač 216; Brela
    213; Drvenik Veli 198; Dubrovnik 246; Dugi
    Otok 178; Elafiti Islands 255; Jelsa 223;
    Lovran 144; Lubenice 155; Lumbarda 230;
    Makarska Riviera 214–215; Mali Lošinj 156;
    Novalja 165; nude 162, 165, 177, 223; Opatija
    Riviera 141; Pag 164, 165; Pelješac Peninsula
    256; Poreč 119; Primošten 193; private 196;
    Pula 107; Rab 160, 162; Rabac 101; Rijeka 137;
    Rovinj 114; Šibenik 188; Silba 178; Split 207;
    Sućuraj 224; Susak 159; Trogir 196; Ugljan
    177; Valun 155; Vela Plaža 149; Vrboska 224;
    Zadar 173
Beccadelli, Dubrovnik Lodovico: 256
beer: 268, 348
Bela Krajina: 298-299
Belec: 62
Beli: 154
best-of itinerary: 14–17
beverages: 348
Bijela vila (White Villa): 111
biking: Bohinj 305; Bovec 307; Cape Kamenjak
    107; Karlovac 91; Kranjska Gora 306;
    Kumrovec 67; Ljubljana 273; Maribor 286;
    Marjan Peninsula 206; Mljet 232; mountain
    295, 306; Mount Sljeme 48; Veli Brijun 111;
    Velika Planina 295; Zagorje 66; Zagreb 46;
    Zlatni Rt (Golden Cape) 114
Bilo Idro: 16, 223
bird-watching: Caput Insuae Eco Centre 154;
    Kopački rit 86; Lonjsko polje 96; Sečovlje
    Salina Nature Park 316
Biševo: 24, 227
Biskupovo (Bishop's House): 256
Biskupska palača (Bishop's Palace): 154
Bistro Apetit: 15, 51
Bitoraj: 21, 95
Bjeloasica: 94
Black Madonna: 62
Bled: 14, 22, 300-304
Blue Cave (Modra špilja): 24, 227
Blue World Institute of Marine Research and
    Conservation: 157
boat travel: 334, 335, 336
Bogojina: 292
Bogovićeva: 14, 53
Bohinj: 22, 304-306
Bol: 23, 217

Boškinac: 165
Bosnia-Herzegovina: 214
Botanički vrt (Botanical Gardens): 38
Bovec: 20, 307
Brač: 23, 216-218
Brački muzej (Brač Museum): 218
Branislav Dešković Gallery: 217
Brda region: 317
Brela: 213
Brewery Museum (Pivovarski muzej): 268
Brijuni Islands: 23, 111-112
Britanski trg: 44
Brod Fortress: 82
Brodsko Kolo Festival: 82
Brtonigla: 19, 123
Buffet Škola: 17, 251
Bukaleta: 19, 153
Bukovac, Vlaho: 254
Bundek: 47
bura winds: 179
Burglars' Tower (Kula lotrščak): 36
business hours: 350
bus travel: 13, 334, 335, 336, 338
butterflies: 95
Buzet: 109

C

cable cars: 305
Čakovec: 77
Calvary Hill (Kalvarija): 62
camping: 345
canoeing: 232-233
canyoning: 305
Cape Kamenjak: 107
Caput Insuae Eco Centre: 19, 154
Carinthian Museum of Ravne (Koroški
    pokrajinski muzej): 290
carnival season: 138, 164
Carpe Diem: 16, 24, 219
car travel: 334, 335, 336-338, 339
castles: Bled 301; Čakovec 77; Celje 292;
    Grad Podsreda 294; Historical Museum of
    Istria (Povijesni muzej Istre) 106; Kamnik
    295; Ljubljanski Grad (Ljubljana Castle)
    265; Metlika 298; Murska Sobota 291;
    Novo Mesto 297; Ozalj 93; Ptuj Grad 287;
    Ribnica 296-297; Sisak 96; Škofja Loka
    294; Štanjel 318; Stari Grad, Varaždin 73;
    Trakošćan 70; Trsatska gradina (Trsat
    Castle) 136; Veliki Tabor 68
Cathedral (Katedrala), Dubrovnik: 243
Cathedral of St. Anastasia (Katedrala svete
    Stošlje): 170

Cathedral of St. Domnius (Katedrala svetog Dujma): 204

Cathedral of St. Mary (Katedrala svete Marije): 106

Cathedral of St. Nicholas (Stolnica sveti Nikolaja): 265

Cathedral of the Ascension (Katedrala Marijinog Uznesenja): 74

Cathedral of the Assumption (Katedrala Uznesenja), Krk Town: 146

Cathedral of the Assumption (Stolnica Marijinega vnebovzetja), Koper: 312

Cathedral of the Assumption of the Blessed Virgin Mary (Katedrala Marijina Uznesenja): 32

Catholicism: 330, 331

caves: Blue Cave (Modra špilja) 227; exploring 94, 305; Karst Region 316; Manita Peć 179; Pazin 124; Pekel Cave 293; Postojna Cave (Postojnska Jama) 318; Škocjanske Jame (Škocjan Caves) 318; Vela Luka 230

Cavtat: 254

Celje: 292

Celje Castle (Stari Grad Celje): 292

Celje Regional Museum (Pokrajinski muzej Celje): 292

cell phones: 356

cemeteries: 41, 73, 106, 225

Centar Kaptol: 32

Centar za istraživanje mora (Marine Biological Institute): 114

Centromerkur: 262

Cerkev Marijinega Vnebovzetja (Church of the Assumption): 302

Cerkev Sveti Janez (Church of St. John): 305

Cerkev sveti Trojice (Church of the Holy Trinity): 313

Čevljarski Most (Cobblers' Bridge): 267

Chapel of Our Lady of Carmel (Crkvica Gospe od Karmene): 101

Chapel of Our Lady on the Rocks (Crkvica Majka Bojža na škrijinah): 124

Chapel of St. George (Kapelica sv. Jurga): 60

Chapel of St. Hieronymous (Crkvica svetog Jeronima): 130

Chapel of St. Mary of Formosa (Crkvica Marije od Trstika): 105

children's activities: 22-23, 350; Aquarium Poreč 119; Caput Insuae Eco Centre 154; Etnoland 187; Hiša Eksperimentov (House of Experiments) 264; Kobilarna Lipica (Lipica Stud Farm) 319; Puppet Theater (Lutkovno Gledališče) 265; Railway Museum (Železniški muzej) 267; Slovenski gasilski muzej (Fire Brigade Museum) 299; Trakoščan 70; Zagreb City Museum (Muzej grada Zagreba) 33; zoos 46, 268

Christie, Agatha: 82

Church and Convent of St. John the Baptist (Bazilika svetog Ivana Evandeliste): 160

Church of Our Lady (Crkva velike Gospe): 256

Church of Our Lady of Trsat (Crkva gospel trsatske): 136

Church of St. Andrew (Crkva svetog Andrije): 160Church of St. Blaise (Crkva svetog Blaža): 110

Church of St. Catherine (Crkva svete Katerine): 36

Church of St. George (Stolna Cerkev Sv. Jurija): 315

Church of St. Isidor (Crkva Sv. Izidora): 152Church of St. Jerome (Crkva Sv. Jeronima): 78

Church of St. John (Crkva svetog Ivana), Hvar: 223

Church of St. John (Cerkev Sveti Janez), Bohinj: 305

Church of St. Justine (Crkva svete Justine): 160

Church of St. Mary (Crkva svete Marije): 42

Church of St. Mary of the Snow (Crkva Sveta Marija Snježne): 151

Church of St. Mary the Great (Crkva svete Marije Velike): 159

Church of St. Nicholas (Crkva svetog Nikole), Susak: 158

Church of St. Nicholas (Crkva svetog Nikole), Varaždin: 72

Church of Sts. Cosmas and Damian (Crkvica Sv. Kuzmana i Domjana): 129

Church of Sts. Cosmos and Damian (Crkva svetog Kozme i Damjana), Hvar: 219

Church of Sts. Cosmos and Damian (Crkva svetog Kozme i Damjana), Lastovo Grožnjan: 231

Church of Sts. Vitus and Modestus (Župna crkva Sv. Vida i Modesta): 129

Church of the Annunciation (Crkva svetog Blagovijesta): 93

Church of the Assumption (Cerkev Marijinega Vnebovzetja): 302

Church of the Birth of the Blessed Virgin (Crkva rodenja blažene djevice Marije): 101

Church of the Blessed Virgin Mary (Crkva blažene djevice Marije): 130

Church of the Holy Spirit (Crkva svetog Duha), Hvar: 219

Church of the Holy Spirit (Crkva svetog Duha), Požega: 80
Church of the Holy Trinity (Cerkev sveti Trojice): 313
Cibona tower: 41, 49
Čipiko Palace: 195
Čipkarska šola (Lace-Making School): 20, 308
City Cemetery (Gradsko Groblje), Varaždin: 73
City Gallery (Gradska galerija), Labin: 101
City Tower (Gradski toranj), Rijeka: 135
City Walls (Gradske zidine), Dubrovnik: 238
climate: 12, 320-321, 322
climbing: 94, 179, 305
Club Peek&Poke: 135
Coal-Mining Museum of Slovenia (Muzej premogovništa Slovenije): 294
Coastal Slovenia: 311-316; highlights 310; Hrastovlje 313; Koper 312-313; maps 9, 310; Piran 315-316; planning tips 11, 310; Portorož 315
Cobblers' Bridge (Čevljarski Most): 267
Collection of Sacral Art (Izložbena zbirka sakraine umjetnosti): 146
communications: 355
Community Gallery Hlebine (Galerija Hlebine): 78
concentration camps: 95
consulates: 340, 341
Convent of St. Nicholas (Samostan svetog Nikole): 196
convents, Dubrovnik: 245
costume parades: 74
crafts: Đakovo 83; Etnoland 187; International Folklore Festival 44; Rab 161; Slovenian 332; Varaždin 74
Cres: 19, 151-155
Cres Town: 151
Crkva blažene djevice Marije (Church of the Blessed Virgin Mary), Hum: 130
Crkva Blažene Djevice Marije, Lepoglava: 70
Crkva gospel trsatske (Church of Our Lady of Trsat): 136
Crkva presvetog Trojstva (Holy Trinity Church): 90
Crkva rodenja blažene djevice Marije (Church of the Birth of the Blessed Virgin): 101
Crkva Sv. Jeronima (Church of St. Jerome): 78
Crkva Sv. Anastazije: 60
Crkva Sveta Marija Snježne (Church of St. Mary of the Snow): 151
Crkva svete Eufemije (St. Euphemia's Church): 113
Crkva svete Justine (Church of St. Justine): 160

Crkva svete Katerine (Church of St. Catherine): 36
Crkva svete Lucije (St. Lucy's Church): 149
Crkva svete Marije (Church of St. Mary), Zagreb: 42
Crkva svete Marije (St. Mary's Church), Vrboska: 223
Crkva svete Marije (St. Mary's Church), Zadar: 171
Crkva svete Marije Velike (Church of St. Mary the Great): 159
Crkva Sveti Jurja (St. George's Church): 164
Crkva Sveti Kristofor (St. Christopher's Church): 160
Crkva svetog Andrije (Church of St. Andrew): 160
Crkva svetog Antuna (St. Anthony's Church): 157
Crkva svetog Blagovijesta (Church of the Annunciation): 93
Crkva svetog Blaža (Church of St. Blaise): 110
Crkva svetog Ciprijana (St. Cyprian's Church): 225
Crkva svetog Donata (St. Donat's Church): 170
Crkva svetog Duha (Church of the Holy Spirit), Hvar: 219
Crkva svetog Duha (Church of the Holy Spirit), Požega: 80
Crkva svetog Ivana (Church of St. John): 223
Crkva svetog Ivana Krstitelja (Franciscan Church of St. John the Baptist): 73
Crkva svetog Jurja (St. George's Church): 144
Crkva svetog Kozme i Damjana (Church of Sts. Cosmos and Damian), Hvar: 219
Crkva svetog Kozme i Damjana (Church of Sts. Cosmos and Damian), Lastovo Grožnjan: 231
Crkva svetog Kvirina (St. Quirinus's Church): 146
Crkva svetog Lovre (St. Lawrence's Church), Požega: 81
Crkva svetog Lovre (St. Lawrence's Church), Vrboska: 224
Crkva svetog Marka (St. Mark's Church): 34
Crkva svetog Mihovila (St. Michael's Church): 257
Crkva svetog Nikole (Church of St. Nicholas), Susak: 158
Crkva svetog Nikole (Church of St. Nicholas), Varaždin: 72
Crkva svetog Nikole (St. Nicholas's Church), Cavtat: 254
Crkva svetog Šimuna (St. Simeon's Church): 173

Crkva svetog Stjepana (St. Stephen's Church): 126
Crkva svetog Vida (St. Vitus's Church): 135
Crkva svetog Vlaha (St. Blasius's Church): 241
Crkva Sv. Izidora (Church of St. Isidor): 152
Crkva velike Gospe (Church of Our Lady): 256
Crkvica Gospe od Karmene (Chapel of Our Lady of Carmel): 101
Crkvica Majka Božža na škrijinah (Chapel of Our Lady on the Rocks): 124
Crkvica Marije od Trstika (Chapel of St. Mary of Formosa): 105
Crkvica svetog Jeronima (Chapel of St. Hieronymous): 130
Crkvica Sv. Kuzmana i Domjana (Church of Sts. Cosmas and Damian): 129
Črnomelj: 299
Croatia: culture 330; economy 328; food 345-346; geography 320-322; government 328; inland 63-96; money 354; social customs 352; transportation 333-335, 336-338; visas 340; wine 18
Croatian History Museum (Hrvatski povijesni muzej): 35
Croatian Maritime Museum (Hrvatski pomorski muzej): 24, 207
Croatian Museum of Naive Art (Hrvatski muzej naivne umjetnosti): 34
Croatian National Theater (Hrvatsko Narodno Kazalište), Rijeka: 137
Croatian National Theater (Hrvatsko Narodno Kazalište), Zagreb: 36-37
Croatian Natural History Museum (Hrvatski prirodoslovni muzej): 35
cross-country skiing: 281, 306
Crvendać: 20, 87
Crveni Otok: 114
Cukarin: 16, 230
culinary tour: 17-19
customs: 340, 341
Cvjetni trg (Flower Square): 36

D

Dakovo: 83
Dalmantinac, Juraj: 186
Damir i Ornela: 19, 123
dance, folk: 82
d'Annunzio, Gabriele: 135
Dan Vina (Wine Day): 109
death paintings: 313
demography: 330, 331
design, interior: 37
Desnićka, Veronika: 68

dialects, Slovenian: 289
Dilj mountain: 82
Dinamo: 343
dinosaur footprints: 111
Diocletian, Emperor: 202, 205
Diocletian's Palace: 16, 24, 204
disabilities, travelers with: 349
Zavičajni muzej (District Museum), Poreč: 119
diving: 342; Bled 302; Dubrovnik 247; Kornati Islands 183; Krk 150; Mljet 232-233; Portorož 314; sponge 192
Dobra Vila: 20, 307
Dolac Market (Tržnica Dolac): 15, 31, 51
Dolenjska: 296-298
Dolenjski Muzej (Dolenjska Museum): 297
dolphin watching: 158
Dom hrvatskih likovnih umjetnika (House of Croatian Artists): 40
Dominikanski samostan (Dominican monastery), Bol: 217
Dominikanski samostan (Dominican monastery), Dubrovnik: 244
Dominikanski samostan (Dominican monastery), Ptuj: 287
Donja jezera (Lower Lakes), Plitvice Lakes National Park: 182
Donji Grad (Lower Town), Zagreb: 36
Dordić-Mayner Park (Perivoj Dordić-Mayner): 255
Dragon Bridge (Zmajski Most): 264
Drašković Palace (Palača Drašković): 73
Dražen Petrović Memorial Center Museum: 41
drinks: 348
driving: 334, 335, 336-338
Drvenik Mali: 198
Drvenik Veli: 198
Državni arhiv (State Archives): 38
Držić, Marin: 244
Dubovac: 91
Dubrovnik: 16, 234-258; accommodations 248-249; entertainment 246-247; food 250-252; highlights 235; history 235-237; maps 9, 236; old town 238-244; planning tips 10, 237; services 252; sights 238-246; summer crowds 246; transportation 253
Dubrovnik Art Gallery (Umjetnička Galerija): 245
Dubrovnik Summer Festival: 247
Dugi Otok: 178
Duke's Palace (Knežev dvor), Pag Town: 164
Duke's Palace (Kneževa palača), Šibenik: 186
Dulčić-Masle-Pulitika Gallery (Galerija Dulčić-Masle-Pulitika): 243

Dvorac: 86
Dvorac Eltz (Eltz Castle): 89

E

economy: 328-329
Elafiti Islands: 255-256
El Greco: 39
Eltz Castle (Dvorac Eltz): 89
embassies: 340, 341
emergency numbers: 352
employment: 349
English-language media: 356
Enjingi: 20, 81
Entomološki muzej (Entomology Museum): 72
environmental issues: 321, 322
Etnografski muzej (Ethnographic Museum),
    Split: 205
Etnografski muzej (Ethnographic Museum),
    Zagreb: 38
Etnografski muzej Istre (Ethnographic Museum
    of Istria): 124
Etnografski muzej Rupe (Rupe Ethnographic
    Museum): 244
Etnoland: 187
Eufrazijeva basilica (Basilica of Euphrasius): 118
Euphrasius, Bishop: 118
Exhibition Pavilion: 38

F

farmer's markets: Đakovo 83; Dolac Market
    (Tržnica Dolac) 31; Tourist Farm Vinski hram
    kupljen 291; Zadar 172
fauna: 321, 322
Fažanska škola soljenja sardela (Fažana School
    of Sardine Salting): 109
ferries: 334
Fešta istarske malvazije (Istrian Malvasia
    Festival): 109, 123
Fešta miadega vina (Festival of New Wine): 109
film: Animafest: World Festival of Animated
    Films 44; Croatian Festival of One-
    Minute Films 81; International Festival
    of Documentary Film 272; Libertas Film
    Festival 247; Motovun Film Festival 127; Pula
    Film Festival 107; Slovenian 332; Teatro
    Fenice 136; Trash Film Festival 75; Zagreb 43
Filovci: 292
Fire Brigade Museum (Slovenski gasilski
    muzej): 299
fish: 346
Fisherman's festivals (Ribarske fešte): 109, 155
fishing: Bjeloasica 94; Bohinj 305; Fužine 94; Iž
    177; Jarun 47

Fishing Museum (Ribarski muzej): 226
fjords: 116
flora: 321, 322
Flower Square (Cvjetni trg): 36
folk dance: 82
folklore festival: 146
Fonticus Gallery: 129
food: 109, 191, 345-349; see also specific place
foreign embassies: 340, 341
Fortica: 15, 101
fortress (Kaštel), Krk: 146
Forum, Pula: 106
Forum, Zadar: 170
Fotogalerija Lang: 59
Franciscan Church of St. John the Baptist
    (Crkva svetog Ivana Krstitelja): 73
Franciskanska cerkev (Franciscan Church of
    the Annunciation): 262
Franjevački samostan (Franciscan Monastery),
    Cres: 152
Franjevački samostan (Franciscan Monastery),
    Dubrovnik: 240
Franjevački samostan (Franciscan Monastery),
    Krapanj Island: 192
Franjevački samostan (Franciscan Monastery),
    Pelješac Peninsula: 256
Franjevački samostan (Franciscan Monastery),
    Pula: 106
Franjevački samostan (Franciscan Monastery),
    Punat: 148-149
Franjevački samostan (Franciscan Monastery),
    Rijeka: 136
Franjevački samostan (Franciscan Monastery),
    Samobor: 60
Franjevački samostan (Franciscan monastery),
    Vukovar: 89
Franjevački samostan (Franciscan Monastery),
    Zadar: 171
Franjevački trg (Franciscan Square): 73
Freedom Square (Trg Slobode): 72
frescoes: 332; see also specific place
funicular: 36
Fužine: 21, 22, 94-95

G

Galerija Dulčić-Masle-Pulitika (Dulčić-Masle-
    Pulitika Gallery): 243
Galerija Hlebine (Community Gallery Hlebine):
    78
Galerija Ivana Meštrovića (Ivan Meštrović
    Gallery): 206
Galerija Ivana Rangera (Gallery of Ivan
    Ranger): 70

Galerija likovnih umjetnosti (Gallery of Fine Arts): 84
Galerija Miha Maleš (Miha Maleš Gallery): 295
Galerija Prica: 60
Galerija starih i novih majstora (Gallery of Old and New Masters): 73
Galerija zatvorskih radova (Gallery of Prisoner's Work): 70
Gallery Alvona: 101
Gallery Rigo: 122
gardens: Karlovac 91; Lokrum 246; Prirodoslovni muzej (Natural History Museum) 136; Srdenjovje kovni samostanski mediteranski vrt Sv. Lovre (Medieval Mediterranean Garden of St. Lawrence's Monastery) 187; Trsteno 254; Tvrdalj 222; Veli Lošinj 157-158; Villa Angiolina 141; Volčji Potok 295; Zagreb 38
Gavelac: 177
gay travelers: 351
Generalić, Ivan: 78
Generalić Gallery: 78
geography: 320, 322
Gil's: 17, 250
Glagolitic script: 150
Glagolitic Script Exhibition (Izložba glagoljice): 136
Glavna tržnica (Main Market), Ljubljana: 264
Glavni kolodvor (Main Train Station), Zagreb: 39
Gliptoteka Hazu (Glyptotheque of the Croatian Academy of Sciences and Arts): 32
Golden Cape (Zlatni Rt): 114
Golden Gate (Porta Aurea), Split: 206
Golden Gate (Zlatna vrata), Pula: 104-105
Golf Hotel Castle Mokrice: 14, 298
Goli Otok: 160
Gornja jezera (Upper Lakes), Plitvice Lakes National Park: 182
Gornji Grad (Upper Town), Osijek: 84
Gornji Grad (Upper Town), Zagreb: 15, 22, 33
Gornji trg (Upper Square), Ljubljana: 266
Gorski Kotar: 21, 22, 94-96
Gospa Gusarica (Our Lady of the Pirates): 226
Gospa od Šunja (Our Lady of Šunja): 255
Gostilna Lectar: 20, 303
gourmet food festivals: 109
government: 328
Governor's Palace (Guvernerova palača): 135
Gradska galerija (City Gallery), Labin: 101
Gradska loža (Town Loggia), Trogir: 195
GradsKavana: 17, 250
Gradske zidine (City Walls), Dubrovnik: 238
Gradski muzej (Town Museum), Karlovac: 91

Gradski muzej (Town Museum), Korčula: 229
Gradski muzej (Town Museum), Pag: 165
Gradski muzej (Town Museum), Požega: 81
Gradski muzej (Town Museum), Samobor: 59
Gradski muzej (Town Museum), Vukovar: 88
Gradski toranj (City Tower), Rijeka: 135
Gradsko Groblje (City Cemetery), Varaždin: 73
Gračišće: 125
Graphic Art Gallery (Kabinet grafike): 39
graphic arts: 268
Great Bell Tower (Veli zvonik): 160
griffon vultures: 154
Gripe Fortress (Tvrđava Gripe): 207
Groda: 219
Grožnjan: 17, 129-130
Gubec, Ambroz Matija: 69
Gundulić, Ivan: 243
Guvernerova palača (Governor's Palace): 135

H

Hajduk: 208, 343
handicrafts: see crafts
health: 351-352
herdsmen's settlements: 295
Herzegovina: 214
hiking: 341; Bjeloasica 94; Bled 302; Bohinj 305; Bosnia-Herzegovina 214; Bovec 307; Cape Kamenjak 107; Caput Insuae Eco Centre 154; Celje 292; Dilj mountain 82; Gračišće 125; Iški Vintgar 281; Iž 177; Klek mountain 94; Kobarid Historical Walk 308; Krk 150; Krka National Park 192; Labin to Rabac 100; Lubenice 155; Marjan Peninsula 206; Mount Sljeme 48; Northern Žumberak 93; Opatija 140; Paklenica National Park 179; Park prirode Učka (Učka Nature Park) 141; Plitvice Lakes National Park 182; Risnjak National Park 94; Samobor 60; Šipan 256; Stara Baška 149; Susak 158; Velika Planina 295; Vis 225; Wire Walk 272; Zbiljsko jezero 281; Žumberak 93
Hiša Eksperimentov (House of Experiments): 22, 264
Historical Museum of Istria (Povijesni muzej Istre): 106
history: 323-328
History and Maritime Museum of the Croatian Littoral (Povijesni i pomorski muzej hrvatskog): 135
Histria Festival: 107
Hlebine: 78
Hodočasnička crkva Marije Bistričke (Pilgrimage Church of St. Mary of Bistrica): 62
holidays: 353

Holy Trinity Church (Crkva presvetog Trojstva): 90
Homeland Altar (Oltar domovine): 48
Homeland War: 327-328; Dubrovnik siege 240; museum 91; in Slavonia 79; Vukovar siege 88, 89
Hostel Celica: 22, 274
hostels: 345
hot-air ballooning: 273
Hotel Grad Otočec: 20, 298
Hotel San Rocco: 19, 123
hot springs: 292, 294, 302
House of Croatian Artists (Dom hrvatskih likovnih umjetnika): 40
House of Experiments (Hiša Eksperimentov): 22, 264
House of Marco Polo: 229
House of Workers (Radnički Dom): 88
Hrastovlje: 313
Hrelić: 44
Hrvatski muzej naivne umjetnosti (Croatian Museum of Naive Art): 34
Hrvatski pomorski muzej (Croatian Maritime Museum): 24, 207
Hrvatski povijesni muzej (Croatian History Museum): 35
Hrvatski prirodoslovni muzej (Croatian Natural History Museum): 35
Hrvatsko Narodno Kazalište (Croatian National Theater), Rijeka: 137
Hrvatsko Narodno Kazalište (Croatian National Theater), Zagreb: 36-37
Hum: 23, 130
human fish: 318
Humska Konoba: 17, 23, 130
Hvar: 15, 16, 218-224
Hvar Town: 23, 218-222

I

ice skating: 281
Idrija: 20, 308
Ilirski trg: 34
Illyricus, Matija Vlačić: 101
Ilok wineries: 89-90
Inland Croatia: 63-96; highlights 64; Karlovac Region 90-96; maps 9, 65; Međimurje 71-79; planning tips 8, 66; Slavonia 79-90; Zagorje 66-71
Inland Slovenia: 282-308; highlights 283; Julian Alps 300-308; maps 9, 284; planning tips 10, 283; Pohorje Region 285-290; Pomurje Region 291-292; Savinjska Valley 292-294
insurance: health 352; travel 351

interior design: 37
International Festival of Puppet Theater: 44
International Folklore Festival: 44
International Lace-Making Festival: 70
International Theater Festival: 107
Internet access: 356
Iški Vintgar: 281
Istria: 23, 97-130; culinary tour 17-19; highlights 98; inland 124-130; Labin 100-104; maps 9, 99; planning tips 8, 100; Poreč 117-124; Pula 104-110; wine 119, 120
Istrian Malvasia Festival (Fešta istarske malvazije): 123
itineraries: 14-24; Bosnia-Herzegovina side trip 214; Dubrovnik 238; Kvarner Islands 147; Ljubljana 263; Šibenik 187; Slavonia wine roads 80; time-constrained 8; village visits 20-21; Zagreb 30
Ivan Meštrović Gallery (Galerija Ivana Meštrovića): 206
Ivica i Marica: 22, 50
Iž: 177
Izložba glagoljice (Glagolitic Script Exhibition): 136
Izložbena zbirka sakralne umjetnosti (Collection of Sacral Art): 146
Izola: 313-314

J

janjetina (lamb): 191, 192
Jarun: 47
Jasenovac: 95
jazz: 272
Jelačić family tomb: 62
Jelačić Novi dvori: 61
Jelsa: 220, 223
Jesuit's Square (Jezuitski trg): 36
jet skiing: 314
Jeunesse Musicales International Cultural Centre: 129
Jewish Square (Židovski trg): 285
Jezero mira: 178
Jezuitski trg (Jesuit's Square): 36
Joyce, James: 106
Julian Alps: 300-308
Juraj Šporer Art Pavilion: 141
Jurandvor: 149
Jurin Podrum: 16, 222
Jurjevanje festival: 299
Jurlinovi Dvori: 15, 192, 193

K

Kabinet grafike (Graphic Art Gallery): 39

Kalvarija (Calvary Hill), Marija Bistrica: 62
Kalvarija (Stations of the Cross), Zbiljsko
jezero: 281
Kamanjo's: 220
Kamenita vrata (Stone Gate): 33
Kamerlengo: 196
Kamnik: 295
Kandarola Cove: 162
Kapelica sv. Jurga (Chapel of St. George): 60
Kapetanova kuća: 16, 257
Kaptol neighborhood: 30, 49
Karlovac: 90
Karst Region: 9, 11, 316-319
Kaštela: 198
Kaštel (fortress), Krk: 146
Kaštel svetog Mihovila (St. Michael's Fortress):
187
Katarina: 77
Katedrala (Cathedral), Dubrovnik: 243
Katedrala Marijina Uznesenja (Cathedral
of the Assumption of the Blessed Virgin
Mary): 32
Katedrala Marijinog Uznesenja (Cathedral of
the Ascension): 74
Katedrala svete Marije (Cathedral of St. Mary):
106
Katedrala svete Stošlje (Cathedral of St.
Anastasia): 170
Katedrala sveti Stjepan (St. Stephen's
Cathedral): 15, 218
Katedrala svetog Dujma (Cathedral of St.
Domnius): 204
Katedrala svetog Jakova (St. Jacob's
Cathedral): 186
Katedrala svetog Lovrijenca (St. Lawrence's
Cathedral): 194
Katedrala svetog Marka (St. Mark's Cathedral):
229
Katedrala Uznesenja (Cathedral of the
Assumption): 146
kayaking: 232-233, 247, 273, 305, 307
kažuni (stone shelters): 129
Kendov Dvorec: 20, 308
King Tomislav Square (Trg Kralja Tomislava),
Samobor: 59
King Tomislav Square (Trg kralja Tomislava),
Varaždin: 73
klapa festival: 211, 330
Klek mountain: 94
Kneževa palača (Duke's Palace), Šibenik: 186
Knežev dvor (Duke's Palace), Pag Town: 164
Knežev dvor (Rector's Palace), Dubrovnik: 17,
242

Kobarid: 307
Kobariški muzej (Kobarid Museum): 308
Kobilarna Lipica (Lipica Stud Farm): 319
Kod Ruže: 20, 86
Kod Žaca: 51
Koločep: 255
Komiža: 24, 226-227
Komrčar: 160
Konoba Corrado: 19, 157
Konoba Jastožera: 24, 226-227
Konoba Volta: 21, 95
Kopački rit: 21, 86
Koper: 312-313
Kopnena vrata (Land Gate): 194
Korčula: 15, 16, 228-231
Korčula Town: 228
Kornati Islands: 16, 183-184
Koroški pokrajinski muzej (Carinthian Museum
of Ravne): 290
Korzo: 135
Kotež: 112
Kotlić: 23, 130
Krajina: 298
Krakovo: 268
Kranjska Gora: 306-307
Krapanj Island: 192
Krapina: 69
Križni: 60
Krk: 146-151
Krka Monastery: 192
Krka National Park: 190
Krk Folklore Festival (Smotra folklore otoka
Krka): 146
Krk Town: 146
Krstionica (Baptistry), Split: 205
Krvavec: 295
Kuća o batani (Batana House): 23, 113
Kuća Sobol: 23, 95
Kukuriku: 17, 142
Kula lotrščak (Burglars' Tower), Zagreb: 36
Kula skrivanat (Town Tower), Pag Town: 164
Kula stražarnica (Watchtower), Varaždin: 73
Kumrovec: 67
Kupelweiser, Paul: 111
Kurentovanje: 288
Kutjevo cellars: 20, 81
Kvarner Gulf: 131-166; culinary tour 17-19;
highlights 132; Kvarner Islands 146-166;
maps 9, 133; Opatija Riviera 140-145;
planning tips 9, 132; Rijeka 134-140
Kvarner Islands: 146-166; best-of itinerary 147;
Cres 151-155; Krk 146-151; Lošinj 155-157; Pag
163-166; Susak 158-159

L

Labin: 100-104
Labin National Museum (Narodni muzej Labin): 101
lace: 70
Lace-Making School (Čipkarska šola): 20, 308
Lace Museum: 164
Lake Bled: 301, 302
Land Gate (Kopnena vrata): 194
land mines: 86, 214
language: 289, 330, 331
Lastovo: 231-232
Law Faculty: 37
Lazareti: 245
legends: 302
Le Mandrać: 17, 142
Lent: 285
Lepoglava: 69, 69-70
lesbian travelers: 351
Levan Island: 107
Lička kuća: 15, 182
lighthouses: 108, 232
Likovnih Umetnosti Slovenj Gradec (Slovenj Gradec Art Gallery): 290
Limski Kanal: 116
Lipica Stud Farm (Kobilarna Lipica): 319
Lipizzaner stud farms: 83, 319
Lippica: 319
Livade: 128
Livio Benvenuti: 17, 127
Ljubljana: 22, 259-281; accommodations 274-275; architecture 263; entertainment 269-272; food 275-278; highlights 260; history 260; maps 9, 261; old town 266-267; planning tips 10, 261; recreation 273; services 278; shopping 272; sights 262-268; transportation 279-281
Ljubljana Castle: 265
Ljubljana City Museum (Mestni Muzej Ljubljana): 267
Ljubljana dragon: 264
Ljubljanski Grad (Ljubljana Castle): 265
Lojzekova hiža: 62
Lokrum: 17, 245
Lokve: 21, 94
Lonjsko polje: 21, 90, 96
Lopud: 255
Lošinj: 155-157
Lovran: 144-145
Lower Lakes (Donja jezera), Plitvice Lakes National Park: 182
Lower Town (Donji Grad), Zagreb: 36
Lubenice: 154

Lumbarda: 230
Lungomare: 140
Lutkovno Gledališče (Puppet Theater): 22, 265

M

mail: 355
Main Market (Glavna tržnica), Ljubljana: 264
Main Train Station (Glavni kolodvor), Zagreb: 39
Majka Bojža na Placu (St. Mary's-on-the-square): 125
Makarska Riviera: 213-215, 214-215
Maksimir: 22, 46
Maleš, Miha: 295
Mali Brijun: 112
Mali Lošinj: 19, 155
Mali Salon: 135
Mali Ston: 257
Maneštrijada: 109, 125
maps: 356
Marafor Square (Trg Marafor): 119
Maribor: 285
Marija Bistrica: 62
Marija Jurić Zagorka: 32
Marija Snježna (Our Lady of the Snow): 62
Marine Biological Institute (Centar za istraživanje mora): 114
Marjan Peninsula: 16, 206
Market Hall, Pula: 106
Markov trg (St. Mark's Square): 34
Marshal Tito Square (Trg maršala Tita), Rovinj: 112
Marshal Tito Square (Trg maršala Tita), Zagreb: 36
Marton Museum (Muzej Marton): 59
Marulićev trg (Marulić Square): 38
Maslinica: 101
Matija Skurjeni Museum: 62
Matija vlačič Illyricus Memorijalna zbirka (Memorial Collection of Matija Vlačić Illirik): 101
media: 355
Medieval Mediterranean Garden of St. Lawrence's Monastery (Srdenjovje kovni samostanski mediteranski vrt Sv. Lovre): 16, 187
Međimurje: 71-79
Medugorje: 214
Medvedgrad: 48
Medveja: 142
Memorial Collection of Matija Vlačič Illirik (Matija vlačič Illyricus Memorijalna zbirka): 101

Mestna hiša (Town Hall), Ljubljana: 266
Mestni Muzej Ljubljana (Ljubljana City
    Museum): 267
Mestni trg (Town Square), Ljubljana: 266
Meštrović, Ivan: 34, 37, 206, 254
Meštrović Atelier (Meštrović Studio): 34
Metlika: 298
metric system: 357
Middle Ages: 323-324
Miha Maleš Gallery (Galerija Miha Maleš): 295
Mimara, Ante Topić: 38
Mimara Museum (Muzej Mimara): 38
mines: 290, 294, 308, 316
Mirogoj: 41
mistletoe brandy: 17
Mljet: 15, 232-233
Moderna galerija (Modern Gallery), Ljubljana:
    267
Moderna galerija (Modern Gallery), Zagreb: 39
Modra špilja (Blue Cave): 24, 227
Monastery of Our Lady of the Snow (Samostan
    snježne Gospe): 254
money: 354
Moravske Toplice: 291
Moreno Coronica: 19, 124
Mornaričko groblje (Naval Cemetery): 106
Morske orgulje (Sea Organ): 172
Mostar: 214
Motovun: 126-128
Motovun Film Festival: 127
mountain biking: 295, 306
Mount Kopa Area: 290
Mount Medvednica: 47
Mount Sljeme: 22, 46, 47, 48
movies: see film
M. Stančić Square (Trg M. Stančića): 73
Murder on the Orient Express (Christie): 82
Murska Sobota: 291
Murska Sobota Regional Museum (Pokrajinski
    muzej Murska Sobota): 291
Murter: 183
Museum Lapidarium: 122
Museum of Arts and Crafts (Muzej za
    umjetnost i obrt): 37
Museum of Contemporary and Modern Art
    (Muzej moderne i suvremene umjetnosti):
    136
Museum of Frogs (Muzej Žaba): 21, 22, 94-95
Museum of Slavonia (Muzej Slavonije): 84
Museum Square (Muzejski trg): 135
music: Dubrovnik Summer Festival 247;
    Grožnjan 129; Istrian 130; jazz 272; klapa
    festival 211; Ljubljana 270, 271; Lubenice

154; Osor 154; Poreč 119; Rab 160; Slovenian
    331-332; Slovenska Filharmonija (Slovenian
    Philharmonic Hall) 267; St. Donat's Musical
    Evenings 174; Tartini's House (Tartinijeva
    Hiša) 315; Turbo-Folk 270; Varaždin 74;
    Zagreb 43; Zrinjevac 39; see also specific
    place
Muzej grada Rijeke (Rijeka City Museum): 136
Muzej grada Zagreba (Zagreb City Museum):
    33
Muzej Marton (Marton Museum): 59
Muzej međimurja (Museum of Međimurje): 77
Muzej Mimara (Mimara Museum): 38
Muzej moderne i suvremene umjetnosti
    (Museum of Contemporary and Modern Art):
    136
Muzej premogovništa Slovenije (Coal-Mining
    Museum of Slovenia): 294
Muzej seljačkih buna (Peasant's Revolt
    Museum): 69
Muzejski trg (Museum Square): 135
Muzej Slavonije (Museum of Slavonia): 84
Muzej Staro Selo (Old Village Museum),
    Kumrovec: 67
Muzej Žaba (Museum of Frogs): 21, 22, 94-95
Muzej za umjetnost i obrt (Museum of Arts and
    Crafts): 37

N

naive art movement: 35, 78
Napoleonic rule: 325
Narodna galerija (National Gallery): 267
Narodni muzej Labin (Labin National Museum):
    101
Narodni muzej (National Museum): 267
Narodni trg (National Square): 172
National Gallery (Narodna galerija): 267
National Museum (Narodni muzej): 267
National Square (Narodni trg): 172
Natural History Museum (Prirodoslovni muzej):
    136
northern Dalmatia: 167-198; highlights 168;
    maps 9, 169; Murter 183; Paklenica National
    Park 179-181; planning tips 9, 168; Plitvice
    Lakes National Park 181-183; Primošten
    192-193; Trogir 194-198; Zadar 170-176
Naval Cemetery (Mornaričko groblje): 106
northern Krk: 148
Novalja: 165
Novigrad: 122
Novo Mesto: 297
nude sunbathing: 114, 162, 165, 177, 223
Nun Čika Square (Trg Opatice Čike): 171

O

Odescalchi castle: 21, 90
Od Puča: 244
Ogulin: 94
Old Town (Stari Grad), Hvar: 16, 220, 222-223
Old Town (Stari Grad), Rijeka: 135
Old Town (Stari Grad), Samobor: 60
Old Town (Stari Grad), Varaždin: 73
Old Village Museum (Muzej Staro Selo), Kumrovec: 67
Oleum Olivarum: 109
Olimijski centar (Olympic Center): 94
olive oil: 109, 110, 228
Olive Oil Exhibition: 109, 110
Oltar domovine (Homeland Altar): 48
Olympic Center: 94
Omiš: 211-213
Onofrio's Little Fountain: 242
Opatija: 140-144
Opatija Riviera: 17, 140-145
opera: 43
Oprtalj: 128-129
Orebić: 256
Orlando: 242
Orlando's Column: 241
Osijek: 20, 83
Osor: 151, 154
Ottoman wars: 324
Our Lady of Šunja (Gospa od Šunja): 255
Our Lady of the Pirates (Gospa Gusarica): 226
Our Lady of the Snow (Marija Snježna): 62
oysters: 257
Ozalj: 93

P

packing tips: 354
Pag: 163-166
Pag Town: 164
Paklenica National Park: 179-181
Palača Drašković (Drašković Palace): 73
Palača Patačić (Patačić Palace): 73
Palača Prassinsky-Sermage: 73
Palača Sponza (Sponza Palace): 241
Palace Solomon: 125
Palmižana: 220, 222
Papalićeva Palača (Papalić Palace): 206
parachuting: 302
paragliding: 302
Parish Church of St. Peter and Paul (Župna crkva svetog Petra i Pavia): 84
Parish Church (Zborna crkva), Pag Town: 164
Park prirode Učka (Učka Nature Park): 141

Pašman: 177
passports: 13, 340
Patačić Palace (Palača Patačić): 73
Pazin: 124-125
peasants' revolt: 69
Peasant's Revolt Museum (Muzej seljačkih buna): 69
Pekel Cave: 293
Pelegrini: 15, 189
Pelješac Peninsula: 16, 256-258
performing arts: Art Republika festival 100; Dubrovnik Summer Festival 247; International Theater Festival 107; Teatro Fenice 136; Zadar 174; Zagreb 43; see also specific place
Perivoj Dordić-Mayner (Dordić-Mayner Park): 255
Petrović, Dražen: 41
Pharos: 129
phone services: 355
photography: 59, 240
Pilgrimage Church of St. Mary of Bistrica (Hodočasnička crkva Marije Bistričke): 62
piracy: 212
Piran: 315-316
Pivovarski muzej (Brewery Museum): 268
Pjaca: 218
Pjaceta: 229
plague, 1729: 84
plague columns: 84, 90, 285
plane travel: 13, 333-334
planning tips: 8-14
plants: 321, 322
Plavi Podrum: 17, 142
Plešivička wine route: 61
Plitvice Lakes National Park: 15, 181-183
Podsreda: 294
Pojoda: 24, 225
Poklad festival: 231
Pokrajinski muzej (Regional Museum), Koper: 312
Pokrajinski muzej Celje (Celje Regional Museum): 292
Pokrajinski muzej Murska Sobota (Murska Sobota Regional Museum): 291
police: 340, 341
Pomorski muzej Sergej Mašera (Sergej Mašera Maritime Museum): 315
Pomurje Region: 291-292
Poreč: 19, 117-124
Porta Aurea (Golden Gate): 206
Portorož: 314
Postojnska Jama (Postojna Cave): 318

Povijesni i pomorski muzej hrvatskog (History and Maritime Museum of the Croatian Littoral): 135
Povijesni muzej Istre (Historical Museum of Istria): 106
Požega: 79
Praetorian Palace (Pretorska Palaca): 312
Pravoslavna crkva (Serbian Orthodox Church): 36
Premantura: 107
Prešeren, France: 262
Prešernov trg (Prešeren Square): 262
Pretorska Palaca (Praetorian Palace): 312
Pribić: 93
Primošten: 192-193
Prirodoslovni muzej (Natural History Museum): 136
prisons: 160
Pristava Lepena: 20, 307
Protestantism: 101
Pršuta Tri Wine Bar: 16, 219-220
Ptuj: 287-288
Puconci: 292
Pula: 19, 104-110
Punat: 148-149
Punta Verudela: 107
Puntijarka: 48
Puppet Theater (Lutkovno Gledališče), Ljubljana: 22, 265
puppet theater festival, Zagreb: 44
Pustijerna: 243

QR
Rab: 159-163
Rabac: 100
Rabac Summer Festival: 101
Račićev mauzolej (Račić Mausoleum): 254
Radnički Dom (House of Workers): 88
rafting: Bjeloasica 94; Bled 302; Bohinj 305; Dubrovnik 247; Ljubljana 273; Soča River 300, 307
Railway Museum (Železniški muzej): 22, 267
railways: 13, 82
Rakitna: 281
Ranger, Ivan: 42, 69, 71
Ravlić house: 21, 96
Ravne: 290
recreation: 341-343
Rector's Palace (Knežev dvor), Dubrovnik: 17, 242
Regent Esplanade hotel: 14, 38, 39, 54
Regional Museum (Pokrajinski muzej), Koper: 312

religion: 330, 331
Remete: 42
Republic of Croatia Square (Trg Republike Hrvatske), Rijeka: 136
Republic of Croatia Square (Trg Republike Hrvatske), Šibenik: 187
restaurants: 347-348; *see also specific place*
Restoran Milan: 19, 108
Revelin Fortress: 245
Ribarske fešte (Fisherman's festivals): 109
Ribarski muzej (Fishing Museum): 226
Ribčev Laz: 305
Ribnica: 296-297
Ribnjak: 32
Rijeka: 134-140
Rijeka City Museum (Muzej grada Rijeke): 136
Risnjak National Park: 94
Riva: 135, 196, 204
Robbov Vodnjak (Robba's Fountain): 266
Robinson: 220
rock climbing: 94, 179, 305
Rogaška Slatina: 294
Roland: 242
Roman amphitheater (Amfiteatar): 23, 104
Romanička kuća (Romanesque House): 119
Roman necropolis archaeological park (Arheološki park Rimska nekropola): 293
Romuald's Cave: 116
Rosalnice: 299
Rotovški trg: 285
Rotovž (Town Hall), Maribor: 285
Rovinj: 23, 112-117
Rovinj Heritage Museum (Zavičajni muzej Rovinj): 113
Rožanec: 299
Rukavac: 227
rural itinerary: 20-21

S
safety: 351-352
sailing: 23-24, 342
salt mining: 316
Samobor: 21, 59-61
Samoborski fašnik: 59
Samostan snježne Gospe (Monastery of Our Lady of the Snow): 254
Samostan svetog Nikole (Convent of St. Nicholas): 196
Šapiun: 231
Sarajevo: 214
Savinjska Valley: 292-294
Savinjske Alps Region: 294-296
Savska: 40

scuba diving: see diving
sculpture: Bogovićeva 53; Croatian 330-331; Joyce, James 106; Koroški pokrajinski muzej (Carinthian Museum of Ravne) 290; Meštrović, Ivan 34, 37, 206, 254; Mirogoj 41; Slovenian 332
sea, travel by: 334, 335, 336
Sea Organ (Morske orgulje): 172
seasons, best travel: 12
Sečovlje Salina Nature Park: 316
Selo: 291
Šempeter: 293
Serbian Orthodox Church (Pravoslavna crkva): 36
Sergej Mašera Maritime Museum (Pomorski muzej Sergej Mašera): 315
Sergia family: 104-105
Šetalište braće Radić: 82
Šetalište Fra Odorika Badurine: 160
Šetalište Kardinala Frane Šepera: 83
Šetalište Stari Grad: 81
7.Future Nature: 107
Šibenik: 15, 185-192
Silba: 178
Šipan: 256
Šipanska Luka: 256
Sisak: 96
skating: 47
skiing: 46, 295, 306, 342
Sklepić house: 21, 88
Škocjanske Jame (Škocjan Caves): 318
Škofja Loka: 294
Skoji Islands: 231
Škola: 52
Škrip: 218
skydiving: 286
Slavonia: 79-90
Slavonski Brod: 82-83
Sljeme: 46, 47
Slovene Ethnographic Museum (Slovenski etnografski muzej): 264
Slovenia: coastal 311-316; culture 331-332; economy 329; food 346-347; geography 322-323; government 328; inland 282-308; money 355; social customs 353; transportation 335, 338-339; visas 340-341; wineries 18
Slovenj Gradec: 290
Slovenj Gradec Art Gallery (Likovnih Umetnosti Slovenj Gradec): 290
Slovenska Filharmonija (Slovenian Philharmonic Hall): 267
Slovenske Konjice: 289

Slovenski etnografski muzej (Slovene Ethnographic Museum): 264
Slovenski gasilski muzej (Fire Brigade Museum): 299
Smotra folklore otoka Krka (Krk Folklore Festival): 146
snorkeling: 216
snowboarding: 296
soccer: 342; Hajduk 208; Ljubljana 273; Varteks 75; Zagreb 49
social customs: 352-354
Soča River: 307
Soča River Valley: 300
Song of Roland: 242
southern Dalmatia: 199-233; highlights 200; islands 216-233; itinerary 15; Makarska Riviera 213-215; maps 9, 201; Omiš 211-213; planning tips 10, 199; Split 202-210
spas: 49, 148, 292, 294, 344
spelunking: see caves
Špilja Vrelo: 94
Split: 16, 23, 202-210
sponge diving: 192
Sponza Palace (Palača Sponza): 17, 241
Square of Five Walls (Trg pet bunara): 173
Srdenjovje kovni samostanski mediteranski vrt Sv. Lovre (Medieval Mediterranean Garden of St. Lawrence's Monastery): 16, 187
Štanjel: 318
St. Anthony's Church (Crkva svetog Antuna): 157
Stara Baška: 149
Stari Grad (Old Town), Hvar: 16, 220, 222-223
Stari Grad (Old Town), Rijeka: 135
Stari Grad (Old Town), Samobor: 60
Stari Grad (Old Town), Varaždin: 73
Stari Grad Celje (Celje Castle): 292
Starigrad Paklenica: 179
State Archives (Državni arhiv): 38
Stations of the Cross (Kalvarija): 281
St. Blasius (Sveti Vlaho): 241
St. Blasius's Church (Crkva svetog Vlaha): 241
St. Christopher's Church (Crkva Sveti Kristofor): 160
St. Cyprian's Church (Crkva svetog Ciprijana): 225
St. Donat's Church (Crkva svetog Donata): 170
steam train: 305
St. Euphemia's Church (Crkva svete Eufemije): 113
St. George's Church (Crkva Sveti Jurja), Pag Town: 164
St. George's Church (Crkva svetog Jurja), Lovran: 144

Stična: 281
Stična Samostan (Stična Monastery): 281
St. Jacob's Cathedral (Katedrala svetog Jakova): 186
St. John's Fortress (Tvrđava Sv. Ivan): 243
St. Lawrence's Cathedral (Katedrala svetog Lovrijenca): 194
St. Lawrence's Church (Crkva svetog Lovre), Požega: 81
St. Lawrence's Church (Crkva svetog Lovre), Vrboska: 224
St. Lawrence's Monastery, Medieval Mediterranean Garden of (Srdenjovje kovni samostanski mediteranski vrt Sv. Lovre): 16, 187
St. Lucy's Church (Crkva svete Lucije): 149
St. Mark's Cathedral (Katedrala svetog Marka): 229
St. Mark's Church (Crkva svetog Marka): 34
St. Mark's Square (Markov trg): 34
St. Mary's Church (Crkva svete Marije), Vrboska: 223
St. Mary's Church (Crkva svete Marije), Zadar: 171
St. Mary's-on-the-square (Majka Bojža na Placu): 125
St. Michael's Church (Crkva svetog Mihovila): 257
St. Michael's Fortress (Kaštel svetog Mihovila): 187
St. Nicholas's Church (Crkva svetog Nikole): 254
Stolna Cerkev Sv. Jurija (Church of St. George): 315
Stolnica Marijinega vnebovzetja (Cathedral of the Assumption): 312
Stolnica sveti Nikolaja (Cathedral of St. Nicholas): 265
Ston: 257
Stončića: 227
Stone Gate (Kamenita vrata): 33
stone shelters (kažuni): 129
St. Quirinus's Church (Crkva svetog Kvirina): 146
Stradun: 16, 238
Street Museum, Izola: 313
Strossmayerova galerija starih majstora (Strossmayer Gallery of Old Masters): 39
Strossmayerovo šetalište (Strossmayer's path): 36
Strossmayerov trg (Strossmayer Square): 39
St. Simeon's Church (Crkva svetog Šimuna): 173

St. Stephen's Cathedral (Katedrala sveti Stjepan): 15, 218
St. Stephen's Church (Crkva svetog Stjepana): 126
study abroad: 349
Stupica: 107
St. Vitus's Church (Crkva svetog Vida): 135
Sućuraj: 224
Subotina uz divovsku fritadu s tartufima (Subotina with giant truffle omelet): 109
summer sledding: 286, 306
Sunset Lounge: 17, 246
Supetar: 216
Susak: 158-159
Sveta Katarina: 114
Sveta Nedelja: 223
Sveti Jerolim: 112
Sveti Vlaho (St. Blasius): 241
Svirče: 223
synagogues: 241

T
Tartini's House (Tartinijeva Hiša): 315
Teatro Fenice: 136
Tehnički muzej (Technical Museum): 41
Telašćica Bay: 178
Telegrin: 206
telephone services: 355
Temple of Augustus: 106
tennis: 94
terme (thermal spas): 344
Tesla, Nikola: 40
Three Parishes (Tri fare): 299
Tikveš: 86
Tintoretto: 39
Tito, Josip Broz: 37, 67, 111, 326
Titov trg (Tito's Square): 101
Tivoli Mansion: 268
Tivoli Park: 268
Tkalčićeva Street: 15, 22, 32
Tkon: 177
Tobačni muzej (Tobacco Museum): 268
Tomislavov trg (Tomislav Square): 38
Torcida: 192
Torte i to: 32, 50
tourism: 329
tourist information: 357
tours: Etnoland 187; Kopački rit boat 86; Krka National Park 190; Ljubljana 263, 273, 278; Lonjsko polje 96; Paklenica National Park 179; Romauld's Cave 116; Slavonia wine roads 80; Vukovar wine country 88; Zagreb 55; see also specific place

Town Hall (Mestna hiša), Ljubljana: 266
Town Hall (Rotovž), Maribor: 285
Town Hall (Vijećnica), Varaždin: 74
Town Loggia (Gradska loža), Trogir: 195
Town Museum (Gradski muzej), Karlovac: 91
Town Museum (Gradski muzej), Korčula: 229
Town Museum (Gradski muzej), Pag: 165
Town Museum (Gradski muzej), Požega: 81
Town Museum (Gradski muzej), Samobor: 59
Town Museum (Gradski muzej), Vukovar: 88
Town Square (Mestni trg), Ljubljana: 266
Town Tower (Kula skrivanat), Pag Town: 164
train, steam: 305
train travel: 13, 334, 335, 336, 338
Trajbar Team: 62
Trakoščan: 70
transportation: 13, 333-339; *see also specific place*
Trash Film Festival: 75
Trattoria Bora Bar: 19, 158
travel insurance: 351
Treaty of Vienna: 325
Trg bana Jelačića (Ban Jelačić Square), Krk: 146
Trg bana Jelačića (Ban Jelačić Square), Zagreb: 30-31
Trg F. Petrića: 151
Trg I.B. Mažuranić: 82
Trg kralja Petra Krešimira IV: 164
Trg Kralja Tomislava (King Tomislav Square), Samobor: 59
Trg kralja Tomislava (King Tomislav Square), Varaždin: 73
Trg Marafor (Marafor Square): 119
Trg maršala Tita (Marshal Tito Square), Rovinj: 112
Trg maršala Tita (Marshal Tito Square), Zagreb: 36
Trg M. Stančića (M. Stančić Square): 73
Trg Opatice Čike (Nun Čika Square): 171
Trg pet bunara (Square of Five Walls): 173
Trg Republike Hrvatske (Republic of Croatia Square), Rijeka: 136
Trg Republike Hrvatske (Republic of Croatia Square), Šibenik: 187
Trg Slobode (Freedom Square): 72
Trg svetog Trojstva: 81
Trg sv Stjepana: 218
Trg Valdibora (Valdibor Square): 114
Trg žrtava fašizma (Victims of Fascism Square): 40
Trieste: 314
Tri fare (Three Parishes): 299

Triglav National Park: 20, 307
Triple Bridge (Tromostovje): 262
Trogir: 194-198
Tromostovje (Triple Bridge): 262
Trsat: 136
Trsatska gradina (Trsat Castle): 136
Trsteno: 254
truffles: 125
Tržnica Dolac (Dolac Market): 15, 31, 51
Turbo-Folk: 270
Tvrđa: 20, 84
Tvrdalj: 222
Tvrđava Gripe (Gripe Fortress): 207
Tvrđava Sv. Ivan (St. John's Fortress): 243

U

Učka Nature Park (Park prirode Učka): 141
Ugljan: 177
Ukanc: 305
Umjetnička Galerija (Dubrovnik Art Gallery): 245
Umjetničke zbirke (Art Collections): 155
Umjetnički paviljon (Art Pavilion): 39
UNESCO sites: 181, 204, 313, 318
Upper Dolenjska Wine Road: 20, 298
Upper Lakes (Gornja jezera), Plitvice Lakes National Park: 182
Upper Square (Gornji trg), Ljubljana: 266
Upper Town (Gornji Grad), Osijek: 84
Upper Town (Gornji Grad), Zagreb: 15, 22, 33
Urania Cinema: 84
Uršulinska crkva (Ursuline Church): 72
uspinjača (funicular): 36
Užičić Palace: 219

V

Valdibor Square (Trg Valdibora): 114
Valkane: 107
Valsabbion: 19, 108
Valsaline: 107
Valun: 155
Vanka, Maksimilian: 229
Varaždin: 71-77
Varoš Quarter: 173
Varteks: 75
vegetation: 321, 322
Vela Luka: 230
Vela Plaža: 149
Velenje: 294
Veli Brijun: 111
Velika Planina: 295
Veliki Tabor: 68
Veli Lošinj: 19, 157-158

Veli zvonik (Great Bell Tower): 160
Venice: 314
Venice-Simplon Orient Express: 82
Victims of Fascism Square (Trg žrtava fašizma): 40
Vijećnica (Town Hall), Varaždin: 74
Villa Angiolina: 141
Vinarija Zdelarević: 21, 82
Vinistra: 109, 119
Vintgar Gorge: 302
Vis: 15, 24, 224-228
visas: 13, 340-341
Vis Town: 24, 224
Vodnikov trg (Vodnik Square): 264-265
Vodnjan: 110
Vodnjanka: 110
Volčji Potok: 295
volleyball: 94
Vrboska: 223
Vukovar: 88

W

War Photo Limited: 240
Watchtower (Kula stražarnica), Varaždin: 73
waterfalls: Gračišće 125; Iški Vintgar 281; Krka National Park 190; Plitvice Lakes National Park 182; underground 293
waterskiing: 314
weather: 179
Well of Life: 37
White Villa (Bijela vila): 111
white-water rafting: 247
wildlife: 321, 322
wildlife viewing: dolphins 158; Kopački rit 86; Lonjsko polje 96; Plitvice Lakes National Park 181; Veli Brijun 111
windsurfing: 107
wine: 18, 349; Istrian 120; Malvasia 109; Pelješac Peninsula 256; shopping for 45; Vinistra 119
Wine Day (Dan Vina): 109
wineries: 18; Baranja, the 87-88; Brač 218; Brda region 317; Brtonigla 123; Hvar 16; Ilok 89-90; Ivica Matošević 117; Maribor 285; Međimurje 78; Motovun 127; Pelješac Peninsula 258; Poreč 119; Požega 81; Primošten 193; Ptuj 288; Slavonski Brod 82; Susak 159; Sveta Nedelja 223; Svirče 223; Vis 227
wine roads: Bela Krajina 299; Dolenjska 298; Koper 312; Maribor 286; Međimurje 77; Plešivička wine route 61; Pomurje Region 292; Slavonia 80; Slovenia 297

Winter harbor (Zimska luka): 83
Wire Walk: 272
women travelers: 351
World War I: 325
World War II: 95, 308, 325-326

XYZ

Zadar: 170-176
Zagreb: 22, 25-62; accommodations 49-50; entertainment 42-44; food 50-55; highlights 26; history 27; maps 9, 28; planning tips 8, 27-29; recreation 46-49; services 55-56; shopping 44-46; sights 30-42; tours 55; transportation 57-58
Zagreb City Museum (Muzej grada Zagreba): 33
Zagreb Film Festival: 44
Zagreb Summer Festival: 44
Zagreb Zoo: 46
Zajarki Lake: 62
Zavičajni muzej (District Museum), Poreč: 119
Zavičajni muzej Rovinj (Rovinj Heritage Museum): 113
Zavjetni stup (plague column): 84
Zbiljsko jezero: 281
Zborna crkva (Parish Church), Pag Town: 164
Železniški muzej (Railway Museum): 22, 267
Žička kartuzija (Žiče Carthusian monastery): 289
Židovski trg (Jewish Square): 285
Zigante Tartufi: 17, 128
Zimska luka (Winter harbor): 83
Zlatan Plenković: 15, 16, 223
Zlatna vrata (Golden Gate): 104-105
Zlatni Rt (Golden Cape): 23, 114
Zmajski Most (Dragon Bridge): 264
zoos: 46, 268
Zrinjevac: 39
ŽSD Stadium: 273
Žudioska: 241
Žumberak: 93
Župna crkva svetog Petra i Pavia (Parish Church of St. Peter and Paul): 84
Župna crkva Sv. Vida i Modesta (Church of Sts. Vitus and Modestus): 129

List of Maps

Front color map
Croatia & Slovenia: 2-3

Discover Croatia & Slovenia
chapter divisions map: 9

Zagreb
Zagreb: 28

Inland Croatia
Inland Croatia: 65
Varaždin: 72
Wine Roads Tour of Slavonia: 80
Osijek: 84
Karlovac: 91

Istria
Istria: 99
Pula: 105
Rovinj: 113
Poreč: 118

Kvarner Gulf
Kvarner Gulf: 133
Opatija Riviera: 141
Cres: 152
Lošinj: 156

Northern Dalmatia
Northern Dalmatia: 169
Zadar: 171
Šibenik: 185
Trogir: 194

Southern Dalmatia
Southern Dalmatia: 201
Split: 203
Brač: 216
Hvar: 219
Vis: 225
Korčula: 229

Dubrovnik
Dubrovnik: 236
Old Town Dubrovnik: 239

Ljubljana
Ljubljana: 261

Inland Slovenia
Inland Slovenia: 284
Julian Alps: 301

Coastal Slovenia and the Karst Region
Coastal Slovenia and the Karst Region: 311

Acknowledgments

Thanks so much to all the wonderful people who helped me bring this book to life. For those I haven't thanked enough, I figure this is my chance so here it goes: First, to all of my caring, intelligent professors—Mrs. Thomas, Professor Alix Ingber, and Professor Eija Celli, for inspiring me and teaching me. Next to my friends who've kept me laughing and listened throughout the years, good and bad—Dyan, Jane, Slavica, Yvonne, and Desiree, to name a few—as well as the teacher that believed in me, taught me a ton about writing, and gave me a chance—the brilliant editor John Newton—and my kind editors Lisa Gill and Alicia Miller, who keep work fun. Also a huge thank you to all the teachers at The Learning Tree in Zagreb—Josmar, Nancy, Joy, Ella, Snjezana, and Kate—who not only took excellent care of my kids at school from 9 to 3 while I was writing this book, but became excellent friends as well. To Ema, my right-hand woman and second mother, much, much love and thanks. To my editors at Avalon, who have been outstanding, kind, and professional—Kathryn, Brice, and Kathryn—thank you for making my first book such a joy. To my family—my in-laws, Stipe and Jela, who accepted me as one of their own; my grandmothers, Go and Mama, for giving me creativity; my parents, Beth and Eddie, who have always believed in me, supported me, and answered the phone at 3 A.M. with a smile when needed; my sweet babies, Noemi and Andre, who teach me something every day and always make me a better person; and my Tomo, who has stuck with me through it all and always, buzz tons.

www.moon.com

DESTINATIONS | ACTIVITIES | BLOGS | MAPS | BOOKS

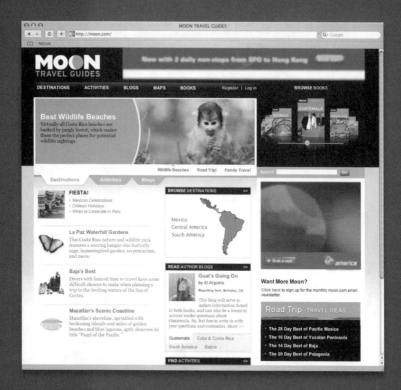

MOON.COM is all new, and ready to help plan your next trip! Filled with fresh trip ideas and strategies, author interviews, informative blogs, a detailed map library, and descriptions of all the Moon guidebooks, Moon.com is all you need to get out and explore the world—or even places in your own backyard. As always, when you travel with Moon, expect an experience that is uncommon and truly unique.

MAP SYMBOLS

▓▓▓ Expressway	**◖** Highlight	✗ Airfield	⚓ Golf Course
─── Primary Road	○ City/Town	✈ Airport	**P** Parking Area
═══ Secondary Road	◉ State Capital	▲ Mountain	◢ Archaeological Site
▪▪▪▪ Unpaved Road	⊛ National Capital	✚ Unique Natural Feature	⛪ Church
------- Trail	★ Point of Interest		⛽ Gas Station
.... Ferry	• Accommodation	⚐ Waterfall	⟳ Glacier
▬▬▬ Railroad	▾ Restaurant/Bar	▲ Park	▨ Mangrove
▓▓▓ Pedestrian Walkway	▪ Other Location	▣ Trailhead	▧ Reef
▥▥▥ Stairs	∆ Campground	�skiing Skiing Area	▭ Swamp

CONVERSION TABLES

°C = (°F − 32) / 1.8
°F = (°C x 1.8) + 32
1 inch = 2.54 centimeters (cm)
1 foot = 0.304 meters (m)
1 yard = 0.914 meters
1 mile = 1.6093 kilometers (km)
1 km = 0.6214 miles
1 fathom = 1.8288 m
1 chain = 20.1168 m
1 furlong = 201.168 m
1 acre = 0.4047 hectares
1 sq km = 100 hectares
1 sq mile = 2.59 square km
1 ounce = 28.35 grams
1 pound = 0.4536 kilograms
1 short ton = 0.90718 metric ton
1 short ton = 2,000 pounds
1 long ton = 1.016 metric tons
1 long ton = 2,240 pounds
1 metric ton = 1,000 kilograms
1 quart = 0.94635 liters
1 US gallon = 3.7854 liters
1 Imperial gallon = 4.5459 liters
1 nautical mile = 1.852 km

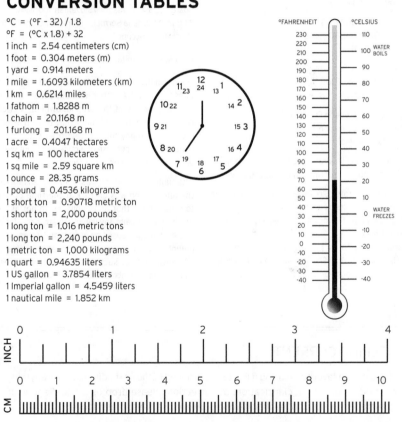

MOON CROATIA & SLOVENIA

Avalon Travel
a member of the Perseus Books Group
1700 Fourth Street
Berkeley, CA 94710, USA
www.moon.com

Editor and Series Manager: Kathryn Ettinger
Copy Editor: Amy Scott
Graphics Coordinator: Kathryn Osgood
Production Coordinator: Darren Alessi
Cover Designer: Kathryn Osgood
Map Editor: Brice Ticen
Cartographers: Kat Bennett, Chris Markiewicz
Proofreader: Julie Littman
Indexer: Rachel Kuhn

ISBN-10: 1-59880-198-8
ISBN-13: 978-1-59880-198-9
ISSN: 1947-8798

Printing History
1st Edition — June 2009
5 4 3 2 1

Front cover photo: Prešeren Square, Ljubljana, Slovenia © digitalrailroad.com
Title page photo: Rovinj, Istria, Croatia © Jay Beiler/dreamstime.com
Interior color photos: p. 4: © B. Kladnik/Slovenian Tourist Board, p. 5: © Shann Fountain Čulo, p. 6 top: © Carlyle Calhoun, bottom: © Miroslav Beneda/dreamstime.com, p. 7 upper left: © Shann Fountain Čulo, upper right: © Carlyle Calhoun, bottom left: © Carlyle Calhoun, bottom right: © dreamstime.com, p. 8: © Robert Lerich/dreamstime.com, p. 10: Dario Bajurin/bigstockphoto.com, p. 11 top: © J. Skok/Slovenian Tourist Board, bottom: © B. Bajželj/Slovenian Tourist Board, p. 12: © Josef Bosak/dreamstime.com, p. 13: © A. Fevžar/Slovenian Tourist Board, p. 14: © A. Fevžer/Slovenian Tourist Board, p. 15: © Mirsad Mehulic/dreamstime.com, p. 16: © dreamstime.com, p. 17: © Holger Mette/dreamstime.com, p. 18: © Shann Fountain Čulo, p. 19: © Danijel Micka/dreamstime.com, p. 20: © B. Kladnik/Slovenian Tourist Board, p. 21: © D. Mladenovič/Slovenian Tourist Board, p. 22: © J. Skok/Slovenian Tourist Board, p. 23: © B. Kladnik/Slovenian Tourist Board, p. 24 top: © Gordana Sermek/dreamstime.com, bottom: © dreamstime.com

Printed in the United States by RR Donnelley

KEEPING CURRENT

If you have a favorite gem you'd like to see included in the next edition, or see anything that needs updating, clarification, or correction, please drop us a line. Send your comments via email to feedback@moon.com, or use the address above.